D1555084

LDS
BELIEFS

LDS
BELIEFS

A DOCTRINAL REFERENCE

ROBERT L. MILLET • CAMILLE FRONK OLSON
ANDREW C. SKINNER • BRENT L. TOP

DESERET
BOOK

SALT LAKE CITY, UTAH

Library of Congress Cataloging-in-Publication Data
Millet, Robert L., author.
    LDS beliefs : a doctrinal reference / Robert L. Millet, Camille Fronk Olson, Andrew C. Skinner, and Brent L. Top.
        p. cm.
    Includes bibliographical references and index.
    ISBN 978-1-60908-059-4 (hardbound : alk. paper)
    1. The Church of Jesus Christ of Latter-day Saints—Doctrines—Encyclopedias.
2. Mormon Church—Encyclopedias. I. Olson, Camille Fronk, author. II. Skinner, Andrew C., 1951– author. III. Top, Brent L. IV. Title.
    BX8605.5.M55 2011
    230'.93—dc23   2011019590

Printed in the United States of America
Publishers Printing, Salt Lake City, UT

10   9   8   7   6   5   4   3   2   1

CONTENTS

ACKNOWLEDGMENTS

As with any project, but particularly with one as extensive and complex as this one, there are many people whose contributions have been crucial. First, we are grateful to our faculty colleagues in Religious Education at Brigham Young University, many of whom served as sounding boards to our ideas, read our entries, and suggested changes that have improved this work. It is wonderful to have experts in so many fields just down the hall who are willing to share ideas and provide valuable critique.

We also appreciate the help of our research assistants and student secretaries who helped us organize the topics, check the sources, and prepare the manuscript for publication: Connie Lankford Brace, Adele Gabriel, Mia Gabriel, KateLyn Jenkins, Karra King, Camilla Schulte, Rachel Thompson, Shealyn Moon, and Dana Kendall.

We are especially grateful to Sheri Dew and Cory Maxwell for their encouragement, support, and careful oversight of this project. Our editor, Suzanne Brady, is without peer. We are most appreciative of her efforts and those of her associates Michael Morris and Derk Koldewyn in producing a book that is so much better than the submitted manuscript. We likewise appreciate the efforts of Shauna Gibby as designer and Rachael Ward as typographer. In short, we have been blessed by the kind professionalism of the staff of Deseret Book Company.

INTRODUCTION

Joseph Smith wrote, "We believe all that God has revealed, all that He does now reveal, and we believe that He will yet reveal many great and important things pertaining to the Kingdom of God" (Articles of Faith 1:9). Truth is eternal, but our grasp of that truth, our insight into its application, and the way our leaders emphasize the implications of that truth may expand as time goes by.

It is precisely for that reason that we have written this volume. Because the Lord is revealing himself and his plan of salvation line upon line, precept upon precept (Isaiah 28:10; 2 Nephi 28:30), few published works within Latter-day Saint literature—other than the scriptures themselves—will have an eternal shelf life. Elder Jeffrey R. Holland taught: "In our heartfelt devotion to Jesus of Nazareth as the very Son of God, the Savior of the world, we invite all to examine what we have received of Him, to join with us, drinking deeply at the 'well of water springing up into everlasting life' [John 4:14], these constantly flowing reminders that God lives, that He loves us, and that He speaks. I express the deepest personal thanks that His works never end and His 'words . . . never cease'" (94).

In the revelation we call the Olive Leaf, the Lord instructed the early Latter-day Saints: "I give unto you *a commandment that you shall teach one another the doctrine of the kingdom. Teach ye diligently and my grace shall attend you,* that you may be instructed more perfectly in theory, in principle, in doctrine, in the law of the gospel, in all things that pertain unto the kingdom of God, that are expedient for you to understand" (D&C 88:77–78; emphasis added). Saints from the beginning of this dispensation have listened and learned from their leaders and from one another. Almost everything we do in the restored Church entails teaching and training, with repeated reference to the words of the prophets.

There is a vital need in our day for committed and competent disciples who not only know the gospel is true but also know the gospel. Our quest to comprehend the tenets of the restored gospel is practical and experiential as well as theological: what we know affects what we do, and what we do affects who and what we become (Oaks, 32–34). "True doctrine, understood, changes attitudes and behavior," Elder Boyd K. Packer explained. "The study of the doctrines of the gospel will improve behavior quicker than a study of behavior will improve behavior. . . . That is why we stress so forcefully the study of the doctrines of the gospel" ("Children," 17). Elder Neal A. Maxwell pointed out that "doctrines believed and practiced do change and improve us, while ensuring our vital access to the Spirit. Both outcomes are crucial" (page x).

The Lord's house is a house of order (D&C 132:8). Modern apostles and prophets have been called and put in place "for the perfecting of the saints, for the work of the ministry, for the edifying of the body of Christ: till we all come in the unity of the faith, and of the knowledge of the Son of God, unto a perfect [meaning whole, complete, mature] man, unto the measure of the stature of the fulness of Christ: *that we henceforth be no more children, tossed to and fro, and carried about with every wind of doctrine,* by the sleight of men, and cunning craftiness, whereby they lie in wait to deceive; but speaking the truth in love, may grow up into him in all things, which is the head, even Christ" (Ephesians 4:12–15; emphasis added).

President J. Reuben Clark Jr. taught that "some of the General Authorities have had assigned to them a special calling; they possess a special gift: they [the apostles] are sustained as prophets, seers, and revelators, which gives them a special spiritual endowment in connection with their teaching of the people. They have the right, the power, and authority to declare the mind and will of God to his people, subject to the overall power and authority of the President of the Church. Others of the General Authorities are not given this special spiritual endowment and authority covering their teaching; they have a resulting limitation, and the resulting limitation upon their power and authority in teaching applies to every other officer and member of the Church, for none of them is spiritually endowed as a prophet, seer, and revelator." President Clark added that the president of the Church "alone has the right to receive revelations for the Church, either new or amendatory, or to give authoritative interpretations of scriptures that shall be binding on the Church, or change in any way the existing doctrines of the Church" (9–10; or Packer, "Apostles," 6).

And so we look to those upon whom the keys of the kingdom have been conferred to establish doctrine, interpret doctrine, clarify doctrine, and explicate doctrine. In this volume we have not sought to be novel or creative in our presentation but rather to defer to the Lord's anointed, saying "none other things than that which the prophets and apostles have written" (D&C 52:9). To determine whether something is a part of the doctrine of the Church, we have asked ourselves and one other: Is it in the four standard works? Is it in official declarations or proclamations? Is it taught in general conference or other official gatherings by general authorities or general officers of the Church today? Is it in the current general handbooks or approved curriculum of the Church? If it meets one or more of these criteria, we have felt safe in drawing upon it ("Approaching").

LDS Beliefs is unusual in several ways, including the following:

1. Although this volume is encyclopedic in scope, it is not a typical encyclopedia. Scores of topics have been addressed but not by dozens of contributors, as is often the case; rather, four individuals have done the writing. We have often used the less formal *we* to refer to those of us (authors and readers) who are Latter-day Saints. In addition, some entries contain both a recitation of facts and a discussion. For example, the entry "Apocalypse" does more than define the Apocalypse as the book of Revelation written by John the Beloved; it also discusses several themes and doctrines in this New Testament book. Similarly, the entry "Cross/Crucify/Crucifixion" does more than explain that this was the manner in which our Savior Jesus Christ was put to death; it also provides a brief historical background for the practice of crucifixion as a means of torture and execution in the ancient world.

2. We have used the standard system of parenthetical references for quotations from scripture, but we have used an abbreviated system for parenthetical references to sources other than scripture. If the author of a quoted passage is named in the text, only the page number of the relevant source is cited parenthetically. When two or more sources by the same author are used, a short reference to the title is included with

the page number. Complete bibliographic information for each source is found at the end of each topic.

3. At the end of the book is an index to the topics we have addressed. There *See* directs the reader to the entry in which a specific matter is treated. For example, in the Index of Topics under "Birth Control," we find "*See* Procreation"; under "Feminism," "*See* Woman." Where additional entries in the book may provide further insight, we have used *See also*. For example, in the Index of Topics under "Propitiation," we find "*See also* Atonement"; under "War in Heaven," "*See also* Premortal existence."

4. We have chosen to confine ourselves to discussing beliefs, teachings, and doctrines of The Church of Jesus Christ of Latter-day Saints. We do not address policies, procedures, or programs, but we have allotted space to topics of special interest in modern Mormonism and today's larger religious world.

5. We have treated a few subjects that would not of themselves be considered beliefs or doctrines but may be historically important or indirectly related to doctrinal matters. Examples include such entries as "Dead Sea Scrolls" and "Ecumenism."

6. The length of an article does not indicate its doctrinal significance. Such vital doctrines as faith, repentance, and charity are deeply significant and are, of course, deserving of more space than we have given them. Thus, for example, the fact that the entry "Constitution of the United States of America" is lengthier than "Man of Holiness" is no indication that the former subject is more important than the latter.

We have been selective in the subjects we have chosen to address; this work is not intended to be exhaustive. Deeper insight into matters pertaining to the Book of Mormon, for example, can be found in the excellent work edited by our colleague Dennis L. Largey, *Book of Mormon Reference Companion* (Salt Lake City: Deseret Book, 2003). Moreover, no book on Latter-day Saint beliefs is a substitute for holy scripture. It is our desire to motivate readers to turn frequently to the scriptures as well as to the words of the prophets and apostles charged to guide the destiny of the Church in our day.

"How blessed we are to have the restored gospel of Jesus Christ," President Thomas S. Monson declared. "It provides answers to questions concerning where we came from, why we are here, and where we will go when we pass from this life. It provides meaning and purpose and hope to our lives" (112).

We have written here of the beliefs and teachings of the Restoration because we believe deeply in them and are fully committed to what God has wrought through modern prophets and apostles in these last days. While we have sought earnestly to be in harmony with scripture and with the teachings of our leaders, this work is not an official publication of either The Church of Jesus Christ of Latter-day Saints or Brigham Young University.

SOURCES

"Approaching Mormon Doctrine." In *Newsroom: The Official Resource for News Media, Opinion Leaders, and the Public.* Salt Lake City, 4 May 2007. Available at http://newsroom.lds.org/article/approaching-mormon-doctrine.

Clark, J. Reuben, Jr. "When Are Church Leaders' Words Entitled to Claim of Scripture?" *Church News,* 31 July 1954, 9–11.

Holland, Jeffrey R. "'My Words . . . Never Cease.'" *Ensign,* May 2008, 91–94.

Maxwell, Neal A. *One More Strain of Praise.* Salt Lake City: Bookcraft, 1999.

Monson, Thomas S. "Till We Meet Again," *Ensign,* Nov. 2010, 111–12.

Oaks, Dallin H. "The Challenge to Become." *Ensign,* Nov. 2000, 32–34.

Packer, Boyd K. "Little Children." *Ensign,* Nov. 1986, 16–18.

———. "The Twelve Apostles." *Ensign,* Nov. 1996, 6–8.

AARON

The Old Testament Aaron was the son of Amram and Jochebed of the tribe of Levi (Exodus 6:16–20), the brother of Miriam the prophetess (Exodus 15:20), and the older brother of the great Israelite deliverer and lawgiver, Moses (Exodus 6:20; 7:7). Aaron was chosen by Jehovah to assist Moses in his ministry and to be a spokesman for him (Exodus 4:10–16). He climbed Mount Sinai with Moses, Nadab, Abihu, and seventy elders and "saw the God of Israel" (Exodus 24:9–10). He held the Melchizedek Priesthood before the lesser priesthood was instituted (Taylor, 5). Aaron was an acknowledged leader among the people. He was given a presiding position over the elders and appointed as judge, along with Hur, in Moses' absence (Exodus 24:14; 32:1). Aaron's lasting stature is confirmed by his name being attached to the lesser priesthood for all time in order to distinguish it from the greater or Melchizedek Priesthood (D&C 84:18–27; 107:1, 20). "Why it is called the lesser priesthood is because it is an appendage to the greater, or the Melchizedek Priesthood, and has power in administering outward ordinances" (D&C 107:14).

Before Israel's great sin involving the golden calf, Aaron and his sons were chosen by the Lord to be the first to officiate in the priest's office, according to the directions received by Moses on Mount Sinai. They were clothed in "holy garments" made "for glory and for beauty," including a breastplate, ephod, robe, girdle, and bonnet (Exodus 28:2, 4, 40). They were then anointed with oil, consecrated, and sanctified "that they [might] minister unto me [the Lord] in the priest's office" (Exodus 28:41). Aaron's position then is comparable to that of presiding bishop in the Church today (Taylor, 5–6). After the Israelites transgressed against God at Mount Sinai by worshipping the golden calf, God removed from Israel as a whole the keys of the Melchizedek Priesthood, the higher law, and the ordinances thereof, and Aaron and his sons administered the law of carnal commandments, which was added to the gospel "because of transgression" (Galatians 3:19).

Aaron was apparently a skilled craftsman, for it was he of whom certain Israelites demanded the creation of images of false gods. He instructed the people to take off their gold earrings, from which he fashioned a golden calf and built an altar (Exodus 32:1–5). Moses destroyed the golden calf by burning it, grinding it to powder, scattering it on water, and then making the "children of Israel drink of it" (Exodus 32:20).

The full extent of Aaron's involvement in Israel's act of apostasy is not known (Exodus 32:4–5, 21–22, 25), but his sin was not a sin unto death as it was for others (Exodus 32:26–28). Though he seems to have repented of his wrongdoing (Exodus 32:29–33), he was later involved in other misdeeds. After leaving Sinai on the way to the plains of Moab, Aaron joined with his sister, Miriam, in murmuring against Moses' authority. Aaron repented, but Miriam continued in her errant ways for a time and was cursed with leprosy (Numbers 12:1–15). Later, both Aaron and Moses were forbidden to enter the promised land because they had failed to honor the Lord and had exalted themselves in finding water, though it was really God who had provided the water when Israel thirsted in the wilderness of Zin (Numbers 20:1–12, 24).

After the Israelites journeyed to Mount Hor, according to the Lord's command Moses led Aaron to the top of the mountain, stripped him of his priestly garments, and put them on Aaron's son Eleazar and on Eleazar's son. Aaron died on the mount in the sight of all the people at the age of 123 years. All the house of Israel mourned thirty days for him (Numbers 20:22–29).

The pattern of Aaron's call to the priesthood was the model and pattern in the Church of Jesus Christ of the meridian dispensation: "And no man taketh this honour unto himself, but he that is called of God, as was Aaron" (Hebrews 5:4). That is how priesthood holders must be chosen and ordained today, as Aaron was: by God through his authorized administrators (D&C 27:8; 132:58–59). Those who magnify their calling in the priesthood "become the sons of Moses and of Aaron" (D&C 84:33–34).

In the Book of Mormon, *Aaron* is the name of three prominent individuals: a Jaredite king (Ether 1:16), a king of the Lamanites

(Mormon 2:9; 3:4; Moroni 9:17), and a son of King Mosiah (Mosiah 27:34). Aaron, the son of Mosiah, was at first an unbeliever who sought to destroy the Church of God (Mosiah 27:8–10, 34). He was converted after an angel appeared to him and his companions, including Alma the Younger (Mosiah 27:11, 32). He repented and began to preach the word of God with power (Mosiah 27:32–28:8). Aaron refused to be named king (Mosiah 29:3), choosing instead to teach the gospel in the land of the Lamanites. He and his brethren are excellent models of sacrifice for God's kingdom, missionary service, and gospel teachers. They had "searched the scriptures diligently" and "given themselves to much prayer, and fasting," possessing the "spirit of prophecy, and the spirit of revelation, and when they taught, they taught with power and authority of God" (Alma 17:2–3).

A most impressive example of Aaron's power, authority, and wisdom as a teacher is demonstrated in the dramatic conversion story of King Lamoni's father (Alma 22). "When Aaron saw that the king would believe his words, he began from the creation of Adam, reading the scriptures" to him (Alma 22:12), teaching him the three pillars of eternity—the Creation, the Fall, and the Atonement (Alma 22:13–16)—with profound and transforming results for the king, the queen, and their household (Alma 22:17–23). Aaron demonstrated both the instructional pattern and the standard of personal worthiness to be emulated by all gospel teachers.

SOURCE
Taylor, John. *Items on Priesthood.* Salt Lake City: Deseret News, 1881.

ACS

AARONIC PRIESTHOOD

The Aaronic Priesthood was revealed to and established by Moses as a separate order of priesthood because ancient Israel rebelled against God, refused to be sanctified by participation in the ordinances of the Melchizedek Priesthood, and committed an act of apostasy in worshipping the golden calf (Exodus 32). Therefore, God in his wrath took away from Israel as a whole the Melchizedek Priesthood, his "holy order, and the ordinances thereof," as well as his divine presence (JST, Exodus 34:1). He "swore that they should not enter into his rest while in the wilderness, which rest is the fulness of his glory" (D&C 84:24).

What continued with Israel was a lesser priesthood (lesser in power and authority to the Melchizedek Priesthood), to which was added a lesser law, the "law of a carnal commandment," administered by the lesser priesthood (JST, Exodus 34:2; D&C 84:26). This lesser priesthood was conferred upon Aaron and his sons (Exodus 28) as "an everlasting priesthood throughout their generations" (Exodus 40:15). They were consecrated and anointed (ordained) to officiate in the office of priest (Exodus 28:41; 40:12–16), to administer the sacrificial system in ancient Israel (Leviticus 1:11; 3:2, 5), and to possess the keys of, or the administrative power over, the lesser priesthood. Therefore, the lesser priesthood is called the Aaronic Priesthood "because it was conferred upon Aaron and his seed, throughout all their generations" (D&C 107:13). The lesser priesthood is also called the Levitical Priesthood because the lesser priesthood was conferred upon members of the tribe of Levi (Aaron's tribe) between the ages of thirty and fifty (Numbers 3–4).

The two names, Aaronic and Levitical, are sometimes used interchangeably today (D&C 107:6). In ancient times, however, three offices in the lesser priesthood were differentiated: Levites (any worthy male member of the tribe of Levi), priests (Aaron and his male descendants), and the high priest (chosen from among the eligible firstborn male descendants of Aaron). Thus, Aaron and his descendants held greater offices and possessed greater responsibilities in the Levitical Priesthood than the other Levites. The high priest was the presiding officer (or president) of the Aaronic or Levitical Priesthood. Aaron was the first high priest (Exodus 28–29; Leviticus 8; D&C 84:18).

John the Baptist was a descendant of Aaron (Luke 1:5, 13), held the keys of the Aaronic Priesthood, and served as the last legal administrator of the Aaronic order before the restoration of the Melchizedek Priesthood by Jesus Christ in the meridian dispensation (*Joseph Smith,* 81–82; JST, John 1:15–28). During another period of apostasy ensuing at the death of apostles and prophets in the Old and New Worlds, the Melchizedek and Aaronic Priesthoods were taken from the earth. When the Lord determined the time was right, the two priesthoods were brought back to the earth. The lesser priesthood, which is a preparatory priesthood—preparing and training its worthy possessors to receive the Melchizedek Priesthood—was restored first. As a resurrected being, John the Baptist came to Joseph Smith and Oliver Cowdery and conferred upon them the Levitical Priesthood in this final dispensation on 15 May 1829 (D&C 13:1; 27:8). When John the Baptist appeared to perform this task, he explained that he was acting under the direction of Peter, James, and John, the ancient apostles who held the keys of the higher priesthood, called the Priesthood of Melchizedek. He promised Joseph and Oliver that in due time the higher priesthood would be conferred upon them (Smith, *History,* 1:39–42). As revealed and recorded in modern revelation, the offices in the Aaronic Priesthood now include bishop, priest, teacher, and deacon, each with distinct responsibilities (D&C 20:38–60, 64; 68:14–21). Each ordained deacon, teacher, and priest belongs to a quorum of his peers, presided over by a quorum president (D&C 107:85–87). In this dispensation, "the bishopric is the presidency of this priesthood, and holds the keys or authority of the same" (D&C 107:15), with the bishop officiating as the president of the Aaronic Priesthood in each ward (D&C 107:87–88).

There are important contrasts between the lesser or Aaronic Priesthood and the greater or Melchizedek Priesthood. The Aaronic Priesthood deals with the temporal matters and outward ordinances of the law and the gospel (D&C 107:20; see also 1 Chronicles 23:27–32), including "the keys of the ministering of angels, and of the gospel of repentance, and of baptism by immersion for the remission of sins" (D&C 13:1). The Melchizedek Priesthood holds the "keys of all the spiritual blessings of the church—to have the privilege of receiving the mysteries of the kingdom," "even the key of the knowledge of God" (D&C 107:18–19; 84:19). Through its ordinances "the power of godliness is manifest," and the face of God may be beheld (D&C 84:20, 22).

In ancient times, receipt of the lesser priesthood was based on heredity, bestowed on individuals because of the lineage of their father and mother. But the Melchizedek Priesthood came without respect to parents, or "without descent" (JST, Hebrews 7:3). The lesser priesthood was a "schoolmaster" to bring or prepare Israel to understand and receive Christ (Galatians 3:24). The Melchizedek Priesthood is the very priesthood of the Son of God, and "all other authorities or offices" (including those of the Aaronic Priesthood) are appendages to it (D&C 107:3, 5). Perfection does not come through the lesser or Levitical Priesthood but only through the Melchizedek Priesthood (Hebrews 7:11). The lesser priesthood is not received with an oath, but the high priesthood is (JST, Hebrews 7:19–21; D&C 84:35–38). In modern times the Lord has made clear that whosoever is faithful in "obtaining these two priesthoods, . . . and the magnifying their calling, are sanctified by the Spirit" and "become the sons of Moses and of Aaron and the seed of Abraham, and the church and kingdom, and the elect of God" (D&C 84:34).

SOURCES

Joseph Smith [manual]. Teachings of Presidents of the Church series. Salt Lake City: The Church of Jesus Christ of Latter-day Saints, 2007.

Smith, Joseph. *History of The Church of Jesus Christ of Latter-day Saints.* Edited by B. H. Roberts. 7 vols. 2d ed. rev. Salt Lake City: The Church of Jesus Christ of Latter-day Saints, 1932–51.

ACS

ABBA

The word *Abba* means "father" in Aramaic, one of the languages spoken in Palestine in Jesus' day. Grammatically, it is an emphatic form meaning "the father," but when used personally, especially in prayer, it means "my father" (*Interpreter's,* 1:3). It is found three times in the New Testament: Mark 14:36; Romans 8:15; and Galatians 4:6. During New Testament times, even though "Greek was becoming the *lingua franca* of the whole Near East, Aramaic continued both as a literary language and as the household language of most Jews" (Meyers, 65). Thus, the word *Abba* "is assumed to have been a common colloquial one, doubtless derived from use in the family circle" (*Interpreter's,* 1:3).

Theologically, this usage is important because it lends a tone of intimacy to Mark's report of Jesus' prayer in Gethsemane at the time of his suffering (Mark 14:36). Jesus is addressing his literal Father, the Father of both his physical and his spirit body, in the hour of his great extremity. His use of *Abba,* a word most likely learned in the family setting, emphasizes his closeness to his Father. The Joseph Smith Translation of John 3:34 likewise emphasizes the closeness that existed between God the Father and his Son, our Savior, when it reports: "For he whom God hath sent speaketh the words of God: for God giveth him [Jesus] not the Spirit by measure, for he dwelleth in him, even the fulness."

Significantly, the apostle Paul uses the term *Abba* in his epistles to teach the profound doctrine of our closeness to the Father and our joint heirship through Jesus Christ. Through the Savior's atonement, we inherit all the Father possesses (D&C 84:38). To the Romans, Paul wrote: "For as many as are led by the Spirit of God, they are the sons of God. For ye have not received the spirit of bondage again to fear; but ye have received the Spirit of adoption, whereby we cry, Abba, Father. The Spirit itself beareth witness with our spirit, that we are the children of God: and if children, then heirs; heirs of God, and joint-heirs with Christ; if so be that we suffer with him, that we may be also glorified together" (Romans 8:14–17).

Thus, to members of the early Church of Jesus Christ, *Abba* had important theological implications, pointing to both Jesus' suffering and his relationship to his Father as well as to the disciples' sought for relationship with God the Father through the sacrifice of Jesus Christ. Among the Jews living after Jesus' mortal ministry, especially the rabbis, the term *Abba* is used as a title of great honor.

SOURCES

The Interpreter's Dictionary of the Bible: An Illustrated Encyclopedia. Edited by George Arthur Buttrick. 5 vols. Nashville, Tenn.: Abingdon Press, 1962.

Myers, Eric M., and James F. Strange. *Archaeology, the Rabbis, and Early Christianity.* Nashville, Tenn.: Abingdon, 1981.

ACS

ABORTION

In "The Family: A Proclamation to the World," the First Presidency and Council of the Twelve Apostles declared, "We affirm the sanctity of life and of its importance in God's eternal plan" (102). From Mount Sinai, God declared, "Thou shalt not kill" (Exodus 20:13). In this dispensation he added an important phrase to that divine decree: "nor do anything like unto it" (D&C 59:6). Elective abortion—the premeditated termination of the life of an unborn child—is, as President Spencer W. Kimball taught, "one of the most revolting and sinful practices in this day" (7). Although abortion is "like unto" murder, the Church has declared that there are rare circumstances in which an abortion could be considered justifiable. The circumstances include "incest or rape, when the life or health of the mother is judged by competent medical authority to be in serious jeopardy, or when the fetus is known . . . to have serious defects that will not allow the baby to survive beyond birth." Because of the serious nature of such an action, persons facing that decision are counseled to "consult with their local ecclesiastical leaders and to pray in great earnestness, receiving a confirmation through prayer before proceeding" (Hinckley, 70).

Although abortion is a sin for which forgiveness may be obtained, members of the Church who encourage, financially support, perform, or submit to abortion may be subject to Church discipline, including excommunication. A person may not be baptized into the Church who has been involved with an abortion until he or she is judged by the proper Church authority to have truly repented.

SOURCES

First Presidency and Council of the Twelve Apostles. "The Family: A Proclamation to the World." *Ensign,* Nov. 1995, 102.

Hinckley, Gordon B. "What Are People Asking about Us?" *Ensign,* Nov. 1998, 70–72.

Kimball, Spencer W. "Guidelines to Carry Forth the Work of God in Cleanliness." *Ensign,* May 1974, 4–8.

BLT

ABRAHAM

Abraham was one of the greatest prophets and patriarchs who ever lived. He entered into the gospel covenant with Jehovah, promising obedience and righteous behavior and, in return, securing to himself and his posterity the promises of priesthood power, lands of everlasting inheritance, an innumerable posterity, and all the blessings of the gospel, including eternal life (Abraham 2:6, 9–11). Through Abraham and his posterity, all the nations of the earth would be blessed. Thus, the covenant he received included the responsibility of missionary labor (Abraham 2:9–10, 15; Genesis 17:4–7; Galatians 3:8).

Abraham was born in Ur of the Chaldees (Genesis 11:27–28) into a family that had turned to idolatry and human sacrifice (Abraham 1:5–7). This was true even of Abraham's own father, Terah (Abraham 2:5). Yet Abraham rose above such false teachings and sought earnestly to know the Lord (Abraham 2:12), to be "a follower of righteousness," to receive the high priesthood, "to be a father of many nations" and "a prince of peace" (Abraham 1:2)—in other words, a type of Jesus Christ. Abraham did not wait for God to come to him with these blessings. He sought for them, actively and intensely (Abraham 1:2, 4). Ultimately, Jehovah appeared to Abraham and conferred upon him the promises of the covenant (Abraham 2:6, 8).

The biblical story of Abraham's life is found in Genesis 11:26–25:10. He was originally known as Abram (Hebrew, "exalted father"), but with the covenant came a new name, Abraham (Hebrew, perhaps meaning "father of a multitude"; Bible Dictionary, "Abraham"). Three of the great religions of the world—Judaism, Christianity, and Islam—trace their literal and spiritual ancestry back to him, and are sometimes referred to as the "Abrahamic religions." He is known in scripture as the "Friend of God" (James 2:23) and the "father of the faithful" (D&C 138:41). Jews regard Abraham as both the first Hebrew and the first Jew (Genesis 14:13). Muslims regard Abraham as *Khalil Ullah,* "friend of God."

Abraham had three wives: Sarah (Hebrew, "princess," though in Genesis 11:29–17:15 she is called Sarai; Bible Dictionary, "Sarah"); Hagar (Hebrew, "flight"; Genesis 16; 21:9–21; 25:12; Bible Dictionary, "Hagar"); and Keturah (Hebrew, "incense"; Genesis 25:1–4; 1 Chronicles 1:32–33; Bible Dictionary, "Keturah"). With them Abraham became the founding patriarch of the Israelites, Ishmaelites, Midianites, and many other groups. According to the Bible, the fulness of the Abrahamic covenant came through his son Isaac (Genesis 17:21; 21:12; 22:16–18; 25:5), who, in the sense of the covenant, is called Abraham's "only son" (Genesis 22:16; Hebrews 11:17). Nonetheless, Ishmael was also given the promise of becoming a great nation (Genesis 17:20; 21:13; 25:16) and is accounted with Abraham's seed. In truth, all individuals become the seed of Abraham—lineal descendants by birth and others by adoption—if they accept the gospel covenant through priesthood ordinances (Galatians 3:7–29; Smith, 3:380). All men who receive the Aaronic and Melchizedek Priesthoods, and are faithful, are specifically designated "the seed of Abraham" (D&C 84:34).

From the record kept by Abraham and translated by Joseph Smith, now called the book of Abraham, we learn much about Abraham's life that is not recorded in the Bible. The book of Abraham describes the hardships Abraham suffered under his idolatrous father, which culminated in an attempt to make him a human sacrifice by handing him over to the priest of Pharaoh then residing in the land of Chaldea (Abraham 1:5–8). Abraham described the altar on which he was offered as possessing "the form of a bedstead" (Abraham 1:13). Facsimile no. 1 in the book of Abraham shows a lion couch altar (in the form of a bedstead) of the type seen today among the ruins and artifacts of ancient Egypt. The name of Abraham has been found in papyrus documents, one attestation "accompanied by a picture, a lion couch scene similar to the one in facsimile no. 1 of the book of Abraham, but this picture is oriented in reverse" (Gee, 60).

Though that papyrus document with the lion couch image is removed from Abraham's time by two millennia (it dates from the third century A.D.), it came from Thebes in Egypt, where the Joseph Smith papyri originated. The text does not explain the connection between Abraham and the lion couch, but there is no doubt that the papyrus document implies one. In fact, "the figure on the lion couch in this papyrus is a woman. . . . Elements on this papyrus remind one of the three virgins Abraham wrote of who 'were offered up because of their virtue; they would not bow down to worship gods of wood or of stone, therefore they were killed upon this altar, and it was done after the manner of the Egyptians' (Abr. 1:11)" (Gee, 61).

Abraham was spared death as he prayed to the Almighty, and "the angel of his presence" stood by him and immediately unloosed his bands (Abraham 1:15). The wickedness of human sacrifice and Abraham's divinely effected rescue stand in stark contrast to the supreme test of the patriarch's life—God's seemingly contradictory request that Abraham take his only son, Isaac, go to the land of Moriah, "and offer him there for a burnt offering upon one of the mountains" the Lord would show him (Genesis 22:1–2). Abraham proved his unwavering loyalty to God by not withholding his son. The Prophet Joseph Smith stated: "The sacrifice required of Abraham in the offering up of Isaac, shows that if a man would attain to the keys of the kingdom of an endless life; he must sacrifice all things" (5:555).

Of Abraham's sacrifice the Lord himself said: "Abraham was commanded to offer his son Isaac; nevertheless, it was written: Thou shalt not kill. Abraham, however, did not refuse, and it was accounted unto him for righteousness" (D&C 132:36). The prophet Jacob called Abraham's sacrifice of Isaac a similitude of the sacrifice of our Father in Heaven of his Only Begotten Son (Jacob 4:5). The Lord upholds Abraham's behavior in this regard as the standard for all to emulate. Speaking of Church members who had been afflicted, persecuted, and cast out from the land of their inheritance, the Lord said: "Yet I will own them, and they shall be mine in that day when I shall come to make up my jewels. Therefore, they must needs be chastened and tried, even as Abraham, who was commanded to offer up his only son" (D&C 101:3–4).

Muslims believe it was Ishmael, rather than Isaac, who was almost sacrificed by Abraham. The event is commemorated yearly in the celebration of Eid al-Adha, one of the most important festivals (some say the most important) in Islam. On that occasion each Muslim family sacrifices a domestic animal—a sheep, goat, or even a camel—as a symbol of Abraham and Ishmael's sacrifice. The meat of the sacrificed animal is divided among the family members participating in the sacrifice and shared with the poor. This feast celebrates God's sparing the son of Abraham as it focuses on the patriarch's test and his willingness to obey God's command.

We also learn in the book of Abraham that Abraham was told by God to leave his homeland in Ur and travel to Canaan (Abraham 2:3–4), "for I have purposed to take thee away . . . and to make of thee a minister to bear my name in a strange land which I will give unto thy seed after thee for an everlasting possession, when they hearken to my voice" (Abraham 2:6). Thus, obedience to God is the key element for Abraham's posterity to practice in order to possess the land of inheritance promised under the Abrahamic covenant.

When famine intensified in Canaan, Abraham traveled south to Egypt (Abraham 2:21). In preparation for his visit there, the Lord showed the great patriarch a vision of the heavens so that he could better declare God's word to the Egyptians by teaching from a common point of reference (Abraham 3:15). He saw the order of the planets and the stars and their times, seasons, and revolutions. He saw that one planet is above another in a great chain of existence extending to Kolob, the governing body of the heavens, the planet nigh unto the throne of God, which is after the reckoning of the Lord's time. He saw that one revolution of that sphere (a day unto the Lord) is as a thousand years of earth's time (Abraham 3:1–9). He was then shown the organized intelligences in the kingdom of heaven, one more intelligent than another in a grand order of existence extending to the Lord himself, who is "more intelligent than they all" (Abraham 3:19, 22).

All of this was to teach Abraham a profound lesson that he could then teach to the Egyptians, who were noted observers of the heavens. As the stars in heaven are ordered, so are the spirits of God's vast kingdom. As the stars are governed, so is God's kingdom. As is Kolob, so is Christ. "The heavens are the pattern for the Church, the Church is the pattern for the home, the home is the pattern for the individual. The principle of unity and order is equally important in each sphere. Further, Abraham's vision illustrates that without gradation of assignment and responsibility, there can be no order. Two people cannot occupy the same position at the same time any more than can planets. . . . Each is to assume his or her own divinely given sphere of responsibility. All serve in capacities in which there are those who are greater and lesser in authority. If we have been called to preside over someone, then someone else has been called to preside over us, and so on until we come to the very throne of heaven itself. As the stars are governed, so the heavens are governed; as the heavens are governed, so the kingdom of heaven is governed; as the kingdom of heaven is governed, so all who would be its citizens must learn to govern themselves" (McConkie, "Heavens," 245). In this context, Abraham learned of his chosen status, that he was among the noble and great spirits in the premortal existence whom God made his rulers. He came to understand the Savior's status as one "like unto God" (Abraham 3:24) and his offer to become the Redeemer of all and the executor of the Father's plan. And he learned of Lucifer's expulsion from the Father's presence because he "kept not his first estate" (Abraham 3:28).

In the revelation on the new and everlasting covenant, including eternal marriage (D&C 132), the Lord described Abraham's valiance and admonished Joseph Smith to follow him: "Abraham received all things, whatsoever he received, by revelation and commandment, by my word, saith the Lord, and hath entered into his exaltation and sitteth upon his throne. Abraham received promises concerning his seed, and of the fruit of his loins—from whose loins ye are, namely, my servant Joseph—which were to continue so long as they were in the world; and as touching Abraham and his seed, out of the world they should continue; both in the world and out of the world should they continue as innumerable as the stars; or, if ye were to count the sand upon the seashore ye could not number them.

"This promise is yours also, because ye are of Abraham, and the promise was made unto Abraham; and by this law is the continuation of the works of my Father, wherein he glorifieth himself. Go ye, therefore, and do the works of Abraham; enter ye into my law and ye shall be saved" (D&C 132:29–32).

Furthermore, the Lord promised Joseph Smith the same exaltation Abraham now enjoys: "For I am the Lord thy God, and will be with thee even unto the end of the world, and through all eternity; for verily I seal upon you your exaltation, and prepare a throne for you in the kingdom of my Father, with Abraham your father" (D&C 132:49).

Abraham received the high priesthood from his presiding leader, Melchizedek (D&C 84:14). He was also blessed by Melchizedek on the occasion of Abraham's rescue of Lot and the recovery of his material goods. At that time he paid tithes to Melchizedek (Genesis 14:13–20). Elder Bruce R. McConkie believed that because of what happened next, the sacrament "may well have been prefigured, some two thousand years before its formal institution among men, when 'Melchizedek, king of Salem, brought forth bread and wine; and he brake bread and blest it, and he blest the wine, he being the priest of the most high God. And he gave to Abram' (JST, Genesis 14:17–18)" (384).

After a life of exact obedience, Abraham died at the age of 175 years and was buried in the cave of Machpelah. There he was "gathered to his people" (Genesis 25:7–9), for Machpelah was also the final resting place of Sarah (Genesis 23:19), Isaac and Rebekah (Genesis 49:30–31), and Jacob and Leah (Genesis 49:31; 50:13). Herod the Great built over the Tomb of the Patriarchs the huge shrine that can still be seen in Hebron. Abraham's purchase of the burial plot is a story that emphasizes his absolute integrity (Genesis 23).

In all things Abraham was faithful. He established the pattern for Isaac and Jacob to follow. Because God could not withhold the realization of promised blessings, "they have entered into their exaltation, according to the promises, and sit upon thrones, and are not angels but are gods" (D&C 132:37).

SOURCES

Gee, John. "Research and Perspectives: Abraham in Ancient Egyptian Texts." *Ensign,* Jul. 1992, 60–62.

McConkie, Bruce R. *The Promised Messiah: The First Coming of Christ.* Salt Lake City: Deseret Book, 1978.

McConkie, Joseph F. "The Heavens Testify of Christ." In Robert L. Millet and Kent P. Jackson, eds., *The Pearl of Great Price,* 239–45. Vol. 2 of Studies in Scripture series. Salt Lake City: Randall Book, 1985.

Smith, Joseph. *History of The Church of Jesus Christ of Latter-day Saints.* Edited by B. H. Roberts. 7 vols. 2d ed. rev. Salt Lake City: The Church of Jesus Christ of Latter-day Saints, 1932–51.

ACS

ABRAHAM, BOOK OF

The book of Abraham was first published in 1842 in the Church periodical *Times and Seasons* and appeared in 1851 in the first edition of the Pearl of Great Price, prepared in Great Britain by Elder Franklin D. Richards of the Quorum of the Twelve Apostles. In the summer of 1835 members of the Church purchased from Michael Chandler four mummies and two or more papyrus scrolls that had been discovered in Egypt by a man named Antonio Lebolo. The Prophet Joseph Smith showed little interest in the mummies but was fascinated by the papyri. Through the Urim and Thummim and with W. W. Phelps and Oliver Cowdery as scribes, Joseph began to translate "some of the characters or hieroglyphics, and much to our joy found that one of the rolls contained the writings of Abraham, another the writings of Joseph of Egypt, etc.,—a more full account of which will appear in its place as I proceed to examine or unfold them. Truly we can say, the Lord is beginning to reveal the abundance of peace and truth" (Smith, 2:236).

In his journal entry of 1 October 1835, the Prophet recorded that "during the research, the principles of astronomy as understood by Father Abraham and the ancients unfolded to our understanding" (2:286). The book of Abraham and the three facsimiles, as we have them in the Pearl of Great Price, were published in the *Times and Seasons* in March 1842. Nearly a year later, in the 1 February 1843 issue, *Times and Seasons* editor John Taylor encouraged the Saints to renew their subscriptions to the paper, adding, "We would further state that we had the promise of Br. Joseph, to furnish us with further extracts from the Book of Abraham" (4: 95).

The history of the papyri after the death of the Prophet is sketchy. The Egyptian relics were kept by Lucy Mack Smith until her death and were then sold by Emma Smith Bidamon to a Mr. A. Combs. Combs sold two of the mummies and some papyri to the Saint Louis Museum in 1856; in 1863 they were sold to the Chicago Museum (later renamed the Woods Museum). It had generally been assumed that all of the papyri were destroyed in the Great Chicago Fire of 1871, but in 1967 it was announced that Dr. Aziz Atiya, a professor of Middle Eastern Studies at the University of Utah, had found eleven papyrus fragments, including Facsimile One, in the New York Metropolitan Museum of Art. Not being a Latter-day Saint himself (he was a Coptic Christian) but being somewhat familiar with Latter-day Saint culture and the Pearl of Great Price, Dr. Atiya recognized Facsimile One and contacted Church leaders, who eventually acquired the papyrus fragments.

Committed Latter-day Saints and critics of the faith alike were intrigued with what would come of the find. The latter group exulted that once and for all the book of Abraham would be exposed as a figment of Joseph Smith's fertile imagination. The translation of the eleven fragments and the facsimile by trained Egyptologists revealed parts of the ancient Egyptian Book of Breathings, which is an excerpt of the larger Book of the Dead. It is actually a funerary text—material associated with the burial and future state of the dead. In other words, the fragments seem to have nothing to do with the person and work of Abraham.

H. Donl Peterson, former professor of ancient scripture at Brigham Young University and dedicated student of the book of Abraham, observed: "The Book of Abraham and Joseph's papyri were described as 'beautifully written on papyrus, with black, and a small part red, ink or paint, in perfect preservation.' The eleven fragments recovered from the Metropolitan Museum of Art in New York City do not fit that description at all. What was discovered was Facsimile One and some other fragments unrelated to the published account of the present Book of Abraham. They were part of the original scrolls once owned by Joseph Smith but not directly related to the Abrahamic text. The partial text of the Book of Breathings returned to the Church in 1967 was not the text for the Book of Abraham" (173).

Professor Peterson said that the book of Abraham "was not finished. In fact it was hardly begun. The Book of Abraham was a lengthy record. . . . Oliver Cowdery spoke of volumes necessary to contain it. Only two short installments were published during Joseph Smith's lifetime, although more was promised. Had not Joseph Smith's last sixteen months been so turbulent, no doubt more of the translation would have been forthcoming, as he had promised. We have but a small fraction of a rather lengthy record" (174).

"Is the book of Abraham true?" Elder Bruce R. McConkie asked. "Yes, but it is not complete; it stops almost in midair. Would that the Prophet had gone on in his translation or revelation as the case may be" (21).

SOURCES
"The Book of Abraham." *Times and Seasons* 3, no. 9 (1 Mar. 1842): 703–6.
"The Book of Abraham." *Times and Seasons* 3, no. 10 (15 Mar. 1842): 719–22.
McConkie, Bruce R. "The Doctrinal Restoration." In Monte S. Nyman and Robert L. Millet, eds. *The Joseph Smith Translation: The Restoration of Plain and Precious Things,* 1–22. Provo, Utah: Brigham Young University, 1985.
Peterson, H. Donl. "The History and Significance of the Book of Abraham." In Robert L. Millet and Kent P. Jackson, eds. *The Pearl of Great Price,* 161–81. Vol. 2 of Studies in Scripture series. Salt Lake City: Randall Book, 1985.
Smith, Joseph. *History of The Church of Jesus Christ of Latter-day Saints.* Edited by B. H. Roberts. 7 vols. 2d ed. rev. Salt Lake City: The Church of Jesus Christ of Latter-day Saints, 1932–51.
Taylor, John. "Notice." *Times and Seasons* 4, no. 6 (1 Feb. 1843): 95.

RLM

ABRAHAM, SEED OF

Every book of scripture makes reference to Abraham's posterity as the heirs and stewards of the Abrahamic covenant (Abraham 2:8–11). Frequently, these "children of the prophets" (Acts 3:25) or "children of the promise" (Romans 9:8; see also Galatians 4:28) are collectively named "Israel" or the "house of Israel" in reference to Jacob, Abraham's grandson, whose name God changed to Israel (Genesis 32:28).

John the Baptist warned those who falsely assumed that only literal, lineal descendants of Abraham would qualify for God's covenant promises. John boldly declared, "God is able of these stones to raise up children unto Abraham" (Luke 3:8; Matthew 3:9). Similarly, the apostle Paul cautioned the Roman Saints that "they are not all Israel, which are of Israel" (Romans 9:6). Those of non-Israelite lineage are adopted into the family of Abraham through their faith and obedience to the principles and ordinances of the gospel of Jesus Christ.

More binding than literal descent from Abraham, Abraham's children are those who "do the works of Abraham" (John 8:39) and have the faith of Abraham, whether they are Abraham's literal descendants or not (Galatians 3:6–9; Romans 4:13). Nephi explained that "as many of the Gentiles as will repent are the covenant people of the Lord; and as many of the Jews as will not repent shall be cast off; for the Lord covenanteth with none save it be with them that repent and believe in his Son, who is the Holy One of Israel" (2 Nephi 30:2). Through modern revelation, the Lord has taught that magnifying callings within or under the direction of the priesthood further secures our place as Abraham's seed (D&C 84:33–34).

Being the seed of Abraham does not automatically signify chosenness or election but identifies the responsibility to take the gospel to all the families of the earth (Genesis 12:3). Various groups of people at different times in the history of the world have been specifically identified with the responsibilities of Abraham's seed, including the people of Lehi at the time of the Savior's visit (3 Nephi 20:25), as well as the Latter-day Saints (D&C 103:17). Truly, the Lord "covenanted with Abraham that [He] would remember his seed forever" (2 Nephi 29:14) and that his promises to Abraham's seed would "continue so long as they were in the world; and . . . out of the world they should continue" (D&C 132:30).

In addition to the descendants of Sarah's son, Isaac (Genesis 21:2–3), Abraham's seed are to be found among the descendants of Hagar's son, Ishmael (Genesis 16:15), and Keturah's sons, Zimran, Jokshan, Medan, Midian, Ishbak, and Shuah (Genesis 25:1–2). Through their posterity, these sons of Abraham, individually and collectively, inaugurated multiple nations and religions of the world. Because Jews, Christians, and Muslims all look to Abraham as their father, Abraham has literally become the "father of many nations" (Abraham 1:2; Genesis 17:4, 5).

CFO

ABRAHAMIC COVENANT

The Abrahamic covenant is an important aspect of the new and everlasting covenant, the fulness of the gospel of Jesus Christ. God entered into a covenant with Abraham, promising him that he and his posterity would receive the gospel (Galatians 3:8), the priesthood, eternal life, and a land inheritance (Genesis 13:14–16; 15:1–6; 17:1–7; JST, Genesis 13; 15; Abraham 2:8–11, 19). These promises are often called "the promises made to the fathers" (D&C 2:2; see also 27:10; 98:32), inasmuch as they were perpetuated through Isaac, Jacob, Joseph, and their descendants.

In fulfillment of part of the covenant, Abraham's posterity has been scattered throughout the earth in order that God's covenant people may serve as a leavening influence among all his children. A person who joins The Church of Jesus Christ of Latter-day Saints, entering into covenant with Christ through accepting the restored gospel and being baptized by those having proper authority, enters into the Abrahamic covenant. To become a son or daughter of Christ is tantamount to becoming a son or daughter of Abraham (Galatians 3:27–29; 2 Nephi 30:1–2). Furthermore, those who continue faithful and enter the holy temple to be endowed and married for eternity qualify, through faithfulness to their covenants, for all the blessings of Abraham, Isaac, and Jacob.

RLM

ABRAHAM'S BOSOM

In the parable of the rich man and Lazarus, Jesus speaks of a rich man who finds himself in hell while a beggar named Lazarus goes to "Abraham's bosom" when they die (Luke 16:22). Abraham's bosom refers to that portion of the spirit world where the righteous await resurrection after they die. It is the same place that Alma called "paradise" and described as "a state of happiness, . . . a state of rest, a state of peace, where they shall rest from all their troubles, and from all care, and sorrow" (Alma 40:12).

According to the parable, "a great gulf" separated hell from Abraham's bosom, precluding any interaction between the two realms (Luke 16:26). One consummate blessing of the Savior's ministry came as he bridged that gulf by organizing and commissioning righteous spirits in paradise to "carry the light of the gospel to them that were in darkness, even to all the spirits of men" (D&C 138:30). Abraham is named among the "great and mighty ones who were assembled in this vast congregation of the righteous" dead in paradise, none of whom were yet resurrected (D&C 138:38).

Describing paradise as Abraham's bosom communicates the importance of family and the close sociality and felicity the righteous spirits share in this temporary abode of peace, rest, and gospel teaching.

CFO

ACCOUNTABILITY

In his work "to bring to pass the immortality and eternal life" of his children, God the Father holds each of us accountable for our words, works, and thoughts during mortality (Moses 1:39; Exodus 32:33; Alma 12:14). Through his great plan of happiness, the Father prepared a world where we could learn and grow by being responsible for our choices and for the property and opportunities over which he has made us stewards (D&C 42:32; 134:1). He gives laws that teach us good from evil, provides conditions in which opposing options are available for us to choose freely, and then allows us to experience the consequences of those choices (2 Nephi 2:5–19). After the fall of Adam and Eve, God "saw that it was expedient" that his children "should know concerning the things whereof he had appointed unto them" (Alma 12:28). Therefore, God first made the plan of salvation known to them, and then he gave them commandments for which he would hold them accountable (Alma 12:30–32).

At the final judgment, we will give an accounting of what we said and did in our time of probation, either to our justification or condemnation (Matthew 12:36–37). There the dead will stand before God to be judged out of the "books, according to their works" (Revelation 20:12).

If we repent, manifest faith in Jesus Christ, and rely on his infinite atonement, our idle and sinful choices will not condemn us before God (Mosiah 3:21; Isaiah 53:10–11). The Father will consecrate our sincere faith in the Savior and our repentance for our mistakes, shortcomings, and sins "for the welfare of [our] soul" (2 Nephi 32:9). Likewise, through the mercy, merits, and grace of the Redeemer, the Lord does not hold accountable little children, those who are incapable of understanding God's requirements, or those who sin because they have not been taught the laws of God (2 Nephi 9:25–27; Romans 2:3–12).

CFO

ADAM

The first man created on earth was Adam, who was formed in the image and likeness of God (Genesis 1:26–27). As the head of the first dispensation of the everlasting gospel, Adam was instructed by God himself, by ministering angels, and by the power of the Holy Ghost (Moses 5:58–59). "God conversed with [Adam] face to face," the Prophet Joseph Smith taught. "In his presence he was permitted to stand, and from his own mouth he was permitted to receive instruction. He heard his voice, walked before him and gazed upon his glory, while intelligence burst upon his understanding, and enabled him to give names to the vast assemblage of his Maker's works" (*Lectures,* 13). As the Lord's first anointed prophet on earth, Adam was ordained to the holy priesthood (D&C 84:16) and taught and administered the principles and ordinances of the everlasting gospel (Moses 6:51–67). Many in the Judeo-Christian world view Adam and Eve, because of the Fall, as the reason for sin and suffering in the world; their actions are viewed as unfortunate at best and evil at worst. Because of modern revelation, however, Latter-day Saints reject this view and rejoice in the righteousness of Adam and Eve. The Book of Mormon teaches us that Adam knowingly and obediently "fell that men might be" (2 Nephi 2:25). It was Adam's faithful fall that initiated mortality, beginning the process by which all of God's children are able to participate in the plan of salvation and progress toward immortality and eternal life, which are God's work and glory (Moses 1:39).

Not only does the restored gospel teach us concerning Adam's mortal role as the first man, head of the first dispensation, and preacher of righteousness but it also teaches us through modern revelation concerning his premortal and postmortal missions. Before the world was created, Adam was known as "Michael, the prince, the archangel" (D&C 107:54). In Hebrew the name *Michael* means "who is like God." It was Michael, the premortal Adam, who "contended with the devil" (Jude 1:9) and led the forces of righteousness in the war in heaven (JST, Revelation 12:6–7).

Undoubtedly, the archangel joined with the Father and the Son in governing the kingdom of heaven and preparing the earth. President Brigham Young taught that "Father Adam came to assist in organizing the earth out of the crude material that was found" (16:167). Likewise, President Joseph Fielding Smith taught: "It is true that Adam helped to form this earth. He labored with our Savior Jesus Christ. I have a strong view or conviction that there were others also who assisted them" (1:74–75; see also Abraham 4).

Just as Michael helped prepare the earth, so will the postmortal Adam play a deeply significant role in preparing the earth for the Second Coming and the ultimate triumph of God's kingdom. He ministered to the Prophet Joseph Smith "on the banks of the Susquehanna, detecting the devil when he appeared as an angel of light!" (D&C 128:20). The Prophet taught that Adam was given the responsibility to oversee the ordinances of the gospel and "to reveal them from heaven, or to send angels to reveal them. . . . These angels are under the direction of Michael or Adam, who acts under the direction of the Lord" (4:207–9). Thus, the postmortal Adam was involved in the work of the Restoration and helps to oversee the earthly kingdom of God (D&C 78:16).

The Prophet Joseph Smith taught, as Daniel of old saw in vision, that the resurrected Adam—Michael, the prince, the archangel, and Ancient of Days—will hold a council at Adam-ondi-Ahman to prepare the human family for the coming of the Son of Man (D&C 116:1; Daniel 7:9–10, 13–14). "He (Adam) is the father of the human family and presides over the spirits of all men and all that have had the keys must stand before him in this grand council," the Prophet taught. "The Son of Man stands before him, and there is given him glory and dominion. Adam delivers up his stewardship to Christ, that which was delivered to him as holding the keys of the universe, but retains his standing as head of the human family" (3:386–87).

At the Savior's return, it will be Adam who "shall sound his trump and then shall all the dead awake, for their graves shall be opened, and they shall come forth—yea, even all" (D&C 29:26). As the father of the human family, Adam is also linked to the keys of the resurrection. Elder Bruce R. McConkie stated: "It also could well be that *Adam, who brought mortality and death into the world, was also permitted to restore the power that brings immortality and life to his descendants.* Christ, of course, in the ultimate sense holds the keys of the resurrection and of raising souls in immortality, but, as we also know, it is his practice to operate through his servants, and righteous persons will, in due course, participate in calling their loved ones forth in the resurrection" (120; emphasis added).

At the end of the earth—meaning at the end of the Millennium (D&C 88:101; Joseph Smith–Matthew 1:55)—the final great battle between good and evil, known as the "battle of the great God" (D&C 88:114) or the battle of Gog and Magog (Revelation 20:8), will take place. Once again, the mighty Michael, the eternal captain of Jehovah's army, will come face-to-face with his foe, Satan. "The devil and his armies shall be cast away into their own place, that they shall not have power over the saints any more at all. For Michael shall fight their battles, and shall overcome him who seeketh the throne of him who sitteth upon the throne, even the Lamb. This is the glory of God, and the sanctified; and they shall not any more see death" (D&C 88:114–16). Michael's final victory is in preparation for the earth to be made celestial.

SOURCES

Lectures on Faith. Salt Lake City: Deseret Book, 1985.

McConkie, Bruce R. *The Millennial Messiah: The Second Coming of the Son of Man.* Salt Lake City: Deseret Book, 1982.

Smith, Joseph. *History of The Church of Jesus Christ of Latter-day Saints.* Edited by B. H. Roberts. 7 vols. 2d ed. rev. Salt Lake City: The Church of Jesus Christ of Latter-day Saints, 1932–51.

Smith, Joseph Fielding. *Doctrines of Salvation.* Compiled by Bruce R. McConkie. 3 vols. Salt Lake City: Bookcraft, 1954–56.

Young, Brigham. In *Journal of Discourses.* 26 vols. London: Latter-day Saints' Book Depot, 1854–86.

BLT

ADAMIC LANGUAGE

We call the language spoken and written by Adam and his posterity the Adamic language. During the early generations of mortals on this earth, a book of remembrance was kept among them "in the language of Adam" (Moses 6:5). It was a "language which was pure and undefiled," and with it "children were taught to read and write" (Moses 6:6). It was a language especially suited to writing that which was revealed by the spirit of inspiration (Moses 6:5). Moroni's statement to the Lord about the brother of Jared bespeaks the power of the original, pure language: "Thou madest him that the things which he wrote were mighty even as thou art, unto the overpowering of man to read them" (Ether 12:24). Though a change was instituted with the confounding of languages after the Tower of Babel was constructed—up to that point all people spoke the same language (Genesis 11:1, 6–9)—the Lord promised that during the Millennium he would again "turn [return] to the people a pure language, that they may all call upon the name of the Lord, to serve him with one consent" (Zephaniah 3:9).

"In the language of Adam," the name of God the Father is "Man of Holiness" and the "name of his Only Begotten is the Son of Man [of Holiness]" (Moses 6:57). Because we know that the Son is also called Son Ahman (D&C 78:20; 95:17), perhaps we possess vestiges of the Adamic language in such scriptural terms and phrases as Adam-ondi-Ahman (D&C 116:1; 107:53).

ACS

ADOPTION

Adoption is the process by which one is received legally into a family that he or she was not born into naturally. In the gospel sense, there are two adoptions.

First, through faith, repentance, baptism, and the reception of the Holy Ghost, we are adopted into the family of the Lord Jesus Christ. We become his sons and daughters, and he becomes the Lord of our spiritual rebirth, the Head of the family of the sanctified and redeemed, the Father of our salvation (Mosiah 5:7–8). By virtue of his atoning blood and through the medium of the Holy Spirit, which is the Sanctifier, we are born again and become new creatures in Christ

(2 Corinthians 5:17; Mosiah 27:26). We take upon us the family name, the name of Christ, which we are expected to bear with fidelity and devotion. We receive his image in our countenances and experience a mighty change of heart (Alma 5:14).

Second, those who join the Church of Jesus Christ and who are not literal descendants of Abraham, Isaac, and Jacob are adopted into the house of Israel. This adoption refers to those who are not already of the chosen lineage.

RLM

ADULTERY

"Thou shalt not commit adultery," the Lord God declared in the Ten Commandments (Exodus 20:14; see also Deuteronomy 5:18). A sexual relationship between a married person and someone other than his or her lawfully wedded spouse is generally referred to as adultery. In the scriptures, however, the word *adultery*, like *fornication*, can be used to refer to any sexual immorality (Matthew 15:19; 1 Corinthians 6:9–18; Hebrews 13:4; Revelation 22:15; Jacob 2:23–28; Alma 16:18). In ancient times the penalty for adultery was death (Leviticus 20:10; Deuteronomy 22:22). In this dispensation, the Lord has reiterated the seriousness of adultery and other sexual sin and declared that "he that committeth adultery, and repenteth not, shall be cast out"—meaning excommunicated from the Church (D&C 42:24). Although adultery and other forms of immorality are "most abominable above all sins save it be the shedding of innocent blood or denying the Holy Ghost" (Alma 39:5), the Lord has promised that "he that has committed adultery and repents with all his heart, and forsaketh it" shall be forgiven (D&C 42:25).

The Savior taught his disciples that avoiding the sin of adultery entails more than merely abstaining from illicit sexual behaviors; it also entails keeping our minds and hearts pure, free from sexual lust. Calling for an inward righteousness higher than just avoiding outward immoral behavior, Jesus taught "that whosoever looketh on a woman to lust after her hath committed adultery with her already in his heart" (Matthew 5:28). In our day the Lord has equated lust with mental and emotional infidelity and warned against the spiritual consequences of such: "He that looketh upon a woman to lust after her shall deny the faith, and shall not have the Spirit; and if he repents not he shall be cast out" (D&C 42:23; see also 63:16). God's prohibition of adultery and warnings against lustful desires and thoughts protect the sanctity of marriage and family and preserve the companionship of the Holy Ghost in our lives. The command not to commit adultery is likewise a commandment to have complete devotion to one's spouse, both sexually and emotionally, temporally and spiritually. "Thou shalt love thy wife [or husband] with all thy heart," the Lord stated, "and shalt cleave unto her [or him] and none else" (D&C 42:22). President Spencer W. Kimball wrote: "The words *none else* eliminate everyone and everything. The spouse then becomes pre-eminent in the life of the husband or wife and neither social life nor occupational life nor political life nor any other interest nor person nor thing shall ever take precedence over the companion spouse" (250).

In the scriptures, adultery—a tangible evidence of breaking one's covenants and of a lack of complete devotion—is sometimes used as a metaphor for apostasy, the turning from one's devotion to God and the breaking of covenants with him. This apostasy can be both individual and national. The Old Testament contains many references to peoples who, like an adulterous spouse, are unfaithful to Christ the Bridegroom (Numbers 25:1–3; Jeremiah 3:6–10; Ezekiel 16:15–59). Similarly, adultery is often equated with idolatry—worshipping other gods and allowing anyone or anything else to become more important to us than our covenantal relationships.

SOURCE

Kimball, Spencer W. *The Miracle of Forgiveness.* Salt Lake City: Bookcraft, 1969.

BLT

ADVOCATE

Because no unclean thing can enter into the presence of God, each of us needs an advocate to plead our case before the Father. Jesus Christ is our Advocate before God the Father and the only One who can intercede on our behalf (D&C 110:4; 1 John 2:1). Specifically, the Savior intervenes for all those who "sin and repent" (JST, 1 John 2:1), or, as Mormon explained, for "those who have faith in him" and "cleave unto every good thing" (Moroni 7:28).

Affirming that he will be our Advocate throughout our mortal lives, as well as at the final judgment, the Lord Jehovah appeared in glory to the Prophet Joseph Smith and Oliver Cowdery in the newly dedicated Kirtland Temple on 3 April 1836, declaring: "I am the first and the last; I am he who liveth, I am he who was slain; I am your advocate with the Father. Behold, your sins are forgiven you; you are clean before me; therefore, lift up your heads and rejoice" (D&C 110:4–5). Similarly, the Lord spoke to members of the Church through the Prophet Joseph to "hearken to his voice" during their challenges, remembering that he is "the advocate with the Father, who is pleading your cause before him" (D&C 45:2–3), a passage that again reflects his advocacy even now.

As the only "high priest" who "was in all points tempted like as we are, yet without sin" (Hebrews 4:15), the Redeemer alone can plead our cause, "saying: Father, behold the sufferings and death of him who did no sin, in whom thou wast well pleased; behold the blood of thy Son which was shed, the blood of him whom thou gavest that thyself might be glorified; wherefore, Father, spare these my brethren that believe on my name, that they may come unto me and have everlasting life" (D&C 45:4–5). Reflecting our complete confidence in the Savior's advocacy, righteousness, and purifying power, we are entitled to "come boldly unto the throne of grace" (Hebrews 4:16), thereby bearing witness that it is by his grace and righteousness that we are saved.

CFO

AGENCY

"Next to the bestowal of life itself," President David O. McKay taught, "the right to direct our lives is God's greatest gift to man. Freedom of choice is more to be treasured than any possession earth can give. It is inherent in the spirit of man. . . . It is the impelling source of the soul's progress" (1072). Agency is the power to choose; it is an eternal principle, a God-given gift to all of his children, an essential condition to the overall purpose and operation of the plan of salvation. Father Lehi, in the Book of Mormon, teaches that "the Lord God gave unto man that he should act for himself" (2 Nephi 2:16). All men are "free according to the flesh" to "choose liberty and eternal life, through the great Mediator of all men, or to choose captivity and death, according to the captivity and power of the devil; for he seeketh that all men might be miserable like unto himself" (2 Nephi 2:27).

The scriptures, particularly the Book of Mormon, teach that there are four imperative principles that likewise must exist for agency to be exercised and to ensure accountability. First, there must be sufficient knowledge of good and evil (2 Nephi 2:5; see also Moroni 7:16–17). Second, there must be opposition, or enticements. Lehi taught, "Wherefore, man could not act for himself save it should be that he was enticed by the one or the other" (2 Nephi 2:16). Third, eternal laws must exist that cannot be compromised or ignored—eternal laws of cause and effect, action and consequence. "And if ye shall say there is no law, ye shall also say there is no sin. If ye shall say there is no sin, ye shall also say there is no righteousness. And if there be no righteousness there be no happiness. And if there be no righteousness nor happiness there be no punishment nor misery. And if these things are not there is no God" (2 Nephi 2:13; see also Alma 12:31–32). Fourth, there must be freedom to choose between opposites—freedom to choose righteousness or wickedness, good or bad—and everything in between. "Ye are free; ye are permitted to act for yourselves," the prophet Samuel the Lamanite declared, "for behold, God hath given unto you a knowledge and he hath made you free. He hath given unto you that ye might know good from evil, and he hath given unto you that ye might choose life or death; and ye can do good and be restored unto that which is good, or have that which is good restored unto you; or ye can do evil, and have that which is evil restored unto you" (Helaman 14:30–31; see also 2 Nephi 10:23).

Agency, the power to choose, is inextricably linked to freedom, the power and privilege to carry out our choices (Oaks, 37–47). Every choice has a fixed consequence. A person can exercise agency to make a choice, but agency does not mean that the person is able to choose, change, or be free from the attendant consequences. That is why agency and accountability always go hand in hand. Thus, a person's freedom to make additional choices is affected by the use of his agency. One who chooses to use harmful drugs, for example, may retain his agency but lose his freedom to make other choices because of addictions or other restrictions, such as prison or death. Thus, the proper use of agency through correct choices always expands our freedom, whereas disobedience and wickedness always restrict it and, as Lehi said, "giveth the spirit of the devil power to captivate, to bring you down to hell" (2 Nephi 2:29). "The further one goes in the making of wrong decisions in the exercise of free agency," President Marion G. Romney taught, "the more difficult it is for him to recover the lost ground. One can, by persisting long enough, reach the point of no return. He then becomes an abject slave. By the exercise of his free agency, he has decreased the area in which he can act, almost to the vanishing point" (45). In contrast, President Romney taught, exercising agency to choose the Savior and follow in his way leads to "liberty and eternal life, through the great Mediator of all men," not only in mortality but also in eternity. Eternal life is a perfect liberty—"the freedom of the soul"—where one is completely free to do whatever he wants because his wants are in perfect harmony with God's will (45; see also Helaman 10:4–10).

SOURCES

McKay, David O. "Man's Free Agency—an Eternal Principle of Progress." *Improvement Era,* Dec. 1965, 1072–73, 1096–98.

Oaks, Dallin H. "Free Agency and Freedom." In *Brigham Young University 1987–88 Devotional and Fireside Speeches,* 37–47. Provo, Utah: Brigham Young University, 1988.

Romney, Marion G. "The Perfect Law of Liberty." *Ensign,* Nov. 1981, 43–45.

BLT

AHMAN

Ahman is one of the names of Elohim, our Father in Heaven (D&C 78:20; 95:17). It may well be a remnant of the Adamic language (Pratt, 2:342).

SOURCE

Pratt, Orson. In *Journal of Discourses.* 26 vols. London: Latter-day Saints' Book Depot, 1854–86.

RLM

ALMIGHTY

The name and title *Almighty* rightly designates both God the Father and his Son, Jesus Christ (Genesis 49:25; Revelation 1:8; 2 Nephi 23:6; Helaman 10:11; D&C 84:96; 121:33). Both are all-mighty—their might is all-encompassing. What is said of one can be said of the other (D&C 35:2; 93:3). Both are all-knowing Gods (2 Nephi 2:24; 9:20), and both possess all power to accomplish their purposes (Mosiah 4:9; Alma 26:35). Gospel writers Matthew, Mark, and Luke testified that "with God all things are possible" (Matthew 19:26; Mark 10:27; see also Luke 1:37), and John declared that "the Lord God omnipotent reigneth" (Revelation 19:6). *Omnipotent* means all-powerful. Nothing is too hard for the Lord (Genesis 18:14). Because the Father and the Son possess infinite understanding (Psalm 147:5), and because their power is not restrained by forces that affect mortals, we may exercise complete faith and trust in them (*Lectures,* 54–56).

Other name-titles of Deity using the term *Almighty* abound in scripture: Almighty God (Genesis 17:1; 28:3; 1 Nephi 17:48; D&C 20:21; 87:6; 88:106); Lord Almighty (D&C 84:118; 2 Corinthians 6:18); Lord God Almighty (Revelation 4:8; 11:17; 21:22; 1 Nephi 1:14; 2 Nephi 9:46; D&C 109:77; 121:4).

SOURCE

Lectures on Faith. Salt Lake City: Deseret Book, 1985.

ACS

ALPHA AND OMEGA

The phrase "Alpha and Omega" is one of the many name-titles of Jesus Christ found in both the New Testament and the Doctrine and Covenants (Revelation 1:8–17; 21:6; 22:13; D&C 19:1; 63:60; 68:35; 75:1; 81:7; 112:34; 132:66). The two words are, respectively, the first and last letters of the Greek alphabet, the beginning and the end. They symbolize the nature and roles of Jesus Christ: he is the beginning and the end in that he holds all power over our salvation from creation through the end of the world (D&C 19:1, 3); all created things center in him (D&C 88:6–13); he is timeless and eternal—the "beginning and the ending . . . [he] which is, and which was, and which is to come" (Revelation 1:8); he is constant and unchanging, "from eternity to eternity he is the same, and his years never fail" (D&C 76:4). To the Nephites after his resurrection, Christ testified: "I am the light and the life of the world. I am Alpha and Omega, the beginning and the end" (3 Nephi 9:18). Isaiah recorded similar truths: "Thus saith the

Lord the King of Israel, and his redeemer the Lord of hosts; I am the first, and I am the last; and beside me there is no God" (Isaiah 44:6; see also 48:12).

ACS

AMEN

The word *amen* derives from a Hebrew root meaning "yes," "truly," "surely," "certainly," "so be it," or the like. It is most often used as a term of unequivocal confirmation or solemn affirmation uttered by listeners who wish to pledge their support to a prayer, blessing, sermon, or proposal they have heard. By uttering this affirmation, they acknowledge their commitment to bear the consequences of the prayer or blessing or to work to bring about the conditions requested or the pronouncements made.

The scriptures are replete with examples of how the term has been and should be used. We are commanded to conclude our prayers or expressions of thanksgiving with "amen" (Matthew 6:13). Affirmation of support or allegiance to a statement of worship, praise, or solemn declaration should conclude with *amen* (D&C 88:135; 1 Corinthians 14:16). The word *amen* ends a blessing at the conclusion of one of Paul's letters (Galatians 6:18) and at the end of a declaration of praise in Jude's letter (Jude 1:25).

The Lord himself used *amen* when making declarations about his messianic role (Revelation 1:18). He also used the term to introduce some of his own sayings given during his mortal ministry: "Amen I say to you" (*NAB,* Matthew 5:18, 26; 6:2) and "Amen, amen, I say to you" (*NAB,* John 1:51). The King James Version renders these uses as "verily." John the Revelator saw four beasts of heaven adding their amen to statements of blessing and praise offered to the Lord by all creatures (Revelation 5:13–14). It seems a fitting way to conclude the New Testament record by uttering *amen* (Revelation 22:21).

In addition to our righteous uses of *amen,* the Hebrew text of Isaiah 65:16 presents it as one of the names of God: "God of Amen" (*'elohe amen*), translated as "God of Truth" in the King James Version. One of Christ's name-titles is *Amen* (Revelation 3:14), presumably indicating his being full of truth, constancy, steadfastness, firmness, power, and commitment to the Father. This usage is possibly related to the name-title Son Ahman, used to designate Jesus Christ in our dispensation (D&C 78:20; 95:17) and deriving from a common ancient root found not only in the Adamic, Hebrew, and Greek languages but also in Egyptian. One of the supreme gods of the Egyptians was Amun (also Amon or Amen), later known as Amun-Ra.

The term *amen* is also used by the Lord as a statement of damnation, finality, or even cursing upon those who misuse priesthood authority—"Amen to the priesthood or the authority of that man" (D&C 121:37). This is not unlike two specific uses of the term in Old Testament times, when, at a certain feast, the members of the congregation answered the curses pronounced by the Levites with *amen* in order to call ill-fate upon themselves should they be guilty of unrighteousness (Deuteronomy 27:15–26). The listeners to Nehemiah's curses against the stiff-necked nobles of his day also responded with *amen* (Nehemiah 5:13). Members of the Dead Sea Scroll community living at Qumran (during the last century B.C. and the first century A.D.) likewise were required to respond *amen* to both blessings and curses pronounced by the priests of their day (1Q-Serekh Scroll 1:20; 2:10, 18; Charlesworth, 1:9, 11).

SOURCES

Charlesworth, James H. *The Dead Sea Scrolls: Hebrew, Aramaic, and Greek Texts with English Translations.* 2 vols. Louisville, Ky.: Westminster John Knox Press, 1994–95.
New American Bible. Rev. compact ed. New York: Oxford University Press, 2011.

ACS

AMERICA

Scriptural pronouncements declare the American continent to be "a land which is choice above all other lands" (Ether 2:10; 1 Nephi 13:30); a land consecrated to those whom the Lord brings to it (2 Nephi 1:7); a land in which peoples are established by the Lord to fulfill the covenant he made with Israel; a land where "the powers of heaven" are manifested (3 Nephi 20:22); a land of liberty guaranteed protection against all other nations, provided its inhabitants are righteous (2 Nephi 1:7); a land whose citizens must "serve the God of the land, who is Jesus Christ" or "be swept off" the face of it (Ether 2:12, 10); the land upon which the New Jerusalem will be established

(3 Nephi 20:22). Modern revelation declares that America is the land where Adam and Eve first dwelt and where Adam-ondi-Ahman was located, "the place where Adam shall come to visit his people, or the Ancient of Days shall sit, as spoken of by Daniel the prophet" (D&C 116:1). It is the place where "the God of heaven shall again visit His people" (Whitney, 205). America is the land that shall receive the city of Enoch, which will come down out of heaven to be joined with the earthly New Jerusalem (Ether 13:3; Moses 7:21, 62; Revelation 21:2).

Modern apostles and prophets have taught that "the Lord prepared America as the site for the restoration of his truth in the latter days, laying a groundwork for it over a period of nearly two thousand years" (Petersen, 7). In April 1976, during "the first general conference in the bicentennial year of the United States of America," President N. Eldon Tanner of the First Presidency declared that "the discovery of the Americas was not an accident. The event had been foreordained in the eternal councils. The prophets of old had it in view. Jacob foresaw it when he blessed his son Joseph, calling him 'a fruitful bough by a well, whose branches run over the wall . . . unto the utmost bound of the everlasting hills.' (Gen. 49:22, 26.)" (48). President Joseph Fielding Smith taught that America is "the land of Joseph," where "the city Zion, or the New Jerusalem" will be built (3:67, 72). While ministering in the Americas, the resurrected Christ testified that the Gentiles "should be established in this land, and be set up as a free people by the power of the Father" that the gathering of a remnant of the house of Jacob might take place, that Zion might be established, "that the covenant of the Father may be fulfilled which he hath covenanted with his people, O house of Israel" (3 Nephi 21:4).

President Joseph Fielding Smith also noted, "The Book of Mormon informs us that the whole of America, both North and South, is a choice land above all other lands, in other words—Zion" (3:73). The Book of Mormon powerfully confirms that God's hand has been intimately involved in the history of America. The first people led to America by the Lord were the Jaredites, who came at the time of the confusion of languages during the building of the tower of Babel (Ether 1:33–43). They knew of the choice status of the land and of the divine decree that the inhabitants of the land must live in righteousness in order to possess it (Ether 2:9–12). But they eventually proved to be wicked, and all were destroyed in fulfillment of the Lord's promises and warnings (Ether 15:29, 33).

Another important group of people led to America by the Lord was the family of Lehi, who arrived six hundred years before the coming of the Messiah in mortality. The Lord revealed to them that he was keeping the land hidden from other nations in order to fulfill his purposes. He also promised that those inhabitants of America who would keep the commandments would prosper and possess the land "unto themselves" (2 Nephi 1:9). The prophet Nephi saw in vision the events that would transpire in preparation for the establishment of the American republic (1 Nephi 13:10–19). He "beheld a man among the Gentiles" upon whom the Spirit of God rested and then guided him in his discovery of the Western Hemisphere (1 Nephi 13:12). Modern prophets have identified this person as Christopher Columbus. Furthermore, Nephi beheld many other multitudes of Gentiles whom the Lord guided as they settled the Americas. And he saw how the Lord delivered a certain group of Gentiles "out of the hands of all other nations," giving to the colonists of North America ultimate victory against "their mother Gentiles" in the American Revolution (1 Nephi 13:13–19). The history of the United States of America has vindicated the prophetic statements of Nephi. All of this was accomplished in preparation for the restoration of the Church of Jesus Christ, which was organized in the United States on 6 April 1830 (D&C 20:1).

To the Prophet Joseph Smith the Lord revealed the reason behind His involvement in the divinely inspired Constitution of the United States as well as the reason for the redemption of the land of the United States of America: "Therefore, it is not right that any man should be in bondage one to another. And for this purpose have I established the Constitution of this land, by the hands of wise men whom I raised up unto this very purpose, and redeemed the land by the shedding of blood" (D&C 101:80). That this was done to establish America as the Lord's base of operations in all the world was further confirmed to Joseph Smith: "That law of the land which is constitutional, supporting that principle of freedom in maintaining rights and privileges, belongs to all mankind, and is justifiable before me" (D&C 98:5). Speaking in April 1976 general conference, apostle and future Church president Ezra Taft Benson said, "Every Latter-day Saint should love the inspired Constitution of the United States—a nation with a spiritual foundation and a prophetic history—which nation the Lord has declared to be his base of operations in these latter days" (91).

In 1787 the Constitution of the United States was drafted. Two years later, in 1789, it was put into operation, and the electoral college voted George Washington the first president of the new nation. Washington vehemently squelched any effort to have himself or any other person made king in America. In fulfillment of Book of Mormon prophecy, latter-day America would have no kings: "And this shall be a land of liberty unto the Gentiles, and there shall be no kings upon the land, who shall raise up unto the Gentiles" (2 Nephi 10:11). Modern prophets have testified of the greatness of America's founding fathers who signed the Declaration of Independence and the Constitution. In 1877 they appeared to President Wilford Woodruff in a vision in the Saint George Utah Temple, insisting that baptisms be performed on their behalf. President Woodruff testified "that those men who laid the foundation of this American government . . . were the *best spirits* the God of heaven could find on the face of the earth. . . . General Washington and all the men that labored for the purpose were inspired of the Lord" (89; emphasis added).

The government of the United States has not always supported the Saints in their petitions for redress stemming from violent persecutions and other wrongs. Perhaps the most well-known example of that failure is President Martin Van Buren's statement: "Your cause is just, but I can do nothing for you" (Smith, *History,* 4:80; see also 4:40). Nevertheless, Church members have always been encouraged to support the laws of the land and work within the system of government to effect change.

America is a land with not only a prophetic destiny and sacred history but also a tremendous responsibility to serve as a beacon of hope to the oppressed (Hyde, 6:367–71). It must stand for and teach principles of liberty and righteousness in all the world.

SOURCES

Benson, Ezra Taft. "The Constitution—A Glorious Standard." *Ensign,* May 1976, 91–93.

Hyde, Orson. In *Journal of Discourses.* 26 vols. London: Latter-day Saints' Book Depot, 1854–86.

Petersen, Mark E. *The Great Prologue.* Salt Lake City: Deseret Book, 1975.

Smith, Joseph. *History of The Church of Jesus Christ of Latter-day Saints.* Edited by B. H. Roberts. 7 vols. 2d ed. rev. Salt Lake City: The Church of Jesus Christ of Latter-day Saints, 1932–51.

Smith, Joseph Fielding. *Doctrines of Salvation.* Compiled by Bruce R. McConkie. 3 vols. Salt Lake City: Bookcraft, 1954–56.

Tanner, N. Eldon. "If They Will but Serve the God of the Land." *Ensign,* May 1976, 48–51.

Whitney, Orson F. *Life of Heber C. Kimball.* Salt Lake City: Bookcraft, 1945.

Woodruff, Wilford. In Conference Report, Apr. 1898, 88–90.

ACS

ANCIENT OF DAYS

The prophet Daniel "beheld till the thrones were cast down, and the Ancient of days did sit. . . . One like the Son of man came with the clouds of heaven, and came to the Ancient of days, and they brought him near before him" (Daniel 7:9, 13).

Most commentators in the Christian world believe this to be a reference to God, but Joseph Smith learned by revelation that it is in fact a reference to Michael, who is Adam. In chronicling the persons who will be in attendance at the council at Adam-ondi-Ahman, the revelation mentions Moroni, Elias, John the Baptist, Elijah, Joseph, Jacob, Isaac, and Abraham, "and also . . . Michael, or Adam, the father of all, the prince of all, the ancient of days" (D&C 27:5–11). In a revelation given to the Prophet in May 1838, "Spring Hill is named by the Lord Adam-ondi-Ahman, because, said he, it is the place where Adam shall come to visit his people, or the Ancient of Days shall sit, as spoken of by Daniel the prophet" (D&C 116:1). In his vision of the redemption of the dead, President Joseph F. Smith observed that "among the great and mighty ones who were assembled in this vast congregation of the righteous [in paradise] were Father Adam, the Ancient of Days and father of all" (D&C 138:38).

Joseph Smith declared that "Daniel in his seventh chapter speaks of the Ancient of Days; he means the oldest man, our Father Adam, Michael, he will call his children together and hold a council with them to prepare them for the coming of the Son of Man. He (Adam) is the father of the human family, and presides over the spirits of all men, and all that have had the keys must stand before him in this grand council. . . . The Son of Man stands before him, and there is given him [Christ] glory and dominion" (3:386–87).

SOURCE

Smith, Joseph. *History of The Church of Jesus Christ of Latter-day Saints.* Edited by
B. H. Roberts. 7 vols. 2d ed. rev. Salt Lake City: The Church of Jesus Christ of
Latter-day Saints, 1932–51.

RLM

ANGEL

The Hebrew word that is translated "angel" is *malakh,* meaning
"messenger." Angels are not, as traditional Christians aver, special creations of God. Rather, they are human beings who minister for the
Lord. An angel may be a resurrected being (D&C 129:1); a translated
being; an unembodied spirit, one who has not yet taken a physical
body; a disembodied spirit, one who has lived and died and now awaits
the resurrection; a mortal who is attentive to the Spirit of God and
follows divine direction to assist or bless another; or the Lord himself.
Joseph Smith taught that "an angel of God never has wings" (3:392).

Angels are subject unto Christ "to minister according to the word
of his command, showing themselves unto them of strong faith and a
firm mind in every form of godliness. And the office of their ministry
is to call men unto repentance, and to fulfil and to do the work of
the covenants of the Father . . . by declaring the word of Christ unto
the chosen vessels of the Lord, that they may bear testimony of him"
(Moroni 7:30–31). Indeed, one of the signs of the times, and one of the
spiritual indicators of a people's worthiness, is the extent to which angels continue to minister, inasmuch as "it is by faith that angels appear
and minister unto men; wherefore, if these things have ceased wo be
unto the children of men, for it is because of unbelief" (Moroni 7:37).

"The keys of the ministering of angels" were restored by John the
Baptist on 15 May 1829 (D&C 13:1). Further, the ministry of angels is a gift of the Spirit (Moroni 10:14), a gift the Saints of God
are encouraged to seek (D&C 46:8). Angels, both seen and unseen,
continue to appear to bestow authority; bear witness; bring protection,
comfort, and assurance; and deliver warnings.

Satan also sends messengers (Alma 30:53)—angels who, like their
master, are striving to overthrow the kingdom of God and spread confusion, conflict, fear, discord, and destruction. Those who followed
Lucifer in the premortal existence were cast to the earth as fallen

angels, consigned forever to an incorporeal state: they have no physical body and cannot receive the fulness of joy that comes through the inseparable union of body and spirit in the resurrection (D&C 93:33). They work to distract, deceive, tempt, pervert, and pollute goodness and truth in order to make the children of men miserable like themselves (2 Nephi 2:18, 27).

SOURCE

Smith, Joseph. *History of The Church of Jesus Christ of Latter-day Saints.* Edited by B. H. Roberts. 7 vols. 2d ed. rev. Salt Lake City: The Church of Jesus Christ of Latter-day Saints, 1932–51.

RLM

ANNIHILATION

Some well-meaning Christians have concluded that God is too kind, too caring, too merciful to allow his children who do not accept Jesus Christ and his gospel to burn in an endless hell, to be forever subject to a world of fire and brimstone. Consequently, they have chosen instead to believe in a kind of conditional immortality in which life forever will be granted only to those who choose Christ. All others will be snuffed out of existence, annihilated, at the time of death. The restoration of the gospel brought a flood of intelligence into this world concerning the world to come. As to the suffering of the wicked in the next life, the Prophet Joseph Smith declared: "A man is his own tormenter and his own condemner. Hence the saying, They shall go into the lake that burns with fire and brimstone. The torment of disappointment in the mind of man is as exquisite as a lake burning with fire and brimstone. I say, so is the torment of man" (224). We are immortal beings—we had no beginning, and we will have no end. All persons who receive a physical body will be resurrected to a kingdom of glory. Those who live on this earth and commit the unpardonable sin will be resurrected to a kingdom of no glory (D&C 88:32), subject to the second and final spiritual death, banished to outer darkness.

SOURCE

Joseph Smith [manual]. Teachings of Presidents of the Church series. Salt Lake City: The Church of Jesus Christ of Latter-day Saints, 2007.

RLM

ANTICHRIST

Any individual or institution that rejects Christ and his gospel, the plan of salvation, and the Church of Jesus Christ could be characterized as *antichrist* (1 John 4:1–4). "He that is not with me," Jesus taught, "is against me" (Matthew 12:30; see also 2 Nephi 10:16). The ultimate antichrist is Lucifer, who rejected the Only Begotten and openly rebelled against God in the premortal War in Heaven. Those who followed him in that rebellion were cast out of heaven to the earth. In every imaginable way, they continue their efforts to destroy the work of God and torment those who love and follow the Lord. They are, likewise, *antichrist.* The apostle John wrote that "even now are there many antichrists" (1 John 2:18) who deny "the Father and the Son" (1 John 2:22) and are "deceivers" (2 John 1:7; Revelation 13:13–14). The antichrist deceivers are both spirit beings—Satan and those "angels to a devil" (2 Nephi 9:9) who were thrust down to the earth with him—and mortals who enter into league with them in fighting against God, his gospel, and his faithful disciples.

There are many antichrists whose names never appear in holy writ, but the Book of Mormon identifies three influential men who openly sought to destroy faith, lead men astray, and undermine the earthly kingdom of God: Sherem (Jacob 7), Nehor (Alma 1), and Korihor (Alma 30). These earthly antichrists learned their deceptive and destructive craft from *the* antichrist himself (Alma 30:53). Nephi taught that "there are save two churches only; the one is the church of the Lamb of God, and the other is the church of the devil" (1 Nephi 14:10). The church of the Lamb of God is composed of true followers of Christ; the church of the devil is composed of antichrists. Therefore, the institutions that fight against the Church and faithful believers are also referred to in the scriptures as the antichrist, "which is the mother of abominations; and she is the whore of all the earth" (1 Nephi 14:10). Ultimately, all that is antichrist, whether institutional or individual, will be destroyed, "and the great and abominable church, which is the whore of all the earth, shall be cast down by devouring fire" (D&C 29:21; see also Ezekiel 38–39; 1 Nephi 22:23; Revelation 18).

BLT

APOCALYPSE

The Greek word *apocalypse* means "uncovering" or "revelation." The Apocalypse is the book of Revelation in the New Testament. It was an important book in the first century of the Christian era, one that provided hope and perspective for the former-day Saints. When properly approached and understood, it provides a similar hope for Latter-day Saints who live in the twenty-first century. Although it is not likely that even the most serious students of scripture will uncover every symbol and thereby come to understand every particular of Revelation, certain doctrinal refrains, recurring lessons, and basic principles may be grasped by all of us. Even if we are uncertain about the meanings of many of the unusual symbols in the Apocalypse, we can understand and appreciate the overarching messages of this book of holy scripture. Some of these messages in the book of Revelation include the following:

1. Those Saints who overcome the world will receive from Christ the supernal rewards of the faithful: they will eat of the tree of life, meaning they will gain eternal life (2:7; see also Alma 32:41–42); they will not be overcome by the second death (2:11); they will come to know all things, even as God does (2:17; D&C 130:9–11); they will gain power over many kingdoms and rule with the word of God, even as Christ, who is the bright and morning star (JST, 2:26–27; 22:16); they will be adorned in white robes of righteousness (3:4; 19:8); they will have the name of God written upon them (3:12); and they will sit with Christ on his throne, even as Christ also overcame and sits down on the throne of the Father (3:21; see also D&C 93:20).

2. Jesus Christ, who is the Lion of the tribe of Judah, the root of David, has power to loose the seals on the record of men's dealings on earth (5:1–10). In other words, the Master knows the end from the beginning—he knows what was, what is, and what is to be. His is the eternal perspective, and we can trust in and rely on his omniscient and all-loving wisdom to orchestrate the events of our lives.

3. "Worthy is the Lamb that was slain to receive power, and riches, and wisdom, and strength, and honour, and glory, and blessing" (5:12). Indeed, if any people in all the world have reason to rejoice in the Lord, it is the Latter-day Saints. When we contemplate what has been restored to earth—knowledge and power and gifts abounding—we

ought to lift our voices to heaven and exult with John the Revelator, "Alleluia: for the Lord God omnipotent reigneth" (19:6).

4. The war that began in heaven continues on earth; it will be waged until the Savior returns in glory. Many in our day are afflicted with the same poison that afflicts Lucifer and his followers: they are the "accuser of our brethren" (12:10). But the faithful overcome dissidence and opposition and persecution "by the blood of the Lamb, and by the word of their testimony," for they love "not their lives unto the death" (12:1–11).

5. Despite rising tides of wickedness, the Lord saw fit to restore the fulness of his gospel. John "saw another angel fly in the midst of heaven, having the everlasting gospel to preach unto them that dwell on the earth, and to every nation, and kindred, and tongue, and people" (14:6). President Gordon B. Hinckley testified: "That angel has come. His name is Moroni. His is a voice speaking from the dust, bringing another witness of the living reality of the Lord Jesus Christ. We have not as yet carried the gospel to every nation, kindred, tongue, and people. But we have made great strides. We have gone wherever we are permitted to go. God is at the helm and doors will be opened by His power according to His divine will. Of that I am confident. Of that I am certain" (70).

6. All people will be judged by their works out of the books that are written on earth and in heaven (20:11–13; see also D&C 128:6–7). "He that overcometh shall inherit all things; and I will be his God, and he shall be my son" (21:7). The faithful will become kings and priests, queens and priestesses unto God forever (1:5–6; 5:10; 20:6).

7. Wickedness will expand, malevolence will multiply, and the forces of evil will cover the globe. But the great and abominable church will eventually fall, and satanic influences will be no more (chapters 17–19). Eventually good will triumph over evil on this earth. A day of righteousness will be ushered in at the time of our Savior's return in glory. Satan will be bound, and the work of God will go forward without distraction for a thousand years. At the end of that glorious era, the devil will be loosed for a little season, but he and his minions will be defeated by the powers of God, and a final cleansing will take place. The earth will then become the celestial kingdom (chapters 21–22; D&C 88:17–20).

Joseph Smith taught, "The book of Revelation is one of the plainest books God ever caused to be written" (5:342). Surely Joseph referred less to the seemingly infinite number of symbolic details than to the key themes and the unmistakable principles that are found in Revelation. These central messages we can all understand. We can, like the former-day Saints, watch and be ready (3:3; 16:15). We can be vigilant, ever alert to evil in all its diverse and divisive forms. We can take heart that the God of heaven is in charge, that he presides over the affairs of humankind, and that divine justice and pardoning mercy will yet deliver and reward the Saints.

SOURCES

Hinckley, Gordon B. "Stay the Course—Keep the Faith." *Ensign,* Nov. 1995, 70–72.

Smith, Joseph. *History of The Church of Jesus Christ of Latter-day Saints.* Edited by B. H. Roberts. 7 vols. 2d ed. rev. Salt Lake City: The Church of Jesus Christ of Latter-day Saints, 1932–51.

RLM

APOCRYPHA AND PSEUDEPIGRAPHA

The Greek plural noun *apocrypha* ("hidden" or "hidden things") refers to a collection of fourteen or fifteen scripture-like books (or portions of books) found in some translations and editions of the Bible. They are related to the Old Testament. The books of the Apocrypha are 1 and 2 Esdras; Tobit; Judith; Additions to Esther; Wisdom of Solomon; Ecclesiasticus, or Wisdom of Jesus ben Sirach; Baruch, including the Letter of Jeremiah; the Prayer of Azariah and Song of the Three Young Men; Susanna; Bel and the Dragon; the Prayer of Manasseh; and 1 and 2 Maccabees (*Interpreter's,* 1:161).

The books of the Apocrypha were never included in the canon of the Hebrew Bible (finalized circa A.D. 90), being regarded as either nonauthoritative, of spurious origin, or, by a few, as containing material too sacred or esoteric for common consumption. Some modern scholars believe "they were all written during the last two centuries B.C. and the first century A.D." (*Interpreter's,* 1:161). There was debate among ancient Jewish authorities over the canon, specifically which books should be included and which excluded and for what reasons. The books of the Apocrypha are among those that did not receive full authoritative status; however, they were included in later editions of the

Septuagint (the Greek version of the Old Testament), which was the version used by the apostles living in Roman Judea.

Three basic attitudes toward the Apocrypha emerged in the early Christian church and found support later in different denominations:

1. During the second century, certain authorities (Irenaeus and Tertullian, for example) tagged certain books as unworthy of use and began to identify each as an *apocryphon* (singular form of the Greek word) to designate their questionable nature. By the third century, Julius Africanus and others advocated complete omission of these books from the Christian canon. This view was embraced by Calvinists and other Reformed Protestants.

2. Though Jerome (circa A.D. 347–420) included the books of the Apocrypha in his new translation, the Latin Vulgate, he did not regard them as being canonical. This is the stance later taken by Lutherans and Anglicans. It was during Jerome's time the term *apocrypha* was used as a general category for these books.

3. Various other theologians of the Roman Catholic Church, including Origen (circa A.D. 185–254) and Augustine (354–430), pressed for full canonical status of the books of the Apocrypha. The Roman Catholic Church councils, especially the Council of Hippo (393) and the Council of Trent (1546), supported this position and emphasized the canonicity of all books in the Vulgate. Martin Luther's German Bible (1534) grouped the books of the Apocrypha all together at the end of the Old Testament under the heading "Apocrypha: books not equal to sacred Scriptures but which are useful and good for reading."

The Authorized or King James Version (1611) initially scattered the books of the Apocrypha among canonical books. However, as early as 1629, some English Bibles appeared without the Apocrypha. Since 1827, editions published by the British and Foreign Bible Society excluded the Apocrypha, as did editions published by the American Bible Society. However, since the King James Bible from which the Prophet Joseph Smith worked contained the Apocrypha, it is obvious that questions regarding its value and authenticity had not been settled definitively.

In 1833, while working on his inspired revision of the Old Testament, the Prophet Joseph Smith came to the books of the Apocrypha and inquired of the Lord about the necessity to revise them. He was told that the Apocrypha contained many things that are true, that it was mostly translated correctly, but that it also contained many things that are not true and that it was not necessary to translate it (D&C 91:1–3). The Lord concluded his revelation to Joseph with counsel that is profitable for our approach to most religious literature: "Therefore, whoso readeth it, let him understand, for the Spirit manifesteth truth; and whoso is enlightened by the Spirit shall obtain benefit therefrom; And whoso receiveth not by the Spirit, cannot be benefited" (D&C 91:4–6).

The Pseudepigrapha is a category of books very much like the Apocrypha. "Pseudepigrapha" ("false writings") refers to works deemed to have been falsely ascribed to an important or famous figure in the history of Judaism or early Christianity, or works with a false title. These writings were excluded from the official canon of scripture on the basis of their questionable authenticity, though they may contain profound truths. They include such works as the Testaments of the Twelve Patriarchs, the Book of Enoch, the Martyrdom of Isaiah, the Assumption of Moses, the Life of Adam and Eve, the Apocalypse of Abraham, and many others. Several of these have been translated into English and published in various collections.

With the increased academic attention that has been focused on the Apocrypha and Pseudepigrapha in recent decades has come increased appreciation for them. New archeological and manuscript discoveries, particularly the Dead Sea Scrolls, have shown how various works of the Apocrypha and Pseudepigrapha were part of the canon of some ancient communities or, at the very least, were regarded as possessing special status among them. These discoveries have revealed that some works in the Apocrypha and Pseudepigrapha existed in multiple copies and variant forms. We also know that passages from works in the Apocrypha and Pseudepigrapha were being quoted in canonical works. The New Testament book of Jude, for example, quotes from the Assumption of Moses (also called the Testament of Moses) concerning a dispute between Michael the Archangel and the devil about the body of Moses (Jude 1:9). It is also likely that Jude uses material once found in writings or oral traditions attributed to Enoch regarding the second coming of the Messiah (compare Jude 1:14 and Moses 7:62–66).

Apocryphal and pseudepigraphal works have helped confirm that some doctrines and concepts emphasized in Latter-day Saint theology, such as apostasy, revelation, resurrection, eternal life, temple teachings, and eschatological beliefs regarding the last days, have an ancient setting. The books of 1 and 2 Maccabees, for example, are invaluable in helping to clarify the historical picture of intertestamental Judaism and provide detailed descriptions of the apostasy of the Maccabean (Hasmonean) period. The reality of the early patriarchs Adam, Enoch, and Abraham is confirmed and their eras illuminated within certain sections of the Apocrypha and Pseudepigrapha. Cosmic visions, mysteries of the kingdom and secrets of heaven revealed to man, and washings and anointings are themes found more than once in the Apocrypha and Pseudepigrapha.

Of significant value is how the Apocrypha and Pseudepigrapha have informed our understanding of the concept of canon—that the canon of scripture in certain eras of Israel's past was more open, diverse, and expansive than in Christianity today; just as Latter-day Saints profess an expanded and legitimate collection of inspired, authoritative books of scripture, so too did some of the ancients; scripture was buried in the earth for preservation; books once regarded as part of the canon were lost; and some writings of the Apocrypha and Pseudepigrapha should not have been as easily dismissed or ignored as they were by various earlier communities of faith.

Latter-day Saints have an affinity for the Apocrypha and Pseudepigrapha. The Prophet Joseph Smith revealed teachings and entire books that find parallels among the works of the Apocrypha and Pseudepigrapha. He restored portions of the books of Abraham and Moses, which in turn point to once-extant copies of a book of Enoch and a memoir of Adam and Eve—writings found in the Apocrypha and Pseudepigrapha. According to revelation, we know that there is much value in the Apocrypha and also in the Pseudepigrapha, but as students of the gospel, we also know that to gain the greatest and most lasting benefit, we must first possess a knowledge of the doctrines of the kingdom and study under the influence of the Spirit of the Lord. It must be remembered that the Apocrypha and the Pseudepigrapha do not form part of the Latter-day Saint canon.

SOURCE

The Interpreter's Dictionary of the Bible: An Illustrated Encyclopedia. Edited by George Arthur Buttrick. 5 vols. Nashville, Tenn.: Abingdon Press, 1962.

ACS

APOSTASY

Apostasy means "away from standing" or "falling away." Whenever an individual or a group begins to entertain critical thoughts or feelings or to act in ways meant to condemn or fight against the truth, those individuals thereby begin the sure decline toward apostasy. President George Q. Cannon observed: "[A friend] wished to know whether we . . . considered an honest difference of opinion between a member of the Church and the authorities of the Church apostasy. . . . We replied that we had not stated that an honest difference of opinion between a member of the Church and the authorities constituted apostasy; for we could conceive of a man honestly differing in opinion from the authorities of the Church and yet not be an apostate; but we could not conceive of a man publishing those differences of opinion and seeking by arguments, sophistry and special pleading to enforce them upon the people to produce division and strife and to place the acts and counsels of the authorities of the Church, if possible, in a wrong light and not be an apostate, for such conduct was apostasy as we understood the term" ("Apostasy," 457).

President Cannon explained on another occasion: "If the breach is daily widening between ourselves and the world . . . we may be assured that our progress is certain, however slow. On the opposite hand, if our feelings and affections, our appetites and desires, are in unison with the world around us and freely fraternize with them . . . we should do well to examine ourselves. Individuals in such a condition might possess a nominal position in the Church but would be lacking the life of the work, and, like the foolish virgins who slumbered while the bridegroom tarried, they would be unprepared for his coming" ("Second," 645–46).

Moral agency is an imperative ingredient in the Father's great plan of happiness, and next to life itself, nothing is to be treasured or defended more than the freedom to choose. God does not expect all members of the Church of Jesus Christ to think alike, to see things in exactly the same way, or to come to identical conclusions. Blind sheep cannot provide the kind of intelligent and dynamic discipleship needed to sustain and defend the kingdom of God on earth. Yet there are proper ways to express concern and voice disagreement. Indeed, the Lord Jehovah hates "feet that be swift in running to mischief" and "he that soweth discord among brethren" (Proverbs 6:18–19). The Prophet Joseph Smith declared that "man who rises up to condemn others, finding fault with the Church, saying that they are out of the way, while he himself is righteous, then know assuredly, that that man is in the high road to apostasy; and if he does not repent, will apostatize, as God lives" (318).

SOURCES

Cannon, George Q. "Second Advent of the Messiah." *Millennial Star* 23 (5 Oct. 1861): 643–46.

———. "What Is Apostasy?" Editorial in *Deseret News*, 3 Nov. 1869, 457.

Joseph Smith [manual]. Teachings of Presidents of the Church series. Salt Lake City: The Church of Jesus Christ of Latter-day Saints, 2007.

RLM

APOSTASY, GREAT

The concept of a restoration through the calling of modern prophets necessarily implies a belief in an apostasy, or a falling away. The apostasy of the early Christian church after the death of the apostles is sometimes referred to as the Great Apostasy because of its duration (more than a millennium and a half) and its depth. It was foreseen by ancient prophets (Amos 8:11–12; Isaiah 24:5), was universal in scope, and was a time when the powers of God and the doctrines of salvation were either not on earth or existed in an altered form. Warnings of this apostasy can be found in the New Testament (Acts 20:28–30; 2 Thessalonians 2:1–4; 1 Timothy 4:1–3; 2 Timothy 4:1–4; 1 John 2:18–19).

In the centuries following the death of Jesus Christ and his apostles, many plain and precious truths were lost (1 Nephi 13:26). Most biblical scholars acknowledge that scribal errors inevitably took place in the transmission of the Bible and even that thousands of errors were introduced purposefully by scribes adding to or taking from the manuscripts. The Prophet Joseph explained: "From sundry revelations which had been received, it was apparent that many important points touching the salvation of men had been taken from the Bible, or lost before it was compiled" (*Joseph Smith,* 217). "From what we can draw from the Scriptures relative to the teaching of heaven," he declared later, "we are induced to think that much instruction has been given to man since the beginning which we do not possess now. . . . We have what we have, and the Bible contains what it does contain" (*History,* 2:18). In short, Joseph said, "I believe the Bible, as it ought to be, as it came from the pen of the original writers" (*Words,* 256).

During the years that followed the death and resurrection of the Lord, Christians sought earnestly to "contend for the faith which was once delivered unto the saints" (Jude 1:3). The Epistles of Paul, Peter, Jude, and John suggest that the falling away of the Christian church was well under way by the close of the first century. With the deaths of the apostles and the loss of the priesthood and its keys, or directing power, the institutional power to perform saving ordinances, learn the mind of God, and interpret scripture was gone from the earth. To be sure, throughout the centuries that followed, there were noble men and women, religious persons of goodwill, learned individuals who sought to hold the church together and to preserve holy writ. These acted, however, without prophetic or apostolic authority.

The New Testament clearly teaches the need for divine authority. Jesus ordained the Twelve Apostles (John 15:16), gave to them the keys of the kingdom of God (Matthew 16:18–19; 18:18), and empowered his servants to perform miracles and take the gospel to all nations (Matthew 10:1, 5–8; 28:19–20). Later, after the Lord's death, the apostles commissioned others to serve in the ministry (Acts 6:1–6; 13:1–3; 14:23; 1 Timothy 4:14; 2 Timothy 1:6; Titus 1:5) to ensure that the saving ordinances (sacraments) were performed only by those properly ordained (Acts 19:1–6, 13–16). Priesthood power was something no man could assume or purchase; it came only through the laying on of hands by those holding proper authority (Acts 8:18–20; Hebrews 5:4). With the death of the apostles, within one hundred years of the crucifixion of Jesus, the power and authority to act in the name of God was lost from the earth.

Although Catholics claim apostolic succession (that the bishops of the ancient Church conveyed their priesthood powers down to the Pope in our time), Latter-day Saints teach that God's divine authority was not to be found in the Old World by the middle of the second century A.D. or in the New World by the middle of the fifth century A.D. The Roman church had control of the Christian faith until the sixteenth century, at which point courageous men and women objected to, opposed, and broke away from Catholicism.

Roger Williams, the man known as the founder of the Baptist faith, later in his life renounced the views of the Baptists and "turned seeker, i.e., to wait for new apostles to restore Christianity." He felt the need "of a special commission, to restore the modes of positive worship, according to the original institution" (Backman, 181). "Williams concluded that the Protestants were 'not . . . able to derive the authority . . . from the apostles, . . . [but] conceived God would raise up some apostolic power'" (Backman, 180). In short, Williams held that there was "no regularly constituted church of Christ, on earth, nor any person authorized to administer any church ordinance, nor can there be until new apostles are sent by the great head of the Church, for whose coming I am seeking" (Richards, 29). Joseph Smith said concerning the situation in the Christian world in regard to divine authority: "I will illustrate it by an old apple tree. Here jumps off a branch and says, I am the true tree, and you are corrupt. If the whole tree is corrupt, are not its branches corrupt? If the Catholic religion is a false religion, how can any true religion come out of it?" (*History,* 6:478).

In speaking of the passing of the primitive Church, President Boyd K. Packer observed that "the flame flickered and dimmed. Ordinances were changed or abandoned. The line was broken, and the authority to confer the Holy Ghost as a gift was gone. . . . But always, as it had from the beginning, the Spirit of God inspired worthy souls.

"We owe an immense debt to the protesters and the reformers who preserved the scriptures and translated them. They knew something had been lost. They kept the flame alive as best they could. Many of them were martyrs. But protesting was not enough; nor could reformers restore that which was gone. In time, a great diversity of churches arose" ("Tongues," 8). On another occasion President Packer taught: "The line of priesthood authority was broken. But mankind was not left in total darkness or completely without revelation or inspiration. The idea that with the Crucifixion of Christ the heavens were closed and they opened in the First Vision is not true. The Light of Christ would be everywhere present to attend the children of God; the Holy Ghost would visit seeking souls. The prayers of the righteous would not go unanswered" ("Light," 11). Similarly, Elder Dallin H. Oaks explained: "We are indebted to the men and women who kept the light of faith and learning alive through the centuries to the present day. We have only to contrast the lesser light that exists among peoples unfamiliar with the names of God and Jesus Christ to realize the great contribution made by Christian teachers through the ages. We honor them as servants of God" (85).

Elder Alexander B. Morrison wrote: "The view that changes in the early church resulted in the descent of a blanket of stygian darkness over the entire earth, such that humankind had no contact with God or the Spirit for nearly two millennia, simply doesn't stand up to the scrutiny of modern scholarship. Scholars of today, benefiting from perspectives and information not readily available a century ago, understand that the 'Dark Ages' were not nearly so dark as previously had been thought" (2).

And yet, although the Protestant Reformation provided some measure of correction to the Christian church, it was not sufficient. A complete restoration was needed. The Prophet declared, "We don't ask any people to throw away any good they have got; we only ask them to come and get more" (*Joseph Smith*, 155).

President Gordon B. Hinckley said: "If we will go forward, never losing sight of our goal, speaking ill of no one, living the great principles we know to be true, this cause will roll on in majesty and power to fill the earth. Doors now closed to the preaching of the gospel will be opened. The Almighty, if necessary, may have to shake the nations to humble them and cause them to listen to the servants of the living God. Whatever is needed will come to pass. . . . Let us love the Lord, yes, with all our strength and power. And let us also love our neighbors. Let us banish from our lives any elements of self-righteousness. . . . Let us be friendly. Let us be helpful. Let us live the Golden Rule. Let us be neighbors of whom it might be said, 'He or she was the best neighbor I ever had'" (69).

SOURCES

Backman, Milton V. *American Religions and the Rise of Mormonism.* Salt Lake City: Deseret Book, 1965.

Hinckley, Gordon B. "Look to the Future." *Ensign,* Nov. 1997, 67–69.

Joseph Smith [manual]. Teachings of Presidents of the Church series. Salt Lake City: The Church of Jesus Christ of Latter-day Saints, 2007.

Morrison, Alexander B. *Turning from Truth: A New Look at the Great Apostasy.* Salt Lake City: Deseret Book, 2005.

Oaks, Dallin H. "Apostasy and Restoration." *Ensign,* May 1995, 84–87.

Packer, Boyd K. "The Cloven Tongues of Fire." *Ensign,* May 2000, 7–9.

———. "The Light of Christ." *Ensign,* Apr. 2005, 8–14.

Richards, LeGrand. *A Marvelous Work and a Wonder.* Salt Lake City: Deseret Book, 1990.

Smith, Joseph. *History of The Church of Jesus Christ of Latter-day Saints.* Edited by B. H. Roberts. 7 vols. 2d ed. rev. Salt Lake City: The Church of Jesus Christ of Latter-day Saints, 1932–51.

The Words of Joseph Smith. Compiled and edited by Andrew F. Ehat and Lyndon W. Cook. Provo, Utah: Brigham Young University Religious Studies Center, 1980.

RLM

APOSTLE

The word *apostle* derives from the Greek word *apostolos* and means "one who is sent forth." Though it may be used in various ways, in the Church today the term almost always is used to refer to a man ordained to that specific office in the Melchizedek Priesthood. Apostles are special witnesses of the name of Christ—his divinity and reality—in all the world (D&C 107:23). As in the ancient Church, when Jesus chose from among his disciples twelve whom he named apostles (Luke 6:13) and sent them forth to be his witnesses and leaders after his ascension (Acts 1:2–6), the Church of Jesus Christ in this last dispensation is guided by the Quorum of Twelve Apostles, which regulates the affairs of God's kingdom on earth under the direction of three presiding high priests who form the First Presidency. As they did in Jesus' day, the apostles in the Quorum of the Twelve (and in the First Presidency) hold the keys of the priesthood, the controlling authority of the Church delegated to men on earth by God (D&C 107:35; see also John 15:16). President Brigham Young said of this authority: "The keys of the eternal Priesthood, which is after the order of the Son of God, are comprehended by being an apostle. All the Priesthood, all the keys, all the gifts, all the endowments, and everything preparatory to entering into the presence of the Father and of the Son, are in, composed of, circumscribed by, or I might say incorporated within the circumference of, the Apostleship" (1:134–35).

The senior apostle of God on the earth is the president of the Church, the only individual authorized to exercise all priesthood keys in their fulness (D&C 132:7). He and two counselors form the First Presidency, the supreme governing body or presiding quorum over the whole Church, separate and apart from the Quorum of the Twelve Apostles, though the latter is designated as a body, or "quorum, equal in authority and power" to the First Presidency (D&C 107: 24). This means that when the First Presidency is dissolved upon the death of the president of the Church, the Twelve are authorized to exercise all of the power, authority, and prerogatives previously vested in the First Presidency.

Anciently, Peter, James, and John served as the chief apostles, being privileged to receive special instructions and witness certain events according to the Lord's own choosing, including those on the Mount of Transfiguration (Matthew 17:1–9) and the Savior's agony in Gethsemane (Mark 14:32–33). The first apostles in our dispensation were ordained under the hands of the resurrected Peter, James, and John (D&C 27:12). President Joseph Fielding Smith said: "The keys of the ministry which John says . . . were given to Peter, James, and himself [D&C 7:7], constituted the authority of Presidency of the Church in their dispensation. . . . These keys were given at the transfiguration to these Apostles, and they in turn gave them to Joseph Smith and Oliver Cowdery in this dispensation. (D&C 27:12–13; 128:20)" (1:49). President Brigham Young testified that "Joseph Smith, Oliver Cowdery, and David Whitmer were the first Apostles of this dispensation" (6:320). Heber C. Kimball indicated that Martin Harris was also ordained at some point (6:29). Subsequently, the Three Witnesses to the Book of Mormon were commissioned to select and ordain twelve other men to form the first Quorum of the Twelve Apostles in the latter days (D&C 18:26–30, 37–40; Kimball, 6:29). This quorum was organized in February 1835.

Others besides the members of the Quorum of the Twelve may be ordained apostles, called to serve as special witnesses of Jesus Christ. Paul consistently spoke of himself as one called to be an apostle (Romans 1:1; 1 Corinthians 1:1; 9:1; Galatians 1:1), and he applied the title to James, brother of the Lord (Galatians 1:19) and probably to Barnabas (1 Corinthians 9:5–6). We do not know with certainty, however, that they were members of the Quorum of the Twelve Apostles. The Lord has indicated that the number of official members of the Quorum of the Twelve should be maintained by filling vacancies as they arise (D&C 118:1). This fits exactly the inspired pattern established in the first-century Church (Acts 1:15–26).

When the Savior visited the Nephites in the New World after his resurrection, he chose twelve special disciples to lead his Church and administer his ordinances in the Americas (3 Nephi 12:1). The Prophet Joseph Smith indicated that these men were apostles (4:538). The twelve New World leaders were to judge their own people, and they in turn would be judged by the twelve apostles Jesus had chosen in the Old World. These original twelve apostles would also judge the rest of the twelve tribes of Israel (Mormon 3:18–19).

SOURCES

Kimball, Heber C. In *Journal of Discourses.* 26 vols. London: Latter-day Saints' Book Depot, 1854–86.

Smith, Joseph. *History of The Church of Jesus Christ of Latter-day Saints.* Edited by B. H. Roberts. 7 vols. 2d ed. rev. Salt Lake City: The Church of Jesus Christ of Latter-day Saints, 1932–51.

Smith, Joseph Fielding. *Church History and Modern Revelation.* 2 vols. Salt Lake City: The Council of the Twelve Apostles, 1953.

Young, Brigham. In *Journal of Discourses.* 26 vols. London: Latter-day Saints' Book Depot, 1854–86.

ACS

ARMAGEDDON

The Greek term *Armageddon* is a transliteration of two combined Hebrew words, *Har Megedon* or *Megiddon,* which mean "Mountain of Megiddo." Armageddon is the name of the last great battle on the earth that will be raging when the Savior comes again.

Anciently, Megiddo was a city overlooking the Jezreel Valley or Plain of Esdraelon (the Greek form of Jezreel), about sixty miles north of Jerusalem. Because of Megiddo's commanding position, the valley it controlled was known as the valley of Megiddon in Old Testament times (Zechariah 12:11). The city of Megiddo guarded the important highways and trade routes that crossed the valley and, therefore, was often the site of significant battles. Over time, as the city was destroyed and rebuilt on top of previous levels, it began to resemble a small mountain as one approached it from the valley. The Israelites fought at Meggido (Joshua 12:7, 21; 17:11; Judges 5:19–20; 1 Kings 9:15; 2 Kings 9:27; 23:29–30; 2 Chronicles 35:20–24), as did many other armies, including the Egyptians, Canaanites, Philistines, Assyrians, and Syrians. The great warrior-pharaoh, Thutmose III, was one of the first to take Megiddo from the native population, and he boasted in 1468 B.C. that capturing Megiddo was like capturing a thousand cities. By the time the apostle John wrote his Apocalypse (the book of Revelation), Megiddo had become a symbol for war.

In his vision of the last days, the end of the world, and the second coming of Christ, John saw that Megiddo would again be involved in war, specifically the last great battle before the coming of Christ: "The kings of the earth and of the whole world, . . . gather them to the battle of that great day of God Almighty. . . . And he gathered them together into a place called in the Hebrew tongue Armageddon" (Revelation 16:14–16). John also saw that the army was of enormous proportions: "And the number of the army of the horsemen were two hundred thousand thousand [two hundred million]: and I heard the number of them" (Revelation 9:16). Elder Bruce R. McConkie stated, "Armageddon is the place where the final war will be fought, meaning, as we suppose, that it will be the focal point of a worldwide conflict, and also that as a place of ancient warfare, it will be a symbol of the conflict that will be raging in many nations and on many battlefronts. . . . All nations are at war; some are attacking Jerusalem and others are defending the once holy city" (464).

Thus we understand that the battle of Armageddon will encompass many areas but especially the land from ancient Megiddo to Jerusalem. As Zechariah testified, however, Jerusalem is the ultimate prize, and the carnage will be terrible: "For I will gather all nations against Jerusalem to battle; and the city shall be taken, and the houses rifled, and the women ravished; and half of the city shall go forth into captivity, and the residue of the people shall not be cut off from the city. Then shall the Lord go forth, and fight against those nations, as when he fought in the day of battle. And his feet shall stand in that day upon the mount of Olives, which is before Jerusalem on the east, and the mount of Olives shall cleave in the midst thereof toward the east and toward the west, and there shall be a very great valley; and half of the mountain shall remove toward the north, and half of it toward the south" (Zechariah 14:2–4).

Elder Orson Pratt stated that Satan would be the promoter of this final great battle. "He [Satan] will gather up millions upon millions of people into the valleys around about Jerusalem in order to destroy the Jews after they have gathered. How will the Devil do this? He will perform miracles to do it. The Bible says the kings of the earth and the great ones will be deceived by these false miracles. . . . What will they do? Gather them up to battle unto the great day of God Almighty. Where? Into the valley of Armageddon" (7:188–89). It appears that the valley of Megiddo will be something of a staging area for the gigantic armies fighting for control of Jerusalem and for the destruction of the Jewish people.

President Joseph Fielding Smith indicated that "before the coming of Christ, the great war, sometimes called Armageddon, will take place as spoken of by Ezekiel, chapters 38 and 39. Another war of Gog and Magog will be after the millennium" (3:45). In other words, Armageddon is the name of the great war seen by Ezekiel as centering in Jerusalem with Gog and Magog as Israel's opponents. At the end of the Millennium another battle of the great God will occur, also involving Gog and Magog. The apostle John describes the latter battle this way: "And when the thousand years are expired, Satan shall be loosed out of his prison, and shall go out to deceive the nations which are in the four quarters of the earth, Gog and Magog, to gather them together to battle: the number of whom is as the sand of the sea. And they went up on the breadth of the earth, and compassed the camp of the saints about, and the beloved city: and fire came down from God out of heaven, and devoured them" (Revelation 20:7–9; see also D&C 88:111–16).

SOURCES

McConkie, Bruce R. *The Millennial Messiah: The Second Coming of the Son of Man.*
    Salt Lake City: Deseret Book, 1982.
Pratt, Orson. In *Journal of Discourses.* 26 vols. London: Latter-day Saints' Book
    Depot, 1854–86.
Smith, Joseph Fielding. *Doctrines of Salvation.* Compiled by Bruce R. McConkie.
    3 vols. Salt Lake City: Bookcraft, 1954–56.

ACS

ASCENSION OF CHRIST

Though there have been many ascensions of Christ (each time he has appeared to mortals as a resurrected being has involved a subsequent ascension), the scriptures speak primarily of two. Most Christians consider the formal ascension as that which occurred after the resurrected Christ completed his forty-day ministry (Acts 1:3) among the disciples in the Old World. Acts 1:9–11 records: "And when he had spoken these things, while they beheld, he was taken up; and a cloud received him out of their sight. And while they looked stedfastly toward heaven as he went up, behold, two men stood by them in white apparel; which also said, Ye men of Galilee, why stand ye gazing up into heaven? this same Jesus, which is taken up from you into heaven, shall so come in like manner as ye have seen him go into heaven."

From Luke's account we glean at least three important facts:

1. The Lord's formal ascension was attested by two heavenly messengers, thus validating the ancient law of witnesses.

2. All of the disciples present on that occasion were Galileans who had been with him during his earthly ministry (Acts 1:1–8).

3. The Lord's formal ascension set the pattern for his formal return at his Second Coming, which will also take place on the Mount of Olives (Zechariah 14:4–5; D&C 45:48; 133:20).

This formal ascension was preceded by Jesus' first ascension immediately after his resurrection, which was a private event involving only Mary Magdalene, the first human to see Jesus alive again. On that first Easter morn Jesus said to her: "Touch me not; for I am not yet ascended to my Father: but go to my brethren, and say unto them, I *ascend* unto my Father, and your Father; and to my God, and your God" (John 20:17; emphasis added). That very evening Jesus appeared to the disciples assembled in a room (John 20:19). But to them he said something different from what he had said to Mary that morning: "Handle me and see; for a spirit hath not flesh and bones, as ye see me have" (Luke 24:39). His invitation implies that he had by then ascended to God the Father and returned for the visit to his disciples. John records that when Jesus had shown to the disciples "his hands and his sides," then "were the disciples glad" (John 20:20). Apparently, this unmistakable demonstration that Jesus possessed again the same body that had been laid in the tomb brought gladness. They saw that he was truly a resurrected being.

Since his formal ascension, the Lord has returned to earth several times to minister to both ancient and modern prophets and apostles and give them instruction (Acts 9:1–9; Revelation 1:10–19; Joseph Smith–History 1:16–20; D&C 110:1–10). After each of these appearances he has returned to heaven.

ACS

ATONEMENT

In his last address to the members of the Church, only days before his death, Elder Bruce R. McConkie explained that "the atonement of Christ is the most basic and fundamental doctrine of the gospel, and it is the least understood of all our revealed truths. Many of us have a superficial knowledge and rely upon the Lord and his goodness to see us through the trials and perils of life. But if we are to have faith like Enoch and Elijah we must believe what they believed, know what they knew, and live as they lived. May I invite you to join with me in gaining a sound and sure knowledge of the Atonement. We must cast aside the philosophies of men and the wisdom of the wise and hearken to that Spirit which is given to us to guide us into all truth. We must search the scriptures, accepting them as the mind and will and voice of the Lord and the very power of God unto salvation" (10).

President Boyd K. Packer testified: "Truth, glorious truth, proclaims there is . . . a Mediator. Through Him mercy can be fully extended to each of us without offending the eternal law of justice. This truth is the very root of Christian doctrine. You may know much about the gospel as it branches out from there, but if you only know the branches and those branches do not touch that root, if they have been cut free from that truth, there will be no life nor substance nor redemption in them" (56).

These two prophetic proclamations affirm the simple yet profound word of the Prophet Joseph Smith that the apostolic witness of the resurrection and Atonement are indeed the fundamental principles of our religion. Truly, "all other things which pertain to our religion are only appendages" to the central verity of our Lord's mediational mission (3:30).

Holy scripture has set forth the sobering reality that "all have sinned, and come short of the glory of God" (Romans 3:23) and that God "cannot look upon sin with the least degree of allowance" (D&C 1:31). "For your iniquities have ye sold yourselves," Jehovah stated to ancient Israel (Isaiah 50:1). Because of the fall of our first parents in Eden, and because we as mortals occasionally choose to disobey the commandments of God, every son and daughter of God on earth is in a spiritually precarious position—we are both lost and fallen (1 Nephi 10:6; Alma 42:6). We are lost, for "we like sheep have gone astray; we have turned every one to his own way" (Isaiah 53:6). We are in desperate need of a map, a way back home. We need a guide, a leader, one who walks ahead and can see afar off. And we need to be found, to be rescued. Because we are fallen, we need to be lifted up, washed and renewed, and reoriented toward life and things as they really are.

"Since man had fallen he could not merit anything of himself" (Alma 22:14). No amount of human effort can rescue us. Mortals cannot forgive their own sins, cannot cleanse their own hearts, cannot through works alone behave themselves into righteousness, cannot raise themselves from the grave, and cannot, worlds without end, glorify themselves beyond death's door. We have not the strength so to do. We are powerless.

But there is a way back. Indeed, God himself, our Father in Heaven, prepared a plan of salvation, a great plan of happiness by which we may be rescued, redeemed, reconciled, and restored to the family of God. At the heart of that grand plan of salvation is the Atonement of Jesus Christ. The Atonement is the means by which fallen, sinful men and women may be put back into a right relationship with our Father and God. Jesus is the Means, the Way, the Mediator, the Intercessor between a perfectly righteous and infinite God and a flawed, finite humanity. It was decreed in the councils of heaven, long before the earth was formed, that Jesus would "descend from his throne divine" (*Hymns,* no. 193) and take a "tabernacle of clay," a mortal body (Mosiah 3:5). He would live as we live, would "be like man, almost" (*Hymns,* no. 175), yet he would not—he could not—yield to sin (2 Corinthians 5:21; Hebrews 4:15; 1 Peter 2:22). He would live a perfect life, would learn obedience by the things he suffered (Hebrews 5:8), and would, through having met every obstacle and engaged every pain and barrier and thereby perfected his empathy, be in a position to succor the children of God in their sorrows, infirmities, and temptations (Alma 7:11–12; D&C 62:1).

While in a sense the Savior's atonement would encompass his entire life, the climax of his work of redemption began in the Garden of Gethsemane and was completed on the Cross of Calvary. In a way incomprehensible to mortal minds, during those hours of atonement in Gethsemane and on Golgotha, the Father transferred to his Beloved Son the sins and pains and frustrations and fears that had been, were then, and would yet be experienced by the whole of humankind. Our Lord "descended in suffering below that which man can suffer; or, in other words, suffered greater sufferings, and was exposed to more powerful contradictions than any man can be" (*Lectures*, 59; compare Hebrews 12:3). Jesus the Christ descended below all, that he might overcome the world and ascend above all (2 Corinthians 8:9; Ephesians 4:8; D&C 88:6). He who had never taken a detour or a backward step, he whose every word was proper and whose every action was right, even he tasted the bitterness of sin and came to know the awful alienation from God that comes in the wake of disobedience; he took our place and assumed our burdens. Jesus could say, as he did in modern revelation, "I have . . . trodden the wine-press alone, even the wine-press of the fierceness of the wrath of Almighty God" (D&C 76:107; compare D&C 88:106; 133:50; Isaiah 63:3). In the Garden of Gethsemane—meaning the garden of the oil press or the garden of the wine-press—our Divine Redeemer became subject to God's wrath, the withdrawal of God's sacred and sustaining Spirit. Without that sustaining Spirit, the intensity of the impact of that wrath caused Jesus to sweat blood, "to bleed at every pore, and to suffer both body and spirit" (D&C 19:18; compare Luke 22:44; Mosiah 3:7; Young, 3:206). Through his willingness to have the sins of humanity heaped upon his own soul, he became "sin for us" (2 Corinthians 5:21). As Paul taught, "Christ hath redeemed us from the curse of the law, being made a curse for us" (Galatians 3:13). Jesus "was made a little lower than the angels for the suffering of death, crowned with glory and honour; that he by the grace of God should taste death for every man" (Hebrews 2:9). In short, Christ came into the world not only to *change* us (which is fundamental and foundational to the Christian faith) but also to effect an *exchange* with us: for when we receive him through the gospel covenant, Jesus takes our sin and offers us his righteousness.

In a very real sense, the gospel or glad tidings (good news) is that Jesus Christ came to earth, lived a perfect life, suffered and died for us, and three days later rose from the dead in glorious immortality. The gospel is the Atonement (1 Corinthians 15:1–4; 3 Nephi 27:13–14; D&C 76:40–42). In another sense, the gospel is the good news that through receiving the first principles and ordinances, what Joseph Smith called the "articles of adoption" (6:58), we may receive and apply the powers of the Atonement and qualify for eternal life (D&C 33:10–12; 39:6).

SOURCES

"How Great the Wisdom and the Love." *Hymns of The Church of Jesus Christ of Latter-day Saints,* no. 195. Salt Lake City: The Church of Jesus Christ of Latter-day Saints, 1985.

Lectures on Faith. Salt Lake City: Deseret Book, 1985.

McConkie, Bruce R. "The Purifying Power of Gethsemane." *Ensign,* May 1985, 9–11.

Packer, Boyd K. "The Mediator." *Ensign,* May 1977, 54–56.

Smith, Joseph. *History of The Church of Jesus Christ of Latter-day Saints.* Edited by B. H. Roberts. 7 vols. 2d ed. rev. Salt Lake City: The Church of Jesus Christ of Latter-day Saints, 1932–51.

"While of These Emblems We Partake." *Hymns of The Church of Jesus Christ of Latter-day Saints,* no. 173. Salt Lake City: The Church of Jesus Christ of Latter-day Saints, 1985.

Young, Brigham. In *Journal of Discourses.* 26 vols. London: Latter-day Saints' Book Depot, 1854–86.

RLM

ATONEMENT, INFINITE

The Atonement of Jesus Christ is infinite and eternal, in at least the following ways:

1. It engages and overcomes the most common and prevalent facet of mortality, namely, physical death, which we share with every other mortal creature (2 Nephi 9:7).

2. It is timeless. Jesus Christ is the Lamb "slain from the foundation of the world" (Revelation 13:8; Moses 7:47), and his atonement is in effect for all who live on this earth—those who lived before he came to earth, those who lived during the time of his ministry, and those

who come to earth after the meridian of time (Jarom 1:11; Mosiah 3:13; 16:6; Alma 24:13; 39:17–19; D&C 20:25–27).

3. It was performed by One who is an "infinite and eternal" Being (Alma 34:14). Jesus Christ was the son of Mary, a mortal woman, and from her he inherited mortality, including the capacity to die. Jesus was also the son of God, and from him he inherited immortality, including the power to live forever. "No man taketh [my life] from me, but I lay it down of myself. I have power to lay it down, and I have power to take it again" (John 10:18; see also Helaman 5:11).

4. It defies human (mortal) law and logic. Jesus did what no mortal person could do. The touch of his hand and the unspeakable power of his mediation transcend what most mortals understand about justice and mercy, right and wrong, restitution and punishment. Note Amulek's words to the errant Zoramites: "It is expedient that there should be a great and last sacrifice; yea, not a sacrifice of man, neither of beast, neither of any manner of fowl; for it shall not be a human sacrifice; but it must be an infinite and eternal sacrifice. Now there is not any man that can sacrifice his own blood which will atone for the sins of another. Now, if a man murdereth, behold will our law, which is just, take the life of his brother? I say unto you, Nay. But the law requireth the life of him who hath murdered; therefore there can be nothing which is short of an infinite atonement which will suffice for the sins of the world" (Alma 34:10–12).

5. Christ, or Jehovah, redeems all he creates. He has created worlds without number, and a limitless collection of worlds have "passed away"—gone though their mortal, postmortal, and glorified states—by the word of God's power, meaning, by the power of his Only Begotten Son (Moses 1:32–33, 35; 7:30).

"And now, after the many testimonies which have been given of him," Joseph Smith and Sidney Rigdon affirmed, "this is the testimony, last of all, which we give of him: That he lives! For we saw him, even on the right hand of God; and we heard the voice bearing record that he is the Only Begotten of the Father—that by him, and through him, and of him, the worlds are and were created, and the inhabitants thereof are begotten sons and daughters unto God" (D&C 76:22–24). In 1843 the Prophet Joseph wrote the following poetic parallel to the verses just cited; called "A Vision," it was published in the *Times and Seasons* (82–83):

> *And I heard a great voice, bearing record from heaven,*
> *He's the Saviour, and only begotten of God—*
> *By him, of him, and through him, the worlds were all made,*
> *Even all that career in the heavens so broad,*
>
> *Whose inhabitants, too, from the first to the last,*
> *Are sav'd by the very same Saviour of ours;*
> *And, of course, are begotten God's daughters and sons,*
> *By the very same truths, and the very same powers.*

In our day Elder Russell M. Nelson likewise taught: "His [Christ's] Atonement is infinite—without an end. It was also infinite in that all humankind would be saved from never-ending death. It was infinite in terms of his immense suffering. It was infinite in time, putting an end to the preceding prototype of animal sacrifice. It was infinite in scope—it was to be done once for all. And the mercy of the Atonement extends not only to an infinite number of people, but also to an infinite number of worlds created by Him" (167).

SOURCES

Nelson, Russell M. *Perfection Pending.* Salt Lake City: Deseret Book, 1998.
"A Vision." *Times and Seasons* 4, no. 6 (1 Feb. 1843): 81–85.

RLM

BAAL

A Hebrew word that occurs many times in the Old Testament, *Baal* (plural, *baalim*) refers to the false god or gods worshipped principally among the Phoenician, Philistine, and Canaanite peoples. In this sense, the term is best translated as "lord" or "master."

Baal was the name of the supreme male deity thought to control nature, storms, agriculture, and fertility and whose rites of worship involved degrading and abhorrent practices that corrupted true worship.

The type of Baal worship encountered by ancient Israel,

especially the northern kingdom, seems to have had its principal seat in Phoenicia. The sins of King Ahab in this regard were particularly notorious: "Ahab the son of Omri did evil in the sight of the Lord above all that were before him. . . . he took to wife Jezebel the daughter of Ethbaal king of the Zidonians [Phoenicians], and went and served Baal, and worshipped him. And he reared up an altar for Baal in the house of Baal, which he had built in Samaria" (1 Kings 16:30–32). It was during this time that Elijah's dramatic contest with the 450 prophets of Baal occurred (1 Kings 18). The cult of Baal was prominent in Israel until Jehu put an end to it (2 Kings 10:23–26).

As a name, *Baal* was sometimes used in compound constructions, as in the names of other deities, such as Baal-peor, god of the Moabites (Numbers 25:1–3, 17–18), Baal-berith, a god worshipped at Shechem (Judges 8:33; 9:4), and Baal-zebub, god of the Philistines at Ekron (2 Kings 1:2); and in the names of persons, such as Ethbaal, king of the Zidonians, or Phoenicians (1 Kings 16:31). Baal was also the name of two other individuals: a Reubenite (1 Chronicles 5:5) and a Benjamite (1 Chronicles 8:30).

ACS

BABYLON

At the Savior's second coming, "all the proud . . . and all that do wickedly, shall be stubble" (Malachi 4:1) because, the Lord declared, "I will not spare any that remain in Babylon" (D&C 64:24). After the inhabitants of Judah, the southern kingdom, were taken captive by armies of the Babylonian Empire (about 605–598 B.C.), the empire's capital city, Babylon, was figuratively used in scripture to mean the corrupt world that is ruled and influenced by Satan. The inhabitants of this symbolic worldly city are described as those who "seek not the Lord to establish his righteousness, but every man walketh in his own way, and after the image of his own god, whose image is in the likeness of the world" (D&C 1:16). Therefore, the Lord declares, "Go ye out from among the nations, even from Babylon, from the midst of wickedness, which is spiritual Babylon" (D&C 133:14; see also Revelation 18:4–5).

In his Apocalypse, John saw Babylon as "the mother of harlots and abominations of the earth" and the "habitation of devils, and the hold of every foul spirit" (Revelation 17:5; 18:2). But in the end, after making "war with the Lamb, . . . the Lamb [Christ] shall overcome them," and "Babylon the great" will fall, to arise no more (Revelation 17:14; D&C 1:16; see also Revelation 14:8).

CFO

BAPTISM

The Father has commanded everyone to repent and receive the saving ordinance of baptism (John 3:3–5; 2 Nephi 31:11). Together with repentance, baptism is the gate to the strait and narrow path that leads us back to God the Father (2 Nephi 31:17). Baptism is essential for salvation (Mark 16:16; Acts 2:38; D&C 18:22). As Jesus taught Nicodemus, "Except a man be born of water and of the Spirit, he cannot enter into the kingdom of God" (John 3:5).

Jesus Christ gave his authorized servants specific instructions to follow whenever they baptized a repentant believer: "Behold, ye shall go down and stand in the water, and in my name shall ye baptize them" (3 Nephi 11:23). The Savior has also specified the prayer accompanying the ordinance of baptism (D&C 20:73). The person being baptized is then laid under the water and brought up straightway out of it (D&C 20:74; Moses 6:64; Colossians 2:12). The imagery associated with baptism is powerful and instructive. "We are buried with [Christ] by baptism into death; that like as Christ was raised up from the dead by the glory of the Father, even so we also should walk in newness of life" (Romans 6:4). As a newborn babe springs to life upon emerging from the womb, so through baptism we are born again as new creatures, sons and daughters of Christ (Moses 6:59; Mosiah 5:7).

Indeed, even the holy Lamb of God submitted to the ordinance of baptism to fulfill all righteousness. He did not see himself as an exception to the commandment but instead "humbl[ed] himself before the Father, and witness[ed] unto the Father that he would be obedient unto him in keeping his commandments" (2 Nephi 31:7). As the great Exemplar, the Lord then tells us, "Follow thou me" (2 Nephi 31:10). Therefore, we must also be baptized to witness "unto the Father that [we] are willing to keep [his] commandments" (2 Nephi 31:14) and "to put on Christ" (Galatians 3:27), that we become "heirs according to the [Abrahamic] promise" (Galatians 3:29).

The Lord has specified the qualities that a person needs to have in order to be baptized. "All those who humble themselves before God, and desire to be baptized, and come forth with broken hearts and contrite spirits, and witness before the church that they have truly repented of all their sins, and are willing to take upon them the name of Jesus Christ, having a determination to serve him to the end, and truly manifest by their works that they have received of the Spirit of Christ unto the remission of their sins, shall be received by baptism into his church" (D&C 20:37). Preparation for baptism includes recognition that one has not spiritually progressed that far without "relying wholly upon the merits of him who is mighty to save" (2 Nephi 31:19).

When we are baptized, we make a covenant with God and retain it afterward. Through baptism we demonstrate to God our individual commitment to join the fold of Christ and our willingness to be called after his name—as "his sons and his daughters," we covenant to serve God, keep his commandments "unto the end of [our] lives," and always remember him (Mosiah 5:7–8; Moroni 4:3; see also 3 Nephi 7:24–25; Mosiah 18:8–10). In return, God will pour out his Spirit upon us in greater abundance, remit our sins, cleanse us through the baptism of fire and the Holy Ghost, and make of us new creatures (2 Nephi 31:13, 17; Moroni 6:4; 2 Corinthians 5:17). We renew that covenant through partaking of the sacrament of the Lord's Supper.

Little children and those not capable of understanding the commandments of God are covered by the righteousness of the Redeemer and therefore need no baptism (Moroni 8:20, 22; D&C 20:71; 29:49–50). The Lord has been adamant on this point, for the ordinance of baptism has been misunderstood, disputed, and distorted in the past (JST, Genesis 17:5–7; Moroni 8:4; D&C 74:6–7). Because of the atonement of Christ, "power is not given unto Satan to tempt little children, until they begin to become accountable before [God]," or at about eight years of age (D&C 29:46–47; 68:27).

In his mercy the Lord is also mindful of those who die without receiving a testimony of Christ and his gospel. During the three days his spirit was in the postmortal spirit world, Jesus Christ prepared the way for the gospel to be preached "to those who had died in their sins, without a knowledge of the truth, or in transgression, having rejected the prophets" (D&C 138:32; 1 Peter 3:18–21; 4:6). Authorization was then given to his representatives on earth to perform baptisms for the dead in temples, sacred edifices appropriate for this ordinance (D&C 124:29–30; 1 Corinthians 15:29).

When the resurrected Christ told his disciples in Jerusalem, "Go ye therefore, and teach all nations, baptizing them in the name of the Father, and of the Son, and of the Holy Ghost" (Matthew 28:19–20), he was clearly inviting everyone, in every era and in every land, to come to him and, beginning with baptism, follow his path, which leads back to the Father

CFO

BAPTISM OF FIRE

Synonymous with the scriptural terms "born again," "born of the Spirit," "second birth," and "spiritual rebirth," the baptism of fire is the actual reception of the Holy Ghost by an individual. Nephi explained that after one has followed the Savior "with full purpose of heart, acting no hypocrisy and no deception before God, but with real intent, repenting of your sins, witnessing unto the Father that ye are willing to take upon you the name of Christ, by baptism," only then will that person truly "receive the Holy Ghost; yea, then cometh the *baptism of fire* and of the Holy Ghost; and then can ye speak with the tongue of angels, and shout praises unto the Holy One of Israel" (2 Nephi 31:13; emphasis added). In the scriptures, fire is a symbol both of purification and of the presence of God. The term "refiner's fire" (Malachi 3:2) denotes a transformation of something from a lower state to a higher through a process that eliminates impurities and coarser elements. Spiritually speaking, the Holy Ghost refines and purifies us and brings about a "mighty change" of heart and soul (Mosiah 5:2, 7).

Elder Bruce R. McConkie taught that "sins are remitted not in the waters of baptism, as we say in speaking figuratively, but when we receive the Holy Ghost. It is the Holy Spirit of God that erases carnality and brings us into a state of righteousness. We become clean when we actually receive the fellowship and companionship of the Holy Ghost. It is then that sin and dross and evil are burned out of our souls *as though by fire*. The baptism of the Holy Ghost is the baptism of fire" (290; emphasis added).

SOURCE

McConkie, Bruce R. *A New Witness for the Articles of Faith.* Salt Lake City: Deseret Book, 1985.

BLT

BEELZEBUB

Beelzebub is a name for Satan in the New Testament. Some Jews applied the epithet to Jesus (Matthew 10:25). The Pharisees and scribes accused Jesus of being in league with this "prince of the devils" (Matthew 9:34), by whose power they claimed the Savior cast out demons and healed people. Knowing their thoughts, Jesus responded that such a view was impossible because a kingdom divided against itself cannot stand. If Satan casts out Satan, how will his kingdom survive? Rather, Jesus performed his miracles by the power of God (Matthew 12:24–28; Mark 3:22–26; Luke 11:15–20).

The term *Beelzebub,* or Ba'alzebub, comes from combining two Hebrew words: *Ba'al* ("Lord") *zebub* ("of flies"). Originally Ba'alzebub was the Philistine god of the city of Ekron. It is mentioned in 2 Kings 1:2 when Ahaziah fell ill and sent messengers to inquire of Ba'alzebub whether Ahaziah would recover from the disease. False gods, however, do not give inspired counsel.

ACS

BIBLE

The English word *bible* derives from the Greek term *biblia,* meaning "books." The Bible is a divine library of sixty-six individual books divided into the Old and New Testaments, collected and edited over many centuries. The books were written by divinely inspired authors about Israel's sacred history and theology, her covenants with God, her faith and loyalty to him, her patriarchs and prophets, her expectation of a Messiah, and the fulfillment of that expectation in the advent of Jesus Christ. The New Testament (twenty-seven books) is named in relation to the Old Testament (thirty-nine books); the original word from which we get *testament* was understood in ancient times to mean "covenant" (Jeremiah 31:31–34). The compilation of the Old Testament was completed and the final authoritative status of its current books confirmed in the first century, probably at Jamnia or Yavneh (an ancient city of Palestine) around A.D. 90. The New Testament canon was likely complete by the end of the second century A.D or the beginning of the third.

In general terms the Old Testament tells the Israelites who they are and how God interacted with them. The New Testament records testimonies of Christ's mortal ministry and his atoning acts as well as the history of the early Church and some of the writings of its apostles and prophets. The original language of the Old Testament was Hebrew; that of the New Testament was Greek.

The Bible "has had a greater influence on the world for good than any other book ever published" (Smith, *Doctrines,* 3:184). It has been at the heart of major developments in world history, especially the Protestant Reformation, which helped to free the Bible from the bondage of inaccessible monasteries and the libraries of elite institutions. The history of efforts to give the world the complete Bible in English, beginning with John Wycliffe's first translation from Latin in 1381 or 1382, shows how much the adversary hates the Bible and tries to prevent it from going forth to all people. Men such as John Wycliffe (1320–84) and William Tyndale (1492–1536), upon whose translation the King James Version was based, paid a dear, sometimes ultimate, price for their work. They have been honored by latter-day prophets and apostles as divinely inspired heroes worthy of our gratitude. In the main, the Reformers and Bible translators were "honest men with yearning hearts, [who] at the peril of their very lives, attempted to establish points of reference, that they might find the true way. . . . The reformers were pioneers, blazing wilderness trails in a desperate search for those lost points of reference which, they felt, when found would lead mankind back to the truth Jesus taught. John Wycliffe, Martin Luther, Jan Hus, Zwingli, Knox, Calvin, and Tyndale all pioneered the period of the Reformation. Significant was the declaration of [William] Tyndale to his critics: 'I will cause a boy that driveth the plough shall know more of the scripture than thou doest'" (Monson, 51).

Not only those who labored to bring forth translations of the Bible in the vernacular of the people but even those humble souls who earnestly hungered to understand God's word in their own tongue were sometimes burned at the stake, with copies of the Bible tied mockingly around their necks as cruel and ironic punishment for their righteous desires.

The Bible stands as a foundation stone of the Lord's true Church in the latter days. The Prophet Joseph Smith was reared with Bible stories and teachings, and it was as a result of his reading a passage in the Epistle of James that he was prompted to ask God which of all the Christian denominations he should join (Joseph Smith–History 1:11–14). In his adult years, the mature Prophet of the Restoration taught that the Bible was the inspired word of God, that every person of common intelligence could see God's "own handwriting" in the Bible, and that "he who reads it oftenest will like it best, and he who is acquainted with it, will know the hand [of God] wherever he can see it" (*Joseph Smith,* 66). He frequently quoted from or paraphrased the Bible in his sermons, and "much of the Prophet's teaching focused on passages from the Bible, which was frequently his tool for explaining doctrine" (Jackson, x).

The version Joseph Smith used was the King James Version. First published in 1611, it remains the official English language version of the Church. Though many other versions have been produced over the years, few if any have equaled the majesty and richness of expression found in the King James Version. The First Presidency declared in 1992: "While other Bible versions may be easier to read than the King James Version, in doctrinal matters latter-day revelation supports the King James Version in preference to other English translations. All of the Presidents of the Church, beginning with the Prophet Joseph Smith, have supported the King James Version by encouraging its continual use in the Church. In light of the above, it is the English language Bible used by The Church of Jesus Christ of Latter-day Saints" (80).

Notwithstanding the great value Joseph Smith placed on the Bible, he also acknowledged the errors it contained. In February 1832 he stated "that many important points touching the salvation of men, had been taken from the Bible, or lost before it was compiled" (*Joseph Smith,* 217). Consequently, when asked in 1842 about the history of the Church and its beliefs by Mr. John Wentworth, the Prophet included statement number eight in the list that is now called the Articles of Faith: "We believe the Bible to be the word of God as far as it is translated correctly." This statement complements an ancient prophetic declaration in the Book of Mormon that warned of "many plain and precious things taken away" from the Bible before it went forth "unto all nations of the Gentiles" (1 Nephi 13:28–29).

Joseph Smith also undertook the study of biblical languages to better understand the text. He observed, for example, that "our [doctrinal] latitude and longitude can be determined in the original Hebrew with far greater accuracy than in the English version. There is a grand distinction between the actual meaning of the prophets and the present translation" (*History,* 5:342–43). The Prophet was commanded by the Lord to undertake, through inspiration, a new translation of the Bible, now known as the Joseph Smith Translation, which he began in June 1830. Of this enterprise the Lord said, "The scriptures shall be given, even as they are in mine own bosom, to the salvation of mine own elect" (D&C 35:20).

The Church honors and reveres the Bible; it is one of the standard works of our faith. Members of the Church are commanded to teach the principles of the gospel "which are in the Bible and the Book of Mormon" (D&C 42:12). President Heber J. Grant, who served as president of the Church from 1918 to 1945, reflected the attitude of the faithful regarding the Bible: "All my life I have been finding additional evidences that the Bible is the Book of books, and that the Book of Mormon is the greatest witness for the truth of the Bible that has ever been published" (660). The First Presidency similarly noted in 1992: "The most reliable way to measure the accuracy of any biblical passage is not by comparing different texts, but by comparison with the Book of Mormon and modern-day revelation" (80).

SOURCES

First Presidency. "First Presidency Statement on the King James Version of the Bible." *Ensign,* Aug. 1992, 80.

Grant, Heber J. "The President Speaks." *Improvement Era,* Nov. 1936, 659–60.

Jackson, Kent P., ed. *Joseph Smith's Commentary on the Bible.* Salt Lake City: Deseret Book, 1994.

Joseph Smith [manual]. Teachings of Presidents of the Church series. Salt Lake City: The Church of Jesus Christ of Latter-day Saints, 2007.

Monson, Thomas S. "They Showed the Way." *Ensign,* May 1997, 50–52.

Smith, Joseph. *History of The Church of Jesus Christ of Latter-day Saints.* Edited by B. H. Roberts. 7 vols. 2d ed. rev. Salt Lake City: The Church of Jesus Christ of Latter-day Saints, 1932–51.

Smith, Joseph Fielding. *Doctrines of Salvation.* Compiled by Bruce R. McConkie. 3 vols. Salt Lake City: Bookcraft, 1954–56.

ACS

BIRTHRIGHT

During the patriarchal era of the Bible, every son was entitled to a share of his father's estate. One son, however, was named the birthright son with particular responsibilities and privileges beyond those that his brothers received. As the patriarch of his clan, the birthright son inherited presiding authority in the Abrahamic covenant and twice the wealth that his brothers were given. His responsibilities and additional resources extended to the care and sustenance of his mother, childless wives of his father, unmarried sisters, or sisters returning home because of divorce or widowhood without children. For example, just as Rebekah's brother, Laban, acted in proxy for their absent father in arranging her marriage to Isaac, so the birthright son acted in proxy for his father in helping unmarried sisters find husbands and providing them a dowry (Genesis 24).

The firstborn son was traditionally expected to receive the birthright, but often in biblical history a younger son was named the birthright recipient. For example, the Lord identified Abraham's second son, Isaac, as the covenant son rather than the firstborn son, Ishmael (Genesis 21). Esau "despised his birthright" (Genesis 25:34), so the responsibility was given to his younger brother, Jacob (Genesis 26–27). Jacob begot twelve sons, but the eleventh one, Joseph, became the birthright son (Genesis 37). As a result, Joseph received a double portion of inheritance; that double portion was recognized when his two sons, Manasseh and Ephraim, each received an inheritance when the promised land was divided among the tribes of Israel (Numbers 26:28–37; Joshua 16–17). Finally, although Ephraim was the younger son, the patriarch Jacob put him ahead of his elder brother, Manasseh, for the birthright (Genesis 48:8–22). The Lord called the birthright son, who was a type of Christ, "his firstborn" and assigned him the leadership responsibilities of maintaining the covenant in his stead: "I am a father to Israel," Jehovah declared, "and Ephraim is my firstborn" (Jeremiah 31:9).

The declaration of the birthright son was often made by the father (or grandfather) in a formal, official manner, much like a patriarchal blessing today. The father or patriarch depended on inspiration from heaven in giving the right blessing for each son. Therefore, we read that "by faith Isaac blessed Jacob and Esau concerning things to come. By faith Jacob, when he was a dying, blessed both the sons of Joseph" (Hebrews 11:20–21).

CFO

BISHOP

The word *bishop* is a translation of the Greek *episcopos,* meaning "overseer." It is used in three ways in the Lord's Church in this dispensation. First, it is a name-title of Jesus Christ, who is called "the Shepherd and Bishop of [our] souls" by the apostle Peter (1 Peter 2:25). Second, it is the title of all members of the Presiding Bishopric. Third, and most common, the title *bishop* designates the ecclesiastical leader, holding keys of presidency, over a ward. Each ward bishop serves simultaneously as president of the Aaronic Priesthood in the ward and as the president of the priests quorum (D&C 107:87–88). As the presiding high priest in the ward, he is responsible for all its members (D&C 107:17–18) and is a judge in Israel (D&C 58:17; 107:74), who judges, counsels, and delegates among his congregation just as Moses judged, led, and delegated (Exodus 18). "And whoso . . . is appointed to be a judge in Israel, like as it was in ancient days . . . [is] to judge his people by the testimony of the just, and by the assistance of his counselors, according to the laws of the kingdom which are given by the prophets of God" (D&C 58:17–18).

Therefore, although *bishop* is an office in the Aaronic Priesthood, it is a necessary appendage belonging to the high priesthood (D&C 84:29). And though worthy members of the Church who are literally and demonstrably descendants of Aaron have the legal right to the office of Presiding Bishop (D&C 68:20), other worthy high priests are appointed bishops over wards and also Presiding Bishop (D&C 68:15, 19; 107:17, 69–76). A bishop is given the gift to discern all the gifts of the Spirit in order that every member of his ward may be benefited thereby (D&C 46:27, 29). Bishops are to search out and care for the poor (D&C 84:112) and administer "all temporal things" (D&C 107:68). For these and other reasons, the apostle Paul taught:

"A bishop then must be blameless, the husband of one wife, vigilant, sober, of good behaviour, given to hospitality, apt to teach; not given to wine, no striker, not greedy of filthy lucre; but patient, not a brawler, not covetous; one that ruleth well his own house, having his children in subjection with all gravity; (For if a man know not how to rule his own house, how shall he take care of the church of God?) not a novice, lest being lifted up with pride he fall into the condemnation of the devil. Moreover he must have a good report of them which are without; lest he fall into reproach and the snare of the devil" (1 Timothy 3:2–7; see also Titus 1:7–9).

Each bishop must be ordained to the office (D&C 20:67; 107:17) and set apart to his specific field of labor, usually the ward in which he is authorized to work (Smith, 166). Edward Partridge was the first bishop ordained in our dispensation (D&C 41:9), and Newel K. Whitney the second (D&C 72:7–8).

SOURCE

Smith, Joseph F. *Gospel Doctrine.* Salt Lake City: Deseret Book, 1939.

ACS

BISHOPRIC

The term *bishopric* is used two different ways in scripture. The first, more general way refers to priesthood leaders who hold positions or offices of authority in the Lord's Church and serve with colleagues in administering their responsibilities. For example, when the apostle Peter met with the other disciples to choose a replacement for Judas Iscariot in the Quorum of the Twelve, Peter said, "For it is written in the book of Psalms, Let his habitation be desolate . . . and his bishop-rick let another take" (Acts 1:20). In this dispensation the Lord also used the term to refer to the Twelve: "For verily thus saith the Lord, that inasmuch as there are those among you who deny my name, others shall be planted in their stead and receive their bishopric" (D&C 114:2).

The second, specific usage of *bishopric* refers to three high priests of the order of Melchizedek, a bishop and two counselors, who administer all the affairs of their ward (D&C 84:29; 68:19) or, in the case of the Presiding Bishopric, the temporal affairs of the Church. The Presiding Bishopric is responsible to aid in the disposition of Church tithing funds (D&C 120:1). All bishops are ordained; counselors in ward bishoprics are set apart.

ACS

BLASPHEMY

The English word *blasphemy* derives from the Greek *blasphemein,* meaning "to speak evil of," or "to slander." Any profane or mocking speech, writing, or action directed toward or about Deity or other sacred things is blasphemy. Likewise, anything that shows contempt, disdain, or deliberate disrespect for God or sacred things is blasphemy.

In the Old Testament, blasphemy usually involves speech that is disrespectful of God, especially cursing, uttering profane oaths and imprecations, damning, or calling down evil upon someone or something in a way that connects the utterance to Deity. The Mosaic code gives strict prohibitions about blasphemy and harsh punishments for it. "He that blasphemeth the name of the Lord, he shall surely be put to death, and all the congregation shall certainly stone him: as well the stranger, as he that is born in the land, when he blasphemeth the name of the Lord, shall be put to death" (Leviticus 24:16). By contrast, Job was an example of one who, though taunted to curse God and die, maintained complete loyalty to him and refused to blaspheme (Job 2:9–10). In Old Testament times some actions were considered clearly blasphemous, such as the Israelites building the golden calf, which is referred to as casting the Lord's law "behind their backs" (Nehemiah 9:18, 26).

In the New Testament, blasphemy is, again, most often associated with speech. But, ironically, it is Jesus who not infrequently is accused of committing blasphemy, as when he is perceived to be assuming prerogatives reserved for Deity—such as being able to forgive sins: "Why doth this man thus speak blasphemies? who can forgive sins but God only?" (Mark 2:7; see also Luke 7:37–50). Likewise, when he declares himself to be one with his Father, he is accused of blasphemy (John 10:30–33).

The most significant charges of blasphemy leveled against Jesus came during his arraignment before the Sanhedrin and high priest; these charges led directly to his crucifixion. "Then the high priest rent his clothes, saying, He hath spoken blasphemy; what further need have we of witnesses? behold, now ye have heard his blasphemy. What think ye? They answered and said, He is guilty [deserving] of death" (Matthew 26:65–66; see also Mark 14:64). Of course Jesus did nothing but tell the truth in testifying that he was "the Christ, the Son of God" (Matthew 26:63).

The apostle Paul identified blasphemy as a sign of apostasy (2 Timothy 3:2). And John the Revelator described the great church led by the devil in the latter days as being made up of the kingdoms of the earth and possessing the "name of blasphemy" (Revelation 13:1).

In our dispensation the Lord has warned, "Let all men beware how they take my name in their lips" (D&C 63:61). One sign of the times is that the Lord's "disciples shall stand in holy places, and not be moved; but among the wicked, men shall lift up their voices and curse God and die" (D&C 45:32). The Lord also reiterated the warning issued during his mortal ministry that "blasphemy against the Holy Ghost . . . shall not be forgiven in the world nor out of the world" (D&C 132:27; see also Matthew 12:31–32; Mark 3:28–29). It is the unpardonable sin because it means denying and rebelling against Jesus Christ and sacred things *after* the Holy Ghost has given an individual a sure and certain knowledge of their reality.

ACS

BLOOD ATONEMENT

The only form of blood atonement that is a part of the teaching and practice of The Church of Jesus Christ of Latter-day Saints is the blood atonement of the Lord Jesus Christ. Forgiveness for sin, cleansing and renewal from the effects of sin, and the divine empowerment associated with a change of disposition toward sin— all come through the atoning blood of Christ, shed for us in the Garden of Gethsemane and on the cross of Calvary. During a period of the restored Church's history, especially during the era known as the "Mormon Reformation" (1857–67), Church leaders made extensive efforts to encourage the Saints to sanctify themselves, to reenthrone spiritual discipline in their lives, and to avoid worldly and immoral practices. In some instances, Church leaders delivered fiery sermons with sober and even harsh language concerning the consequences of serious sin, even stating that for some sins it might be necessary for the offender to be put to death ("blood atoned") in order to receive remission of sins.

Two things should be kept in mind when seeking to understand this period of Church history:

1. Such teachings were largely a kind of revival rhetoric and had the same effect of harsh preaching among the Saints in ancient America: "And there was nothing save it was exceeding harshness, preaching and prophesying of wars, and contentions, and destructions, and continually reminding them of death, and the duration of eternity, and the judgments and the power of God, and all these things—stirring them up continually to keep them in the fear of the Lord . . . and exceedingly great plainness of speech, would keep them from going down speedily to destruction" (Enos 1:23). Such language is "more express . . . that it might work upon the hearts of the children of men" (D&C 19:7).

2. In a statement prepared in August 1835 to explain Latter-day Saint views on government and laws in general, we read the following: "We believe that all religious societies have a right to deal with their members for disorderly conduct, according to the rules and regulations of such societies; provided that such dealings be for fellowship and good standing; but we do not believe that any religious society has authority to try men on the right of property or life, to take from them this world's goods, or to put them in jeopardy of either life or limb, or to inflict any physical punishment upon them. They can only excommunicate them from their society, and withdraw from them their fellowship" (D&C 134:10).

We read of instances of individuals in ancient times being put to death for violating the law of God, such as in the days of Moses and the children of Israel, but that was a completely different situation than we have now. They lived in a theocratic society where there was no separation of church and state, no division between religious and civil powers. Because we do not live in such a society, we are subject to the principles set forth in our inspired Constitution and in Doctrine and Covenants 134:10. There is no historical evidence of anyone being subject to some form of blood atonement (other than cleansing through the blood of the Savior) in the restored Church. Capital punishment is not to be equated with blood atonement; capital punishment is the purview of civil magistrates, not Church leaders, and the courts choose how duly convicted criminals may be executed.

RLM

BONDAGE

The scriptures speak of two kinds of bondage—temporal and spiritual. Deliverance from both kinds is a recurring theme in holy writ. The Old Testament records that ancient Israel was often in bondage to foreign powers that oppressed and plundered them. Likewise, the Book of Mormon records many examples of peoples who were put in bondage to another people. Often such captivity came about because of the people's pride, wickedness, and disregard for prophetic counsel. The scriptural accounts of the bondage of God's people are accompanied by prophetic promises of deliverance and accounts of how those promises were fulfilled. Temporal bondage and deliverance are thus a type or symbol of spiritual bondage and redemption. Death and sin are the two main kinds of spiritual bondage found in the scriptures.

The fall of Adam brings the ultimate bondage—what Jacob in the Book of Mormon calls "this awful monster; yea, that monster, death and hell" (2 Nephi 9:10)—from which man cannot be delivered without divine assistance. Death is characterized in the scriptures in such terms as "bands of death" and "chains of death." This universal bondage is destroyed by the infinite atoning sacrifice and resurrection of Jesus Christ, which "breaketh the bands of death, having gained the victory over death" (Mosiah 15:8). Resurrection is thus characterized as "deliverance" and "liberty to the captives" (D&C 138:18).

In like manner, sin is a real form of bondage. The Book of Mormon repeatedly describes sin with such phrases as "awful chains" (2 Nephi 1:13), "chains of hell" (Alma 13:30), and "bands of iniquity" (Mosiah 23:12). Sin and the loss of the Spirit that results are a bondage from which we can escape only through faith in Jesus Christ, repentance, and obedience to the principles and ordinances of the gospel.

BLT

BOOK OF MORMON

The Book of Mormon is another testament of Jesus Christ, a companion volume of scripture with the Bible. Like the Bible, it was written by "holy men of God" who spoke or wrote by the power of the Spirit (2 Peter 1:21). It is a chronicle of men and women who left the Old World and journeyed to the New, directed and guided by that same God who prompted and led Noah and Abraham, Jacob and Moses, Isaiah and Malachi, Peter and John. It contains a timeless message—a repeated reminder that unless people acknowledge their weakness, confess their sins, and surrender their lives to God our Eternal Father and his Son, Jesus Christ, they will continue to wrestle with reality, struggle with priorities, and wander in the morass of misery and meaninglessness. The Book of Mormon affirms the biblical theme that man's purpose in life can be discovered only through turning heavenward and seeking to know and follow the counsel of the Almighty. In short, "If men do not comprehend the character of God, they do not comprehend themselves" (Smith, 6:303).

The Book of Mormon is filled with redemptive theology, with teachings and testimonies of the plight of fallen man, of the absolute necessity of a spiritual rebirth, and of thundering proclamations that peace in this world and eternal life in the world to come can be enjoyed only "in and through the atoning blood of Christ, the Lord Omnipotent" (Mosiah 3:18). The Book of Mormon attests, with other scriptural texts of the Restoration, of Christ's eternal gospel—that Christian prophets have declared Christian doctrine and participated in Christian ordinances, or sacraments, since the beginning of time. Thus Book of Mormon prophetic personalities, even those who lived centuries before the mortal ministry of Jesus in the Old World, call upon God the Eternal Father, in the name of his Son Jesus Christ, by the power of the Holy Ghost. This unusual scriptural record declares that not only did Abraham have the gospel of Jesus Christ almost two millennia before the Savior came (Galatians 3:8) but of this Redeemer "give all the prophets witness" (Acts 10:43). Or, as one prophet and record-keeper in the Book of Mormon testified six centuries before Christ: "For, for this intent have we written these things, that they [their descendants] may know that we knew of Christ, and we had a hope of his glory many hundred years before his coming; and not only we ourselves had a hope of his glory, but also all the holy prophets which were before us. Behold, they believed in Christ and worshipped the Father in his name, and also we worship the Father in his name.

And for this intent we keep the law of Moses, it pointing our souls to him; and for this cause it is sanctified unto us for righteousness, even as it was accounted unto Abraham in the wilderness to be obedient unto the commands of God in offering up his son Isaac, which is a similitude of God and his Only Begotten Son" (Jacob 4:4–5; see also Jarom 1:11; Mosiah 3:13; 16:6).

Joseph Smith taught that the Book of Mormon is "the most correct of any book on earth" (4:461). This is because of the undiluted and penetrating message it presents—the way it establishes in no uncertain terms that "there is a God in heaven, who is infinite and eternal, from everlasting to everlasting the same unchangeable God, the framer of heaven and earth, and all things which are in them" (D&C 20:17); the way it highlights the nature of fallen humanity; the way it focuses repeatedly upon man's utter inability to forgive or cleanse or resurrect or save himself; the way it places Jesus Christ center stage and testifies of the infinite and eternal scope of his atoning sacrifice. In the Book of Mormon, Christ is the Lord God Omnipotent, who saves "not only those who believed after he came in the meridian of time, in the flesh, but all those from the beginning, even as many as were before he came, who believed in the words of the holy prophets, . . . as well as those who should come after" (D&C 20:26–27).

The Book of Mormon is the most correct book on earth because it teaches us who God is; what the Godhead is; how the Father, the Son, and the Holy Ghost are infinitely more one than they are separate; and how the love and unity among them are of such magnitude that the Nephite record speaks of them several times simply as "one God, infinite and eternal, without end" (D&C 20:28; see also 2 Nephi 31:21; Alma 11:44; 3 Nephi 9:15; 11:27, 36; 28:10; Mormon 7:7). The Book of Mormon is the most correct book because it presents with consistent clarity the delicate balance between the grace of our Lord and God and the works of righteousness that must always characterize and identify true disciples of the Master (2 Nephi 2:2–8; 25:23; 31:19; Alma 22:14; Helaman 14:13; Moroni 6:4).

The Book of Mormon assists us to span the chasm that many feel exist between the God of the Old Testament and the God of the New. "I make my own heartfelt declaration of God our Eternal Father this morning," Elder Jeffrey R. Holland stated, "because some in the contemporary world suffer from a distressing misconception of Him. Among these there is a tendency to feel distant from the Father, even estranged from Him, if they believe in Him at all. And if they do believe, many moderns say they might feel comfortable in the arms of Jesus, but they are uneasy contemplating the stern encounter of God" (71).

Elder Holland observed further that "one of the remarkable contributions of the Book of Mormon is its seamless, perfectly consistent view of divinity throughout that majestic book. Here there is no Malachi-to-Matthew gap, no pause while we shift theological gears, no misreading the God who is urgently, lovingly, faithfully at work on every page of that record from its Old Testament beginning to its New Testament end. Yes, in an effort to give the world back its Bible and a correct view of Deity with it, what we have in the Book of Mormon is a uniform view of God in all His glory and goodness, all His richness and complexity—including and especially as again demonstrated through a personal appearance of His Only Begotten Son, Jesus Christ" (71).

Finally, Elder Holland pointed out, "Jesus did not come to improve God's view of man nearly so much as He came to improve man's view of God and to plead with them to love their Heavenly Father as He has always and will always love them. The plan of God, the power of God, the holiness of God, yes, even the anger and the judgment of God they had occasion to understand. But the love of God, the profound depth of His devotion to His children, they still did not fully know—until Christ came" (72).

Do we desire to know how to handle wayward children; how to deal justly yet mercifully with transgressors; how to bear pure testimony; how to teach and preach in such a manner that people cannot go away unaffected; how to detect the enemies of Christ; how to withstand those who seek to destroy our faith; how to discern and expose secret combinations that seek to destroy the works of the Lamb of God; how to deal properly with persecution and anti-Mormonism; and how to establish Zion? Then we must search and study the Book of Mormon.

Do we desire to know more about how to avoid pride and the perils of the prosperity cycle; how to avoid priestcraft and acquire and embody charity, the pure love of Christ; how our sins may be remitted and how we can know when they have been forgiven; how to retain a remission of sins from day to day; how to come unto Christ, receive his holy name, partake of his goodness and love, and be sanctified by his Spirit? Do we desire to know how to prepare for the second coming of the Son of Man? Then we must search and study the Book of Mormon.

President Ezra Taft Benson stated: "It is not just that the Book of Mormon teaches us truth, though it indeed does that. It is not just that the Book of Mormon bears testimony of Christ, though it indeed does that, too. But there is something more. There is a power in the book which will begin to flow into your lives the moment you being a serious study of the book. You will find greater power to resist temptation. You will find the power to avoid deception. You will find the power to stay on the strait and narrow path. The scriptures are called 'the words of life' (see D&C 84:85), and nowhere is that more true than it is of the Book of Mormon. When you begin to hunger and thirst after those words, you will find life in greater and greater abundance" (21–22).

The Book of Mormon is far more than a theological treatise, more than a collection of great doctrinal sermons. It is not just a book that helps us feel good; it is a heavenly document that has been given to help us *be* good. Stated differently, this volume is not just a book about religion. It *is* religion. Our challenge, therefore, is not just to read and study the Book of Mormon but to live it and accept and apply its doctrines and philosophy.

The Book of Mormon presses us for a decision. We cannot simply dismiss it with a wave of the hand and a turn of the head; it must be explained. Thus, as Elder Bruce R. McConkie pointed out, "the time is long past for quibbling about words and for hurling unsavory epithets against the Latter-day Saints. These are deep and solemn and ponderous matters. We need not think we can trifle with sacred things and escape the wrath of a just God.

"Either the Book of Mormon is true, or it is false; either it came from God, or it was spawned in the infernal realms. . . . It is not and cannot be simply another treatise on religion; it either came from heaven or from hell. And it is time for all those who seek salvation to find out for themselves whether it is of the Lord or of Lucifer" (73).

And as far as members of the Church are concerned, President Ezra Taft Benson has declared boldly: "Every Latter-day Saint should make the study of this book a lifetime pursuit. Otherwise he is placing his soul in jeopardy and neglecting that which could give spiritual and intellectual unity to his whole life" (7–8).

SOURCES

Benson, Ezra Taft. *A Witness and a Warning: A Modern-day Prophet Testifies of the Book of Mormon.* Salt Lake City: Deseret Book, 1988.

Holland, Jeffrey R. "The Grandeur of God." *Ensign,* Nov. 2003, 70–73.

McConkie, Bruce R. "What Think Ye of the Book of Mormon?" *Ensign,* Nov. 1983, 72–74.

Smith, Joseph. *History of The Church of Jesus Christ of Latter-day Saints.* Edited by B. H. Roberts. 7 vols. 2d ed. rev. Salt Lake City: The Church of Jesus Christ of Latter-day Saints, 1932–51.

RLM

BORN AGAIN

To Nicodemus the Pharisee, Jesus declared, "Except a man be born again, he cannot see the kingdom of God" (John 3:3). The spiritual rebirth of which the Savior spoke involves both the ordinance of baptism ("born of water") and the mighty change of heart that comes through the sanctifying power of the Holy Ghost ("born of . . . the Spirit") (John 3:5). Both are required for salvation.

"Baptism by water is but half a baptism," the Prophet Joseph Smith taught, "and is good for nothing without the other half—that is the baptism of the Holy Ghost" (95). Being born again is the spiritual transformation that results when we have actually received the Holy Ghost and experienced the remission of sins that accompanies it. Nephi explained that *after* we have followed the Savior "with full purpose of heart, acting no hypocrisy and no deception before God, but with real intent, repenting of your sins, witnessing unto the Father that ye are willing to take upon you the name of Christ, by baptism," only then will we "receive the Holy Ghost; yea, then cometh the baptism of fire and of the Holy Ghost" (2 Nephi 31:13). Being born again comes through the actual reception of the Holy Ghost—the fulfillment of the command given to every baptized member of the Church upon confirmation: "Receive the Holy Ghost."

The Book of Mormon clearly teaches that while the ordinance of baptism allows us to enter in at the gate, salvation cannot be obtained without also experiencing spiritual rebirth: "The gate by which ye should enter is repentance and baptism by water; and then cometh a remission of your sins by fire and by the Holy Ghost" (2 Nephi 31:17). Several Book of Mormon passages illustrate as well as define what it means to be born again (Enos 1:1–6; Mosiah 5:1–7; 27:25–26; Alma 13:1–12; 18:41–43; 19:6, 33; Helaman 5:41–49; 3 Nephi 9:20–22). Being born again is, as King Benjamin taught, being "spiritually be-gotten" unto Christ through faith in his atoning sacrifice, whereby our "hearts are changed" (Mosiah 5:7). Spiritual rebirth brings "a mighty change in us, or in our hearts, that we have no more disposition to do evil, but to do good continually" (Mosiah 5:2). Elder Orson Pratt explained the process: "Water baptism is only a preparatory cleansing of the believing penitent, whereas, the Baptism of fire and the Holy Ghost cleanses more thoroughly, by renewing the inner man, and by purifying the affections, desires, and thoughts which have long been habituated in the impure ways of sin" (57).

This spiritual rebirth may come in dramatic ways, as in the cases of Paul (Acts 9), Alma (Mosiah 27; Alma 36), King Benjamin's people (Mosiah 5), King Lamoni and his wife (Alma 18–19), and the large number of people who were converted on the day of Pentecost (Acts 2). This same spiritual transformation may occur less visibly as a grad-ual process rather than as a singular event. Today, as anciently, there are those who receive the Holy Ghost and become "new creatures" (Mosiah 27:26; 2 Corinthians 5:17) in Christ through sudden, mi-raculous conversions, and yet others are born again gradually, step-by-step, being "quickened in the inner man" (Moses 6:65–66), and like the Lamanites of old, they may not even recognize it (3 Nephi 9:20). A person may be born again numerous times and from one level of spiri-tual conversion to a higher level. Elder Bruce R. McConkie explained:

"We are born again when we die as pertaining to unrighteousness and when we live as pertaining to the things of the Spirit. But that doesn't happen in an instant, suddenly. That . . . is a process. Being born again is a gradual thing, except in a few isolated instances that are so miraculous they get written up in the scriptures. As far as the gen-erality of the members of the Church are concerned, we are born again by degrees, and we are born again to added light and added knowledge and added desires for righteousness as we keep the commandments. . . .

"As members of the Church, if we chart a course leading to eternal life; if we begin the processes of spiritual rebirth, and are going in the right direction . . . ; if we chart a course of becoming perfect, and, step by step and phase by phase, are perfecting our souls by overcoming the world, then it is absolutely guaranteed—there is no question whatever about it—we shall gain eternal life. Even though we have spiritual rebirth ahead of us, perfection ahead of us, the full degree of sanctification ahead of us, if we chart a course and follow it to the best of our ability in this life, then when we go out of this life we'll continue in exactly the same course" (399–401).

Thus there is no real difference in the quality of the experience of being born again, whether it comes gradually or suddenly. The *process* may differ, but the *results* are the same. Whether the transformation is sudden or a slow process of growth with almost imperceptible changes, being born again brings with it fruits that can be felt and discerned within our hearts and observed in our lives. The degree to which we experience these things is an indication of the degree to which we have experienced the "mighty change" of heart (Alma 5:14). The indicators of the baptism of fire in our lives include peace of conscience (Enos 1:6; Mosiah 4:2–3; 27:29; Alma 36:19), feelings of divine joy and love (2 Nephi 4:21; Mosiah 4:3; Alma 19:29–30; 36:20–21; Moroni 8:26), a desire to do good continually, with no desire to do evil (Mosiah 5:2; Alma 13:11–12; 19:33), increased love for fellowmen and desire to serve others (Enos 1:9–13; Mosiah 4:11, 13, 16; 28:3; Alma 36:24), increased spiritual understanding (Mosiah 5:3; Alma 19:6; 26:19–22), and having God's image—his will and ways—engraven upon our countenances, or in other words, reflected in how we live (Alma 5:41; 3 Nephi 21; 27).

As physical birth is a beginning, so too is spiritual rebirth. Once we have been born again, had our hearts "changed through faith on [Christ's] name" (Mosiah 5:7), and have received a remission of sins by the power of the Holy Ghost, we must continue pressing forward with "a steadfastness in Christ, having a perfect brightness of hope, and a love of God and of all men" (2 Nephi 31:20).

SOURCES

Joseph Smith [manual]. Teachings of Presidents of the Church series. Salt Lake City: The Church of Jesus Christ of Latter-day Saints, 2007.

McConkie, Bruce R. "Jesus Christ and Him Crucified." In *1976 Devotional Speeches of the Year,* 391–405. Provo, Utah: Brigham Young University Press, 1977.

Pratt, Orson. *Orson Pratt: Writings of an Apostle.* Salt Lake City: Mormon Heritage Publishers, 1976.

BLT

BRAZEN SEA

The brazen sea (1 Chronicles 18:8), also called the molten sea (1 Kings 7:23), was an enormous basin (ten cubits, or approximately 180 inches, from rim to rim) cast of brass under Solomon's leadership for the Jerusalem temple (2 Chronicles 4:2; 1 Kings 7:23). It corresponded with the brass basin made for the Tabernacle, which the children of Israel had used in the wilderness (Exodus 30:17–21), and rested on the backs of twelve oxen, arranged in sets of three facing outward toward the cardinal points of the compass (1 Kings 7:25, 44). Solomon placed the brazen sea on the south side of the temple, at the southeast corner of the courtyard of the priests (2 Chronicles 4:9–10).

The Bible says only that the brazen sea was used by priests for ritual cleansing (2 Chronicles 4:6). By commandment, these washings followed the same practice involving the brass laver of the earlier Tabernacle, in which Aaron and his sons were commanded to "wash their hands and their feet, that they die not: and it shall be a statute for ever to them, even to him and to his seed throughout their generations" (Exodus 30:21). Elder Bruce R. McConkie stated that the "brazen sea was used for performing baptisms for the living" (104). The washings performed in the brazen sea foreshadowed the atonement of Christ, which "saved us, by the washing of regeneration" (Titus 3:5).

Latter-day Saint temples have a large font patterned after the brazen sea of Solomon's temple. There baptisms for the dead are performed by proxy. The twelve oxen supporting each of these fonts (Mazar, 377) represent the twelve tribes of Israel. In ancient times salvation was not preached in the spirit world, nor were vicarious baptisms performed for the dead until after the death and resurrection of Jesus Christ (Moses 7:37–39; D&C 138).

SOURCES

Mazar, Amihai. *Archaeology of the Land of the Bible.* New York: Doubleday, 1992.

McConkie, Bruce R. *Mormon Doctrine.* 2d ed. Salt Lake City: Bookcraft, 1966.

ACS

BREAD OF LIFE

Even as the children of Israel were miraculously sustained by manna from heaven during their forty-year sojourn in the wilderness, they were reminded that physical nourishment was not enough to truly live. Moses warned them that "man doth not live by bread only, but by every word that proceedeth out of the mouth of the Lord" (Deuteronomy 8:3). The day after feeding the five thousand, Jesus taught the Galilean multitude that he was the "bread of life" that "cometh down from heaven, and giveth life unto the world" (John 6:35, 33). Whereas the Israelites "did eat manna in the wilderness, and are dead," those who eat of the Bread of Life, or believe on and come unto Christ, will "live for ever" (John 6:48–51).

As we symbolically and with faith eat of the Savior's flesh and drink of his blood, exemplified by the emblems of the sacrament of the Lord's Supper, the Lord will eventually grant us eternal life and raise us up "at the last day" (John 6:54; 1 Corinthians 11:27). Alma taught that we "eat and drink of the bread and the waters of life freely" when we come unto Christ, repent, and "bring forth works of righteousness" (Alma 5:34–35). When we feast on the Bread of Life, our robes are washed "white in the blood of the Lamb," and we "hunger no more, neither thirst any more . . . for the Lamb which is in the midst of the throne shall feed [us]" (Revelation 7:14, 16–17). Because of his atoning sacrifice, Jesus Christ is the "[only] meat which endureth unto everlasting life" (John 6:27).

CFO

BRIDEGROOM

The bridegroom is used in the scriptures, both ancient and modern, as a symbol for the Lord Jesus Christ. The Church (covenant Israel) is represented as the bride. Marriage is symbolic of the covenant relationship between God and man. In the Old Testament, numerous passages portray Jehovah as a loving bridegroom whose love and mercy for his bride—even when she has been unfaithful—is infinite and eternal. This symbolism is used to call ancient Israel to repentance and to extend a merciful invitation to return in strict faithfulness to the Bridegroom—the Lord (Psalm 19:5–6; Isaiah 54:5–8; Jeremiah 3:14; 31:1, 6–8; Ezekiel 16:8–9, 14–15, 60–62; 34:11–25; Hosea 1–3). Similarly, in the New Testament, John the Baptist referred to Jesus as the Bridegroom (John 3:27–30), and the Savior himself used this same symbolism in his parable of the ten virgins (Matthew 25:1–3). John the Revelator symbolically spoke of the Church as the bride who would be made ready through repentance and righteousness to receive the Bridegroom at his glorious second coming (Revelation 19:7–9; 21:9). The Lord has reemphasized to the modern Church this redemptive relationship by using the symbolism of marriage. The message is both instructional and invitational. Individual members of the Church, who collectively are covenant Israel, are like a bride waiting for the groom to come and take her to himself and are thus commanded to be spiritually prepared to meet the Bridegroom (D&C 33:17–18; 109:73–74; 133:10).

BLT

BUFFETINGS OF SATAN

The Holy Ghost is the Comforter, charged by the Father and the Son to inspire, lift, warn, teach, testify, and lead us into all truth. While salvation, or eternal life, is "the greatest of all the gifts of God" in eternity (D&C 6:13; 14:7), the gift of the Holy Ghost is the most vital heavenly gift we can receive in this life. We may not realize just how precious an endowment it is until we lose it through serious sin or are severed from the Church through formal excommunication. It is then, void of the Spirit, alienated from things of righteousness and thus subject to spiritual death, that we may experience what the scriptures describe as the buffetings of Satan. To buffet is to shove, push, strike, or knock about. The devil and his minions unloaded their spiritual artillery of temptings and tauntings upon One who was left so very alone—our Lord and Savior during his hours of atonement. Elder James E. Talmage taught: "In that hour of anguish Christ met and overcame all the horrors that Satan, 'the prince of this world' [John 14:30] could inflict. The frightful struggle incident to the temptations immediately following the Lord's baptism was surpassed and overshadowed by this supreme contest with the powers of evil" (613).

In speaking to the early leaders of the Church, the Lord declared: "Wherefore, a commandment I give unto you, to prepare and organize yourselves by a bond or everlasting covenant that cannot be broken. And he who breaketh it shall lose his office and standing in the church, and shall be delivered over to the buffetings of Satan until the day of redemption" (D&C 78:11–12). On another occasion he said, "And the soul that sins against this covenant, and hardeneth his heart against it, shall be dealt with according to the laws of my church, and shall be delivered over to the buffetings of Satan until the day of redemption" (D&C 82:21).

SOURCE

Talmage, James E. *Jesus the Christ*. Salt Lake City: Deseret Book, 1973.

RLM

CAIN

From the book of Moses, Joseph Smith's inspired translation of the early chapters of Genesis, we learn that Adam and Eve may well have been grandparents before Cain and Abel were born (Moses 5:2–3, 16). One generation of Adam and Eve's posterity chose to love Satan more than God and "began from that time forth to be carnal, sensual, and devilish" (Moses 5:13). Then Eve conceived and bore Cain. She said, "I have gotten a man from the Lord; wherefore he may not reject [God's] words. But behold, Cain hearkened not, saying: Who is the Lord that I should know him?" (Moses 5:16).

Cain loved Satan more than God and entered into an alliance with the evil one. As a part of his wicked oath, Cain agreed to become the father of Satan's lies, to become "Mahan, the master of this great secret, that I may murder and get gain" (Moses 5:31). Covetous of his brother Abel's flocks and jealous because his own sacrifice was rejected by God—it was given for all the wrong reasons and was contrary to the Lord's instructions that Adam's posterity should offer an animal sacrifice (Moses 5:5; Smith, 2:15–16)—Cain allowed his anger to fester and his soul to canker. He slew Abel, incurred the wrath of God, became a fugitive and a vagabond in the earth, and was the coauthor of secret combinations (Moses 5:16–55; Helaman 6:26–27). Both Satan and Cain are called Perdition (D&C 76:26; Moses 5:24), which means ruin or destruction. Their followers—those who sin against truth and knowledge by denying and defying the Son after walking in his light—are called sons of perdition.

SOURCE

Smith, Joseph. *History of The Church of Jesus Christ of Latter-day Saints.* Edited by B. H. Roberts. 7 vols. 2d ed. rev. Salt Lake City: The Church of Jesus Christ of Latter-day Saints, 1932–51.

RLM

CALLING AND ELECTION

The Lord has declared in our dispensation that "he who doeth the works of righteousness shall receive his reward, even peace in this world, and eternal life in the world to come" (D&C 59:23). Isaiah had written some twenty-six hundred years earlier, "And the work of righteousness shall be peace; and the effect of righteousness quietness and assurance for ever" (Isaiah 32:17). Those in this life who conduct themselves with fidelity and devotion to God and his laws will eventually know that peace "which passeth all understanding" (Philippians 4:7), the calming but powerful assurance that one has successfully met the challenges of mortality. These are they who have lived "by every word of God" (Luke 4:4) and are willing to serve the Lord at all hazards. They have made their calling and election sure (Smith, 3:380). For them the Day of Judgment has been advanced, and the blessings associated with the glories of the celestial kingdom are assured. They receive what the Prophet Joseph Smith called the "more sure word of prophecy" (5:389). He explained: "The more sure word of prophecy means a man's knowing that he is sealed up unto eternal life, by revelation and the spirit of prophecy, through the power of the Holy Priesthood. It is impossible for a man to be saved in ignorance" of this truth (D&C 131:5–6). Though it is true, as President Marion G. Romney observed, that "the fullness of eternal life is not attainable in mortality, . . . the peace which is its harbinger and which comes as a result of making one's calling and election sure is attainable in this life" (20).

The Prophet Joseph Smith extended a challenging invitation to the Saints: "I would exhort you to go on and continue to call upon God until you make your calling and election sure for yourselves, by obtaining this more sure word of prophecy, and wait patiently for the promise until you obtain it" (5:389). Latter-day Saints who have received the ordinances of salvation, including the blessings of the temple, may thus press forward in the work of the Lord and with quiet dignity and patient maturity seek to be worthy of gaining the certain assurance of salvation before the end of their mortal lives. But should a person not formally receive the more sure word of prophecy in this life, he or she has the scriptural promise that faithfully enduring to the end—keeping the covenants and commandments from baptism to the end of mortality (Mosiah 18:8–9)—eventuates in the promise of eternal life, whether that promise be received here or hereafter (D&C 14:7; 53:7; 2 Nephi 31:20; Mosiah 5:15).

"Blessed are they who are faithful and endure, whether in life or in death, for they shall inherit eternal life" (D&C 50:5). Elder Bruce R. McConkie expressed the following sentiments at the funeral of Elder S. Dilworth Young: "If we die in the faith, that is the same thing as saying that our calling and election has been made sure and that we will go on to eternal reward hereafter. As far as faithful members of the Church are concerned, they have charted a course leading to eternal life. This life is the time that is appointed as a probationary estate for men to prepare to meet God, and as far as faithful people are concerned, if they are in the line of their duty, if they are doing what they ought to do, although they may not have been perfect in this sphere, their probation is ended. Now there will be some probation for some other people hereafter. But for the faithful saints of God, now is the time and the day, and their probation is ended with their death, and they will not thereafter depart from the path. It is true, as the Prophet Joseph Smith said, that there are many things that have to be done 'even beyond the grave' to work out our salvation, but we'll stay in the course and we will not alter from it, if we have been true and faithful in this life" (5).

Salvation is a reality and a possibility, a goal within the reach of all humankind. The precious promises made available through the atoning sacrifice of Jesus our Lord give focus and direction to our actions. Salvation, eternal life, exaltation—all expressions connoting the glories of the celestial kingdom and a life that is similar to God's own life— represent the grand ends to our myriad means, the reason we do what we do in the Church and in the home. To those who have developed "precious faith" (2 Peter 1:1) like that of the ancients come the blessings enjoyed by the ancients: the fulness of the glory of the Father and a continuation of the family unit forever and ever (D&C 132:19).

SOURCES

McConkie, Bruce R. Address delivered at the funeral of S. Dilworth Young, Salt Lake City, 13 July 1981.

Romney, Marion G. In Conference Report, Oct. 1965, 20–23.

Smith, Joseph. *History of The Church of Jesus Christ of Latter-day Saints.* Edited by B. H. Roberts. 7 vols. 2d ed. rev. Salt Lake City: The Church of Jesus Christ of Latter-day Saints, 1932–51.

RLM

CANON OF SCRIPTURE

The canon of scripture may be defined as the list or collection of authoritative, divinely approved, sacred books upon which a community of believers is based. The word *canon* derives from the Greek noun *kanon*, meaning "reed" or "cane" and thus by extension "rule" or "measure." The Greek word is probably derived from the Hebrew *qaneh*, a reed used for measuring, as described in Ezekiel 40:3, 5. The canon is also the standard against which texts are measured to determine scriptural authority. "Its technical use with reference to books of the Bible seems to have become current among Greek and Latin authors by A.D. 350" (Sperry, 7).

Canons may be closed or open. The Jewish canon is closed, meaning that material cannot be added to or removed from the longstanding, specific collection of books constituting the Hebrew Bible (what Christians call the Old Testament). Most Christian denominations believe in a closed canon, accepting the twenty-seven books of the New Testament and the thirty-nine books of the Old Testament as the complete canon of scripture, although some denominations also accept the Old Testament Apocrypha as canonical. The notion of a closed canon ultimately reflects a belief that institutional or public revelation has ceased.

Some Christians have attempted to justify the notion of a closed canon by referring to Revelation 22:18–19: "If any man shall add unto these things . . . and if any man shall take away from the words of the book of this prophecy, God shall take away his part out of the book of life." This passage, however, can hardly mean that only the Bible as presently constituted is all that God intended for his children to have. First of all, much of the same language appears in Deuteronomy 4:2: "Ye shall not add unto the word . . . , neither shall ye diminish ought from it" (see also Deuteronomy 12:32). What is the entire New Testament, then, if not an addition "unto the word" of God?

Moreover, various biblical texts themselves attest to the existence of books now lost from the present biblical canon but at one time regarded as authoritative by prophets and inspired writers. Those who oppose the idea that additional institutional revelation is possible, those who are adamant that the Bible is complete and exists exactly the way God intended, or those who condemn scripture not found in the Bible as being necessarily spurious, false, and evil, should consider the many biblical references to records not found in the Bible. For example, Numbers 21:14 speaks of the book of the wars of the Lord; Joshua 10:13 and 2 Samuel 1:18 speak of the book of Jasher (Hebrew, "upright"); 1 Kings 11:41 speaks of the book of the acts of Solomon; 1 Chronicles 29:29 speaks of the book of Nathan the prophet and the book of Gad the seer; 2 Chronicles 20:34 speaks of the book of Jehu; and 1 Corinthians 5:9 speaks of a missing epistle of Paul. All these are just some of the texts that help make the case for lost scripture and an incomplete biblical canon.

Our understanding remains hazy about how some books were declared authoritative (part of the canon) and others were not. Evidence suggests that the canonizing of the Old Testament occurred in stages, the latest developments happening between 200 B.C. and A.D. 100. By Jesus' day, the three-fold division of the Law, the Prophets, and the Writings had been established (Matthew 22:40; Luke 24:44). In Hebrew these are, respectively, the *Torah,* the *Nevi'im,* and the *Khetuvim,* which is why the Jewish people refer to the Hebrew Bible as the *Tanakh*—an acronym formed by combining the first letter of each of the three division names. In addition, comparisons of our modern Old Testament with the biblical books found among the Dead Sea Scrolls (extant roughly between 150 B.C. and A.D. 68) show a remarkably close correspondence and thus indicate just how early the canon of the Hebrew Bible, specifically the content, was fixed. It may be that final decisions about specific books were reached by a council at Jamnia or Yavneh around A.D. 90.

The New Testament canon also developed over time. Most scholars believe the Pauline epistles were the first to circulate among branches of the early Church. Other epistles were added, and various lists of authoritative books circulated for many decades. Some of our present New Testament books were purposely left off the various canonical lists at different stages, while other books not now considered canonical appeared on the lists. Perhaps the oldest extant list of New Testament writings is called the Muratorian Canon, which is believed to date to the second century A.D. It mentions all of the current New Testament books except Hebrews, James, and 1 and 2 Peter. It adds the Apocalypse of Peter and the Wisdom of Solomon. The earliest known list of exactly the same books found in our present New Testament dates from A.D. 367 in an Easter letter of Athanasius, bishop of Alexandria.

One task of Church councils convened during the first three centuries of the Christian era was to determine which of the writings purporting to be scriptural were, in fact, orthodox, authoritative, and acceptable and which were spurious and heretical. It is miraculous that so many of the authentic writings were preserved and the noncanonical dismissed. Among the criteria used to determine canonicity were the following:

Apostolic origin. Was the text written by or based on the teachings of a first-generation apostle or a genuine eyewitness?

General acceptance. Was the text acknowledged as authentic by the principal Christian communities of the early Church?

Church use. Was the text read aloud or used in worship by the larger Christian communities?

Consistency. Was the content of the text consistent with known and accepted doctrines of the early Church?

In northern Africa in A.D. 393 the Synod of Hippo approved the

New Testament as it appears today. To suppose that the establishment of the biblical canon was without challenges is patently erroneous.

Latter-day Saint knowledge of the scriptural canon clarifies many questions and issues. In contrast to a closed canon, we know the canon is open, by God's design, and far more expansive than the traditional Judeo-Christian canon. Our canon is composed of what we call the standard works: the Bible, the Book of Mormon, the Doctrine and Covenants, and the Pearl of Great Price. Additions have been made to that canon over time. The vision of the celestial kingdom (D&C 137) and the vision of the redemption of the dead (D&C 138) were not part of the standard works until the general conference of April 1976, when Church members voted to accept President Spencer W. Kimball's proposal that those revelations be accepted as scripture. Another example is the June 1978 revelation received by President Kimball that extended the priesthood to all worthy male members of the Church. In general conference, 30 September 1978, Church members voted to "accept this revelation as the word and will of the Lord"; the revelation on priesthood now appears as Official Declaration 2 found at the end of the Doctrine and Covenants.

Joseph Smith laid out the Church's position on the nature of continuing revelation in a statement that has significant implications for the concept of canon. It is preserved as the ninth article of faith: "We believe all that God has revealed, all that He does now reveal, and we believe that He will yet reveal many great and important things pertaining to the Kingdom of God." Thus, the canon of scripture of The Church of Jesus Christ of Latter-day Saints remains open and is always expanding, as described in a revelation given in November 1831: "And whatsoever they shall speak when moved upon by the Holy Ghost shall be scripture, shall be the will of the Lord, shall be the mind of the Lord, shall be the word of the Lord, shall be the voice of the Lord, and the power of God unto salvation" (D&C 68:4). This does not mean, however, that the canon is error-free. Joseph Smith also explained, "We believe the Bible to be the word of God as far as it is translated correctly; we also believe the Book of Mormon to be the word of God" (Articles of Faith 1:8).

History teaches us that errors were introduced in the formation and translation of scripture. Saint Jerome, one of the Fathers of the

Roman Catholic Church, undertook his translation of the Vulgate precisely because of errors that existed in the version of the Bible used in his day. In a letter to Pope Damasus in A.D. 383, seeking permission for his translation project, Jerome argued: "For if we are to pin our faith to the Latin texts, it is for our opponents to tell us *which;* for there are almost as many forms of texts as there are copies. If, on the other hand, we are to glean the truth from a comparison of many, why not go back to the original Greek and correct the mistakes introduced by inaccurate translators, and the blundering alterations of confident but ignorant critics, and further all that has been inserted or changed by copyists more asleep than awake?" (Stevenson, 183). Indeed, God has given us living oracles in part to correct error in scripture and keep the wellspring of doctrine pure.

SOURCES

Sperry, Sidney B. *The Spirit of the Old Testament.* 2d ed. Salt Lake City: Deseret Book, 1980.

Stevenson, J., ed. *Creeds, Councils and Controversies: Documents Illustrating the History of the Church A.D. 337–461.* Nashville, Tenn.: Abingdon Press, 1990.

ACS

CARNAL

Deriving from the Latin *carnis* ("flesh"), *carnal* means "of the flesh," or "sensual." It connotes the fallen, worldly, spiritually unregenerate condition of all mortals who have not experienced the life-changing and regenerating power of Jesus Christ. Since the time of the Fall, when Satan came among the posterity of Adam and Eve, "men began from that time forth to be carnal, sensual, and devilish" (Moses 5:13; see also 6:49). As Paul taught, "The works [characteristics] *of the flesh* . . . are . . . adultery, fornication, uncleanness, lasciviousness, idolatry, witchcraft, hatred, variance, emulations, wrath, strife, seditions, heresies, envyings, murders, drunkenness, revellings, and such like: . . . they which do such things shall not inherit the kingdom of God" (Galatians 5:19–21; emphasis added).

The carnal man, or man "of the flesh," is the natural man, the man who lives by his natural, animal-like, worldly instincts and impulses. The problem with this condition is that "the natural man is an enemy to God, and has been from the fall of Adam, and will be, forever and ever, unless he yields to the enticings of the Holy Spirit, and putteth off the natural man and becometh a saint through the atonement of Christ the Lord, and becometh as a child, submissive, meek, humble, patient, full of love, willing to submit to all things which the Lord seeth fit to inflict upon him, even as a child doth submit to his father" (Mosiah 3:19).

Thus, the only way for us to change our carnal condition into a state of godly approval is through the atonement of Jesus Christ. The Atonement offers and brings about a rebirth if we accept it. The Lord taught, "Marvel not that all mankind, yea, men and women, all nations, kindreds, tongues and people, must be born again; yea, born of God, changed from their carnal and fallen state, to a state of righteousness, being redeemed of God, becoming his sons and daughters; and thus they become new creatures; and unless they do this, they can in nowise inherit the kingdom of God" (Mosiah 27:25–26).

The qualities of someone who has been born of God, become a son or daughter of Christ, and overcome the natural man are "love, joy, peace, longsuffering, gentleness, goodness, faith, meekness, temperance. . . . And they that are Christ's have crucified the flesh with [its] affections and lusts" (Galatians 5:22–24).

God's plan of salvation provides, ultimately, two options for Adam and Eve's posterity: remain in a carnal state and suffer spiritual death, or embrace the Atonement, become a new creature in Christ, and receive eternal life. "For to be carnally minded is death; but to be spiritually minded is life and peace. Because the carnal mind is enmity against God. . . . So then they that are *after the flesh* cannot please God" (JST, Romans 8:6–8; emphasis added).

ACS

CELESTIAL KINGDOM

Every person who has ever lived on this earth will be resurrected through the atonement of Jesus Christ. Only those who have adhered strictly to the gospel of Jesus Christ, however, will inherit a celestial glory (Alma 11:40–45; D&C 88:16–24), which is the highest of the three kingdoms of glory (D&C 76:50–113). President Joseph Fielding taught: "The celestial kingdom is prepared for the righteous, those who have been faithful in the keeping of the commandments of the

Lord, and have been cleansed of all their sins. These dwell in the presence of the Father and the Son" (2:208).

The Prophet Joseph Smith saw in vision the celestial kingdom, where God the Father dwells in great glory like fire. "The heavens were opened upon us, and I beheld the celestial kingdom of God, and the glory thereof, whether in the body or out I cannot tell. I saw the transcendent beauty of the gate through which the heirs of that kingdom will enter, which was like unto circling flames of fire; also the blazing throne of God, whereon was seated the Father and the Son. I saw the beautiful streets of that kingdom, which had the appearance of being paved with gold" (D&C 137:1–4).

There are also three levels, or degrees, within the celestial kingdom itself (D&C 131:1). Only those who exercise faith in the Lord Jesus Christ and subscribe to the principles and ordinances that follow therefrom will enjoy the full glory of that kingdom in which the Father dwells. Jesus Christ said that "no unclean thing can enter into his kingdom; therefore nothing entereth into his rest save it be those who have washed their garments in my blood, because of their faith, and the repentance of all their sins, and their faithfulness unto the end" (3 Nephi 27:19). Modern revelation defines the rest spoken of here as "the fulness of his [the Lord's] glory" (D&C 84:24). This is what is meant by exaltation.

Participation in the new and everlasting covenant of marriage, administered in the Lord's temples, opens the door to exaltation. The Prophet Joseph explained: "In the celestial glory there are three heavens or degrees; and in order to obtain the highest, a man must enter into this order of the priesthood [meaning the new and everlasting covenant of marriage]; and if he does not, he cannot obtain it. He may enter into the other, but that is the end of his kingdom; he cannot have an increase" (D&C 131:1–4). Those entering the rest of the Lord, who receive a fulness of celestial glory, will enjoy a continuation of fatherhood and motherhood in the family organization (D&C 132:19–20). Those who prove true and faithful in all things "become like the Son and joint heirs with him in the Father's kingdom" (Smith, *Answers*, 2:208).

Our Heavenly Father's glory is a function of who he is—a divine, exalted personage possessing every good quality, power, attribute, and characteristic in a perfected state—and is also the infinite kingdom over which he presides. He will always be our exalted Father in Heaven and the ultimate object of our worship. His celestial kingdom is so vast it is incomprehensible to mortals: "For behold, there are many worlds that have passed away by the word of my power. And there are many that now stand, and innumerable are they unto man; but all things are numbered unto me, for they are mine and I know them" (Moses 1:35).

The apostle John saw in vision the celestial kingdom and described it: "After this I beheld, and, lo, a great multitude, which no man could number, of all nations, and kindreds, and people, and tongues, stood before the throne, and before the Lamb, clothed with white robes, and palms in their hands; and cried with a loud voice, saying, Salvation to our God which sitteth upon the throne, and unto the Lamb. . . . And one of the elders answered, saying unto me, What are these which are arrayed in white robes? And whence came they? and I said unto him, Sir, thou knowest. And he said to me, These are they which came out of great tribulation, and have washed their robes, and made them white in the blood of the Lamb. Therefore are they before the throne of God, and serve him day and night in his temple: and he that sitteth on the throne shall dwell among them" (Revelation 7:9–15).

This earth upon which we dwell "will become a celestial kingdom when it is sanctified" (Smith, *Answers,* 2:210). This truth suggests that the whole of the celestial kingdom is made up of many parts and planets (and there are many; Moses 1:33), including the earth upon which we dwell. The Lord expounded this unique doctrine—the celestial glorification of the earth—to the Prophet Joseph Smith: "The redemption of the soul is through him that quickeneth all things, in whose bosom it is decreed that the poor and the meek of the earth shall inherit it. Therefore, it must needs be sanctified from all unrighteousness, that it may be prepared for the celestial glory; for after it hath filled the measure of its creation, it shall be crowned with glory, even with the presence of God the Father; that bodies who are of the celestial kingdom may possess it forever and ever; for, for this intent was it made and created, and for this intent are they sanctified" (D&C 88:17–20).

The apostle Paul taught that all humans will be resurrected with the kind of body they will possess in the eternities, according to the kingdom of glory they are worthy to inherit. Those who are worthy of a celestial glory will be resurrected with a celestial body. These are they who will inherit this earth. Those worthy of the terrestrial glory will rise with a terrestrial body; those worthy of a telestial glory will have a telestial body (1 Corinthians 15:40–42). Those who obtain a celestial inheritance "shall dwell in the presence of God and his Christ forever and ever. . . . These are they who shall have part in the first resurrection. These are they who shall come forth in the resurrection of the just. . . . These are they whose bodies are celestial, whose glory is that of the sun, even the glory of God, the highest of all, whose glory the sun of the firmament is written of as being typical" (D&C 76:62–70).

That the different categories of resurrected bodies have different characteristics and potentials is obvious from a statement by the Prophet Joseph Smith that "in the resurrection, some are raised to be angels; others are raised to become Gods" (5:427). Therefore, there will be no movement from lower kingdoms to higher ones in eternity. In describing those who inherit a telestial glory, the Lord declared, "They shall be judged according to their works, and every man shall receive according to his own works, his own dominion, in the mansions which are prepared; and they shall be servants of the Most High; but *where God and Christ dwell they cannot come, worlds without end*" (D&C 76:111–12; emphasis added).

The fundamental principle undergirding the law that operates in the celestial kingdom is unity. Speaking of the early Church in this present dispensation, the Lord stated: "Behold, I say unto you, were it not for the transgressions of my people, speaking concerning the church and not individuals, they might have been redeemed even now. But behold, they have not learned to be obedient to the things which I required at their hands, but are full of all manner of evil, and do not impart of their substance, as becometh saints, to the poor and afflicted among them; and are not united according to the union required by the law of the celestial kingdom; and Zion cannot be built up unless it is by the principles of the law of the celestial kingdom; otherwise I cannot receive her unto myself" (D&C 105:2–5). Thus we learn that the law of the celestial kingdom is also fundamental to the establishment of Zion, as Enoch's people understood (Moses 7:18–19). Those who cannot abide the law of the celestial kingdom "must inherit another kingdom, even that of a terrestrial kingdom, or that of a telestial kingdom. For he who is not able to abide the law of a celestial kingdom cannot abide a celestial glory" (D&C 88:21–22).

SOURCES

Smith, Joseph. *History of The Church of Jesus Christ of Latter-day Saints.* Edited by B. H. Roberts. 7 vols. 2d ed. rev. Salt Lake City: The Church of Jesus Christ of Latter-day Saints, 1932–51.

Smith, Joseph Fielding. *Answers to Gospel Questions.* 5 vols. Salt Lake City: Deseret Book, 1957–66.

ACS

CHARITY

The great Nephite prophet Mormon said, "Charity is the pure love of Christ" (Moroni 7:47). That simple definition has profound implications and might well be understood as (1) the pure love we can and should feel, in undying gratitude, for our Lord and Savior; (2) the pure love that Jesus has shown, does now show, and will yet show for all of us; and (3) the pure love we are charged to demonstrate toward our Heavenly Father's children. "Love is one of the chief characteristics of Deity," the Prophet Joseph Smith taught, "and ought to be manifested by those who aspire to be the sons of God [Moroni 7:48]. A man filled with the love of God, is not content with blessing his family alone, but ranges through the whole world, anxious to bless the whole human race" (*Joseph Smith,* 330–31).

The word *charity* is never used in scripture to denote action or service, although such love is consistently the motivating force behind Christlike service. Rather, charity is a gift of the Spirit, a "fruit of the Spirit" (Galatians 5:22). While such marvelous gifts as faith, healing, miracles, prophecy, revelation, wisdom, knowledge, discernment, tongues, and the ministry of angels are all evidences of the true Church and signs of God's tender mercies upon the sheep of his fold, charity is "a more excellent way" (1 Corinthians 12:31–13:13). Moroni, speaking to our Lord, stated: "And I also remember that thou hast said that thou hast prepared a house for man, yea, even among the mansions of thy Father, in which man might have a more excellent hope; wherefore man must hope, or he cannot receive an inheritance in the place which thou hast prepared. And again, I remember that thou hast said that thou hast loved the world, even unto the laying down of thy life for the world, that thou mightest take it again to prepare a place for the children of men. And now I know that this love which thou hast had for the children of men is charity; wherefore, except men shall have charity they cannot inherit that place which thou hast prepared in the mansions of thy Father" (Ether 12:32–34).

We should exercise all the grit and willpower and faith we can to keep the commandments, demonstrate the discipline associated with denying ourselves of ungodliness and worldly lusts, and draw upon all the feelings of compassion and empathy within us. But charity is an endowment of the Spirit, a heavenly gift for which we are counseled to "pray unto the Father with all the energy of heart, that [we] may be filled with this love, which he hath bestowed upon all who are true followers of his Son, Jesus Christ; that [we] may become the sons [and daughters] of God; that when he shall appear we shall be like him, for we shall see him as he is; that we may have this hope; that we may be purified even as he is pure" (Moroni 7:48). Elder Jeffrey R. Holland wrote:

"It is instructive to note that the charity, or 'the pure love of Christ,' we are to cherish can be interpreted two ways. One of its meanings is the kind of merciful, forgiving love Christ's disciples should have one for another. That is, all Christians should try to love as the Savior loved, showing pure, redeeming compassion for all. Unfortunately, few, if any, mortals have been entirely successful in this endeavor, but it is an invitation that all should try to meet.

"The greater definition of 'the pure love of Christ,' however, is not what we as Christians try but largely fail to demonstrate toward others but rather what Christ totally succeeded in demonstrating toward us. True charity has been known only once. It is shown perfectly and purely in Christ's unfailing, ultimate, and atoning love for us. It is Christ's love for us that 'suffereth long, and is kind, and envieth not.' It is his love for us that is not 'puffed up . . . , not easily provoked, thinketh no evil.' It is Christ's love for us that 'beareth all things, believeth all things, hopeth all things, endureth all things.' It is as demonstrated in Christ that 'charity never faileth.' It is that charity—his pure love for us—without which we would be nothing, hopeless, of all men and women most miserable. Truly, those found possessed of the blessings of his love at the last day—the Atonement, the Resurrection, eternal life, eternal promise—surely it shall be well with them."

Elder Holland continued: "This does not in any way minimize the commandment that we are to try to acquire this kind of love for one another. We should 'pray unto the Father with all the energy of heart that [we] may be filled with this love.' We should try to be more constant and unfailing, more longsuffering and kind, less envious and puffed up in our relationships with others. As Christ lived so should we live, and as Christ loved so should we love. But the 'pure love of Christ' Mormon spoke of is precisely that—Christ's love. With that divine gift, that redeeming bestowal, we have everything; without it we have nothing and ultimately are nothing, except in the end 'devils [and] angels to a devil.'

"Life has its share of fears and failures. Sometimes things fall short. Sometimes people fail us, or economies or businesses or governments fail us. But one thing in time or eternity does not fail us—the pure love of Christ" (336–37).

Ethical deeds, works of faith, and acts of kindness toward others are much more effective and pure when the source of our good actions is the Holy One. As we begin to become new creatures in Christ, we begin to serve out of proper motives. Both Mormon and Paul wrote of charity as the greatest of all the fruits of the Spirit, the one that will endure forever (Moroni 7:45–48; 1 Corinthians 13:1–13).

It should go without saying that disciples of Christ ought to love one another. Their view of reality, their goals and ambitions, their hopes and dreams for here and hereafter—all these they share with other members of the Church far and wide. They are welded together, clothed in the "bond of charity," a "mantle, which is the bond of perfectness and peace" (D&C 88:125). The expression of the love of God is not to be limited, however, to the "household of faith" (D&C 121:45). We have a duty beyond the fold as well, and the Holy Spirit, which is the source of pure love, expands our vision to see and feel as we ought. The Prophet Joseph Smith said: "There is a love from God that should be exercised toward those of our faith, who walk uprightly, which is peculiar to itself, but it is without prejudice; it also gives scope to the mind, which enables us to conduct ourselves with greater liberality towards all that are not of our faith, than what they exercise towards one another. These principles approximate nearer to the mind of God, because [they are] like God, or Godlike" (*History*, 3:304).

Indeed, as Mormon and Paul wrote, charity endures forever. It never fails (Moroni 7:46–47; 1 Corinthians 13:8). Though there may come a day when such gifts of the Spirit as prophecy or tongues or knowledge will have served their useful function, charity—the pure love of Christ—will still be in operation, burning brightly in the hearts and souls of the sons and daughters of Almighty God. "When that which is perfect is come" (1 Corinthians 13: 10), the true followers of Jesus Christ will have become like unto him who is the embodiment of love. They will be "filled with charity, which is everlasting love" (Moroni 8:17).

Charity is "the highest pinnacle the human soul can reach and the deepest expression of the human heart" (Hunter, 170). Truly, as the apostle Paul wrote, receiving from God the gift of charity is evidence of our spiritual growth and maturity, a sign that we are growing unto Christ: "When I was a child, I spake as a child, I understood as a child, I thought as a child: but when I became a man, I put away childish things" (1 Corinthians 13:11).

We must pray for charity. We must plead for it. We must ask with all the energy of heart to be so endowed. As we do so, there will come moments of surpassing import, sublime moments in which our whole souls seem to reach out to others with a kind of fellowship and affection that we would not otherwise know. Such love is beyond anything earthly, above and beyond anything that mortals can explain or produce. It provides moral courage to those who face difficult challenges. It unites husbands, wives, and children and grants them a foretaste of eternal life. It welds classes and congregations and wards and stakes in a union that is the foundation for Zion. And it comes from the Lord, who is the source of all that is godlike. To the degree that we trust in the Lord and yield our hearts to him (Helaman 3:35), "neither death, nor life, nor angels, nor principalities, nor powers, nor things present, nor things to come, nor height, nor depth, nor any other creature, shall be able to separate us from the love of God, which is in Christ Jesus our Lord" (Romans 8:38–39).

SOURCES

Holland, Jeffrey R. *Christ and the New Covenant: The Messianic Message of the Book of Mormon.* Salt Lake City: Deseret Book, 1997.
Hunter, Howard W. *That We Might Have Joy.* Salt Lake City: Deseret Book, 1994.

Joseph Smith [manual]. Teachings of Presidents of the Church series. Salt Lake City: The Church of Jesus Christ of Latter-day Saints, 2007.

Smith, Joseph. *History of The Church of Jesus Christ of Latter-day Saints.* Edited by B. H. Roberts. 7 vols. 2d ed. rev. Salt Lake City: The Church of Jesus Christ of Latter-day Saints, 1932–51.

RLM

CHASTEN

Because of our "ease" and "great prosperity" (Helaman 12:2), we have a natural tendency to harden our hearts, travel a path that takes us away from the Lord, and assume we can succeed by our own intellect and strength. Consequently, God often chastens his children to help them remember him. Chastening may range from a mild rebuke to afflictions for disobedience or even death, terror, famine, and destruction to turn us again to him (Helaman 12:3).

God chastens us because of our sins (D&C 61:8). The scriptures contain many examples of specific reasons that God chastens a son or daughter, but these are not all-inclusive lists. God chastens us when we fail to forgive one another in our hearts (D&C 64:8), when we murmur against him or those whom he calls (1 Nephi 16:25; D&C 75:7–8), when we neglect family members (D&C 93:50), when we fail to pray as the Lord asks us to do (Ether 2:14), when we disobey his commands and counsel (D&C 103:4–5), or when we try to hide our sins (D&C 58:60). The Prophet Joseph Smith told the early Saints, "We have been chastened by the hand of God heretofore for not obeying His commands, although we never violated any human law, or transgressed any human precept; yet we have treated lightly His commands, and departed from His ordinances, and the Lord has chastened us sore" (161). At times, being chastened by the Lord is the only way we learn to be obedient (D&C 105:6).

The apostle Paul learned that God chastens us to bring us to a sense of our own nothingness, lest we become puffed up with our own sense of importance. Paul described his own chastening as being given "a thorn in the flesh . . . lest I should be exalted above measure." As a result, he learned to "glory in [his] infirmities, that the power of Christ may rest on [him]." Paul concluded, "For when I am weak, then am I strong" (2 Corinthians 12: 9–10).

The immediate blessing from God's chastening is that it will lead us to repent of our sins if we choose to accept his correction (1 Nephi 16:39; D&C 1:27; 98:21). Even when we are living obedient lives, the Lord may chasten us to strengthen and purify us (D&C 90:36). The people of Alma established a Zion-like community in which they made and kept sacred covenants with God, but the Lord allowed them to be brought into bondage to try "their patience and their faith" (Mosiah 23:21).

Scripture provides evidence that God chastens us because he loves us (Proverbs 3:11–12; Revelation 3:19; Helaman 15:3; D&C 95:1). "For whom the Lord loveth he chasteneth, and scourgeth every son whom he receiveth. If ye endure chastening, God dealeth with you as with sons; for what son is he whom the father chasteneth not? . . . We have had fathers of our flesh which corrected us, and we gave them reverence: shall we not much rather be in subjection unto the Father of spirits, and live?" (Hebrews 12:6–7, 9).

Knowing that challenges can strengthen us to become more like him, God chastens us "for our profit, that we might be partakers of his holiness" (Hebrews 12:10). In fact, chastening is essential to the process of our becoming sanctified (D&C 101:5; 136:31). The trait of the believers lauded in Hebrews 11 is their unshakable faith in God that sustained them through intense times of chastening. Therefore, while "no chastening for the present seemeth to be joyous, but grievous: nevertheless afterward it yieldeth the peaceable fruit of righteousness unto them which are exercised thereby" (Hebrews 12:11). Seeing the positive results of chastening is why Job declared, "Happy is the man whom God correcteth: therefore despise not thou the chastening of the Almighty" (Job 5:17).

SOURCE

Joseph Smith [manual]. Teachings of Presidents of the Church series. Salt Lake City: The Church of Jesus Christ of Latter-day Saints, 2007.

CFO

CHASTITY

Human sexuality, with its accompanying power of procreation, is a sacred, God-given gift. President Boyd K. Packer has taught that "it is essential to the plan of redemption and is the source of human happiness. Through the righteous exercise of this power, as through nothing else, we may come close to our Father in Heaven and experience a fulness of joy. . . . The power of procreation is not an incidental part of the plan of happiness; it is the key—the very key" (208). Because of their importance to his plan, the Lord has given commandments to protect and preserve these sacred powers. The Lord's law of chastity is that "the sacred powers of procreation are to be employed only between man and woman, lawfully wedded as husband and wife" (First Presidency, 102). Chastity, often referred to by Latter-day Saints as moral cleanliness, involves abstaining from all sexual behaviors or relationships outside the bonds of marriage. President Joseph F. Smith taught: "Sexual union is lawful in wedlock, and if participated in with right intent is honorable and sanctifying. But without the bonds of marriage, sexual indulgence is a debasing sin, abominable in the sight of Deity" (309). The scriptures testify that chastity—sexual purity—is "most dear and precious above all things" (Moroni 9:9) and that God "delights in the chastity of women [and men]" (Jacob 2:28).

SOURCES

First Presidency and Council of the Twelve Apostles. "The Family: A Proclamation to the World." *Ensign,* Nov. 1995, 102.

Packer, Boyd K. *Mine Errand from the Lord: Selections from the Sermons and Writings of Boyd K. Packer.* Salt Lake City: Deseret Book, 2008.

Smith, Joseph F. *Gospel Doctrine.* Salt Lake City: Deseret Book, 1939.

BLT

CHERUBIM

The word *cherubim* is the English form of the Hebrew plural noun *keruvim* (singular, *keruv*) and represents some type of heavenly beings, but its complete and specific meaning has been lost. The King James Bible adds the English plural *s* to *cherubim,* even though the term is already a plural form. Restoration scripture, however, consistently uses *cherubim* correctly. For example, the book of Alma confirms the report of Genesis 3:24 that God placed cherubim and a flaming sword to guard the tree of life and protect our first parents from partaking of its fruit and living forever in their sins (Alma 12:21; 42:2–3; see also Moses 4:31).

Several Old Testament passages portray cherubim as having wings. These include descriptions of the mercy seat in the Tabernacle used by the children of Israel in the wilderness (Exodus 25:17–22; 37:6–9), discussions of the interior of Solomon's temple (1 Kings 6:23–28; 2 Chronicles 3:10–11), the ark of the covenant (1 Kings 8:7–8; 2 Chronicles 5:8), and Ezekiel's unusual vision (Ezekiel 10:14; see also 41:18–25). Some kind of winged creation is implied in David's psalm of praise describing how the Lord "rode upon a cherub, and did fly: and he was seen upon the wings of the wind" (2 Samuel 22:11; see also Psalm 18:10).

Similarly, John's Apocalypse describes four beasts in heaven, full of eyes and each possessing six wings about him, worshipping and praising God round about his celestial throne (Revelation 4:6–9). In a revelation given to Joseph Smith to help us understand John's sweeping vision, it was made known that the eyes of these beasts "are a representation of light and knowledge, that is, they are full of knowledge; and their wings are a representation of power, to move, to act, etc." (D&C 77:4). Thus, it seems reasonable to believe that David's language depicting the Lord riding upon a cherub is symbolic of his power to move, act, and accomplish his purposes in great power.

Though we do not completely understand the meaning of the term *cherubim,* we do know that humans who are now angels of God do not possess wings (Smith, 3:392). And, as Elder John A. Widtsoe taught, "Little is known about the beings known under the above name [cherubim] beyond the fact that they are creatures in the service of the Lord" (3:182). We also know that cherubim are beings who dwell in the presence of the Lord.

SOURCES

Smith, Joseph. *History of The Church of Jesus Christ of Latter-day Saints.* Edited by B. H. Roberts. 7 vols. 2d ed. rev. Salt Lake City: The Church of Jesus Christ of Latter-day Saints, 1932–51.

Widtsoe, John A. *Evidences and Reconciliations.* Arranged by G. Homer Durham. 3 vols. Salt Lake City: Bookcraft, 1965.

ACS

CHILDREN, INNOCENCE OF

Are children pure? The answer to this question is a resounding yes! Children are pure because of the Atonement, because Jesus Christ declared them so. In the words of Lehi, children are redeemed "because of the righteousness of [our] Redeemer" (2 Nephi 2:3). King Benjamin, declaring the words of an angel, said: "The law of Moses availeth nothing except it were through the atonement of [Christ's] blood. And even if it were possible that little children could sin they could not be saved" (Mosiah 3:15–16). That is, if Christ required children to be responsible for wrong and sinful actions, they could not be saved without the Atonement. "But I say unto you," Benjamin explains, "they are blessed; for behold, as in Adam, or by nature, they fall, even so the blood of Christ atoneth for their sins" (Mosiah 3:16).

The revelations state that little children "cannot sin, for power is not given unto Satan to tempt little children, until they begin to become accountable before me" (D&C 29:47). All of us know of deeds performed by little children that may be described as evil. But children's actions are not counted as sin. Why? Because, in the words of God, "Little children are redeemed from the foundation of the world through mine Only Begotten" (D&C 29:46). Christ explained that "the curse of Adam is taken from [children] in me, that it hath no power over them" (Moroni 8:8). Little children are subject to the effects of the Fall, just as all of us are; they are not, however, held accountable for their actions.

In summary, little children are saved without condition—without faith, repentance, or baptism. Their innocence is decreed by and through the tender mercies of an all-loving Lord. Children are innocent through the Atonement, and we are called upon to become as innocent as little children in the very same way—through applying the atoning blood of our Savior (Moroni 8:10).

RLM

CHILDREN OF GOD

God is our Father in Heaven, the Father of the spirits of all humankind (Numbers 16:22; 27:16; Hebrews 12:9). We are his spirit children. Because of the Fall, however, we come forth into a world of sin, a fallen world in which we are alienated from things of righteousness, including the royal family of God. Through faith in the Lord Jesus Christ—which brings forth repentance, baptism, and the reception of the Spirit—we are forgiven of our sins and become innocent before God. In addition, through the Atonement we are reinstated into the family of God. That is, we become "children of God" in this sense by rebirth, by adoption, by regeneration.

The apostle John wrote, as a part of the prologue to his Gospel, that Jesus "came unto his own, and his own received him not. But as many as received him, to them gave he power to become the sons of God, even to them that believe on his name" (John 1:11–12; see also 3 Nephi 9:16–17). We must be given power—gospel power, Atonement power—to become a son or daughter of God. "Behold, what manner of love the Father hath bestowed upon us, that we should be called the [children] of God: therefore the world knoweth us not, because it knew him not. Beloved, now are we the [children] of God, and it doth not yet appear what we shall be [in the resurrected, glorified state]: but we know that, when he shall appear, we shall be like him; for we shall see him as he is. And every man that hath this hope in him purifieth himself, even as he is pure" (1 John 3:1–3). By Christ "and through him, and of him, the worlds are and were created, and the inhabitants thereof are begotten sons and daughters unto God" through the Atonement (D&C 76:24).

RLM

CHRIST

There is only one Christ (2 Nephi 25:18), and Jesus of Nazareth is that Christ (Matthew 16:16, 20; Acts 10:38; 18:5). The term *Christ*, from the Greek *christos,* means "anointed one." It is the equivalent of the Hebrew *mashiakh* or Aramaic *mashikha,* which is the origin of the word *Messiah*. The Gospel of John mentions this equivalence: "We have found the Messias, which is, being interpreted, the Christ" (John 1:41; see also 4:25). As seen in the New Testament, Christ is a name-title applied by the Jews, in general, to an anticipated king-conqueror-savior who would be anointed, just as their ancient kings were, to provide deliverance from all of Israel's enemies, political and military. They also understood that Christ would come through the lineage of David (Matthew 22:42; John 7:42) and be called the Son of God, as is evident when Caiaphas, the high priest, said to Jesus, "I adjure thee by the living God, that thou tell us whether thou be the Christ, the Son of God" (Matthew 26:63). But to most, especially the leaders of the Jews, Christ's surpassing role and mission were lost or misunderstood.

The spiritually attuned, however, understood Christ to be much more than a great and powerful temporal ruler, as Jesus himself testified: "The Spirit of the Lord is upon me, because he hath *anointed* me to preach the gospel to the poor; he hath sent me to heal the brokenhearted, to preach deliverance to the captives, and recovering of sight to the blind, to set at liberty them that are bruised, to preach the acceptable year of the Lord" (Luke 4:18–19; emphasis added).

Only by personal revelation can we understand the identity, nature, purpose, importance, role, and place of Christ. A man who received such revelation was Simeon, to whom Jesus was brought as an infant. "And it was revealed unto him [Simeon] by the Holy Ghost, that he should not see death, before he had seen the Lord's Christ. And he came by the Spirit into the temple: and when the parents brought in the child Jesus, . . . then took he him up in his arms, and blessed God, and said, Lord, now lettest thou thy servant depart in peace, according to thy word: for mine eyes have seen thy salvation" (Luke 2:26–30). Peter was able to testify that Jesus was the Christ, the Son of the living God, only through revelation (Matthew 16:13–18). The apostle Paul affirmed that no one can know and testify of Jesus' purpose and exalted status except by the Holy Ghost (1 Corinthians 12:3). Eternal life is predicated upon *knowing* that Jesus is the Christ, whom the Father sent (John 17:3).

There are so many aspects of Jesus' role as Christ and so many activities and actions in which he was and is involved, "the which, if they should be written every one . . . even the world itself could not contain the books that should be written" (John 21:25). Suffice it to say that all things center in Christ. All things are before Christ (D&C 88:6, 41). Salvation comes only "through the name of Christ" (Mosiah 3:17). All things are the "typifying of him" (2 Nephi 11:4). Every man, woman, and child must come unto Christ (Mosiah 3:17; Moroni 7:16; 10:30, 32–33; see also Topical Guide and Bible Dictionary in the Latter-day Saint edition of the King James Version of the Bible, particularly the entries on Jesus Christ, to learn more about Jesus Christ and the significance of this name-title).

ACS

CHRISTIAN

A Christian is one who accepts the scriptural, prophetic, and Spirit-delivered testimony of the divinity of Jesus of Nazareth. A Christian believes in our Lord's virgin birth; that he is the Son of God and God the Son; that he performed miracles, such as healing the sick, causing the lame to walk and the blind to see, and raising the dead; that in a way incomprehensible to mortal minds, Jesus Christ took upon himself the burden of the sins and sufferings of all humankind and made forgiveness and deliverance available through faith on his name and through acceptance of the terms and conditions of his gospel; that he rose from the dead and thereby made resurrected immortality available to every living soul. Truly, "as in Adam all die, even so in Christ shall all be made alive" (1 Corinthians 15:22). A Christian is one who acknowledges his or her sin and weakness and recognizes that peace and happiness and salvation come only through applying the atoning blood of Jesus Christ. A Christian knows full well that there is no other name by which salvation comes except the name of Jesus Christ (Acts 4:12; 2 Nephi 31:21; Mosiah 3:17; Moses 6:52).

Luke wrote that the name *Christian* was first used in Antioch of Syria (Acts 11:26) to describe those who received Jesus Christ as Lord. The Book of Mormon speaks of a time in the New World about a century earlier when followers of Jesus were called Christians (Alma 46:13–15). In fact, Latter-day Saints recognize that Christ's gospel is eternal, for Christian prophets have proclaimed Christian doctrine and administered Christian ordinances since the earliest times on earth. Adam and Eve were taught the gospel, accepted it, received baptism and confirmation, and became earth's first Christians (Moses 6:51–67; Smith, 92–93, 107–8).

Christians are persons striving to put off the natural man and "put on Christ" (Galatians 3:27; see also Romans 13:14; Mosiah 3:19), to gain the mind of Christ (1 Corinthians 2:16), laboring to become new creatures in Christ (2 Corinthians 5:17; Mosiah 27:26), and to be imitators of the life of Christ (3 Nephi 27:27), both as individuals and as members of the Church, the body of Christ (1 Corinthians 12:11–20).

Latter-day Saints are Christians. We love Christ, we admire Christ, we worship Christ, we look to Christ, we treasure the words of Christ spoken by him and his anointed servants, and we have given our lives to Christ. We rejoice in his mercy and exult in his grace. His atoning sacrifice is the fundamental principle of Mormonism (Smith, 49). He is the center of our faith.

SOURCE
Joseph Smith [manual]. Teachings of Presidents of the Church series. Salt Lake City:
The Church of Jesus Christ of Latter-day Saints, 2007.

RLM

CHURCH

For Latter-day Saints, the Church is vital. It not only represents what the scriptures call the body of Christ or the body of believers—the congregation of the faithful, the household of faith—but it is also the means by which the ordinances (sacraments), messages, worship, evangelization, and associations so central to Christian life are made available to the people. Let there be no question about it: peace and joy here, and salvation and eternal reward hereafter, are to be found first and foremost in Jesus Christ. He is indeed the Way, the Truth, and the Life (John 14:6). He has, as the apostle Paul wrote, "brought life and immortality to light through the gospel" (2 Timothy 1:10). Or, as the angel said to King Benjamin, "salvation was, and is, and is to come, in and through the atoning blood of Christ, the Lord Omnipotent" (Mosiah 3:18). The Church proclaims and declares and spreads the gospel, the good news that deliverance from sin and death and hell are available through the merciful plan of salvation, the center of which is Christ the Lord.

The Church serves varied functions, each of which contributes to the gradual sanctification of the soul. The Church is where we go to participate weekly in the sacrament of the Lord's Supper. We partake of the emblems of our Lord's broken body and spilt blood in memory of Christ's life, teachings, love, suffering, death, atonement, and resurrection; we cultivate the appropriate feelings of gratitude and thanksgiving to him and to our Heavenly Father for his sacrificial offering; we meditate upon our own lives, including the covenants we have made with him and our need for his forgiveness of our sins; and we renew the covenant we made at the time of baptism by promising him that we will do all in our power to bring honor to his sacred name by keeping his commandments—these embody our poor effort to manifest a broken heart and a contrite spirit (3 Nephi 9:20; D&C 59:8) and our desire to have our souls cleansed of sin and our lives filled with God's enlivening and enriching Spirit.

The sacrament, as well as the other ordinances of salvation, must be performed by proper authority under the direction of the persons charged to oversee their performance. Babies are blessed; individuals are baptized by immersion, confirmed members of the Church, and given the gift of the Holy Ghost; and worthy men are ordained to office in the priesthood—all beneath the umbrella we call the Church. Latter-day Saints of all ages come to know and love and depend upon the other members of the Church; the sweet brotherhood and sisterhood that comes through regular association with others who feel about the Lord as you do cannot be measured. Praying together, singing hymns as a congregation, listening to and applying the messages of scripture—these activities constitute that corporate worship that epitomizes the work of the Church.

The work of the Church is done through a lay ministry. Such local Church leaders as bishops and stake presidents serve for a limited time without pay or other earthly reward. To join The Church of Jesus Christ of Latter-day Saints is to enlist in an army of workers who have been called by their local Church leaders to serve in a given capacity and to devote the necessary time and energy and prayer to that calling. We are all called to minister to one another, to invite all to come unto Christ, and to encourage and lift and strengthen those within the fold. We promise at the time of baptism to bear one another's burdens, to mourn with those who mourn, to comfort those who stand in need of comfort, and to "stand as witnesses of God at all times and in all things, and in all places that [we] may be in, even until death" (Mosiah 18:8–9). In a systematic fashion within the overall organization of the local congregation, we visit one another, see to one another's needs, and seek to inspire one another. In other words, Church membership entails more than four walls and Sunday preaching. To be a practicing Latter-day Saint is to be involved throughout the week.

Attendance at Church meetings and active involvement is a great antidote to worldliness. In August 1831, Joseph Smith recorded the following: "Thou shalt thank the Lord thy God in all things. Thou shalt offer a sacrifice unto the Lord thy God in righteousness, even that of a broken heart and a contrite spirit. *And that thou mayest more fully keep thyself unspotted from the world, thou shalt go to the house of prayer and offer up thy sacraments upon my holy day;* for verily this is a day appointed unto you to rest from your labors, and to pay thy devotions unto the Most High; nevertheless thy vows shall be offered up in righteousness on all days and at all times; but remember that on this, the Lord's day, thou shalt offer thine oblations [offerings of time, talents, or means] and thy sacraments unto the Most High, confessing thy sins unto thy brethren, and before the Lord" (D&C 59:7–12; emphasis added).

Church callings and assignments—be it serving in Sunday School, Relief Society, Primary, or as a financial clerk or the bishop—come by inspiration. Sometimes persons will be called to serve in organizations or assignments in which they have little or no experience or even aptitude. One does not seek out a calling, lobby for it, or send out resumes. As President J. Reuben Clark Jr. pointed out, in this Church one accepts the position to which one is duly called, a position that the individual neither seeks nor declines. He also said that in the Church, what matters is not *where* we serve but *how* (154).

This is what the kingdom of God is all about—individuals serving where they may or may not have specific training, aptitude, or strength. The Church is neither a factory nor a political organization where people forevermore fill a given role or politic for this or that job. We are led by farmers and plumbers, college presidents and art historians. We are taught by lawyers and accountants and homemakers and custodians. We are called upon to bend and stretch, to reach and try new things. We are called upon to climb higher, to move on.

President Gordon B. Hinckley stated: "This church does not belong to its President. Its head is the Lord Jesus Christ, whose name each of us has taken upon ourselves. We are all in this great endeavor together. We are here to assist our Father in His work and His glory, 'to bring to pass the immortality and eternal life of man' (Moses 1:39). Your obligation is as serious in your sphere of responsibility as is my obligation in my sphere. No calling in this church is small or of little consequence. All of us in the pursuit of our duty touch the lives of others. . . .

"You have as great an opportunity for satisfaction in the performance of your duty as I do in mine. The progress of this work will be determined by our joint efforts. Whatever your calling, it is as fraught with the same kind of opportunity to accomplish good as is mine.

What is really important is that this is the work of the Master. Our work is to go about doing good as did He" (71).

One other purpose of the Church is to learn to live peaceably and work amiably with imperfect people, which makes Christians out of us. One of the ways we know we are growing spiritually, maturing in the qualities of holiness, and preparing ourselves to be with our Maker is the extent to which we become more sensitive to people—to their plights, to their challenges, to their silent struggles.

So what does it mean for an individual member to proclaim, "I know the Church is true"? It does not mean that the Church saves, for it does not; Christ saves. It does not mean, for example, that because baptism is a required ordinance it adds anything to the completed work of Jesus Christ or that it supplements his atoning sacrifice in any way. Baptism, as an ordinance, is an outward manifestation of one's inward, personal covenant to come unto Christ, accept and rely upon the cleansing power of his blood, and make him truly the Lord of one's life. In the truest sense, Jesus Christ forgives our sins.

Thus the foundation of one's faith, that around which all other elements of a testimony revolve, is a witness that God lives, that Jesus Christ is the Son of God, and that he was crucified for the sins of the world. To proclaim that "the Church is true" is to proclaim that the Church is an auxiliary, an aid, a divinely given means whereby we can come unto Christ, receive the covenants and ordinances of salvation at the hands of legal administrators, worship and praise the Almighty in sermon and song and service, and enjoy fellowship with men and women who are just as fallible and spiritually needy as we are. The Church is less a sanctuary for the sanctified than it is a rehabilitation center for sinners. The Church is true in that it does what God intends for it to do. It is true in that it seeks to make of us true disciples of the Lord Jesus Christ.

In writing to the Saints at Ephesus, Paul explained that God had provided help and government to the Church through the appointment of officers—apostles, prophets, evangelists, pastors, and teachers. Why? "For the perfecting of the saints, for the work of the ministry, for the edifying of the body of Christ: Till we all come in the unity of the faith, and of the knowledge of the Son of God, unto a perfect man, unto the measure of the stature of the fulness of Christ:

That we henceforth be no more children, tossed to and fro, and carried about with every wind of doctrine, by the sleight of men, and cunning craftiness, whereby they lie in wait to deceive; but speaking the truth in love, may grow up into him in all things, which is the head, even Christ" (Ephesians 4:12–15). The Church thus helps to promote unity, orthodoxy, strength, and knowledge to withstand error, all in an effort to keep us from conforming to this world by being transformed by the Spirit, even to the renewing of our minds (Romans 12:2), leading eventually to that time when we all have "the mind of Christ" (1 Corinthians 2:16).

SOURCES

Hinckley, Gordon B. "This Is the Work of the Master." *Ensign,* May 1995, 69–71.

Clark, J. Reuben, Jr. In Conference Report, Apr. 1951, 154.

RLM

CHURCH DISCIPLINE

"We believe that all religious societies have a right to deal with their members for disorderly conduct, according to the rules and regulations of such societies," states an official Church declaration on the role of government and of laws in general. This statement was accepted by the vote of the Church on 17 August 1835 and is included in the Doctrine and Covenants as section 134. The Church has the right to discipline Church members "provided that such dealings be for fellowship and good standing; but we do not believe that any religious society has authority to try men on the right of property or life, to take from them this world's goods, or to put them in jeopardy of either life or limb, or to inflict any physical punishment upon them. They can only excommunicate them from their society, and withdraw from them their fellowship" (D&C 134:10). This statement reflects scriptural teachings—both ancient and modern—that true repentance requires spiritual discipline. The literal meaning of the word *discipline* is "to make one a disciple," "to correct, train or shape." In this sense, living the gospel always produces and requires discipline.

Throughout the scriptures the Lord gives his authorized servants the charge to look after and protect the flock of God—to help individuals conform their lives to divine principles and to protect the believers from those who might prey on them in some manner (Alma 5:59–60;

115

Mosiah 26:34–36; 3 Nephi 18:31; 1 Timothy 5:20; 1 Thessalonians 5:14). Alma understood that at times it becomes "expedient that those who committed sin, that were in the church, should be admonished by the church" (Mosiah 26:6). This training, correcting, admonishing, and disciplining are done within the Church today through both informal and formal means.

Informal Church discipline is done privately when a bishop, who is a "judge in Israel" (D&C 107:72), or other authorized presiding Church leader counsels with a person who has transgressed the laws of God. There may be the loss of privileges, such as partaking of the sacrament, serving in a calling, attending the temple, or other activities for a period of time. This is often referred to in the Church as informal probation. The individual may also receive exhortations or counsel to do certain things that will fill his or her life with greater spiritual light and strength, such as personal prayer and scripture study. All of these efforts are designed to give direction and support to the person who desires to become more Christlike in devotion and discipleship. The primary purpose of all we do in the Church, including discipline, is to lead souls to Christ.

The Book of Mormon prophet Alma was instructed of the Lord that "whosoever will not repent of his sins the same shall not be numbered among [his] people" (Mosiah 26:32). Likewise, the apostle Paul taught the Corinthian Saints to "put away from among [themselves] that wicked person" (1 Corinthians 5:13), such as Church members who were fornicators or were guilty of other equally serious sins (1 Corinthians 5:13). In our day the Lord has confirmed that at times persons guilty of serious wrongdoing, covenant breaking, and other spiritually damaging behaviors will need to be brought "to the church, not the members, but to the elders" so "that they may be dealt with according to the law of God" (D&C 42:89, 81; see also Moroni 6:7; D&C 102). "The elders" in this and other similar scriptural passages refers to a council composed of called, ordained, and set-apart Church leaders who are given the responsibility to maintain proper discipline within the body of the Church and to bless the lives of all its members.

"The gospel is to save men, not to condemn them," President Harold B. Lee taught, "but to save, it is sometimes necessary to confront and to discipline as the Lord has directed us" (118). In such cases as apostasy, adultery, incest, child abuse, serious criminal offenses, embezzlement of Church funds, and other serious violations of the accepted standards for Church members, a formal disciplinary council may be required to (1) help the transgressor fully repent, (2) protect the innocent from physical and spiritual dangers, and (3) safeguard the good name, integrity, and influence of the Church. Leaders of the Church—particularly those entrusted with keys of presidency and who are set apart as judges—have a solemn obligation to teach, testify, train, and discipline in such a way that the individual and the institution can be worthy of the companionship of the Holy Spirit. They have been given the charge to "see that there is no iniquity in the church" (D&C 20:54; see also 43:11). To ignore this responsibility will lead to the condemnation both of the transgressor who needs the discipline to fully repent and of the priesthood leader who fails to administer it as the Lord directs (Jacob 1:19).

President John Taylor warned: "I have heard of some Bishops who have been seeking to cover up the iniquities of men; I tell them, in the name of God, they will have to bear . . . that iniquity, and if any of you want to partake of the sins of men, or uphold them, you will have to bear them. Do you hear it, you Bishops and you Presidents? God will require it at your hands. You are not placed in position to tamper with the principles of righteousness, nor to cover up the infamies and corruptions of men" (78).

Church discipline blesses the individuals in the repentance process and enables them to once again have the Holy Ghost guide them, and it also protects the Church from a collective loss of the Spirit. If sin were allowed to go unchecked in the kingdom of God on earth, President George Q. Cannon taught, "the Spirit of God would undoubtedly be so grieved that it would forsake not only those who are guilty of these acts, but it would withdraw itself from those who would suffer them to be done in our midst unchecked and unrebuked" (26:139).

Formal Church disciplinary councils are held on a ward or branch level and on a stake or mission level. The level of the disciplinary council is determined by the stake or mission president in consultation with the bishop or branch president. Counseling together, they consider many factors, such as the seriousness of the transgression, the age and spiritual maturity of the transgressor, the covenants that were violated, the impact of the sin upon others, and the transgressor's attitude. What is best for the individual is always the primary consideration. The disciplinary council is usually composed of the bishopric or branch presidency. However, when a Melchizedek Priesthood holder has committed a sin that may likely result in excommunication, the stake president, as the presiding officer of the Melchizedek Priesthood in the stake, will convene a stake disciplinary council. This council is composed of the stake presidency assisted by the high council or other high priests as appointed. The specific procedures and policies regarding each kind of council are outlined by the Church in a handbook for bishops and stake presidents that is prepared under the direction of the First Presidency and the Quorum of the Twelve Apostles.

Church disciplinary councils are not to be confused with judicial courts of law, either in purpose or in procedure. Church discipline is governed by the laws of God and is more concerned with helping individuals to repent and enjoy the full blessings of the gospel than merely determining guilt or innocence and applying punishment.

When a person has demonstrated true repentance and devotion to the Lord and his Church over time and has met the conditions established by the judge in Israel, a disciplinary council may be reconvened to consider restoring full fellowship and authorizing baptism into the Church. Generally, the council will be convened at the same level as the earlier one. In some cases, only the First Presidency of the Church can authorize a return to full fellowship in the Church.

An additional part of returning to full fellowship is what is known as a "restoration of blessings." An excommunicated member who has met all the conditions of the council and is baptized may request that priesthood and temple blessings be restored by the First Presidency. When that request is approved, the First Presidency will authorize a General Authority or stake president to perform a special ordinance to restore previously held blessings. After the ordinance of restoration of blessings is performed, a new membership record is produced containing all the original dates of priesthood ordinances, with no reference to the excommunication.

A person who desires to have his or her name removed from the records of the Church or who has joined another church is not subject to these procedures of Church discipline. Having one's name removed requires administrative action by the bishop or branch president or by the stake or mission president rather than by a disciplinary council.

The Lord invites all people to repent of their sins, to come unto him, and to know the joy that comes from a clear conscience and righteous living. The Church is an earthly vehicle to assist us in that quest. Counsel, correction, and sometimes formal discipline from the Lord's anointed servants help us focus our efforts and reorient our spiritual compass. Though difficult and painful at times, Church discipline is one of the greatest manifestations of God's love and mercy. Because of the Atonement, it not only has the power to guide the wayward soul back to the strait and narrow path of the gospel but also lifts the burden of sin from the shoulders of the repentant.

SOURCES

Cannon, George Q. In *Journal of Discourses.* 26 vols. London: Latter-day Saints' Book Depot, 1854–86.

Lee, Harold B. *The Teachings of Harold B. Lee.* Edited by Clyde J. Williams. Salt Lake City: Bookcraft, 1996.

Taylor, John. In Conference Report, Apr. 1880, 74–79.

BLT

CHURCH OF THE FIRSTBORN

The scriptures speak of those who qualify for exaltation as being the "church of the Firstborn" (D&C 76:54, 67, 102). The church of the Firstborn is composed of faithful Saints who have proven true and faithful to their covenants. As baptism is the gate to membership in the Church of Jesus Christ on earth, so celestial marriage opens the door to membership in the heavenly church (Smith, 2:42; McConkie, *Promised,* 47; *Witness,* 337). The church of the Firstborn is the Church beyond the veil, the organized body of Saints who qualify for exaltation, or the blessings of the Firstborn. Jesus is the literal Firstborn of the Father and as such is entitled to the birthright. Through his act of consummate mercy and grace (the Atonement), our Savior makes it possible for us to inherit, receive, and possess the same blessings he receives, as though we ourselves were the Firstborn. Those who come into the Church and live worthy of the companionship of the Holy Ghost are born again; they become the sons and daughters of Jesus Christ by adoption. If they continue faithful, receive the covenants and ordinances of the temple, and are true to those higher covenants, they will eventually become the sons and daughters of God, meaning the Father (McConkie, *Doctrinal*, 2:472–75, 491). They become heirs of God, joint-heirs with Christ to all that the Father has, including eternal life. "Wherefore, as it is written, they are gods, even the sons of God" (D&C 76:58). President Brigham Young therefore stated that "the ordinances of the house of God are expressly for the Church of the Firstborn" (8:154).

SOURCES

McConkie, Bruce R. *Doctrinal New Testament Commentary.* 3 vols. Salt Lake City: Bookcraft, 1966–73.

———. *A New Witness for the Articles of Faith.* Salt Lake City: Deseret Book, 1985.

———. *The Promised Messiah: The First Coming of Christ.* Salt Lake City: Deseret Book, 1978.

Smith, Joseph Fielding. *Doctrines of Salvation.* Compiled by Bruce R. McConkie. 3 vols. Salt Lake City: Bookcraft, 1954–56.

Young, Brigham. In *Journal of Discourses.* 26 vols. London: Latter-day Saints' Book Depot, 1854–86.

RLM

COMFORTER

Two Comforters are mentioned in the scriptures: the Holy Ghost and the Lord Jesus Christ himself. At the Last Supper, Jesus promised his disciples the Comforter, "which is the Holy Ghost," who "shall teach you all things, and bring all things to your remembrance" (John 14:26). One of the name-titles of the Holy Ghost is the Comforter because he brings peace and comfort to troubled hearts in times of need (John 14:27); he "filleth with hope and . . . love" (Moroni 8:26). In addition, the Comforter is a testator—testifying of the divinity of Jesus Christ and the power of his atonement (John 15:26; D&C 21:9; 90:11). The Comforter also "showeth all things, and teacheth the peaceable things of the kingdom" (D&C 39:6). The Comforter, who "knoweth all things" (D&C 42:17), also reveals truths "made known from on high" (D&C 75:27), which are "glad tidings of great joy, even the everlasting gospel" (D&C 79:1). All these fruits of the Comforter—peace, joy, love, enlightenment, strength—are but a foretaste of that which God has in store for those who love and serve him (1 Corinthians 2:9; D&C 76:116–18).

The ultimate Comforter is the presence of the Lord Jesus Christ himself. He is known as the Second Comforter, in fulfillment of the Savior's promise to the disciples at the Last Supper: "I will not leave you comfortless: *I will come to you*" (John 14:18; emphasis added). Until we abide in the eternal presence of God, we have the promise, if we are faithful, of the continual companionship of the Holy Ghost in mortality as a Comforter and Guide. This "last Comforter" (Smith, 3:381), the Second Comforter, comes to faithful and sanctified Saints according to God's "own time, and in his own way, and according to his own will" (D&C 88:68).

SOURCE

Smith, Joseph. *History of The Church of Jesus Christ of Latter-day Saints.* Edited by B. H. Roberts. 7 vols. 2d ed. rev. Salt Lake City: The Church of Jesus Christ of Latter-day Saints, 1932–51.

BLT

COMMON CONSENT

"All things shall be done by common consent in the church" (D&C 26:2), the Lord instructed the Prophet Joseph Smith shortly after the Church was organized. Common consent is the process by which members of the Church support and sustain persons called to serve in the Church, as well as decisions and actions made by the presiding officers, both general and local. This foundational principle was included in the Articles and Covenants of the Church found in the Doctrine and Covenants: "No person is to be ordained [or set apart] to any office [calling] in this church, where there is a regularly organized branch of the same, without the vote of that church" (D&C 20:65). The usage of the word *vote* may evoke the image of an election, such as a political one. There is a fundamental difference, however, between what that word means in a Church setting and what it means in a political setting. In the Church, members do not nominate or elect officers; nor do they initiate actions or changes in programs or procedures. That right belongs to the presiding officer, who holds the keys, or right of presidency, and the authority to lead the respective unit of the Church. Under the inspiration of the Lord, the presiding officer selects and calls those who will lead and serve in various capacities in the Church. Under the law of common consent, members then have the right and responsibility to sustain or not sustain—to approve or disapprove—the one called (D&C 124:144).

President J. Reuben Clark Jr. taught: "The body of the Church has no *calling* or 'nominating' power, but only the sustaining, or politically speaking the 'electing' power. When the presiding authority presents any man to the body of the Church to be sustained, the only power which the assembly has is to vote, by uplifted hand, either to sustain or not to sustain" (28–29). The principle of common consent, as practiced in the modern Church, has roots in the practices of the ancient Church, as seen in both the Old Testament and the New Testament. In Moses' day, "all the people answered with one voice" (Exodus 24:3) and sustained the calling of Joshua (Numbers 27:18–20). The membership of the New Testament church, in similar manner, "assembled with one accord" in sustaining the calling of Barnabas and Paul (Acts 15:25).

Although the Church is not a democratic institution, the principle of common consent safeguards individual agency and allows for the "voice of the people" to be heard. The First Presidency affirmed this in 1907: "We deny the existence of arbitrary power in the Church, and this because its government is moral government purely, and its forces are applied through kindness, reason, and persuasion. . . . The members are at liberty to vote as they choose" (487–88).

The Lord has given the members of the Church the right to vote according to their conscience, with the understanding that it is the Lord who directs the calls to service and leadership in the Church. There may be times when a negative vote may be appropriate. President Joseph Fielding Smith taught: "No man has the right to raise his hand in opposition, or with contrary vote, unless he has a reason for doing so that would be valid if presented before those who stand at the head. In other words, I have no right to raise my hand in opposition to a man who is appointed to any position in this Church, simply because I may not like him, or because of some personal disagreement or feeling I may have, but only on the grounds that he is guilty of wrong doing, of transgression of the laws of the Church which would disqualify him for the position which he is called to hold" (123–24).

Common consent—or a sustaining vote—is not so much a vote for a person or action but rather an individual covenant to faithfully support, strengthen, speak well of, and pray for those who are sustained. It is also a reflection of our testimony and an acknowledgment of the mantle and authority of the man who holds the keys and who is called by the Lord to preside. The act of raising our hands in a sustaining vote is an outward sign of our inward commitment to the gospel and a demonstration of our conviction that the Spirit guides our Church leaders.

SOURCES

Clark, J. Reuben, Jr. In Conference Report, Oct. 1940, 28–32.
First Presidency. "An Address." *Improvement Era,* May 1907, 481–95.
Smith, Joseph Fielding. *Doctrines of Salvation.* Compiled by Bruce R. McConkie.
   3 vols. Salt Lake City: Bookcraft, 1954–56.

BLT

CONCEIVED IN SIN

Joseph Smith wrote to John Wentworth, "We believe that men will be punished for their own sins, and not for Adam's transgression" (Articles of Faith 1:2). The Lord affirmed this principle in his statement to Adam: "I have forgiven thee thy transgression in the Garden of Eden" (Moses 6:53).

This declaration must, however, be understood in the proper doctrinal context. Although God forgave our first parents their transgression, although no original sin was entailed upon Adam and Eve's children, and although "the Son of God hath atoned for original guilt, wherein the sins of the parents cannot be answered upon the heads of the children" (Moses 6:54), we are not unaffected by the Fall. King David cried out in agony, "Behold, I was shapen in iniquity; and in sin did my mother conceive me" (Psalm 51:5). Jehovah explained to Adam, "Inasmuch as thy children are conceived in sin, even so when they begin to grow up, sin conceiveth in their hearts, and they taste the bitter, that they may know to prize the good" (Moses 6:55). We do not believe that the whole of humanity is depraved in the sense that everyone is completely evil. We do not believe that human beings, because of intrinsic carnality and sensuality, lack the power to choose good over evil. That power to choose comes as a marvelous benefit of the Atonement (Galatians 5:1; 2 Nephi 2:26; Helaman 14:30–31). We do not believe that children are born in sin or that they inherit the so-called sin of Adam, either by sexual union or by birth.

Children are conceived in sin in that they are conceived into a world of sin. In addition, conception is the means, the vehicle, by which the effects of the Fall—a fallen nature, or mortality, what the scriptures call the flesh—are transmitted to the posterity of Adam and Eve. To be sure, the propensity for sin and susceptibility to it are implanted in our nature at conception, just as death is. Both death and sin are present only as potentialities at conception and are therefore not fully evident at birth. Death and sin do, however, become part of our nature as we grow up. Sin occurs naturally, as does death. In the case of little children, the results of this fallen nature (sinful actions and dispositions) are held in abeyance by virtue of the Atonement until they reach the time of accountability. When children reach that age, they must thereafter repent and come unto Christ by covenant and through the ordinances of the gospel (D&C 18:42; 29:47; 137:10).

RLM

CONDESCENSION OF GOD

Nephi "beheld a virgin, and she was exceedingly fair and white." Then an angel asked Nephi: "Knowest thou the condescension of God?" (1 Nephi 11:13, 16). To condescend means to "go down with" or to "go down among." The angel's question might be restated thus: Nephi, do you fathom the majesty of it all? Can your mortal mind comprehend the infinite wonder and grandeur of the marvelous love made manifest by the Father and the Son?

Nephi answered: "I know that he loveth his children; nevertheless, I do not know the meaning of all things" (1 Nephi 11:17). Those who come to know him who is eternal discover that the infiniteness of God as the Almighty does not preclude either his immediacy or his intimacy as a loving Lord. Enoch learned this precious lesson during his ministry (Moses 7:28–32), and Nephi evidenced his knowledge of the same principle.

The condescension of God the Son consists in the coming to earth of the great Jehovah, the Lord God Omnipotent, the God of the ancients. The condescension of God the Son thus consists in the fact that the Eternal One would "descend from his throne divine"

(*Hymns,* no. 193), to be born in the most humble of circumstances, to become one of the most helpless creatures of all creation—a human infant—and submit to the influences of mortal life. An angel explained to King Benjamin the condescension of God the Son: "The time cometh, and is not far distant," he prophesied, "that with power, the Lord Omnipotent who reigneth, who was, and is from all eternity to all eternity, shall come down from heaven among the children of men, and shall dwell in a tabernacle of clay." Furthermore, Jehovah, the God of Creation, "shall suffer temptations, and pain of body, hunger, thirst, and fatigue, even more than man can suffer, except it be unto death" (Mosiah 3:5, 7). The condescension of the Son—his ministry among the unenlightened and his suffering and death—followed by the persecution and death of his anointed servants, is described by Nephi (1 Nephi 11:27–36).

Inextricably tied to the concept of Christ's incarnation, of the condescension of God the Son, is the awful irony of the suffering and atonement of our Lord. He who was sinless was persecuted and put to death by sinners whom he came to save. He who was sinless suffered anguish as though he himself were the great sinner. In Paul's words, God the Father has "made him to be sin for us, who knew no sin" (2 Corinthians 5:21). In other words, He who deserved least of all to suffer suffered most—more than mortal mind can fathom. He who had brought light and life—in truth, the more abundant life (John 10:10)—was rejected by the powers of darkness. The *Lectures on Faith,* presented to the School of the Elders in Kirtland, Ohio, record that Jesus Christ is called the Son of God because he "descended in suffering below that which man can suffer; or, in other words, suffered greater sufferings, and was exposed to more powerful contradictions than any man can be" (59). All this Nephi saw in vision, including the persecution and deaths of the Twelve Apostles after the crucifixion and ascension of the Master (1 Nephi 11:24–36).

SOURCES

"I Stand All Amazed." *Hymns of The Church of Jesus Christ of Latter-day Saints,* no.
193. Salt Lake City: The Church of Jesus Christ of Latter-day Saints, 1985.
Lectures on Faith. Salt Lake City: Deseret Book, 1985.

RLM

CONFIRMATION

The ordinance of confirmation is performed after a person gains admission to The Church of Jesus Christ of Latter-day Saints through baptism for the remission of sins (D&C 20:41; 33:15). The ordinance is performed by the laying on of hands in the name of Jesus Christ and by the authority of the Melchizedek Priesthood. The baptized person is confirmed a member of the Church and given the gift of the Holy Ghost. In the ordinance, the person being confirmed is told, "Receive the Holy Ghost." It is in essence a command to live in such a way as to be continually guided, instructed, comforted, and blessed by the companionship and influence of the Spirit. As a result, the ordinance of confirmation itself does not actually confer the Holy Ghost but rather gives the person the right to receive that gift upon condition of faithfulness. The ordinance opens the door or gives the gift, figuratively speaking, but the personal faith and righteousness of the individual enables the gift to be realized. The Prophet Joseph Smith taught, "The Gift of the Holy Ghost by the laying on of hands, cannot be received through the medium of any other principle than the principle of righteousness, for if the proposals are not complied with, it is of no use, but withdraws" (96).

SOURCE

Joseph Smith [manual]. Teachings of Presidents of the Church series. Salt Lake City: The Church of Jesus Christ of Latter-day Saints, 2007.

BLT

CONSCIENCE

As spirit children of God, each of us has the innate ability to know right from wrong. That ability, called our conscience, does not remain stagnant throughout mortality. It will grow sharper and increasingly sensitive when we heed its directives, as the apostle Paul experienced after his conversion to Jesus Christ. Before he knew the Savior, Paul viewed himself as "blameless" in the eyes of God, but afterward, with his sharpened conscience, he discovered that many attitudes not forbidden under the law of Moses could nonetheless be offensive to God (Philippians 3:6; JST, Romans 7:9–20). On the other hand, our conscience will become insensitive to influences around us when we consistently ignore it, as Amulek observed: "I did harden my heart, for I was called many times and I would not hear; therefore I knew . . . yet I would not know" (Alma 10:6). The Light of Christ "inviteth and enticeth to do good continually" (Moroni 7:13). This constant divine influence educates our conscience or quickens our understanding (D&C 88:11). By attuning our conscience to the Light of Christ and the promptings of the Holy Ghost, we can eventually learn to see things as God sees them.

Scriptures teach that we can skew or weaken our conscience so that evil no longer seems evil. As a result, our conscience is "seared with a hot iron" (1 Timothy 4:2) until we become "past feeling" (1 Nephi 17:45; Ephesians 4:19). Consider Herod Antipas when he justified an order to execute John the Baptist for his "oath's sake." Later, hearing a rumor that John had "risen from the dead," Herod's guilty conscience haunted him (Mark 6:26–27). Similarly, a group of scribes and Pharisees with numbed consciences brought an adulterous woman to Christ to be judged of him. When Jesus revealed their deceptiveness, they sheepishly slipped away, "being convicted by their own conscience" (John 8:9).

Jesus warned that in the future, individuals would seek to deceive their conscience into concluding that killing the apostles would be doing God a service (John 16:2). Later, Paul acknowledged his guilt in doing just that (Philippians 3:6–7). When he was on the road to Damascus intending to bring harm to Christians, the Savior appeared to him, saying, "It is hard for thee to kick against the pricks" (Acts 9:5)—evidence that Paul's conscience had begun to thaw.

On the other hand, if a skewed conscience persists in condemning us after God has forgiven us, we need the Lord's educating influence on our hearts. "For if our heart condemn us, God is greater than our heart, and knoweth all things" (1 John 3:20; see also Romans 14:22). With the influence of the light and through the atonement of Christ, our conscience will become pure (1 Timothy 3:9), and our remorse will turn to joy (Alma 42:24). Humbled and deeply aware of their need for the Lord's forgiveness, King Benjamin's people were filled with joy and a "peace of conscience, because of the exceeding faith which they had in Jesus Christ" (Mosiah 4:3).

The Church has long maintained that "no government can exist in peace" without securing "to each individual the free exercise of conscience" (D&C 134:2). All should be allowed "the privilege of worshiping Almighty God according to the dictates of [their] own conscience" (Articles of Faith 1:11).

CFO

CONSECRATE/CONSECRATION, LAW OF

The word *consecrate* means "to make sacred" or to do something "with sacredness." A person or thing may be set apart from the common or profane and dedicated to the worship and service of God and the building up of his kingdom on earth. Ancient Israelites were commanded to consecrate themselves in preparation for being in God's presence (Exodus 32:29). For example, priests and Levites in Mosaic times were consecrated to the service of the Lord and were thus expected to live holy and spiritual lives in order to fulfill their sacred calling (Numbers 3:6, 8). In a similar manner, Nazarites such as Samson (Judges 16:17), Samuel (1 Samuel 1:11), and possibly John the Baptist were consecrated by covenant, even before they were born, to fulfill a specific service to God. Their personal consecration involved a voluntary separation from certain things that could make them unclean or unworthy or in any way inhibit their service to God (Numbers 6:1–22). Objects used in the worship of God were consecrated, or made sacred, to that end. Such objects included temples and tabernacles, altars, furnishings, and utensils associated with religious rites. Thus, the word *dedicated* is often used interchangeably with *consecrated*. From the time of Adam until the Law of Moses was fulfilled, sacrifices, whether the firstfruits of the field or the firstlings of flocks, were also consecrated or "set apart" as symbolic reminders of Christ's atoning sacrifice. Consecration and sacrifice thus go hand in hand and are almost always spoken of within the same context. Sacrifice requires giving up something *for* God, while consecration requires giving something *to* God.

For Latter-day Saints the law of consecration calls for us to give unto the Lord our best efforts in his service, to make available all of our time, talents, and means to the furthering of God's work on earth, and to be set apart from the profane things of the world that prevent us from fulfilling our foreordained missions. Consecration is the willingness to lay our all on the altar of God—to not hold back anything spiritual or temporal in our devotion to the Lord and his Church. Latter-day Saints make a solemn covenant to consecrate all that they have and are to God for the building up of his earthly kingdom and the blessing of all of his children. The law of consecration is in operation whenever and wherever this covenant is made. It is an eternal law—a law, as President Ezra Taft Benson said, "for an inheritance in the celestial kingdom" (123).

In every dispensation, the law of consecration as lived by God's people has also had a temporal dimension to it—a means whereby the Saints could be equal in heavenly and earthly bonds (D&C 78:5). Enoch's people "were of one heart and one mind, and dwelt in righteousness; and there was no poor among them" (Moses 7:18). In New Testament times "all that believed were together, and had all things common; And sold their possessions and goods, and parted them to all men, as every man had need" (Acts 2:44–45). We read in the Book of Mormon that the consecration of faithful Nephites produced a condition where "they had all things common among them; therefore there were not rich and poor, bond and free, but they were all made free, and partakers of the heavenly gift" (4 Nephi 1:3). When covenant people are truly consecrated, the spiritual and temporal blessings result in a "prosperity in Christ" (4 Nephi 1:23) that yields "no contention in the land, because of the love of God which [does] dwell in the hearts of the people. And there [are] no envyings, nor strifes, nor tumults, nor whoredoms, nor lyings, nor murders, nor any manner of lasciviousness; and surely there could not be a happier people among all the people who had been created by the hand of God" (4 Nephi 1:15–16).

In this dispensation the Lord revealed to the Prophet Joseph Smith the means whereby the law of consecration could bless the poor and needy Saints as well as further the work of the Church. Nineteenth-century Latter-day Saints lived the law of consecration and stewardship (sometimes referred to as the united order), whereby they voluntarily consecrated by legal deed their possessions to the bishop for the use of the Church. The bishop would then deed back to the person a "stewardship" or an "inheritance" that would amply meet the needs of the family. The member who entered into this covenant of consecration was thus held accountable for how he managed his stewardship. After the needs and just wants had been met for the family, all surplus would go to the "Lord's storehouse," enabling the bishop and his authorized agents to help alleviate suffering and poverty among less fortunate Saints. These surplus resources were also used to build houses of worship and do other things that would expand the kingdom of God on earth, thus bringing spiritual and temporal blessings to more of God's children. Several revelations in the Doctrine and Covenants outlined not only the purpose but also the procedures for this specific practice (D&C 42:30–39; 51:2–19; 58:35–36; 72; 78:3–5; 82:17–19; 104:14–15, 17–18). The law of consecration and stewardship reminds dedicated disciples that all things are the Lord's and we are stewards of that which he has given us. "What have you to consecrate that is actually your own?" President Brigham Young asked. "Nothing" (2:307).

Although the covenant is the same, the specific practices or implementation of it have changed over time "by revelation adapted to the circumstances in which the children of the kingdom are placed" (Smith, 5:135).

President Henry B. Erying stated: "Because the Lord hears their cries and feels your deep compassion for [those in need], He has from the beginning of time provided ways for His disciples to help. He has invited His children to consecrate their time, their means, and themselves to join with Him in serving others.

"His way of helping has at times been called living the law of consecration. In another period His way was called the united order. In our time it is called the Church welfare program.

"The names and the details of operation are changed to fit the needs and conditions of people. But always the Lord's way to help those in temporal need requires people who out of love have consecrated themselves and what they have to God and to His work" (22).

Hence, specific practices or applications of the law of consecration may change, but the law itself, and its associated covenant, does not. It is eternal. President Ezra Taft Benson declared: "The law of consecration is a celestial law, not an economic experiment" (121). President Gordon B. Hinckley likewise testified that "the law of consecration [was] not done away with and [is] still in effect" (639). Neither God nor circumstances, neither programs nor policies, prevent us from living the law of consecration today. That which prevents consecration is our own selfishness, covetousness, worldliness, and faithlessness. In short, we need not look to some future day in order to live the law of consecration. As Elder Neal A. Maxwell taught: "We tend to think of consecration only as yielding up, when divinely directed, our material possessions. But ultimate consecration is the yielding up of oneself to God" (36).

SOURCES

Benson, Ezra Taft. *The Teachings of Ezra Taft Benson.* Salt Lake City: Bookcraft, 1988.
Eyring, Henry B. "Opportunities to Do Good." *Ensign,* May 2011, 22–26.
Hinckley, Gordon B. *Teachings of Gordon B. Hinckley.* Salt Lake City: Deseret Book, 1997.
Maxwell, Neal A. "Consecrate Thy Performance." *Ensign,* May 2002, 36–38.
Smith, Joseph. *History of The Church of Jesus Christ of Latter-day Saints.* Edited by B. H. Roberts. 7 vols. 2d ed. rev. Salt Lake City: The Church of Jesus Christ of Latter-day Saints, 1932–51.
Young, Brigham. In *Journal of Discourses.* 26 vols. London: Latter-day Saints' Book Depot, 1854–86.

BLT

CONSTITUTION OF THE UNITED STATES OF AMERICA

The Constitution of the United States of America is a written standard inspired by God to establish and perpetuate individual freedoms, the rule of law, and government by the consent of the governed. Latter-day Saint scripture affirms that the Constitution is part of God's overall plan for his children living on this earth in the dispensation of the fulness of times.

America was foreordained by God to be a land of liberty in which no kings would rule (2 Nephi 10:11–14). The Gentiles who ultimately came to possess America "were delivered by the power of God out of the hands of all other nations" (1 Nephi 13:19). They settled in this land and were "set up as a free people by the power of the Father" (3 Nephi 21:4). Therefore, "for this purpose," declared the Lord, "have I established the Constitution of this land, by the hands of wise men whom I raised up unto this very purpose, and redeemed the land by the shedding of blood" (D&C 101:80). In the dedicatory prayer for the Kirtland Temple, the Prophet Joseph Smith was inspired to pray as follows: "Have mercy, O Lord, upon all the nations of the earth; have mercy upon the rulers of our land; may those principles, which were so honorably and nobly defended, namely, the Constitution of our land, by our fathers, be established forever" (D&C 109:54).

Indeed, the Constitution was established by God for the benefit not only of the citizens of the United States but also of all humankind, in order to fulfill the purposes of God. Those purposes can be brought to pass only when moral agency is held inviolate and its governmental derivative, freedom based on the rule of law, is firmly established. The Lord plainly explained:

"The laws and constitution of the people, which I have suffered to be established . . . should be maintained for the rights and protection of all flesh, according to just and holy principles; that every man may act in doctrine and principle pertaining to futurity, according to the moral agency which I have given unto him, that every man may be accountable for his own sins in the day of judgment. . . . And for this purpose have I established the Constitution of this land" (D&C 101:77–78, 80; see also 98:5–6).

Moral agency thus stands at the heart of the doctrine of an inspired constitution. The Lord has informed us that constitutionally protected freedoms were not intended to guarantee unrestrained liberty without regard to God's will and desires. Rather, the Constitution and the principles that form it are inseparably connected to God's plan; he is the moving force behind its establishment. The Constitution cannot be disconnected from God; freedom cannot be separated from accountability. In another revelation the Lord reiterated the universality of the principles found in the Constitution: "And that law of the land which is constitutional, supporting that principle of freedom in maintaining rights and privileges, belongs to all mankind, and is justifiable before me" (D&C 98:5).

Many prophets have spoken of the virtues and inspired status of the Constitution. The Prophet Joseph Smith called it a "glorious standard." In poetic imagery, he testified that it was "founded in the wisdom of God. It is a heavenly banner; it is to all those who are privileged with the sweets of its liberty, like the cooling shades and refreshing waters of a great rock in a thirsty and weary land. It is like a great tree under whose branches men from every clime can be shielded from the burning rays of the sun. . . . We say that God is true; that the Constitution of the United States is true; that the Bible is true; that the Book of

Mormon is true; that the Book of Covenants is true; that Christ is true" (*History,* 3:304). Little wonder the Prophet described himself as "the greatest advocate of the Constitution of the United States there is on the earth" (*History,* 6:56–57).

Joseph Smith is not the only latter-day prophet to put the Constitution on a par with the scriptures. President J. Reuben Clark Jr. said: "To me, . . . that statement of the Lord, 'I have established the Constitution of this land,' puts the Constitution of the United States in the position in which it would be if it were written in this book of Doctrine and Covenants itself. This makes the Constitution the word of the Lord to us. That it was given, not by oral utterance, but by the operation of his mind and spirit upon the minds of men, inspiring them to the working out of this great document of human government, does not alter its authority" (93). As President Clark indicated, the United States Constitution is a written document, not a collection of oral traditions or behavioral customs. This, in truth, is one of its great strengths and gives it enduring power.

President David O. McKay affirmed the eternal nature of the principles embodied in the Constitution: "There are some fundamental principles of this republic which, like eternal truths, never get out of date. . . . Such are the underlying principles of the Constitution" (in *Encyclopedia,* 1:318).

President Brigham Young unequivocally pledged the Saints' loyalty to the Constitution and its universal principles: "We will cling to the Constitution of our country, and to the government that reveres that sacred charter of free men's rights; and, if necessary, pour out our best blood for the defense of every good and righteous principle" (358).

Elder Bruce R. McConkie commented on the destiny of the United States: "It is our firm conviction as a people that the stars and stripes will be waving triumphantly in the breeze, as a symbol of the greatness and stability of the United States of America, when the Lord comes. This nation was established to be the Lord's base of operations in this final gospel dispensation. From it the gospel is to go to every other nation and people. The greater its influence among the nations of the world, the more rapidly the gospel spreads. But the Lord has told us that all nations, the United States included, shall cease to be when he comes" (491).

Without question, the idea of a divinely inspired Constitution is rare in public discourse. Even more rare is the phenomenon observed among the Latter-day Saints that the Constitution holds a place of sacred honor among our beliefs.

SOURCES

Benson, Ezra Taft. *The Teachings of Ezra Taft Benson.* Salt Lake City: Bookcraft, 1988.

Clark, J. Reuben, Jr. In Conference Report, Apr. 1935, 89–96.

Encyclopedia of Mormonism. Edited by Daniel H. Ludlow. 4 vols. New York: Macmillan, 1992.

McConkie, Bruce R. *The Millennial Messiah: The Second Coming of the Son of Man.* Salt Lake City: Deseret Book, 1982.

Smith, Joseph. *History of The Church of Jesus Christ of Latter-day Saints.* Edited by B. H. Roberts. 7 vols. 2d ed. rev. Salt Lake City: The Church of Jesus Christ of Latter-day Saints, 1932–51.

Young, Brigham. *Discourses of Brigham Young.* Selected and arranged by John A. Widtsoe. Salt Lake City: Deseret Book, 1954.

ACS

CONVERSION

We convert our allegiance to the Savior when we humble ourselves, allow our hearts and minds to be pricked or awakened from their natural state, desire baptism, and make a covenant of service to God for the rest of our lives (Acts 2:37–38; Psalm 51:13). This mighty change of heart is ignited when we gain a testimony, born of the Spirit, that Jesus Christ is the Redeemer and we turn our broken hearts to God (Alma 5:13–15; Joel 2:13). Conversion is grounded in a belief in "the prophecies of the holy prophets, which are written, which leadeth [an individual] to faith on the Lord, and unto repentance" (Helaman 15:7). Through conversion, therefore, our sins are "blotted out" because of the merciful sacrifice of Jesus Christ (Acts 3:19).

Jesus identified a deeper level of conversion than simply declaring his divinity. During the Savior's ministry, Peter bore witness to Jesus: "Thou art the Christ, the Son of the living God" (Matthew 16:16). But later, during the Last Supper, the Savior revealed that Peter's testimony was only the beginning of conversion, that he was not yet fully converted. "When thou art converted," Jesus told him, "strengthen thy brethren" (Luke 22:32). In this sense, conversion is not an event but a lifelong process. It involves becoming a new creature through the atonement of Christ after "wading through much tribulation" and learning to follow the direction of the Holy Ghost (Mosiah 27:28). Elder Dallin H. Oaks taught that conversion, which is more than knowing and declaring, "requires us to *do* and to *become*." He explained that moving though a process of conversion "is achieved not just by doing what is right, but by doing it for the right reason—for the pure love of Christ" (33). When we have "no more disposition to do evil but to do good continually" (Mosiah 5:2), we can know that we are becoming more like the Savior and progressing toward full conversion.

SOURCE

Oaks, Dallin H. "The Challenge to Become." *Ensign,* Nov. 2000, 32–34.

CFO

COUNCIL(S) IN HEAVEN

The plan of salvation and its attendant laws and principles were "ordained in the midst of the Council of the Eternal God of all other gods before this world was" (D&C 121:32). Abraham saw in vision that before the formation of the earth, "the Gods took counsel among themselves" (Abraham 4:26). The Prophet taught, "At the first organization in heaven we were all present, and saw the Savior chosen and appointed and the plan of salvation made, and we sanctioned it" (*Joseph Smith,* 209). This is commonly referred to as the Grand Council in Heaven. Undoubtedly there were many councils in the premortal world in which the gospel was taught and plans were made. "It was the design of the councils of heaven before the world was," Joseph Smith declared, "that the principles and laws of the priesthood should be predicated upon the gathering of the people in every age of the world" (*History,* 5:423). It is interesting to note that the Prophet used the plural form *councils.* President Joseph F. Smith likewise spoke of many planning meetings or councils where the children of God "were vitally concerned in the carrying out of these great plans and purposes" (25:57). Instruction was a primary purpose for such meetings (D&C 138:55–56). These councils, like earthly councils functioning under the direction of priesthood authority, were a time for organization, preparation, and formal instruction that led us to greater understanding of the laws of God, the role of mortality in the plan of salvation, and other principles designed to bring about "the immortality and eternal life of man" (Moses 1:39).

SOURCES

Joseph Smith [manual]. Teachings of Presidents of the Church series. Salt Lake City: The Church of Jesus Christ of Latter-day Saints, 2007.

Smith, Joseph. *History of The Church of Jesus Christ of Latter-day Saints*. Edited by B. H. Roberts. 7 vols. 2d ed. rev. Salt Lake City: The Church of Jesus Christ of Latter-day Saints, 1932–51.

Smith, Joseph F. In *Journal of Discourses*. 26 vols. London: Latter-day Saints' Book Depot, 1854–86.

BLT

COVENANT

A covenant is a binding agreement—a contract between at least two parties. In a theological sense, a covenant is a sacred compact and promise between God and man. God establishes the conditions of sacred covenants. As mortals, we do not have the right to amend such conditions. We can either choose to enter into a covenantal relationship with the Lord and obey his stipulations or choose to reject and disobey them. "I command and men obey not," declared the Lord, "I revoke and they receive not the blessing" (D&C 58:32). God's people have been and always will be covenant people. The gospel of Jesus Christ is an everlasting covenant given to our Heavenly Father's children in all dispensations. In our day it has been restored to earth and, as such, is known as "the new and everlasting covenant" (D&C 132:6; 133:57). The scriptures teach and record not only God's covenants but also the consequences of abiding or rejecting those covenants. Every gospel ordinance of salvation, such as baptism, the sacrament of the Lord's Supper, ordination to the priesthood, endowments and marriage sealing performed in the temple, have attendant covenants—two-way promises between the Lord and the recipient of the ordinance and covenant. Likewise, obedience to specific commandments, such as Sabbath observance (Exodus 20:8–11; 31:13–17; D&C 59:9–20), payment of tithes and offerings (Isaiah 58:6–11; D&C 119:3–6), and living the Word of Wisdom (D&C 89), is also evidence of a covenantal relationship and yield covenantal blessings. With a solemn and binding oath—"an immutable covenant" (D&C 98:3)—God has promised blessings both here and hereafter to those who keep their covenants, but those who "do not what I say . . . have no promise" (D&C 82:10).

Indeed, Latter-day Saints are charged to "observe to keep all the commandments and covenants" (D&C 42:78) and "walk in all the ordinances of the Lord" (D&C 136:4). President Boyd K. Packer taught: "Ordinances and covenants become our credentials for admission into His presence. To worthily receive them is the quest of a lifetime; to keep them thereafter is the challenge of mortality. . . . [Covenants make] men and women . . . rise above themselves, reach beyond themselves and come within the grasp of celestial exaltation. . . . Surely the Lord is pleased when we are worthy of the title: A keeper of the covenants" (86–87).

SOURCE

Packer, Boyd K. *Mine Errand from the Lord: Selections from the Sermons and Writings of Boyd K. Packer.* Salt Lake City: Deseret Book, 2008.

BLT

COVET

The sin of coveting suggests an ungodly desire, lust, or excessive envy for something or someone that supersedes our devotion to God. The apostle Paul considered covetousness akin to idolatry (Colossians 3:5) and a sin that will disqualify us from the kingdom of God if we do not repent (1 Corinthians 6:10). In one of the Ten Commandments, God condemned coveting a neighbor's home, spouse, or belongings (Exodus 20:17). He has even warned against coveting one's own property, suggesting the evils associated with loving and worshipping possessions more than the Creator who gave them to us (D&C 19:26; Romans 1:25).

Also a catalyst for catastrophes and heartache in "the last days" (2 Timothy 3:1), covetousness was a weakness of the Israelites that led to the Babylonian captivity (Jeremiah 6:13). Covetousness led to the failure of the Saints to live the law of consecration and stewardship during Joseph Smith's day (D&C 104:4, 52–53). During his mortal ministry, Jesus told a man who sought his help in compelling a brother to share his inheritance, "Beware of covetousness: for a man's life consisteth not in the abundance of the things which he possesseth" (Luke 12:15). In the Book of Mormon, King Benjamin cautioned the poor Nephites against coveting "that which [they] have not received" (Mosiah 4:24–25).

The blessing of a prolonged life is associated with opposing covetousness (Proverbs 28:16). Knowing that the Lord will never leave or forsake us, we are therefore invited to resist covetousness in all that we do and "be content with such things as [we] have" (Hebrews 13:5). Like the Psalmist, we can pray, "Incline my heart unto thy testimonies, and not to covetousness" (Psalm 119:36).

Using the term *covet* in a righteous sense, the apostle Paul invited us to sincerely desire and diligently seek the gifts of the Spirit: "Covet earnestly the best gifts," he wrote, to guard against schism in the Church (1 Corinthians 12:31, 25).

CFO

CREATION

The scriptures teach that all things were created first spiritually and then temporally, or physically (D&C 29:30–32). How the earth and all things thereon were created spiritually has not yet been fully revealed. With regard to the spirit creation of mankind, however, the Lord has revealed important information. "Man as a spirit," the First Presidency declared in 1909, "was begotten and born of heavenly parents, and reared to maturity in the eternal mansions of the Father, prior to coming upon the earth in a temporal body" (77).

Many things are known concerning the temporal, or physical, creation of the earth as revealed in the scriptures and the teachings of modern prophets. Many things, however, have not yet been revealed. Any doctrinal discussion of the Creation must acknowledge such limitations in man's understanding. Knowing what we do not know is sometimes as valuable as knowing what we do know.

What we know. To Latter-day Saints, there is no doubt that God is the Creator and that all things are created by his infinite, divine power (Genesis 1:1; Ecclesiastes 11:5; Isaiah 40:28; Abraham 4:1–27; 2 Nephi 2:14). Numerous scriptural passages testify that under the direction of the Father, Jesus Christ is "the Creator of all things from the beginning" (Mosiah 3:8; Helaman 14:12; see also John 1:1–3, 14; Ephesians 3:9; Colossians 1:13–16; Hebrews 1:1–2; Mosiah 4:2; 3 Nephi 9:15; Ether 3:15–16; D&C 14:9; 76:24; 93:9–10; Moses

1:32–33; 2:1, 27). These passages also inform us that God's creations are infinite—"worlds without number," the expanse and nature of which mortal man cannot comprehend (Moses 1:33).

Latter-day Saints reject the traditional Christian view of an *ex nihilo* creation—meaning that God created the world, mankind, and all living things out of nothing. The Prophet Joseph Smith taught: "You ask the learned doctors why they say the world was made out of nothing, and they will answer, 'Doesn't the Bible say He *created* the world?' And they infer, from the word create, that it must have been made out of nothing. Now, the word create came from the [Hebrew] word *baurau,* which does not mean to create out of nothing; it means to organize; the same as a man would organize materials and build a ship. Hence, we infer *that God had materials to organize the world out of chaos*—chaotic matter, which is element, and in which dwells all the glory. Element had an existence from the time He had. The pure principles of element are principles which can never be destroyed; they may be organized and re-organized, but not destroyed. They had no beginning, and can have no end" (6:308; emphasis added). Matter is element, and elements are eternal (D&C 93:33). The Creation was thus a divinely managed organization of matter that had always existed.

We also know that man, different from all other of God's creations, was created in God's image, after his likeness (Genesis 1:26–27; Mosiah 7:27; Ether 3:15; D&C 20:18). Joseph Smith's translation of the Bible is even more precise: "In the day that God created man, in the likeness of God made he him; in the image of his own body, male and female, created he them" (Moses 6:8–9). Because of his distinctive creation and relationship to God, man was also given a unique stewardship, or responsibility, over God's other creations (Genesis 1:28; see also Smith, 3:307).

From the scriptures, particularly the Book of Mormon, we see that the Creation is directly linked to the fall of Adam. "Thus, man is created in such a way that he can fall," Elder Bruce R. McConkie wrote. "He falls and brings mortality and procreation and death into being so that he can be redeemed by the atoning sacrifice of the Lord Jesus Christ. . . . The Creation, the Fall, and the Atonement are bound together as one" (15; see also 2 Nephi 2:22–25).

What we don't know. The scriptures tell us why man and the earth were created, but they do not tell us how. We know that the Creation was done by God in his infinite power, but the exact manner in which he accomplished it and how long it took have not been revealed. Much of the language of scripture concerning the process of the Creation is symbolic. "We do not know the how and why and when of all things," Elder McConkie taught concerning the Creation. "Our finite limitations are such that we could not comprehend them if they were revealed to us in all their glory, fulness, and perfection. What has been revealed is that portion of the Lord's eternal word which we must believe and understand if we are to envision the truth about the Fall and the Atonement and thus become heirs of salvation. This is all we are obligated to know in our day" (10). In the absence of the ultimate revealed word on the subject, many members of the Church, including some leaders, have expressed their views on the subject through the years. Such opinions and theories do not, however, constitute the official doctrine of the Church.

"Our religion is not hostile to real science," the First Presidency declared in 1910. "That which is demonstrated, we accept with joy; but vain philosophy, human theory and mere speculations of men, we do not accept nor do we adopt anything contrary to divine revelation or to good common sense" ("Words," 3). Regarding the Creation, the Lord has promised that all things will be revealed at his coming and during his millennial reign (D&C 101:32–33).

SOURCES

First Presidency. "The Origin of Man." *Improvement Era,* Nov. 1909, 75–81; or *Ensign,* Aug. 2002, 26–30.

McConkie, Bruce R. "Christ and the Creation." *Ensign,* June 1982, 8–15.

Smith, Joseph. *History of The Church of Jesus Christ of Latter-day Saints.* Edited by B. H. Roberts. 7 vols. 2d ed. rev. Salt Lake City: The Church of Jesus Christ of Latter-day Saints, 1932–51.

"Words in Season from the First Presidency." *Deseret Evening News,* 17 Dec. 1910, 3.

BLT

CREEDS

According to one account of the First Vision (1838), Joseph Smith learned that all creeds "were an abomination in [God's] sight; that those professors were all corrupt; that 'they draw near to me with their lips, but their hearts are far from me, they teach for doctrines the commandments of men, having a form of godliness, but they deny the power thereof" (Joseph Smith–History 1:19). Originally the Latin word *credo* meant simply "I believe." In Joseph Smith's day, the word *creed* meant "a brief summary of the articles of Christian faith" or "that which is believed" (Webster, "creed"). A modern dictionary defines a creed as "a system of religious belief," "a set of opinions or principles on any subject," or "belief or confidence in; an article of faith" (*Oxford,* "creed").

"Following the American Revolution, a number of theologians vehemently condemned all the popular creeds of Christendom. Urging all disciples of Christ to return to the purity of New Testament Christianity, these preachers taught that the Bible should be regarded as the only standard of faith, that every congregation should be autonomous, and that all men are endowed with the capacity to accept or reject God's gift of salvation. Although these resolute leaders were divided concerning the doctrine of the Godhead, they rejected the use of the term 'Trinity,' claiming that such a word was unscriptural" (Backman, 159).

Joseph Smith was not necessarily opposed to religious creeds in general. The preface to the first edition of the Doctrine and Covenants (1835) states: "There may be an aversion in the minds of some against receiving any thing purporting to be articles of religious faith, in consequence of there being so many now extant; but if men believe a system, and profess that it was given by inspiration, certainly, the more intelligibly they can present it, the better. It does not make a principle untrue to print it, neither does it make it true not to print it."

To the extent that creeds promote or perpetuate falsehood, then of course our Father in Heaven would be displeased with them. To the extent that creeds divide people, categorize them, exclude them, and lead them to persecute others, we can appreciate why they would be viewed as undesirable. To the extent that they become a badge of belonging, the identifying mark by which a "true Christian" is known, the only way by which we can understand what the scriptures really mean about God and Christ—then to that extent the Christian circle is drawn smaller and smaller and the grace of God that makes salvation available to all humankind is frustrated (Titus 2:11).

It may be that the Prophet Joseph was as concerned with creedalism as he was with incorrect doctrine within the creeds. Two Christian writers have observed: "The early Church creeds were motivated more by political than theological concerns. As William Penn is credited with saying, 'Persecution entered with creed-making.' Like-mindedness became a requirement rather than a goal. Orthodoxy, not love and grace, became the central focus." Further, they said: "The saved were those Christians who shared our doctrinal creed. It wasn't enough to claim you were Christian. You had to be the right kind of Christian, a faithful adherent of our religious code. Those within this tight circle were our brothers and sisters, and we were obliged to love them. Those outside our church, denomination, or religion were unsaved" (Gulley, 56, 61).

The apostle Paul affirmed that our Savior "will have all men to be saved, and to come unto the knowledge of the truth" (1 Timothy 2:4). This is what the Prophet Joseph had in mind when he stated in October 1843: "I cannot believe in any of the creeds of the different denominations, because they all have some things in them I cannot subscribe to, though all of them have some truth. I want to come up into the presence of God, and learn all things; but the creeds set up stakes, and say, 'Hitherto shalt thou come, and no further'; which I cannot subscribe to" (327).

SOURCES

Backman, Milton V., Jr. *Christian Churches of America: Origins and Beliefs.* New York: Charles Scribner's Sons, 1983.

Gulley, Philip, and James Mulholland. *If God Is Love: Rediscovering Grace in an Ungracious World.* New York: HarperCollins, San Francisco, 2004.

Joseph Smith [manual]. Teachings of Presidents of the Church series. Salt Lake City: The Church of Jesus Christ of Latter-day Saints, 2007.

The New Shorter Oxford English Dictionary. 2 vols. 6th ed. New York: Oxford University Press, 2007.

Webster, Noah. *American Dictionary of the English Language.* 1828. Reprint, San Francisco: Foundation for American Christian Education, 1980.

RLM

CROSS/CRUCIFY/CRUCIFIXION

The English word *cross* derives from the Latin *crux* or *crucis*. Thus, *crucify* and *crucifixion* mean "to fasten to a cross." All of these terms are related to the Latin *cruciare,* meaning "torture." Indeed, crucifixion was among the most horrible means of torture a condemned person could endure before succumbing to death. Anciently, a cross was the structure upon which the sentence of execution was carried out. Crosses for crucifixion were used by many peoples of the ancient world, particularly the Seleucids, Carthaginians, and Romans from about the sixth century B.C. to the fourth century A.D. The Romans perfected the practice of crucifixion, but it seems to have originated with the ancient Persians, though at least one source puts its beginnings in Egypt (Hewitt, 40). In the ancient world a cross usually consisted of two parts, an upright pole (Latin, *stipes*) or stake (Greek, *stauros*), with a transverse beam, or crossbar, attached (Latin, *patibulum*). Sources indicate that "the condemned [party] never carried the complete cross. . . . Instead only the crossbar was carried to the place [where] the upright piece was set in the ground" (Zias and Sekeles, 190). The ancient secular writer Plautus refers to a victim carrying a crossbar through the city beyond the gate and then being fastened to a cross at the place of crucifixion (161).

This harmonizes well with what we know about crucifixion practices in first-century Jerusalem. Because no executions were allowed to be performed within Jerusalem's walls, based on ancient regulations (Numbers 15:35; 1 Kings 21:13; Acts 7:58), crucifixion processions led to the site of crucifixion outside the city. In the case of Jesus Christ, the procession began at the judgment hall called the Praetorium, where Jesus was given his cross to carry, most likely the *patibulum* only. Because of its weight and Jesus' exhaustion, one Simon of Cyrene was forced to help. The procession passed through a crowded street, where Jesus addressed certain women and then moved on to the site of crucifixion called Golgotha (Aramaic) or Calvary (Latin), meaning "skull" (Matthew 27:32–33; Mark 15:16–22; Luke 23:26–33; John 19:13–17). This location was outside but near the city and close to a gate, probably the one through which Jesus passed (John 19:17, 20; Hebrews 13:12). The procession was led by a Roman centurion, accompanied by at least a quaternion, or four soldiers (John 19:23).

The weight of biblical evidence implies that the upright piece to which Jesus' *patibulum* was fastened was a tree whose branches may have been trimmed off. The Gospel writers uniformly referred to Jesus' cross as simply *stauros,* or "stake." The apostle Paul says, however,

"Christ hath redeemed us from the curse of the law, being made a curse for us: for it is written, Cursed is everyone that hangeth on a tree" (Galatians 3:13). He was quoting Deuteronomy 21:23, which may be viewed as the ultimate Old Testament prophetic reference to Christ's crucifixion. The apostle Peter speaks of the crucifixion of Jesus, "who his own self bare our sins in his own body on a tree, that we, being dead to sins, should live unto righteousness: by whose stripes ye were healed" (1 Peter 2:24). To Cornelius and his family Peter bore a powerful testimony of Jesus as Messiah: "And we are witnesses of all things which he did both in the land of the Jews, and in Jerusalem; whom they slew and hanged on a tree" (Acts 10:39).

Crucifixion on a "tree" is also mentioned in the Dead Sea Scrolls as punishment for special offenses against the "true" community of Israel. The Temple Scroll, regarded as the sixth book of the Torah, is the longest of the Dead Sea Scrolls and a valuable source of background information on aspects of Jewish life and thought in Jesus' day. The scroll says: "If a man slanders his people and delivers his people to a foreign nation and does evil to his people, you shall hang him on a tree and he shall die. On the testimony of two witnesses and on the testimony of three witnesses he shall be put to death and they shall hang him on the tree. If a man is guilty of a capital crime and flees (abroad) to the nations, and curses his people, the children of Israel, you shall hang him also on the tree, and he shall die. But his body shall not stay overnight on the tree. Indeed you shall bury him on the same day. For he who is hanged on the tree is accursed of God and men. You shall not pollute the ground which I give you to inherit" (Vermes, 217).

From the foregoing we might infer that the use of trees in the process of crucifixion was not an anomaly. We also see some of the crimes for which someone could be crucified among at least one group of Jews living in the Holy Land in Jesus' era.

The horrors of crucifixion are well documented. According to the Roman writer Cicero and the Jewish historian Josephus, crucifixion was the worst or most pitiable form of death. Modern scholars who have studied crucifixion have stated, "Death by crucifixion was not caused by the traumatic injury of nailing; rather, hanging from the cross resulted in a painful process of asphyxiation, in which the two sets of muscles used for breathing—the intercostal muscles *and* the diaphragm—became progressively weakened. In time, the victim expired as a consequence of inability to continue breathing properly" (Zias, 190). Victims of crucifixion drowned in the fluid that accumulated in their lungs. The implication here is clear: it would have been impossible to resuscitate a victim of crucifixion (as some anti-resurrection advocates have claimed about Jesus).

Crucifixion was state-sponsored torture, calculated to produce the greatest amount of suffering over the longest possible time before death occurred. Rome's aim in supporting crucifixion, which was a public event or spectacle, was deterrence or prevention. "Whenever we crucify the condemned, the most crowded roads are chosen, where the most people can see and be moved by this terror. For penalties relate not so much to retribution as to their exemplary effect" (Pseudo-Quintilian, in Hanson, 86).

Written sources record that thousands of people were put to death by crucifixion in Roman Judea during the seventy-four years between the death of Herod the Great in 4 B.C. and the destruction of Jerusalem in A.D. 70. The historian Josephus reported that during a revolt that broke out after Herod's death, the Roman leader Quintilius Varus (46 B.C.–A.D. 9) crucified two thousand rebellious Jews (*Antiquities,* 17.10.10). When Titus laid siege to Jerusalem in A.D. 70, he built earthworks around it, captured those attempting to escape, and crucified them opposite the city walls. The daily tally of crucifixion victims was five hundred, sometimes more. "The soldiers, out of the wrath and hatred they bore the Jews, nailed those they caught, one after one way, and another after another, to the crosses, by way of jest; when their multitude was so great, that room was wanting for the crosses, and crosses wanting for the bodies" (Josephus, *Wars,* 5.11.1). The practice of crucifixion in the empire was finally abolished by Constantine in the fourth century (Zias and Charlesworth, 278).

Several sources assert that nails or spikes were driven through Jesus' wrists, in addition to the palms of his hands, for fear that the weight of his body would cause it to tear away from the cross. Medical authorities attest that it "has been shown that the ligaments and bones of the wrist can support the weight of a body hanging from them, but the palms [alone] cannot" (Edwards, 1460). Thus, the nails driven into the Savior's wrists fastened him securely to the cross and fulfilled

Isaiah's prophecy (Isaiah 22:23). There is hardly a more powerful image in scripture for Latter-day Saints than the one Isaiah uses of the nail in a sure place.

As the victim was nailed to the crossbar and lifted into place on the stake, pole, or tree, the victim's arms would bear the full weight of his body. When the victim sagged and more weight was put on the wrists, excruciating pain would shoot along the fingers and up the arms. "To relieve some of the pain in the hands, wrists, and arms, the victim would push down on his feet to raise himself up with the result that searing pain would shoot up the legs from the nail-wounds in the feet. At some point, waves of cramps would sweep over the muscles of the legs and feet, causing throbbing pain as well as the inability to push upward and relieve the pain and pressure in the arms and wrists. Also, with the arms stretched out on the cross, breathing became increasingly difficult. Air could be drawn into the lungs, but not exhaled and asphyxiation eventually resulted" (Davis, 39). When the legs of victims were broken, as reported in John 19:31–33, death resulted much more quickly because of the inability of the victim to raise up his body and stave off asphyxiation.

Crucifixion, however, was still an agonizingly slow way to die. Under normal circumstances, a crucified body was left hanging on the cross to rot and be picked at by birds and insects. It is believed that this sometimes occurred while the victim was still alive, even if just barely. This, combined with the unnatural and contorted position of the body on the cross, contributed to the victim's misery. Jesus' horrible circumstance was attested to by Israel's ancient psalmist: "I am poured out like water, and all my bones are out of joint: my heart is like wax; it is melted in the midst of my bowels" (Psalm 22:14).

Elder James E. Talmage indicated that while Jesus was on the cross, "in addition to the fearful suffering incident to crucifixion, the agony of Gethsemane had recurred, intensified beyond human power to endure" (661). This suffering included, as it did in Gethsemane, the withdrawal of the Father's Spirit and presence, "leaving to the Savior of men the glory of complete victory over the forces of sin and death" (Talmage, 661).

Restoration scripture testifies that the crucifixion of Jesus the Messiah was known by all the ancient prophets centuries before it occurred (Jacob 4:4–5; Mosiah 13:33–35). Enoch is singled out as having seen vividly "the Son of Man lifted up on the cross after the manner of men" (Moses 7:55). The resurrected Savior testified to the Nephites about the cross: "I came into the world to do the will of my Father, because my Father sent me. And my Father sent me that I might be lifted up upon the cross; and after that I had been lifted up upon the cross, that I might draw all men unto me" (3 Nephi 27:13–14). The crucifixion of our Savior and the plan of our Father in Heaven are inextricably linked.

Truly the cross was a powerful image for Book of Mormon prophet-writers, not only because it symbolizes the Lord's suffering and atonement but also because it represents discipleship itself. It is the symbol of suffering that those who are committed to Christ will experience in the face of worldly opposition to God's plan. Jacob promised that "the saints of the Holy One of Israel, . . . they who have endured the crosses of the world, and despised the shame of it . . . shall inherit the kingdom of God" (2 Nephi 9:18). The righteous, like their Savior, care nothing about the ridicule heaped upon them by the wicked and worldly for following God's will; such ridicule is to be despised or ignored (Hebrews 12:2). Jacob also implored all men to "believe in Christ . . . and suffer his cross" (Jacob 1:8). Alma encouraged his son to "cross" himself in wicked practices, that is, to shun them and repent (Alma 39:9). In similar fashion, Nephi quoted the Savior's teachings regarding wicked and worldly ways: "It is better that ye should deny yourselves of these things, wherein ye will take up your cross" (3 Nephi 12:30). In other words, the symbol of following the Savior's example is the cross. True disciples withstand temptations, trials, and persecutions for their commitment to Christ and his gospel.

Jesus Christ commands his disciples to take up their crosses, just as he took up his, because only total consecration can prepare us to live in the environment in which God dwells—the celestial kingdom—which is so radically different from the world (D&C 105:2–5). Therefore, he said, "If any man will come after me, let him . . . take up his cross. . . . And now for a man to take up his cross, is to deny himself all ungodliness, and every worldly lust, and keep my commandments" (JST, Matthew 16:24–26).

Though the cross is a powerful and important symbol, Latter-day

Saints have not been encouraged to wear crosses or crucifixes or to display them in their homes. Nor are crosses displayed on or within our church buildings. First, there is the danger that any symbol of Christ, whom we worship, can itself become the thing venerated. Such was the case with the image of the brass serpent that Moses set up in the wilderness (Numbers 21; John 3:14–15). After several hundred years, the image had become the object being worshipped and had to be destroyed by righteous King Hezekiah (2 Kings 18:4). Second, even though the cross was a profound theological symbol to the earliest Christians, the idea of wearing a replica of the tool of crucifixion probably would have seemed abhorrent to them. Third, modern prophets have encouraged Church members to keep images of the living Christ uppermost in their minds. President Gordon B. Hinckley recounted an interaction he had with a minister of a Protestant denomination:

"We recently held an open house in the Arizona Temple. Following a complete renovation of that building, nearly a quarter of a million people saw its beautiful interior. On the first day of the opening, clergymen of other religions were invited as special guests, and hundreds responded. It was my privilege to speak to them and to answer their questions at the conclusion of their tours. I told them that we would be pleased to answer any queries they might have. Many were asked. Among these was one which came from a Protestant minister.

"Said he: 'I've been all through this building, this temple which carries on its face the name of Jesus Christ, but nowhere have I seen any representation of the cross, the symbol of Christianity. I have noted your buildings elsewhere and likewise find an absence of the cross. Why is this when you say you believe in Jesus Christ?'

"I responded: 'I do not wish to give offense to any of my Christian brethren who use the cross on the steeples of their cathedrals and at the altars of their chapels, who wear it on their vestments and imprint it on their books and other literature. But for us, the cross is the symbol of the dying Christ, while our message is a declaration of the living Christ.'

"He then asked: 'If you do not use the cross, what is the symbol of your religion?'

"I replied that the lives of our people must become the only meaningful expression of our faith and, in fact, therefore, the symbol of our worship" (92).

Finally, it must be reemphasized that the cross and the crucifixion of Jesus Christ are ultimately symbols of loyalty: of Christ to his Father and of disciples to our Lord. What happened to Jesus at Golgotha did not come because Pilate or the Jewish leaders had the power to impose it but rather because Jesus was willing to accept it (Packer, 69–72). At the Second Coming, as during Christ's appearance to the Nephites, the wounds the Savior received at his crucifixion will bear stunning witness of his messiahship, his divine Sonship, and, ultimately, his love even for those who carried out his crucifixion. Those wounds will convince the Jews and others of both his faithfulness and his identity (D&C 45:51–52).

SOURCES

Davis, C. Truman. "A Physician Testifies about Crucifixion." *Review of the News,* 14 Apr. 1976, 31–40.

Edwards, William D., Wesley J. Gabriel, and Floyd E. Hosmer. "On the Physical Death of Jesus Christ." *Journal of the American Medical Association* 255, no. 11 (21 Mar. 1986): 1455–63.

Hewitt, J. W. "The Use of Nails in the Crucifixion." *Harvard Theological Review* 25, no. 1 (Jan. 1932): 29–45.

Hinckley, Gordon B. "The Symbol of Christ." *Ensign,* May 1975, 92–94.

Josephus, Flavius. *The Antiquities of the Jews.* In *Josephus: Complete Works.* Translated by William Whiston. Grand Rapids, Mich.: Kregel Publications, 1960.

———. *The Wars of the Jews.* In *Josephus: Complete Works.* Translated by William Whiston. Grand Rapids, Mich.: Kregel Publications, 1960.

Packer, Boyd K. "Atonement, Agency, Accountability." *Ensign,* May 1988, 69–72.

Plautus, Titus Maccius. *The Braggart Warrior.* Translated by Paul Nixon. New York: G. P. Putnam's Sons, 1916.

Pseudo-Quintilian. *Declamations* 274. In K. C. Hanson and Douglas E. Oakman. *Palestine in the Time of Jesus: Social Structures and Social Conflicts.* 2d ed. Minneapolis: Fortress Press, 2008.

Talmage, James E. *Jesus the Christ.* Salt Lake City: Deseret Book, 1973.

Vermes, Geza. *The Complete Dead Sea Scrolls in English.* London: Penguin, 1998.

Yadin, Y. "Epigraphy and Crucifixion." *Israel Exploration Journal* 23 (1973): 18–22.

Zias, Joe, and James H. Charlesworth. "Crucifixion: Archaeology, Jesus, and the Dead Sea Scrolls." In *Jesus and the Dead Sea Scrolls,* edited by James H. Charlesworth, 273–89. New York: Doubleday, 1992.

Zias, Joe, and Eliezer Sekeles. "The Crucified Man from Giv'at ha-Mivtar— A Reappraisal." *Biblical Archaeologist* 48, no. 3 (Sept. 1985): 190–91.

ACS

CULT

The New Shorter Oxford English Dictionary offers the following definitions of *cult:* (1) "Worship; reverential homage rendered to a divine being"; (2) "A system of religious worship, especially as expressed in ceremonies, ritual, etc."; (3) "Devotion or homage paid to a person or thing, especially a fashionable enthusiasm"; (4) "A transient fad." It is not until we turn to the word *cultish* that we find this definition: "Of the nature of, resembling, or belonging to a cult, especially one regarded as eccentric or unorthodox." Frankly, any religious group could be considered a cult under any of the first three definitions. The fourth describes a movement that is short-lived. And of course such words as *eccentric* or *unorthodox* are not flattering terms. Moreover, referring to another person's religious faith as a cult has become a considerable insult. Further, some do not distinguish between *cult* and *occult;* thus it is not uncommon for some to associate the so-called cult of Mormonism with cults that practice devil worship or voodoo.

A book entitled *The New Cults* describes cults as follows: (1) they are started by strong and dynamic leaders; (2) they believe in additional scripture; (3) they have rigid standards for membership; (4) they proselyte new converts; (5) the leaders or officials of the cult are not professional clergymen; (6) they believe in ongoing and continual communication from God; and (7) they claim some truth not available to other individuals or groups (Martin, 17–21). Only a moment's reflection will reveal that the first-century Christian church meets all of these requirements. And, indeed, from a Jewish or Roman perspective, that's just what the followers of Jesus were. Not only did they meet all seven requirements but they were also considered eccentric and unorthodox.

A growing number of religious leaders and scholars have chosen to jettison the word *cult* in describing Mormonism, fully cognizant of the offense it causes Latter-day Saints and equally aware of how seriously misleading the word can be to those who know little about the Church. It is easy to dismiss another person who sees things differently, but it is difficult to pay the price to understand what that person *really* believes and feels. It is easy to pigeonhole, categorize, marginalize, or even demonize someone you don't know. On the other hand, it is much more difficult to believe the worst about a friend you have come to trust and love.

SOURCES

Martin, Walter. *The New Cults.* Santa Ana, Calif.: Vision House, 1980.

The New Shorter Oxford English Dictionary. Edited by Leslie Brown. 2 vols. 6th ed. New York: Oxford University Press, 2007.

RLM

CURSE

Individuals who spurn the word of truth, who ignore the promptings and guidance of their consciences, and who revel in the works of the flesh forfeit the comfort and direction of the Holy Spirit. It is with them as though they had been cursed. For example, in discussing the law of chastity, President Boyd K. Packer taught: "Laws were set up to guide all of [God's] children in the use of this gift. He does not have to be spiteful or vengeful in order that punishment will come from the breaking of the moral code. The laws are established of themselves. Crowning glory awaits you if you live worthily. The loss of the crown may well be punishment enough. Often, very often, we are punished as much by our sins as we are for them" (112). Mormon, in writing of the followers of Amlici the dissident, taught, "Now I would that ye should see that they brought upon themselves the curse; and even so doth every man that is cursed bring upon himself his own condemnation" (Alma 3:19).

SOURCE

Packer, Boyd K. "Why Stay Morally Clean?" *Ensign,* July 1972, 111–13.

RLM

———◆———

DAMNATION

"He that believeth and is baptized shall be saved," the resurrected Christ declared to his disciples, "but he that believeth not shall be damned" (Mark 16:16). Damnation is the opposite of salvation and eternal increase; it is having one's spiritual progress halted and the partaking of God's glory, presence, and the fulness of eternal life blocked.

As used in a variety of ways in the scriptures, damnation is experienced in various levels and durations. It is sometimes used synonymously with *hell,* as in those "damned souls" (Mormon 9:4) who "blaspheme against the Holy Ghost" (Mark 3:29). In contrast with those who "received the testimony of Jesus, and believed on his name and were baptized" (D&C 76:51) and those "who are honorable men of the earth, who were blinded by the craftiness of men" (D&C 76:75) who come forth in the first resurrection, there are those "that have done evil" (John 5:29)—"they who are liars, and sorcerers, and adulterers, and whoremongers" (D&C 76:103)—who come forth in the last resurrection, "the resurrection of damnation" (John 5:29). In the ultimate sense, anyone "who is not able to abide the law of a celestial kingdom cannot abide a celestial glory" (D&C 88:22); such individuals experience damnation in that they do not inherit exaltation. Thus, their rewards, powers, privileges, and glories are limited, incomplete, and fixed (D&C 76:112); in other words, they are damned.

In a sense, when individuals deprive themselves through unworthiness and an unwillingness to repent, they experience damnation in that their spiritual progress is stopped and their blessings are forfeited. For this reason the apostle Paul taught that one who partakes of the sacrament unworthily "eateth and drinketh damnation to himself" (1 Corinthians 11:29; see also 3 Nephi 18:28–29). Likewise, the Lord revealed to Joseph Smith in this dispensation that "he that doeth not anything until he is commanded, . . . the same is damned" (D&C 58:29). Thus, escaping the effects of damnation, whether in mortal life or in eternity, requires faith in the Lord Jesus Christ, repentance of sin, and obedience to the commandments, principles, and ordinances of the gospel.

BLT

DARK AGES

The term "Dark Ages" has been used to denote the period of history perceived as the cultural, economic, and demographic deterioration in Western Europe, beginning with the decline of the Western Roman Empire (which officially ended in A.D. 476) up to the beginning of the Renaissance (the rebirth of classical culture) in Italy. The idea that this period was a dark age is generally attributed to the

Renaissance scholar Petrarch in the 1330s. The term was at one point adopted to characterize the whole of the Middle Ages (roughly A.D. 300–1300). The phrase "Dark Ages" employs traditional light-dark dualism, well known to religious writers throughout the centuries. The phrase contrasts earlier and later periods of intellectual brilliance and cultural achievement with the medieval age of decline in learning and literacy in Roman literature, including a decrease in contemporary written history, a diminishing of European population groups, and a lack of significant achievement in material culture.

The sense in which Latter-day Saint Church leaders over the years have used the phrase "Dark Ages" is tied to a decline in spiritual learning and scriptural literacy in the Middle Ages. President Joseph Fielding Smith noted that ignorance prevailed in the Dark Ages: "A man with learning could enter the ministry, and the common people were kept in darkness, more particularly concerning the scriptures, and the idea prevailed that the scriptures were not to be had by the common people" (1:178).

Indeed, a good deal of the deserved negative view inherent in the term "Dark Ages" is directly linked to the efforts of medieval church leaders to keep the Bible out of the hands of the people and to mediate spiritual enlightenment through priests and bishops of the Roman Catholic Church. This long-standing policy is illustrated by the comments of Catholic leader Henry Knighton. He opposed the work of early English reformer, church critic, and parish priest John Wycliffe to translate the Bible into English so that all could study it with the direct assistance of the Holy Spirit and learn personally and individually of God's ways. Said Knighton: "Christ gave his Gospel to the clergy and the learned doctors of the Church so that they might give it to the laity. . . . Wycliffe, by thus translating the Bible, made it the property of the masses and common to all and more open to the laity, and even to women who were able to read. . . . And so the pearl of the gospel is thrown before swine. . . . The jewel of the clergy has been turned into the sport of the laity" (in Miller, 155).

It is against the backdrop of this attitude and environment in the Middle Ages that the great chronicler of Christian martyrs, John Foxe, reinforced the idea of a spiritual dark age when he wrote of the accomplishments of John Wycliffe: "At what time [that] all the world was in most desperate and vile estate, and the lamentable ignorance and darkness of God's truth had overshadowed the whole earth, this man stepped forth like a valiant champion, unto whom that may justly be applied which is spoken of one Simon, the son of Onias: 'Even as the morning-star being in the midst of a cloud, and as the moon being full in her course, and as the bright beams of the sun; so doth he shine and glister in the temple and Church of God'" (50).

Latter-day Saints believe that this kind of darkness had at least part of its roots in the soil of apostasy from the Lord's Church, which began in the first century. The Church of Jesus Christ was "built upon the foundation of the apostles and prophets" (Ephesians 2:20). The institutional revelation inherent in the operation of the true and living Church of Jesus Christ bathed the world in light and truth. It kept darkness at bay. But much spiritual light was lost when that Church was taken from the earth after the deaths of the apostles.

The great prelude to the Restoration was the Renaissance and Protestant Reformation, which followed the Middle Ages and which began to disperse the spiritual darkness that had so often prevailed during that time. President Thomas S. Monson described the reformers in the main as "honest men with yearning hearts, [who] at the peril of their very lives, attempted to establish points of reference, that they might find the true way. . . . The reformers were pioneers, blazing wilderness trails in a desperate search for those lost points of reference which, they felt, when found would lead mankind back to the truth Jesus taught" (51). The religious reformers of the Renaissance and Reformation played a vital role in laying the foundation for the Restoration of the latter days by changing the theological landscape of Christendom, paving the way for copies of the Bible to be placed in the hands of the common people, and drawing attention to the doctrines and teachings of original Christianity.

Although the term "Dark Ages" is in some ways an apt metaphor that resonates with those who know of the destructive and long-term effects of the Apostasy begun in the first century, caution is urged. The term is rarely used by historians today who study the Middle Ages because it is too much of a generalization; it can be misleading and even inaccurate in summing up a period of almost a thousand years. It wasn't a period of total darkness; it demonstrated many bright spots. Interestingly, it was in the nineteenth century (the century of Restoration) that scholars began to recognize the accomplishments of individuals during the so-called Dark Ages.

SOURCES

Foxe, John. *Foxe's Book of Martyrs*. Edited by W. Grinton Berry. New York: Eaton and Main, 1911.

Miller, Stephen M., and Robert V. Huber. *The Bible: A History*. Intercourse, Pa.: Good Books, 2004.

Monson, Thomas S. "They Showed the Way." *Ensign,* May 1997, 50–52.

Smith, Joseph Fielding. *Doctrines of Salvation*. Compiled by Bruce R. McConkie. 3 vols. Salt Lake City: Bookcraft, 1954–56.

ACS

DEAD SEA SCROLLS

Justifiably referred to as one of the most important manuscript discoveries of all time, the Dead Sea Scrolls are a collection of some nine hundred ancient documents (more than a hundred thousand fragments) found about a mile from the northwest shore of the Dead Sea between 1947 and 1956. They are written in Hebrew, Aramaic, and Greek, mostly on parchment (animal skin), some papyrus, and one scroll on thin copper. Of the approximately two hundred caves in the region, only eleven have yielded manuscripts so far. These manuscripts center on the ancient communal center known as Qumran. The manuscripts date, for the most part, between 150 B.C. and A.D. 68—roughly the period when Qumran was occupied. The community was destroyed when the Romans laid waste to the region during the First Jewish Revolt (A.D. 66–70). The scrolls and the associated Qumran community are most often identified with the Essenes, a sect of Judaism extant during the period between the Testaments and discussed by the writers Josephus and Pliny the Elder.

The Dead Sea Scrolls are usually divided into three categories based on content: biblical texts, apocryphal and pseudepigraphal texts, and sectarian texts or documents. About 40 percent of the total number of manuscripts, or portions of manuscripts, are biblical texts. Complete copies or fragments of copies of every book of the Hebrew Bible (the Old Testament) have been found except for the book of Esther. Deuteronomy, Isaiah, and Psalms were the most numerous of the biblical texts discovered: fourteen surviving manuscripts of Deuteronomy were found, twelve of Isaiah, and ten of the Psalms. Interestingly, Jesus quoted more from Deuteronomy, Isaiah, and Psalms than from the other books of the Old Testament.

One of the real treasure troves from Qumran was found in the first cave discovered. It contained two scrolls of Isaiah. The first one, the Great Isaiah Scroll, was found preserved in a clay jar and is a complete manuscript of the entire book, all sixty-six chapters, and measures more than seven meters in length. The second one is only fragmentary. The texts of the two differ in style. The complete scroll is described as being coarser than the second, its scribe less exacting over spelling, exchanging difficult words for more common ones, and sometimes incorporating Aramaic words into the text. The scribe of the second Isaiah scroll copied a text that followed the Masoretic text closely (Eshel, 18). The Masoretic text (Hebrew, *masora,* meaning "traditional") is the standardized version of the Hebrew text from which the King James Old Testament was produced. Obviously, Isaiah was very important to the sect at Qumran. In this regard, Latter-day Saints are reminded of Jesus' words to the Nephites: "A commandment I give unto you that ye search these things diligently; for great are the words of Isaiah" (3 Nephi 23:1).

The second category of documents found, apocryphal and pseudepigraphal, includes such works as the books of Enoch, Jubilees, Tobit, and Sirach. These are texts that were known before the discovery of the Dead Sea Scrolls, but that were not ultimately canonized in the Hebrew Bible. Some of them have been included in different versions of the Bible through the ages in a separate section known as the Apocrypha. Joseph Smith encountered the Old Testament Apocrypha but did not include those books in his inspired translation of the Bible, by divine decree (D&C 91). Some of the texts have parallels in Restoration scripture, such as the Qumran books of Enoch and passages from Moses 6–7.

The third category of texts found at Qumran is called sectarian. They are previously unknown documents that contain some of the history and philosophy of the community, lay out the rules by which the community was governed, and interpret both history and scripture according to the self-awareness and beliefs possessed by the community. These sectarian documents were binding on the covenant members of the community just as the biblical texts were, and they seem to have been regarded as part of their canon. This category comprises approximately 30 percent of all the texts discovered and includes such documents as the Serek Scroll, or Rule of the Community, the War Scroll, the Habakkuk Pesher (Hebrew, *pesher,* "commentary"), and the Temple Scroll, which scholars deem to have been regarded as the sixth book of the Law by Qumran inhabitants.

The Temple Scroll describes, among other things, an ideal temple to be established by God himself at the end of time. It is explicitly linked to a covenant that God made with Jacob at Bethel. This has been of interest to Latter-day Saints because of prophetic statements such as one by President Marion G. Romney, a member of the First Presidency from 1972 to 1985: "Pondering upon the subject of temples and the means therein provided to enable us to ascend into heaven brings to mind the lesson of Jacob's dream. . . . Temples are to us all what Bethel was to Jacob" (16). In fact, the basic ideal of those residing at Qumran anciently was to make of their community a virtual, open-air temple. They referred to the area where they ate their sacred meals as a holy temple. Little wonder that the Temple Scroll was so important at Qumran.

The Qumran covenant-makers "interpreted Scripture above all as relating to themselves in the present" (Freedman, 101). A prime example is the scroll known as Habakkuk Pesher, in which the references to the Assyrians and Egyptians were interpreted as meaning the Seleucid and Ptolemaic empires, which were contemporary with Qumran. Another example is a prophecy of Ezekiel, which the inhabitants of Qumran understood themselves as fulfilling. They selected Qumran as their living place because that is "where Ezekiel's mighty, healing river would flow into the Dead Sea" (Freedman, 103), healing it—as Joseph Smith also said (5:337)—and inaugurating a new Eden, a heaven on earth. This interpretive principle resonates with Latter-day Saints because of the "likening" principle articulated by Nephi: "For I did liken all scriptures unto us, that it might be for our profit and learning" (1 Nephi 19:23).

The significance of the Dead Sea Scrolls to Latter-day Saints is manifold. The scrolls show that the canon of scripture was more expansive anciently than among groups today, comprising more than just the Bible. (The Book of Mormon prophesied that some would say, "A Bible! A Bible! We have got a Bible, and there cannot be any more Bible" [2 Nephi 29:3]). They show that sacred texts were buried in the ground anciently. The Copper Scroll from Cave 3, discovered in 1953, shows that texts really were written on metal anciently. The scrolls present a number of familiar-sounding ideas: a belief in ongoing divine revelation, consecration, temple-worthy behavior, a strict probationary period for prospective community members, a priesthood-oriented hierarchy, a belief in the apostate condition of the world and the need for a restoration and return to truth, the application of the term *Saints* (holy ones) to covenant members, light and dark dualism, and others. But while the scrolls portray a unified community that upheld concepts that make them sound like an early manifestation of the true Church, they also embraced some notions contrary to the teachings of the gospel of Jesus Christ. The scrolls do not contain copies of any New Testament books, nor do they mention any of the known historical figures of Christianity.

Nevertheless, the Dead Sea Scrolls are invaluable because they illuminate the Jewish world in the age of Jesus. They provide the earliest extant copies of the Hebrew Bible, one thousand years older than previous earliest copies. They are of great worth to textual scholars of the Old Testament. They show that two or three versions of the same biblical book existed side by side. They have helped textual historians better understand the history of the Old Testament and its individual books. The scrolls have also helped to correct errors in the biblical text that have come down to us. It is certain that the scrolls will continue to yield important insights into the complex world that produced rabbinic Judaism on the one hand and Christianity on the other, along with their respective bodies of literature. It is not a coincidence that the Dead Sea Scrolls and other ancient literary finds, discovered after the restoration of the gospel in the early nineteenth century, often support principles and doctrines known at first only by revelation given in the early days of this dispensation. Christ's gospel began on this earth with Adam, and it is eternal.

SOURCES

Eshel, Hanan. *Qumran*. Jerusalem: Carta, 2009.

Freedman, David Noel, and Pam Fox Kuhlken. *What Are the Dead Sea Scrolls and Why Do They Matter?* Grand Rapids, Mich.: Eerdmans, 2007.

Romney, Marion G. "Temples—The Gates to Heaven." *Ensign,* Mar. 1971, 12–16.

Smith, Joseph. *History of The Church of Jesus Christ of Latter-day Saints.* Edited by B. H. Roberts. 7 vols. 2d ed. rev. Salt Lake City: The Church of Jesus Christ of Latter-day Saints, 1932–51.

ACS

DEAD WORKS

Dead works are works performed without proper authority. At the time of the organization of the Church, certain Baptist converts who had accepted the message of the restored gospel hesitated to be baptized, inasmuch as they had already been baptized by immersion in their former faith (D&C 22:2; Pratt, 16:293–94). Dead works are also the administration of such ordinances as baptism that are performed unnecessarily, as for such persons as little children who have not yet reached the age of accountability (Moroni 8:23).

SOURCE

Pratt, Orson. In *Journal of Discourses.* 26 vols. London: Latter-day Saints' Book Depot, 1854–86.

RLM

DEATH

Death is the separation of a person's spirit and physical body. Nothing is more common to mortals than birth and death; it is the common lot of all who come into this life to leave it. Every man or woman is born, and every man or woman must die. All are born as helpless infants, and all depart this sphere equally helpless in the face of death. Death is something most of us fear, something from which we hide, something most of us would choose to avoid if we could. Even among those who read by the lamp of gospel understanding, death is frequently viewed with fear and trembling. Wilford Woodruff once "referred to a saying of Joseph Smith, which he heard him utter (like this), That if the people knew what was behind the veil, they would try by every means to . . . get there, but *the Lord in his wisdom had implanted the fear of death in every person that they might cling to life and thus accomplish the designs of their Creator*" (Walker, 1:465–66; emphasis added).

159

In the purest sense, there is no death and there are no dead. When things die, they do not cease to be; they merely cease to be in this world. Life goes on. Death is a transition, a change in assignment, a transfer to another realm. When we die, the spirit continues to see and act and feel and associate; it is only the physical body that becomes inactive and lifeless for a season. And so it is that we use a term—*death*—to describe things from our limited perspective. From an eternal vantage point, there is only life. We speak often of a person's "untimely death." Generally we mean that it is untimely for those who remain behind. Though it is true that individuals may hasten their death and thus shorten their day of probation, for the faithful there is nothing untimely about death. President Joseph Fielding Smith thus explained: "May I say for the consolation of those who mourn, and for the comfort and guidance of all of us, that no righteous man is ever taken before his time. In the case of the faithful saints, they are simply transferred to other fields of labor. The Lord's work goes on in this life, in the world of spirits, and in the kingdoms of glory where men go after their resurrection" (10).

In a sense, we die as to premortality in order to be born into mortality. Likewise, we must die as pertaining to time in order to be born into eternity. The separation of the physical body and the eternal spirit is a necessary part of the plan of God, for, as Alma explained, to reclaim man from this temporal death would destroy the great plan of happiness (Alma 42:8). Truly, death passes upon all men and women to fulfill "the merciful plan of the great Creator" (2 Nephi 9:6). It is merciful in the sense that it delivers us from the toils and agonies and pains of this life. "When men are prepared," the Prophet Joseph Smith observed, "they are better off to go hence" (6:52).

SOURCES

Smith, Joseph. *History of The Church of Jesus Christ of Latter-day Saints.* Edited by B. H. Roberts. 7 vols. 2d ed. rev. Salt Lake City: The Church of Jesus Christ of Latter-day Saints, 1932–51.

Smith, Joseph Fielding. "Funeral Services for Elder Richard L. Evans." *Ensign,* Dec. 1971, 10–11.

Walker, Charles L. *The Diary of Charles L. Walker.* Edited by Andrew Karl Larson and Katherine Miles Larson. 2 vols. Logan, Utah: Utah State University Press, 1980. Spelling and punctuation modernized.

RLM

DISCIPLE/DISCIPLESHIP

While the term *disciple* can be broadly applied to any follower of a discipline, body of ideas, philosophy, way of life, or course of action, the most important discipleship anyone can embrace is that of Jesus Christ. To be one of his disciples in the full sense of the word requires making covenants to try to follow with exactness his gospel and his example. It means commitment over convenience, as Elder Jeffrey R. Holland explained (68–73). Discipleship means following the Lord's commands (2 Nephi 31:7). Discipleship requires the submission of one's own will to the will of the Lord, which is "really the only uniquely personal thing we have to place on God's altar" (Maxwell, 24). While in mortality, Jesus himself described some of the defining characteristics of his disciples: "The disciple is not above his master, nor the servant above his lord. It is enough for the disciple that he be as his master" (Matthew 10:24–25). "If ye continue in my word, then are ye my disciples indeed" (John 8:31). "By this shall all men know that ye are my disciples, if ye have love one to another" (John 13:35). "Herein is my Father glorified, that ye bear much fruit; so shall ye be my disciples" (John 15:8).

In the New Testament, the term *disciple* is most often used to denote "the Twelve," those specific followers chosen and ordained by Jesus to serve as apostles (Matthew 10:1; John 15:16). These became the leaders of his Church, holding the keys of priesthood authority to bind and seal on earth and in heaven, to regulate the affairs of the kingdom of God on earth (Matthew 16:19; 18:18–20). The Twelve Apostles were chosen by Jesus personally from among the larger group of his disciples (Luke 6:13). Thus, all apostles are disciples, but not all disciples are apostles. Many of Jesus' disciples, including members of the original Quorum of the Twelve, were first disciples of John the Baptist, who had the responsibility, as forerunner, to train Jesus' disciples and then to ensure their allegiance had been transferred to the Master (Luke 7:19–22; 11:1; John 1:35–37; 3:25–30).

In the Book of Mormon, the twelve chosen to lead the Church among the Nephites were called the twelve disciples (3 Nephi 12:1; 15:11–12; 19:4). In actuality, these twelve were also apostles, as Moroni indicates (Moroni 2:2; Smith, 4:538). The Book of Mormon is almost entirely about disciples and discipleship. Its closing words unmistakably point to the inseparable relationship between these two concepts: "Yea, come unto Christ, and be perfected in him, and deny yourselves of all ungodliness" (Moroni 10:32). Thus, to be a *disciple* of Jesus Christ requires *discipline*. The two words come from the same Latin root; in order to *follow* Jesus we must implement his *manner of behavior* in our lives.

SOURCES

Holland, Jeffrey R. "The Inconvenient Messiah." *Ensign,* Feb. 1984, 68–73.

Maxwell, Neal A. "'Swallowed Up in the Will of the Father.'" *Ensign,* Nov. 1995, 22–24.

Smith, Joseph. *History of The Church of Jesus Christ of Latter-day Saints.* Edited by B. H. Roberts. 7 vols. 2d ed. rev. Salt Lake City: The Church of Jesus Christ of Latter-day Saints, 1932–51.

ACS

DISPENSATION

Because our Heavenly Father loves all of his children, he desires for them to be happy in mortality and worthy to return to his presence for eternity. As a result, he reveals through prophets the principles and ordinances of the eternal plan of salvation. Each period of time in which God has given or dispensed the keys of the priesthood to a prophet and commanded him to teach gospel truths and administer the saving ordinances of the gospel to the people of the world (D&C 132:7) is called a dispensation. The gospel and its attendant authority and principles are revealed anew at different times so that people of one generation are not totally dependent upon past dispensations for their understanding of gospel principles and the keys of salvation. As a result, many prophets have been dispensational heads, including Adam, Enoch, Noah, Abraham, Moses, and Jesus Christ. No doubt there have also been dispensations of the gospel in the New World, such as among the Jaredites (Ether 1:41–43; 3:6–16) and, later, the Nephites (1 Nephi 2:2–4; 3 Nephi 11:7–40). A dispensation was perhaps had among the lost ten tribes of Israel, whom the resurrected Christ promised to visit and teach and with whom he promised to renew covenants (3 Nephi 16:1–4).

We do not know all of the dispensations (and their respective prophetic heads) that have existed on earth throughout its history. In many cases, dispensations are established and the gospel is restored after previous generations have rejected the prophets and have fallen into apostasy. This was the case of Noah after the Flood. After the death of Christ and his apostles in the meridian of time, the Great Apostasy, with its loss of priesthood authority to administer the principles and ordinances of salvation, a new dispensation and an accompanying restoration was required. The dispensation of the fulness of times, headed by the Prophet Joseph Smith, is the last dispensation because all of the keys and ordinances of salvation have been restored anew, and they "shall never be taken again from the earth" (D&C 13:1; see also D&C 110).

BLT

DIVORCE

"Marriage is ordained of God" (D&C 49:15), and "what therefore God hath joined together, let not man put asunder" (Matthew 19:6). Our Heavenly Father desires that all of his children be able to enjoy supreme happiness in marriage and family life. Living according to his higher law would make divorce nonexistent. Unfortunately, mortal men fall short of that higher law and, as a result, the Lord allows for the dissolution of marriages through proper, legal divorce. Under the law of Moses, divorce would be granted if certain rights and claims were equitably met (Leviticus 21:7, 14; Deuteronomy 24:1–4). As Jesus declared, however, divorce was allowed "because of the hardness of your hearts," but "from the beginning it was not so" (Matthew 19:8). Jesus called his disciples to a higher righteousness wherein divorce, except in the most rare of circumstances, would not be needed or permitted (Matthew 5:31–32). Today, as in ancient times, the Lord's anointed servants counsel against divorce and encourage husbands and wives to reconcile and do all in their power to strengthen their marriages, honor associated covenants, and repent of sins and shortcomings (1 Corinthians 7:10–14; Ephesians 5:22–31; D&C 42:22). Elder Dallin H. Oaks taught:

"The kind of marriage required for exaltation—eternal in duration and godlike in quality—does not contemplate divorce. In the temples of the Lord, couples are married for all eternity. But some marriages do not progress toward that ideal. Because of the 'hardness of [our] hearts,' the Lord does not currently enforce the consequences of the celestial standard. He permits divorced persons to marry again without the stain of immorality specified in the higher law. Unless a divorced member has committed serious transgressions, he or she can become eligible for a temple recommend under the same worthiness standards that apply to other members" (70).

When proper civil authority grants divorces, the Church recognizes and accepts such decrees. The sealings of husbands to wives, performed in holy temples, however, are not dissolved by a civil divorce decree. There is no such thing as a temple divorce. Only the First Presidency, which holds all the keys of the kingdom—including the power to loose as well as to bind (Matthew 16:19)—has the authority to render a cancellation of a temple sealing.

SOURCE
Oaks, Dallin H. "Divorce." *Ensign,* May 2007, 70–73.

BLT

DOCTRINE

Doctrines are teachings. The central, saving doctrine is that Jesus is the Christ, the Son of God, the Savior and Redeemer of humankind; that he lived, taught, healed, suffered, and died for our sins; and that he rose from the dead the third day with a glorious, immortal, resurrected body (1 Corinthians 15:1–4; D&C 76:40–42). The Prophet Joseph Smith spoke of these central truths as the "fundamental principles" of our religion to which all other doctrines are but appendages (3:30). President Boyd K. Packer taught: "Truth, glorious truth, proclaims there is . . . a Mediator. . . . Through Him mercy can be fully extended to each of us without offending the eternal law of justice. This truth is the very root of Christian doctrine. You may know much about the gospel as it branches out from there, but if you only know the branches and those branches do not touch that root, if they have been cut free from that truth, there will be no life nor substance nor redemption in them" ("Mediator," 56).

Such counsel really does point us toward that which is of most worth in sermons and in the classroom, that which should receive our greatest emphasis. There is power in doctrine, power in the word (Alma 31:5): power to heal the wounded soul (Jacob 2:8), power to transform human behavior. "True doctrine, understood, changes attitudes and behavior," President Packer explained. "The study of the doctrines of the gospel will improve behavior quicker than a study of behavior will improve behavior. . . . That is why we stress so forcefully the study of the doctrines of the gospel" ("Children," 17). Elder Neal A. Maxwell also pointed out that "doctrines believed and practiced do change and improve us, while ensuring our vital access to the Spirit. Both outcomes are crucial" (page x).

We are under obligation to learn the doctrines, teach them properly, and bind ourselves to speak and act in harmony with them. Only in this way can we perpetuate truth in a world filled with error, avoid deception, focus on what matters most, and find joy and happiness in the process. In seeking to discern what is the doctrine of the Church today, we might consider:

Is it found within the four standard works or within official declarations or proclamations? Is it taught or discussed in general conference or other official gatherings by general Church leaders today? Is it found in the general handbooks or approved curriculum of the Church today? If it meets at least one of these criteria, we can feel secure in teaching it.

SOURCES
Maxwell, Neal A. *One More Strain of Praise.* Salt Lake City: Bookcraft, 1999.
Packer, Boyd K. "Little Children." *Ensign,* Nov. 1986, 16–18.
———. "The Mediator." *Ensign,* May 1977, 54–56.
Smith, Joseph. *History of The Church of Jesus Christ of Latter-day Saints.* Edited by B. H. Roberts. 7 vols. 2d ed. rev. Salt Lake City: The Church of Jesus Christ of Latter-day Saints, 1932–51.

RLM

DOCTRINE AND COVENANTS

A collection of revelations given to the Prophet Joseph Smith and subsequent presidents of the Church, the Doctrine and Covenants is one of the standard works of the Church. While Latter-day Saints also accept the Bible and the Book of Mormon, along with the Pearl of Great Price, as the scriptural canon, the Doctrine and Covenants is unique in several ways. First, it is not a translation from ancient documents but rather direct revelations and communications from God to his children through his chosen prophets. As President Gordon B. Hinckley characterized it, it is "a conduit for the expressions of the

Lord to His people" (164). It does not contain historical narratives as found in other scriptures but rather the words of the Lord given to the living prophet in response to questions and issues raised by individuals or specific circumstances of the day. Joseph Smith recorded, "In these infant days of the Church, there was a great anxiety to obtain the word of the Lord upon every subject that in any way concerned our salvation" (1:207). The revelations that came in response to those desires came by a variety of means—visitations from heavenly beings (D&C 2, 13, 110), the Urim and Thummim (D&C 3, 6–7, 11, 14–17), visions (D&C 76, 137, 138), the voice of God (D&C 130:12–13), and the voice of the Spirit of God, which conveyed words, thoughts, and ideas that were then recorded by scribes (D&C 88:66). Another unique feature of the Doctrine and Covenants is that it can expand or contract. It is truly an open and flexible canon, as evidenced by its history.

After the organization of the Church in 1830, the revelations contained in sections 20 and 22 served as an early constitution of the Church. They were read often in Church conferences and were subsequently published in the Church's first official newspaper, *The Evening and the Morning Star*. In 1831 it was decided that a compilation of the Prophet Joseph Smith's revelations was to be published as the Book of Commandments. A revelation was given that was to be the preface for the publication. That preface is section 1 of the Doctrine and Covenants.

After eighteen months of preparation—compiling, editing, and revising—the Book of Commandments went to press. During the publication process, a mob destroyed the press and most of the printed pages of the book. Some members of the Church gathered up as many of the pages as could be rescued and bound them. These bound volumes of the Book of Commandments contained sixty-five sections, but more were planned to be included. As a result of the mob action and persecutions in Missouri, the Church never republished this volume.

In 1834 the Lord revealed to the Prophet Joseph Smith that the Church was to publish an even larger collection of the Prophet's revelations, to be known as the Book of Covenants, in order to "arrange the items of doctrine of Jesus Christ, for the government of his church of the Latter-day Saints." This volume was to contain "the revelations which have been given to said church up to this date, or shall be until such arrangement is made" (D&C [1835], 255). It was determined that the title should be expanded to Doctrine and Covenants to reflect the twofold nature of the book. The first part, "the doctrine of the Church of the Latter-day Saints," consisted of the seven lectures given to the School of the Elders during 1834–35, known as the Lectures on Faith. The second part contained "Covenants and Commandments," meaning the revelations given to the Prophet Joseph Smith, and thus the title Doctrine and Covenants. Several significant revelations received since the Book of Commandments was compiled were included in the 1835 edition of the Doctrine and Covenants. These included revelations on priesthood (D&C 84), the Word of Wisdom (D&C 89), and Church organization (D&C 107). In addition to the Lectures on Faith, the 1835 edition contained 102 sections, a statement on marriage (which was subsequently replaced by section 132), and a statement on government (which became section 134).

Shortly after the death of the Prophet Joseph Smith in 1844, the Church published a new edition of the Doctrine and Covenants. Eight additional revelations were included, bringing the total to 111 sections. Also included in this Nauvoo edition was John Taylor's statement concerning the martyrdom of Joseph and Hyrum Smith (now section 135).

The next major revision of the Doctrine and Covenants was done by Elder Orson Pratt under the direction of President Brigham Young. In the 1876 edition, 26 revelations were added, bringing the total to 136 sections. The earlier article on marriage was deleted, replaced by section 132. The sections were divided into shorter verses, and an index was added for the first time. In 1879, Elder Pratt added footnotes, and this version was presented to the Church for a sustaining vote in the October 1880 general conference.

Ten years later, at the October 1890 general conference, President Wilford Woodruff's "Official Declaration," intended to halt the practice of plural marriage in the Church, was accepted as authoritative and binding on the members of the Church. The 1908 edition of the Doctrine and Covenants included this Official Declaration, sometimes referred to as the Manifesto.

Important refinements to the Doctrine and Covenants were made in the 1921 edition. The text of the revelations remained the same as in earlier editions, but under the direction of President Heber J. Grant, Elder James E. Talmage contributed several helpful changes. They included an explanatory introduction, a chronology of the revelations, expanded index and concordances, revised footnotes, and introductory information at the beginning of each section that included a brief summary of the contents of the revelation. Perhaps the most significant change was the omission of the Lectures on Faith; these theological presentations had never been considered to be of the same type or stature as the revelations themselves.

In 1981 a new edition of the Doctrine and Covenants was published. Two additional revelations were included (sections 137 and 138) as well as Official Declaration 2, which announced the receipt of President Spencer W. Kimball's revelation on the priesthood. The two visions had previously been accepted by the Church at the April 1976 conference but were included for the first time in the Doctrine and Covenants in 1981. Excerpts from the teachings of President Wilford Woodruff regarding the revelation ending the practice of plural marriage were added. Several other revisions were included that were designed to help readers more effectively study the scriptures. These included expanded and corrected historical headings, a more complete doctrinal summary for each section, maps showing the geographical location of early Church history sites, extensive footnotes, and a revised index. These were added as companions to the Topical Guide and Bible Dictionary, which were included in the 1979 Latter-day Saint edition of the King James Bible.

Throughout the Doctrine and Covenants, the voice of the Lord is heard speaking not only to the Prophet but also to all who will hear and hearken. The Doctrine and Covenants is, as President Ezra Taft Benson declared, the capstone of our religion, "an essential part of our spiritual life. . . .

"Thus, the Doctrine and Covenants is a glorious book of scripture given directly to our generation. It contains the will of the Lord for us in these last days that precede the second coming of Christ. It contains many truths and doctrines not fully revealed in other scripture" (28). Reflecting the Prophet Joseph Smith's all-encompassing understanding of the plan of salvation and the eternal purposes of God, the Doctrine and Covenants gives both important clarifications to doctrines found in other volumes of scripture and reveals new truths unknown in previous dispensations. By its nature and its history, the Doctrine and Covenants stands as a witness that God "does now reveal, and . . . that He will yet reveal many great and important things pertaining to the Kingdom of God" (Articles of Faith 1:9).

SOURCES

Benson, Ezra Taft. *A Witness and a Warning: A Modern-day Prophet Testifies of the Book of Mormon.* Salt Lake City: Deseret Book, 1988.

Hinckley, Gordon B. *Teachings of Gordon B. Hinckley.* Salt Lake City: Deseret Book, 1997.

Smith, Joseph. *History of The Church of Jesus Christ of Latter-day Saints.* Edited by B. H. Roberts. 7 vols. 2d ed. rev. Salt Lake City: The Church of Jesus Christ of Latter-day Saints, 1932–51.

BLT

DUST OF THE EARTH

The physical bodies of Adam and Eve were created from the "dust of the earth" (Mormon 9:17; Genesis 2:7; Moses 3:7). At death, our corruptible mortal bodies eventually return to dust, befitting the Lord's explanation to Adam: "Thou shalt return unto the ground—for thou shalt surely die . . . : for dust thou wast, and unto dust shalt thou return" (Moses 4:25; Genesis 3:19). Like Job, we will all one day "sleep in the dust" (Job 7:21). The same conclusion to mortality will befall animals on the earth, for "all go unto one place; all are of the dust, and all turn to dust again" (Ecclesiastes 3:20).

Allowing Satan's temptations to pull us down to a degrading, carnal, and sinful lifestyle is at times scripturally depicted as dwelling in the dust. God cursed the serpent in the Garden to "eat" dust throughout his life because he had tempted Adam and Eve (Genesis 3:14; Moses 4:20). Christ called hypocritical Pharisees and scribes "whited sepulchres," or externally attractive receptacles containing mortal flesh turning to dust, suggesting the depths of sin to which they stooped to circumvent the laws of God (Matthew 23:27–28). Finally, Father Lehi told his wayward sons, "Awake! and arise from the dust," meaning they needed to "shake off the chains" that pulled them down and turn away from their debasing attitudes and behaviors. Only then could they enjoy the freedom and heights that come with the "armor of righteousness" (2 Nephi 1:14, 21, 23).

As we come to better know and love Jesus Christ as our Savior and Redeemer, we more clearly understand the reality of our lowly state in contrast to his greatness. Mormon described us in our fallen condition as "less than the dust of the earth" (Helaman 12:7) because whether it be a particle of dust or a majestic mountain, all God's other creations instantly obey him. On the other hand, with our unsteady hearts, we are "slow to do good" but "quick to hearken unto the words of the evil one" (Helaman 12:4). Even though King Benjamin's people had been diligent (Mosiah 1:11) in keeping the Lord's commandments, after they heard their king's witness of their indebtedness to Jesus Christ, they fell to the ground and "viewed themselves in their own carnal state, even less than the dust of the earth" (Mosiah 4:2). In pleading to God for help, Abraham likened himself to merely "dust and ashes" when considering his nothingness without the Lord's help (Genesis 18:27).

Often words of prophets, preserved long after the prophet's death, are described as coming from the dust of the earth, as though these inspired teachers were speaking to us from the grave (Moroni 10:27). Nephi prophesied that long after the destruction of his people, their words would "speak unto [us] out of the ground, and their speech shall be low out of the dust, and their voice shall be as one that hath a familiar spirit" (2 Nephi 26:16; Isaiah 29:4).

CFO

ECUMENISM

Kindhearted persons cannot long endure tension or enmity between themselves and others. As a result, many persons through the years have sought to bridge the divides that inevitably exist between individuals of various religious persuasions. In some cases, unfortunately, these ecumenical efforts have resulted in a dilution of doctrine and a compromise of conscience, especially in settings where it was felt necessary to alter or even expurgate ideas or teachings because resolution between two or more discussants was difficult. Such compromise is always costly and is the reason The Church of Jesus Christ of Latter-day

Saints has generally elected not to be a part of ecumenical movements. When, on the other hand, ecumenical endeavors involve a sincere desire to build deeper understanding, friendship, cooperation, and sensitive respect for those who may differ from the Latter-day Saint point of view—and neither compromise nor disloyalty is called for— Latter-day Saints step forward and speak out. Our voices need to be heard, and our points of view represent a distinctive contribution to the larger religious conversation.

RLM

EDUCATION

Through the Prophet Joseph Smith, the Lord gave the command- ment to "teach one another the doctrine of the kingdom" and the promise that his grace would enable us in the process of becoming educated. He then expanded our earthly educational curriculum to include a study of "things both in heaven and in the earth, and un- der the earth; things which have been, things which are, things which must shortly come to pass; things which are at home, things which are abroad; the wars and the perplexities of the nations, and the judgments which are on the land; and a knowledge also of countries and of king- doms" (D&C 88:77–79).

God's plan for his children in mortality includes literacy. Adam and Eve taught their children to "read and write" (Moses 6:6). The Book of Mormon prophet Nephi acknowledged his parents for provid- ing him with an education in "all the learning of [his] father," thereby preparing him to keep a written record of their history and "the things of God" (1 Nephi 1:1; 6:3). Similarly, the Lord admonishes, "Seek ye out of the best books words of wisdom; seek learning, even by study and also by faith" (D&C 88:118).

Unfortunately, educational opportunities have too often been abused and have thereby served as a source of pride and arrogance. "When they are learned they think they are wise," the prophet Jacob warned, "and they hearken not unto the counsel of God, for they set it aside, supposing they know of themselves, wherefore, their wisdom is foolishness and it profiteth them not" (2 Nephi 9:28). At other times "people began to be distinguished by ranks, according to their riches and their chances for learning" (3 Nephi 6:12). A true education leads to the desire to expand such opportunities to others, that all may learn and in turn lift and strengthen their neighbors.

Education, whether formal or informal, has always been encouraged by Church leaders. Although career training is critical, the importance and fruits of education extend beyond achieving the necessary skills for being gainfully employed. As president of Brigham Young University, Elder Dallin H. Oaks taught: "One of the most important purposes of a university education is to prepare men and women to be responsible and intelligent leaders and participants in the life of their families, their Church, and in their communities. That kind of education is needed by young men and young women alike" (57). Education opens new opportunities to appreciate life and afford others the same blessings. It builds confidence, curiosity, and the ability to value and learn from those whose culture and history is different. The Perpetual Education Fund, established by the Church in 2000, offers academic opportunities to those who would not have access to advanced education otherwise and further testifies to the value the Lord places on education.

God's children may not know until later the specific reason that he has directed them to pursue more education. He has said, however, that whatever education his children receive will help prepare them "to magnify the calling whereunto I have called you, and the mission with which I have commissioned you" (D&C 88:80).

SOURCE
Oaks, Dallin H. "Insights." *Ensign,* Mar. 1975, 56–58.

CFO

ELDER

The term *elder* has both general and specific meanings in the scriptures and practices of the Church. In the Old Testament, the term usually referred to the older and wiser men among the people who may have had responsibilities to govern or judge the affairs of the group. It was not necessarily associated with priesthood or ecclesiastical matters (1 Samuel 15:30; 2 Samuel 17:4; Proverbs 31:23; Ezekiel 8:1). When there is an organized Church, the leaders of the Church—those with presiding and directing responsibilities—are referred to in the scriptures as "the elders" (Exodus 24:9–11; Acts 11:30; 20:17; Alma

4:7; Moroni 3:1; 6:7; D&C 20:2–3, 16, 66, 70; 46:2; 107:60). More specifically, elder is an office in the Melchizedek Priesthood (D&C 107:60, 89). Ordained elders have responsibilities to "baptize; and to ordain other elders, priests, teachers, and deacons; and to administer bread and wine—the emblems of the flesh and blood of Christ—and to confirm those who are baptized into the church, by the laying on of hands for the baptism of fire and the Holy Ghost, according to the scriptures; and to teach, expound, exhort, baptize, and watch over the church; and to confirm the church by the laying on of hands, and the giving of the Holy Ghost; and to take the lead of all meetings" (D&C 20:38–44). They have authority to bless and administer to the sick (James 5:14–15; D&C 42:44), "to preach faith and repentance and remission of sins" to the world (D&C 53:3), to "conduct all meetings as they are directed and guided by the Holy Spirit" (D&C 46:2), to "administer in spiritual things, agreeable to the covenants and commandments of the church," and to "officiate in all the offices of the church when there are no higher authorities present" (D&C 107:12).

The term *elder* may also appropriately be used for any man who holds the Melchizedek Priesthood, regardless of the specific office he holds. For example, full-time male missionaries are referred to as elders, even if they have been ordained to the office of high priest. In a broader sense, all the priesthood of God could be viewed as the "elders of Israel" (*Hymns,* no. 319). The Lord declared that "an apostle is an elder" (D&C 20:38). Because of this and out of reverence for the sacred calling, members of the Quorum of the Twelve Apostles are referred to with the title Elder. Likewise, members of the seventy, as "especial witnesses" who "act in the name of the Lord under the direction of the Twelve" (D&C 107:25, 34), are also addressed with the title Elder.

SOURCE
"Ye Elders of Israel." *Hymns of The Church of Jesus Christ of Latter-day Saints,* no. 319. Salt Lake City: The Church of Jesus Christ of Latter-day Saints, 1985.

BLT

ELDER BROTHER

John the Beloved opened his magnificent Gospel with this statement: "In the beginning was the Word, and the Word was with God, and the Word was God. The same was in the beginning with God. All things were made by him; and without him was not any thing made that was made" (John 1:1–3). That is, in the premortal life, Christ, here designated as the Word, was with our Heavenly Father. In fact, Christ was God in that first estate. As God and leader of the "noble and great ones" (Abraham 3:22; 4:1), he created worlds without number (Moses 1:33; 7:30). It is appropriate, therefore, that we refer to Jesus Christ as our elder brother as pertaining to the premortal life.

It should be of some interest, however, that of the almost one hundred names given to our Lord and Savior by the Nephite prophets, the phrase "elder brother" is never used. Because the Nephites looked upon Christ with such awe and viewed him with such adoration, it may not have seemed appropriate to them to refer to him as elder brother; he was God.

Elder M. Russell Ballard explained: "We occasionally hear some members refer to Jesus as our Elder Brother, which is a true concept based on our understanding of the premortal life with our Father in Heaven. But like many points of gospel doctrine, that simple truth doesn't go far enough in terms of describing the Savior's role in our present lives and His great position as a member of the Godhead. Thus, some non-LDS Christians are uncomfortable with what they perceive as a secondary role for Christ in our theology. They feel that we view Jesus as a spiritual peer. They believe that we view Christ as an implementor for God, if you will, but that we don't view Him as God to us and to all mankind, which, of course, is counter to biblical testimony about Christ's divinity. Let me help us understand, with clarity and testimony, our belief about Jesus Christ. We declare He is the King of Kings, Lord of Lords, the Creator, the Savior, the Captain of our Salvation, the Bright and Morning Star. He has taught us that He is in all things, above all things, through all things and round about all things, that He is Alpha and Omega, the Lord of the Universe, the first and the last relative to our salvation, and that His name is above every name and is in fact the only name under heaven by which we can be saved. . . .

"We can understand why some Latter-day Saints have tended to focus on Christ's Sonship as opposed to His Godhood. As members of earthly families, we can relate to Him as a child, as a Son, and as a Brother because we know how that feels. We can personalize that relationship because we ourselves are children, sons and daughters, brothers and sisters. For some it may be more difficult to relate to Him as a God. And so in an attempt to draw closer to Christ and to cultivate warm and personal feelings toward Him, some tend to humanize Him, sometimes at the expense of acknowledging His Divinity. So let us be very clear on this point: it is true that Jesus was our Elder Brother in the premortal life, but we believe that in this life it is crucial that we become 'born again' as His sons and daughters in the gospel covenant" (66).

SOURCE

Ballard, M. Russell. "Building Bridges of Understanding." *Ensign,* June 1998, 62–68.

RLM

ELECTION

"Remember the days of old," Jehovah said, speaking through Moses, "consider the years of many generations: ask thy father, and he will shew thee; thy elders, and they will tell thee. When the most High divided to the nations their inheritance, when he separated the sons of Adam, he set the bounds of the people according to the number of the children of Israel. For the Lord's portion is his people; Jacob is the lot of his inheritance" (Deuteronomy 32:7–9). This poignant statement embodies what is called the doctrine of election in the flesh, the idea that God has elected or foreordained individuals and nations of people to come to earth at a certain time in the earth's history. As a result of premortal faithfulness, the descendants of Abraham, Isaac, and Jacob have been sent to earth to fulfill a grand and divine mission—to bless the peoples of the earth, to be a light to the nations (Isaiah 49:6) and a leavening influence among all people, to perform a redemptive labor (Alma 13:1–3), to proclaim the true and living God, and to invite all to abide by his teachings and commandments.

To the Athenians the apostle Paul declared: "God that made the world and all things therein, seeing that he is Lord of heaven and earth, dwelleth not in temples made with hands; neither is worshipped with men's hands, as though he needed any thing, seeing he giveth to all life, and breath, and all things; and hath made of one blood all nations of men for to dwell on all the face of the earth, and hath determined the times before appointed, and the bounds of their habitation" (Acts

17:24–26). In the words of the God of the Old Testament, Israel is "mine elect, in whom my soul delighteth" (Isaiah 42:1; see also 45:4). God's special treatment of his chosen people—even though their deeds in this life do not appear to merit special treatment or an ennobled status—is what is called "the election of grace" (Romans 11:5), an acknowledgment that divine partiality is neither whimsical nor cavalier but a providential decision based on previous (premortal) faithfulness (Romans 9:10–15). When the kingdom of God has spread to all corners, when Zion has been established and the New Jerusalem put in place, when our Lord and Savior chooses to return to earth and reign as King of kings and Lord of lords, then will the righteous "lift up their voice, and with the voice together sing this new song, saying: The Lord hath brought again Zion; the Lord hath redeemed his people, Israel, according to the election of grace, which was brought to pass by the faith and covenant of their fathers. The Lord hath redeemed his people; and Satan is bound and time is no longer. The Lord hath gathered all things in one. The Lord hath brought down Zion from above. The Lord hath brought up Zion from beneath" (D&C 84:98–100).

We generally speak of the election of nations and peoples and the foreordination of individuals. Occasionally, however, the terms are used interchangeably. In writing to the Saints at Thessalonica, Paul expressed his abundant gratitude for their "work of faith, and labour of love, and patience of hope in our Lord Jesus Christ, in the sight of God . . . knowing, brethren beloved, your election of God" (1 Thessalonians 1:3–4). For that matter, many were called and elected in their first estate to lineage, family, receipt of the gospel and its saving ordinances, and even eternal life—all conditioned on mortal faithfulness. When persons pursue the course in this life to which they were appointed and learn to serve God "at all hazards," they make their premortal calling and election to eternal life sure, meaning they have passed the tests of mortality and will inherit the highest of eternal rewards hereafter (Smith, 3:380).

SOURCE

Smith, Joseph. *History of The Church of Jesus Christ of Latter-day Saints.* Edited by B. H. Roberts. 7 vols. 2d ed. rev. Salt Lake City: The Church of Jesus Christ of Latter-day Saints, 1932–51.

RLM

ELECT OF GOD

The elect of God are those who hear the voice of the Lord, do not harden their hearts, gather with the Lord and his Church, magnify their callings, and, because of their purity, abide the day of the Savior's second coming (D&C 29:7; 33:6; 35:21; 84:34; Moses 7:62). Further, the elect are those who demonstrate holiness, mercy, kindness, humility, meekness, long-suffering, forgiveness, and charity (Colossians 3:12–14)—in other words, those who embody the "fruit of the Spirit" (Galatians 5:22). In the ultimate sense, the elect are those who qualify for eternal life, those who through their sacrifice come to know that their course in life is pleasing to God, that their salvation hereafter is secure (D&C 97:8; 132:49–50; *Lectures,* 67–70).

Jesus sounded the sobering warning on the Mount of Olives that in the last days the allurement of signs and wonders, together with the appeal of false Christs and false prophets, would be so persuasive that, "if possible, they shall deceive the very elect, who are the elect according to the covenant" (Joseph Smith–Matthew 1:22). On the other hand, those who are truly elect, who treasure up the word of God, will not be deceived (Joseph Smith–Matthew 1:37).

SOURCE
Lectures on Faith. Salt Lake City: Deseret Book, 1985.

RLM

ELIAS

Generally speaking, the word *Elias* is the New Testament form of *Elijah.* The Prophet Joseph Smith introduced another use of the word—a forerunner, one who goes before to prepare the way. John the Baptist was an Elias for the Messiah (JST, Matthew 11:15; 17:11–13; Mark 9:11). The restored gospel is also an Elias for the Messiah, a preparatory work for the second coming of the Son of Man (D&C 45:9), as was the Prophet Joseph himself (JST, Matthew 17:14).

Joseph, in speaking of the spirit of Elias in regard to the priesthood, said: "There is a difference between the spirit and office of Elias and Elijah. . . . The spirit of Elias is to prepare the way for a greater revelation of God, which is the Priesthood of Elias, or the Priesthood that Aaron was ordained unto. And when God sends a man into the world to prepare for a greater work, holding the keys of the power of Elias, it was called the doctrine of Elias, even from the early ages of the world.

"John's mission was limited to preaching and baptizing; but what he did was legal; and when Jesus Christ came to any of John's disciples, He baptized them with fire and the Holy Ghost.

"We find the Apostles endowed with greater power than John: their office was more under the spirit and power of Elijah than Elias" (6:249–50).

SOURCE

Smith, Joseph. *History of The Church of Jesus Christ of Latter-day Saints.* Edited by B. H. Roberts. 7 vols. 2d ed. rev. Salt Lake City: The Church of Jesus Christ of Latter-day Saints, 1932–51.

RLM

ELIJAH

The life and ministry of Elijah, a prophet to the northern kingdom of Israel during the ninth century B.C., is chronicled in 1 Kings 17 through 2 Kings 2. His name in Hebrew means "My God is Jehovah," which also communicates the focus of his mission. With the binding power of the priesthood, Elijah sealed the heavens so it would not rain for three and a half years, resulting in a devastating drought in response to King Ahab and Queen Jezebel's wicked influence over Israel (1 Kings 17:1; Luke 4:25). At the conclusion of his mortal ministry, Elijah was translated and taken up in a chariot of fire as the mantle of leadership fell on his successor, Elisha (2 Kings 2:11–12).

Because Malachi prophesied that Elijah would return to restore the sealing power of the priesthood (Malachi 4:5), some Jews at the time of Christ wondered whether Jesus was in reality Elijah returned to earth (Matthew 16:14). Indeed, Elijah did return as a translated being to bestow the keys of the higher priesthood on Peter, James, and John by the laying on of hands. This bestowal of priesthood keys occurred on the Mount of Transfiguration about six months prior to the Savior's crucifixion (Matthew 17:3).

When the angel Moroni appeared to Joseph Smith in September 1823, he relayed Malachi's prophecy about Elijah four times and with some significant changes: "I will reveal unto you the Priesthood, by the hand of Elijah the prophet, before the coming of the great and dreadful day of the Lord. And he shall plant in the hearts of the children the promises made to the fathers, and the hearts of the children shall turn to their fathers. If it were not so, the whole earth would be utterly wasted at his coming" (D&C 2; Joseph Smith–History 1:38–39). The fulfillment of that promise occurred on 3 April 1836 when Elijah appeared to Joseph Smith and Oliver Cowdery in the Kirtland Temple to bestow the same power to seal families together throughout all generations.

Joseph Smith explained the significance of Elijah's mission in this final dispensation: "The spirit, power, and calling of Elijah is, that ye have power to hold the key of the revelation, ordinances, oracles, powers and endowments of the fulness of the Melchizedek Priesthood and of the kingdom of God on the earth; and to receive, obtain, and perform all the ordinances belonging to the kingdom of God, even unto the turning of the hearts of the fathers unto the children, and the hearts of the children unto the fathers, even those who are in heaven. . . .

" . . . This is the spirit of Elijah, that we redeem our dead, and connect ourselves with our fathers which are in heaven, and seal up our dead to come forth in the first resurrection; and here we want the power of Elijah to seal those who dwell on earth to those who dwell in heaven. This is the power of Elijah and the keys of the kingdom of Jehovah" (6:251–53; spelling modernized).

SOURCE

Smith, Joseph. *History of The Church of Jesus Christ of Latter-day Saints.* Edited by B. H. Roberts. 7 vols. 2d ed. rev. Salt Lake City: The Church of Jesus Christ of Latter-day Saints, 1932–51.

CFO

ELOHIM

The Hebrew plural noun *Elohim* is translated as "gods." The singular *El* is the Hebrew version of the general term for God or "the Divine Being" found in the Semitic family of languages. For example, the word *Allah* is the Arabic cognate for God. Sometimes the plural noun is used as a name-title for God the Father, as in Numbers 16:22: "the God [*Elohim/Elohe*] of the spirits of all flesh." When used in this sense, the plural nature of the noun is understood as the plural of majesty or excellence or intensification (Gesenius, 398) and reflects all the qualities and characteristics possessed by God the Father in their fulness and perfection. He is truly all-mighty, all-powerful, all-knowing, and all-loving.

Sometimes it is impossible to know whether the term *Elohim* is referring to God the Father or to Jehovah, as with Genesis 1:1: "In the beginning God [*Elohim*] created the heaven and the earth." At other times it is clear that *Elohim* is intended as a simple plural noun meaning "gods," as in Deuteronomy 10:17: "The Lord your God [*Elohim*] is God [*Elohe*] of gods [*Elohim*]." Daniel 2:47 has similar phrasing, only in Aramaic (*Elahin*).

In its singular construction, *El* is sometimes joined with similar or related terms to create other descriptive name-titles of Deity. For example, *El Elyon* means "most high God" (Genesis 14:18–20, 22), *El Shaddai* means "God Almighty" (Exodus 6:3), and *El-elohe-Israel* is translated as "the God of Israel" (Genesis 33:20, footnote a). Anciently, compound names with significant meaning were created by attaching *El* to other nouns or adjectives. Hence, such names as Michael ("who is like God"), Eleazar ("God helped"), Daniel ("God is a judge"), and Bethel ("house of God") reminded ancient Israel of the importance of God in their lives.

SOURCE

Gesenius, H. F. W. *Gesenius' Hebrew Grammar*. Edited by E. Kautzsch and A. E. Cowley. Oxford: Clarendon Press, 1910.

ACS

ENDLESS/ETERNAL

The terms *endless* and *eternal* have both quantitative and qualitative meanings in the scriptures and the restored gospel of Jesus Christ. Quantitatively, the terms refer to the infinity of time—something that is eternal in its duration "without beginning of days or end of years" (Moses 1:3). In many places, however, the terms are qualitative descriptions. They may not be speaking of time at all but rather of a nature or kind. For example, God is described as "endless" and "eternal"; thus, his punishments are likewise described as "endless" and "eternal"—but not because they never end (D&C 19:10; 20:17; Moses 1:3). Some of God's punishments do end, as in the case of the repentant and re-deemed. Other punishments do not end, as in the case of the fate of the sons of perdition. Yet both are endless and eternal because they are divine, godly, perfect (D&C 19:6–12). Eternal life would thus be life of eternal duration in a resurrected, glorified state but also endless and eternal in that it is God's life in character and nature.

BLT

END OF THE EARTH

The end of the earth is the end of the Millennium, the thousand years of peace brought by the power of God and maintained by righteousness (1 Nephi 22:15, 26; 2 Nephi 30:18). "For the great Millennium, of which I have spoken by the mouth of my servants, shall come. For Satan shall be bound, and when he is loosed again he shall only reign for a little season, and then cometh the end of the earth" (D&C 43:30–31). "And again, another trump shall sound, which is the third trump; and then come the spirits of men who are to be judged, and are found under condemnation [the telestial]; and these are the rest of the dead; and they live not again until the thousand years are ended, neither again, until the end of the earth" (D&C 88:100–101; see also 38:5).

RLM

END OF THE WORLD

The end of the world is the end of the worldly, the destruction of the wicked that takes place when Christ returns in glory. "And Jesus left [the apostles], and went upon the Mount of Olives. And as he sat upon the Mount of Olives, the disciples came unto him privately, saying: Tell us when shall these things be which thou hast said concerning the destruction of the temple, and the Jews; and what is the sign of thy coming, and of the end of the world, or the destruction of the wicked, which is the end of the world?" (Joseph Smith–Matthew 1:4). The Prophet Joseph Smith explained in 1835: "The end of the world is the destruction of the wicked; the harvest and the end of the world have an allusion directly to the human family in the last days, instead of the earth, as many have imagined" (2:271).

SOURCE

Smith, Joseph. *History of The Church of Jesus Christ of Latter-day Saints.* Edited by
    B. H. Roberts. 7 vols. 2d ed. rev. Salt Lake City: The Church of Jesus Christ of
    Latter-day Saints, 1932–51.

RLM

ENDOWMENT

An endowment is a rich gift. Thus, to be endowed is to be given a
rich gift. In Latter-day Saint temples, worthy members receive such a
gift through a ritual presentation called the endowment. At the heart
of this endowment is the knowledge and power, given through ordinances, that enable faithful participants to receive exaltation and all
that God the Father possesses (D&C 84:33–38). President Brigham
Young stated, "Your endowment is, to receive all those ordinances in
the House of the Lord, which are necessary for you, after you have
departed this life, to enable you to walk back to the presence of the
Father, passing the angels who stand as sentinels, being enabled to
give them the key words, the signs and tokens, pertaining to the Holy
Priesthood, and gain your eternal exaltation in spite of earth and hell"
(2:31).

The temple ordinances administered in Kirtland represented a
partial endowment and consisted of washings, anointings, sealing of
anointings, and the washing of feet. The holy endowment has been defined and described in various ways that, taken together, help explain
it more completely. Of course, as with all concepts, no verbal descriptions can replace personal experience and participation. Elder James E.
Talmage referred to the temple endowment as administered in modern times as a course of instruction—"instruction relating to the significance and sequence of past dispensations, and the importance of
the present as the greatest and grandest era in human history. This
course of instruction includes a recital of the most prominent events of
the creative period, the condition of our first parents in the Garden of
Eden, their disobedience and consequent expulsion from that blissful
abode, their condition in the lone and dreary world . . . , the plan of
redemption by which the great transgression may be atoned, the period of great apostasy, the restoration of the Gospel with all its ancient
powers and privileges. . . . The ordinances of the endowment embody

certain obligations on the part of the individual, such as covenant and promise to observe the law of strict virtue and chastity" (83–84).

President David O. McKay said, "There are few, even temple workers, who comprehend the full meaning and power of the temple endowment. Seen for what it is, it is the step-by-step ascent into the Eternal Presence" (in Parry, 58). President Boyd K. Packer wrote: "To endow is to enrich, to give to another something long lasting and of much worth. The temple endowment ordinances enrich in three ways: (a) The one receiving the ordinance is given power from God. 'Recipients are endowed with power from on high.' (b) A recipient is also endowed with information and knowledge. 'They receive an education relative to the Lord's purposes and plans.' (*Mormon Doctrine,* 227.) (c) When sealed at the altar a person is the recipient of glorious blessings, powers, and honors as part of his endowment" (153).

Elder Carlos E. Asay, former president of the Salt Lake Temple, stated that all of these definitions are worthy of serious study and consideration: the endowment is a preparatory process, a course of instruction, a step-by-step ascent toward God, and an enriching gift of power, knowledge, and glorious blessings. In addition, he regarded "the ordinances of the endowment as *an exchange of love* between God, our Father, and us. . . . [E]very commandment, every ordinance, every covenant, every law, every '*thou shalt,*' every '*thou shalt not,*' and every teaching received from our Father in Heaven and His Son, our Savior—especially those received in the House of the Lord—is an expression of divine love. In the process of receiving the outpourings of love from Deity in the temple, we are invited to covenant that we will obey the laws, keep the commandments and live as we have been taught. Consequently, every covenant or promise we make with God is an expression of our love to him in return" (5).

The Prophet Joseph Smith was clear that every individual who desires to be exalted must receive exactly the same ordinances, including the endowment administered in the house of the Lord. He said, "You need an endowment . . . in order that you may be prepared and able to overcome all things" (2:309). The consistency across dispensations of the Lord's requirements for full salvation is a significant theme in the Prophet's teachings. Said he, "God will deal with all the human family equally" (4:597). He added, "If a man gets a fullness of the priesthood of God, he has to get it in the same way that Jesus Christ obtained it, and that was by keeping all the commandments and obeying all the ordinances of the house of the Lord" (5:424). The Prophet also noted: "The question is frequently asked 'Can we not be saved without going through with all those ordinances &c.?' I would answer, No, not the fullness of salvation . . . ; and any person who is exalted to the highest mansion has to abide a celestial law, and the whole law too" (6:184). Therefore, it follows that "every man who wishes to save his father, mother, brothers, sisters and friends, must go through all the ordinances for each one of them separately, the same as for himself, from baptism to ordination, washings and anointings, and receive all the keys and powers of the Priesthood, the same as for himself" (6:319).

Furthermore, these ordinances of exaltation, including the endowment, were established and firmly set in our premortal existence, according to Joseph Smith: "It was the design of the councils of heaven before the world was, that the principles and laws of the priesthood should be predicated upon the gathering of the people in every age of the world. . . . Ordinances instituted in the heavens before the foundation of the world, in the priesthood, for the salvation of men, are not to be altered or changed. All must be saved on the same principles. It is for the same purpose that God gathers together His people in the last days, to build unto the Lord a house to prepare them for the ordinances and endowments, washings and anointings, etc. One of the ordinances of the house of the Lord is baptism for the dead. God decreed before the foundation of the world that that ordinance should be administered in a font prepared for that purpose in the house of the Lord" (6:423–24).

President Heber C. Kimball taught that the temple endowment administered in the modern Church of Jesus Christ is the same as the endowment administered in the ancient Church of Jesus Christ. Jesus himself "inducted his Apostles into these ordinances" (10:241). President Joseph Fielding Smith and other prophets of this dispensation have also indicated that the ancient Saints received the endowment (2:164–65).

The first complete endowments in this dispensation were administered by Joseph Smith to a small group on 4 May 1842 in the upper room of his red brick store in Nauvoo, Illinois. The participants were Hyrum Smith, Church patriarch; Brigham Young, Heber C. Kimball, and Willard Richards of the Twelve Apostles; Newel K. Whitney, bishop; George Miller, bishop and president of the Nauvoo high priests quorum; and James Adams, president of the Springfield branch. Of this event Joseph Smith said: "I spent the day in the upper part of the store . . . instructing them in the principles and order of the Priesthood, attending to washings, anointings, endowments and the communication of keys pertaining to the Aaronic Priesthood, and so on to the highest order of the Melchizedek Priesthood, setting forth the order pertaining to the Ancient of Days, and all those plans and principles by which any one is enabled to secure the fullness of those blessings which have been prepared for the Church of the First Born, and come up and abide in the presence of the Eloheim in the eternal worlds" (5:1–2).

Over the next two years, the Prophet introduced these ordinances to approximately ninety men and women and instructed the Quorum of the Twelve regarding the keys of the priesthood that administer these sacred matters. He also instructed them to administer the endowment to worthy Church members in the Nauvoo Temple once it was completed. Endowments were given there beginning 10 December 1845, and dozens of people participated. By the end of the month, more than one thousand Saints had been endowed. Joseph Fielding Smith wrote that after the Saints' exodus from Nauvoo and their settlement in the Salt Lake Valley, endowments were administered on Ensign Peak and later in the Endowment House (2:231–57).

Vicarious endowments for deceased persons were performed for the first time on 11 January 1877 in the Saint George Utah Temple after its completion. President Brigham Young reemphasized that work for the dead required a temple. He personally directed the ordinance work for his kindred dead in the Saint George temple as well as the development of a "perfect form of the endowments" (*Church,* 416).

Closely associated with the endowment is the doctrine and practice of eternal marriage, whereby a couple and their children may be sealed together by the power of the priesthood for time and eternity. In May and July 1843, Joseph Smith received two revelations explaining the necessity of eternal marriage for exaltation and the great blessings deriving from that ordinance, which are found in Doctrine and

Covenants 131 and 132. Joseph sealed many of the endowed men and women to their spouses. The best available evidence indicates that children were sealed to their parents for the first time in this dispensation on 25 January 1846 (Cowan, 20).

The glorious endowment of the holy priesthood is available to all worthy members of The Church of Jesus Christ of Latter-day Saints. It is directed on earth by those who hold the keys of the Melchizedek Priesthood, for "the power and authority of the higher, or Melchizedek Priesthood, is to hold the keys of all the spiritual blessings of the church—to have the privilege of receiving the mysteries of the kingdom" (D&C 107:18–19), which mysteries are encompassed in the endowment.

SOURCES

Asay, Carlos E. "Temple Blessings and Applications," lecture to Religious Education faculty, Brigham Young University, 6 Mar. 1998. Unpublished manuscript. Capitalization standardized.

Church History in the Fulness of Times [manual]. Prepared by the Church Educational System. Salt Lake City: The Church of Jesus Christ of Latter-day Saints, 1993.

Cowan, Richard. "The Pivotal Nauvoo Temple." Unpublished manuscript.

Kimball, Heber C. In *Journal of Discourses.* 26 vols. London: Latter-day Saints' Book Depot, 1854–86.

Packer, Boyd K. *The Holy Temple.* Salt Lake City: Bookcraft, 1980.

Parry, Donald W., ed. *Temples of the Ancient World: Ritual and Symbolism.* Salt Lake City: Deseret Book, 1994.

Smith, Joseph. *History of The Church of Jesus Christ of Latter-day Saints.* Edited by B. H. Roberts. 7 vols. 2d ed. rev. Salt Lake City: The Church of Jesus Christ of Latter-day Saints, 1932–51.

Smith, Joseph Fielding. *Doctrines of Salvation.* Compiled by Bruce R. McConkie. 3 vols. Salt Lake City: Bookcraft, 1954–56.

Talmage, James E. *The House of the Lord.* Salt Lake City: Deseret Book, 1968.

Young, Brigham. In *Journal of Discourses.* 26 vols. London: Latter-day Saints' Book Depot, 1854–86.

ACS

ENDURING TO THE END

"Let him that thinketh he standeth take heed lest he fall," the apostle Paul counseled the New Testament Saints (1 Corinthians 10:12). He admonished the Hebrews: "Let us hold fast the profession of our faith without wavering" (Hebrews 10:23). In our day the Lord has declared that "there is a possibility that man may fall from grace and depart from the living God; therefore let the church take heed and pray always, lest they fall into temptation; yea, and even let those who are sanctified take heed also" (D&C 20:32–34). Taking heed of ourselves and holding fast to our faith—remaining vigilant against temptation with faith in the Savior, repenting of our sins, and obeying the commandments—is enduring to the end. Latter-day Saints who have taken the covenant of baptism upon themselves promise to serve the Master "to the end" (D&C 20:37; see also Mosiah 18:8–10; Moroni 6:3). Numerous other scriptural passages specifically use the phrase "endure unto the end" as a principle of the gospel leading unto eternal life and salvation (1 Nephi 13:37; 2 Nephi 9:24; 31:20; 3 Nephi 27:16–17; D&C 10:69; 14:7; 18:22; 20:25, 29; 50:5; 63:20, 47). Enduring to the end is, as Elder Neal A. Maxwell declared, "not merely the passage of time, but the passage of the soul. . . . To endure in faith and [do] God's will . . . therefore involves much more than putting up with a circumstance" (34).

In the literal sense of the term, all people will endure to the end—meaning living until they die. In the doctrinal sense, however, enduring to the end means being true to our covenants, remaining fixed in our faith in the Lord and commitment to his kingdom, continuing to serve God and our fellowmen until the end of our mortal life, even amidst opposition and adversity. It is standing firm and steadfast for the cause of righteousness and against wickedness and worldliness. It is not giving up or giving in. It is pressing forward through the spiritual mists of darkness, "continually holding fast to the rod of iron"—which is the Lord and his word—even as others mock and make life difficult (1 Nephi 8:30; 15:24). The Lord has promised each of us, as he did the Prophet Joseph Smith, that when we face adversity and afflictions, doubts and discouragement, "if thou endure it well, God shall exalt thee on high" (D&C 121:8). Faithful endurance is a fundamental principle of the gospel and a characteristic of devoted disciples of the Lord. Joseph Smith declared that "we have endured many things, and hope to be able to endure all things" (Articles of Faith 1:13). Enduring to the end is hoping for and trusting in the Lord's promise that "all thrones and dominions . . . shall be . . . set forth upon all who have endured valiantly for the gospel of Jesus Christ" (D&C 121:29).

SOURCE

Maxwell, Neal A. "Endure It Well." *Ensign,* May 1990, 33–35.

BLT

ENOCH, BOOK OF

Enoch was the seventh in the line of patriarchs issuing from Adam (Moses 6:10–22). He lived some three millennia before the time of Christ and was among the greatest of seers (Moses 6:35–36). He saw in vision the future of the world, including the atoning sacrifice of Jesus Christ, the coming forth of the Book of Mormon and restoration of the gospel, the Second Coming, and the millennial reign of the Messiah (Moses 7:47–65). Enoch was so righteous that ultimately he and his people were taken into heaven while still in mortality (Moses 7:18–21). Before he was translated, however, Enoch participated in a great gathering with Adam and his righteous posterity three years prior to the death of our first father. A brief account of this event was given by the Prophet Joseph Smith (D&C 107:53–56), who concluded with this statement: "These things were all written in the book of Enoch, and are to be testified of in due time" (D&C 107:57).

In a future day the contents of the ancient, authentic record written by the patriarch Enoch will be made available. Speaking of this anticipated record, Elder Orson Pratt said, "When we get that, I think we shall know a great deal about the ante-diluvians [patriarchs before the Flood], of whom at present we know so little" (19:218). We have a foretaste of the profound information contained in Enoch's writings. Excerpts from this record are found in narrative sections of the Book of Moses, particularly Moses 6–7, given by revelation to the Prophet Joseph Smith as he translated the King James Bible.

The anticipated book of Enoch should not be confused with the existing pseudepigraphal, noncanonical Jewish writings ascribed to Enoch. (Some denominations do hold some Enoch texts to be canonical: the Beta Israel Jewish community, Ethiopian Orthodox Church, and Eritrean Orthodox Church.) These texts were composed between the fourth and first centuries B.C. The main text, 1 Enoch (also called the Book of Enoch), exists in complete form only in the Ge'ez (Ethiopic) language, with substantial Aramaic fragments found among the Dead Sea Scrolls and some fragments in Greek and Latin. First

Enoch was extant by the time the New Testament Epistle of Jude was composed, as it was quoted in Jude 1:14–15 (see also 1 Enoch 1:9). Some scholars argue that most, if not all, of the New Testament writers were familiar with 1 Enoch and influenced by it.

To what extent 1 Enoch is based on the much older, authentic record of Enoch the Seer is a debated question. Hugh Nibley wrote extensively on the similarities between the pseudepigraphal Enoch texts and Moses 6–7, indicating that the Jewish pseudepigraphal texts were based, in part, on information surviving from the distant past when Enoch actually lived.

Even though the pseudepigraphal Enoch texts are not the equivalent of the great seer's ancient record, they possess value (D&C 91)—not the least of which is their demonstration of the credibility of Joseph Smith's Enoch texts as authentic, ancient testimony.

SOURCES

Nibley, Hugh. *Enoch the Prophet.* Volume 2 of Collected Works of Hugh Nibley. Salt Lake City: Deseret Book and Provo, Utah: Foundation for Ancient Research and Mormon Studies, 1986.

Pratt, Orson. In *Journal of Discourses.* 26 vols. London: Latter-day Saints' Book Depot, 1854–86.

ACS

ETERNAL FATHER

Both God the Father and his Son Jesus Christ are properly called Eternal Father. They are infinite and eternal in nature, and our relationship with each is infinite and eternal, both in quality and duration.

We pray to God the Eternal Father throughout the day and also each week when we partake of the sacrament. He is the Father of our spirits forever, and the Savior is his Only Begotten Son forever (Hebrews 12:9; 1 Nephi 11:21). God the Eternal Father is also the first member of the Godhead, as designated in our first article of faith.

Because Jesus Christ is "the Father of heaven and earth, the Creator of all things from the beginning" (Helaman 14:12), and the Father of our spiritual rebirth when our "hearts are changed through faith on his name" (Mosiah 5:7), he is also appropriately called Eternal Father or "Everlasting Father," as Isaiah prophesied of him (Isaiah 9:6). Jesus Christ declared: "I am the Father and the Son. In me shall all mankind have life, and that eternally, even they who shall believe on my name;

and they shall become my sons and my daughters" (Ether 3:14). The Book of Mormon prophet Abinadi described the second member of the Godhead as both "Father and Son" because of the dual qualities he alone possesses: mortal and immortal, human and divine, flesh and spirit (Mosiah 15:1–8). Therefore only he could suffer as he did in mortality, finally to die only when he had completed his work, "the will of the Son being swallowed up in the will of the Father" (Mosiah 15:7). Abinadi thereby concluded that he who atoned and redeemed us may be called the "Eternal Father" (Mosiah 16:15).

CFO

ETERNAL LIFE

Eternal life refers not to the duration of our lives hereafter, for that is what is entailed in immortality (living forever); rather it refers to the kind and quality of life we will enjoy: God's life, for Eternal is one of God's names (D&C 19:11; Moses 7:35). To gain eternal life is to qualify for the highest and most profound reward a benevolent Lord can bestow upon men and women. There is no purer aspiration or grander expectation a disciple of Christ can have. To have eternal life is to be fully redeemed. To have eternal life is to enjoy the fulness of salvation. To have eternal life is to qualify for exaltation. Specifically, according to the revelation, to gain eternal life is to enjoy (1) the fulness of the glory of the Father and (2) the continuation of the family unit into eternity (D&C 132:19–20).

God's children are called upon to come unto Christ, acknowledge their sins and apply unto his atoning blood, receive the ordinances of salvation, strive to deny themselves of ungodliness, and become obedient disciples, coming unto him and seeking to emulate his matchless example. But eternal life remains a gracious offering, a gift, the greatest of all the gifts of God (D&C 14:7). It may not be earned, bartered for, or purchased, except by the Savior himself, who bought us with his blood (1 Corinthians 6:19–20; 7:23; 1 Peter 1:18–19). It is a gift that must be received. Had there been no Atonement, no amount of good works would make up for its absence, and eternal life would be an utter impossibility for every son and daughter of God.

RLM

ETERNAL LIVES

To gain eternal lives is to be saved in the highest heaven, to receive exaltation. It is the same as receiving eternal life, but eternal *lives* stresses the "continuation of the seeds forever and ever" (D&C 132:19), meaning the everlasting perpetuation of the family unit. While salvation or eternal life is an individual matter, exaltation or eternal lives is a family affair. The Prophet Joseph Smith declared, "Except a man and his wife enter into an everlasting covenant and be married for eternity, while in this probation, by the power and authority of the Holy Priesthood, they will cease to increase when they die; that is, they will not have any children after the resurrection. But those who are married by the power and authority of the priesthood in this life, and continue without committing the sin against the Holy Ghost, will continue to increase and have children in the celestial glory" (5:391).

SOURCE

Smith, Joseph. *History of The Church of Jesus Christ of Latter-day Saints.* Edited by B. H. Roberts. 7 vols. 2d ed. rev. Salt Lake City: The Church of Jesus Christ of Latter-day Saints, 1932–51.

RLM

ETERNAL PROGRESSION

The concept embodied in the phrase *eternal progression* is that men and women have been engaged in spiritual development and moral expansion from eternity past and will do so into eternity future. Those who kept their first estate are "added upon" (Abraham 3:26): they come to earth, receive a physical body, confront new opportunities and challenges, establish sacred and eternal relationships, exercise saving faith in the Lord Jesus Christ, and grow in spiritual graces beyond what they could have enjoyed in the premortal world. Further, those who achieve in this life what they were sent here to achieve and who pass the tests of mortality are, again, "added upon"; they qualify for eternal life or exaltation in the celestial kingdom of God. "Though our outward man perish," the apostle Paul declared, "yet the inward man is renewed day by day. For our light affliction, which is but for a moment, worketh for us a far more exceeding and eternal weight of glory" (2 Corinthians 4:16–17). In other words, followers of Christ are gradually "changed into the same image [as their Lord] from glory to glory, even as by the Spirit of the Lord" (2 Corinthians 3:18). From spirit birth to mortality to death to resurrected and glorified immortality, life with and like God (1 John 3:1–2)—this is the path of divine glory, the process of eternal progression.

RLM

ETERNITY TO ETERNITY, FROM

The scriptures declare that "from eternity to eternity" and "from everlasting to everlasting," God is the same (D&C 76:4; 20:17). From one premortal existence to the next (McConkie, 166), God's qualities, attributes, and character are constant, trustworthy, and dependable; they never change. He is and always will be a God of truth, justice, judgment, mercy, long-suffering, and love. Joseph Fielding Smith explained: "From eternity to eternity means from the spirit existence through the probation which we are in, and then back again to the eternal existence which will follow. Surely this is everlasting, for when we receive the resurrection, we will never die. We all existed in the first eternity. I think I can say of myself and others, we are from eternity; and we will be to eternity everlasting, if we receive the exaltation" (1:12; see also McConkie, 166).

SOURCES

McConkie, Bruce R. *The Promised Messiah: The First Coming of Christ.* Salt Lake City: Deseret Book, 1978.

Smith, Joseph Fielding. *Doctrines of Salvation.* Compiled by Bruce R. McConkie. 3 vols. Salt Lake City: Bookcraft, 1954–56.

RLM

ETHICS

Ethics is a system of good deeds, a program of noble endeavors. Ethics is not necessarily righteousness. The very word *ethics* has come to connote socially acceptable standards based on current consensus, as opposed to absolute truths based on God's eternal laws. Ethics is too often to virtue and righteousness what theology is to religion—a pale substitute. Indeed, ethics without the virtue that comes through the cleansing powers of the Redeemer is like religion without God, at least the true and living God.

"It is one thing," Elder Bruce R. McConkie wrote, "to teach ethical principles, quite another to proclaim the great doctrinal verities, which are the foundation of true Christianity and out of which eternal salvation comes. True it is that salvation is limited to those in whose souls the ethical principles abound, but true it is also that Christian ethics, in the full and saving sense, automatically become a part of the lives of those who first believe Christian doctrines." In summary, "It is only when gospel ethics are tied to gospel doctrines that they rest on a sure and enduring foundation and gain full operation in the lives of the saints" (699).

Elder Bruce C. Hafen pointed out, "The ultimate purpose of the gospel of Jesus Christ is to cause the sons and daughters of God to become as Christ is. Those who see religious purpose only in terms of ethical service in the relationship between man and fellowmen may miss that divinely ordained possibility. It is quite possible to render charitable—even 'Christian'—service without developing deeply ingrained and permanent Christlike character. Paul understood this when he warned against giving all one's goods to feed the poor without true charity. . . .

" . . . While religious philosophies whose highest aim is social relevance may do much good, they will not ultimately lead people to achieve the highest religious purpose, which is to become as God and Christ are" (235–36).

SOURCES

Hafen, Bruce C. *The Broken Heart: Applying the Atonement to Life's Experiences.* Expanded edition. Salt Lake City: Deseret Book, 2008.

McConkie, Bruce R. *A New Witness for the Articles of Faith.* Salt Lake City: Deseret Book, 1985.

RLM

EVANGELIST

An evangelist is a patriarch. "Wherever the Church of Christ is established in the earth, there should be a Patriarch for the benefit of the posterity of the Saints, as it was with Jacob in giving his patriarchal blessing unto his sons" (Smith, 3:381). Philip, one of the seven special assistants to the apostles in the meridian of time (Acts 6:1–6), later settled in Caesarea and became an evangelist, or patriarch (Acts 21:8).

In a broad sense, an evangelist is a preacher, a teacher, an articulator of the word of God (2 Timothy 4:5). Thus many in the Christian world refer to Matthew, Mark, Luke, and John as evangelists, inasmuch as they proclaimed the word through the power of their written testimonies of the Savior. In addition, an evangelist in today's larger Christian world is a preacher charged to bring about change in people's lives through the spoken word, one whose message sobers listeners to their sinful plight and points them to the need for spiritual transformation through Jesus Christ. Dwight L. Moody traveled thousands of miles to deliver the word during the middle to late nineteenth century, while Billy Sunday was a colorful spokesman in America who fought unceasingly against the evils of alcohol during Prohibition. Billy Graham would be considered by many to be the best known evangelist of the twentieth century.

SOURCE

Smith, Joseph. *History of The Church of Jesus Christ of Latter-day Saints.* Edited by B. H. Roberts. 7 vols. 2d ed. rev. Salt Lake City: The Church of Jesus Christ of Latter-day Saints, 1932–51.

RLM

EVE

As the "mother of all living," Eve is connected to each of us (Genesis 3:20; Moses 4:26). Her use of reasoning and agency initiated life in a fallen world, where her children would encounter pain, sorrow, and joy beyond anything she and Adam could imagine in the Garden of Eden. Eve was divinely designated to be a heroine and role model for her daughters. When she was brought to Adam in the Garden of Eden, he declared, "This I know now is bone of my bones, and flesh of my flesh. . . . Therefore shall a man leave his father and his mother, and shall cleave unto his wife; and they shall be one flesh" (Moses 3:23–24).

By placing the tree of knowledge in the midst of the Garden of Eden and giving the warning, "Thou shalt not eat of it, nevertheless, thou mayest choose for thyself, for it is given unto thee" (Moses 3:17), God created an environment in which Adam and Eve were free to discover the only way they and their posterity could access the full power of Christ's Atonement and thereby reach their divine potential. Eve partook of the fruit of the tree of knowledge before her husband did and thereby commenced the consequences of a fallen world. Nowhere in scripture did God punish Eve for her actions in the garden; nor did he require her to repent of partaking of the forbidden fruit (Moses 6:53). In contrast to cursing the ground and the serpent, God strengthened and empowered Adam and Eve after they ate from the tree of knowledge, giving them opportunities for growth, not punishment. Elder Russell M. Nelson has taught: "We and all mankind are forever blessed because of Eve's great courage and wisdom. By partaking of the fruit first, she did what needed to be done. Adam was wise enough to do likewise" (34).

Everything God does is "for the benefit of the world" (2 Nephi 26:24). The consequences that he pronounced after Adam and Eve's transgression underscore that he always intended them to leave the garden. He told Eve that he would "greatly multiply thy sorrow," meaning that he would require her to do painful things over and over again. Additionally, God told Eve that he would multiply her conception, meaning that she would repeatedly experience pain associated with bearing and rearing each of her children (Genesis 3:16; Moses 4:22). As a "help meet" (Genesis 2:18; Moses 3:18) for Adam, Eve magnified the supernal gift of life, provided only through the grace and merits of Jesus Christ, when she gave mortal life to God's children. Finally, God blessed Eve that "thy desire shall be to thy husband, and he shall rule over thee" (Genesis 3:16; Moses 4:22). God's design is grounded in family and required that Adam and Eve be united. By turning Eve's desires toward her husband, God fostered an interdependent companionship in which the woman needs the man as much as the man needs the woman (1 Corinthians 7:11).

Eve and her husband's equal yet complementary responsibilities are evident in their relationship and activities after their departure from the garden. Together Adam and Eve worked the soil, reared children, prayed to God, heard his response, received his commandments concerning sacrifice, and taught their children (Moses 5:1–12). Never is it implied that Eve worked *for* her husband or *against* him or *around* him or *because* of him. But Eve "did labor *with* him" (Moses 5:1; emphasis added). She rejoiced in her husband's testimony of the joy and understanding that would come because of their transgression (Moses 5:11). In response to her husband's witness and their challenging experiences in a fallen world, Eve was glad and declared, "Were it not for our transgression we never should have had seed, and never should have known good and evil, and the joy of our redemption, and the eternal life which God giveth unto all the obedient" (Moses 5:11).

An acceptance of and appreciation for the mutual dependence that God designed to exist between man and woman is one of the most important messages of the scriptural record. Adam and Eve's example from the beginning ranks as a hallmark of marital partnership.

SOURCE

Nelson, Russell M. "Constancy and Change." *Ensign,* Nov. 1993, 33–36.

CFO

EVERLASTING BURNINGS

The supernal light that attends God and is associated with his person and the place where he dwells is so grand, so magnificent, so glorious that it can be understood only by referring to the brightness of the sun (Joseph Smith–History 1:16). In describing the celestial kingdom, Joseph Smith remarked: "I saw the transcendent beauty of the gate through which the heirs of that kingdom will enter, which was like unto circling flames of fire; also the blazing throne of God, whereon was seated the Father and the Son" (D&C 137:2–3). Two months later the Savior appeared in the Kirtland Temple. "His eyes were as a flame of fire; the hair of his head was white like the pure snow; his countenance shown above the brightness of the sun" (D&C 110:3). In posing the question of who will qualify for life in the highest heaven, the celestial glory, Isaiah asked: "Who among us shall dwell with the devouring fire? who among us shall dwell with everlasting burnings?" (Isaiah 33:14). "How consoling to the mourners," the Prophet stated at the memorial service for King Follett, "when they are called to part with a husband, wife, father, mother, child, or dear relative, to know that, although the earthly tabernacle is laid down and dissolved, they shall rise again to dwell in everlasting burnings in immortal glory, not to sorrow, suffer, or die any more; but they shall be heirs of God and joint heirs with Jesus Christ" (6:306).

SOURCE

Smith, Joseph. *History of The Church of Jesus Christ of Latter-day Saints.* Edited by

B. H. Roberts. 7 vols. 2d ed. rev. Salt Lake City: The Church of Jesus Christ of Latter-day Saints, 1932–51.

RLM

EVIL

The word *evil* has several meanings in scripture. Evil is that which is corrupt, undesirable, bad, worthless, ugly, and painful (Genesis 21:11–12; 26:29; 28:8; 31:7; 41:19–20; Deuteronomy 26:6; 28:35; 1 Samuel 18:10; 2 Samuel 12:18; 2 Kings 2:19; Nehemiah 2:3; Ecclesiastes 7:3; Proverbs 11:15; 20:14; 25:19; Jeremiah 24:2; Matthew 6:23; 7:17; Revelation 16:2). Evil also represents challenges, trials, and mortal vicissitudes (Genesis 19:19; 47:9; Psalm 90:15; Matthew 6:34; Ephesians 5:16), and even divine punishment for sin (Deuteronomy 31:17; Jeremiah 26:19; Amos 9:4). In addition, evil is the wrong that individuals do to one another (Genesis 19:7; 44:5; Judges 11:27; James 3:8). Evil is that which flows spontaneously from the heart of fallen people, the "works of the flesh" (Galatians 5:19–21); it is the natural workings of the natural man, the enemy of God (Mosiah 3:19). The brother of Jared confessed in prayer that "because of the fall our natures have become evil continually" (Ether 3:2). Modern revelation teaches us that wicked men "love darkness . . . because their deeds are evil" (D&C 10:21).

Moral agency is an eternal principle. The power of choice is fundamental and foundational to human personality, spiritual development, and eventual exaltation. The right to make decisions has been, is now, and will forevermore be a vital part of our existence. As a result, some of God's children choose the way of "liberty and eternal life, through the great Mediator of all [humankind]." Others, however, choose the path of captivity and death, "according to the captivity and power of the devil; for he seeketh that all men might be miserable like unto himself" (2 Nephi 2:27). In doing so, they choose unwisely and contrary to their best interest (Alma 41:11). That is, they choose evil.

The Prophet observed, "The devil has no power over us only as we permit him" (*Joseph Smith,* 214). The Prophet also said "that Satan was generally blamed for the evils which we did, but if he was the cause of all our wickedness, men could not be condemned. The devil could not compel mankind to do evil; all was voluntary" (*History,* 4:358). Truly, "as well might the devil seek to dethrone Jehovah, as overthrow an innocent soul that resists everything which is evil" (*History,* 4:605).

Satan is a specialist in evil and labors incessantly to spread it far and wide. As pertaining to mortality and life here in our second estate, "that which is evil cometh from the devil" (Omni 1:25; see also Alma 5:40; Moroni 7:12, 17).

SOURCES

Joseph Smith [manual]. Teachings of Presidents of the Church series. Salt Lake City: The Church of Jesus Christ of Latter-day Saints, 2007.

Smith, Joseph. *History of The Church of Jesus Christ of Latter-day Saints.* Edited by B. H. Roberts. 7 vols. 2d ed. rev. Salt Lake City: The Church of Jesus Christ of Latter-day Saints, 1932–51.

RLM

EXALTATION

To Moses the Lord said, "For behold, this is my work and my glory—to bring to pass the immortality and eternal life of man" (Moses 1:39). Immortality is living forever with a resurrected, glorified body. Eternal life is living forever in the presence of God and enjoying the kind of life, attributes, glory, and power he possesses. Both immortality and eternal life are made possible through the infinite atonement of Jesus Christ. All will be resurrected, but only those who exercise saving faith in the Savior, repent of their sins, and strive to live in accordance with the principles and ordinances of the gospel will become exalted or, as the apostle Paul taught, "joint-heirs with Christ" (Romans 8:17). As the Savior himself taught, those who obtain exaltation receive "my Father's kingdom; therefore all that my Father hath shall be given unto him" (D&C 84:38; see also D&C 76:50–60).

Jesus taught that "he that believeth and is baptized shall be saved" (Mark 16:16), and "he that endureth to the end shall be saved" (Matthew 10:22). The apostle Paul described the gospel as the "power of God unto salvation" (Romans 1:16) and Christ as the "author of eternal salvation" (Hebrews 5:9). Peter spoke of "faith unto salvation" (1 Peter 1:5). Numerous passages in the Book of Mormon likewise speak of salvation as the ultimate heavenly reward for the righteous (2 Nephi 25:23; 31:17–20; Mosiah 3:9, 17; 4:6–8; Alma 34:15; Helaman 14:8; Moroni 8:17).

A finer distinction between the varying degrees of salvation and ultimate exaltation and a more comprehensive understanding of the celestial kingdom (D&C 131; 132) comes from the additional light of the Restoration as found in Joseph Smith's vision of the glories in heaven (D&C 76). From these latter-day revelations, we learn that all but the sons of perdition are "saved" to a kingdom of glory, whereas those who inherit the highest glory in God's celestial kingdom are "exalted." To be exalted means to "dwell in the presence of God and his Christ forever and ever" (D&C 76:62) and to possess the fulness of the glory of the Father—to be among those "into whose hands the Father has given all things" (D&C 76:55). Those who are exalted become gods (D&C 76:58) because "all things are theirs" (D&C 76:59), and they shall "be above all, because all things are subject unto them" (D&C 132:20). Exaltation means to possess as joint–heirs with Jesus Christ all of the Father's "thrones, kingdoms, principalities, and powers, dominions, all heights and depths." Perhaps the most important distinction between exaltation and all other forms of salvation and glory is the "continuation of the seeds forever and ever" (D&C 132:19). That is, exalted beings will enjoy eternal family relationships. "And in order to obtain [exaltation], a man must enter into this order of the priesthood [meaning the new and everlasting covenant of marriage]; and if he does not, he cannot obtain it" (D&C 131:2–3). The Prophet Joseph Smith called exaltation "the fullness of salvation," which is obtained only by abiding the celestial law and "going through with all those ordinances [of the temple]" (6:184).

SOURCE

Smith, Joseph. *History of The Church of Jesus Christ of Latter-day Saints.* Edited by B. H. Roberts. 7 vols. 2d ed. rev. Salt Lake City: The Church of Jesus Christ of Latter-day Saints, 1932–51.

BLT

FAITH

Faith is the complete trust, confidence in, and reliance upon the merits, mercy, and grace of Jesus Christ for salvation. It is a gift of the Spirit (Moroni 10:11), a divine endowment that affirms to the human heart the identity and redemptive mission of the Savior. Though one might speak of faith in a broad sense as the underlying reason that people live and move and go about their daily activities, the faith of which the scriptures speak is faith in the Lord Jesus Christ.

The apostle Paul wrote that "faith is the substance ["assurance," according to the JST] of things hoped for, the evidence [or proof] of things not seen" (Hebrews 11:1). Alma declared to the Zoramites that to have faith is "not to have a perfect knowledge of things; therefore if ye have faith ye hope for things which are not seen, which are true" (Alma 32:21; see also Ether 12:6). Sincerity and devotion to a cause are not sufficient; saving faith can only be exercised in that which is true. Thus, no matter how committed the Zoramites were to their unusual liturgy atop the Rameumptom (Alma 31), their false beliefs concerning God could not result in faith unto life and salvation. Their refusal to believe in the coming condescension of God the Son (Alma 31:16) precluded salvation, no matter how consistently they cried out to their deity in their weekly rituals.

We see also from this passage that faith is intimately connected with hope: to have true faith in Christ is to have hope in Christ. When we come to know who Jesus is—how great and marvelous are his powers and his knowledge and the nature of his sacrificial offering—and when we gain faith in him, then we gain a hope in Christ. No one can attain unto faith without also having hope. We need not speak of faith as something one either has in its fulness or does not have. Gaining faith is a process. And so it is with hope. Individuals like the humble Zoramites begin with the simple hope that there is a Savior (see Alma 32:27). On the other end of the continuum are those who know their Lord, have treasured up his word, and have been valiant in their witness. Their hope is for eternal life, for exaltation in the celestial kingdom.

"And what is it that ye shall hope for?" Mormon asked. "Behold I say unto you that ye shall have hope through the atonement of Christ and the power of his resurrection, to be raised unto life eternal, and this because of your faith in him according to the promise. Wherefore, if a man have faith he must needs have hope; for without faith there cannot be any hope" (Moroni 7:41–42). The disciple of Christ has hope, not in the worldly sense (wishing or yearning) but rather in the sense of anticipation, expectation, and assurance that through the

Divine Redeemer he will be saved in the highest heaven. He is motivated and directed, not by self-confidence but by his confidence or hope in Christ.

The scriptures make no distinction between true faith and true belief; belief is a synonym for faith. To have faith in Christ is to believe in Christ, to "believe that he is, and that he created all things, both in heaven and in earth; [to] believe that he has all wisdom, and all power, both in heaven and in earth" (Mosiah 4:9). The Nephite prophets labored diligently to invite their people "to believe in Christ, and to be reconciled to God" (2 Nephi 25:23), "for the Lord covenanteth with none save it be with them that repent and believe in his Son, who is the Holy One of Israel" (2 Nephi 30:2). The Nephites were called upon to "believe in Christ, and view his death, and suffer his cross and bear the shame of the world" (Jacob 1:8). Truly, "whosoever shall believe on the Son of God, the same shall have everlasting life" (Helaman 14:8). In summarizing the first principles and ordinances of the gospel, Mormon wrote, "And if it so be that ye believe in Christ, and are baptized, first with water, then with fire and with the Holy Ghost, following the example of our Savior, . . . it shall be well with you in the day of judgment" (Mormon 7:10).

Trust and reliance are likewise synonyms for faith. To have faith in Christ is to trust in him, to rely completely upon him. The Lord Jesus extends his arms of mercy toward those who trust in him; "the same shall be lifted up at the last day" (Mosiah 23:22). Of the two thousand stripling warriors, Helaman noted, "Now this was the faith of these of whom I have spoken; they are young, and their minds are firm, and they do put their trust in God continually" (Alma 57:27). Nephi explained that the Saints of God are able to come unto Christ through "relying wholly upon the merits of him who is mighty to save" (2 Nephi 31:19). Moroni likewise wrote that people are "nourished by the good word of God, to keep them in the right way, . . . relying alone upon the merits of Christ, who was the author and the finisher of their faith" (Moroni 6:4). Jacob added a sobering conclusion to the matter: Only those who have "perfect faith in the Holy One of Israel"—meaning, presumably, a wholehearted belief in, a complete trust in, and a total reliance upon his redeeming blood—can be saved in the kingdom of God (2 Nephi 9:23). Again, because we cannot save ourselves, our absolute dependence cannot be in ourselves, no matter how impressive our accomplishments; rather, it must be in Him who bought us with his blood. Like Jacob, we are redeemed "because of the righteousness of [our] Redeemer" (2 Nephi 2:3).

Faith is more than a tenet, more than a doctrine, more than a belief. *Lectures on Faith* states that faith is a principle of power, the power by which God and men bring to pass divine purposes (3–4, 72; see also Hebrews 11:3). When the former-day Saints, especially those in the Book of Mormon, operated by faith, they operated according to the mind and will of God. Faith is not merely the power of suggestion, the power of positive thinking. The faithful, though filled with hope in Christ, are not just more optimistic than the world. People do not exercise faith by wishing and willing something to be. Men and women operate by faith when they seek to know the mind of God on a matter and then proceed confidently; they first obtain their "errand from the Lord" (Jacob 1:17) and then move forward with a quiet but dynamic assurance that God will work his wonders through them.

True faith always manifests itself in faithfulness, in sustained obedience and endurance to the end (1 Nephi 7:12; Alma 44:4; 48:15). The risen Lord declared that "no unclean thing can enter into [God's] kingdom; therefore nothing entereth into his rest save it be those who have washed their garments in my blood, because of their faith, and the repentance of all their sins, and their faithfulness unto the end" (3 Nephi 27:19). The missionary Ammon pointed out that "he that repenteth and exerciseth faith, and bringeth forth good works, and prayeth continually without ceasing—unto such it is given to know the mysteries of God" (Alma 26:22).

Some have supposed that faith and knowledge are on opposite ends of a continuum—that once they have knowledge, they no longer have or need faith. Actually, faith and knowledge build upon one another. A certain degree of knowledge is necessary in order to exercise faith, even "a particle of faith" (Alma 32:27). Then, after one has begun to develop faith, new and added knowledge comes—new insights, new perspectives, new feelings, new desires. There is a sense in which one might speak, as Alma did to the Zoramites, of one's faith being replaced by knowledge whenever a testimony of a particular principle has been obtained (Alma 32:34; Ether 3:19). In reality, however, faith has not disappeared but instead has been added upon.

Faith is a principle of power and thus a divine attribute possessed by God in perfection. God is the embodiment of faith, just as he is the embodiment of love and justice and judgment and mercy (*Lectures,* 3–4, 72). And so we are not working toward that day when we will no longer live and act by faith but rather toward that day, beyond the resurrection, when we will operate by perfect faith. "In the eternal sense," Elder Bruce R. McConkie wrote, "because faith is the power of God himself, it embraces within its fold a knowledge of all things. This measure of faith, the faith by which the worlds are and were created and which sustains and upholds all things, is found only among resurrected persons. It is the faith of saved beings" (209).

The final great fruit of faith is eternal life. In the first estate we walked by sight and by faith. Those who were valiant in the premortal existence demonstrated "exceeding faith and good works" there and were foreordained and appointed to significant assignments here (Alma 13:3). In this life we walk by faith (2 Corinthians 5:7). That is, we proceed through life with the Spirit-given assurance that our actions are approved of God and will result in the salvation of our souls. To see with an "eye of faith" (Alma 5:15; 32:40) is thus to act according to the witness of the Spirit, to act as though we had seen and thus had perfect knowledge. The Saints of God view things with an eye of faith in this life until one day, because of their faithful endurance, they see "with their eyes the things which they had beheld with an eye of faith" (Ether 12:19).

"The very name of the kind of life [God] lives is eternal life, and thus eternal life consists in living and being as he is. In other words, eternal life is to gain the power of God, which power is faith, and thus to be able to do what he does and to live as he lives. And the great and eternal plan of salvation that he has ordained and established consists of those laws, ordinances, and powers whereby faith is acquired and perfected until it is possessed in the same degree and to the same extent that it exists in Deity. Faith will thus dwell independently in every person who gains eternal life" (McConkie, 169).

The *Lectures on Faith* state that "when men begin to live by faith they begin to draw near to God; and when faith is perfected they are like him; and because he is saved they are saved also; for they will be in the same situation he is in, because they have come to him; and when he appears they shall be like him, for they will see him as he is" (74). In this sense, the plan of salvation is "a system of faith—it begins with faith, and continues by faith; and every blessing which is obtained in relation to it is the effect of faith, whether it pertains to this life or that which is to come. To this all the revelations of God bear witness" (80).

Alma taught that if we will nourish the word—especially the proposition concerning the redemptive reality of Jesus the Christ—the fruits of faith will be forthcoming in our lives and the seed of faith in Christ "shall take root; and behold it shall be a tree springing up unto everlasting life. And because of your diligence and your faith and your patience with the word in nourishing it, that it may take root in you, behold, by and by ye shall pluck the fruit thereof, which is most precious, which is sweet above all that is sweet, and which is white above all that is white, yea, and pure above all that is pure; and ye shall feast upon this fruit even until ye are filled, that ye hunger not, neither shall ye thirst" (Alma 32:41–42).

SOURCES

Lectures on Faith. Salt Lake City: Deseret Book, 1985.

McConkie, Bruce R. *A New Witness for the Articles of Faith.* Salt Lake City: Deseret Book, 1985.

RLM

FALL

Latter-day Saints believe that Adam and Eve went into the Garden of Eden to fall, that what they did had the approbation of God and was thus a transgression (a "going across") and not a sin, and that their fall was as much a part of the foreordained plan of the Father as was the Atonement. We believe in the words of the Prophet Joseph Smith that "Adam was made to open the way of the world" (1:282). Although the Fall was a move downward, it was a move forward in the eternal scheme of things because it "brought man into the world and set his feet upon progression's highway" (Cowley, 287).

To fail to teach the Fall is to lessen our understanding of the importance of the Atonement. President Ezra Taft Benson observed: "Just as a man does not really desire food until he is hungry, so he does not desire the salvation of Christ until he knows why he needs Christ. No one adequately and properly knows why he needs Christ until he understands and accepts the doctrine of the Fall and its effect upon all mankind" (33).

The Fall and the Atonement are a package deal: the one creates the need for the other. We do not appreciate and treasure the medicine until we appreciate the seriousness of the malady. We cannot look earnestly and longingly to the Redeemer if we do not sense the need for redemption. Jesus came to earth to do more than offer sage advice. He is not merely a benevolent consultant or a spiritual adviser. He is our Savior. He came to save us. The following are a few of the principles that may be learned from scripture regarding the effects of the Fall and the nature of fallen humanity:

1. *All mankind are lost and fallen.* In what seems to be the first reference in the Book of Mormon to the Fall, Nephi taught that "six hundred years from the time that my father left Jerusalem, a prophet would the Lord God raise up among the Jews—even a Messiah, or, in other words, a Savior of the world. And he [Lehi] also spake concerning the prophets, how great a number had testified of these things, concerning this Messiah, . . . or this Redeemer of the world. Wherefore, all mankind were in a lost and in a fallen state, and ever would be save they should rely on this Redeemer" (1 Nephi 10:4–6; see also Alma 42:6).

Note carefully those two words so descriptive of mortals—*lost* and *fallen.* Truly, as Isaiah declared (and Abinadi quoted), "All we, like sheep, have gone astray; we have turned every one to his own way" (Isaiah 53:6; Mosiah 14:6). The Good Shepherd comes on a search-and-rescue mission after all of his lost sheep. He who never took a moral detour or a backward step reaches out and reaches down to lift us up. We are lost in that we do not know our way home without a guide, in that we are alienated from God and separated from things of righteousness. We are fallen in that we have chosen, like our Exemplar, to condescend to enter a telestial tenement. Because our eternal spirit has taken up its temporary abode in a tabernacle of clay, we must be lifted up, quickened, and resuscitated spiritually if we are to return to the divine presence.

Individuals are lost and fallen in that they are subject to spiritual death, which is the separation from God (Alma 42:7, 9) and the separation from the things of righteousness (Alma 12:6, 32; 40:26). Alma explained to his son Corianton that after they partook of the forbidden fruit, our first parents were "cut off from the tree of life" and thereby "became lost forever, yea, they became fallen man. And now, we see by this that our first parents were cut off both temporally and spiritually from the presence of the Lord; and thus we see they became subjects to follow after their own will." Alma pointed out that inasmuch as "the fall had brought upon all mankind a spiritual death as well as a temporal, that is, they were cut off from the presence of the Lord, it was expedient that mankind should be reclaimed from this spiritual death. Therefore, as they had become carnal, sensual, and devilish, by nature, this probationary state became a state for them to prepare; it became a preparatory state" (Alma 42:6–7, 9–10).

2. *We inherit a fallen nature through our conception into mortality.* God spoke to Father Adam in the dawn of history: "Inasmuch as thy children are conceived in sin, even so when they begin to grow up, sin conceiveth in their hearts, and they taste the bitter, that they may know to prize the good" (Moses 6:55). To say that we are not responsible for the fall of Adam and Eve is not to say that we are unaffected by it. To say that we do not inherit an original sin through the Fall is not to say that we do not inherit a fallen nature and thus the capacity to sin. Fallenness and mortality are inherited. They come to us as a natural consequence of the second estate we call earth life.

Lehi explained to Jacob that after the Fall, "the days of the children of men were prolonged, according to the will of God, that they might repent while in the flesh; wherefore, their state became a state of probation, and their time was lengthened, according to the commandments which the Lord God gave unto the children of men. For he gave commandment that all men must repent; for he showed unto all men that they were lost, because of the transgression of their parents" (2 Nephi 2:21).

Abinadi likewise explained to the priests of Noah that yielding to Lucifer's temptation in the Garden of Eden "was the cause of [Adam and Eve's] fall; which was the cause of all mankind becoming carnal, sensual, devilish, knowing evil from good, subjecting themselves to the devil. Thus, all mankind were lost; and behold, they would have been endlessly lost were it not that God redeemed his people from their lost and fallen state." Continuing, Abinadi points out that a fallen nature is not just something we descend into through personal sin but something out of which we must be extracted through divine regenerating powers: "Remember that he that persists in his own carnal nature, and goes on in the ways of sin and rebellion against God, remaineth in his fallen state and the devil hath all power over him. Therefore he is as though there was no redemption made, being an enemy to God" (Mosiah 16:3–5).

3. *We may be faithful and pure hearted and yet still be buffeted by the pulls of a fallen world.* There is a difference between the natural man and the spiritual man who is taunted by the natural world in which he lives. Perhaps there is no better illustration of this in scripture than Nephi, son of Lehi. He was a man who was obedient and submissive, a man who was led and empowered by the Spirit of Almighty God: "My heart pondereth continually upon the things which I have seen and heard." Now note the words that follow, words spoken by a man who was surely as pure and virtuous as anyone we know: "Nevertheless, notwithstanding the great goodness of the Lord, in showing me his great and marvelous works, my heart exclaimeth: O wretched man that I am! Yea, my heart sorroweth because of my flesh; my soul grieveth because of mine iniquities. I am encompassed about, because of the temptations and the sins which do so easily beset me. And when I desire to rejoice, my heart groaneth because of my sins" (2 Nephi 4:16–19).

The people of Benjamin were described by their great king as "a diligent people in keeping the commandments of the Lord" (Mosiah 1:11). We suppose that they were followers of our Lord and Savior, people who had come out of the world by covenant. King Benjamin delivered to his people one of the most significant addresses in all the Book of Mormon. He announced his retirement and his son Mosiah as his successor. He gave an accounting of his reign and ministry, encouraged the people to serve one another and thereby serve God, and counseled them (in the words of an angel) to put off the natural man and put on Christ through the Atonement. The people were electrified by the power of the message. Benjamin "cast his eyes round about on the multitude, and behold they had fallen to the earth, for the fear of the Lord had come upon them. And they had viewed themselves in their own carnal state, even less than the dust of the earth" (Mosiah 4:1–2). They cried unto the Lord for forgiveness and deliverance. They were a noble people, a diligent people who viewed themselves in their own carnal state.

The brother of Jared went to the top of Mount Shelem with sixteen transparent stones, eager to have the Lord touch them and thereby light his people's barges. He presented the stones to the Lord and prayed: "O Lord, thou hast said that we must be encompassed about by the floods. Now behold, O Lord, and do not be angry with thy servant because of his weakness before thee; for we know that thou art holy and dwellest in the heavens, and that we are unworthy before thee; because *of the fall our natures have become evil continually*" (Ether 3:2; emphasis added). Then he called upon God for divine assistance.

We can grow in spiritual graces to the point "that we have no more disposition to do evil, but to do good continually" (Mosiah 5:2) and that we cannot look upon sin save it be with abhorrence (Alma 13:12; 2 Nephi 9:49; Jacob 2:5). We can, like Nephi, delight in the things of the Lord (2 Nephi 4:16). But as long as we dwell in the flesh, we will be subject to the pulls of a fallen world.

"Will sin be perfectly destroyed?" President Brigham Young asked. "No, it will not, for it is not so designed in the economy of Heaven. . . . Do not suppose that we shall ever in the flesh be free from temptations to sin. Some suppose that they can in the flesh be sanctified body and spirit and become so pure that they will never again feel the effects of the power of the adversary of truth. Were it possible for a person to attain to this degree of perfection in the flesh, he could not die neither remain in a world where sin predominates. . . . I think we shall more or less feel the effects of sin so long as we live, and finally have to pass the ordeals of death" (10:173).

4. *Little children are innocent by virtue of the Atonement, not by nature.* Little children are innocent as one of the unconditional blessings of the Atonement because Jesus Christ decreed them so (Mosiah 3:16; Moroni 8:10, 12, 22; D&C 29:46; 74:7).

5. *The natural man is an enemy to God and to all righteousness.* "There is a natural birth, and there is a spiritual birth," Elder Bruce R. McConkie wrote. "The natural birth is to die as pertaining to premortal life, to leave the heavenly realms where all spirits dwell in the

Divine Presence, and to begin a new life, a mortal life, a life here on earth. The natural birth creates a natural man, and the natural man is an enemy to God. In his fallen state he is carnal, sensual, and devilish by nature. Appetites and passions govern his life, and he is alive— acutely so—to all that is evil and wicked in the world" (282).

The angel explained to King Benjamin that "men drink damnation to their own souls except they humble themselves and become as little children, and believe that salvation was, and is, and is to come, in and through the atoning blood of Christ, the Lord Omnipotent. For the natural man is an enemy to God, and has been from the fall of Adam, and will be, forever and ever, unless he yields to the enticings of the Holy Spirit, and putteth off the natural man and becometh a saint through the atonement of Christ the Lord" (Mosiah 3:18–19; see also 1 Corinthians 2:11–14).

The Latter-day Saint view of man—his nature and destiny—is remarkably optimistic. We are the sons and daughters of God Almighty; we are his spirit offspring (Numbers 16:22; 27:16; Hebrews 12:9). We have the capacity through drawing upon the powers of the Atonement to grow in spiritual graces and in Christlike attributes so as to be "partakers of the divine nature" (2 Peter 1:4). But despite our divine heritage, despite our spiritual potentialities, we cannot save ourselves. We cannot forgive our own sins, cleanse our souls, renew our hearts, raise ourselves from the dead, or prepare a heavenly mansion on our own. Elder Dallin H. Oaks observed: "Man unquestionably has impressive powers and can bring to pass great things by tireless efforts and indomitable will. But after all our obedience and good works, we cannot be saved from the effect of our sins without the grace extended by the atonement of Jesus Christ" (67).

SOURCES

Benson, Ezra Taft. *A Witness and a Warning: A Modern-day Prophet Testifies of the Book of Mormon.* Salt Lake City: Deseret Book, 1988.

Cowley, Matthias, and Orson F. Whitney. *Cowley & Whitney on Doctrine.* Compiled by Forace Green. Salt Lake City: Bookcraft, 1963.

McConkie, Bruce R. *A New Witness for the Articles of Faith.* Salt Lake City: Deseret Book, 1985.

Oaks, Dallin H. "'What Think Ye of Christ?'" *Ensign,* Nov. 1988, 65–68.

Smith, Joseph. *History of The Church of Jesus Christ of Latter-day Saints.* Edited by B. H. Roberts. 7 vols. 2d ed. rev. Salt Lake City: The Church of Jesus Christ of Latter-day Saints, 1932–51.

Young, Brigham. In *Journal of Discourses.* 26 vols. London: Latter-day Saints' Book Depot, 1854–86.

RLM

FALSE CHRISTS

False Christs may be spiritual frauds, deceived or deceiving individuals who claim to be the Lord and Redeemer. Similarly, false Christs may be false systems of salvation. Satan provided the pattern for false Christs to follow, either by designing persons or by false systems of salvation. In premortality, he petitioned the Father, "Here am I, send me, I will be thy son, and I will redeem all mankind, that one soul shall not be lost" (Moses 4:1). He later appeared to Moses "and commanded, saying: I am the Only Begotten, worship me" (Moses 1:19). False Christs echo Satan's selfish and defaming voice, becoming expert in the practice of priestcraft, in that they "preach and set themselves up for a light unto the world, that they may get gain and praise of the world; but they seek not the welfare of Zion" (2 Nephi 26:29).

Leaders of the early Christian church knew of the existence of those who teach against Jesus Christ as though they could save us (1 John 2:18; 2 Peter 2:1). Shortly before his crucifixion, Jesus alerted his apostles to the deceptive powers of antichrists or false Christs who should come in their day as well as in the latter days: "For many shall come in my name, saying—I am Christ—and shall deceive many" (Joseph Smith–Matthew 1:6).

Likewise, Book of Mormon peoples knew of these dangers. Nephi warned us against false Christs, saying that we "need not look forward any more for a Messiah to come, for there should not any come, save it should be a false Messiah which should deceive the people; for there is save one Messiah spoken of by the prophets, and that Messiah is he who should be rejected of the Jews" (2 Nephi 25:18).

CFO

FAMILY

In the history of The Church of Jesus Christ of Latter-day Saints, the First Presidency and the Quorum of the Twelve Apostles have issued official proclamations to the world only a handful of times. On 23 September 1995, "The Family: A Proclamation to the World" was introduced by President Gordon B. Hinckley in a general Relief Society meeting. This monumental proclamation outlines the Church's view on the eternal significance of families. It declares that "the family is central to the Creator's plan for the eternal destiny of His children" (102). Latter-day Saints have a unique understanding of how "the family is ordained of God" because of our belief that we lived in a family setting as spirits before we came to earth, that the family is the basic unit of society on earth, that at death the righteous will also be organized by families in the post-earth spirit world, and that family relationships will continue for those resurrected and exalted in God's celestial kingdom.

Before we were born on earth, we lived in the family of God, where we were taught, reared, and nurtured by Heavenly Parents (First Presidency, "Origin," 26). We observed and were part of a celestial family—seeing how perfect parents love and nurture their beloved children. We understood that the plan of salvation provided the means whereby we could be united as families throughout all eternity in a state of perfect happiness and joy.

To help our Heavenly Father's children learn, progress, and be responsible and happy in this life, God has given to all parents "a sacred duty to rear their children in love and righteousness, to provide for their physical and spiritual needs, to teach them to love and serve one another, to observe the commandments of God and to be law-abiding citizens wherever they live. Husbands and wives—fathers and mothers—will be held accountable before God for the discharge of these obligations" (First Presidency, "Family," 102). In addition to biblical teachings concerning families, Latter-day Saints look to scriptural injunctions in the Book of Mormon and the Doctrine and Covenants that explicitly command parents to raise their children in righteousness and to make their homes places of love and respect, where the Spirit of the Lord abides (Mosiah 4:14–15; 3 Nephi 18:21; D&C 68:25–27; 93:47–50).

Leaders of the Church from the days of the Prophet Joseph Smith to the present have unequivocally taught of the eternal significance of the family and the sacred role of parents. "No other success can compensate for failure in the home" was a maxim often cited by President David O. McKay (116). Likewise, President Harold B. Lee often taught Church members that "the most important of the Lord's work you will ever do will be within the walls of your own homes" (280). It is because of these prophetic admonitions—ancient and modern— coupled with the knowledge that families are indeed intended to be eternal, that Latter-day Saints place so much emphasis on strengthening family relationships. We believe that what we do in our homes here will affect our progress and family relationships in the hereafter. President Joseph F. Smith taught:

"The very foundation of the kingdom of God, of righteousness, of progress, of development, of eternal life and eternal increase in the kingdom of God, is laid in the divinely ordained home; and there should be no difficulty in holding in the highest reverence and exalted thought, the home, if it can be built upon the principles of purity, of true affection, of righteousness and justice. The man and his wife who have perfect confidence in each other, and who determine to follow the laws of God in their lives and fulfill the measure of their mission in the earth, would not be, and could never be, contented without the home. Their hearts, their feelings, their minds, their desires would naturally trend toward the building of a home and family and of a kingdom of their own; to the laying of the foundation of eternal increase and power, glory, exaltation and dominion, worlds without end" (304).

Latter-day Saints believe that after death, the spirit of a deceased righteous person enters a postmortal spirit world, where there is a reunion with other departed loved ones. One of the distinguishing characteristics of this realm is the continuation of family relationships. "These righteous spirits are close by us," taught President Ezra Taft Benson. "They are organized according to priesthood order in family organizations as we are here; only there they exist in a more perfect order. This was revealed to the Prophet Joseph" (35–36).

With regard to family relationships after the resurrection, the Lord has revealed that righteous men and women who enter into the new and everlasting covenant of marriage and are true and faithful to that covenant will be able, after they are resurrected to celestial glory, to live in an eternal family unit (D&C 131:1–4; 132:19). In this manner, the eternal family comes full circle—premortal spirit sons and daughters organized in a heavenly family, born and reared in earthly homes, reunited with and organized by families in the postmortal spirit world, and, if true to their covenants, resurrected to celestial glory, sealed to their earthly family, and endowed with power to create an eternal family unit. Thus, as Elder Bruce R. McConkie taught:

"Salvation is a family affair. . . . It is written that neither is the man without the woman nor the woman without the man in the Lord [1 Corinthians 11:11]. In the perfected church family it might also be said that neither are the parents without the children nor the children without the parents in the Lord's type of family.

"The true gospel is family centered. Full salvation consists of the continuation of the family unit in celestial glory. Those for whom the family unit continues have eternal life; those for whom it does not continue do not have eternal life, for heaven itself is but the projection of a [righteous] family into eternity.

"That power by which salvation comes is so great that it can make of earth a heaven, and of man, a god.

"The noblest concept that can enter the heart of man is the concept that the family unit continues in eternity, and that salvation is a family affair" (26, 27–28).

SOURCES

Benson, Ezra Taft. *The Teachings of Ezra Taft Benson.* Salt Lake City: Bookcraft, 1988.

First Presidency. "The Origin of Man." *Improvement Era,* Nov. 1909, 75–81; or *Ensign,* Feb. 2002, 26–30.

First Presidency and Council of the Twelve Apostles. "The Family: A Proclamation to the World." *Ensign,* Nov. 1995, 102.

Lee, Harold B. *The Teachings of Harold B. Lee.* Edited by Clyde J. Williams. Salt Lake City: Bookcraft, 1996.

McConkie, Bruce R. In Conference Report, Apr. 1970, 26–28.

McKay, David O. In Conference Report, Apr. 1935, 110–16, quoting J. E. McCulloch, *Home: The Savior of Civilization,* 42. Washington, D.C.: Southern Co-Operative League, 1924.

Smith, Joseph F. *Gospel Doctrine.* Salt Lake City: Deseret Book, 1939.

BLT

FATHER IN HEAVEN

Standing outside the empty tomb, the resurrected Christ declared to Mary Magdalene, "I ascend unto my Father, and your Father; and to my God, and your God" (John 20:17). On several other occasions, Jesus taught that his Father in Heaven is likewise our Father in Heaven. In the Sermon on the Mount, Jesus taught the disciples that "if ye forgive men . . . , *your* heavenly Father will also forgive you" (Matthew 6:14; emphasis added) and charged them to "be ye therefore perfect, even as *your* Father which is in heaven is perfect" (Matthew 5:48; emphasis added). Teaching the power and pattern of prayer, the Savior taught that "*thy* Father which seeth in secret himself shall reward thee openly" (Matthew 6:4; emphasis added) and that "*your* Father knoweth what things ye have need of, before ye ask him" (Matthew 6:8; emphasis added). The Lord's Prayer likewise teaches that God the Almighty—the divine, eternal Father of Jesus Christ—is to be addressed in prayer simply as "*our* Father" (Matthew 6:9; emphasis added).

Numerous other passages in the Bible and the Book of Mormon also speak of God as Father in Heaven (Psalm 82:6; Ephesians 1:3; 4:6; Colossians 1:19; Hebrews 12:9; 1 Nephi 11:21; Mosiah 2:34; Mormon 6:22). While much of the world may think of God as the universal Father because he is the Creator, Latter-day Saints believe that God is literally the father of all humankind. The First Presidency and Quorum of the Twelve Apostles have declared: "All human beings—male and female—are created in the image of God. Each is a beloved spirit son or daughter of heavenly parents. . . . In the premortal realm, spirit sons and daughters knew and worshipped God as their Eternal Father" (102). To Latter-day Saints, the phrases "fatherhood of God" and "brotherhood of man" and the Lord's admonition to "pray to thy Father" are taken literally because of that premortal relationship. President Brigham Young emphatically taught: "I want to tell you, each and every one of you, that you are all well acquainted with God our heavenly Father, or the great Eloheim. You are well acquainted with Him, for there is not a soul of you but what has lived in His house and dwelt with Him year after year. . . . There is not a person here to-day but what is a son or a daughter of that Being. In the spirit world their spirits were first begotten and brought forth, and they lived there with their parents for ages before they came here. This, perhaps, is hard for many to believe, but it is the greatest nonsense in the world not to believe it. If you do not believe it, cease to call Him Father; and when you pray, pray to some other character" (4:216).

SOURCES

First Presidency and Council of the Twelve Apostles. "The Family: A Proclamation to the World." *Ensign,* Nov. 1995, 102.

Young, Brigham. In *Journal of Discourses*. 26 vols. London: Latter-day Saints' Book Depot, 1854–86.

BLT

FATHER OF LIGHTS

The apostle James uses the phrase "Father of lights" as a summary of all the godly attributes and characteristics possessed by God the Father in their fulness, qualities that we may receive as his children. "Every good gift and every perfect gift is from above, and cometh down from the *Father of lights,* with whom is no variableness, neither shadow of turning" (James 1:17; emphasis added). "God is light, and in him is no darkness at all" (1 John 1:5). Light may be understood as enlightenment, knowledge, intelligence, glory, and power. The apostle Paul spoke of "the light of the knowledge of the glory of God" (2 Corinthians 4:6). Light is another way of describing God's omnipotence, omniscience, and omnipresence.

What is said of God the Father is also true of his Beloved Son. Jesus Christ testified that "he that hath seen me hath seen the Father. . . . I am in the Father, and the Father in me" (John 14:9–10). Thus, Jesus is legitimately and in every way "the light of the world" (John 8:12). Just as important, those who accept and live the gospel of Jesus Christ are "called . . . out of darkness into his marvellous light" (1 Peter 2:9). Then, if we, God's children, become focused wholly on God's work and glory (Moses 1:39), ultimately our whole body will be filled with light and no darkness will dwell in us. "That body which is filled with light comprehendeth all things" (D&C 88:67). This is another way of saying that all who are focused singly on God will become as he is.

ACS

FEAR OF GOD

The phrases "fear of God" and "fear of the Lord" mean having respect for, reverence for, or awe toward God and sacred things. In its most common usage, *fear* is defined as a feeling of anxiety, agitation, or apprehension caused by the presence or nearness of danger, pain, or the like. Fear in this sense is incompatible with faith, as Jesus taught

(Mark 4:40). On the other hand, "fear of God" or "fear of the Lord" is an attitude of profound respect mingled with love directed toward the Supreme Being. Rather than competing with faith or diminishing it, such an attitude complements and increases our faith.

Thus, the "fear of the Lord is the beginning of knowledge" (Proverbs 1:7). When we exhibit fear of God, we are on the path leading to perfection. As indicated by the proverb, we are then capable of progressing, step by step, to that state or stage of knowledge that is a precursor to exaltation. "And beside this," the apostle Peter said, "giving all diligence, add to your faith virtue; and to virtue knowledge; and to knowledge temperance; and to temperance patience; and to patience godliness; and to godliness brotherly kindness; and to brotherly kindness charity. For if these things be in you, and abound, they make you that ye shall neither be barren nor unfruitful in the knowledge of our Lord Jesus Christ. . . . Wherefore . . . , give diligence to make your calling and election sure" (2 Peter 1:5–8, 10).

All of these things begin with and flow from the fear of God. Fear of God increases our ability to trust him (Psalm 115:11; Proverbs 14:26). Abraham's willingness to sacrifice his son Isaac came from, and was a manifestation of, his fear of God. The angel said to him, "For now I know that thou fearest God" (Genesis 22:12). And Abraham's willingness to serve God "at all hazards," not even withholding his son, allowed God to bless him with exaltation (Smith, 3:380). When the apostle Paul tells the Saints to work out their own salvation with fear and trembling, he is really teaching true disciples to cultivate the profound respect, awe, and love for God that ultimately lead to exaltation as a natural course (Philippians 2:12; Mormon 9:27). The prophet Isaiah points out the mutually reinforcing blessings and gifts associated with the fear of the Lord (Isaiah 11:2–5).

It is now easier to see why the author of Ecclesiastes designated the fear of God as "the whole duty of man" (Ecclesiastes 12:13). God's mercy is upon those who fear him, as Mary, the mother of Jesus, expressed in her psalm of praise, sometimes called the *Magnificat* (Luke 1:50). Conversely, when the fear of God is absent from individuals' lives, their minds become darkened and they treat lightly sacred things (D&C 84:54).

SOURCE

Smith, Joseph. *History of The Church of Jesus Christ of Latter-day Saints.* Edited by
   B. H. Roberts. 7 vols. 2d ed. rev. Salt Lake City: The Church of Jesus Christ of
   Latter-day Saints, 1932–51.

ACS

FIRE AND BRIMSTONE

The scriptures frequently speak of the suffering of the wicked
in hell as eternal burning in a lake of fire and brimstone (Revelation
14:10; 19:20; 2 Nephi 9:16; 28:23; Jacob 3:11; Mosiah 3:27; Alma
12:17; D&C 63:17; 76:36). This is, to be sure, a graphic and sobering
description, but it is symbolic. "A man is his own tormenter and his
own condemner," the Prophet Joseph Smith stated. "Hence the saying, They shall go into the lake that burns with fire and brimstone.
The torment of disappointment in the mind of man is as exquisite
as a lake burning with fire and brimstone. I say, so is the torment of
man" (6:314). Most all suffering of this kind will take place in hell,
within the postmortal spirit world. When the price of suffering has
been paid, the uttermost farthing rendered, the disembodied spirit will
be released from suffering to participate in the last resurrection and be
assigned to a kingdom of glory. Only the sons of perdition, those who
sinned against the Holy Ghost, who denied and defied the light of the
Son, will suffer in hell or outer darkness eternally (D&C 76:44–48).
The Prophet Joseph taught that "those who sin against the Holy Ghost
cannot be forgiven in this world or in the world to come [Matthew
12:31–32]; they shall die the second death. Those who commit the unpardonable sin are doomed to *Gnolom*—to dwell in hell, worlds without end" (6:317).

SOURCE

Smith, Joseph. *History of The Church of Jesus Christ of Latter-day Saints.* Edited by
   B. H. Roberts. 7 vols. 2d ed. rev. Salt Lake City: The Church of Jesus Christ of
   Latter-day Saints, 1932–51.

RLM

FIRST ESTATE

An estate is an abode or place of habitation or condition (Ecclesiastes 3:16; Ezekiel 16:55). The premortal existence is referred to as

the first estate. Abraham, having seen the premortal spirits in vision, learned of the first and second estates (Abraham 3:26). Those spirits who rebelled against God and who were expelled from the premortal realm, including Perdition himself, "kept not their first estate" (Jude 1:6; see also Abraham 3:26, 28). In contrast, Abraham learned that those who remain faithful in the premortal world "keep their first estate." He further learned that those who "keep their second estate"—meaning they are faithful, obedient, and repentant during their probationary period on earth—"shall have glory added upon their heads for ever and ever" (Abraham 3:26). The first estate is thus the premortal probationary period, while the second estate is one's mortal life on earth.

BLT

FIRST FLESH

"And I, the Lord God, formed man from the dust of the ground, and breathed into his nostrils the breath of life; and man became a living soul, the first flesh upon the earth, the first man also" (Moses 3:7). Man was not the first living thing on earth, for both ancient and modern scripture attest that plants and animals preceded him in the Creation. But Adam was in fact the first *mortal flesh,* the first natural flesh, the first (with Eve) to partake of the forbidden fruit and fall.

RLM

FIRST VISION

God the Eternal Father and his Son, the Lord Jesus Christ, appeared to Joseph Smith in a grove of trees in upstate New York in the spring of 1820. This is what Latter-day Saints refer to as the First Vision. Camp meetings and revivals were held throughout what came to be known as the "Burned-over District" because of the large number of religious revivals that swept over the area; there are more reports of revivals in upstate and western New York in 1819 and 1820 than in any other section of the country. At the time of the First Vision only about 11 percent of the people in the nation and in the immediate vicinity where Joseph Smith lived were members of a Christian organization. But in his 1838 account of the First Vision (in the Pearl of Great Price), the Prophet stated that great multitudes were joining churches not just in Palmyra but rather in the whole region or district or country (Joseph Smith–History 1:5). Methodism was the fastest growing religion in America at the time; the Methodists held more camp meetings than any other group.

Lessons that can be learned from the First Vision include the following:

1. *The power of pondering.* One tradition holds that young Joseph Smith heard the Reverend George Lane encourage the seekers to "ask of God" and that James 1:5–6 was a part of some of his sermons (Madsen, 8; McConkie, 5). There may be no more instructive statement about the power of pondering than that contained in the Prophet's words: "I was one day reading the Epistle of James, first chapter and fifth verse, which reads: 'If any of you lack wisdom, let him ask of God, that giveth to all men liberally, and upbraideth not; and it shall be given him.' Never did any passage of scripture come with more power to the heart of man than this did at this time to mine. It seemed to enter with great force into every feeling of my heart. I reflected on it again and again, knowing that if any person needed wisdom from God, I did; for how to act I did not know, and unless I could get more wisdom than I then had, I would never know" (Joseph Smith–History 1:11–12).

Joseph had confidence in the word of God, so this was no superficial inquiry. He obviously had been taught by his parents that holy writ has eternal relevance. Young Joseph took an idea, a phrase written sometime around A.D. 50, and likened it to himself. He appropriately wrenched James's words from their original New Testament context and sensed that they had specific reference and application to a farm boy in 1820 in upstate New York. "The Spirit of God rested mightily upon him. Not even Enoch and Abraham and Moses and the ancient prophets had been empowered by such yearnings for truth and salvation as then filled Joseph's soul. As guided from on high, he retired to the place before appointed by the Lord of heaven and there began to offer up to God the desires of his heart" (McConkie, 5).

2. *The reality of Satan.* There was a vital truth to be learned by Joseph Smith early in his prophetic training—a painful and poignant truth but one that he would need to understand clearly: the reality of Satan and of his eternal hatred for God and his plan of salvation. It was as though the father of lies sensed that he needed to act quickly to

confront Joseph Smith directly, to nip his inquiry in the bud, to frustrate and even stop the marvelous work and a wonder before it had a chance to get off the ground. Joseph explained that after he had knelt in the grove to offer up the yearnings of his soul, he "was seized upon by some power which entirely overcame me, and had such an astonishing influence over me as to bind my tongue so that I could not speak. Thick darkness gathered around me, and it seemed to me for a time as if I were doomed to sudden destruction" (Joseph Smith–History 1:15).

We have four accounts of the First Vision that Joseph dictated: an 1832 account, an 1835 account, an 1838 account, and the 1842 account found in the Wentworth Letter. In his 1835 account of the First Vision, the Prophet related: "Information was what I most desired at this time, and with a fixed determination to obtain it, I called on the Lord for the first time in the place above stated, or in other words, I made a fruitless attempt to pray. My tongue seemed to be swollen in my mouth, so that I could not utter. I heard a noise behind me like someone walking towards me. I strove again to pray, but could not; the noise of walking seemed to draw nearer. I sprang upon my feet and looked around, but saw no person or thing that was calculated to produce the noise of walking. I kneeled again. My mouth was opened and my tongue loosed; I called on the Lord in mighty prayer. A pillar of fire appeared above my head, which presently rested down upon me and filled me with unspeakable joy. A personage appeared in the midst of this pillar of flame, which was spread all around and yet nothing consumed. Another personage soon appeared like unto the first. He said unto me, 'Thy sins are forgiven thee.' He testified also unto me that Jesus Christ is the Son of God. I saw many angels in this vision. I was about 14 years old when I received this first communication" (in Backman, *First*, 159).

3. *The greater power of God.* Joseph became aware at an early age of the power of the Arch-Deceiver—an "actual being from the unseen world, who had such marvelous power as I had never before felt in any being" (Joseph Smith–History 1:16)—but he also learned firsthand that the power of God Almighty is greater. He is the Omnipotent One, "the God of glory" (Moses 1:20).

In what was actually the first published account of the First Vision, in Scotland in 1840, Elder Orson Pratt described the First Vision as follows: "And while thus pouring out his soul, anxiously desiring an answer from God, he at length saw a very bright and glorious light in the heavens above, which, at first, seemed to be a considerable distance. He continued praying, while the light appeared to be gradually descending towards him; and as it drew nearer, it increased in brightness and magnitude, so that, by the time that it reached the tops of the trees, the whole wilderness, for some distance around, was illuminated in a most glorious and brilliant manner. He expected to have seen the leaves and boughs of the trees consumed as soon as the light came in contact with them; but perceiving that it did not produce that effect, he was encouraged with the hope of being able to endure its presence" (in Backman, *First,* 172). In the 1842 Wentworth Letter, Joseph pointed out that "while fervently engaged in supplication, my mind was taken away from the objects with which I was surrounded, and I was enwrapped in a heavenly vision and saw two glorious personages who exactly resembled each other in features and likeness, surrounded with a brilliant light which eclipsed the sun at noonday" (in Backman, *First,* 169).

We Latter-day Saints tend to emphasize our distinctive belief in God's physical or corporeal nature (how God is like man), but we must never forget that he whom we worship is also an exalted, glorified Being possessing a divine nature—unlike man's physical body. Moses wrote that "the sight of the glory of the Lord was like devouring fire on the top of the mount in the eyes of the children of Israel" (Exodus 24:17). Similarly, in speaking through Isaiah, Jehovah asked: "Who among us shall dwell with the devouring fire? who among us shall dwell with everlasting burnings?" (Isaiah 33:14). In his vision of the celestial kingdom, received in January 1836, Joseph Smith said, "I saw the transcendent beauty of the gate through which the heirs of that [celestial] kingdom will enter, which was like unto circling flames of fire; also the blazing throne of God, whereon was seated the Father and the Son" (D&C 137:2–3).

4. *Redemption through Jesus Christ.* Joseph Smith also learned first-hand of the life beyond and of the immortality of the soul. Early in his ministry he became a witness of the Resurrection, for before him stood the resurrected Lord Jesus, attesting that indeed life did continue beyond the grave and that immortality does come through the

inseparable union of body and spirit. In fact, according to the earliest account of the First Vision in 1832, the testimony of Jesus and the efficacy of his redeeming labor were among the first things Joseph was taught.

"I cried unto the Lord for mercy," he stated, "for there was none else to whom I could go and obtain mercy. And the Lord heard my cry in the wilderness, and while in the attitude of calling upon the Lord . . . a pillar of light above the brightness of the sun at noonday came down from above and rested upon me, and I was filled with the Spirit of God. And the Lord opened the heavens upon me, and I saw the Lord, and he spake unto me, saying, 'Joseph, my son, thy sins are forgiven thee. Go thy way, walk in my statutes, and keep my commandments. Behold, I am the Lord of glory. I was crucified for the world, that all those who believe on my name may have eternal life. . . . ' My soul was filled with love, and for many days I could rejoice with great joy and the Lord was with me" (in Backman, *First,* 157).

5. *The nature of the Father and the Son.* Joseph Smith learned that the Father and the Son were separate and distinct personages, separate Gods, and thus that the creedal statements concerning a triune Deity were incorrect. While Unitarians believed that the first and second members of the Godhead were distinct beings, most Christians subscribed to the doctrine of the Trinity, meaning three beings in one. Only eleven days before his death, the Prophet declared, "I have always declared God to be a distinct personage, Jesus Christ a separate and distinct personage from God the Father, and that the Holy Ghost was a distinct personage and a Spirit: and these three constitute three distinct personages and three Gods" (6:474).

We are uncertain what the young prophet learned at the time of the First Vision relative to the corporeality or physical nature of God the Father. Joseph certainly may have been taught or recognized that God has a physical body, but he did not say so. On the other hand, note the following from Joseph Smith's translation of Genesis, now found in the sixth chapter of Moses (November–December 1830): "In the day that God created man, in the likeness of God made he him; *in the image of his own body, male and female, created he them,* and blessed them" (Moses 6:8–9; emphasis added). In 1836, the Reverend Truman Coe, a Presbyterian minister who had lived among the Saints in Kirtland for four years, wrote in a local newspaper of some of the beliefs of the Latter-day Saints. "They believe that the true God is a material being," he explained, "composed of body and parts; and that when the Creator formed Adam in his own image, he made him about the size and shape of God himself" (in Backman, "Truman," 354). William Clayton records that on 5 January 1841 the Prophet Joseph declared: "That which is without body and parts is nothing. There is no other God in heaven but that God who has flesh and bones" (*Words,* 60). On 9 March 1841 the Prophet spoke of the ministries of Jesus as the Mediator and the Holy Ghost as the Witness or Testator. He then stated that "the Son had a tabernacle and so had the Father" (*Words,* 64). Finally, on 2 April 1843 in Ramus, Illinois, Joseph the Prophet delivered instructions on this matter that are the basis for D&C 130:22: "The Father has a body of flesh and bones as tangible as man's; the Son also; but the Holy Ghost . . . is a personage of Spirit."

6. *Order in the kingdom of God.* The young prophet recorded that "just at this moment of great alarm, I saw a pillar of light exactly over my head, above the brightness of the sun, which descended gradually until it fell upon me. It no sooner appeared than I found myself delivered from the enemy which held me bound. When the light rested upon me I saw two Personages, whose brightness and glory defy all description, standing above me in the air. One of them spake unto me, calling me by name and said, pointing to the other—*This is My Beloved Son. Hear Him!*" (Joseph Smith–History 1:16–17).

There is order in the kingdom of God. Note that the Father introduced the Son. The King James Version of John 1:18 states, "No man hath seen God at any time; the only begotten Son, which is in the bosom of the Father, he hath declared him."

Under inspiration, Joseph the Seer altered that verse as follows: "And no man hath seen God at any time, *except he hath borne record of the Son;* for except it is through him no man can be saved" (JST, John 1:19, emphasis added; see also JST, Psalm 14:1; JST, 1 John 4:12).

"We have a wonderful illustration," President Joseph Fielding Smith taught, "of how revelation comes through Christ presented to us in the Vision given to the Prophet Joseph Smith. The Father and the Son appeared unto him, but it was not the Father who answered his question! The Father introduced Joseph to his Son, and it was the Son who answered the important question and gave the instruction.

"Had Joseph Smith come home from the grove and declared that the Father and the Son appeared to him and that the Father spoke to him and answered his question while the Son stood silently by, then we could have accepted the story as a fraud. Joseph Smith was too young and inexperienced to know this at the time, but he made no mistake, and his story was in perfect harmony with divine truth, with the divine law that Christ is the Mediator between God and man" (1:28).

7. The fulness of the gospel was not on the earth. Joseph Smith learned that the Church of Jesus Christ, as established by the Savior and his apostles in the meridian of time, had not continued during the centuries in its pristine purity. He was therefore instructed to join none of the churches in the area. "They told me that all religious denominations were believing in incorrect doctrines, and that none of them was acknowledged of God as his church and kingdom. And I was expressly commanded to 'go not after them,' at the same time receiving a promise that the fulness of the gospel should at some future time be made known unto me" (in Backman, *First,* 169; see also Smith, 4:536).

Joseph Smith's introduction to Jesus Christ came in the Sacred Grove in the spring of 1820. That monumental theophany reaffirmed the fundamental Christian teaching—that Jesus of Nazareth lived, died, was buried, and rose from the tomb in glorious immortality. In the midst of the light that shone above the brightness of the sun stood the resurrected Lord Jesus in company with his Father, the Almighty Elohim. Joseph knew from the time of the First Vision that death was not the end, that life continues after one's physical demise, that another realm of existence—a postmortal sphere—does in fact exist. Through open vision, by visitations, and by voice, Joseph Smith came to know his Lord as few men have ever known him. The revelations that came through the Prophet acquainted him with the mind and voice and will of the Master. Joseph came to know firsthand how to commune with Jehovah.

The First Vision is fundamental. It is foundational to the faith of Latter-day Saints. It represents the beginning of renewed revelation of God to man in this final dispensation. Elder Orson Pratt testified: "Now here was a certainty; here was something that he saw and heard;

here were personages capable of instructing him, and of telling him which was the true religion. How different this from going to an uninspired man . . . ! One minute's instruction from personages clothed with the glory of God coming down from the eternal worlds is worth more than all the volumes that ever were written by uninspired men" (12:354).

"Nothing short of this total vision to Joseph could have served the purpose to clear away the mists of the centuries," President Spencer W. Kimball attested. "Merely an impression, a hidden voice, a dream could [not] have dispelled the old vagaries and misconceptions. . . . The God of all these worlds and the Son of God, the Redeemer, our Savior, in person attended this boy. He saw the living God. He saw the living Christ" (430).

President Gordon B. Hinckley declared: "To me it is a significant and marvelous thing that in establishing and opening this dispensation our Father did so with a revelation of himself and of his Son Jesus Christ, as if to say to all the world that he was weary of the attempts of men, earnest though these attempts might have been, to define and describe him. . . . The experience of Joseph Smith, in a few moments in the grove on a spring day in 1820, brought more light and knowledge and understanding of the personality and reality and substance of God and his Beloved Son than men had arrived at during centuries of speculation" (236).

SOURCES

Backman, Milton V., Jr. *Joseph Smith's First Vision: Confirming Evidences and Contemporary Accounts.* 2d ed. Salt Lake City: Bookcraft, 1980. Spelling and punctuation standardized.

———. "Truman Coe's 1836 Description of Mormonism." *BYU Studies* 17, no. 3 (Spring 1977): 347–54.

Hinckley, Gordon B. *Teachings of Gordon B. Hinckley.* Salt Lake City: Deseret Book, 1997.

Kimball, Spencer W. *The Teachings of Spencer W. Kimball.* Edited by Edward L. Kimball. Salt Lake City: Deseret Book, 1982.

Madsen, Truman B. *Joseph Smith the Prophet.* Salt Lake City: Bookcraft, 1989.

McConkie, Bruce R. *A New Witness for the Articles of Faith.* Salt Lake City: Deseret Book, 1985.

Pratt, Orson. In *Journal of Discourses.* 26 vols. London: Latter-day Saints' Book Depot, 1854–86.

Smith, Joseph. *History of The Church of Jesus Christ of Latter-day Saints.* Edited by

B. H. Roberts. 7 vols. 2d ed. rev. Salt Lake City: The Church of Jesus Christ of Latter-day Saints, 1932–51.

Smith, Joseph Fielding. *Doctrines of Salvation*. Compiled by Bruce R. McConkie. 3 vols. Salt Lake City: Bookcraft, 1954–56.

The Words of Joseph Smith. Compiled and edited by Andrew F. Ehat and Lyndon W. Cook. Provo, Utah: Brigham Young University Religious Studies Center, 1980. Spelling and punctuation standardized.

RLM

FLATTERY

A form of manipulation to gain favor, followers, and success or to offer false hope, flattery is insincere speech or dishonest promises to compel or persuade others to believe and comply with our wishes. As the father of lies, Satan is the model of flattery, using it to deceive God's children into sin and denying the existence of the devil and hell (2 Nephi 28:22; D&C 10:25–26, 29).

The Book of Mormon contains multiple examples of antichrists and anarchists who used flattery and vain words to usurp power, inspire dissension, and offer false claims or false hopes to the people. Sherem hoped to shake the prophet Jacob through "much flattery . . . according to the power of the devil" (Jacob 7:4); many Nephites became idolatrous "because they were deceived by the vain and flattering words" of King Noah and his wicked priests (Mosiah 11:7); and Korihor led many "to lift up their heads in their wickedness" through his "lying and . . . flattering words" (Alma 30:18, 47). Conspiring to become king, Amalickiah became popular among the Nephites through flattery, telling them "that if they would support him and establish him to be their king that he would make them rulers over the people" (Alma 46:5). Before his repentance and conversion to Christ, Alma the son of Alma "was a man of many words, and did speak much flattery to the people; therefore he led many of the people to do after the manner of his iniquities" (Mosiah 27:8).

The rich young ruler may well have been using flattery when he addressed Jesus as "Good Master" to warrant the Savior's quick response: "Why callest thou me good? None is good, save one, that is, God" (Luke 18:18–19). By contrast the early Christian missionaries boldly preached the gospel of Christ without ever using flattering words. In other words, they did not use deceit, guile, or words they knew the people wanted to hear in order to build a following but rather bore witness of the truth through the power of the Holy Spirit (1 Thessalonians 2:5).

The scriptures caution that "a flattering mouth worketh ruin" (Proverbs 26:28). The Prophet Joseph Smith taught that being "frank and open" in communication will strengthen friendships in times of need, whereas "flattery is . . . a deadly poison" (3:295).

SOURCE

Smith, Joseph. *History of The Church of Jesus Christ of Latter-day Saints.* Edited by B. H. Roberts. 7 vols. 2d ed. rev. Salt Lake City: The Church of Jesus Christ of Latter-day Saints, 1932–51.

CFO

FLESH

The word *flesh* as used in scripture is not so much a reference to the physical body as it is a reference to mortality or the fallen nature of humankind. To say that the flesh wars against the spirit (Romans 8:5–9) is to say that the mortal elements of our identity do battle constantly with our immortal spirit. In this light, Jesus is the "Only Begotten Son of the Father" in that he is the Only Begotten Son in the flesh, meaning, born into mortality.

RLM

FLESH AND BLOOD

"Flesh and blood" is a scriptural phrase describing the mortal body. Thus when Paul declares that "flesh and blood cannot inherit the kingdom of God," he follows up with "neither doth corruption inherit incorruption" (1 Corinthians 15:50). "God Almighty Himself dwells in eternal fire," Joseph Smith explained; "flesh and blood cannot go there, for all corruption is devoured by the fire. 'Our God is a consuming fire.' When our flesh is quickened by the Spirit [in the resurrection], there will be no blood in this tabernacle" (6:366). He said on another occasion, "Flesh and blood cannot go there; but flesh and bones, quickened by the Spirit of God, can" (6:52).

SOURCE

Smith, Joseph. *History of The Church of Jesus Christ of Latter-day Saints.* Edited by

B. H. Roberts. 7 vols. 2d ed. rev. Salt Lake City: The Church of Jesus Christ of Latter-day Saints, 1932–51.

RLM

FLOOD OF NOAH

The book of Genesis describes a great and catastrophic flood upon the earth, sent by God "to destroy all flesh" (Genesis 6:17) because "all flesh had corrupted his way upon the earth" (Genesis 6:12). Joseph Smith's translation is more specific, attributing the Flood to a fulfilled prophecy of Noah: "And it came to pass that Noah continued his preaching unto the people, saying: Hearken, and give heed unto my words; believe and repent of your sins and be baptized in the name of Jesus Christ, the Son of God, even as our fathers, and ye shall receive the Holy Ghost, that ye may have all things made manifest; and if ye do not this, the floods will come in upon you; nevertheless they hearkened not" (Moses 8:23–24). The Prophet Joseph also taught that "Noah was born to save seed of everything, when the earth was washed of its wickedness by the flood" (1:283). Theologically, the flood of Noah represented the baptism of the earth, as affirmed by Church leaders, including President Brigham Young and Elder Orson Pratt (1:333; 8:83). Conversely, the symbolic nature of baptism is captured in the Flood, whereby "eight souls were saved by water," the "like figure whereunto even baptism doth also now save us" (1 Peter 3:20–21).

The seer Enoch saw in vision that "upon the residue of the wicked the floods came and swallowed them up" (Moses 7:43). He wept bitterly over his brethren and refused to be comforted until he was shown the coming of Jesus Christ, whose shed blood can make all things right. Enoch prayed that God would have "mercy upon Noah and his seed, that the earth might never more be covered by the floods" (Moses 7:50). As noted by Isaiah and others, God answered his plea (Isaiah 54:9).

During his mortal ministry, Jesus Christ made reference to the Flood when describing conditions of the latter days before the Second Coming, for "as it was in the days of Noe, so shall it be also in the days of the Son of man" (Luke 17:26; see also Joseph Smith–Matthew 1:42–43). The apostle Peter also mentioned the flood of Noah when teaching the doctrine of Christ's redemptive visit to the spirits in prison

(1 Peter 3:18–20). The Book of Mormon repeatedly speaks of the great Flood (Alma 10:22; 3 Nephi 22:9; Ether 6:7; 13:2).

President John Taylor taught that the Lord had more than one reason for sending the flood. It was actually an act of divine love, to prevent premortal spirits from having to be born into such wicked circumstances as existed in Noah's day. He explained: "This antediluvian people were not only very wicked themselves, but having the power to propagate their species, they transmitted their unrighteous natures and desires to their children, and brought them up to indulge in their own wicked practices. And the spirits that dwelt in the eternal worlds knew this, and they knew very well that to be born of such parentage would entail upon themselves an infinite amount of trouble, misery and sin. . . . But, says the caviller [frivolous debater], is it right that a just God should sweep off so many people? Is that in accordance with mercy? Yes, it was just to those spirits that had not received their bodies, and it was just and merciful too to those people guilty of the iniquity. Why? Because by taking away their earthly existence he prevented them from entailing their sins upon their posterity and degenerating them, and also prevented them from committing further acts of wickedness" (19:158–59).

Outside of scripture, stories of cataclysmic inundations or floods are found in many cultures across time and geographic locales. Various historians and scientists also indicate "that a historical event lies behind the flood tradition" (*New,* 2:465).

SOURCES
The New Interpreter's Dictionary of the Bible. 5 vols. Nashville, Tenn.: Abingdon Press, 2006–9.
Pratt, Orson. In *Journal of Discourses.* 26 vols. London: Latter-day Saints' Book Depot, 1854–86.
Smith, Joseph. *History of The Church of Jesus Christ of Latter-day Saints.* Edited by B. H. Roberts. 7 vols. 2d ed. rev. Salt Lake City: The Church of Jesus Christ of Latter-day Saints, 1932–51.
Taylor, John. In *Journal of Discourses.* 26 vols. London: Latter-day Saints' Book Depot, 1854–86.
Young, Brigham. In *Journal of Discourses.* 26 vols. London: Latter-day Saints' Book Depot, 1854–86.

ACS

FORBIDDEN FRUIT

The fruit of the tree of knowledge of good and evil was forbidden to Adam and Eve (2 Nephi 2:15–19; Mosiah 3:26; Alma 12:22–23). "Of every tree of the garden thou mayest freely eat, but of the tree of the knowledge of good and evil, thou shalt not eat of it, nevertheless, thou mayest choose for thyself, for it is given unto thee; but, remember that I forbid it, for in the day thou eatest thereof thou shalt surely die" (Moses 3:16–17). Essentially God was saying to our first parents: Of every tree of the garden thou mayest freely [without consequence] eat. But of the tree of the knowledge of good and evil, thou shalt not [freely, without consequence] eat of it, nevertheless, thou mayest choose for thyself, for it is given unto thee; but, remember that I forbid it, for in the day thou eatest thereof, thou shalt surely die.

In other words, the only question to be decided by Adam and Eve was whether they desired to remain in the Garden of Eden. If they did—and there were certainly many things to recommend staying there—then they were not to partake of the forbidden fruit. For if they partook of the fruit, the Lord would forbid them from staying in the garden. As President Joseph Fielding Smith put it: "The Lord said to Adam, here is the tree of the knowledge of good and evil. If you want to stay here then you cannot eat of that fruit. If you want to stay here then I forbid you to eat it. But you may act for yourself, and you may eat of it if you want to" ("Atonement," 124).

"It was Eve," Elder Dallin H. Oaks observed, "who first transgressed the limits of Eden in order to initiate the conditions of mortality. Her act, whatever its nature, was formally a transgression but eternally a glorious necessity to open the doorway toward eternal life. Adam showed his wisdom by doing the same" (73). Elder Bruce R. McConkie suggested that when our first parents partook of this fruit, they "complied with whatever the law was that brought mortality into being" (86). Thus, God's prohibition against partaking of the forbidden fruit may have been essentially a statement of consequences—what would come about if and when they did partake.

We speak of our first parents' actions in Eden as a *transgression,* not as a sin (Articles of Faith 1:2). Indeed, the Nephite prophets were consistent in their expressions that Adam's act was a transgression (2 Nephi 2:22; 9:6; Mosiah 3:11; Alma 12:31). The Prophet Joseph

Smith taught that "Adam did not commit sin in eating the fruits, for God had decreed that he should eat and fall" (*Words*, 63). President Joseph Fielding Smith stated: "Just why the Lord would say to Adam that he forbade him to partake of the fruit of that tree is not made clear in the Bible account, but in the original as it comes to us in the book of Moses it is made definitely clear. It is that the Lord said to Adam that if he wished to remain as he was in the garden, then he was not to eat the fruit, but if he desired to eat it and partake of death he was at liberty to do so. . . . Adam made the wise decision, in fact the only decision that he could make" ("Necessary?" 231).

Elder Oaks has also explained: "Some acts, like murder, are crimes because they are inherently wrong. Other acts, like operating without a license, are crimes only because they are legally prohibited. Under these distinctions, the act that produced the Fall was not a sin—inherently wrong—but a transgression—wrong because it was formally prohibited. These words [transgression and sin] are not always used to denote something different, but this distinction seems meaningful in the circumstances of the Fall" (73). President Joseph Fielding Smith expressed his views on this matter as follows: "I am very, very grateful for Mother Eve. If I ever get to see her, I want to thank her for what she did and she did the most wonderful thing that ever happened in this world and that was to place herself where Adam had to do the same thing that she did or they would have been separated forever. . . . They had to partake of that fruit or you wouldn't be here. I wouldn't be here. No one would have been here except Adam and Eve; and they would have stayed there and been there today and been there forever. . . . Adam and Eve did the very thing they had to. I tell you, I take my hat off to Mother Eve" (*Take,* 291–92).

SOURCES

McConkie, Bruce R. *A New Witness for the Articles of Faith.* Salt Lake City: Deseret Book, 1985.

Oaks, Dallin H. "'The Great Plan of Happiness.'" *Ensign,* Nov. 1993, 72–75.

Smith, Joseph Fielding. "Fall—Atonement—Resurrection—Sacrament." In *Charge to Religious Educators,* 2d ed. Salt Lake City: The Church of Jesus Christ of Latter-day Saints, 1982.

———. In Conference Report, Oct. 1967, 121–22.

———. *Take Heed to Yourselves!* Salt Lake City: Deseret Book, 1966.

———. "Was the Fall of Adam Necessary?" *Improvement Era,* Apr. 1962, 230–31.

The Words of Joseph Smith. Compiled and edited by Andrew F. Ehat and Lyndon W.

Cook. Provo, Utah: Brigham Young University Religious Studies Center, 1980. Spelling and punctuation standardized.

RLM

FOREKNOWLEDGE OF GOD

The scriptures clearly attest to the omniscience of God. The apostle Paul said, "Known unto God are all his works from the beginning of the world" (Acts 15:18; see also Abraham 2:8). Nephi taught that "the Lord knoweth all things from the beginning" (1 Nephi 9:6). Jacob likewise declared: "O how great the holiness of our God! For he knoweth all things, and there is not anything save he knows it" (2 Nephi 9:20; see also Helaman 8:8). In this dispensation, the Lord has stated, "All things are present before mine eyes" (D&C 38:2). Numerous other passages speak of the infinite knowledge of God. *Lectures on Faith* indicates that God's ability to save his children is directly related to his omniscience: "Without the knowledge of all things God would not be able to save any portion of his creatures; . . . and if it were not for the idea existing in the minds of men that God had all knowledge it would be impossible for them to exercise faith in him" (51–52).

The doctrine of foreordination is based on God's foreknowledge. Without an understanding of the nature of God, the conditions of the premortal world, and the principles of the plan of salvation revealed through latter-day revelation, some might understandably interpret *predestinate* and *God's foreknowledge* to mean that there is absolute determinism in all things.

Elder James E. Talmage wrote: "The doctrine of absolute predestination, resulting in a nullification of man's free agency, has been advocated with various modifications by different sects. Nevertheless, such teachings are wholly unjustified by both the letter and spirit of sacred writ. . . . This heretical doctrine [of predestination] seeks to rob Deity of mercy, justice, and love; it would make God appear capricious and selfish, directing and creating things solely for His own glory. . . . It leads to the absurd conclusion that mere knowledge of coming events must act as a determining influence in bringing about those occurrences. God's knowledge of spiritual and of human nature enables Him to conclude with certainty as to the actions of any of His children under given conditions; yet that knowledge is not of compelling force upon the creature" (*Articles,* 191; see also *Great,* 19–20).

That God "foresees but does not fix the outcome" (Maxwell, 71) is reflected in Alma's testimony concerning those chosen in the premortal world to be leaders on earth. They were "called and prepared from the foundation of the world according to the foreknowledge of God, *on account of their exceeding faith and good works;* in the first place [in the premortal world] being left to choose good or evil; therefore they having chosen good, and exercising exceedingly great faith, are called with a holy calling" (Alma 13:3; emphasis added).

SOURCES

Lectures on Faith. Salt Lake City: Deseret Book, 1985.

Maxwell, Neal A. "A More Determined Discipleship." *Ensign,* Feb. 1979, 69–73.

Talmage, James E. *Articles of Faith.* Classics in Mormon Literature series. Salt Lake City: Deseret Book, 1981.

———. *The Great Apostasy.* Salt Lake City: Deseret Book, 1965.

BLT

FOREORDINATION

Foreordination is the premortal selection of individuals to come forth in mortality at specified times, under certain conditions, and to fulfill predesignated responsibilities. To Latter-day Saints, foreordination does not mean absolute determinism with a fixed, immutable outcome. This latter notion, promoted by Saint Augustine, John Calvin, and others, is generally referred to as *predestination,* "a sectarian substitute for the true doctrine of foreordination" (McConkie, 588). Although the word *predestinate* appears in the writings of Paul (Romans 8:29–30; Ephesians 1:5, 11), the Greek word which the King James translators rendered *predestinate* has a variety of meanings. The Greek word suggests the foreknowledge of God but not necessarily absolute determination of all things, thereby excluding man's agency. For this reason many Bible revisions and newer translations replace the word *predestinate* with such words as *foreordain* or *appoint.*

Numerous examples of foreordination are mentioned in the scriptures. Abraham was told that he was included among the "noble and great" spirits of the premortal world who were chosen before birth to be leaders in God's kingdom on earth (Abraham 3:22). The Lord likewise informed Jeremiah, "Before I formed thee in the belly I knew thee; and

. . . I ordained thee a prophet unto the nations" (Jeremiah 1:5). Alma taught that priests belonging to a "holy order" were foreordained "according to the foreknowledge of God, on account of their exceeding faith and good works" (Alma 13:1, 3). The Prophet Joseph Smith concluded that "every man who has a calling to minister to the inhabitants of the world was ordained to that very purpose in the Grand Council of heaven before this world was" (6:364). In addition to these foreordinations to priesthood callings, many spirits may have been elected or foreordained to specific nations and generations, which the apostle Paul characterized as the "bounds of [our] habitation" (Acts 17:26), as well as to families and to various assignments, circumstances, and missions on earth.

While each of these foreordained appointments is ultimately based on the omniscience and foreknowledge of God, several factors may influence one's earthly circumstances. First, foreordination comes as a blessing or reward for premortal righteousness and valiant commitment to Jehovah, the Lord Jesus Christ. Birth into the house of Israel and heirship to all the blessings of Abraham, Isaac, and Jacob is also a foreordination or birthright of the faithful (Ephesians 1:4–5). Through faithfulness on earth, whatever one's premortal foreordination or prior covenants, one may, as Paul taught, be "adopted" into the house of Israel and receive all the promised blessings of the ancient fathers and mothers (Romans 9:4). On the other hand, one may be foreordained to important missions and blessings in mortality but through sin and rebellion fail to fulfill those foreordinations and thus forfeit the blessings. Thus, faithful obedience to the covenants and ordinances of the gospel is a primary factor in determining ultimate association with the chosen lineage and the fulfillment of foreordination to other rights and responsibilities.

Second, Latter-day Saints further believe that time, place, and circumstance of birth, and associated foreordained responsibilities may be the outcome of former covenants and divine decisions by an infinitely wise and compassionate Father. Thus, foreordination may include those opportunities and challenges that would foster the individual's ultimate growth and spiritual development.

A third principle that must be emphasized in any discussion of foreordination is that God designates individuals to come into mortality through specific nations, races, cultures, circumstances, and at specific times in the world's history with specific roles and responsibilities to help bring to pass God's plans for his children. These foreordinations include not only those whose missions are to bring souls to Christ and lead them to ultimate salvation but also those whose deeds and teachings are designed to elevate all mankind. The First Presidency said that such would be the case for "the great religious leaders of the world . . . and the Reformers, as well as philosophers . . . and others" who taught moral truths "to enlighten whole nations and to bring a higher level of understanding to individuals" ("Love"). The specifics of these factors remain unclear. As a result, a person's premortal character cannot be judged by his or her present station in life. Some of the most bitter and arduous circumstances may be, in the perspective of eternity, the most blessed and perhaps even the situations individuals elected and agreed to enter.

Foreordination, however, does not preclude the exercise of agency, and it carries with it heavy responsibilities. Because a person was noble and great in the premortal life and foreordained to important blessings and duties in this life does not ensure either ultimate salvation or the earthly fulfillment of one's foreordination. The fulfillment of any predesignated responsibility or reward is conditioned upon one's continued faithfulness and devotion to God and his kingdom.

SOURCES

McConkie, Bruce R. *Mormon Doctrine.* 2d ed. Salt Lake City: Bookcraft, 1966.

Smith, Joseph. *History of The Church of Jesus Christ of Latter-day Saints.* Edited by B. H. Roberts. 7 vols. 2d ed. rev. Salt Lake City: The Church of Jesus Christ of Latter-day Saints, 1932–51.

Statement of the First Presidency. 15 Feb. 1978. In Spencer J. Palmer, "God's Love for All Mankind." *The Expanding Church.* Salt Lake City: Deseret Book, 1978.

BLT

FORGIVENESS

There are two kinds of forgiveness taught in the scriptures and the gospel of Jesus Christ: (1) God's forgiveness or remission of the sins of the penitent, and (2) the mercy and forgiveness that men are commanded to extend to each other. This twofold nature of forgiveness is clearly seen in the Savior's words in the Lord's Prayer: "Forgive us our debts, as we forgive our debtors" (Matthew 6:12). Each form of forgiveness—forgiveness *received from* God and forgiveness *extended to* those who sin against us—is related to the other and comes because of the atonement of Jesus Christ.

Forgiveness of sins. A complete remission of sins is available to all "who have not sinned unto death" (D&C 64:7; see also D&C 42:18, 79), upon the conditions of "faith unto repentance" (Alma 34:15; see also D&C 1:32). "Though your sins be as scarlet, they shall be as white as snow; though they be red like crimson, they shall be as wool," the Lord lovingly declared through the prophet Isaiah, for "I am he that blotteth out thy transgressions" (Isaiah 1:18; 43:25). Numerous passages throughout the standard works testify of God's willingness to forgive sins and spiritually restore those who truly love him, turn from their sins, and seek to obey the commandments (Ezekiel 18:22; Daniel 9:9; Ephesians 1:7; Hebrews 8:12; 1 John 1:9; Mosiah 4:2; 26:22; Moroni 6:1–2). In our day, the Lord has promised: "Behold, he who has repented of his sins, the same is forgiven, and I, the Lord, remember them no more" (D&C 58:42).

The scriptures not only contain God's merciful promise to forgive sins and transform souls but also provide us with important insights concerning how we may know if we have obtained forgiveness of sins. One of the most significant indicators is found in Enos's declaration: "My guilt was swept away" (Enos 1:6). Likewise, King Benjamin's people experienced forgiveness of sins and spiritual rebirth accompanied by a "peace of conscience, because of the exceeding faith which they had in Jesus Christ" (Mosiah 4:3). In addition to peace of conscience, forgiveness of sins almost always brings feelings of joy and love. Alma contrasted this joy of forgiveness with the pains of wickedness. "And oh, what joy, and what marvelous light I did behold; yea, my soul was filled with joy as exceeding as was my pain" (Alma 36:20; see also Mosiah 4:1, 3; Alma 5:26; 19:13–30; Moroni 8:26).

With forgiveness of sins comes a change in one's disposition. Forgiveness brings, as King Benjamin's people testified, "a mighty change in us, or in our hearts, that we have no more disposition to do evil, but to do good continually" (Mosiah 5:2). Similarly, Alma spoke of the ancient high priests whose "garments were washed white through the blood of the Lamb" as being so changed by God's forgiving grace that they "could not look upon sin save it were with abhorrence" (Alma

13:11–12). When we are forgiven of our sins and enjoy accompanying peace of conscience, divine love and joy, and increased desires for righteousness, a natural outgrowth of those fruits of forgiveness is the desire to share that love with and serve our fellowmen. "If ye have known of [God's] goodness and have tasted of his love," King Benjamin declared, "and have received a remission of your sins, which causeth such exceedingly great joy in your souls, . . . ye yourselves will succor those that stand in need of your succor; ye will administer of your substance unto him that standeth in need" (Mosiah 4:11, 16). Receiving forgiveness of sins not only affects our feelings of love, gratitude, and devotion to God but also intensifies our feelings for our fellowmen (Enos 1:5–12; Mosiah 28:2–3; Alma 36:24). In this way, God's forgiveness of us affects our willingness and capacity to forgive others.

Forgiveness of others. "I, the Lord, will forgive whom I will forgive," Christ declared in a revelation through the Prophet Joseph Smith, "but of you it is required to forgive all men" (D&C 64:10). The scriptures, both ancient and modern, make it clear that God's willingness to forgive us is tightly intertwined with our willingness to forgive others (Matthew 6:14–15; 18:21–35; Mosiah 26:31; D&C 64:7–11). True repentance requires a "broken heart and a contrite spirit" (3 Nephi 9:20), which must also include a merciful heart and forgiving spirit toward others. Unwillingness to forgive others who have transgressed against us is an indication of insufficient "faith unto repentance" (Alma 34:15; see also D&C 1:32) and of a heart that has yet to be completely softened by the healing and transforming power of Christ's mercy. For this reason, the Lord stated that "he that forgiveth not his brother his trespasses *standeth condemned before the Lord;* for there *remaineth in him the greater sin*" (D&C 64:9; emphasis added). We stand "condemned before the Lord" because without forgiveness of others there can be no remission of sins. To have our sins remitted is to be justified before the Lord, which is the opposite of being condemned by him.

An unwillingness to let go of grudges and forgive—a hardened and vindictive heart—indicates that we have not fully experienced the mighty change of heart—the softened heart—that accompanies a remission of sins through the "tender mercies" (1 Nephi 1:20) of Christ's infinite atonement. In addition, our refusal to forgive others, as reflected in our actions and the intents of our hearts, may be more offensive than the offenses we have suffered. It may be that the "greater sin" remains in us because an unforgiving spirit reflects a desire on our part to deny or withhold the healing effects of the Atonement in the lives of others. Refusing to forgive those who have offended us is presumptuously assuming the right to judge, which belongs to Jesus Christ.

Attempting to usurp Christ's right to judge also reflects a lack of faith in the justice of God and a reluctance on our part to allow Christ, in his divine role as a perfectly just judge, to balance the books. The truth of the matter is that no attempt on our part, whether through our actions or our feelings, can have any impact on the role of the Atonement in the lives of others. Our failure to forgive will not preclude others from partaking of the fruit of the tree of life—which fruit is the love and mercy of Christ. We can only prevent ourselves from partaking of it. On the other hand, forgiving others opens the door for our own forgiveness of sins, spiritual progress, and service, which could not be obtained without it. President Gordon B. Hinckley taught: "If there be any who nurture in their hearts the poisonous brew of enmity toward another, I plead with you to ask the Lord for strength to forgive. This expression of desire will be of the very substance of your repentance. It may not be easy, and it may not come quickly. But if you will seek it with sincerity and cultivate it, it *will* come. . . . There will come into your heart a peace otherwise unattainable" (229).

SOURCE

Hinckley, Gordon B. *Teachings of Gordon B. Hinckley.* Salt Lake City: Deseret Book, 1997.

BLT

FORNICATION

To many Latter-day Saints, the term *fornication* usually refers to sexual intercourse between unmarried people. The scriptures tend to use the term in a broader sense, however, applying it to any form of sexual immorality. "Flee fornication," the apostle Paul admonished the Corinthian Saints (1 Corinthians 6:18). The Greek word from which the word *fornication* is translated is *porneia,* which implies any sexual sin or perversion. The word is often used interchangeably with the word adultery (Matthew 5:32; 19:9; 1 Corinthians 7:2; 10:8;

Jude 1:7). In the Book of Mormon, *fornication* is synonymous with "whoredoms"—sexual immorality in all its forms (Jacob 2:23–33; 3:12; Helaman 8:26). Abstaining from fornication and unchastity was a condition for admission into the Church in New Testament times (Acts 15:20, 29) and remains so in the Church today (D&C 42:74–78).

Metaphorically, the word *fornication* is used to describe general moral corruption. It is closely associated with idolatry—how God's covenant people break their vows, are unfaithful to him, and turn to other gods (Jeremiah 2:20–36; Ezekiel 16:15–43). John the Revelator describes the devil's kingdom as Babylon, the "mother of harlots and abominations," with whom the wicked and worldly "have been made drunk with the wine of her fornication" (Revelation 17:2, 5; see also 2:14, 20–22; 18:2–9).

BLT

FREEDOM

The words *freedom* and *free* are used many times in the scriptures in two general contexts—spiritual freedom and temporal freedom. All mankind has been given spiritual freedom by our Maker. Spiritual freedom involves the God-given right to choose—the eternal gift of agency. "Men are free according to the flesh," Father Lehi taught in the Book of Mormon. "And they are free to choose liberty and eternal life, through the Great Mediator of all men, or to choose captivity and death, according to the captivity and power of the devil; for he seeketh that all men might be miserable like unto himself" (2 Nephi 2:27). Although we often use the terms freedom and agency interchangeably, there seems to be a doctrinal distinction between the two words. Elder Dallin H. Oaks explained: "Because *free agency* is a God-given precondition to the purpose of mortal life, no person or organization can take away our free agency in mortality. . . . What can be taken away or reduced by the conditions of mortality is our *freedom,* the power to act upon our choices. Free agency is absolute, but in the circumstances of mortality freedom is always qualified. Freedom may be qualified or taken away (1) by physical laws, including the physical limitations with which we are born, (2) by our own action, and (3) by the action of others, including governments" (43).

The scriptures are replete with examples of how freedom is lost through wickedness and indifference. The destruction and captivity that came upon ancient Israel is a prime example. Both the Old Testament and the Book of Mormon illustrate how the freedom of individuals can be sorely restricted or destroyed by the reign of wicked kings and unjust civil governments. For this reason the Lord revealed in our day that governments and civil laws should protect freedom of conscience and preserve freedom to pursue life, liberty, and happiness (D&C 134). Temporal freedom can also be affected—both negatively and positively—by factors that are neither political nor governmental. Economic conditions can restrict or expand one's freedom. Likewise, physical conditions such as sickness, handicaps, and addictions can restrict an individual's temporal freedom. As a result, a person may be spiritually free in the sense that he or she has agency—the unqualified right to choose—and yet not be free politically, physically, or emotionally.

It is spiritual freedom, more than any form of temporal freedom, that Jesus promised when he declared, "The truth shall make you free" (John 8:32). Through abiding his gospel and partaking of his atoning sacrifice, we become free from the bondage of sin and the captivity of the devil (Mosiah 5:8; Romans 6:19–23). Regardless of one's level of political independence or temporal freedom, freedom from wickedness and worldliness is possible. Possessing the Spirit of God in our lives provides us with "the spirit of freedom" (Alma 61:15). It is this spiritual freedom that President Marion G. Romney called "freedom of the soul" and "perfect liberty." He taught: "Freedom thus obtained—that is, by obedience to the law of Christ—is freedom of the soul, the highest form of liberty. And the most glorious thing about it is that it is within the reach of every one of us, regardless of what people about us, or even nations, do. All we have to do is learn the law of Christ and obey it. To learn it and obey it is the primary purpose of every soul's mortal life" (45).

Eternal life—freedom from sin, death, temptation, and tribulation—is ultimate freedom, freedom that never fails and never ends.

SOURCES

Oaks, Dallin H. "Free Agency and Freedom." In *Brigham Young University 1987–88*

Devotional and Fireside Speeches, 37–47. Provo, Utah: Brigham Young University, 1988.

Romney, Marion G. "The Perfect Law of Liberty." *Ensign,* Nov. 1981, 43–45.

BLT

FRUIT OF THE SPIRIT

As we seek to cultivate the influence and direction of the Spirit, we will gradually begin to notice a change in our nature—our personality, our feelings, our desires and ambitions, what we love and what we abhor. More than anything else, we will begin to acquire Christlike attributes and become more people conscious—more attentive to their needs, more sensitive to their feelings, more eager to love and serve them. In short, we will begin to embody what the apostle Paul called the "fruit of the Spirit," namely, "love, joy, peace, longsuffering, gentleness, goodness, faith, meekness, temperance" (Galatians 5:22–23). These are the most powerful signs of personal spiritual growth, the greatest evidence that we are beginning to emulate the Master.

RLM

FULNESS OF THE FATHER

Those who rise in the morning of the First Resurrection, who inherit exaltation and eternal life, are said to receive the fulness of the Father, meaning the fulness of the glory and power of God, our Heavenly Father. Of those who so receive, the revelations declare, "Therefore all that my Father hath shall be given unto him" (D&C 84:38; see also 76:55). "They who dwell in [God's] presence are the church of the Firstborn; and they see as they are seen, and know as they are known, having received of his fulness and of his grace; and he makes them equal in power, and in might, and in dominion" (D&C 76:94–95). "And then shall the angels be crowned with the glory of his might, and the saints shall be filled with his glory, and receive their inheritance and be made equal with him" (D&C 88:107). "And of his fulness have all we received, even immortality and eternal life, through his grace" (JST, John 1:16).

RLM

FULNESS OF TIMES, DISPENSATION OF THE

Throughout the history of the world, the Lord has revealed his word and will to prophets (Amos 3:7). With priesthood authority from God, these prophets have established the Church of Jesus Christ and administered the ordinances of salvation. The various periods when the gospel has been restored to earth after times of rejection and apostasy are known as dispensations. The final dispensation of the gospel is known as the dispensation of the fulness of times. It commenced with the First Vision to Joseph Smith, the restoration of all priesthood authority, and the establishment of The Church of Jesus Christ of Latter-day Saints. It will continue until the end of time—the second coming of Christ, destruction of the wicked, the Millennium, resurrection of the dead, and the triumphal consummation of all the work of Christ.

This final dispensation is a fulness in that all the powers and principles of previous dispensations are "gather[ed] together in one" (D&C 27:13). In short, the dispensation of the fulness of times is the dispensation of dispensations—with all keys and knowledge necessary for salvation restored or revealed (D&C 101:32–34; 110:11–16; 112:32). The Prophet Joseph Smith spoke of the dispensation of the fulness of times as "a whole and complete and perfect union, and welding together of dispensations, and keys, and powers, and glories . . . from the days of Adam even to the present time. And not only this, but those things which have never been revealed from the foundation of the world, but have been kept hid from the wise and prudent, shall be revealed unto babes and sucklings in this, the dispensation of the fulness of times" (D&C 128:18). The work that must be completed during this dispensation—on both sides of the veil—is of such magnitude that urgency and total dedication on the part of members of the Church are required for this dispensation to fulfill its prophetic destiny. President Wilford Woodruff was taught this by way of vision. In his vision he spoke with the martyred Prophet Joseph Smith:

"I saw him at the door of the temple in heaven. He came to me and spoke to me. He said he could not stop to talk with me because he was in a hurry. The next man I met was Father Smith [Joseph Smith Sr.]; he could not talk with me because he was in a hurry. I met half a dozen brethren who had held high positions on earth, and none of them could stop to talk with me because they were in a hurry. I was much astonished. By and by I saw the Prophet again and I got the privilege of asking him a question.

"'Now,' said I, 'I want to know why you are in a hurry. I have been in a hurry all my life; but I expected my hurry would be over when I got into the kingdom of heaven, if I ever did.'

"Joseph said: 'I will tell you, Brother Woodruff. Every dispensation that has had the priesthood on the earth and has gone into the celestial kingdom has had a certain amount of work to do to prepare to go to the earth with the Savior when he goes to reign on the earth. Each dispensation has had ample time to do this work. We have not. We are the last dispensation, and so much work has to be done, and we need to be in a hurry in order to accomplish it'" (288–89). In our day, all the streams and rivers of the past flow into the grand ocean of revealed truth that is the dispensation of the fulness of times.

SOURCE

Woodruff, Wilford. *The Discourses of Wilford Woodruff.* Compiled by G. Homer Durham. Salt Lake City: Bookcraft, 1946.

BLT

GABRIEL

The Prophet Joseph Smith taught that the angel known as Gabriel was the great patriarch Noah, father of the human race in his day, second only to Michael (Adam) in priesthood hierarchy among mortals, and standing in third position from the Lord himself (3:386). His name in Hebrew means either "man of God" or "God is my mighty one."

Gabriel is named four times in the Bible, twice in Daniel (8:16; 9:21) and twice in Luke (1:19, 26). He functioned as interpreter of Daniel's vision and of scripture. Perhaps his greatest mission was to announce the impending birth of John the Baptist and of Jesus to, respectively, Zacharias and Mary. He spoke with tremendous power. In the temple, when Zacharias asked for proof of the announcement, Gabriel cited his name and authority—one who stood "in the presence of God" (Luke 1:19). He then laid a temporary curse on the aged priest for his sign-seeking (Luke 1:20–22).

In latter-day revelation, Gabriel has been called Elias (D&C 27:7), one with whom the Lord will drink of the fruit of the vine in a great sacramental service held at the time of the Second Coming, as promised during the Last Supper (Luke 22:18). There is no evidence that Gabriel will announce the resurrection at the Second Coming as is sometimes mentioned in popular culture. Rather, Michael will sound the trump at the times of resurrection (D&C 88:106–112). In Jewish writings of the Second Temple period (circa 200 B.C.–A.D. 70), Gabriel is mentioned as one of four archangels who interact with God's people on earth, along with Michael, Sariel, and Raphael. Interestingly, in an epistle to the Church written in 1842, now Doctrine and Covenants 128, the Prophet named the voices heard in visions and revelations of this last dispensation, including "the voice of Michael, the archangel; the voice of Gabriel, and of Raphael, . . . all declaring . . . their rights, their keys, their honors, their majesty and glory, and the power of their priesthood" (v. 21). Among God's ministers who have walked the earth, there are few who match Gabriel.

SOURCE

Smith, Joseph. *History of The Church of Jesus Christ of Latter-day Saints.* Edited by B. H. Roberts. 7 vols. 2d ed. rev. Salt Lake City: The Church of Jesus Christ of Latter-day Saints, 1932–51.

ACS

GAMBLING

From the earliest days of the Restoration to the present, prophets and apostles have denounced all forms of gambling as morally wrong and spiritually destructive. As early as 1842 the Prophet Joseph Smith condemned "Sabbath breaking, horse racing and gambling" (Clark, 1:139). Likewise, President Brigham Young in October 1844 spoke of the need to root out evil practices that had crept in among the Saints in Nauvoo. "We wish to suppress all grogshops, gambling houses, and all other disorderly houses and proceedings in our city, and to tolerate no intemperance or vice in our midst" (Clark, 1:242). On more than one occasion, the First Presidency of the Church has issued official statements, declaring: "The Church has been and now is unalterably opposed to gambling in any form whatever. It is opposed to any game of chance, occupation, or so-called business, which takes money from the person who may be possessed of it without giving value received in return. It is opposed to all practices the tendency of which is to . . . degrade or weaken the high moral standard which the members of the Church, and our community at large, have always maintained" (Clark, 5:245).

In the Doctrine and Covenants the Lord rebuked those "whose bellies are not satisfied, and whose hands are not stayed from laying hold upon other men's goods, whose eyes are full of greediness, and who will not labor with [their] own hands" (D&C 56:17). Gambling reflects these attitudes in that it "undermines the virtues of work and thrift and the desire to give honest effort in all we do" with the idea that we "can give little or nothing and receive something of value in return" (*True*, 72).

With the advent of legalized gambling and state-run lotteries in many places, the First Presidency in 1986 further clarified the Church's position on gambling. "There can be no question about the moral ramifications of gambling. As it has in the past, The Church of Jesus Christ of Latter-day Saints stands opposed to gambling, including government-sponsored lotteries" ("Church," 104). In counseling members not to participate in state lotteries or engage in other forms of gambling, the Brethren have reiterated that gambling is a "moral evil" (Oaks, 69). In more recent times there has been an influx of many different forms of gambling, including alluring games and activities on the Internet. Disguised as harmless forms of entertainment, these games of chance, as President Gordon B. Hinckley described, possess "an intensity that actually shows on the faces of those who are playing. And in all too many cases this practice, which appears innocent, can lead to an actual addiction." Gambling, like any addiction, is spiritually destructive in that it lessens one's "capacity to do worthwhile things" and adversely affects one's companionship with and sensitivity to the Holy Spirit. "That companionship," President Hinckley concluded, "is incompatible with indulgence of games of chance" (66).

SOURCES

"Church Opposes Government-Sponsored Gambling." *Ensign,* Nov. 1986, 104–5.

Clark, James R., comp. *Messages of the First Presidency of The Church of Jesus Christ of Latter-day Saints.* 6 vols. Salt Lake City: Bookcraft, 1965–75.

Hinckley, Gordon B. "Gambling." *Ensign,* May 2005, 58–61.

Oaks, Dallin H. "Gambling—Morally Wrong and Politically Unwise." *Ensign,* June 1987, 69–75.

True to the Faith: A Gospel Reference. Salt Lake City: The Church of Jesus Christ of Latter-day Saints, 2004.

BLT

GARDEN OF EDEN

At the time of the Creation, our first parents were placed in the Garden of Eden. Adam, Eve, and all forms of life existed in a paradisiacal, nonmortal condition—they were not subject to decay or death. In the case of Adam and Eve, blood had not entered their bodies, nor were they capable of procreation. They would have remained in that existence forever (physical but not subject to death) had there been no fall (2 Nephi 2:22–23; Moses 5:11). The tenth article of faith indicates that when the Lord Jesus returns to earth to initiate the Millennium and reign as King of kings and Lord of lords, "the earth will be renewed and receive [again] its paradisiacal glory."

RLM

GATES OF HELL

The gates of hell represent "the power and dominion of the devil" (Webster, "gate"). After Peter had borne a perfect testimony of the divine Sonship of the Master at Caesarea Philippi, Jesus said: "Blessed art thou, Simon Bar-jona: for flesh and blood hath not revealed it unto thee, but my Father which is in heaven. And I say also unto thee, That thou art Peter, and upon this rock I will build my church; and the gates of hell shall not prevail against it" (Matthew 16:17–18). At the time of the organization of the restored Church, the Lord spoke to the early Saints: "For [the living prophet's] word ye shall receive, as if from mine own mouth, in all patience and faith. For by doing these things the gates of hell shall not prevail against you" (D&C 21:5–6). The Lord's promise to us is that if we cling to the rock of revelation (Smith, 5:258) and exercise intelligent and patient obedience to the counsel of the Lord's anointed, neither Satan nor his nefarious hosts will be allowed to overthrow us.

SOURCES

Smith, Joseph. *History of The Church of Jesus Christ of Latter-day Saints.* Edited by

B. H. Roberts. 7 vols. 2d ed. rev. Salt Lake City: The Church of Jesus Christ of Latter-day Saints, 1932–51.

Webster, Noah. *American Dictionary of the English Language.* 1828. Reprint, San Francisco: Foundation for American Christian Education, 1980.

RLM

GATHERING OF ISRAEL

The mission and destiny of the Lord's chosen people are inextricably tied to the destiny of the earth and its inhabitants (Deuteronomy 32:8; 3 Nephi 23:1–2; Mormon 5:10), a message that is heralded in the Old Testament (Isaiah 45; Jeremiah 16, 31–32; Ezekiel 11) as well as in the Book of Mormon. The people of the covenant are scattered whenever they reject the true Messiah, his gospel, and the true points of his doctrine, and fall into apostasy (2 Nephi 6:8–11; 10:5–6; Helaman 7:17–19). They are scattered in the sense that they alienate themselves from the Lord and from those associations, covenants, and ordinances that lead to salvation. This is first and foremost a spiritual phenomenon; scattered Israelites are as scattered in regard to their identity—who they are and Whose they are—as they are to their geography. On the other hand, when the people of God repent and exercise saving faith in Christ the Lord, whenever they forsake their false traditions and their false gods, whenever they "come to the knowledge of their Redeemer and the very points of his doctrine" (1 Nephi 15:14), they are gathered. The gathering is a twofold process: first, spiritual, and second, temporal—in that order. Israel is gathered first to a person (Jesus Christ) and second to a place (2 Nephi 6:8–11; 10:3–8; 3 Nephi 5:23–26). The branches of Israel (Israelite groups of people) are grafted into the mother tree whenever they "come to the knowledge of the true Messiah" (1 Nephi 10:14).

Whenever those of our Father's children are baptized and confirmed by proper authority and associate thereafter with the Saints in the wards and stakes of Zion, they are gathered. People are gathered through the preaching of the gospel, through missionary work, and thereafter through the receipt of the ordinances of the temple (Smith, 5:423). President Spencer W. Kimball thus explained that "we are concerned with the gathering of Israel. This gathering shall continue until the righteous are assembled in the congregations of the Saints in the nations of the world. . . . Now, the gathering of Israel consists of joining the true church and their coming to the knowledge of the true God. . . . Any person, therefore, who has accepted the restored gospel, and who now seeks to worship the Lord in his own tongue and with the Saints in the nations where he lives, has complied with the law of the gathering of Israel and is heir to all of the blessings promised the Saints in these last days" (438–39). The work of gathering began at the time the Church was organized in April 1830. That work was formalized in the Kirtland Temple on 3 April 1836 through Moses' bestowal of priesthood keys associated with the gathering of Israel (D&C 110:11). Thereby, "Israel shall be saved in mine own due time; and by the keys which I have given shall they be led, and no more be confounded at all" (D&C 35:25).

The Book of Mormon describes the gathering of various branches of Israel. In speaking of the gathering of the descendants of Lehi, Nephi said: "And the gospel of Jesus Christ shall be declared among them; . . . and their scales of darkness shall begin to fall from their eyes; and many generations shall not pass away among them, save they shall be a pure and a delightsome people" (2 Nephi 30:5–6). Nephi spoke of a time when "the Jews which are scattered also shall begin to believe in Christ; and they shall begin to gather in upon the face of the land; and as many as shall believe in Christ shall also become a delightsome people" (2 Nephi 30:7). That is, one of a city and two of a family from among the Jews shall be converted before our Lord's coming (Jeremiah 3:14), but the great day of Jewish conversion will not come until after the Lord Jesus, who is the Messiah, appears on the Mount of Olives and delivers his people from their enemies at the time of the battle of Armageddon (Zechariah 12:9–10; 13:6; D&C 45:48–53). And as it is with all other branches of Israel, the gathering will be first to Christ and his gospel and then to the lands of their inheritance. They will be "washed in the blood of the Lamb" (Ether 13:11), will receive the Book of Mormon and the message of the restored gospel (Mormon 3:21), and will thereby be "restored to the true church and fold of God" (2 Nephi 9:2).

During the Millennium's thousand years of peace and rest and righteousness, the work of the Father—the work of the gathering of Israel—will *commence* (2 Nephi 30:7–15; 3 Nephi 25–26). It will commence in the sense that the gathering and conversions during that day will be of such magnitude as to cause all previous efforts at gathering to pale into insignificance. For one thing, it is principally in the Millennium that the lost tribes—those ten northern tribes that have for generations been scattered among the nations (1 Nephi 22:3–5; Mormon 3:17–18)—will be gathered. "And then shall the power of heaven come down among them; and I also will be in the midst. And then shall the work of the Father commence at that day, . . . among all the dispersed of my people, yea, even the tribes which have been lost, which the Father hath led away out of Jerusalem" (3 Nephi 21:25–26).

SOURCES

Kimball, Spencer W. *The Teachings of Spencer W. Kimball.* Edited by Edward L. Kimball. Salt Lake City: Deseret Book, 1982.

Smith, Joseph. *History of The Church of Jesus Christ of Latter-day Saints.* Edited by B. H. Roberts. 7 vols. 2d ed. rev. Salt Lake City: The Church of Jesus Christ of Latter-day Saints, 1932–51.

RLM

GENDER

"Gender is an essential characteristic of individual premortal, mortal, and eternal identity and purpose," the First Presidency declared in "The Family: A Proclamation to the World" (102). The Church teaches that as children of God, men and women are equal in his eyes. Such equality, however, does not mean sameness. "A full and equal partnership between men and women does not imply the roles played by the two sexes are the same in God's grand design for His children. As the proclamation clearly states, men and women, though spiritually equal, are entrusted with different but equally significant roles," Elder M. Russell Ballard explained. "These stewardships, equally sacred and important, do not involve any false ideas about domination or subordination" (29–30). Both men and women are essential in the plan of salvation. Each gender, with its inherent characteristics and strengths, complements the other and plays a vital role in God's work and glory. The apostle Paul taught that "neither is the man without the woman, neither the woman without the man, in the Lord. For as the woman is of the man, even so is the man also by the woman; but all things of God" (1 Corinthians 11:11–12). Other translations of the Bible provide us with an interesting perspective on the doctrine of equality and interdependence of the sexes with such phrases as "In God's plan men and women need each other" (LB), "In the Lord woman is not independent of man nor man of woman" (NIV), and "In Christ's fellowship woman is as essential to man as man to woman" (NEB). Modern prophets have likewise taught this doctrine.

President Gordon B. Hinckley taught, "I am satisfied that [our Father in Heaven] loves his daughters as much as he loves his sons. . . . Each complements the other. Each is needed by the other. God has created us male and female, each unique in his or her individual capacities and potential" (690).

From the earliest history of the Church, prophets have taught that women, although different in their gifts and responsibilities, are equal to men in the sight of God and entitled to all of the same blessings as men. "The Lord offers to his daughters," President Joseph Fielding Smith taught, "every spiritual gift and blessing that can be obtained by his sons" (66). In 1842, the Prophet Joseph Smith organized the women of the Church into an organization known as the Relief Society. Latter-day Saint women have been involved from the very outset of the Church "in helping build up the Church by supporting missionary efforts, contributing to the construction of temples, and establishing communities where the Saints could worship together. The organization of Relief Society in 1842 mobilized the collective power of the women and their specific assignments to build the Lord's kingdom, just as the organization of priesthood quorums gave men specific responsibilities" (Beck, 108). Teaching the doctrine of the spiritual equality of men and women, the Prophet Joseph Smith said, "The Church was never perfectly organized until the women were thus organized" (451).

Latter-day Saints were among the first in the United States to advocate voting rights for women. Our history is replete with examples of accomplished women who made contributions not only to society but also in the home and Church. Brigham Young, in the mid-nineteenth century, declared, "We have sisters here who, if they had the privilege of studying, would make just as good mathematicians or accountants as any man" (13:61). Latter-day Saints believe strongly in the equality of the sexes but have through the years resisted many social trends and political efforts that would promote sameness of the sexes, denigrate the family, or advocate notions contrary to eternal principles. "No legislation can alter the sexes," President Hinckley taught. "Legislation should provide equality of opportunity, equality of compensation, equality of political privilege. But any legislation which is designed to create neuter gender of that which God created male and female will bring more problems than benefits" (690). Because of our unique understanding of the eternal nature of gender and its vital role in God's plans and purposes for his children, Latter-day Saints strive to eliminate discrimination or mistreatment of any kind based on gender and to support those measures that would promote fair treatment of all God's children. We do, however, reject "many political, legal, and social pressures for changes that confuse gender and homogenize the differences between men and women" or that would seek to "alter those separate duties and privileges of men and women that are essential to accomplish the great plan of happiness" (Oaks, 73).

SOURCES

Ballard, M. Russell. "The Sacred Responsibilities of Parenthood." *Ensign,* Mar. 2006, 26–33.

Beck, Julie B. "Fulfilling the Purpose of Relief Society." *Ensign,* Nov. 2008, 108–11.

First Presidency and Council of the Twelve Apostles. "The Family: A Proclamation to the World." *Ensign,* Nov. 1995, 102.

Hinckley, Gordon B. *Teachings of Gordon B. Hinckley.* Salt Lake City: Deseret Book, 1997.

Joseph Smith [manual]. Teachings of Presidents of the Church series. Salt Lake City: The Church of Jesus Christ of Latter-day Saints, 2007.

Oaks, Dallin H. "The Great Plan of Happiness." *Ensign,* Nov. 1993, 72–75.

Smith, Joseph Fielding. "Magnifying Our Callings in the Priesthood." *Improvement Era,* June 1970, 65–66.

Young, Brigham. In *Journal of Discourses.* 26 vols. London: Latter-day Saints' Book Depot, 1854–86.

BLT

GENTILE

The term *Gentile* means "the nations" and is generally used in reference to the nations of the world that have not been taught the laws and covenants of God. The descendants of Noah's son Japheth were the first to be called Gentiles (Genesis 10:2–5). In later eras the term has been used to designate those who are not of the house of Israel or not of the kingdom of Judah. Members of scattered Israel are at times considered Gentiles because they have lost their identity as God's covenant people and have culturally become like the nations of the world.

Because the more part of all the house of Israel has been scattered among all nations (1 Nephi 22:3–4), we are all Gentiles in a sense, even though we may be lineal descendants of Abraham; that is, we are Israelite by lineage and Gentile by culture. When we come to a knowledge of our Redeemer, we are gathered to Christ and are no longer of "the nations." We are then known as Israel, whether we literally are blood Israel or not. As the apostle Paul observed, "For they are not all Israel, which are of Israel" (Romans 9:6). This perspective is particularly prevalent in the Book of Mormon. "As many of the Gentiles as will repent are the covenant people of the Lord; and as many of the Jews as will not repent shall be cast off; for the Lord covenanteth with none save it be with them that repent and believe in his Son, who is the Holy One of Israel" (2 Nephi 30:2).

The law of Moses contains frequent reminders for the Israelites to be compassionate to Gentiles or "stranger[s]" in their midst (Exodus 22:21; Leviticus 19:33–34). Remembering that God had taken them by the hand to lead them out of Egypt, the Israelites were commissioned to be "a light of the Gentiles; to open the blind eyes" (Isaiah 42:6–7) and to bring them also to God. Oftentimes Gentiles who "do by nature the things contained in the law" are better examples of living the laws of God than those to whom the law was given (Romans 2:14). Through Christ and his covenant, the wall of partition between Jew and Gentile is removed, and they who were once aliens to the covenant "are no more strangers and foreigners, but fellowcitizens with the saints, and of the household of God" (Ephesians 2:12–19).

According to modern-day scripture, Gentiles have an important role in the restoration of the gospel in the latter days, including bringing forth scripture that "shall make known the plain and precious things which have been taken away" (1 Nephi 13:40). Gentiles who repent, come unto Christ, are baptized, and know the doctrine of Christ are divinely appointed to gather Israel and restore them to the Lord (3 Nephi 21:1–6, 22–29; D&C 90:9–11).

CFO

GENTILES, TIMES OF

The Savior taught his meridian Twelve Apostles that "the last shall be first, and the first last" (Matthew 20:16; see also 19:30; Luke 13:30). Jesus was referring to the manner and the order in which individuals and whole nations of people are to receive the gospel. In Christ's mortal ministry the gospel went first to the Jews, "the lost sheep of the house of Israel" (Matthew 15:24; see also 10:5–6); later, as a result of the vision given to Peter, the president of the Church (Acts 10), and largely through the work of Paul (Romans 11:13), the gospel went to the Gentiles.

In our day, the order is reversed: the gospel has been restored in a great Gentile nation, meaning in a nation other than the land of Israel (2 Nephi 30:8; 33:9), through the instrumentality of a Gentile prophet, Joseph Smith (1 Nephi 22:7; 2 Nephi 3:7), who is Israelite by lineage and descent but Gentile by nation and culture (D&C 109:60). President Ezra Taft Benson said: "The Lord has designated these days in which we live as 'the times of the Gentiles.' The Gentile nations are essentially the so-called Christian nations—North and South America and the European nations from which we came. 'The times of the Gentiles' refers to that period of time extending from when the gospel was restored to the world (1830) to when the gospel will again be preached to the Jews—after the Gentiles have rejected it" (110–11).

In modern revelation the Lord has declared: "When the times of the Gentiles is come in, a light shall break forth among them that sit in darkness, and it shall be the fulness of my gospel; but they [the generality of the people] receive it not; for they perceive not the light, and they turn their hearts from me because of the precepts of men. And in that generation shall the times of the Gentiles be fulfilled" (D&C 45:28–30; see also 3 Nephi 16:10–12). This seems to refer to that time when the long-awaited Messiah of the Jews manifests himself to his people on the Mount of Olives and discloses his true identity as the Lord and Redeemer of all humankind (D&C 45:48–53). "When will the Lord take the gospel from the unbelieving Gentiles?" Elder Bruce R. McConkie asked. "It will be when the fulness of the Gentiles is come in, when he remembers the covenant made with his own people, when the hour for millennial glory has arrived" (241).

SOURCES

Benson, Ezra Taft. *Come unto Christ.* Salt Lake City: Deseret Book, 1983.

McConkie, Bruce R. *The Millennial Messiah: The Second Coming of the Son of Man.* Salt Lake City: Deseret Book, 1982.

RLM

GETHSEMANE

The name *Gethsemane,* referring to a garden located on the Mount of Olives east of Jerusalem's Old City across the brook Kedron, is the anglicized form of two combined Hebrew words, *gath* ("press") and *shemen* ("oil"), and means "the place of the oil press." Anciently, it was a site of olive oil production. An early tradition convincingly identifies its location on the west slope of the Mount of Olives, opposite the east gate of the Temple Mount. It is the place to which Jesus retired after leaving the upper room following the Last Supper with his disciples (Matthew 26:36; Mark 14:32; Luke 22:39; John 18:1).

Latter-day Saint theology regarding Gethsemane harmonizes with early postapostolic church writers who regarded the events of Gethsemane as constituting part of Jesus' redemptive act for humankind. The church father Irenaeus (circa A.D. 180) wrote that Jesus "sweated great drops of blood . . . , tokens of the flesh which had been derived from the earth, which He had recapitulated in Himself, bearing salvation to His own handiwork" (3:22:2).

Each of the four Gospels contributes significant information to our understanding of Jesus' experience in Gethsemane. John reports that Judas Iscariot, the betrayer, who was not with Jesus and the other apostles when they arrived at the garden, also "knew the place: for Jesus oft times resorted thither with his disciples" (John 18:2). In other words, Jesus and the Twelve had gone to Gethsemane many times before that night. Perhaps it was a place conducive to prayer and spiritual reflection. Mark reports that at the garden, Jesus took Peter, James, and John farther into the interior of Gethsemane, where Jesus began "to be very heavy" (Mark 14:33; JST, Mark 14:36–38). The prophet Alma identifies the cause of Jesus' feeling of heaviness, even "unto death" (Mark 14:34), when he prophesied that the Son of God would "take upon him" the sickness, suffering, and sin that mortals on this earth experience (Alma 7:11). President Boyd K. Packer testified that "upon Him was the burden of all human transgression, all human guilt. . . .

By choice, [Christ] accepted the penalty . . . for brutality, immorality, perversion, and corruption; for addiction; for the killings and torture and terror—for all of it that ever had been or all that ever would be enacted upon this earth" (69). Elder Neal A. Maxwell referred to this as "the awful arithmetic of the Atonement" ("Willing," 73).

Mark also states that Jesus was "sore amazed" in Gethsemane (Mark 14:33). This phrase is a translation of the Greek *ekthambeisthai*. According to a respected New Testament scholar, the word is best rendered as "terrified surprise" (Murphy-O'Connor, 36). This feeling came about because of Jesus' sinless state. He had never experienced sin before, and at that moment in Gethsemane he experienced for himself infinite sin, sorrow, and suffering. Elder Maxwell summarized the point of Mark 14:33: "Imagine, Jehovah, the Creator of this and other worlds, 'astonished'! Jesus knew cognitively what He must do, but not experientially. He had never personally known the exquisite and exacting process of an atonement before. Thus, when the agony came in its fulness, it was so much, much worse than even He with his unique intellect had ever imagined!" ("Willing," 72–73).

Luke indicates that Jesus' experience in Gethsemane became so intense that he cried out to his Father, "If thou be willing, remove this cup from me: nevertheless not my will, but thine, be done" (Luke 22:42). The Father's will was that the Son suffer and thereby put into effect all the terms and conditions of his plan (3 Nephi 11:11). In his agony, Jesus received the company of an angel to strengthen him (Luke 22:43). Elder Bruce R. McConkie believed this angelic minister to have been Michael, or Adam, the father of the human race (9). Indeed, Jesus' atoning act in the Garden of Gethsemane is directly linked to Adam's transgression in the Garden of Eden. For as Paul taught, "For since by man came death, by man came also the resurrection of the dead. For as in Adam all die, even so in Christ shall all be made alive" (1 Corinthians 15:21–22).

Still, the unrelenting pain and pressure of Jesus' experience became so intense, Luke reports, that "being in an agony he prayed more earnestly: and his sweat was as it were great drops of blood falling down to the ground" (Luke 22:44). Jesus' bloody sweat has been discussed by physicians and attributed to a known but rare condition called hematidrosis, in which the small blood vessels just under the skin hemorrhage due to extreme distress (Edwards, 1456). President Brigham Young states that it was the withdrawal of the Spirit of our Father in Heaven from his Son that caused Jesus to sweat blood: "If he had had the power of God upon him, he would not have sweat blood; but all was withdrawn from him, and a veil was cast over him" (3:206). Such withdrawal plunged Jesus into the depths of hell and caused him to experience, even if only for a time, spiritual death, which is defined as spiritual separation from God. Jesus became completely vulnerable to the powers of Satan (Mosiah 3:7; D&C 122:7–8; Talmage, 613).

Jesus also became subject to the full demands of justice. The scriptures teach that he absorbed the full force of the punishment deserved by each mortal. Elder Maxwell stated: "Jesus always deserved and always had the Father's full approval. But when He took our sins upon Him, of divine necessity required by justice He experienced instead 'the fierceness of the wrath of Almighty God' (D&C 76:107; 88:106)" (*Lord,* 13).

Jesus learned by his own experience in Gethsemane the effect that the powers of Satan can have on human beings. Elder James E. Talmage described Satan's work in the garden that awful night: "Christ's agony in the garden is unfathomable by the finite mind, both as to intensity and cause. . . . He struggled and groaned under a burden such as no other being who has lived on earth might even conceive as possible. It was not physical pain, nor mental anguish alone, that caused Him to suffer such torture as to produce an extrusion of blood from every pore; but a spiritual agony of soul such as only God was capable of experiencing. . . . In that hour of anguish Christ met and overcame all the horrors that Satan, 'the prince of this world' could inflict [John 14:30]. The frightful struggle incident to the temptations immediately following the Lord's baptism was surpassed and overshadowed by this supreme contest with the powers of evil" (613).

Matthew's Gospel reveals Jesus' justifiable concern for the apostles—that they enter not into temptation precisely because of the intensity of Satan's ravages that night. At least twice Jesus interrupted his prayer to encourage the apostles to "watch and pray, that ye enter not into temptation" (Matthew 26:41). The Joseph Smith Translation of Mark 14:36 states that "the disciples began to be sore amazed, and to be very heavy, and to complain in their hearts, wondering if this be the Messiah." Their weariness and slumber in Gethsemane were perhaps induced, at least in part, by their doubt, depression, and temptation.

The intensity of Jesus' experience in Gethsemane seems to have abated somewhat after he prayed the same prayer the third time. He then noticed the approach of those sent to arrest him, led by Judas Iscariot (Matthew 26:44–47). And though his excruciating suffering was far from over, considering the rest of the events of the Atonement still to unfold, in Gethsemane Jesus seems to have fulfilled the declaration of Doctrine and Covenants 88:6: "He descended below all things, in that he comprehended all things"—things he had not known beforehand through personal experience. *Lectures on Faith* states that Jesus Christ "descended in suffering below that which man can suffer; or, in other words, suffered greater sufferings, and was exposed to *more powerful contradictions* than any man can be. But, notwithstanding all this, he kept the law of God, and remained without sin, showing thereby that it is in the power of man to keep the law and remain also without sin" (59–60; emphasis added).

Joseph Smith could speak to this principle because he also knew something about contradictions, as well as the powers of darkness and Lucifer's attempts to destroy body and soul (Joseph Smith–History 1:15–17). Jesus endured these things—but to an infinite degree. President Boyd K. Packer said: "He, by choice, accepted the penalty for all mankind for the sum total of all wickedness and depravity. . . . In choosing, He faced the awesome power of the evil one who was not confined to flesh nor subject to mortal pain. That was Gethsemane" (69).

Because of what took place in Gethsemane and on Golgotha, "we have not an high priest which cannot be touched with the feeling of our infirmities; but was in all points tempted like as we are, yet without sin. Let us therefore come boldly unto the throne of grace, that we may obtain mercy, and find grace to help in time of need" (Hebrews 4:15–16). Because of Gethsemane, Jesus Christ knows each of us perfectly and intimately, and he knows how to help us. In Gethsemane Jesus suffered the sins, sorrows, and sicknesses of all those living and who have lived on millions of earths like ours (Moses 1:33; 7:30). In Gethsemane the work of redemption was begun for all that he created under the Father's direction (D&C 76:42–43). As the revelation states, "By him, and through him, and of him, the worlds are and were created, and the inhabitants thereof are begotten sons and daughters unto God" (D&C 76:24). It is not possible to overstate the magnitude of the suffering experienced by Jesus Christ that began in Gethsemane, nor the infinite power unleashed and made available to all as a result of the Atonement.

SOURCES

Edwards, William D., Wesley J. Gabriel, and Floyd E. Hosmer. "On the Physical Death of Jesus Christ." *Journal of the American Medical Association* 225, no. 11 (21 Mar. 1998): 1455–63.

Irenaeus. *Against Heresies and Fragments.* Whitefish, Mont.: Kessinger Publishing, n.d.

Lectures on Faith. Salt Lake City: Deseret Book, 1985.

Maxwell, Neal A. *Lord, Increase Our Faith.* Salt Lake City: Bookcraft, 1994.

———. "Willing to Submit." Ensign, May 1985, 70–73.

McConkie, Bruce R. "The Purifying Power of Gethsemane." *Ensign,* May 1985, 9–11.

Murphy-O'Connor, Jerome. "What Really Happened at Gethsemane." *Bible Review* 14 (Apr. 1998): 28–39, 52.

Packer, Boyd K. "Atonement, Agency, Accountability." *Ensign,* May 1988, 69–72.

Talmage, James E. *Jesus the Christ.* Salt Lake City: Deseret Book, 1973.

Young, Brigham. In *Journal of Discourses.* 26 vols. London: Latter-day Saints' Book Depot, 1854–86.

ACS

GIFT OF THE HOLY GHOST

The Light of Christ is given to every soul who comes into this life (John 1:9; D&C 84:46). It is a moral monitor, an inherent guide to truth and goodness, an inner capacity that enables persons to discern right from wrong, good from evil, the significant from the irrelevant. It is a form of what might be called general revelation, that which God bestows upon the whole world. To the extent that individuals give heed to this light and hearken to its guidance, they will in time be led to the covenant gospel, wherein they may receive, following baptism, the gift of the Holy Ghost (D&C 84:47–48). Before repenting and receiving baptism, persons may receive of the influence of the Spirit when they read or hear the word of God, but this influence is temporary and fleeting; if it is not acted upon, it will soon depart.

The gift of the Holy Ghost is the right to the companionship, guidance, and cleansing power of the third member of the Godhead, a heavenly endowment that comes only after baptism performed by one who holds the priesthood of God and is authorized to carry out the ordinance. The gift of the Holy Ghost is given by the laying on of hands (Acts 8:14–17) by one who holds the Melchizedek Priesthood. This gift is a divine bestowal of the Spirit that is more constant and more intense than was enjoyed before baptism. The Holy Ghost is the source of specific revelation. Salvation and eternal life are "the greatest of all the gifts of God" in eternity (D&C 6:13; 14:7), the gift of the Holy Ghost is the greatest gift we can receive from a gracious Lord in this life. "You may have the administration of angels," President Wilford Woodruff explained, "you may see many miracles; you may see many wonders in the earth; but I claim that the gift of the Holy Ghost is the greatest gift that can be bestowed upon man" (5).

SOURCE

Woodruff, Wilford. *The Discourses of Wilford Woodruff.* Edited by G. Homer Durham. Salt Lake City: Bookcraft, 1990.

RLM

GLORY

In the Old Testament, the English word *glory* is used to translate the Hebrew *kavodh* and its derivatives; in the New Testament, it is used to translate the Greek *doxa* or *doxazo*.

Kavodh appears about four hundred times in the Hebrew Bible and possesses "an extraordinarily wide range of meaning," including but not limited to wealth, respect, intelligence, beauty, greatness, power, honor, exalted position, abundance, weight, and importance (*New*, 2:576). It also has negative meanings such as burden or something difficult and to harden or boast. The most important uses of *kavodh* in scripture refer to deity.

A significant expression that occurs some thirty-six times in the Old Testament is "Glory of the Lord [Yahweh]" (*New*, 2:576). Sometimes it is used to connote God's influence, which fills the earth (Numbers 14:20–21; Isaiah 6:3), or his majesty and divinity (Psalm 104:31; 138:5; Isaiah 66:19). At other times it denotes a visible manifestation of his presence or appearance (Exodus 24:16–18; 33:14–23; 40:34–35; 1 Kings 8:11; 2 Chronicles 7:2; Ezekiel 1:28; 10:4, 18–19;

11:23; 43: 2–5). The book of Moses and the Doctrine and Covenants also use the phrase in both senses in which it is found in the Old Testament (Moses 1:31; 7:17; D&C 45:67; 64:41; 76:19; 84:5, 32). The similar expression "Glory of God [*el*]" is also found, though only twice (Psalm 19:1; Proverbs 25:2).

The New Testament word *doxa* likewise possesses a number of meanings, including but not limited to favorable or exalted status; someone's reputation or position; a measurement such as "brightness" of light, "beauty" of a flower, "wealth" of nations; power; or even that which is worthy of praise. Again, we see its most important and impressive usage as a way to characterize the divine presence, sometimes coordinated with other characteristics and expressions, such as wisdom and power. "Glory thus formed part of the semantic field of words signifying God's revealed presence" in the person of Jesus Christ (*New*, 2:576).

All the positive meanings embedded in the terms *kavodh* and *doxa* compose the characteristics of God. *Lectures on Faith* teaches that his attributes and characteristics include knowledge, power, justice, judgment, mercy, and truth (50–51). These constitute, in part, his glory. *Lectures* also links "the fullness of the blessing of the gospel of Jesus Christ" with "eternal glory" (49).

As the New Testament makes plain, Jesus' glory is tied to his redemptive sacrifice. On the eve of his great suffering, Jesus prayed to the Father, saying: "I have glorified thee on the earth: I have finished the work which thou gavest me to do. And now, O Father, glorify thou me with thine own self with the glory which I had with thee before the world was" (John 17:4–5). Here Jesus references the exalted position he enjoyed with his Father before his condescension, and he prays for that condition again because, as he said, he finished work entrusted to him by his Father—which work is the Atonement. The accomplishment of that work "glorified" the Father. It set into operation all the terms and conditions of the Father's plan. Thus, not only did Jesus glorify the Father by securing his kingdom for eternity but his completed work also added to his own stature and position as the first resurrected Being. Hebrews tells us that Jesus was "crowned with glory and honour" because of the Atonement (Hebrew 2:9). After his resurrection, Jesus had the ability to withhold or reveal his glory, his identity as the

Holy One of Israel, as evidenced by his encounter with certain disciples on the road to Emmaus (Luke 24:13–35).

While in mortality, anticipating the completion of his atonement, Jesus associated glory with godly power. He prophesied that he would return some day "in the glory of his Father" (Mark 8:38), "in the clouds with great power and glory" (Mark 13:26), and "in his own glory, and in his Fathers', and of the holy angels" (Luke 9:26).

The apostle John specifically associated Jesus' glory with light, as when he spoke of the New Jerusalem: "And the city had no need of the sun, neither of the moon, to shine in it: for the glory of God did lighten it, and the Lamb is the light thereof. And the nations of them which are saved shall walk in the light of it: and the kings of the earth do bring their glory and honour into it" (Revelation 21:23–24).

An important theme in all of John's writings is the fact that Jesus is the Light of the world, the Light of men, and the Being full of grace and truth (John 1:4–9; 8:12; 9:5; 1 John 1:5). After discussing Jesus as the embodiment of light in his prologue to his Gospel, John says, "and we beheld his glory, the glory as of the only begotten of the Father, . . . full of grace and truth" (John 1:14).

Latter-day revelation also connects light and truth with God's glory: "The glory of God is intelligence, or, in other words, light and truth" (D&C 93:36). Another revelation describes this light as the power by which all things in the universe are created, governed, and maintained (D&C 88:6–13). This same revelation extends the promise of this power—and thus glory—to all steadfast disciples of Jesus Christ: "And if your eye be single to my glory, your whole bodies shall be filled with light, and there shall be no darkness in you; and that body which is filled with light comprehendeth all things" (D&C 88:67).

Finally, glory may also be equated with the acts of praise, worship, and godly living that are due our God. John saw angels at the time of the Restoration declaring to the inhabitants of the world, "Fear God, and give glory to him" (Revelation 14:7).

SOURCES

New Interpreter's Dictionary of the Bible. Volume 2. Nashville, Tenn.: Abingdon Press, 2009.

Lectures on Faith. Salt Lake City: Deseret Book, 1985.

ACS

GOD

Joseph Smith taught that "God is the only supreme governor and independent being in whom all fulness and perfection dwell; who is omnipotent, omnipresent and omniscient; without beginning of days or end of life; and that in him every good gift and every good principle dwell; and that he is the Father of lights; in him the principle of faith dwells independently, and he is the object in whom the faith of all other rational and accountable beings center for life and salvation" (*Lectures,* 10). God is infinite, while men and women on earth are finite. God is perfect and complete, while men and women are imperfect and incomplete. There is no knowledge God does not possess, no power he does not have, no divine quality or attribute he lacks. All things are and were with him "one eternal 'now'" (Smith, 4:597). He is the standard against which we judge and determine right and wrong, good and evil. Humans may be complimented and praised, but God is worshipped. God is forevermore immortal, glorified, and exalted. His is a status he cannot forfeit or lose; his is a condition from which he cannot fall; his is a holy throne that cannot be usurped.

Yet despite God's grandeur and magnificence, despite his transcendent life and eternal existence, the scriptures teach that it is life eternal to know God the Father and his Son, Jesus Christ (John 17:3). We read and study the scriptures in an effort to come to understand the mind and will and ways of the Almighty. We love and serve God and our fellow beings in our quest to know him (Mosiah 5:13), but we yield to the ever-present reality that it is only by faith, only by the power of the Holy Spirit, that God can be known (1 Corinthians 2:11–14). He stands revealed, or he remains forever unknown.

"In the ultimate and final sense of the word," Elder Bruce R. McConkie has written, "there is only one true and living God. He is the Father, the Almighty Elohim, the Supreme Being, the Creator and Ruler of the universe. . . . Christ is God; he alone is the Savior. The Holy Ghost is God; he is one with the Father and the Son. But these two are the second and third members of the Godhead. The Father is God above all, and is, in fact, the God of the Son" (51). This understanding can be balanced with the fact that to love the Father is to love the Son; to have faith in the Father is to have faith in the Son; to serve the Father is to serve the Son; and to worship the Father is to worship the Son. And we draw near unto both the Father and the Son through the Spirit.

SOURCES

Lectures on Faith. Salt Lake City: Deseret Book, 1985.

McConkie, Bruce R. *A New Witness for the Articles of Faith.* Salt Lake City: Deseret Book, 1985.

Smith, Joseph. *History of The Church of Jesus Christ of Latter-day Saints.* Edited by B. H. Roberts. 7 vols. 2d ed. rev. Salt Lake City: The Church of Jesus Christ of Latter-day Saints, 1932–51.

RLM

GODHEAD

The Godhead consists of three personages: God the Eternal Father, Jesus Christ the Redeemer, and the Holy Ghost. The Prophet referred to these three as "God the first, the Creator; God the second, the Redeemer; and God the third, the Witness or Testator" (*Joseph Smith*, 42). "The Father has a body of flesh and bones as tangible as man's; the Son also; but the Holy Ghost has not a body of flesh and bones, but is a personage of spirit" (D&C 130:22). These three are separate and distinct personages and beings. This understanding was delivered by revelation to Joseph Smith and stands in stark contrast to efforts on the part of traditional Christian thinkers to maintain the ontological oneness of Father, Son, and Holy Spirit through appealing to Greek philosophical terms such as *homoousios,* meaning "one essence" or "of the same substance."

The Latter-day Saints' belief in three separate persons and three beings within the Godhead—a doctrine taught by Joseph Smith throughout his entire ministry (*History*, 6:474)—is not to say that we are polytheistic. Rather, Mormon monotheism might be stated as follows: We believe the Godhead consists of three persons—Father, Son, and Holy Ghost. Each of these persons possesses all of the attributes of godliness in perfection. The love and unity that exist among the Father, Son, and Holy Ghost are of such magnitude—indeed, we may appropriately say that they are infinitely more one than they are separate—that they form a divine community that is frequently referred to in scripture as "one God" (2 Nephi 31:21; Alma 11:44; Mormon 7:7; 3 Nephi 11:27, 36; 28:10; D&C 20:28; 50:43).

"This unity is a type of completeness," Elder James E. Talmage observed. "The mind of any one member of the Trinity is the mind of the others; seeing as each of them does with the eye of perfection, they see and understand alike. Under any given conditions each would act in the same way, guided by the same principles of unerring justice and equity. The oneness of the Godhead, to which the scriptures so abundantly testify, implies no mystical union of substance, nor any unnatural and therefore impossible blending of personality. Father, Son, and Holy Ghost are as distinct in their persons and individualities as are any three persons in mortality. Yet their unity of purpose and operation is such as to make their edicts one, and their will the will of God" (41).

SOURCES

Joseph Smith [manual]. Teachings of Presidents of the Church series. Salt Lake City: The Church of Jesus Christ of Latter-day Saints, 2007.

Smith, Joseph. *History of The Church of Jesus Christ of Latter-day Saints.* Edited by B. H. Roberts. 7 vols. 2d ed. rev. Salt Lake City: The Church of Jesus Christ of Latter-day Saints, 1932–51.

Talmage, James E. *Articles of Faith.* Classics in Mormon Literature series. Salt Lake City: Deseret Book, 1981.

RLM

GODHOOD

God the Father and his Son, Jesus Christ, are glorified, exalted, perfected personages. They yearn to forgive our sins and purify our hearts, and they delight to honor those who serve them in righteousness and in truth to the end (D&C 76:5). That is, they are neither possessive of their powers nor hesitant about dispensing spiritual gifts or sharing their divine attributes. Joseph Smith taught the School of the Elders that all those who keep God's commandments "shall grow up from grace to grace, and become heirs of the heavenly kingdom, and joint heirs with Jesus Christ; possessing the same mind, being transformed into the same image or likeness" (*Lectures,* 60).

All men and women, like Christ, are made in the image and likeness of God (Genesis 1:27; Moses 2:27), and so Latter-day Saints feel it is neither audacity nor heresy for the children of God to aspire to be like God. Consider the implications of the following scriptural passages:

"Be ye therefore perfect, *even as your Father* which is in heaven is perfect" (Matthew 5:48; emphasis added).

"For as many as are led by the Spirit of God, they are the [children] of God. For ye have not received the spirit of bondage again to fear; but ye have received the Spirit of adoption, whereby we cry, Abba, Father. The Spirit itself beareth witness with our spirit, that we are the children of God: And *if children, then heirs; heirs of God, and joint-heirs with Christ;* if so be that we suffer with him, that we may be also glorified together" (Romans 8:14–17; emphasis added).

"Where the Spirit of the Lord is, there is liberty. But we all, with open face beholding as in a glass [mirror] the glory of the Lord, are changed into the same image [of Christ] from glory to glory, even as by the Spirit of the Lord" (2 Corinthians 3:17–18).

"Grace and peace be multiplied unto you through the knowledge of God, and of Jesus our Lord, according as his divine power hath given unto us all things that pertain unto life and godliness, through the knowledge of him that hath called us to glory and virtue: whereby are given unto us exceeding great and precious promises: that by these *ye might be partakers of the divine nature,* having escaped the corruption that is in the world through lust" (2 Peter 1:2–4; emphasis added).

"Behold, what manner of love the Father hath bestowed upon us, that we should be called the [children] of God: therefore the world knoweth us not, because it knew him not. Beloved, now are we the [children] of God, and it doth not yet appear what we shall be: but we know that, *when he shall appear, we shall be like him;* for we shall see him as he is" (1 John 3:1–2; emphasis added).

It appears that the first revelation of the doctrine of deification—that we can become like our Heavenly Father—to the restored Church came in the vision of the glories of heaven (D&C 76) on 16 February 1832 at Father John Johnson's home. Those who attain unto the highest heaven are described as people who "overcome by faith, and are sealed by the Holy Spirit of promise, which the Father sheds forth upon all those who are just and true. They are they who are the church of the Firstborn. They are they into whose hands the Father has given all things—they are they who are priests and kings, who have received of his fulness and of his glory; . . . wherefore, as it is written [presumably in Psalm 82:6 and John 10:34], *they are gods, even the sons of God*" (D&C 76:53–56, 58; emphasis added).

Between the time of this vision in 1832 and the King Follett sermon on 7 April 1844, Joseph Smith and the early brethren took part in a training program known as the School of the Elders. In the winter of 1834–35 in Kirtland, the Lectures on Faith were delivered. Lecture Five is not only a deep and profoundly significant discussion of the Godhead but also a specific reference to men and women becoming like God through being graced and endowed with the power and might and glory and mind of Deity (61).

"Man is made an agent to himself before his God," President Brigham Young declared. "He is organized for the express purpose, that he may become like his master. You recollect one of the Apostle's sayings, that when we see Him, we shall be like Him [1 John 3:1–2]; and again, We shall become Gods, even the sons of God [D&C 76:88]. . . . We are created, we are born for the express purpose of growing up from the low estate of manhood, to become Gods, like unto our Father in heaven" (3:93).

On the one hand, we worship a divine Being with whom we can in some degree identify. That is to say, his infiniteness does not preclude either his immediacy or his intimacy. "In the day that God created man," the Prophet's inspired translation of Genesis attests, "in the likeness of God made he him; in the image of his own body, male and female, created he them" (Moses 6:8–9). We believe that God is not simply a spirit influence, a force in the universe, or the Great First Cause; when we pray, "Our Father which art in heaven" (Matthew 6:9), we mean what we say. We believe God is comprehensible, knowable, approachable, and, like his Beloved Son, "touched with the feeling of our infirmities" (Hebrews 4:15).

Our God is God. Scriptural passages that speak of him being the same yesterday, today, and forever clearly refer to his divine attributes—his love, justice, constancy, and willingness to bless his children. He is our Heavenly Father, the Father of our spirits (Numbers 16:22; 27:16; Hebrews 12:9). He is a glorified, exalted man, a "Man of Holiness" (Moses 6:57), possessing a body of flesh and bones as tangible as man's (D&C 130:22). We are created in his image and likeness. God is in every way a divine Being. He possesses in perfection every godly attribute. There is no truth he does not know and no power he does not possess. He is omnipotent, omniscient, and, by the power of his Holy Spirit, omnipresent.

Many Christians find the Latter-day Saint concept of deification, or *theosis,* to be problematic at best and perverse at worst. Why? Simply because of the LDS belief that God is not the "Wholly Other" or the distant Deity but rather our literal Father in Heaven. Our belief that finite human beings may relate to and come to be like the infinite and eternal Being borders on blasphemy, they contend, for it shortens the otherwise infinite chasm between Creator and creation. Yes, we would have to agree that one of Joseph Smith's most significant prophetic endeavors was, under inspiration, to make the Father of the universe more accessible to his family members within that universe, to retrieve the unreachable, unknowable, timeless, and impassible Deity that had been pushed to the grand beyond by creedal Christianity.

Some have described our view of Deity as a belief in a finite God. The scriptures say otherwise. From the Doctrine and Covenants, for example, we learn that Latter-day Saints worship "a God in heaven, who is infinite and eternal, from everlasting to everlasting the same unchangeable God, the framer of heaven and earth, and all things which are in them" (D&C 20:17). The Almighty sits "enthroned, with glory, honor, power, majesty, might, dominion, truth, justice, judgment, mercy, and an infinity of fulness" (D&C 109:77). He is not a student, an apprentice, or a novice.

Previous and current Church leaders have spoken little concerning which of God's attributes are communicable and which are incommunicable—that is, which qualities or powers may be conveyed to his children and which are retained as a part of his supreme sovereignty. While we believe that becoming like God is entailed in eternal life (D&C 132:19–20), we do not believe we will ever unseat God the Eternal Father or his Only Begotten Son, Jesus Christ; those holy beings are and forever will be the Gods we worship. Even though we believe in the ultimate deification of man, no authoritative statement within LDS literature suggests that men and women will ever worship any being other than the ones within the Godhead. Elder Parley P. Pratt, in describing those who are glorified and attain eternal life, stated, "The difference between Jesus Christ and another immortal and celestial man is this: the man is subordinate to Jesus Christ and does nothing in and of himself, but does all things in the name of Christ and by his authority, being of the same mind and ascribing all the glory to him and his Father" (32).

Elder Hyrum M. Smith and Janne M. Sjodahl offer the following commentary on the statement "Then shall they be gods" (D&C 132:20): "What a wonderful Revelation this is, when compared with the narrow ideas held in the world! Children of kings are princes and princesses, associating on terms of equality with their royal parents, and having a good chance of becoming kings and queens themselves. But when we say that the privilege of God's children is to associate with Him in the eternal mansions, and that they may become gods, then the world does not understand us, and many deem us guilty of blasphemy. *They seem to think that they honor God by supposing that His children are infinitely inferior to Him. What kind of father is He, then, that He should feel it an honor to be the progenitor of an inferior offspring?* Is there a king on earth who would feel honored by having degenerates and beggars for children? Do not fathers and mothers rejoice in the progress of their children? Is it not their ambition to educate and train their loved ones, until these shall reach the highest possible degree of intelligence and efficiency? Surely, we can do no greater honor to God, our Father, than to admit the divine possibilities which He has implanted in His offspring, and which will be developed under His tuition in this life and hereafter, until His children are perfect as He is perfect" (826–27).

We do not believe we can work ourselves into glory or godhood or that we can gain eternal life through human effort alone. One does not become more Christlike through sheer grit and willpower. Central to all spiritual progress is the atonement of Jesus Christ, and it is only by and through his righteousness that we may be declared righteous. It is only by the power of his precious blood that we may be cleansed and sanctified from the taint and tyranny of sin. And it is only by and through the power of his everlasting life that we receive life—energy, strength, vitality, renewal, enabling power—to accomplish what we could never accomplish on our own.

Whether Latter-day Saint doctrines of exaltation and deification are the same as those delivered by fathers of the early Church, Eastern Orthodox thinkers of the past and present, or modern Christians is immaterial. Joseph Smith did not align himself with practices and beliefs of his day in order to gain legitimacy—nor do we in the twenty-first century. We do not seek or require a theological imprimatur from Catholic, Orthodox, or Protestant Christians. The point is that the doctrine of deification, divinization, or *theosis* has been around for a long time, and it should require more than a tiny bit of cognitive or spiritual dissonance to dismiss or ignore it outright.

"The whole design of the gospel," President Gordon B. Hinckley declared, "is to lead us onward and upward to greater achievement, even, eventually, to godhood. This great possibility was enunciated by the Prophet Joseph Smith in the King Follett sermon and emphasized by President Lorenzo Snow. . . . Our enemies have criticized us for believing in this. Our reply is that this lofty concept in no way diminishes God the Eternal Father. He is the Almighty. He is the Creator and Governor of the universe. He is the greatest of all and will always be so. But just as any earthly father wishes for his sons and daughters every success in life, so I believe our Father in Heaven wishes for his children that they might approach him in stature and stand beside him resplendent in godly strength and wisdom" (48).

Does God want his children to be like him, or is this something that repulses him? Is this idea inappropriate? Does God possess the power to recreate men and women in his own image? What scriptural injunctions preclude the children of God from aspiring to be like him in every way possible?

Through the Savior's blood, according to *Lectures on Faith*, God's children "have a forgiveness of sins, and also a sure reward laid up for [us] in heaven, even that of partaking of the fullness of the Father and the Son through the Spirit. As the Son partakes of the fullness of the Father through the Spirit, so the saints are, by the same Spirit, to be partakers of the same fullness, to enjoy the same glory; for as the Father and the Son are one, so, in like manner, the saints are to be one in them. Through the love of the Father, the mediation of Jesus Christ, and the gift of the Holy Spirit, they are to be heirs of God, and joint heirs with Jesus Christ" (61).

SOURCES

Hinckley, Gordon B. "Don't Drop the Ball." *Ensign,* Nov. 1994, 46–49.

Lectures on Faith. Salt Lake City: Deseret Book, 1985.

Pratt, Parley P. *Key to the Science of Theology; A Voice of Warning.* Salt Lake City: Deseret Book, 1978.

Smith, Hyrum Mack, and Janne M. Sjodahl. *The Doctrine and Covenants Commentary.* Rev. ed. Salt Lake City: Deseret Book, 1972.

Young, Brigham. In *Journal of Discourses.* 26 vols. London: Latter-day Saints' Book Depot, 1854–86.

RLM

GOG AND MAGOG

"Gog and Magog" is a phrase used to identify the last two great battles of earth's seven-thousand-year temporal history, one before the Millennium and one after. Though the first of these battles is usually called Armageddon, Gog and Magog are also names sometimes applied to the great battle of the last days, raging at the very moment the Second Coming of Jesus Christ occurs on the Mount of Olives in Jerusalem. Though John the Revelator calls the premillennial conflict "the battle of that great day of God Almighty" as well as the more common "Armageddon" (Revelation 16:14, 16), Ezekiel refers to it as the battle of "Gog, the land of Magog" (Ezekiel 38:2). In Ezekiel's vision, Gog, the chief prince of Meshech and Tubal, leads a massive coalition of world powers, a combination of nations. Gog invades Israel and seeks to destroy the people of God. But the savage hordes that come against Israel from the north are defeated by the hand of the Lord on the mountains of Israel (Ezekiel 38–39).

Other prophets describe a similar scenario for the premillennial battle. Zechariah was vivid in his portrayal. The battle involves "all nations" (Zechariah 14:2). They lay siege to Jerusalem and Judah (Zechariah 12:2–3). Jerusalem is "taken, and the houses rifled, and the women ravished," and half the city goes forth in captivity (Zechariah 14:2). However, the Lord will come as a thief, "his feet shall stand . . . upon the mount of Olives," which will split in two, and he then will fight against the nations who are attacking Jerusalem, defeat them, and become the "king over all the earth" (Zechariah 14:4, 9).

Ezekiel adds significant details about this worldwide military engagement. The battle of Gog and Magog will take place after the Lord has gathered "the children of Israel from among the heathen" and brought them "into their own land" (Ezekiel 37:21). It will occur "in the latter years" (Ezekiel 38:8), meaning the latter days. The hordes will invade a land whose inhabitants have gathered or been "brought forth out of the nations," and who, at the time, "dwell safely" in a "land of unwalled villages" (Ezekiel 38:8, 11)—unlike ancient times, when all towns and villages were built within great walls for protection. Gog and all his troops and the many nations that are with him will "be like a cloud to cover the land" (Ezekiel 38:9). They will be "a mighty army" coming from the north (Ezekiel 38:15). When Gog invades, the fury of the Lord will rise up against the invaders (Ezekiel 38:18). A "great shaking in the land of Israel" will occur (Ezekiel 38:19), and "the mountains shall be thrown down" (Ezekiel 38:20). John the Revelator also mentions "a great earthquake" during the period before the Second Coming (Revelation 6:12). The Lord will execute judgment against the invaders "with pestilence and with blood" and with "an overflowing rain, and great hailstones, fire, and brimstone" (Ezekiel 38:22). Said he, "Thus will I magnify myself, and sanctify myself; and I will be known in the eyes of many nations, and they shall know that I am the Lord" (Ezekiel 38:23).

The forces of Gog will be destroyed upon the mountains of Israel and then be given to "the ravenous birds of every sort, and to the beasts of the field to be devoured" (Ezekiel 39:4; see also D&C 29:18–21). Those who live in the towns of Israel will go out and use the weapons of their opponents for fuel. And they will plunder those who plundered them (Ezekiel 39:9–10). So great will be the carnage among the forces of Gog that it will take the house of Israel seven months to bury those destroyed by the hand of the Lord (Ezekiel 39:12–13). Such are the things that surely will come to pass. Little wonder that during his mortal ministry, Jesus referred to the events of the last days and those associated with the Second Coming as a repeat of the abomination of desolation: "And again, this Gospel of the Kingdom shall be preached in all the world, for a witness unto all nations, and then shall the end come, or the destruction of the wicked; and again shall the abomination of desolation, spoken of by Daniel the prophet, be fulfilled" (Joseph Smith–Matthew 1:31–32).

Nevertheless, after the events of horror and destruction have run their course, as described by Ezekiel, glorious days of peace and plenty will abound. The Lord will reign on the earth, and all will know that he is in control of all things. "And I will set my glory among the heathen, and all the heathen shall see my judgment that I have executed, and my hand that I have laid upon them. So the house of Israel shall know that I am the Lord their God from that day and forward" (Ezekiel 39:21–22). This is the prophesied time when the Jewish people will be redeemed and know that Jesus of Nazareth was and is their Messiah.

President Joseph Fielding Smith described the scene: "At that particular time will the Savior come as their Deliverer and show them his hands and his feet. They will look upon him and ask him where he received his wounds, and he will tell them they were received in the house of his friends; he is Jesus Christ, their Redeemer. Then will they fall to the ground and mourn, every family apart, because their ancestors persecuted their King and the children have followed in the footsteps of the fathers" (3:47; see also D&C 45:51–53).

While the Jews anciently did not believe that Jesus of Nazareth was the Messiah and thus did not believe in the second coming of Christ, they did believe that a battle of Gog and Magog would precede the coming of their Messiah. "Gog and Magog also appear in the Dead Sea Scrolls and are vividly portrayed in Talmudic literature, where the war against Gog and Magog is identified with the 'messianic wars' preceding the advent of the Messiah" (Werblowsky, 279).

It is interesting that the complete phrase "Gog and Magog" does not appear in Ezekiel but only in John's apocalyptic Revelation (Revelation 20:8); however, John applies the name not to Armageddon but to another great conflict, a final battle that will take place at the *end* of the Millennium (Smith, *Doctrines*, 3:45). The Prophet Joseph Smith stated: "The battle of Gog and Magog will be after the millennium. The remnant of all the nations that fight against Jerusalem were commanded to go up to Jerusalem to worship in the millennium" (5:298). John the Revelator describes the final battle of Gog and Magog in these words: "And when the thousand years are expired, Satan shall be loosed out of his prison, and shall go out to deceive the nations which are in the four quarters of the earth, Gog and Magog, to gather them together to battle: the number of whom is as the sand of the sea. And they went up on the breadth of the earth, and compassed the camp of the saints about, and the beloved city: and fire came down from God out of heaven, and devoured them" (Revelation 20:7–9; see also D&C 88:111–16).

By knowing the scriptures and studying "the wars and the perplexities of the nations, and the judgments which are on the land" (D&C 88:79), the Lord's disciples can be prepared for the future and need not fear (D&C 38:30). They can come to appreciate that the Lord knows all things and possesses all power and ability to bring about his righteous and just purposes in the end.

SOURCES

Josephus, Flavius. *Jewish Antiquities.* Translated by Ralph Marcus and Allen Wikgren. Cambridge, Mass: Harvard University Press, 1963.

Smith, Joseph. *History of The Church of Jesus Christ of Latter-day Saints.* Edited by B. H. Roberts. 7 vols. 2d ed. rev. Salt Lake City: The Church of Jesus Christ of Latter-day Saints, 1932–51.

Smith, Joseph Fielding. *Doctrines of Salvation.* Compiled by Bruce R. McConkie. 3 vols. Salt Lake City: Bookcraft, 1954–56.

Werblowsky, R. J. Zwi, and Geoffrey Wigoder, eds. *The Oxford Dictionary of the Jewish Religion.* New York: Oxford University Press, 1997.

ACS

GOLGOTHA

The word *Golgotha* is the anglicized form of the Aramaic *gulgaltha,* which means "skull." Its Latin equivalent is *calvaria,* or Calvary. Both are found in the canonical Gospels as the name of the place where Jesus Christ was crucified. Matthew 27:33, Mark 15:22, and John 19:17 use Golgotha, while Luke 23:33 uses Calvary. Its location was outside Jerusalem's city walls because no executions were allowed within the city, based on ancient regulation (Numbers 15:35; 1 Kings 21:13; Acts 7:58). Processions involving the condemned person led from the place of sentencing to the site of execution. In Jesus' case, the procession was led by a Roman centurion and accompanied by at least a quaternion (four soldiers) to keep the procession moving (John 19:16, 23; Luke 23:26–27).

John states that Golgotha was close to the city, thus many of the Jews could read the *titulus* ("title"), or placard, placed on the cross that bore the words "JESUS OF NAZARETH THE KING OF THE JEWS," written in three languages—Hebrew, Greek, and Latin (John

19:19). Other scriptures also indicate that Golgotha was situated outside of one of the city gates (Hebrews 13:12–13), all of which fits with Roman penal philosophy. The primary purpose of crucifixion was deterrence of crime, which was why "Romans placed crosses along well-traveled highways, on tops of hills, and at city gates" (*New,* 1:806). The Romans themselves said, "Whenever we crucify the condemned, the most crowded roads are chosen, where the most people can see and be moved by this terror. For penalties relate not so much to retribution as to their exemplary effect" (*New,* 1:807).

The reason that the Savior's crucifixion site was named Golgotha or "skull" remains unclear. Elder James E. Talmage lists some possibilities. Perhaps the name denoted topographical features (some have proposed it was a round, bare spot resembling a skull). Maybe it was a symbolic name representing death, much the same way the image of a skull and crossbones connotes death in modern times. It has even been suggested, beginning with Jerome (A.D. 347–420), that Golgotha was so named because the skulls and bones from executed criminals, interred nearby, became exposed due to the ravages of animals or the elements. Of course, leaving any portion of a corpse unburied was contrary to Jewish law and would have been rectified immediately (Talmage, 667). One tradition proposes that because the site was an old stone quarry, excavations caused its surrounding terrain to resemble a skull.

Beyond its specific association with the crucifixion and burial of Jesus, the term *Golgotha* is not attested in ancient sources. It could well have been a local term, contemporary with Jesus' time only. It seems significant that Joseph Smith's translation of Matthew 27:35, Mark 15:22, and John 19:17 changes "skull" to "burial"—"Golgotha . . . the place of a burial"—indicating that Golgotha was associated with the nearby entombment of crucifixion victims and not with how it looked topographically. The Joseph Smith Translation thus seems to substantiate the view that the place of Jesus' crucifixion was close to his burial, which is the testimony of John: "Now in the place where he was crucified there was a garden; and in the garden a new sepulchre, wherein was never man yet laid. There laid they Jesus" (John 19:41–42).

The four Gospels make no explicit mention of Golgotha being situated on a hill or a mountain. But some have proposed that it was so because it could be seen from "afar off," according to Mark 15:40. Some Latter-day Saint hymns speak of Calvary as being on a hill (*Hymns,* nos. 181, 182, 194).

A traditional site for the location of Golgotha is inside the Church of the Holy Sepulchre, which places the spot where the Savior's cross was located on top of a bedrock rise of about fifteen feet, which would have been a hill anciently. Christians showed little interest in the location of the Crucifixion prior to the fourth century A.D. But according to writers of the age, when the emperor Constantine's mother, Helena, went to the Holy Land in A.D. 326, she identified the true sites of our Lord's ministry, including Golgotha, through a vision she was given. After removing a temple dedicated to Aphrodite, built on the site during the time of Roman emperor Hadrian, Constantine erected two churches where the present Church of the Holy Sepulchre stands.

Another proposed location of Golgotha is near the present-day Garden Tomb, in east Jerusalem. The vicinity of the Garden Tomb as a possibility for Golgotha should not be cavalierly dismissed, even though long-held tradition favors the Church of the Holy Sepulchre. From Mosaic times onward, Levitical requirements for animal sacrifices and offerings dictated that they be made on the north side of the tabernacle or temple altar (Leviticus 1:11). In other words, sacrificial animals were to be slaughtered north of the great altar of burnt offering, the brazen altar, during the days when the tabernacle and first temple existed (Exodus 27:1–2; 39:39), and north of the great altar of sacrifice, "in the area of the north of the Court of the Israelites" (Vamosh, 23), during the days of the second temple, the temple associated with Zerubbabel and Herod. Because all animal sacrifices (burnt, peace, or sin offerings, and so forth) symbolized the "great and last sacrifice" of the Son of God (Alma 34:13–14) down to exact details, it seems appropriate to look for the location of the Crucifixion and entombment of Jesus north of the great altar of the temple at Jerusalem, outside the city walls, and near a thoroughfare constructed in harmony with rules pertaining to ritual purity. Considering all these facts, a location for Golgotha near the Garden Tomb is favored.

Additionally, the issue of ritual purity must be considered when attempting to locate the ancient site of Golgotha because the place of Jesus' crucifixion and the place of his burial were so close to each other

(John 19:41–42). Scholars have concluded that since "burial customs in the first half of the first century C.E. [A.D.] preclude burials and their attendant impurities west (windward) of the Temple, then the crucifixion and burial of Jesus could not have taken place at the site of the Church of the Holy Sepulchre, which is almost exactly due west of the Holy of Holies" (Rousseau, 169). The Holy of Holies was the most sacred portion of the Jerusalem temple, the holiest spot on earth, and was to be guarded above all else.

Amidst some points of uncertainty about Golgotha, one fact stands out. There, at 3 P.M. (the ninth hour) on the eve of Passover, Jesus of Nazareth took his final breath in mortality (Matthew 27:46, 50; Luke 23:44–46) and passed into the world of spirits to continue his ministry to humankind (D&C 138). He endured the torture of the cross at Golgotha for six hours, having been nailed to it at the third hour, or 9 A.M. (Mark 15:25). Unlike the circumstances associated with other victims of crucifixion, the name of the specific and special place where the Son of God carried out a vital part of his atoning sacrifice has been preserved for us.

SOURCES

"Jesus of Nazareth, Savior and King." *Hymns of The Church of Jesus Christ of Latter-day Saints,* no. 181. Salt Lake City: The Church of Jesus Christ of Latter-day Saints, 1985.

The New Interpreter's Dictionary of the Bible. 5 vols. Nashville, Tenn.: Abingdon Press, 2006–9.

Rousseau, John J., and Rami Arav. *Jesus and His World: An Archaeological and Cultural Dictionary.* Minneapolis: Fortress Press, 1995.

Talmage, James E. *Jesus the Christ.* Salt Lake City: Deseret Book, 1973.

"There Is a Green Hill Far Away." *Hymns of The Church of Jesus Christ of Latter-day Saints,* no. 194. Salt Lake City: The Church of Jesus Christ of Latter-day Saints, 1985.

Vamosh, Miriam Feinberg. *Daily Life at the Time of Jesus.* Herzlia, Israel: Palphot, n.d.

"We'll Sing All Hail to Jesus' Name." *Hymns of The Church of Jesus Christ of Latter-day Saints,* no. 182. Salt Lake City: The Church of Jesus Christ of Latter-day Saints, 1985.

ACS

GOOD SHEPHERD

Jesus likened himself to the Good Shepherd and thereby depicted unique characteristics of himself as our Savior. In contrast to the hireling who cares nothing for the sheep but scrambles to save himself when predators threaten to scatter or kill the sheep, the Good Shepherd sacrifices his own life in order to preserve the sheep (John 10:11–13). He will go after a sheep that goes astray, searching until the lost one is found (Luke 15:3–7). The Good Shepherd goes ahead of the sheep, "gently" showing them the way (Isaiah 40:11; John 10:4). He knows each of his sheep, and his sheep know him (John 10:4, 14). The Good Shepherd knows which of the sheep are his because they trust and follow him; they will not follow a stranger because they do not know the stranger's voice (John 10:4–5, 27).

Using the same imagery, the apostle Peter referred to Christ as "the chief Shepherd," suggesting that undershepherds may assist the Good Shepherd in his labors (1 Peter 5:4). The apostle Paul called Jesus "the great shepherd" (Hebrews 13:20). The psalmist referred to him as the "Shepherd of Israel" and the only One who gives us hope, comfort, and complete satisfaction for our needs (Psalm 80:1; 23:1–6). A setting that illustrates the Savior's role as the ultimate Shepherd of our souls occurred the night before the Crucifixion, when Jesus warned his apostles at the Last Supper that they would be "offended because of me this night" and become like scattered sheep without their shepherd (Matthew 26:31). We would be forever lost without the guidance and protection of the Good Shepherd.

The Lord's work to gather his sheep, bringing them to a true knowledge of him, continues until they are numbered and brought in from "the four quarters of the earth" (1 Nephi 22:25; 10:14). Then there will be "one fold and one shepherd; and he shall feed his sheep, and in him they shall find pasture" (1 Nephi 22:25).

CFO

GOOD WORKS

Good works always characterize the followers of the Lord Jesus Christ. Because they have been "called . . . out of darkness into his marvellous light" (1 Peter 2:9), they "walk in the light" and have fellowship with the Father and the Son through the Spirit (1 John 1:7). They may err in judgment, make mistakes, and sin, but they do not continue in sin, for they have been born of the Spirit (1 John 3:9). Rather, they do their best to love and serve God and their fellowmen, accept and magnify Church callings, and strive to make a difference in a world that is desperately in need of goodness. The works of righteousness do not save us of themselves, although they do manifest our gratitude for the Savior's love. Salvation is in Christ and comes through trusting in and relying upon his merits, mercy, and grace (2 Nephi 2:8; 31:19; Moroni 6:4). Salvation, or eternal life, is "the greatest of all the *gifts* of God" (D&C 6:13; 14:7; emphasis added) and must be received by faith and the fruits of faith—repentance, baptism, the reception of the Holy Ghost, and enduring obediently to the end of our days.

The following passages of scripture illustrate that the Lord expects his people to be obedient, to keep his commandments:

"Not every one that saith unto me, Lord, Lord, shall enter into the kingdom of heaven; but he that doeth the will of my Father which is in heaven" (Matthew 7:21).

"For the Son of Man shall come in the glory of his Father with his angels; and then he shall reward every man according to his works" (Matthew 16:27).

"And [Jesus] said to them all, If any man will come after me, let him deny himself, and take up his cross daily, and follow me" (Luke 9:23).

"If ye love me, keep my commandments" (John 14:15).

"Of a truth I perceive that God is no respecter of persons: but in every nation he that feareth him, and worketh righteousness, is accepted with him" (Acts 10:34–35).

"[God] will render to every man according to his deeds" (Romans 2:6; see also Jeremiah 17:10).

"Not the hearers of the law are just before God, but the doers of the law shall be justified" (Romans 2:13).

"This is a faithful saying, and these things I will that thou affirm constantly, that they which have believed in God might be careful to maintain good works. These things are good and profitable unto men" (Titus 3:8).

"But be ye doers of the word, and not hearers only, deceiving your own selves" (James 1:22).

"Thou believest that there is one God; thou doest well: the devils also believe, and tremble. But wilt thou know, O vain man, that faith without works is dead? . . . For as the body without the spirit is dead, so faith without works is dead also" (James 2:19–20, 26).

"And I saw the dead, small and great, stand before God; and the books were opened: and another book was opened, which is the book of life: and the dead were judged out of those things which were written in the books, according to their works" (Revelation 20:12).

"And it came to pass that I said unto them that . . . the day should come that they must be judged of their works, yea, even the works which were done by the temporal body in their days of probation" (1 Nephi 15:32).

"Yea, they are grasped with death, and hell; and death, and hell, and the devil, and all that have been seized therewith must stand before the throne of God, and be judged according to their works" (2 Nephi 28:23).

"Therefore the wicked remain as though there had been no redemption made, except it be the loosing of the bands of death; for behold, the day cometh that all shall rise from the dead and stand before God, and be judged according to their works" (Alma 11:41; see also 12:12).

"And it is requisite with the justice of God that men should be judged according to their works; and if their works were good in this life, and the desires of their hearts were good, that they should also, at the last day, be restored unto that which is good" (Alma 41:3).

"And for this cause I write unto you, that ye may know that ye must all stand before the judgment-seat of Christ, yea, every soul who belongs to the whole human family of Adam; and ye must stand to be judged of your works, whether they be good or evil" (Mormon 3:20).

The holy word certifies that we will be judged by our works, not by the merits of our works, for the prophets proclaim that it is by the merits of Christ that we are saved (2 Nephi 2:8; 31:19; Moroni 6:4). Rather, our works manifest unto God and mortals what kind of people we are, that is, what we are becoming through the cleansing and renovating powers of the Atonement.

RLM

GOSPEL

The gospel is the good news or glad tidings that Jesus Christ came into the world and suffered, bled, and died as an offering for our sins (3 Nephi 27:13–15; D&C 76:40–42), and then rose again from the dead, thus making resurrected immortality and eternal life available to every man, woman, and child on earth (Moses 1:39). The scriptures also refer to the means whereby we receive and appropriate the Atonement as the gospel—namely, by the first principles and ordinances (D&C 33:10–12; 39:5–6). The Book of Mormon is said to contain "the fulness of the gospel of Jesus Christ" (D&C 20:9; 27:5; 42:12; 135:3), but it does not do so in the sense that it contains the fulness of gospel doctrine or a complete recitation of all doctrinal matters revealed as a part of the Restoration; rather, it teaches consistently and powerfully the centrality of the Atonement and the path by which we may apply the atoning blood of Christ and receive peace in this world and eternal life in the world to come.

RLM

GOSPEL, FIRST PRINCIPLES OF

In response to an inquiry concerning the beliefs of Latter-day Saints, the Prophet Joseph Smith penned the Wentworth Letter, the last part of which contains what became the Articles of Faith. These thirteen statements succinctly outline the fundamental teachings of The Church of Jesus Christ of Latter-day Saints. The fourth of these declares, "We believe that the first principles and ordinances of the Gospel are: first, Faith in the Lord Jesus Christ; second, Repentance; third, Baptism by immersion for the remission of sins; fourth, Laying on of hands for the gift of the Holy Ghost" (Articles of Faith 1:4).

The "first principles" refer to those basic, foundational principles that are first and foremost in significance in the gospel of Jesus Christ and in making the Atonement efficacious in our lives. Indeed, these principles grow out of and have meaning because of the Atonement. The resurrected Savior himself identified these principles in defining his gospel when he ministered among his people on the American continent (3 Nephi 11–26; 27:13–21; 2 Nephi 31). The Prophet Joseph Smith taught, "The Doctrine of the Resurrection of the Dead and the

Eternal Judgment are necessary to preach among the first principles of the Gospel of Jesus Christ" (3:379). Latter-day prophets and apostles have also identified enduring to the end, implicit in the scriptures, as "an integral element in the doctrine of Christ" (Holland, 54). Upon these first principles all other doctrines, ordinances, covenants, and practices of the Church are established.

SOURCES

Holland, Jeffrey R. *Christ and the New Covenant: The Messianic Message of the Book of Mormon.* Salt Lake City: Deseret Book, 1997.

Smith, Joseph. *History of The Church of Jesus Christ of Latter-day Saints.* Edited by B. H. Roberts. 7 vols. 2d ed. rev. Salt Lake City: The Church of Jesus Christ of Latter-day Saints, 1932–51.

BLT

GOSPELS, THE

The word *gospel* derives from the Anglo-Saxon term *godspellian* (*god* + *spel,* "story") and means the "good news (of God)." The four New Testament Gospels are compositions that present the good news of the atonement of Jesus Christ, which makes possible the redemption of all humankind from the effects of physical and spiritual death. Thus, some have described the Gospels as "passion narratives [Latin, *passus,* "to suffer"] with long biographical introductions," meaning "their central message was the death and resurrection of Jesus" (Brown, 25). While the Gospels do provide us with the fullest account of the mortal ministry of Jesus found in scripture, they are not really biographies. The Joseph Smith Translation changes their titles to "The Testimony of St Matthew," "The Testimony of St Mark," "The Testimony of St Luke," and "The Testimony of St John." Their message underscores this change.

Latter-day Saints assert that the four Gospels are inspired documents, that the Spirit of God prompted and guided their authors. Both LDS and non-LDS scholars have shown that there is good reason to believe in the reliability of the canonical Gospels. This means that the portrayal of Jesus in Matthew, Mark, Luke, and John "isn't only historically reliable. It's also God's way of helping us know who Jesus really is" (Roberts, 195). Noted New Testament scholar F. F. Bruce, who called the "good news" of the Gospels the story of how "God entered into history" to redeem the world (2), has laid out the evidence for their authenticity and reliability. This includes such matters as the number of surviving early manuscripts, archeological corroboration, the testimony of other ancient nonbiblical writers, and the interval of time between the composition of the Gospels and the actual events they describe. Professor Bruce dates the appearance of the original Gospels as follows: Mark around A.D. 64 or 65; Luke shortly before A.D. 70; Matthew shortly after A.D. 70; and John A.D. 90–100 (7). He quotes another authority on ancient manuscripts, Sir Frederic Kenyon, as saying: "The interval then between the dates of original composition and the earliest extant evidence becomes so small as to be in fact negligible. . . . Both the *authenticity* and the general *integrity* of the books of the New Testament may be regarded as finally established" (Bruce, 15).

All of this does not mean, however, that the Gospels are free of error, as some other Christians argue. Latter-day Saints do not believe in the concept of scriptural inerrancy. Our eighth article of faith declares: "We believe the Bible to be the word of God as far as it is translated correctly" (Articles of Faith 1:8). Joseph Smith further stated that he believed "the bible, as it ought to be, as it came from the pen of the original writers" (*Words,* 256). Still, the Prophet observed, "he that can mark the power of Omnipotence, inscribed upon the heavens, can also see God's own handwriting in the sacred volume: and he who reads it oftenest will like it best" (2:14).

Each of the Gospels contains some unique material, episodes or teachings of the Savior not found in the others. However, Matthew, Mark, and Luke present much of the same material, even using phraseology common to all three. Therefore, they are called the synoptic Gospels, from the Greek *synoptikos,* meaning "common view" or "view together." John's Gospel is very different, containing more than 90 percent unique material (Bible Dictionary, "Gospels"). Perhaps this is a reflection of John's intended audience and purpose—members of the Church of Jesus Christ (Bible Dictionary, "Gospels") already possessing a deeper understanding of and commitment to Jesus, his commandments, and his covenants.

Each Gospel author comes from a different background and appears to be writing with a different primary audience in mind. Matthew, also known as Levi, was a publican, or tax collector

(Matthew 9:9; Luke 5:27, 29). From the beginning of his Gospel, it is obvious he wants to show that Jesus is a son of Abraham through the lineage of David in order to persuade Israel (particularly the Jews) that Jesus is the promised Davidic Messiah (Bible Dictionary, "Gospels"). Matthew cites almost one hundred Old Testament prophecies in support of his testimony. His is the only Gospel to describe the visit of the wise men and the star in the east (Matthew 2:1–12; see also Bible Dictionary, "Gospels"). Matthew was one of the original members of the Quorum of the Twelve Apostles (Luke 6:13, 15).

The early church historian Eusebius (circa A.D. 260–340) reports that Mark was scribe to and interpreter of Peter the chief apostle, and that Mark got his information for his Gospel account directly from Peter (3.39.14–16). Indeed, Peter mentions Mark's being with him in "Babylon," or Rome (1 Peter 5:13). Mark's fast-paced, succinct gospel—which emphasizes Jesus' doings rather than his sayings—is thought to be written for a gentile (Roman) audience (Bible Dictionary, "Gospels," "Mark"). Mark emphasizes Jesus' miracles and sometimes gives geographical and cultural explanations for non-Jewish readers (Mark 2:26; 5:41; 7:2–13). Mark's Gospel is the only one that gives an account of the young man who, after Jesus' arrest, followed Him wearing only a sheet and fleeing naked when almost apprehended (Mark 14:50–52). Mark was not an apostle as far as we know.

Luke was a physician and beloved missionary companion of the apostle Paul (Colossians 4:14; 2 Timothy 4:11; see also Bible Dictionary, "Luke"). His intended audience for both his Gospel and its sequel, the Acts of the Apostles, was the "most excellent Theophilus" (Luke 1:3; Acts 1:1). The identity of this person is not known, but the salutation suggests an individual of distinction or authority (Acts 23:26). It is possible, though not likely, that Luke was generically addressing an educated Greek audience, since the Greek word *theophilus* translates as "one who loves God." Luke's Gospel is a polished literary account and a superb chronological summary of Jesus' ministry. Luke gives more stories about specific women who helped build the kingdom than the other Gospel writers (for example, Luke 8:1–3). Luke's is the only Gospel that describes Jesus' bloody sweat in Gethsemane, perhaps a function of a physician's interest in the physical effects of the Atonement on Jesus (Luke 22:44). He also describes Jesus eating food after his resurrection (Luke 24:42–43). Luke was not an eyewitness to our Lord's majesty and power, nor was he an apostle. But he received his information from those who were eyewitnesses (Luke 1:1–3).

John was in the fishing business with his brother, James, and seems to have been financially comfortable, if not rich (Mark 1:20). That he and his brother possessed strong, intense personalities may be inferred from the fact that Jesus gave them the name Boanerges, "the sons of thunder" (Mark 3:17). We get other insights into their excitable temperaments from the different Gospel accounts (Luke 9:51–56). James and John were original members of the Quorum of the Twelve (Luke 6:13–14; Mark 3:14–17). John, James, and Simon Peter formed the inner circle of three who enjoyed special and sacred experiences with Jesus that the other apostles did not, such as the raising of Jairus's daughter (Mark 5:37–43), the Transfiguration (Mark 9:2), and Gethsemane (Matthew 26:36–37; see also Bible Dictionary, "John"). These three "acted as the First Presidency of the Church in their day" (Smith, *Doctrines,* 3:152). They received the keys of the kingdom on the Mount of Transfiguration (Matthew 17:1–9; Smith, *History,* 3:387). Thus, it is to be expected that John's Gospel would be different from the others. He emphasizes that Jesus was God before he came to earth, that he is the Only Begotten of the Father, and that he is the Light of the world (John 1:1–18). John is the only Gospel writer to describe Nicodemus's night visit to Jesus (John 3:1–21); Jesus' encounter with the Samaritan woman at the well (4:1–30, 39–42); Jesus' raising of Lazarus from the dead (11:1–46); Jesus' special instruction to the Twelve before Gethsemane (John 13–16); Jesus' washing of the apostles' feet (13:1–16); and Jesus' promise that John would tarry on the earth (21:20–24). In his own Gospel, John never refers to himself by name but as "the disciple whom Jesus loved" (13:23; 19:26; 20:2; 21:7, 20, 24). This designation may well be based on a family connection rather than some privileged status. It appears that Jesus' mother and the mother of John (Salome) were sisters, making Jesus and John first cousins (compare Matthew 27:56; Mark 16:1; and John 19:25).

As Luke implies, after Jesus' death there were many attempts to collect accounts of Jesus' life and ministry (Luke 1:1). These attempts continued for centuries, sometimes resulting in the creation of apocryphal gospels that lost their way by discounting or focusing on matters other than the redemptive suffering, physical death, and bodily resurrection of the literal Son of God as the only means of salvation. Many of these apocryphal texts allege that the real basis for salvation was veiled teachings or secret knowledge about the complete evil of the material world (including the physical body and a literal resurrection), and which, they say, Jesus imparted to special disciples initiated into these mysteries. In our current New Testament texts there are indications that early Church leaders were already aware of these apostate trends and were forcefully trying to correct errant views (1 John 1).

How different are the true, orthodox, canonical Gospels from those apocryphal texts. By their content, these four Gospels help us to see what is most important about the mortal life and ministry of Jesus Christ and what the Gospel writers understood to be the essential reason for the Messiah's earthly sojourn. Clearly, their focus is on the last week of his ministry—particularly the last twenty-four hours of his life and his postresurrection appearances. Depending on the Gospel, anywhere from one-fourth to almost one-half of the text concentrates on this time frame (Matthew 21–28; Mark 11–16; Luke 19–24; and John 12–21). As John himself testified, all these things "are written, that ye might believe that Jesus is the Christ, the Son of God; and that believing ye might have [eternal] life through his name" (John 20:31).

SOURCES

Brown, S. Kent. "I Have a Question." *Ensign,* Aug. 1975, 25.

Bruce, F. F. *The New Testament Documents: Are They Reliable?* Grand Rapids, Mich.: Eerdmans, 1985.

Eusebius. *Ecclesiastical History.* Vol. 1. Translated by Kirsopp Lake. 2 vols. Cambridge, Mass.: Harvard University Press, 1992.

Roberts, Mark D. *Can We Trust the Gospels?* Wheaton, Ill.: Crossway Books, 2007.

Smith, Joseph. *History of The Church of Jesus Christ of Latter-day Saints.* Edited by B. H. Roberts. 7 vols. 2d ed. rev. Salt Lake City: The Church of Jesus Christ of Latter-day Saints, 1932–51.

Smith, Joseph Fielding. *Doctrines of Salvation.* Compiled by Bruce R. McConkie. 3 vols. Salt Lake City: Bookcraft, 1954–56.

The Words of Joseph Smith. Compiled and edited by Andrew F. Ehat and Lyndon W. Cook. Provo, Utah: Brigham Young University Religious Studies Center, 1980.

ACS

GOVERNMENT

The concept of government comes from God. It is a divine principle. In that inspired declaration of beliefs about government recorded in Doctrine and Covenants 134, we read that "governments were instituted of God for the benefit of man; and that he holds men accountable for their acts in relation to them, both in making laws and administering them, for the good and safety of society" (v. 1). The purpose of government is to "secure to each individual the free exercise of conscience, the right and control of property, and the protection of life" (v. 2). Governments and their laws must protect the moral agency of humankind, which is a foundational, inviolable principle of existence, given by God to ensure personal accountability (D&C 101:78). To the extent that a government does not fulfill this purpose, it is out of harmony with God's purposes and plans.

All secular governments, to one degree or another, are imperfect. Only the government of God is perfect. As noted by Elder Hyrum M. Smith and Janne M. Sjodahl: "The Lord in the very beginning revealed to Adam a perfect form of government, and this was 'instituted of God for the benefit of man'; but we do not hold that all governments, or any man-made government, was instituted of God although the Lord holds a controlling hand over them. It was not long after the Lord established His government with Adam, and had commanded him to teach correct principles to his children, that men began to rebel and turn away. . . . 'And Satan came among them, saying: I am also a son of God; and he commanded them, saying: Believe it not; and they believed it not, and they loved Satan more than God. And men began from that time forth to be carnal, sensual, and devilish' [Moses 5:13]. From that time forth the authority to rule was usurped by men and, with few exceptions ever since, the governments in the earth have been and are the governments of men, and the guiding hand of the Lord by revelation and authority vested in his servants has been ignored" (852).

That being said, however, it should be noted that LDS Church leaders have taught that even poor governments are preferable to no government at all. Elder Erastus Snow stated: "Anarchy is the absence of all government; it is the antipodes [opposite] of order; it is the acme of confusion; it is the result of unbridled license, the antipodes of true liberty. . . . Even the monopoly of the one-man-power as in Russia [the

Czar], or the monopoly of the aristocracy as in other parts of Europe, or the imbecility and sometimes stupidity of a republic like our own, is far better than no government at all. And for this reason, says the apostle Paul, 'The powers are ordained of God,' not that they are always the best forms of government for the people, or that they afford liberty and freedom to mankind, but that any and all forms of government are better than none at all. . . . One monopoly is better than many; and the oppression of a king is tolerable, but the oppression of a mob, where every man is a law to himself . . . is the worst form of government" (22:151).

The Lord commanded his people to "be subject to the powers that be, until he reigns whose right it is to reign, and subdues all enemies under his feet" (D&C 58:22). Therefore, Latter-day Saints "believe that all men are bound to sustain and uphold the respective governments in which they reside" (D&C 134:5). It naturally follows that we hold "that sedition and rebellion are unbecoming every citizen" who is "protected in their inherent and inalienable rights by the laws of such governments" (D&C 134:5). President N. Eldon Tanner addressed the question of dealing with unjust laws: "There are many who question the constitutionality of certain acts passed by their respective governments, even though such laws have been established by the highest courts in the land as being constitutional, and they feel to defy and disobey the law. Abraham Lincoln once observed: 'Bad laws, if they exist, should be repealed as soon as possible; still, while they continue in force, they should be religiously observed.' This is the attitude of the Church in regard to law observance. . . .

"There is no reason or justification for men to disregard or break the law or try to take it into their own hands. . . .

"It is the duty of citizens of any country to remember that they have individual responsibilities, and that they must operate within the law of the country in which they have chosen to live" (83).

Latter-day Saints do not believe it is just or proper "to mingle religious influence with civil government." No religious group should be supported in its spiritual privileges and another proscribed (D&C 134:9). In 1907 the First Presidency issued this statement: "The Church of Jesus Christ of Latter-day Saints holds to the doctrine of the separation of church and state; the non-interference of church authority in political matters; and the absolute freedom and independence of the individual in the performance of his political duties. . . .

"We declare that from principle and policy, we favor:

"The absolute separation of church and state;

"No domination of the state by the church;

"No church interference with the functions of the state;

"No state interference with the functions of the church, or
    with the free exercise of religion;

"The absolute freedom of the individual from the domination
    of ecclesiastical authority in political affairs;

"The equality of all churches before the law" (Clark, 4:153).

Civil governments can be of great benefit to their citizens. The apostle Peter wrote to the early Church about the importance of submitting to secular rule and allowing civil government to bring judgment upon the wicked: "Submit yourselves to every ordinance of man for the Lord's sake: whether it be to the king, as supreme; or unto governors, as unto them that are sent by him for the punishment of evildoers" (1 Peter 2:13–14). In a similar vein, the apostle Paul wrote concerning the role of government in God's plan: "For rulers are not a terror to good works, but to the evil. Wilt thou then not be afraid of the power? do that which is good, and thou shalt have praise of the same: For he is the minister of God to thee for good. But if thou do that which is evil, be afraid; for he beareth not the sword in vain: for he is the minister of God, a revenger to execute wrath upon him that doeth evil" (Romans 13:3–4).

In the future a perfect form of government will be established on the earth. Jesus Christ "will come in his power and make an end of all man-made governments and take His rightful place as King of kings, and Lord of lords. He has decreed to make a 'full end of all nations'" (Smith, 852–53). The prophet Isaiah spoke of that glorious millennial era when there would be two world capitals from which the Lord will govern all the earth, "for out of Zion shall go forth the law, and the word of the Lord from Jerusalem" (Isaiah 2:3).

SOURCES

Clark, James R., comp. *Messages of the First Presidency of The Church of Jesus Christ of Latter-day Saints.* 6 vols. Salt Lake City: Bookcraft, 1965–75.

Smith, Hyrum Mack, and Janne M. Sjodahl. *The Doctrine and Covenants Commentary.* Rev. ed. Salt Lake City: Deseret Book, 1972.

Snow, Erastus. In *Journal of Discourses.* 26 vols. London: Latter-day Saints' Book Depot, 1854–86.

Tanner, N. Eldon. "The Laws of God." *Ensign,* Nov. 1975, 82–85.

ACS

GRACE

From a doctrinal perspective, God's grace is his mercy, his love, his condescension toward the children of men. Grace is unmerited favor, unearned divine assistance, goodwill, heavenly benefit, loving-kindness, tender mercy. As explained in the Bible Dictionary of the Latter-day Saint edition of the King James Bible, grace is a "divine means of help or strength, given through the bounteous mercy and love of Jesus Christ. It is through the grace of the Lord Jesus, made possible by his atoning sacrifice, that mankind will be raised in immortality, every person receiving his body from the grave in a condition of everlasting life. It is likewise through the grace of the Lord that individuals, through faith in the atonement of Jesus Christ and repentance of their sins, receive strength and assistance to do good works that they otherwise would not be able to maintain if left to their own means. This grace is an enabling power. . . . Divine grace is needed by every soul in consequence of the fall of Adam and also because of man's weaknesses and shortcomings. . . . It is truly the grace of Jesus Christ that makes salvation possible" (697).

The great plan of happiness is a gift. Salvation, which is exaltation, or eternal life, is free. It is not something for which we can barter, nor is it something we may purchase with money. Neither is it, in the strictest sense, something that may be *earned.* More correctly, salvation is a *gift,* a most precious gift, something gloriously transcendent that may only be inherited (D&C 6:13; 14:7). In commending his son Jacob on the manner in which he had learned wisdom and followed righteousness in his youth, Lehi said: "Thou hast beheld in thy youth his [Christ's] glory; wherefore, thou art blessed even as they unto whom he shall minister in the flesh; for the Spirit is the same, yesterday, today, and forever. And the way is prepared from the fall of man, and *salvation is free*" (2 Nephi 2:4; emphasis added).

When the prophets who lived before the coming of the Lord in the flesh spoke of salvation being free, they were in effect declaring the same doctrine that would come from the apostles and prophets after the ministry of Jesus—that we are saved by the grace of Christ. That is to say, free salvation is salvation by grace. Elder Bruce R. McConkie asked: "What salvation is free? What salvation comes by the grace of God? With all the emphasis of the rolling thunders of Sinai, we answer: All salvation is free; all comes by the merits and mercy and grace of the Holy Messiah; there is no salvation of any kind, nature, or degree that is not bound to Christ and his atonement" (*Promised,* 346–47).

Nephi taught that the people of the earth are summoned to the waters of life to partake of the milk and honey of the gospel without money and without price. "Hath he [the Lord] commanded any that they should not partake of his salvation? . . . Nay; but he hath given it free for all men. . . . Behold, hath the Lord commanded any that they should not partake of his goodness? Behold I say unto you, Nay; but all men are privileged the one like unto the other, and none are forbidden" (2 Nephi 26:27–28).

Sometimes in our efforts to emphasize the importance of good works—of receiving the ordinances of salvation, of living by every word of God, of standing as witnesses of God at all times, and of involving ourselves in acts of Christian service that always characterize the disciples of Jesus in any age—we are wont to overlook the simple yet profound reality that the plan of salvation, the gospel of Jesus Christ, is truly a gospel of grace. Through the atonement of Christ, numerous blessings accrue to mortal men and women, blessings that are unconditional benefits of the work of redemption, acts of pure grace. No works or labors or mortal deeds are necessary to bring these eventualities to pass. They come from a gracious Lord who desires to save all the children of the Father. Truly, we are recipients of graces without number and are beneficiaries of the Lord's love and condescension, of gifts that are beyond our power to work for, earn, or even adequately express gratitude for. Like Nephi, we joy in the covenants of the Lord, we delight "in his grace, and in his justice, and power, and mercy in the great and eternal plan of deliverance from death" (2 Nephi 11:5).

"Some gifts coming from the Atonement are universal, infinite, and unconditional," Elder Jeffrey R. Holland declared. "Other aspects of Christ's atoning gift are conditional. They depend on one's diligence in keeping God's commandments. . . . Of course neither the unconditional nor the conditional blessings of the Atonement are available except through the grace of Christ. Obviously the unconditional blessings of the Atonement are unearned, but the conditional ones are not fully merited either. By living faithfully and keeping the commandments of God, one can receive additional privileges; but they are still given freely, not technically earned" (203–4).

The word *grace* is frequently linked with a companion word. For example, grace is tied to such concepts as truth (2 Nephi 2:6; Alma 5:48; 9:26; 13:9), mercy (2 Nephi 9:8; Alma 5:48), equity (Alma 9:26; 13:9), goodness (Moroni 8:3), greatness (2 Nephi 9:53), assurance (D&C 106:8), fulness (D&C 76:94), justice (2 Nephi 11:5), power (2 Nephi 11:5), and condescension (Jacob 4:7).

Note also the different ways *grace* is used in scripture:

Grace as favor or acceptance in God's eyes (Genesis 6:8; 19:19; Exodus 33:13; 34:9; Luke 2:40)

Grace as a blessing from God (Psalm 84:11; 2 Corinthians 9:8; 13:14; Mosiah 18:26; 27:5; D&C 88:78)

Grace as an outpouring of the Holy Spirit or spiritual gifts (Acts 4:33; Romans 12:6; Ephesians 4:7; Mosiah 18:16; D&C 46:15)

Grace as a calling to preach the gospel (Romans 1:5; 1 Corinthians 3:10; Galatians 1:15; Ephesians 3:7–8; 1 Peter 4:10; Moroni 7:2)

Grace as blessings associated with one's lineage (Amos 5:15; Zechariah 12:10; D&C 84:99)

Grace as that which God gives to the weak, including strength to overcome and endure (Proverbs 3:34; 2 Corinthians 8:9; 12:7–10; James 4:5–6; 1 Peter 5:5; Jacob 4:7; Ether 12:27)

Grace as that which brings salvation (Ephesians 2:8; 2 Timothy 1:9; Titus 2:11; 1 Peter 1:13; 2 Nephi 10:24–25; 25:23; D&C 138:14)

The following passages illustrate how often the doctrine of grace is presented in the scriptures of the Restoration:

"And since man had fallen he could not merit anything of himself; but the sufferings and death of Christ atone for their sins, through faith and repentance" (Alma 22:14).

"Wherefore, I know that thou art redeemed, because of the righteousness of thy Redeemer" (2 Nephi 2:3).

"And thou hast beheld in thy youth his glory; wherefore thou art blessed even as they unto whom he shall minister in the flesh; for the Spirit is the same, yesterday, today, and forever. And the way is prepared from the fall of man, and salvation is free" (2 Nephi 2:4).

"Wherefore, how great the importance to make these things known unto the inhabitants of the earth, that they may know that there is no flesh that can dwell in the presence of God, save it be through the merits, and mercy, and grace of the Holy Messiah" (2 Nephi 2:8).

"Wherefore, my beloved brethren, reconcile yourselves to the will of God, and not to the will of the devil and the flesh; and remember, after ye are reconciled unto God, that it is only in and through the grace of God that ye are saved" (2 Nephi 10:24).

"For we labor diligently to write, to persuade our children, and also our brethren, to believe in Christ, and to be reconciled to God; for we know that it is by grace that we are saved, after all we can do" (2 Nephi 25:23).

"And now, my beloved brethren, after ye have gotten into this strait and narrow path, I would ask if all is done? Behold, I say unto you, Nay; for ye have not come thus far save it were by the word of Christ with unshaken faith in him, relying wholly upon the merits of him who is mighty to save" (2 Nephi 31:19).

"The Lord God showeth us our weakness that we may know that it is by his grace, and his great condescensions unto the children of men, that we have power to do these things" (Jacob 4:7).

"And if ye believe on [Christ's] name ye will repent of all your sins, that thereby ye may have a remission of them through his merits" (Helaman 14:13).

"And if men come unto me I will show unto them their weakness. I give unto men weakness that they may be humble; and my grace is sufficient for all men that humble themselves before me; for if they humble themselves before me, and have faith in me, then will I make weak things become strong unto them" (Ether 12:27; see also D&C 17:8; 18:31).

"And after they had been received unto baptism, and were wrought upon and cleansed by the power of the Holy Ghost, they were numbered among the people of the church of Christ; and their names were taken, that they might be remembered and nourished by the good word of God, to keep them in the right way, to keep them continually watchful unto prayer, relying alone upon the merits of Christ, who was the author and the finisher of their faith" (Moroni 6:4).

"Yea, come unto Christ, and be perfected in him . . . ; and if by the grace of God ye are perfect in Christ, ye can in nowise deny the power of God. And again, if ye by the grace of God are perfect in Christ, and deny not his power, then are ye sanctified in Christ by the grace of God, through the shedding of the blood of Christ" (Moroni 10:32–33).

"And that the Lamanites might come to the knowledge of their fathers, and that they might know the promises of the Lord, and that they may believe the gospel and rely upon the merits of Jesus Christ, and be glorified through faith in his name, and that through their repentance they might be saved" (D&C 3:20).

"If thou wilt do good, yea, and hold out faithful to the end, thou shalt be saved in the kingdom of God, which is the greatest of all the gifts of God; for there is no gift greater than the gift of salvation" (D&C 6:13).

"And, if you keep my commandments and endure to the end you shall have eternal life, which gift is the greatest of all the gifts of God" (D&C 14:7).

"These are they who are just men made perfect through Jesus the mediator of the new covenant, who wrought out this perfect atonement through the shedding of his own blood" (D&C 76:69).

Elder Bruce R. McConkie taught: "Suppose we have the scriptures, the gospel, the priesthood, the Church, the ordinances, the organization, even the keys of the kingdom—everything that now is down to the last jot and tittle—and yet there is no atonement of Christ. What then? Can we be saved? Will all our good works save us? Will we be rewarded for all our righteousness?

"Most assuredly we will not. We are not saved by works alone, no matter how good; we are saved because God sent his Son to shed his blood in Gethsemane and on Calvary that all through him might ransomed be. We are saved by the blood of Christ.

"To paraphrase Abinadi [in Mosiah 13:27–28]: 'Salvation doth not come by the Church alone: and were it not for the atonement, given by the grace of God as a free gift, all men must unavoidably perish, and this notwithstanding the Church and all that appertains to it'" ("Grace," 48).

"Men and women unquestionably have impressive powers and can bring to pass great things," Elder Dallin H. Oaks said. "But after all our obedience and good works, we cannot be saved from death or the effects of our individual sins without the grace extended by the atonement of Jesus Christ. . . . In other words, salvation does not come simply by keeping the commandments. . . . Man cannot earn his own salvation" (75).

SOURCES

Holland, Jeffrey R. *Broken Things to Mend.* Salt Lake City: Deseret Book, 2008.
McConkie, Bruce R. *The Promised Messiah: The First Coming of Christ.* Salt Lake City: Deseret Book, 1978.
———. "What Think Ye of Salvation by Grace?" In *Brigham Young University 1983–84 Fireside and Devotional Speeches,* 44–50. Provo, Utah: Brigham Young University Press, 1984.
Oaks, Dallin H. *With Full Purpose of Heart.* Salt Lake City: Deseret Book, 2002.

RLM

GREAT AND ABOMINABLE CHURCH

The great and abominable church, or church of the devil, is any organization—religious, philosophical, social, economic, or political—that persecutes the Saints of God, revels in riches and immorality, tampers with holy scripture and its meaning, and in general fights against Zion and the establishment of the kingdom of God (Revelation 17–18; 1 Nephi 13:4–9; 2 Nephi 10:16). Mormon taught the following guiding principle: "For behold, the Spirit of Christ [the Light of Christ or Spirit of Jesus Christ] is given to every man, that he may know good from evil; wherefore, I show unto you the way to judge; for every thing which inviteth to do good, and to persuade to believe in Christ, is sent forth by the power and gift of Christ; wherefore ye may know with a perfect knowledge it is of God" (Moroni 7:16).

In June 1829, Oliver Cowdery and David Whitmer were instructed to "contend against no church, save it be the church of the devil" (D&C 18:20). Elder B. H. Roberts offered this insightful commentary on this passage: "I understand the injunction to Oliver Cowdery to 'contend against no church, save it be the church of the devil [D&C 18:20],' to mean that he shall contend against evil, against untruth, against all combinations of wicked men. They constitute the church of the devil, the kingdom of evil, a federation of unrighteousness; and the servants of God have a right to contend against that which is evil, let it appear where it will. . . . But, let it be understood, we are not brought necessarily into antagonism with the various sects of Christianity as such. So far as they have retained fragments of Christian truth—and each of them has some measure of truth—that far they are acceptable unto the Lord: and it would be poor policy for us to contend against them without discrimination. . . . Our relationship to the religious world is not one that calls for the denunciation of sectarian churches as composing the church of the devil" (15).

Elder Roberts further observed: "All that makes for untruth, for unrighteousness constitutes the kingdom of evil—the church of the devil. All that makes for truth, for righteousness, is of God; it constitutes the kingdom of righteousness—the empire of Jehovah; and, in a certain sense at least, constitutes the Church of Christ. With the latter—the kingdom of righteousness—we have no warfare. On the contrary both the spirit of the Lord's commandments to His servants and the dictates of right reason would suggest that we seek to enlarge this kingdom of righteousness both by recognizing such truths as it possesses and seeking the friendship and co-operation of the righteous men and women who constitute its membership" (15).

As wickedness spreads, the church of the devil, or mother of abominations, will continue to grow in all lands and among all peoples until she has "dominion over all the earth." Satan's multimillennia battle against God and the covenant people will continue throughout the earth's temporal existence until, in the closing stages of this mortal realm, the "power of the Lamb of God" will descend "upon the saints of the church of the Lamb, and upon the covenant people of the Lord, . . . and they [will be] armed with righteousness and with the power of God in great glory" (1 Nephi 14:11, 14). "For the time speedily shall come," Nephi wrote, "that all churches which are built up to get gain, and all those who are built up to get power over the flesh, and those who are built up to become popular in the eyes of the world, and those who seek the lusts of the flesh and the things of the world, and to do all manner of iniquity; yea, in fine, all those who belong to the kingdom of the devil are they who need fear, and tremble, and quake; they are those who must be brought low in the dust; they are those who must be consumed as stubble" (1 Nephi 22:23).

SOURCE

Roberts, B. H. In Conference Report, Apr. 1906, 13–17.

RLM

GUILT/REMORSE

Because we all "have sinned, and come short of the glory of God" (Romans 3:23), we have experienced guilt or a "remorse of conscience" (Alma 42:18). Guilt is a natural consequence of knowingly choosing contrary to God's law or setting "at defiance the commandments of God" (Alma 5:18). Nephi knew remorse when his heart sorrowed and his soul grieved because of his flesh and iniquities (2 Nephi 4:17, 28). Guilt is how we feel when we are cut off from the influence or presence of the Spirit. Failure to positively respond to these guilty feelings can lead to denying the truth wherever it is taught, thereby compounding the consequences of our sin (1 Nephi 16:2).

When feelings of guilt and remorse lead us to godly sorrow or deep regret for having offended God and others, we will desire to repent and feel increased faith and love for Jesus Christ. Through the miraculous power of the Atonement when we repent, our guilt is "swept away" (Enos 1:6), whether our sins are relatively small or heinous. The converted Lamanites thanked God, who "hath forgiven us of those our many sins and murders which we have committed, and taken away the guilt from our hearts, through the merits of his Son" (Alma 24:10). Although we may likely remember our offense to God, we will not remember the pains of remorse or be "harrowed up by the memory of [our] sins" when we sincerely repent and exercise faith in the Savior (Alma 36:19).

At the Final Judgment, "we shall be brought to stand before God, knowing even as we know now, and have a bright recollection of all our guilt" (Alma 11:43). Those who have repented through faith in Jesus Christ will be "clothed with purity," being covered by the Atonement and filled with enjoyment rather than guilt (2 Nephi 9:14).

CFO

HADES

In Greek mythology, Hades is the god of the underworld. Thus, in the Greek New Testament, *Hades,* in the broad, general sense, refers to the "place of departed spirits" (Hickie, 3). It corresponds to the Hebrew word *Sheol,* found in the Old Testament. Speaking of this broad meaning, the Prophet Joseph Smith taught, "Hades, the Greek, or Shaole, the Hebrew . . . mean a world of spirits. Hades, Shaole, paradise, spirits in prison, are all one: it is a world of spirits. The righteous and the wicked all go to the same world of spirits until the resurrection" (5:425).

As the Prophet's statement implies, the spirit world contains many parts, just as the Father's house contains "many mansions" (John 14:2). In a more specific sense, then, Hades refers to hell, to that part of the spirit world separated from the place of the righteous, where the wicked await their day of deliverance. These are "those who had died in their sins, without a knowledge of the truth, or in transgression having rejected the prophets" (D&C 138:32).

The apostle John testified that Hades will have an end for most of God's children: "death and hell [Greek, *Hades*] delivered up the dead which were in them" (Revelation 20:13). The prophet Jacob taught that this means bringing the body out of the grave through resurrection and bringing the spirit out of hell, or spirit prison (2 Nephi 9:10–12). Of course, there are those whose sins are of such a nature that they cannot inherit a kingdom of glory. They are sons of perdition. They experience hell everlastingly. "Wherefore, he saves all except them—they shall go away into everlasting punishment, which is endless punishment, which is eternal punishment, to reign with the devil and his angels in eternity, where their worm dieth not, and the fire is not quenched, which is their torment" (D&C 76:44).

SOURCES

Hickie, W. J. *Greek-English Lexicon to the New Testament.* New York: Cosimo, 2007.
Smith, Joseph. *History of The Church of Jesus Christ of Latter-day Saints.* Edited by B. H. Roberts. 7 vols. 2d ed. rev. Salt Lake City: The Church of Jesus Christ of Latter-day Saints, 1932–51.

ACS

HAPPINESS

The scriptures often speak of the supreme happiness that comes from living the principles of the gospel of Jesus Christ. In this context, the word *happiness* is often used interchangeably with the word *joy,* which Lehi says is the intended objective of the plan of salvation (2 Nephi 2:25). Reflecting on this doctrine, the Prophet Joseph Smith stated:

"Happiness is the object and design of our existence; and will be the end thereof, if we pursue the path that leads to it; and this path is virtue, uprightness, faithfulness, holiness, and keeping all the commandments of God. . . . In obedience there is joy and peace unspotted, unalloyed; and as God has designed our happiness—and the happiness of all His creatures, He never has—He never will institute an ordinance or give a commandment to His people that is not calculated in its nature to promote that happiness which He has designed, and which will not end in the greatest amount of good and glory to those who become the recipients of his law and ordinances" (5:134–35).

The Book of Mormon prophet Alma referred to God's plan of salvation for his children as the "plan of happiness" (Alma 42:16). He also taught that the nature of God is "the nature of happiness" (Alma 41:11). His work and glory (Moses 1:39) is to assist his children, through the atonement of Jesus Christ, to partake of his nature and become like him. Eternal life—exaltation in God's celestial kingdom—is to obtain a fulness of joy, a fulness of our Father in Heaven's divine nature of happiness. For this reason, Alma taught his son Corianton that "wickedness never was happiness" (Alma 41:10), because those who ultimately reject God's ways and words "are without God in the world, and they have gone contrary to the nature of God; therefore, they are in a state contrary to the nature of happiness" (Alma 41:10–11).

SOURCE

Smith, Joseph. *History of The Church of Jesus Christ of Latter-day Saints.* Edited by B. H. Roberts. 7 vols. 2d ed. rev. Salt Lake City: The Church of Jesus Christ of Latter-day Saints, 1932–51.

BLT

HEATHEN NATIONS

In the scriptures the phrase "heathen nations" generally refers to those nations or peoples who do not believe in the God of Israel and are not part of the gospel covenant. They are those who believe in false gods or no God. They supplant the "everlasting gospel" with man-made belief systems that have no power to save. In the Old Testament, idol worshippers are referred to as "heathen" (2 Kings 16:3; 17:8, 11; Psalm 135:15; Jeremiah 10:2). The New Testament generally uses the term *heathen* to refer to Gentiles—those not of the lineage of Abraham, Isaac, and Jacob. The apostle Paul spoke of his mission to "preach . . . among the heathen" (Galatians 1:16). In modern revelation the term is used for those, regardless of lineage or religious tradition, who have not had the opportunity to hear and embrace the gospel of Jesus Christ (D&C 45:54; 75:22; 90:7–11). Many passages of scripture declare that the heathens will eventually be given a full opportunity to repent of their ways, turn to the true God, accept the gospel covenant, and be saved in the kingdom of God (Ezekiel 39:21; Zechariah 9:10; Malachi 1:11; Galatians 3:8; 2 Nephi 26:33; D&C 45:54). But as a body the heathen nations, those who "died without law," will qualify only for a terrestrial degree of glory hereafter (D&C 76:72).

BLT

HEAVEN

There are two general ways the term *heaven* is used in the scriptures. First, it is used to refer to the sky, or space above the earth. For example, the first verse of the Bible says, "In the beginning God created the heaven and the earth" (Genesis 1:1; see also 1:8, 17; Moses 2:8). Other verses speak of the space above the earth as "the heavens" (Isaiah 55:9; Joel 2:30; Matthew 3:16; Acts 1:11; Helaman 5:48; see also D&C 45:16; 133:17; 2 Kings 1:10; 2:11; Ezekiel 8:3; 1 Thessalonians 4:16).

The second and most common usage of the term is for the abode of God—the heavenly realm of the Almighty (Isaiah 66:1; Matthew 6:9; Colossians 4:1; 1 Peter 3:22). Thus, God is referred to as our Heavenly Father (Matthew 6:14; Mosiah 2:34). Heaven "is a place where God dwells and all his holy angels" (Alma 18:30). Generally,

299

heaven is a term used to describe the eternal reward for the righteous Saints of God after their resurrection. For example, King Benjamin in the Book of Mormon taught that those who "keep the commandments of God" and "hold out faithful to the end" are "received into heaven, that thereby they may dwell with God in a state of never-ending happiness" (Mosiah 2:41).

There are instances in the scriptures, however, where heaven is used to describe a temporary yet blissful place or state prior to the resurrection of all men. For example, Enoch's city of Zion was "taken up into heaven" (Moses 7:21). Likewise, Moses, Elijah, John, and the three Nephite disciples were translated or "caught up to heaven" in a sense, albeit not to an eternal state. The Prophet Joseph Smith taught: "There are two kinds of beings in heaven, namely: Angels, who are resurrected personages, having bodies of flesh and bones. . . . Secondly: the spirits of just men made perfect, they who are not resurrected, but inherit the same glory" (D&C 129:1, 3). Even before the creation of the earth, Lucifer and his followers who rebelled against the Almighty were "fallen from heaven"—meaning they were cast out of God's presence and his heavenly kingdom (Isaiah 14:12; see also Revelation 12:6–11; D&C 76:25–29). Thus, those who were in God's presence "before the foundation of the world" (1 Peter 1:20) were also, in a sense, in heaven.

In regard to eternal rewards or punishments, Latter-day Saints differ from other Christians in that they believe there are varying levels or degrees of heaven—not just the traditional "heaven or hell" paradigm. Jesus taught: "In my Father's house are many mansions" (John 14:2). The Prophet Joseph Smith explained that the term "mansions" means "kingdoms" (1:245; 6:365). Thus, in heaven, or in the kingdom of heaven there are many kingdoms of glory and eternal rewards (D&C 76; 131:1–3). In that context, all who are redeemed by Jesus Christ and are resurrected to a kingdom of glory inherit heaven in a general sense. In the most precise use of the term, only those who "dwell in the presence of God and his Christ forever and ever" (D&C 76:62) and who have "received of his fulness, and of his glory" (D&C 76:56) are in heaven—meaning they have eternal life in the highest heaven (D&C 132:4, 19–24).

SOURCE

Smith, Joseph. *History of The Church of Jesus Christ of Latter-day Saints.* Edited by
B. H. Roberts. 7 vols. 2d ed. rev. Salt Lake City: The Church of Jesus Christ of
Latter-day Saints, 1932–51.

BLT

HEBREW

The term *Hebrew* has two principal meanings in scripture: it is used to denote a group of people, namely a specific line of Abraham's descendants, but it also refers to the language written and spoken by that lineage. The origins of the term remain unclear. The biblical Hebrew word *'avar* means to "traverse, cross, or pass over." From this root comes the word *'ivri,* usually translated as *Hebrew* in English. The root *'avar* is believed to have been applied to the patriarch Abraham, who traversed significant distances in the Fertile Crescent of western Asia to reach and settle the land promised to him by God as part of the covenant (Genesis 12:1–10; 17:7–8; Abraham 2:6). Thus, Abraham was the first Hebrew (Genesis 14:13), and all of his descendants could technically be designated as Hebrews.

However, in the Old Testament one specific line of Abraham's descendants came to be regarded as the Hebrews: the lineage of Jacob, or Israel. Many scholars regard the term *Hebrew* as synonymous with *Israelite.* The term occurs as both a name used by foreigners to refer to the Israelites and as a designation used by the Israelites to refer to themselves. The Egyptian pharaoh who arose and "knew not Joseph" (Exodus 1:8) spoke of "the Hebrew women" to the midwives (Exodus 1:16, 19). Other passages present the term as one of self-identification (Exodus 2:11, 13; Deuteronomy 15:12; Jeremiah 34:9). The Israelite prophet Jonah called himself a Hebrew (Jonah 1:9). It has been proposed that the term was used generally to refer to the people of Israel before their conquest of the promised land, and the term *Israelite* was used afterward. However, in the New Testament era the apostle Paul referred to himself as "an Hebrew of the Hebrews" (Philippians 3:5). The biblical evidence indicates that the terms *Hebrew, Israelite,* and, later, *Jew,* describe the same people. Attempts on the part of a few historians to associate the word *Hebrew* with the seminomadic people called the Habiru or Apiru, mentioned in Egyptian inscriptions of the thirteenth and twelfth centuries B.C., are unconvincing.

The Hebrew language is that branch of the Semitic family of languages spoken first by the tribes of Israel and, later, by their descendants, called, indiscriminately, the Jews. Before the Israelites conquered the biblical promised land, known also as the land of Canaan, the area was dominated by Canaanite, Phoenician, Aramean, and Philistine tribes who spoke languages related to Hebrew. The Israelites, or Hebrews, brought with them to the land of their conquest their own dialect, which was called Hebrew. Hebrew became the language of the royal court as well as of literary achievement, especially for their sacred record, the Hebrew Bible.

Hebrew diminished in usage significantly after the Israelites (or some of them) returned from the Babylonian captivity in 538 B.C. Also after their return from the exile, the Israelites began to be known as the Jews because most of those who returned were from the southern kingdom of Judah or were members of the other tribes that had merged with the inhabitants of Judah. Hebrew largely became lost to the masses over time, though it remained the language of liturgy and scholarship. It was replaced by Aramaic as the *lingua franca* of the Holy Land in the rabbinic age, roughly 200 B.C. to A.D. 400. When the New Testament speaks of Paul's speech to his fellow Jews "in the Hebrew tongue" (Acts 21:40; 22:2), most authorities, ancient and modern, believe this to have been Aramaic. Aramaic is a sister language to Hebrew, possessing many cognates and being written in the same script after the eighth century B.C.

The Hebrew language was not spoken to any significant degree after the Second Jewish Revolt (Bar Kokhba Revolt), ending in A.D. 135. It continued to be read in synagogues and homes but was sometimes not understood. In the late nineteenth century, however, Hebrew underwent a revival and is now one of the official languages of the state of Israel, which was established in modern times (1948) in fulfillment of prophecy.

ACS

HELL

The scriptures speak of hell in a number of ways. First, a person who is subject to "spiritual death," who is separated from the presence of the Lord (his Spirit) and from things of righteousness, is in hell

(2 Nephi 9:12). Second, hell is that dimension of the postmortal spirit world where the wicked are consigned following their death and before their resurrection. It is variously called "spirit prison" or "outer darkness" (Alma 40:13), though spirit prison may also be used to refer to the entire spirit world (1 Peter 3:18–20; D&C 45:17; 138:20, 29, 37, 50). The Hebrew word *Sheol* and the Greek word *Hades* both refer to "the world of the departed" following death. Thus, Joseph Smith could teach: "Hades, the Greek, or Shaole, the Hebrew, these two significations mean a world of spirits. Hades, Shaole, paradise, spirits in prison, are all one: it is a world of spirits" (5:425). Third, at the end of the thousand years we know as the Millennium and the last resurrection that follows it (the resurrection of telestial persons and the sons of perdition), hell as we know it in the spirit world will be no more and will be vacated by all who are entitled to a kingdom of glory. The only ones who will not be resurrected to a kingdom of glory—who suffer hell endlessly, who experience the second spiritual death, and who dwell in outer darkness forever—are the sons of perdition, the "vessels of wrath" who deny and defy God's power (D&C 76:33).

SOURCE

Smith, Joseph. *History of The Church of Jesus Christ of Latter-day Saints.* Edited by B. H. Roberts. 7 vols. 2d ed. rev. Salt Lake City: The Church of Jesus Christ of Latter-day Saints, 1932–51.

RLM

HERESY

A heresy is "a fundamental error in religion, or an error of opinion respecting some fundamental doctrine of religion" (Webster, "heresy"). This is a word Latter-day Saints do not use a great deal; instead, we speak of a false doctrine or an incorrect teaching. The apostle Paul wrote: "I hear that there be divisions among you; and I partly believe it. For there must be also heresies among you, that they which are approved may be made manifest among you" (1 Corinthians 11:18–19). Similarly, John the Beloved observed that "it is the last time [literally, the "end of the age," or the winding up scene of the dispensation]: and as ye have heard that antichrist shall come, even now are there many antichrists; whereby we know that it is the last time. They went out from us, but they were not of us; for if they had been of us, they would no doubt have continued with us: but they went out, that they might be made manifest that they were not all of us" (1 John 2:18–19).

Because mortals can perceive the things of God only "through a glass, darkly" (1 Corinthians 13:12), it is inevitable that we will, from time to time, misunderstand or articulate a given doctrinal matter incorrectly, even when we have no intention of doing so. No true follower of the Lord Jesus Christ would want to teach or write anything that might mislead, create a false impression, or cause another to stumble. As the Prophet Joseph Smith explained, "None but fools will trifle with the souls of men" (3:295). And so we strive to cultivate the Spirit in our lives, to read and ponder and internalize the words of holy scripture and living prophets, and to do everything in our power to ensure that our beliefs and teachings are in harmony with those prophets and apostles who are charged to guide the destiny of the Lord's kingdom.

SOURCES

Smith, Joseph. *History of The Church of Jesus Christ of Latter-day Saints.* Edited by B. H. Roberts. 7 vols. 2d ed. rev. Salt Lake City: The Church of Jesus Christ of Latter-day Saints, 1932–51.

Webster, Noah. *American Dictionary of the English Language,* 1828. Reprint, San Francisco: Foundation for American Christian Education, 1980.

RLM

HIGH PRIEST

Jesus Christ is the great High Priest, "the Apostle and High Priest of our profession" (Hebrews 3:1). He is the presiding officer in the kingdom of God, the One from whom all priesthood powers and endowments and blessings and spiritual gifts flow.

In our day, high priest is an ordained office within the Melchizedek Priesthood, one to which men must be ordained before serving in a bishopric, high council, stake presidency, or as a patriarch. "The duty of a High Priest," Joseph the Seer declared, "is to administer in spiritual and holy things, and to hold communion with God." Further, he stated, "It is the High Priests' duty to be better qualified to teach principles and doctrines, than the Elders" (1:338; see also D&C 107:10). The president of the Church is designated by revelation as the "President of the High Priesthood of the Church; or, in other words, the Presiding High Priest over the High Priesthood of the Church" (D&C 107:65–66).

Adam, Seth, Enos, Cainan, Mahalaleel, Jared, Enoch, Methuselah, Lamech, and Noah were all high priests (D&C 107:53) and served as presiding patriarchs. "All of these patriarchs [from Adam through Methuselah] were ordained and blessed under the hand of Adam. Perhaps we might be permitted the reflection that it may have been possible that these men received some lesser office in the Priesthood before the authority of the evangelist [patriarch] was conferred upon them by father Adam. . . . We are not to understand that these ten men were the only ones who held the divine authority before the flood, but that they were called to positions of responsibility, or presiding authority, among their fellows" (Smith, *Way,* 73).

Abraham sought for and obtained "the right whereunto [he] should be ordained to administer" the "blessings of the fathers" (Abraham 1:2)—what we know as the keys, or directing power, of the priesthood in his day. In other words, the high priest among the former-day Saints was the presiding officer in the kingdom. For example, Melchizedek, a contemporary of Abraham and the one who ordained the father of the faithful (D&C 84:14; see also Smith, 5:555; *Words,* 246), was the high priest after the holy order of God. Melchizedek exercised mighty faith among a wicked people in Salem and was instrumental in their spiritual transformation and ultimate translation (Alma 13:14–19; JST, Genesis 14:25–34). Many of the ancients "were called after this holy order, and were sanctified, and their garments were washed white through the blood of the Lamb. Now they, after being sanctified by the Holy Ghost, having their garments made white, being pure and spotless before God, could not look upon sin save it were with abhorrence; and there were many, exceedingly great many, who were made pure and entered into the rest of the Lord their God" (Alma 13:11–12).

SOURCES

Smith, Joseph. *History of The Church of Jesus Christ of Latter-day Saints.* Edited by B. H. Roberts. 7 vols. 2d ed. rev. Salt Lake City: The Church of Jesus Christ of Latter-day Saints, 1932–51.

Smith, Joseph Fielding. *The Way to Perfection.* Salt Lake City: Deseret Book, 1966.

The Words of Joseph Smith. Compiled and edited by Andrew F. Ehat and Lyndon W. Cook. Provo, Utah: Brigham Young University Religious Studies Center, 1980.

RLM

HOLINESS

Holiness is a preeminent attribute of godliness, sanctity, and purity. It is spiritual or moral wholeness or perfection—purity of one's heart and motives. To be holy is to be set apart and consecrated for a sacred purpose. Holiness is the opposite of profane or common. "I am the Lord your God," Jehovah declared unto the ancient Israelites. "Ye shall therefore sanctify yourselves, and ye shall be holy; for I am holy" (Leviticus 11:44). To keep their minds focused on becoming more holy and godlike, the Lord provided the Old Testament people with sacred rituals, practices, and places. Sabbath observance and laws of purification and diet reminded the people that they must be different from the wicked and unbelieving peoples who surrounded them (Leviticus 10:10; Exodus 20:8; 31:14). Although there were immediate temporal benefits, the primary purpose of these practices was spiritual—pointing the people to God and separating them from worldliness and wickedness. In addition to these practices, there were sacred objects associated with the temple, including the golden band on the high priest's cap that had the words "holiness to the Lord." Today those words are found above the entrance to all Latter-day Saint temples.

Gospel covenants, teachings, and ordinances, including those of the temple, remind us that we need to become more like God—"a kingdom of priests and an holy nation" (Exodus 19:5–6; 1 Peter 2:9). Just as God commanded the ancient disciples to become more holy, he has likewise commanded modern disciples to "bind yourselves to act in all holiness before me" (D&C 43:9) and "practise virtue and holiness" (D&C 38:24). We do that by striving to become more like the Savior in our thoughts, words, deeds, and desires. As he did in past dispensations, the Lord has provided the Church with means whereby we can regularly "practise virtue and holiness" and keep "an eye single to the glory of God," including Sabbath observance, church attendance, personal and family prayer, scripture reading, fasting, singing hymns, and temple worship. Repentance is a quest for greater holiness. It consists of denying ourselves of ungodliness (Moroni 10:32–33), including attitudes of pride and selfishness—all that which is completely foreign to the holiness of God. The more we become comfortable with these practices of holiness and the more we yearn for the things of God, the more holy we become and the more comfortable we will be in God's holy presence. One of the name-titles for God is "Man of Holi~~n~~ (Moses 6:57; 7:35). Hence, when the resurrected Christ decla~~red~~. "Therefore, what manner of man ought ye to be? Verily I say unto you, even as I am" (3 Nephi 27:27), he was inviting us to "give unto the Lord the glory due unto his name," to "bring an offering" of a broken heart and a contrite spirit, and to "worship the Lord in the beauty of holiness" (1 Chronicles 16:29).

BLT

HOLY GHOST

The Holy Ghost, the third member of the Godhead, is a male spirit personage, the minister of the Father and the Son. The Holy Ghost is a revelator, a teacher, a converter, a comforter, a sanctifier, and a sealer. He is one with the Father and the Son in mind, purpose, character, attributes, and glory. At the same time, the Holy Ghost is not an independent Being in the sense of speaking his own mind and delivering an original message. Jesus taught: "When he, the Spirit of truth, is come, he will guide you into all truth: for he shall not speak of himself; but whatsoever he shall hear [from the Father or the Son], that shall he speak: and he will shew you things to come. He shall glorify me: for he shall receive of mine, and shall shew it unto you" (John 16:13–14). The three separate members of the Godhead are one—they bear the same witness and teach the same truths (1 John 5:7).

The revelations of the Restoration set forth the singular truth that the gift of the Holy Ghost was first conferred upon Adam, our first father (Moses 6:64–66), and that throughout the Old Testament "holy men of God spake as they were moved upon by the Holy Ghost" (2 Peter 1:21). For reasons that are not completely clear in the New Testament, the full powers and gifts of the Holy Ghost were not given in the Old World meridian Church until the day of Pentecost. "He that believeth on me," Jesus stated, "as the scripture hath said, out of his belly shall flow rivers of living water. (But this spake he of the Spirit, which they that believe on him should receive; for the Holy Ghost was promised unto them who believe, after that Jesus was glorified)" (JST, John 7:38–39). While the Bridegroom was present with his disciples in the flesh, he was their Comforter, their Revelator, their Testator. He was their Life and Light, their source of power and might.

But because of the vital role that the Spirit would play thereafter in the growth, development, and expansion of the early Church of Jesus Christ, Jesus said, "It is expedient for you that I go away: for if I go not away, the Comforter will not come unto you; but if I depart, I will send him unto you" (John 16:7).

Joseph Smith explained that an "everlasting covenant was made between three personages before the organization of this earth and relates to their dispensation of things to men on the earth. These personages . . . are called God the first, the Creator; God the second, the Redeemer; and God the third, the Witness or Testator" (42).

Clearly we owe everything to our Heavenly Father, who created us. In addition, our everlasting gratitude must always be offered to our Lord and Savior, who was sent to earth on a search-and-rescue mission to retrieve the wandering sheep and redeem us from death and hell and endless torment. Had there been no Atonement, no amount of labor on our part could ever compensate for its absence. Truly, as Jesus proclaimed at the Last Supper, without him we can do nothing (John 15:1–5). Finally, one of the priceless blessings extended to the Saints is the gift of the Holy Ghost, a sacred endowment of power, a supernal privilege of enjoying companionship with a member of the eternal Godhead. Thanks be to God that the Spirit, about which the world knows precious little (John 14:17), is sent to quicken, inspire, teach, testify, reprove, sanctify, comfort, and seal.

"You may have the administrations of angels," President Wilford Woodruff declared, "you may see many miracles; you may see many wonders in the earth; but I claim that the gift of the Holy Ghost is the greatest gift that can be bestowed upon man" (5). And so we worship, we pray, we labor, and we trust in the merits and mercy of the Holy Messiah. And we rejoice in the reality that the Holy Ghost is given to prepare us for association with God and holy beings hereafter.

SOURCES

Joseph Smith [manual]. Teachings of Presidents of the Church series. Salt Lake City: The Church of Jesus Christ of Latter-day Saints, 2007.

Woodruff, Wilford. *The Discourses of Wilford Woodruff.* Compiled by G. Homer Durham. Salt Lake City: Bookcraft, 1946.

RLM

HOLY SPIRIT OF PROMISE

The Holy Spirit of Promise is the Holy Ghost, the Holy Spirit promised to the Saints (John 14:16, 26; D&C 88:3–4). The Holy Ghost is a comforter, a revelator, a sanctifier, a sealer, a member of the Godhead, who knows all things (D&C 42:17; Moses 6:61). It is through the influence of the Holy Spirit of Promise in people's lives that they gain what Paul called the "earnest of their inheritance," that they know they are on course for eternal life, that they are living in a saved condition (2 Corinthians 1:21–22; 5:5; Ephesians 1:13–14; Young, 8:125–26).

Because every contract, vow, or obligation we make before God must be entered into and approved by the Holy Spirit of Promise to have "efficacy, virtue, or force in and after the resurrection from the dead" (D&C 132:7), every covenant we make and ordinance we receive must have the Spirit's ratifying seal upon it before it can be bound on earth and in heaven. Using marriage as an illustration, we might appropriately say that if a young couple enter the holy temple to be married for eternity, if they earnestly and sincerely desire theirs to be an eternal union, and if they do so worthily, trusting their hope in the Lord their Redeemer, their marriage has been "sealed by the Holy Spirit of promise" (D&C 132:7; Ephesians 1:13). It is a conditional sealing, to be sure, contingent upon their faithfulness to the terms set forth in the new and everlasting covenant of marriage. When through the years God finds that the couple has truly made Christ their ideal and grown into a Christlike character, a final sealing is placed upon that marriage, and they are sealed by the Holy Spirit of Promise in the final and ultimate sense—their exaltation is secure, they receive eternal life, and the family unit is perpetuated everlastingly. They thereby receive "a fulness of the Holy Ghost" (D&C 109:15; Christofferson, 19–22).

SOURCES

Christofferson, D. Todd. "The Power of Covenants." *Ensign,* May 2009, 19–23.

Young, Brigham. In *Journal of Discourses.* 26 vols. London: Latter-day Saints' Book Depot, 1854–86.

RLM

HOMOSEXUALITY

The Church of Jesus Christ of Latter-day Saints proclaims that "the sacred powers of procreation are to be employed only between man and woman, lawfully wedded as husband and wife" (First Presidency, 102). Outside these parameters, all sexual relations, whether heterosexual or homosexual, are considered sinful and a violation of God's revealed law of moral cleanliness. Prophets and apostles, both anciently and in modern times, have decried such behaviors as adultery, fornication, homosexuality, and "anything like unto it" (D&C 59:6). Both the Old and New Testaments specifically characterize homosexual relationships—sexual relations between people of the same gender—as evil. The apostle Paul, in the New Testament, boldly declared that "neither fornicators, idolaters, nor adulterers, nor effeminate, nor abusers of themselves with mankind" shall "inherit the kingdom of God" (1 Corinthians 6:9–10). There is no discrimination in the Lord's law of chastity. Violating that law may result in Church disciplinary action, whether such immoral behaviors are homosexual or heterosexual.

God condemns all violations of the law of chastity and calls upon transgressors to exercise faith in the cleansing power of Jesus Christ, repent of their sins, and strive to live their lives in accordance with the principles and ordinances of the great "plan of happiness" (Alma 42:16). Though the Lord condemns transgression, he continues to love transgressors and invites them to return to him. As Latter-day Saints, we are commanded to follow the same pattern. Specifically addressing the issues of homosexuality and same-gender attraction, the First Presidency of the Church has urged "Church leaders and members to reach out with love and understanding to those struggling with these issues. Many will respond to Christlike love and inspired counsel as they receive an invitation to come back and apply the atoning and healing power of the Savior" (Letter; see also Oaks, 12–13).

The First Presidency clearly stated: "There is a distinction between immoral thoughts and feelings and participating in either immoral heterosexual or any homosexual behavior" (Letter). Thus, a person may struggle with same-gender feelings of attraction and still be a faithful member of the Church, worthy and able to enjoy all the blessings of the gospel; however, a person who acts upon those feelings and engages in homosexual behavior or publicly advocates the same may be subject to disciplinary action and loss of Church blessings and privileges. President Gordon B. Hinckley stated,

"Those who consider themselves so-called gays and lesbians . . . may have certain inclinations which are powerful and which may be difficult to control. . . . If they do not act upon these inclinations, then they can go forward as do all other members of the Church. If they violate the law of chastity and the moral standards of the Church, then they are subject to the discipline of the Church, just as others are" (1:208).

The foundational doctrine of agency teaches us that all accountable men and women are "free according to the flesh" (2 Nephi 2:27) to choose whether to entertain unworthy thoughts and act upon those thoughts and feelings. Although many things may influence feelings and tendencies, including biological and sociological factors, each person is responsible for his or her actions. Elder Dallin H. Oaks taught:

"Just as some people have different feelings than others, some people seem to be unusually susceptible to particular actions, reactions, or addictions. Perhaps such susceptibilities are inborn or acquired without personal choice or fault, like the unnamed ailment the apostle Paul called a 'thorn in the flesh' [2 Corinthians 12:7]. . . .

"'Most of us are born with [or develop] thorns in the flesh, some more visible, some more serious than others. We all seem to have susceptibilities to one disorder or another, but whatever our susceptibilities, we have the will and the power to control our thoughts and our actions. This must be so. God has said that he holds us accountable for what we do and what we think, so our thoughts and actions must be controllable by our agency. Once we have reached the age or condition of accountability, the claim "I was born that way" does not excuse actions or thoughts that fail to conform to the commandments of God. We need to learn how to live so that a weakness that is mortal will not prevent us from achieving the goal that is eternal'" (9–10).

The Church teaches that homosexual practice undermines the sanctity of marriage and family and society in general. An official Church document states: "Strong, stable families, headed by a father and mother, are the anchor of civilized society. When marriage is undermined by gender confusion and by distortions of its God-given meaning, the rising generation of children and youth will find it increasingly difficult to develop their natural identity as a man or a woman. Some will find it more difficult to engage in wholesome courtships, form stable marriages, and raise yet another generation imbued with moral strength and purpose" ("Divine"). As a result, the Church condemns homosexual behavior and has opposed efforts to legalize same-sex marriage.

SOURCES

"The Divine Institution of Marriage." In *Newsroom: The Official Resource for News Media, Opinion Leaders, and the Public.* Salt Lake City, 13 Aug. 2008. http://newsroom.lds.org/article/the-divine-institution-of-marriage.

First Presidency and Council of the Twelve Apostles. "The Family: A Proclamation to the World." *Ensign,* Nov. 1995, 102.

Hinckley, Gordon B. *Discourses of President Gordon B. Hinckley.* 2 vols. Salt Lake City: Deseret Book, 2005.

Letter of the First Presidency of The Church of Jesus Christ of Latter-day Saints. 14 Nov. 1991. Available at institute.lds.org.

Oaks, Dallin H. "Same-Gender Attraction." *Ensign,* Oct. 1995, 7–14.

BLT

HOPE

Our hope is in Christ. Hope is more than wishing, more than yearning for some eventuality or some possession. Gospel hope is a solid and sure conviction. Hope is expectation, anticipation, assurance. The Saints of the Most High, who have come out of the world, put off the natural man, and put on Christ are entitled to "a more excellent hope" (Ether 12:32). Hope flows from faith in the Lord Jesus Christ. When we have faith in him, we believe in him—who he is and what he has done. Further, we believe he can do what he says he can do—make us clean and whole; make us pure before God the Father; make us happy, productive, and contributing members of his grand kingdom. Mormon taught: "And again, my beloved brethren, I would speak unto you concerning hope. How is it that ye can attain unto faith, save ye shall have hope? And what is it that ye shall hope for? Behold I say unto you that ye shall have hope through the atonement of Christ and the power of his resurrection, to be raised unto life eternal, and this because of your faith in him according to the promise" (Moroni 7:40–41; see also Ether 12:4).

RLM

HOSANNA

The term *hosanna* is the transliterated form of the Aramaic phrase *hosha-na,* which is the equivalent of the Hebrew *hoshiah-na,* found in the opening words of Psalm 118:25–26: "*Save now,* I beseech thee, O Lord: O Lord, I beseech thee, send now prosperity. Blessed be he that cometh in the name of the Lord: we have blessed you out of the house of the Lord" (emphasis added).

From this passage four points become clear. First, the phrase *hosha-na* or *hoshiah-na* means "Save now!" or "Help us now!" Second, the term is a request for help, a plea for salvation, safety, or redemption. Third, Psalm 118:25–26 presents a temple context. A clearer translation of the last clause of verse 26 could read, "From the house of the Lord we bless you." Fourth, portions of Psalm 118:25–26 were shouted out to greet the Lord as he made his triumphal entry into Jerusalem and the temple on Palm Sunday. "And they that went before, and they that followed, cried, saying, Hosanna; blessed is he that cometh in the name of the Lord: . . . And Jesus entered into Jerusalem, and into the temple: and when he had looked round about upon all things, and now the eventide was come, he went out unto Bethany with the twelve" (Mark 11:9, 11).

Thus, Jesus' entry into the temple complex was heralded by a temple psalm. In addition, because both the word *hosanna* as well as the original Hebrew form of the name *Jesus* derive from the verb translated as "to save," it is almost certain that "the cry *hosanna* was specifically directed to Jesus, rather than to God," as some scholars have thought (*New,* 2:894).

Examples of shouts of hosanna being directed to earthly kings are found in scripture. A woman of Tekoa "fell on her face to the ground . . . and said, Help [Hebrew, *Hoshiah*], O king" (2 Samuel 14:4). In the days of Elisha, a famished woman cried out to the king of Israel, "Help [*Hoshiah*], my lord, O king" (2 Kings 6:26). Thus, in Old Testament times, *hosanna* (or its Hebrew equivalent) added a sense of intensity and urgency to a petition.

Modern scripture helps us to see that in addition to being an entreaty, *hosanna* is also an expression of praise to and glorification of God. Nephi saw the Spirit of God exclaim, "Hosanna to the Lord, the most high God; for he is God over all the earth" (1 Nephi 11:6). The

Nephites praised the Lord for their victories in battle: "Yea, they did cry: Hosanna to the Most High God. And they did cry: Blessed be the name of the Lord God Almighty, the Most High God" (3 Nephi 4:32). Several sections of the Doctrine and Covenants proclaim the goodness and greatness of God with the phrase "Hosanna, blessed be the name of the Lord God" or "most high God" (D&C 19:37; 36:3; 39:19). The dedicatory prayer of the Kirtland Temple ends: "And help us by the power of thy Spirit, that we may mingle our voices with those bright, shining seraphs around thy throne, with acclamations of praise, singing Hosanna to God and the Lamb" (D&C 109:79).

SOURCE

The New Interpreter's Dictionary of the Bible. 5 vols. Nashville, Tenn.: Abingdon Press, 2006–9.

ACS

HOSANNA SHOUT

Based on the pattern demonstrated when Jesus entered the Jerusalem temple to acclamations of "Hosanna" the last Sunday of his mortal life (Matthew 21:9; Mark 11:9–10; John 12:13), the Hosanna Shout is offered at temple dedicatory services and other solemn occasions in our dispensation. The Prophet Joseph Smith explained the purpose and established the wording for the Hosanna Shout at the dedication of the Kirtland Temple. He recorded that after some concluding remarks "and a short prayer, at the close of which we sealed the proceedings of the day by shouting hosanna, hosanna, hosanna to God and the Lamb, three times, sealing it each time with amen, amen, and amen" (2:427–28). The Hosanna Shout is performed to welcome the Lord's presence and to seal the proceedings of the day.

The Hosanna Shout is performed by all members of the congregation at a temple dedication. Each stands in unison with the rest of the congregation, takes a white handkerchief in hand, and waves it in synchronization with each word or phrase in the attitude and exclamation of praise.

SOURCE

Smith, Joseph. *History of The Church of Jesus Christ of Latter-day Saints.* Edited by

B. H. Roberts. 7 vols. 2d ed. rev. Salt Lake City: The Church of Jesus Christ of Latter-day Saints, 1932–51.

ACS

I AM/THE GREAT I AM

"I AM" is one of the name-titles of Jesus Christ; it is used consistently over dispensations. In his role as Jehovah, the premortal Christ used this phrase to identify himself to Moses on Mount Sinai. When Moses asked by what name he should identify the God who had sent him to be Israel's deliverer, Jehovah responded, "I AM THAT I AM: and he said, Thus shalt thou say unto the children of Israel, I AM hath sent me unto you." Moreover, he said, "This is my name for ever, and this is my memorial unto all generations" (Exodus 3:14–15).

Thus, the mortal Christ used the phrase "I AM" to identify himself to his Jewish listeners as their God. In Jerusalem he boldly stated to those who were claiming pride of place based on their Abrahamic lineage, "Verily, verily, I say unto you, Before Abraham was, I am" (John 8:58). The term "I am" used here to translate the original Greek text of the New Testament, *ego eimi,* is identical to the phrase found in the declaration to Moses recorded in Exodus 3:14 of the Septuagint (Greek translation of the Old Testament). When Jesus stood before the contingent of men sent to arrest him at the entrance to the Garden of Gethsemane, he identified himself as "I am" (*ego eimi*)—the pronoun "he" found in this verse in the King James Version is italicized, meaning it was not found in the original Greek text (John 18:6). Finally, in this present dispensation the resurrected Christ declared himself to be "the Great I Am" (D&C 38:1; 39:1).

The phrase "I AM" in its original Hebrew form is a first-person, future tense of the verb "to be" and is translated as "I exist," "I will be," "I exist eternally," "I am everlasting," or the like. This is consistent with the explanation in Doctrine and Covenants 39:1: "[the Lord] who is from all eternity to all eternity." Thus, I AM is closely related to the Hebrew version of the name-title Jehovah (Yahweh), which also derives from the Hebrew verb "to be." It has been suggested that I AM "represents a word play on the root of the word 'Yahweh'" (*Interpreter's,*

315

2:671). Many passages of restoration scripture affirm Christ's eternal, unchanging existence and nature—he never varies (1 Nephi 10:17–20), and from "eternity to eternity he is the same, and his years never fail" (D&C 76:4).

SOURCE

The Interpreter's Dictionary of the Bible: An Illustrated Encyclopedia. Edited by George Arthur Buttrick. 5 vols. Nashville, Tenn.: Abingdon Press, 1962.

ACS

IDOLATRY

The first of the Ten Commandments is "Thou shalt have no other gods before me" (Exodus 20:3). Jesus identified the "first and great commandment" as "Thou shalt love the Lord thy God with all thy heart, and with all thy soul, and with all thy mind" (Matthew 22:36–38). Our first article of faith states: "We believe in God the Eternal Father, and in his Son Jesus Christ, and in the Holy Ghost." If God is not first in our lives, someone or something else is first, and we fall prey to idolatry. President Spencer W. Kimball warned that we can easily transfer our hope from God to the "arm of flesh," thereby becoming idolatrous. He taught, "Whatever thing a man sets his heart and his trust in most is his god; and if his god doesn't also happen to be the true and living God of Israel, that man is laboring in idolatry" (4). The apostle Paul, for example, identified covetousness as idolatry (Colossians 3:5).

Scriptures give evidence of the pervasiveness and frequency of idolatry in nearly every era and people. Isaiah observed the deterioration and vulnerability that befell his people because they removed "their heart far from [Jehovah]" (Isaiah 29:13). In the prophet Micah's day, instead of worshipping God, many worshipped "the work of [their] hands" (Micah 5:13). The apostle Paul cautioned of dangers that would follow Christians because of "worshipping of angels" instead of "holding the Head," or giving Jesus Christ the preeminence (Colossians 2:18–19). He warned of God's wrath for those "who changed the truth of God into a lie, and worshipped and served the creature more than the Creator" (Romans 1:25). The sin of pride is an indication that we give ourselves credit for our successes rather than confessing God's "hand in all things" (D&C 59:21). Likewise, greed and the love of power, status, and fame signal that we are falling into the grasp of idolatry. Certainly, "the love of money is the root of all evil" because we cannot love and serve two masters; if we love money, we no longer love God with all of our hearts (1 Timothy 6:10; Matthew 6:24). If the Lord is not our first love, he will soon fall out of our lives altogether.

SOURCE
Kimball, Spencer W. "The False Gods We Worship." *Ensign,* June 1976, 3–6.

CFO

IDUMEA

The place-name Idumea has both a literal and a symbolic meaning. In the Old Testament it is another name for Edom, the land south of Israel occupied by the descendants of Esau, Jacob's brother (Genesis 32:3; 36:9; Deuteronomy 2:5, 12, 22). In the three passages where the King James Old Testament uses *Idumea* (Isaiah 34:5–6; Ezekiel 35:15; 36:5), the Hebrew text uses *Edom.* In the New Testament (Mark 3:8) Idumea refers to a smaller region immediately south of the district of Judea and not to the entire Edomite territory of earlier times.

King Herod the Great was from Idumea and thus seems to have been viewed with suspicion by Jews because the district of Idumea had been forced to convert to Judaism by the Hasmonean ruler John Hyrcanus (135–104 B.C.). According to Josephus (13:257–58), Herod was, therefore, called a "half-Jew" by some (14:403–4).

Symbolically, because the Edomites, or Idumeans, were a wicked, non-Israelite group of people, their territory came to symbolize the world and its wicked ways. For Isaiah, Edom or Idumea represented all the enemies of God and his people. Therefore, when talking about the judgments that would descend upon the nations of the world at the second coming of Jesus Christ, the prophet specifically described how the sword of the Lord would fall upon Edom/Idumea with a great slaughter (Isaiah 34:5–6). Likewise, in this dispensation the Lord uses Idumea as a great symbol of worldliness and wickedness: "And [he] shall come down in judgment upon Idumea, or the world" (D&C 1:36).

SOURCE

Josephus, Flavius. *Jewish Antiquities.* Translated by Ralph Marcus and Allen Wikgren. Cambridge, Mass.: Harvard University Press, 1963.

ACS

IMMACULATE CONCEPTION

The belief in the immaculate conception is a Roman Catholic doctrine that Mary, the mother of our Lord, was preserved free from the taint of original sin at the time she was conceived in her mother's womb. This was accomplished, according to Catholic tradition, by grace through the eternal merits of her son, Jesus Christ. Latter-day Saints do not accept this belief because we do not believe in original sin; we know from modern revelation that God forgave Adam and Eve their transgression in the Garden of Eden (Moses 6:53). Although Mary was one of the greatest women who ever lived, we do not believe she lived a fully sinless life, given that "all have sinned and come short of the glory of God" (Romans 3:23). Further, it would not be necessary for Mary to be completely sinless in order to give birth to One who would live a sinless life; she is saved through the grace of her Son.

RLM

IMMANUEL

The prophet Isaiah called Jesus Christ "Immanuel," a Hebrew title that means "God with us" or "God [is] with us" (Isaiah 7:14; 2 Nephi 17:14). The Gospel of Matthew identifies Mary's unborn child as the Immanuel prophesied by Isaiah (Matthew 1:20–23), reminding us that Jesus is the God who condescended to come to earth as a mortal and was slain for the sins of the world (1 Nephi 11:16–33).

In this dispensation the Prophet Joseph Smith referred to the Savior as "King Immanuel," who possesses the infinite power to redeem the dead (D&C 128:22). Because God lived among us and "was in all points tempted like as we are, yet without sin," we can "come boldly unto the throne of grace" and receive eternal life (Hebrews 4:15–16).

CFO

IMMORTALITY

To possess immortality is to have the power to live forever. Based upon a faulty translation or understanding of 1 Timothy 6:16, Christians for generations have taught that only God enjoys immortality by nature and that Jesus Christ brought immortality to us through his atonement and resurrection. For them, the immortality of the soul is unidirectional—following death and resurrection. Latter-day Saints understand, however, that we are eternal beings and that we have always lived; we are in fact immortal by nature. What Jesus makes available is resurrected, glorified immortality. Our great hope is to be "raised in immortality unto eternal life" (D&C 29:43), which is to inherit the fulness of the Father (JST, John 1:16). This is God's ultimate work and glory (Moses 1:39).

RLM

INCARNATION/INCARNATE GOD

The term *incarnation* derives from two Latin words, *in,* "into," and *canis,* "flesh," and means "to make into flesh" or "to become flesh." The incarnation is the foundational Christian teaching that Jesus Christ, who was God (Jehovah) in the premortal existence, "was made flesh, and dwelt among us" (John 1:14). The Great Jehovah, the Creator of all things (Mosiah 3:8; 5:15), the very Eternal Father of heaven and earth (Mosiah 15:4), took upon himself the tabernacle of a mortal body. This is the witness of all who possess the spirit of prophecy (Revelation 19:10), but none have given more eloquent voice to this truth than King Benjamin (circa 124 B.C.): "For behold, the time cometh, and is not far distant, that with power, the Lord Omnipotent who reigneth, who was, and is from all eternity to all eternity, shall come down from heaven among the children of men, and shall dwell in a tabernacle of clay" (Mosiah 3:5).

Thus, the incarnation is inextricably linked to the condescension of God, which encompasses two aspects. First, a resurrected, glorified personage (God) descended from his pure and exalted station, scarcely comprehensible to mortals, to become the Father of a mortal offspring (Christ) with a mortal woman (1 Nephi 11:16, 18, 20–21). Second, the Son of God, though he was the Lord Omnipotent, descended from his

319

divine station to enter this fallen, mortal world, to experience "temptations, and pain of body, hunger, thirst, and fatigue, even more than man can suffer, except it be unto death" (Mosiah 3: 7–8), and finally to endure death by the most horrible method imaginable: crucifixion (1 Nephi 11: 32–33). Except for the Atonement, there is no event in history more significant than the incarnation.

ACS

INERRANCY

The question is not whether there have been scribal errors in Bible manuscripts through the centuries—there have been. The question is not whether the Bible is the word of God—it is. The question is not whether the Bible can be relied upon with confidence if in fact there have been errors—it can be. Joseph the Prophet declared: "I believe the Bible, as it ought to be, as it came from the pen of the original writers" (*Words,* 256).

Errors in the Bible do not tarnish its image for Latter-day Saints. For that matter, while Latter-day Saints accept the Book of Mormon, the Doctrine and Covenants, and the Pearl of Great Price as holy scripture from God, we would not rush to proclaim their inerrancy. The marvel is in fact the greater that an infinite and perfect Being can work through finite and imperfect humans to deliver his word to his children. Joseph Smith believed, to be sure, that the message of the Bible is true and from God, that the Bible is God's word, even though it may not be the case that every sentence recorded in the testaments necessarily contains "God's words," meaning a direct quotation or transcription of divine direction.

Joseph taught, and his successors have emphasized, that it is the spirit of revelation within the one called of God that is the energizing force and that in most instances God places the thought into the mind or heart of the revelator, who then assumes the responsibility to clothe the oracle in language. Certainly there are times when a prophet records the words of God directly, but often the "still, small voice" (1 Kings 19:12) whispers to the prophet, who then speaks for God. In short, when God chooses to speak through a person, that person does not become a mindless ventriloquist, an earthly sound system through which the Almighty can voice himself. Rather, that person becomes enlightened and filled with intelligence or truth. "What makes us different from most other Christians in the way we read and use the Bible and other scriptures," Elder Dallin H. Oaks explained, "is our belief in continuing revelation. For us, the scriptures are not the ultimate source of knowledge, but what precedes the ultimate source. The ultimate knowledge comes by revelation" (7).

Nothing could be clearer in the Bible, for example, than that many factors affected the prophetic message—personality, experience, vocabulary, literary talent. The word of the Lord as spoken through Isaiah is quite different from the word of the Lord spoken through Luke, and both are different from that spoken by Jeremiah or Mark. Further, it is worth noting that stone, leaves, bark, skins, wood, metals, baked clay, and papyrus were all used anciently to record inspired messages. Latter-day Saint interest in the ancients is not in the perfection with which such messages were recorded but in the inspiration of the message itself. More specifically, Latter-day Saints are interested in the fact that the heavens were opened to the ancients, that they had messages to record. In other words, knowing that God is the same yesterday, today, and forever (Hebrews 13:8) and the fact that he spoke to them at all (however well or poorly the message may have been recorded) attests that he can speak to men and women in the here and now. After all, the Bible is only black ink on white paper until the Spirit of God illuminates its true meaning to us; if we have obtained that, there is little need to quibble over the Bible's suitability as a history or science text.

The traditions of the past regarding scripture, revelation, and canon were altered dramatically by the First Vision in 1820. God had spoken again, the heavens were no longer sealed, and a new dispensation of truth was under way. The ninth article of faith states: "We believe all that God has revealed, all that He does now reveal, and we believe that He will yet reveal many great and important things pertaining to the Kingdom of God." We feel deep gratitude for the holy scriptures, but we do not worship scripture. Nor do we feel it appropriate to set up stakes and bounds to the works and ways of the Almighty, to tell God, essentially, "Thus far and no more" (Smith, 5:529–30).

Often we encounter religious persons who state emphatically that their position is based entirely upon "the authority of scripture." The fact is, God is the source of any reputable religious authority. In the words of N. T. Wright, "The risen Jesus, at the end of Matthew's gospel, does not say, 'All authority in heaven and on earth is given to the books you are all going to write,' but 'All authority in heaven and on earth is given to me.'" In other words, "scripture itself points—authoritatively, if it does indeed possess authority!—away from itself and to the fact that final and true authority belongs to God himself, now delegated to Jesus Christ" (xi, 24).

We love the Bible. We treasure its teachings and delight in the spirit of worship that accompanies its prayerful study. People's belief in additional scripture does not in any way detract from what they feel toward and learn from the Holy Bible. Studying the Bible lifts our spirits, lightens our burdens, enlightens our mind, and motivates us to seek to live a life of holiness. "When this fact is admitted," Joseph Smith said in 1834, "that the immediate will of heaven is contained in the Scriptures, are we not bound as rational creatures to live in accordance to all [their] precepts?" (*Words*, 2:11).

SOURCES

Oaks, Dallin H. "Scripture Reading and Revelation." *Ensign,* Jan. 1995, 6–9.
Smith, Joseph. *History of The Church of Jesus Christ of Latter-day Saints.* Edited by B. H. Roberts. 7 vols. 2d ed. rev. Salt Lake City: The Church of Jesus Christ of Latter-day Saints, 1932–51.
The Words of Joseph Smith. Compiled and edited by Andrew F. Ehat and Lyndon W. Cook. Provo, Utah: Brigham Young University Religious Studies Center, 1980.
Wright, N. T. *Surprised by Hope: Rethinking Heaven, the Resurrection, and the Mission of the Church.* New York: HarperOne, 2008.

RLM

INFANT BAPTISM

The saving ordinance of water baptism was introduced in the dawn of time. Adam was "caught away by the Spirit of the Lord, and was carried down into the water, and was laid under the water, and was brought forth out of the water. And thus he was baptized" (Moses 6:64–65). Thereby God set the pattern—baptism was to be administered to accountable persons through an immersion. Baptism is symbolic of the death and burial and rise to newness of life of the Lord Jesus Christ (Romans 6:3–5; Colossians 2:12; D&C 128:12–13). The ordinances of the gospel of Jesus Christ are eternal, and they are to remain forever the same (Smith, 2:16–17; 4:208; 5:257).

During the days of Abraham, misunderstanding and confusion ensued concerning the doctrines of atonement and accountability. Consequently, some persons practiced a form of infant baptism (JST, Genesis 17:4–6). In the centuries following the deaths of Christ and his apostles, infant baptism was again reintroduced. We know that in the Old World it came in part because of the prevalent belief in original sin strongly proclaimed by Saint Augustine—the notion that children are carnal and sensual creatures because of the taint they inherit as a result of Adam and Eve's transgression in Eden. Because of a fear that unbaptized children might die and remain eternally depraved and thus forever lost, the practice of infant baptism began to spread.

"The doctrine of baptizing children, or sprinkling them, or they must welter in hell, is a doctrine not true," declared Joseph Smith, "not supported in Holy Writ, and is not consistent with the character of God. All children are redeemed by the blood of Jesus Christ [Mosiah 15:25; Moroni 8:8, 12, 22; D&C 29:46; 74:7; 93:38; 137:10], and the moment that children leave this world, they are taken to the bosom of Abraham" (4:554). Mormon wrote to his son Moroni that it is "solemn mockery before God, that ye should baptize little children. . . . Little children need no repentance, neither baptism. Behold, baptism is unto repentance to the fulfilling the commandments unto the remission of sins. But little children are alive in Christ, even from the foundation of the world. . . . And he that saith that little children need baptism denieth the mercies of Christ, and setteth at naught the atonement of him and the power of his redemption" (Moroni 8:9, 11–12, 20).

SOURCE

Smith, Joseph. *History of The Church of Jesus Christ of Latter-day Saints.* Edited by B. H. Roberts. 7 vols. 2d ed. rev. Salt Lake City: The Church of Jesus Christ of Latter-day Saints, 1932–51.

RLM

INNOCENT BLOOD

Innocent blood is the blood of the pure, the blood of the sanctified. One of the things God hates is the shedding of innocent blood (Proverbs 6:17). Abinadi told the priests of King Noah that if they killed him they would be guilty of shedding innocent blood (Mosiah 17:10). Similarly, in putting to death the wives and children of the believers, the wicked leaders in Ammonihah were accounted as guilty of shedding innocent blood (Alma 14:11).

In the ultimate sense, people shed innocent blood when they betray innocent blood (Matthew 27:4) or, in other words, when they choose to come out in open rebellion against the Son of God. Paul wrote, "It is impossible for those who were once enlightened, and have tasted of the heavenly gift, and were made partakers of the Holy Ghost, and have tasted the good word of God, and the powers of the world to come, if they shall fall away, to renew them again unto repentance; seeing they crucify to themselves the Son of God afresh, and put him to an open shame" (Hebrews 6:4–6). "The blasphemy against the Holy Ghost," the Savior declared in modern revelation, "which shall not be forgiven in the world nor out of the world, is that ye commit murder wherein ye shed innocent blood, and assent unto my death, after ye have received my new and everlasting covenant, saith the Lord God" (D&C 132:27; see also McConkie, 233).

SOURCE

McConkie, Bruce R. *A New Witness for the Articles of Faith.* Salt Lake City: Deseret Book, 1985.

RLM

INTELLIGENCE(S)

The word *intelligence* is used in two different ways in scripture. Each is related to God's power and glory, light and truth, but at the same time, each usage is unique.

1. *Spiritual knowledge and power.* "The glory of God is intelligence," the Lord declared in modern revelation, "or, in other words, light and truth" (D&C 93:36). In the gospel sense, intelligence is much more than intellectual knowledge. It is spiritual enlightenment and power. In this context, intelligence, or God's glory and power, cannot be obtained merely by intellectual pursuits. It must be obtained through faith and righteousness. For this reason the Lord has commanded us to seek intelligence "by study and by faith" (D&C 88:118). Knowledge can be obtained without any spiritual commitment, merely through study or the scientific method. In contrast, acquiring the *intelligence that is God's glory* can be done only through obedience to God's laws and the principles of the gospel. This kind of spiritual knowledge

and power thus enables one to discern more clearly truth from false-hood and to have greater strength to resist temptations. "Light and truth forsake that evil one" (D&C 93:37). Intelligence provides enlightenment and power in this life, but it also has an eternal nature to it. "Whatever principle of intelligence we attain unto in this life, it will rise with us in the resurrection. And if a person gains more knowledge and intelligence in this life through his diligence and obedience than another, he will have so much the advantage in the world to come" (D&C 130:18–19).

2. Spirit element is an eternal part of man. The word *intelligence* is also used synonymously with an eternal spirit element that "was not created or made, neither indeed can be" (D&C 93:29). Refuting the doctrine of creation *ex nihilo* (out of nothing), the Prophet Joseph Smith taught in 1839 that "the Spirit of Man is not a created being; it existed from Eternity and will exist to eternity. Anything created cannot be Eternal. And earth, water, etc.—all these had their existence in an elementary State from Eternity" (3:387). Later, the Prophet further elaborated:

"The mind or the intelligence which man possesses is co-equal [co-eternal] with God himself. . . . I am dwelling on the immortality of the spirit of man. Is it logical to say that the intelligence of spirits is immortal, and yet that it has a beginning? The intelligence of spirits had no beginning, neither will it have an end. . . . Intelligence is eternal and exists upon a self-existent principle. It is a spirit from age to age, and there is no creation about it" (6:310–11).

The Prophet's use of the phrases "self-existent" and "it is a spirit from age to age" has caused some to speculate concerning the specific nature of intelligence as an eternal part of man's spirit. There are two main schools of thought on the subject: (1) Before spirit-birth, there is an eternal entity known as "an intelligence" that possesses identity, agency, and individuality; (2) There is a primal spirit matter that is eternal, from which the spirit body was organized. Although statements from leaders of the Church can be found to support both of these points of view, there is no official doctrine of the Church on the matter. What has been revealed, however, is that there is something called intelligence that is an eternal part of man's nature. What is not known is the specific nature of intelligence. While the word *intelligence* is used in several places in the scriptures, the word *intelligences* appears only once. Abraham sees "the intelligences that were organized before the world was." In the next verse, Abraham says that these organized intelligences "were spirits" (Abraham 3:22–23). Thus, this reference, when viewed in its proper context, cannot be used as evidence that spirits were *intelligences*—with individual identity, personality, and agency—prior to spirit birth. Therefore, it is wise to remember a caution given by President Joseph Fielding Smith: "Some of our writers have endeavored to explain what an intelligence is, but to do so is futile, for we have never been given any insight into this matter beyond what the Lord has fragmentarily revealed" (11).

SOURCES

Smith, Joseph. *History of The Church of Jesus Christ of Latter-day Saints.* Edited by B. H. Roberts. 7 vols. 2d ed. rev. Salt Lake City: The Church of Jesus Christ of Latter-day Saints, 1932–51.

Smith, Joseph Fielding. *Progress of Man.* Salt Lake City: Kessinger Publishing, 2004.

BLT

ISRAEL

Israel is the new name given to Jacob the patriarch at Peniel when he saw God face to face (Genesis 32:28, 30). God reconfirmed the name at Bethel (Genesis 35:10). Its Hebrew meaning is not clear, but perhaps it means "he who prevails with God." Note that the heavenly Being with whom Jacob wrestled said, "Thy name shall be called no more Jacob, but Israel: for as a prince hast thou power with God and with men, and hast *prevailed*" (Genesis 32:28; emphasis added; see also footnote b). Jacob's twelve sons and their posterity are likewise called Israel—the house of Israel or the children of Israel (Genesis 49:28; Exodus 3:10, 15). They are also called the twelve tribes of Israel and include the descendants of the twelve sons: Reuben, Simeon, Levi, Judah, Issachar, and Zebulun (sons of Jacob and Leah), Dan and Naphtali (sons of Jacob and Bilhah), Gad and Asher (sons of Jacob and Zilpah), and Joseph and Benjamin (sons of Jacob and Rachel) (Genesis 29:32; 30:24; 35:16–18).

After the settlement of the twelve tribes in the land of Canaan following the conquest, the kingdom of united Israel had its capital first in Gibeah of Saul. Later, King David moved it from Hebron to

Jerusalem (2 Samuel 5:1–10). After the united kingdom split apart during the reign of Solomon's son Rehoboam (1 Kings 12), the northern tribes formed the kingdom of Israel, headquartered in Samaria. The southern tribes became known as the kingdom of Judah. In modern times the state of Israel (established in 1948), created largely in the land known anciently as Canaan, is sometimes referred to simply as Israel.

As direct descendants of father Abraham (Jacob, also known as Israel, was Abraham's grandson), members of the house of Israel are heirs to all the Abrahamic promises from God through the covenant he made with Abraham. These include promised lands of inheritance, posterity, priesthood, blessings of the gospel, and eternal life. Through Abraham, all the nations of the earth would be blessed (Abraham 2:6–11). Through Abraham and Israel, the Messiah would come and bless the families of the earth. As Paul taught, "Now to Abraham and his seed were the promises made. He saith not, And to seeds, as of many; but as of one, And to thy seed, which is Christ" (Galatians 3:16).

Moses implied that Israel was already an established entity in our premortal existence when he declared that the Lord apportioned to the nations their inheritance in mortality with Israel in mind—that this earthly ordering was based on a heavenly ordering. "When the most High divided to the nations their inheritance, when he separated the sons of Adam, he set the bounds of the people according to the number of the children of Israel. For the Lord's portion is his people; Jacob is the lot of his inheritance" (Deuteronomy 32:8–9). Commenting on this passage, Elder James E. Talmage said, "From this we learn that the earth was allotted to the nations, according to the number of the children of Israel; it is evident therefore that the number was known prior to the existence of the Israelitish nation in the flesh; this is most easily explained on the basis of a previous existence in which the spirits of the future nation were known" (193).

The apostle Paul understood that there was a premortal assignment and arrangement of people's circumstances in this life. Said he, "And [God] hath made of one blood all nations of men for to dwell on all the face of the earth, and hath determined the times before appointed, and the bounds of their habitation" (Acts 17:26). Paul also taught that Israel as a group was foreknown and foreordained by God the Father in our premortal existence (Romans 8:28–30; Ephesians 1:3–5, 11). Therefore, it makes perfect sense that God should command Moses to tell Pharaoh, "Israel is my son, even my firstborn" (Exodus 4:22). Based on premortal activities and assignments, to Israel goes the birthright, the responsibility and obligation to care for the rest of God's family in mortality. Thus, Israel is to be a "peculiar people" (Hebrew, *segullah*) in mortality. A better translation would be God's "special treasure," "prized possession," or "personal property" from among all the people of the earth (Exodus 19:5–6; Deuteronomy 14:2; 1 Peter 2:9).

Elder Melvin J. Ballard taught that Israel existed in our premortal life. Israel, he said, is "a group of souls tested, tried, and proven before they were born into the world. . . . Through this lineage were to come the true and tried souls that had demonstrated their righteousness in the spirit world before they came here" (218–19). President Harold B. Lee explained: "Those born to the lineage of Jacob, who was later to be called Israel, and his posterity, who were known as the children of Israel, were born into the most illustrious lineage of any of those who came upon the earth as mortal beings. All of these rewards were seemingly promised, or foreordained, before the world was. Surely these matters must have been determined by the kind of lives we had lived in that premortal spirit world. Some may question these assumptions, but at the same time they will accept without any question the belief that each one of us will be judged when we leave this earth according to his or her deeds during our lives here in mortality. Isn't it just as reasonable to believe that what we have received here in this earth [life] was given to each of us according to the merits of our conduct before we came here?" (5).

There are natural-born descendants of Israel, and there are those who are adopted into the house of Israel through accepting Jesus Christ and participating in the ordinances of salvation administered by the house of Israel through the true Church. As Paul taught, "That the blessing of Abraham might come on the Gentiles through Jesus Christ; that we might receive the promise of the Spirit through faith. . . . For ye are all the children of God by faith in Christ Jesus. For as many of you as have been baptized into Christ have put on Christ. There is neither Jew nor Greek, there is neither bond nor free, there is neither male nor female: for ye are all one in Christ Jesus. And if ye be Christ's, then are ye Abraham's seed, and heirs according to the promise" (Galatians 3:14–29).

The apostle Paul also taught that even though non-Israelites may be adopted into the house of Israel, mere association with the family by blood does not guarantee the blessings or birthright or chosen status of Israel. "For they are not all Israel, which are of Israel: Neither, because they are the seed of Abraham, are they all children. . . . That is, They which are the children of the flesh, these are not the children of God: but the children of the promise [the gospel] are counted for the seed" (Romans 9:6–8).

To summarize, the term *Israel* can refer to the patriarch Jacob, his literal descendants, the modern nation-state of Israel or the land it occupies today, or any true believer in Christ regardless of lineage who is baptized, adopted into the lineage of Israel, and receives the promises of Abraham. Little wonder that Israel is of such great interest to God the Father and that "the work of the Father" in the latter days is "the fulfilling of the covenant which he hath made unto the people who are of the house of Israel" (3 Nephi 21:7).

Anciently, leadership of the house of Israel was vested in the tribe of Judah until the Messiah came (Genesis 49:10; JST, Genesis 50:24). In the latter days, the tribe of Ephraim will possess the primary leadership role. This includes responsibility for taking the gospel to the world, gathering scattered Israel (including the lost ten tribes), and guarding and administering the ordinances of exaltation (Deuteronomy 33:13–17; Isaiah 11:12–13; D&C 133:25–34). So important is Israel in the family of God that two of God's name-titles are the "God of Israel" and the "Rock of Israel" (2 Samuel 23:3; Deuteronomy 32:4).

SOURCES

Ballard, Melvin J. "The Three Degrees of Glory: A Discourse." In *Crusader for Righteousness*. Salt Lake City: Bookcraft, 1966.

Lee, Harold B. "Understanding Who We Are Brings Self-Respect." *Ensign,* Jan. 1974, 2–6.

Smith, Joseph. *History of The Church of Jesus Christ of Latter-day Saints.* Edited by B. H. Roberts. 7 vols. 2d ed. rev. Salt Lake City: The Church of Jesus Christ of Latter-day Saints, 1932–51.

Talmage, James E. *Articles of Faith.* Classics in Mormon Literature series. Salt Lake City: Deseret Book, 1981.

ACS

ISRAEL, KINGDOM OF

Jacob, or Israel (Genesis 32:28), had twelve sons who became the heads of twelve tribes known as the house of Israel (Genesis 49:28). The house of Israel formed the united kingdom of Israel after the conquest of the land of Canaan. After the death of David's son, King Solomon (circa 922 B.C.), long-standing jealousies, antagonisms, and tensions between the tribes in the north and those in the south erupted violently when rebellion against Rehoboam, Solomon's son and successor, shattered the unity of the Israelite kingdom. The tensions had been aggravated in Solomon's later years by heavy taxation and forced labor. Hence, Ahijah's prophecy of the division of the great Davidic kingdom came to pass: "For thus saith the Lord, the God of Israel, Behold, I will rend the kingdom out of the hand of Solomon. . . . I will take the kingdom out of his son's hand" (1 Kings 11:31, 35). The division of the Davidic kingdom, or house of Israel, was a preparatory step to the scattering of Israel, in which Jehovah took a personal role (Jeremiah 16:13; Ezekiel 5:10; Jacob 5:8).

When the forty-one-year-old Rehoboam traveled to Shechem to be installed as the new king, he met Jeroboam, the Ephraimite adversary of Solomon who had returned from exile in Egypt at the request of the northern tribes of Israel (1 Kings 12:1–3; 2 Chronicles 10:1–3). Rehoboam recognized the need to be confirmed at this important place in order to cement northern allegiance to a united kingdom and to gain Jeroboam's support. The people of the north attached conditions to their acceptance of Rehoboam, asking for a decrease in the severe financial and labor demands that had been instituted by Solomon (1 Kings 12:3–19; 2 Chronicles 10:3–19). When the new king made known his decision to increase their burdens instead, "Israel rebelled against the house of David unto this day" (1 Kings 12:19).

Rehoboam reacted to the secession by mobilizing an army from Judah and Benjamin to quell the rebellion, force the return of the errant northern territories, and preserve political unity. However, "there was war between Rehoboam and Jeroboam all their days" (1 Kings 14:30). The division between their two kingdoms created two separate nations with separate histories from that time on. It will only be in Christ's millennial kingdom that the two will become one again (Ezekiel 37:22). Ten northern tribes established the kingdom of Israel (also called Ephraim because that tribe was the dominant group among the others), while the rest of the tribes formed the southern kingdom of Judah.

The northern kingdom of Israel had its headquarters at Samaria. It was first led by Jeroboam, whose perversions plunged the kingdom into an apostate condition from which it never recovered (1 Kings 12–13). He was followed by a series of eighteen wicked monarchs who ignored or flatly refused to heed the counsel and commands of such mighty prophets as Elijah, Elisha, Amos, and Hosea. Finally, after two hundred years of corruption, the Lord raised up an adversary known as the Assyrians against the kingdom of Israel.

During the reign of King Tiglath-pileser III of Assyria (745–727 B.C.), also referred to in the Bible as Pul (2 Kings 15:19), the Assyrians began to incorporate conquered territories into their empire. Tiglath-pileser's first serious encounter with Israel, during the reign of King Menahem (745–737 B.C.), resulted in Israel's paying a huge sum of tribute money—one thousand talents of silver, or more than thirty-five tons (2 Kings 15:19–20). The tribute was collected by a levy of fifty shekels on every wealthy Israelite citizen (2 Kings 15:20) (Pritchard, 283).

A few years later, in 733 B.C., Tiglath-pileser began absorbing Israel into his kingdom during the reign of Israel's King Pekah (736–732 B.C.)—the same king who had made the alliance with Syria and fought against Judah. This began the deportation of the northern tribes of Israel and was a large part of the scattering that had been foretold by the prophets (Deuteronomy 4:25–27). The year following this Assyrian attack on Israel (732 B.C.), Tiglath-pileser replaced Pekah on the throne of Israel with Hoshea: "They overthrew their king Pekah and I placed Hoshea as king over them" (Pritchard, 284; see also 2 Kings 15:3). Hoshea (732–724 B.C.) seems to have complied with Assyrian demands for the first part of his reign (2 Kings 17:3), but he was the last monarch of the kingdom of Israel.

When Tiglath-pileser died in 727 B.C., revolts broke out in many parts of his empire. It was against this background that the wary Shalmaneser V of Assyria (726–722 B.C.) found evidence that Hoshea had been in communication with Egyptian authorities and had not sent his annual tribute payment. He attacked Israel and besieged the capital city, Samaria (2 Kings 17:4–5). Hoshea the king was captured outside the city before Samaria's fall (2 Kings 17:4).

Shalmaneser died unexpectedly during the three-year siege of Samaria. His successor, Sargon II, boasted of completing the devastation of Israel and conquering the city (2 Kings 17:4–6): "At the beginning of my royal rule . . . the town of the Samarians I besieged, conquered. . . . I led away as prisoners 27,290 inhabitants of it. . . . The town I rebuilt better than it was before and settled therein people from countries which I myself had conquered" (Pritchard, 284).

The destruction of Samaria in 721 B.C. brought to an end the northern kingdom and resulted in the deportation of thousands of its inhabitants to other lands. These Israelites became known as the ten lost tribes of Israel. Latter-day Saints should take special note of these events and what caused them, for their ancestors were likely among those taken away at that time. The scattering was the result of Israel's rebellion; the gathering occurs when the descendants of those ancient Israelites around the world humbly repent, accept the message of the gospel, and return to the Lord through sacred baptismal and temple covenants (1 Nephi 10:14). One of the important tenets of LDS faith centers on Israel in the latter days: "We believe in the literal gathering of Israel and in the restoration of the Ten Tribes" (Articles of Faith 1:10).

From the days of the northern kingdom's first monarch down to the time of its last, every leader in Israel to one degree or another "did that which was evil in the sight of the Lord" (2 Kings 17:2). The wickedness of Jeroboam I was supported and promulgated so much by every one of his successors that the words "the sins of Jeroboam, who made Israel to sin" became a standard phrase used by the biblical writers of this portion of Israel's history (1 Kings 14:16; 2 Kings 10:29; 13:2, 11; 14:24; 15:9, 18, 24).

As both Assyrian and biblical records make clear, after he deported the people of Israel, the king of Assyria, Sargon II, imported and resettled other conquered peoples to replace them. These new colonists intermarried with the remaining Israelites, practiced a corrupt combination of Jehovah worship and idolatry (2 Kings 17:24–34, 40), and became known as Samaritans. Although the Bible tells us that the people of the northern tribes (the ten lost tribes) were resettled in various locations in the Assyrian empire (2 Kings 17:6), the issue of where they were taken is not as important as understanding what they did to merit captivity and exile (2 Kings 17:7–22) nor as important as the Lord's marked involvement in their destiny (2 Kings 17:23, 34–40). The only reliable statements on the location of the descendants of the ancient Israelites come from latter-day revelation. These indicate that Israel is scattered upon the face of all the earth. As Mormon says, "And as surely as the Lord liveth, will he gather in from the four quarters of the earth all the remnant of the seed of Jacob, who are scattered abroad upon all the face of the earth" (3 Nephi 5:24).

Had Israel been humble and honored the true God who had brought them forth from Egypt (2 Kings 17:36), he would have fought their every battle and rescued them from every enemy (2 Kings 17:39). That God delivers his people *from* their enemies when they obey or *to* their enemies when they disobey is documented in several passages of 2 Kings (10:32; 13:3; 17:20). It is a principle also taught in modern revelation: "By hearkening to observe all the words which I, the Lord their God, shall speak unto them, they shall never cease to prevail until the kingdoms of the world are subdued under my feet, and the earth is given unto the saints, to possess it forever and ever. But inasmuch as they keep not my commandments, and hearken not to observe all my words, the kingdoms of the world shall prevail against them" (D&C 103:7–8).

SOURCE

Pritchard, James B., ed. *Ancient Near Eastern Texts Relating to the Old Testament.* 3d ed. Princeton: Princeton University Press, 1969.

ACS

———◦———

JEHOVAH

Jehovah is the name-title by which the premortal Jesus Christ was known in his role as the covenant-making God of Israel in Old Testament times (3 Nephi 15:5; Mosiah 3:5, 8). It is also one of the names by which Joseph Smith referred to Christ in this last dispensation (D&C 110:1–3; 128:9). The name itself is an anglicized form of the Hebrew tetragrammaton, the four-consonant name of

God, YHWH, originally written without vowels in the biblical text and whose ancient pronunciation is probably lost. It may have been something like Yahweh. The name derives from the Hebrew verb "to be" and means "He who was, is, and will be," the "eternally existing one," the "unchanging one," or the like. It is closely tied to the name by which the Lord identified himself to Moses on Mt. Sinai, "I AM" (Exodus 3:13–14), which also derives from the Hebrew verb "to be."

The word *Jehovah* is a product of combining the consonants of the tetragrammaton with the vowels of the word *Adonai* ("Lord"), which the Jews substituted when reading the name YHWH in order to avoid having to pronounce it and thus profane it through too frequent or common usage. It first appears in English in William Tyndale's 1530 translation of Exodus (Malless, 90). Though the King James Version of Exodus 6:3 states that Israel's God was not known in pre-Mosaic (patriarchal) times by his name Jehovah or its Hebrew equivalent, restoration scripture indicates that he was indeed so known (Abraham 1:6; 2:8; JST, Exodus 6:3). Surprisingly, the name Jehovah is found only twice in the Book of Mormon (2 Nephi 22:2; Moroni 10:34).

SOURCE

Malless, Stanley, and Jeffrey McQuain. *Coined by God*. New York: W. W. Norton, 2003.

ACS

JESUS

As the Greek form of the Hebrew names Joshua, Yeshua, or Yehoshua, *Jesus* means "Help of Jehovah," "Jehovah is deliverance," or "Jehovah is salvation." Thus, *Jesus* carries the sense of "Savior-Deliverer." Appropriately, this is the name given to the Babe of Bethlehem by divine decree (Luke 1:31).

Jesus was a common name among the Jews in the first century, so much so in fact that the very criminal released by Pontius Pilate at Passover in place of Jesus of Nazareth was named "Jesus bar-Abba," Aramaic for "Jesus son of father." This criminal is commonly known in the four Gospels as Barabbas. This is a circumstance of such supreme irony as to be much more than mere coincidence—that is, the people called for the release of one son of a father who was guilty, while clamoring for the execution of the true Son of the Father, who was innocent. As has been noted, "An interesting variant occurs in [Matthew 27:16–17], where he is called 'Jesus Barabbas.' . . . Origen implies that most manuscripts in his day (*ca* A.D. 240) included the full name. Many scholars today accept the full name in Matthew as original and suggest that it was probably omitted by later scribes because of the repugnance of having Jesus Christ's name being shared by Barabbas. . . . It is not improbable for Barabbas to have the very common name *Jesus*" (Freedman, 1:607).

The apostles of the meridian Church of Jesus Christ bore powerful witness that "God hath made that same Jesus, whom ye have crucified, both Lord and Christ" (Acts 2:36). There is no question that the name *Jesus* should be used with utmost reverence in our day, for says the Lord himself, "Let all men beware how they take my name in their lips—For behold, verily I say, that many there be who are under this condemnation, who use the name of the Lord, and use it in vain, having not authority" (D&C 63:61–62).

SOURCE

Freedman, David N., editor in chief. *Anchor Bible Dictionary.* 6 vols. New York: Doubleday Dell, 1992.

ACS

JESUS CHRIST, FATHERHOOD OF

Prophesying of the mortal ministry of the Savior, the Book of Mormon prophet Abinadi declared "that God himself shall come down among the children of men, and shall redeem his people. And because he dwelleth in the flesh he shall be called the Son of God, and having subjected the flesh to the will of the Father, *being the Father and the Son*—The Father, because he was conceived by the power of God; and the Son, because of the flesh; thus *becoming the Father and the Son*" (Mosiah 15:1–3; emphasis added). In a doctrinal exposition entitled "The Father and the Son," dated 30 June 1916, the First Presidency and Quorum of the Twelve Apostles clarified how Jesus Christ can be referred to as both Father and Son (Talmage, 466–73). Affirming that God the Eternal Father is the father of the spirits of all humankind, the First Presidency and the Twelve identified three unique ways whereby Jesus Christ is appropriately referred to as the Father and the Son.

1. Jesus Christ is "the Father of the heavens and of the earth, and

all things that in them are" (Ether 4:7). Under the direction of the Father, he is the Creator of this earth and "worlds without number" (Moses 1:32–33; 2:1; John 1:1–3, 14; Colossians 1:16; 3:10; Hebrews 1:2; Mosiah 3:8; Alma 11:38–39; Ether 3:16; D&C 38:1–4; 45:1).

2. Jesus Christ is the Father of the redeemed—the spiritual father of those who receive the gospel and are "born again" through the Atonement of Jesus Christ (Mosiah 27:25). They take his name upon themselves and by the power of the Holy Ghost experience a new birth (Mosiah 5:7–8; 27:25–27; D&C 39:4; 76:24).

3. Jesus Christ is the Father by divine investiture of authority—he speaks as if he were the Father because they are perfectly one in mind, will, and purpose. "In all His dealings with the human family Jesus the Son has represented and yet represents Elohim His Father in power and authority. And so far as power, authority and Godship are concerned His words and acts were and are those of the Father" (Talmage, 465–73; see also John 5:18–19; 14:11; Philippians 2:6; Helaman 5:11; 3 Nephi 9:15; D&C 50:43; 93:4).

Thus, three things are involved in the divine investiture of the Father's authority to the Son. First, the Father has placed upon his Son his name. Jesus speaks and acts in the name of the Father. Second, Jesus speaks the words of the Father because the Father has given those words to him. The Savior himself taught, "The Son can do nothing of himself, but what he seeth the Father do: for what things soever he doeth, these also doeth the Son likewise. For the Father loveth the Son, and sheweth him all things that himself doeth: and he will shew him greater works than these that ye may marvel" (John 5:19–20; see also John 8:28). Third, the Savior has divine investiture of authority because all of the Father's attributes and powers are divinely invested in the Son, who declared, "I am in the Father and the Father in me" (John 14:12). In modern revelation we read that Christ "received a fulness of the glory of the Father; and he received all power both in heaven and on earth, and the glory of the Father was with him, for he dwelt with him" (D&C 93:16–17).

SOURCE

Talmage, James E. *The Articles of Faith.* Classics in Mormon Literature series. Salt Lake City: Deseret Book, 1981.

BLT

JESUS CHRIST, NAMES AND TITLES OF

Jesus Christ, the Redeemer of the world, is known by scores of different names or titles throughout scripture. No one title perfectly describes his magnificent and unique role in the Father's plan, but all of his titles collectively help us better know and reverence him. Portraying the Savior's vast mission, the prophet Isaiah wrote, "For unto us a child is born, unto us a son is given: and the government shall be upon his shoulder: and his name shall be called Wonderful, Counsellor, The mighty God, The everlasting Father, The Prince of Peace" (Isaiah 9:6).

Jesus Christ is also the Rock, the Word, the Love of God, the Creator, the Advocate, the Judge, the Chief Cornerstone, the Only Begotten of the Father, Jehovah, the Great I Am, the Firstfruits of the Resurrection, the Son of Man, Immanuel, the Bread of Life, the Living Water, the King of kings, the Mediator, the Messenger of the Covenant, the Firstborn, and the True Vine. He is the Prophet, our Master and Lord, the Son, the Good Shepherd, the Lamb of God, the Light of the World, the Resurrection and the Life, the Great High Priest, the Second Comforter, and the Great Exemplar. He is Savior, Redeemer, and the source of all hope. He is the Anointed One—Messiah and Christ. He is God.

CFO

JESUS OF NAZARETH

To distinguish our Lord from others during his mortal ministry who bore the common name *Jesus* (the Greek form of the Hebrew names Joshua, Yeshua, and Yehoshua), he is called Jesus of Nazareth. Though born in Bethlehem, Jesus returned to the village of Nazareth in Galilee at a young age and was raised there in fulfillment of a now-unknown prophecy: "And he came and dwelt in a city called Nazareth: that it might be fulfilled which was spoken by the prophets, He shall be called a Nazarene" (Matthew 2:23).

Nonetheless, because Nazareth of Galilee was of such insignificance and backwardness—being one of few Christian place names not found in the Old Testament, the Talmud, or the writings of Josephus—two points may be emphasized. First, many Jews possessed the attitude expressed by Nathanael, who became one of the Twelve Apostles, "Can there any good thing come out of Nazareth?" (John 1:46). Thus, even in the circumstance of his childhood habitation and growth to adulthood, the Savior descended below all things (D&C 88:6). Second, Jesus' Nazarene background contributed to, or at least agreed with, the erroneous notion current in Judaism of his day that "out of Galilee ariseth no prophet" (John 7:52). Perhaps this error further contributed to the refusal of some Jews to accept Jesus of Nazareth as a prophet, let alone the Messiah. The fact that Jesus was from Nazareth was all the evidence some Jews needed to reject him as being a deceiver. He was rejected because of his obscurity.

Whatever the source of this erroneous view, there is no question in the modern world that both disciple and nonbeliever alike understand exactly who is being referred to when the name Jesus of Nazareth is spoken. To every believer it is a name worthy of intense reverence, synonymous with his roles as Savior and King (*Hymns,* no. 181).

SOURCE

"Jesus of Nazareth, Savior and King." *Hymns of The Church of Jesus Christ of Latter-day Saints,* no. 181. Salt Lake City: The Church of Jesus Christ of Latter-day Saints, 1985.

ACS

JEWS

The term *Jew* (Hebrew, *yehudi*) is derived from the name of Judah, fourth son of Jacob and Leah (Genesis 29:35; 37:26–27; 43:3, 8; 44:16). He, his eleven brothers, their wives, and their descendants constituted the house of Israel. Any descendant of Judah was appropriately referred to as a Jew. From Judah's patriarchal blessing, given by his father, Jacob, it was known that his was a tribe of leadership, and it was prophesied that the Messiah would come through his lineage (Genesis 49:8–12, especially 10; JST, Genesis 50:24). During Israel's sojourn in the wilderness after the Exodus, Judah occupied the position of leadership and prominence (Numbers 2:1–3). After the conquest of the holy land (formerly called Canaan), Israel came to be led by descendants of Judah—David and Solomon, Israel's greatest kings (1 Samuel 17:12; 2 Samuel 2:4; 5:1–3; 12:24; 1 Kings 2:12; Matthew 1:1–6).

After the death of King Solomon, the unified nation of Israel (forged earlier at Mount Sinai, as recorded in Exodus 20–23) split into two factions: the southern kingdom of Judah and the northern kingdom of Israel (1 Kings 12; 2 Chronicles 10). Anyone living in the kingdom of Judah, which included the tribes of Judah, the greater part of Benjamin and Simeon (occupying the Negev), and some Levites, was regarded as a Jew. In 721 B.C. the northern kingdom of Israel was conquered by Assyria. Most members of the ten tribes were deported, and foreigners were imported (2 Kings 17; 18:11). They mingled with the remnants of the Israelite people and became known as the Samaritans. Before the destruction of the kingdom of Israel, the southern kingdom of Judah, with its capital at Jerusalem, had received immigrants from the northern kingdom. These included people "out of all the tribes of Israel such as set their hearts to seek the Lord God . . . [and] came to Jerusalem, to sacrifice unto the Lord God of their fathers" (2 Chronicles 11:16). Perhaps Lehi's ancestors participated in this migration, and if not then, certainly at another time. Thus, Lehi and Ishmael, though descendants of Joseph, were Jews (2 Nephi 30:4; 33:8) by virtue of their habitation in Judah.

In 586 B.C. the southern kingdom of Judah was conquered by, and exiled to, Babylon. After the return of some of the exiles, all surviving descendants of the house of Israel, whether back in their homeland or outside of it, were known as Jews. For example, Queen Esther's relative Mordecai, who was from the tribe of Benjamin, was known as a Jew (Esther 2:5; 3:4). This was also true of the apostle Paul, who, though from the tribe of Benjamin, called himself a Jew (Acts 21:37–39; 22:3; Romans 11:1).

The most important of all Jews was the Lord Jesus Christ, who was a lineal descendant of Judah through David (Matthew 1:1–6). He was the fulfillment of Jacob's promise to his son that the scepter would "not depart from Judah, nor a lawgiver from between his feet, until Shiloh come" (Genesis 49:10). Shiloh is Jesus Christ (JST, Genesis 50:24). Jesus taught that "salvation is of the Jews" (John 4:22), meaning that he, a Jew, wrought the infinite and eternal Atonement, the only means whereby anyone can be saved (Alma 34:8–16; Helaman 5:9; 3 Nephi 11:11–14). But this statement also applies to the scriptures, particularly the Bible, which contains the words of life and salvation and which came to all by way of the Jews (2 Nephi 29). The Gentiles must remember the Jews and be grateful to them.

Certain leaders of the Jews engineered the death of Jesus Christ (Matthew 26:3–5; Mark 14:1–2; Luke 22:2). Tragically, the actions of these leaders led most of the Jewish people away from the Savior. However, the New Testament records the lives and actions of many of the noble and great spirits of our Father in Heaven who built the early Church and blessed lives. They were Jews. Among these are the many women who followed Jesus (Luke 8:1–3), the apostles and teachers, and some of the disciples who even sat in the leading councils of first-century Judaism—Nicodemus and Joseph of Arimathaea, for example. Nicodemus defended Jesus in front of the Pharisees, and both Nicodemus and Joseph of Arimathaea gave Jesus a proper burial at great personal sacrifice and aided the grieving family and friends of the Master (Matthew 27:57–60; Mark 15:43–45; Luke 23:50–53; John 3:1; 7:50–53; 19:38–39). We need to remember these exceptions when we read the Book of Mormon prophet Jacob's indictment of "the Jews" as the only "nation on earth that would crucify their God" (2 Nephi 10:3). Any reference to the Jewish people in a derogatory or unkind manner is out of harmony with the teachings of The Church of Jesus Christ of Latter-day Saints.

The scriptures prophesy that in the latter days the Jews will return to Jerusalem and the lands of their forefathers, as the Lord commanded (D&C 133:13; 45:24–25). Another sign of the times is that the Jews will "begin to believe in Christ" and "gather in upon the face of the land" (2 Nephi 30:7). At the time of the Second Coming, the Jews will be engaged in the worldwide conflict known as Armageddon. The Savior's feet will touch the Mount of Olives, and the Jews will be saved by the very same Jesus that their ancestors rejected (Zechariah 12:2–4; 14:2–5). Then the Jews as a people will be converted to Jesus Christ as they recognize him (D&C 45:51–53; Zechariah 12:10–14; 13:6).

In Jewish law, anyone born of a Jewish mother is a Jew. Individuals may convert to the Jewish religion, though Judaism in modern times does not seek out converts as intensely as it once did (see Matthew 23:15, for example). In modern times, the questions of what Judaism is (a religion, a race, a culture, or an ethnic group), as well as who gets to decide who qualifies as a Jew, are complex and sometimes controversial.

ACS

JOINT HEIRS WITH CHRIST

As an act of consummate grace, and as a result of our receipt of God's gift (through faith, repentance, baptism, confirmation, and faithfulness to temple covenants), men and women become the children of God, adopted members of the royal family (Romans 8:14–18; 1 John 2:1–2). As such they become joint heirs or co-inheritors with Christ to all the Father has. Christ is the literal Firstborn, but he manifests his love toward us in granting us an equal status, as though we had been the firstborn. "And now, verily I say unto you, I was in the beginning with the Father, and am the Firstborn; and all those who are begotten through me are partakers of the glory of the same, and are the church of the Firstborn" (D&C 93:21–22).

RLM

JOSEPH SMITH

We believe that Joseph Smith was and is a prophet of God. By that we mean that he was charged by the Almighty to be both a legal administrator and a revealer of truth. As a *legal administrator,* Joseph became the one through whom priesthoods, keys, and authorities were restored to the earth through the appearance and ministration of heavenly messengers—John the Baptist, Peter, James, John, Moses, Elias, Elijah, and "divers angels, from Michael or Adam down to the present time, all declaring their dispensation, their rights, their keys, their honors, their majesty and glory, and the power of their priesthood; giving line upon line, precept upon precept, here a little and there a little; giving us consolation by holding forth that which is to come, confirming our hope!" (D&C 128:21). "Whenever men can find out the will of God and find an administrator legally authorized from God," the Prophet taught, "there is the kingdom of God; but where these are not, the kingdom of God is not. All the ordinances, systems, and administrations on the earth are of no use to the children of men, unless they are ordained and authorized of God; for nothing will save a man but a legal administrator; for none others will be acknowledged either by God or angels" (*History,* 5:259). To those who suppose they can derive their authority from holy scripture, he added, "There is no salvation between the two lids of the Bible without a legal administrator" (*Joseph Smith,* 85).

Joseph Smith was also called to be a *revealer of truth,* a dispenser of doctrinal understanding and eternal principles. Because plain and precious truths and many covenants of the Lord had been taken away or kept back from the Bible, Joseph was appointed to be the principal means by which "other books" (1 Nephi 13:39) of scripture—the Book of Mormon, the Doctrine and Covenants, and the inspired translation of the Bible—were delivered to men on earth for the edification and enlightenment of generations yet unborn (1 Nephi 13:20–40). Specifically, through Joseph Smith the Lord chose to make known such profound theological matters as the premortal existence of man, the significance of the physical body, the vital importance of the fall of our first parents, the infinite scope of the Atonement, the necessity of the priesthood and its ordinances, the unifying concept of Zion, the postmortal state of the soul following death and resurrection, kingdoms of glory hereafter, the fate of those who never have the opportunity to receive the gospel of Jesus Christ in this life, the central place of temples and the eternal family unit, the power of the everlasting covenant to secure those who wander, and many other sacred truths that make the Latter-day Saint system of belief, what has come to be known as Mormonism, distinctive and appealing.

Jehovah spoke to Joseph of old, he who was sold into slavery in Egypt, and prophesied of the coming of Joseph Smith, the *choice seer:* "A seer will I raise up out of the fruit of thy loins [a descendant of Joseph]; and unto him will I give power to bring forth my word unto the seed of thy loins. . . . Wherefore, the fruit of thy loins shall write [the Book of Mormon]; and the fruit of the loins of Judah shall write [the Bible]; and that which shall be written by the fruit of thy loins, and also that which shall be written by the fruit of the loins of Judah, shall grow together, unto the confounding of false doctrines and laying down of contentions, and establishing peace among the fruit of thy loins, and bringing them to the knowledge of their fathers in the latter days, and also to the knowledge of my covenants, saith the Lord" (2 Nephi 3:11–12).

Joseph Smith was also called to serve as a *dispensation head,* to initiate and lead the dispensation of the fulness of times. As such, he stands in these last days as the preeminent prophetic revealer of Jesus Christ and God's plan of salvation. In that sense, he is commissioned and empowered to be a prophet's prophet, a seer's seer, a revelator's revelator. To him the Savior declared in 1829: "This generation [dispensation] shall have my word through you" (D&C 5:10).

"God chose this young man," President John Taylor said. "He was ignorant of letters as the world has it, but the most profoundly learned and intelligent man that I ever met in my life, and I have traveled hundreds of thousands of miles, been on different continents and mingled among all classes and creeds of people, yet I never met a man so intelligent as he was. And where did he get his intelligence from? Not from books, not from the logic or science or philosophy of the day, but he obtained it through the revelation of God made known to him through the medium of the everlasting gospel" (353).

President Lorenzo Snow recalled: "Perhaps there are very few men now living who were so well acquainted with Joseph Smith the Prophet as I was. I was with him oftentimes. I visited with him in his family, sat at his table, associated with him under various circumstances, and had private interviews with him for counsel. I know that Joseph Smith was a prophet of God; I know that he was an honorable man, a moral man, and that he had the respect of those who were acquainted with him. The Lord has shown me most clearly and completely that he was a prophet of God, and that he held the holy priesthood" (55).

President Heber J. Grant attested: "I have met hundreds of men who have said: 'If it were not for Joseph Smith I could accept your religion.' Any man who does not believe in Joseph Smith as a prophet of the true and the living God has no right to be in this Church. That revelation [the First Vision] to Joseph Smith is the foundation stone. If Joseph Smith did not have that interview with God and Jesus Christ, the whole Mormon fabric is a failure and a fraud. It is not worth anything on earth. But God did come, God did introduce His Son; God did inspire that man to organize the Church of Jesus Christ, and all the opposition in the world is not able to withstand the truth. It is flourishing; it is growing, and it will grow more" (15).

President Gordon B. Hinckley declared: "It is a constantly recurring mystery to me how some people speak with admiration for the Church and its work, while at the same time disdaining him through whom, as a servant of the Lord, came the framework of all that the Church is, of all that it teaches, and of all that it stands for. They would pluck the fruit from the tree while cutting off the root from which it grows. . . .

"Great was the Prophet Joseph Smith's vision. It encompassed all the peoples of mankind, wherever they live, and all generations who have walked the earth and passed on. How can anyone, past or present, speak against him except out of ignorance? They have not tasted of his words; they have not pondered about him, nor prayed about him. As one who has done these things, I add my own words of testimony that he was and is a prophet of God, raised up as an instrument in the hands of the Almighty to usher in a new and final gospel dispensation" (501, 503).

Latter-day Saints do not worship Joseph Smith or any of his prophetic successors. Worship is reserved for the Godhead. But the Saints honor him, revere him, and appreciate profoundly the labor he performed and the marvelous work and a wonder he set in motion (Isaiah 29:14; 2 Nephi 25:17; 27:26). The Restoration is far more than the organization of a new church or religious movement. It is a paradigm shift, a corrective, and in a very real sense a religious revolution. Less than two months before his martyrdom, Joseph Smith taught: "I calculate to be one of the instruments of setting up the kingdom of [God foreseen by] Daniel by the word of the Lord, and I intend to lay a foundation that will revolutionize the whole world. . . . It will not be by sword or gun that this kingdom will roll on: the power of truth is such that all nations will be under the necessity of obeying the Gospel" (6:365). It is by this means that William W. Phelps's marvelous hymn of praise to our dispensation head will be fully realized, the means by which "millions shall know Brother Joseph again" (*Hymns*, no. 27).

SOURCES

Grant, Heber J. *Gospel Standards.* Edited by G. Homer Durham. Salt Lake City: Bookcraft, 1998.

Hinckley, Gordon B. *Teachings of Gordon B. Hinckley.* Salt Lake City: Deseret Book, 1997.

Joseph Smith [manual]. Teachings of Presidents of the Church series. Salt Lake City: The Church of Jesus Christ of Latter-day Saints, 2007.

"Praise to the Man." *Hymns of The Church of Jesus Christ of Latter-day Saints*, no. 27. Salt Lake City: The Church of Jesus Christ of Latter-day Saints, 1985.

Smith, Joseph. *History of The Church of Jesus Christ of Latter-day Saints.* Edited by

B. H. Roberts. 7 vols. 2d ed. rev. Salt Lake City: The Church of Jesus Christ of Latter-day Saints, 1932–51.

Snow, Lorenzo. *The Teachings of Lorenzo Snow.* Compiled by Clyde J. Williams. Salt Lake City: Bookcraft, 1984.

Taylor, John. *The Gospel Kingdom.* Edited by G. Homer Durham. Salt Lake City: Bookcraft, 1987.

RLM

JOSEPH SMITH TRANSLATION OF THE BIBLE

Some time before June 1830, Joseph Smith and Oliver Cowdery were called and appointed by God (D&C 42:56; 76:15) to do a "new translation" of the King James Version of the Bible. On 8 October 1829 they purchased a large pulpit-style edition of the King James Version, published in 1828 by the H. & E. Phinney Company in Cooperstown, New York, for use in the translation. The work began in earnest in June 1830 with Moses 1, revealed to Joseph Smith and now contained in the Pearl of Great Price. This revelation was in many ways a preface to the Bible translation and especially to the account of the Creation. Joseph and Oliver proceeded to make their way through the book of Genesis until they had covered essentially the first twenty-four chapters. The Joseph Smith Translation of Genesis 1:1 through 8:18 is now contained in the Pearl of Great Price, known as "Selections from the Book of Moses." On 7 March 1831, Joseph and Oliver received a revelation, now recorded in Doctrine and Covenants 45, which instructed them to lay the Old Testament aside and begin translating the New Testament with Matthew (D&C 45:60–62). They did so and continued until they had completed their translation of the New Testament, at which point they returned to Genesis 24 and resumed work on the Old Testament. The translators wrote to Church leaders in Missouri on 2 July 1833 that they had finished the work of translation (Smith, 1:368).

It appears that the Prophet would read from the Bible and dictate to his scribe, who would write all the words on paper, including alterations the Prophet would make, in the King James text. This longer scribal method continued until the translators reached the Gospel of John. They then began a shorter method in which the scribe wrote only the changes on the manuscript. The Prophet made marks (circles, slashes, dashes, periods, colons) in the Bible itself so that a person looking at the manuscript would know where in the Bible text the changes were to go. In total, 25 verses were added to Genesis for the Moses 1 material; 1,289 verses were altered in the Old Testament; and 2,096 verses were altered in the New Testament, for a total of 3,410 affected verses. Oliver served as a scribe until he was called on a mission in the fall of 1830 (D&C 28:8; 32:2). Others who served as scribes were John Whitmer (D&C 47:1), Emma Smith (D&C 25:6), Frederick G. Williams (D&C 90:19), and Sidney Rigdon. To demonstrate how the Lord felt about this significant branch of Joseph's calling, the word to Elder Rigdon declared: "And a commandment I give unto thee—that thou shalt write for him; and the scriptures shall be given, even as they are in mine own bosom, to the salvation of mine own elect" (D&C 35:20).

It was during the period of the Bible translation (1830–33) that a large number of revelations now contained in the Doctrine and Covenants were received. These divine directions responded either to matters raised in the translation (D&C 74, 76, 77, 91, 132) or were revelations that referred in some way to the translation (D&C 25:6; 45:60–62; 73:3; 76:15–21; 90:13; 93:53; 94:10; 124:89). In fact, the Prophet and his scribes were involved in a concurrent revelatory process—often the insights from the translation and similar insights in the dictated revelations came at about the same time. Sometimes the translation came first; occasionally the revelations preceded the translation. For example, distinctive truths concerning the Creation, Fall, and Atonement came through the early translation of Genesis (Moses 2–4), while at about the same time the Lord delivered these same concepts in Doctrine and Covenants 29. The marvelous detail concerning the patriarch Enoch and his holy city (as contained in Moses 6 and 7) were followed shortly thereafter by revelations that spoke of Enoch and of the need to establish a latter-day Zion (D&C 38:4; 42:29–42). Similarly, vital information concerning the age of accountability as being eight years old was given to Joseph Smith first in his Bible translation (JST, Genesis 17:11) and seven to ten months later in a revelation delivered in November 1831 (D&C 68:27).

The Prophet became intensely interested in the Bible for several reasons: (1) He knew very well that plain and precious truths had been taken away or kept from the Bible before it was compiled (1 Nephi

13:20–40; D&C 6:26; Smith, 1:245); he also knew it was impossible to resolve religious questions by an appeal to the existing Bible (Joseph Smith–History 1:12). (2) He was commanded to complete the translation, and he obeyed. (3) As we have observed, many of the revelations in the Doctrine and Covenants came as a result of the Bible translation. (4) The process of translation proved to be a significant part of the spiritual education of the Prophet. As Church history attests, most of the Prophet's sermons, delivered from 1830 to 1844, were laced with quotations or paraphrasing summaries of biblical passages. Through the translation process, the great latter-day seer became well acquainted with the texts and even the personalities of the Old and New Testaments. Indeed, the Joseph Smith Translation is one of the great evidences of the divine calling of the Prophet Joseph Smith.

Much of the Joseph Smith Translation was included in the 1979 Latter-day Saint edition of the King James Version of the Bible, with short excerpts featured in footnotes and longer excerpts found in the appendix. The Joseph Smith Translation truly is a scriptural treasure.

SOURCE

Smith, Joseph. *History of The Church of Jesus Christ of Latter-day Saints.* Edited by B. H. Roberts. 7 vols. 2d ed. rev. Salt Lake City: The Church of Jesus Christ of Latter-day Saints, 1932–51.

RLM

JOY

The term *joy* is often used synonymously, both in modern vernacular and in the scriptures, with the words *happiness, gladness, rejoicing, felicity, pleasure*. We read in the scriptures that men and women can have joy and rejoicing in both temporal and spiritual things. For example, we can have joy in our posterity (3 John 1:4). We have joy in peace (Psalm 37:11) and in the abundance of blessings we receive from God. There is great joy in sharing the gospel with others and seeing their lives changed thereby (Alma 29:9; D&C 18:15–16). Paul teaches that there can be joy even in tribulations (2 Corinthians 7:4; Colossians 1:11). There is joy in keeping the commandments of God (Mosiah 2:4, 41), in having the Spirit in our lives (Romans 14:17; D&C 11:13), and in receiving a remission of our sins through faith and repentance (Alma 36:20). Numerous other passages testify of the joy that comes through recognizing the hand of God in our lives, trusting in his promises, and partaking of the blessings of the atonement of Jesus Christ. At the other end of the spectrum, the scriptures also state that the wicked can take joy in sin and hypocrites can have joy in their deceptions—but only temporarily or "for a moment" (Job 20:5) or "for a season" (3 Nephi 27:11). In contrast, the joy that "no man taketh from you" (John 16:22) comes to the righteous.

In the Book of Mormon, father Lehi taught, "Men are that they might have joy" (2 Nephi 2:25). The ultimate purpose of man's existence is not to have joy only in this life but to experience in the life to come the supreme, eternal joy that God possesses. Lehi's words reflect the understanding that our Heavenly Father's work and glory is "to bring to pass the immortality and eternal life of man" (Moses 1:39). Eternal life—life with God as joint-heirs with Jesus Christ, inheriting all that the Father has—is the fulness of joy. Although we may experience much joy in life, we receive the fulness of joy—that which is the objective of the plan of salvation—only after the resurrection (D&C 93:33–34; see also Psalm 16:11; Jude 1:24; Alma 4:14; D&C 51:19; 101:36; 138:17). This is the fruit of the tree of life that fills our hearts and souls with "exceedingly great joy" (1 Nephi 8:12; see also 1 Nephi 11:16–23).

BLT

JUDAS

At least six men named Judas (Hebrew, *Yehudah,* meaning "God is praised") are mentioned in the New Testament: (1) the half-brother of Jesus (Matthew 13:55) and author of the epistle of Jude; (2) one of the Twelve, not Iscariot, brother of James (Luke 6:16; John 14:22; Acts 1:13); (3) leader of a revolt in Galilee, who was regarded by some as the Messiah but was killed along with his followers (Acts 5:37); (4) Judas Barsabbas, church leader in Jerusalem, declared to be a prophet (Acts 15:22, 27, 32); (5) a person of Damascus, the host of Paul after the latter's conversion to the Church of Jesus Christ (Acts 9:11); (6) Judas Iscariot, the most famous of them all, a member of the original Quorum of the Twelve Apostles (Bible Dictionary, "Judas").

Judas Iscariot was the son of one Simon (John 6:71). The surname Iscariot is probably a contraction of two Hebrew words meaning "man (*ish*) of Kerioth" (a village in southern Judah; Joshua 15:25; see also Bible Dictionary, "Kerioth"). He was the only one of the Twelve not from Galilee (Acts 1:11; Talmage, 225). He betrayed Jesus by delivering him into the hands of the chief priests, a contractual agreement for which he received thirty pieces of silver (Matthew 26:14–16; Luke 22:4–6). In an episode that foreshadowed the life of the Messiah, Judah, son of Jacob, proposed selling his brother Joseph for the price of a slave (Genesis 37:26–28). Similarly, Judas (Judah) Iscariot sold Jesus for the price of a slave (Matthew 27:3, 9; Talmage, 592), the amount foreseen by prophets (Zechariah 11:12; Exodus 21:32).

The four Gospels paint a uniformly negative picture of Judas Iscariot, all referring to him as a betrayer or traitor even before they describe his carrying out "the blackest deed of treachery of which man is capable" (Talmage, 592; Matthew 10:4; Mark 3:19; Luke 6:16; John 6:71). The Gospels imply that his treachery is all the more shocking precisely because he was one of the Twelve.

The Gospel of John attributes Judas's false concern for the poor to his role as a thief. That is, he "had the bag" (he may have been the treasurer of the Quorum of the Twelve), and because he used to steal from it, he undoubtedly was concerned that his thievery remain secret, covered up by a constant flow of money coming in—in this case by selling costly ointment instead of using it to anoint Jesus (John 12:4–6). John also reports that Jesus referred to Judas as "the son of perdition" (John 17:12). Both John and Luke state that Satan entered into Judas as the conspiracy of betrayal unfolded, though they seem to disagree as to exactly when it occurred (Luke 22:3; John 13:27). It is possible that this demonic possession was literal, since Satan is a spirit personage capable of such a thing and two Gospel witnesses attest to it. Thus, it also seems possible that Satan entered into Judas both before he made his final agreement with the chief priests and during the Last Supper.

It should be observed here that Satan has no power over individuals except as they permit him (*Joseph Smith,* 214). Judas was not predestined to betray Jesus, as explained by Elder James E. Talmage: "It would be contrary to both the letter and spirit of the revealed word to say that the wretched Iscariot was in the least degree deprived of freedom or agency in the course he followed to so execrable an end. His was the opportunity and privilege common to the Twelve of living in the light of the Lord's immediate presence. Judas Iscariot was no victim of circumstances, no insensate tool guided by a superhuman power, except as he by personal volition gave himself up to Satan and accepted a wage in the devil's employ. Had Judas been true to the right, other means than his perfidy would have operated to bring the Lamb to the slaughter. His ordination to the apostleship placed him in possession of opportunity and privilege above that of the uncalled and unordained; and with such blessed possibility of achievement in the service of God came the corresponding capability to fall" (650).

There also seems to be disagreement between the two reports of Judas's death. Matthew says that after he "repented himself" and tried to return the blood money to the priests, he committed suicide by hanging (Matthew 27:3–5). Peter says that Judas purchased a field called Aceldama ("the field of blood") with the conspiracy money, and falling headlong, "burst asunder," and "his bowels gushed out" (Acts 1:18–19). Various attempts have been made to harmonize the two accounts. A reasonable suggestion from the medieval theologian and church father Augustine proposes that Judas hanged himself in the field, and afterward the rope broke and Judas's body fell to the ground and burst open (see also JST, Matthew 27:6).

On the question of Judas's station in the eternities as a son of perdition, President Joseph F. Smith said the following: "If Judas really had known God's power, and had partaken thereof, and did actually 'deny the truth' and 'defy' that power, 'having denied the Holy Spirit after he had received it,' and also 'denied the Only Begotten,' after God had 'revealed him' unto him, then there can be no doubt that he 'will die the second death.' That Judas did partake of all this knowledge—that these great truths had been revealed to him—that he had received the Holy Spirit by the gift of God, and was therefore qualified to commit the unpardonable sin, is not at all clear to me. To my mind it strongly appears that not one of the disciples possessed sufficient light, knowledge nor wisdom, at the time of the crucifixion, for either exaltation or condemnation; for it was afterward that their minds were opened to understand the scriptures, and that they were endowed with power from on high; without which they were only children in knowledge, in comparison to what they afterwards become under the influence of the Spirit" (433).

Either way, Judas Iscariot chose to do evil deeds. He became "Satan's serf, and did his master's bidding" (Talmage, 592). His story is one of great tragedy, filled with valuable lessons for us all.

SOURCES

Joseph Smith [manual]. Teachings of Presidents of the Church series. Salt Lake City: The Church of Jesus Christ of Latter-day Saints, 2007.

Smith, Joseph. *History of The Church of Jesus Christ of Latter-day Saints.* Edited by B. H. Roberts. 7 vols. 2d ed. rev. Salt Lake City: The Church of Jesus Christ of Latter-day Saints, 1932–51.

Smith, Joseph F. *Gospel Doctrine.* Salt Lake City: Deseret Book, 1939.

Talmage, James E. *Jesus the Christ.* Salt Lake City: Deseret Book, 1973.

ACS

JUDGING

The Savior's admonition "Judge not, that ye be not judged" (Matthew 7:1) is often misinterpreted to mean that we should never make judgments regarding people or situations. This is not what the Savior taught. God expects us to be discerning and wise. As a result, we all need to make judgments every day of our lives. Sometimes our very lives—spiritual and physical—depend on those judgments. In addition to the universal responsibility we all have to continually and wisely evaluate people and circumstances, the Lord calls some to be "judges in Israel"—with specific priesthood responsibilities to discern spiritual and temporal matters and make inspired judgments regarding them. The Joseph Smith Translation of the Bible makes this important revision: "Judge not *unrighteously*" (JST, Matthew 7:1; emphasis added). This addition applies not only to called and ordained "common judges in Israel" (bishops and stake presidents) but also to all of us as we make life's important judgments and evaluations.

The Greek word from which "judge" is translated in this passage does not refer to discerning or appraising something in order to make a wise decision but rather means "to condemn." In this context, the word "judge" implies sentencing someone to death or to prison. It connotes a sense of finality. As such, Jesus' words appear to be saying that we are not to condemn or pass "final judgments" regarding someone's spiritual standing before God, based on our personal biases or misconceptions regarding the gospel standard. Although some have callings and keys to pass intermediate judgments of worthiness, the Lord is reminding us that no mortal has the right to declare final or ultimate judgment regarding the souls of men. To do so is unrighteous judgment, and it is always spiritually destructive—both to the judge and the judged.

Two forms of unrighteous judgment—even in necessary, intermediate judgments and evaluations—seem to be especially common in our society: judging by the traditions of men and judging with limited knowledge. The scriptures illustrate and warn against both.

Judging by the traditions of men. The Master taught, "Judge not according to the appearance, but judge righteous judgment" (John 7:24). This form of unrighteous judgment would include making spiritual value judgments based only on how things or people appear to us outwardly, not on how things really are inwardly, at the spiritual core. The Joseph Smith Translation adds another important dimension: "Judge not according to your *traditions*" (JST, Matthew 7:24; emphasis added). This warning is surely against criticizing, demeaning, or condemning another based solely on appearances or on a tradition or cultural expectation that is not a true gospel standard. President Brigham Young offered a similar warning:

"How I regret the ignorance of this people—how it floods my heart with sorrow to see so many Elders of Israel who wish everybody to come to their standard and be measured by their measure. Every man must be just so long, to fit their iron bedstead, or be cut off to the right length: if too short, he must be stretched, to fill the requirement.

"If they see an erring brother or sister, whose course does not comport with their particular idea of things, they conclude at once that he or she cannot be a Saint, and withdraw their fellowship, concluding that, if they are in the path of truth, others must have precisely their weight and dimensions" (8:9).

Judging with limited knowledge. God's judgments are perfectly just because "he knoweth all things" (2 Nephi 9:20), loves infinitely, and "seeth not as a man seeth" but judges "according to the desire of their hearts" (D&C 137:9; see also 1 Samuel 16:7). In contrast, unrighteous judgment occurs when we criticize and condemn another without knowing all the facts, including the desires and intents of the heart. On the other hand, to "judge righteous judgment" (JST, Matthew 7:1) is to give the person every benefit of the doubt, not to excuse what he or she does (if it is truly wrong or unrighteous) but to try to understand it and endeavor as best as mortals can to look upon the heart (1 Samuel 16:7).

Christ's warning about unrighteous judgment also contains this caveat: "For with what judgment ye judge, ye shall be judged: and with what measure ye mete, it shall be measured to you again" (JST, Matthew 7:1–2). How we judge others—whether righteously or un-righteously, with tenderness or anger—will determine to a large degree how we are judged by others and the Lord. This should motivate us to sobering introspection and a determination to seek more earnestly to discern by the Spirit of God and to judge as God judges, not to con-demn as the natural man condemns (3 Nephi 27:27).

SOURCE

Young, Brigham. In *Journal of Discourses.* 26 vols. London: Latter-day Saints' Book Depot, 1854–86.

BLT

JUDGMENT, ETERNAL

Numerous scriptural passages teach of a day of ultimate reckoning when all of God's children will be judged "according to their works" (Revelation 20:12; see also 1 Samuel 2:1–10; Daniel 7:10; Matthew 12:36; Acts 17:31; Romans 14:10; 2 Nephi 9:15; Alma 5:15; 3 Nephi 27:16; Mormon 3:20; D&C 43:29). While this eternal judgment is often referred to as the Final Judgment, God's judging of men and holding them accountable to his laws and commandments actually oc-curs many times during their probation—in premortality, on earth, in the spirit world, and at the resurrection. The eternal judgment involves both intermediate judgments and final judgments.

There was a final judgment for some in the first estate. A third part of the hosts of heaven "rebelled against God, and sought to take the kingdom of our God and his Christ" (D&C 76:28) and were thus condemned to eternally "suffer the wrath of God" (D&C 76:33). On the other end of the spectrum, there were perhaps others who so val-iantly lived in accordance with God's laws that they were foreordained to callings or assignments.

In mortality, intermediate judgments are passed upon us through-out our lives. Worthiness interviews by bishops and stake presidents (common judges in Israel) are part of that process. So also is worthiness to enjoy the companionship of the Holy Ghost. With each we can know to some degree our standing before the Lord. That is a judgment. Just as in the first estate, some may commit unpardonable sins, whereby a final judgment is made concerning their ultimate fate. On the other hand, some may have been so faithful in life that their probation is ended and they are "sealed up unto eternal life" (D&C 131:5; see also Smith, 3:381). That becomes in essence a final judgment. Such was the case with, for example, Lehi (2 Nephi 1:15), Alma (Mosiah 26:20), Mormon (Mormon 2:19), and Joseph Smith (D&C 132:49).

After death there continue to be judgments in preparation for the resurrection. One's entrance into the spirit world—whether into paradise or hell—is an intermediate judgment and a clear indication of one's righteousness or wickedness (Alma 40:11–14). For many, particularly those who did not hear the gospel in mortality, the probationary period continues in the spirit world, and thus judgments in the spirit world would be intermediate.

At the Second Coming, there is also a judgment—intermediate for some and final for "all the proud and they that do wickedly," who shall be burned "as stubble" (D&C 64:24). The righteous—both living and dead—will be caught up to meet the Lord (D&C 88:96–97). That is a judgment as well. For others who will yet repent of their sins and accept the fulness of the gospel during the Millennium, the judgment at the Second Coming is an intermediate one.

The resurrection from the dead is a final judgment in that the glory of a person's resurrected body attests to the law the person has lived and the kingdom the person will inherit (D&C 88:20–31). There will be no doubt as to one's eternal status, for a celestial resurrected person will be as visibly different in glory from those terrestrial and telestial beings as the sun is to the moon and the stars (1 Corinthians 15:40–42).

Although there are various "judgment days"—both intermediate and final—throughout our lives in the premortal, mortal, and postmortal worlds that are all parts of the overall eternal judgment, there is a last judgment after all are resurrected. That last judgment is not so much an assignment to the various kingdoms of glory (since that is already determined by the time of the resurrection) as it is an acknowledgment that God's judgments are indeed just. It is at this last judgment that the spiritual death that came by reason of the Fall—being cast out of the presence of God—is swallowed up by the atonement of Jesus Christ. All mankind are brought back into the presence of God as part of this final judgment scene. The culmination of this judgment is when "all shall bow the knee, and every tongue shall confess to him who sits upon the throne forever and ever" (D&C 76:110; 88:104; see also Philippians 2:9–11; Revelation 5:13). Those who have exercised true faith in Jesus Christ and have lived their lives in accordance with the laws and ordinances of the gospel will remain in the presence of God, inheriting as joint-heirs with Christ all that the Father has—even eternal life. Those who would not live the celestial law "shall return again to their own place, to enjoy that which they are willing to receive, because they were not willing to enjoy that which they might have received" (D&C 88:32). Thus all are judged according to their works and the desires of their hearts against the same standard of judgment—the everlasting gospel of Jesus Christ.

Although others, such as judges in Israel, dispensation heads, and apostles, have a role in intermediate judgments, only Christ can pronounce final judgment. "For the Father judgeth no man, but hath committed all judgment unto the Son," Jesus taught (John 5:22). The Book of Mormon prophet Jacob declared, "The keeper of the gate is the Holy One of Israel; and he employeth no servant there; and there is none other way save it be by the gate; for he cannot be deceived, for the Lord God is his name" (2 Nephi 9:41). Jesus Christ, by virtue of his atoning sacrifice, has "purchased [us] with his own blood" (Acts 20:28) and therefore, he alone has the right to make final judgment—presenting the faithful to the Father (D&C 45:2–3) and rewarding or condemning others "according to his own works, his own dominion, in the mansions which are prepared" (D&C 76:111).

SOURCE

Smith, Joseph. *History of The Church of Jesus Christ of Latter-day Saints.* Edited by B. H. Roberts. 7 vols. 2d ed. rev. Salt Lake City: The Church of Jesus Christ of Latter-day Saints, 1932–51.

BLT

JUSTICE

There are different but complementary aspects of the foundational principle of justice. Broadly speaking, justice is that which is fair, impartial, right, and proper according to the perfect mind and will of God. Justice is a law of consequences—the equitable, consistent, and deserved consequences that follow either obedience to or violation of divinely established law. Divine justice is inviolable and demands perfect adherence to a perfect standard—God's standard. Indeed, justice is an attribute of God himself: "He is the Rock, his work is perfect: for all his ways are judgment: a God of truth and without iniquity, just and right is he" (Deuteronomy 32:4). As the psalmist said, "Justice and judgment are the habitation of thy [God's] throne" (Psalm 89:14). Justice is so fundamental to God's nature and ways that without it, "God would cease to be God" (Alma 42:13).

In order for mortals to exercise faith in God, it is necessary that they "have the idea of the existence of the attribute of justice in him; for without the idea of the existence of the attribute [of] justice in the Deity men could not have confidence sufficient to place themselves under his guidance and direction; for they would be filled with fear and doubt lest the judge of all the earth would not do right, and thus fear or doubt, existing in the mind, would preclude the possibility of the exercise of faith in him for life and salvation" (*Lectures*, 52). When mortals come to understand God's attribute of perfect justice, they can have unshaken confidence in him and his plan.

God's foreordained plan of salvation operates upon the principle of justice. On the one hand, when individuals obey God's commandments, they receive blessings guaranteed by the law of justice: "There is a law, irrevocably decreed in heaven before the foundations of this world, upon which all blessings are predicated—and when we obtain any blessing from God, it is by obedience to that law upon which it is predicated" (D&C 130:20–21). On the other hand, individuals who violate any commandment, once they learn of it, are subject to the accompanying penalty for breaking that commandment because God cannot ignore sin, nor "look upon [it] with the least degree of allowance" (D&C 1:31) because of his justice. Every divine law and every command carries a blessing or a penalty; justice affixes a punishment to each violation (Alma 42:17–18, 22). Thus, justice is essentially tied to the spiritual law of the harvest: "Be not deceived; God is not mocked: for whatsoever a man soweth, that shall he also reap. For he that soweth to his flesh shall of the flesh reap corruption; but he that soweth to the Spirit shall of the Spirit reap life everlasting. And let us not be weary in well doing: for in due season we shall reap, if we faint not" (Galatians 6:7–9).

Because justice is a law of consequences, it underpins the law of restoration. Alma teaches that in the next life we will be restored to what we have become in this life because "that same spirit which doth possess your bodies at the time that ye go out of this life, that same spirit will have power to possess your body in that eternal world" (Alma 34:34). The justice of God divides the wicked from the righteous in the spirit world (1 Nephi 15:30). Every soul who has lived on this earth will return to God as a resurrected being to participate in the Final Judgment, "and if their works have been filthiness they must needs be filthy; and . . . they cannot dwell in the kingdom of God" (1 Nephi 15:33; see also Alma 42:23; Helaman 14:17–19). The unrepentant are "exposed to the whole law of the demands of justice" (Alma 34:16). The principles of justice and judgment go together (2 Nephi 9:14–17).

However, if justice alone operated upon mortals in this world, all people would eventually be lost, barred from God's presence because of the Fall, which subjected the entire human family to physical and spiritual death and inescapable bondage to Satan (2 Nephi 9:6–9; Alma 42:14). But justice is not the only principle that operates in mortality. The atonement of Jesus Christ enables the principle of mercy to operate, which satisfies the demands of justice for all those who repent and lay hold upon the Atonement. Jesus took upon himself—absorbed and suffered—the sinner's deserved punishment (2 Nephi 2:7; Alma 34:15–16; 42:15). His great and last sacrifice brought about "the bowels of mercy, which overpowereth justice" (Alma 34:15). Mercy cannot rob justice (Alma 42:25), but it can intercede and "appease the demands of justice" (42:15). God cannot magically wave away penalties and punishments. Broken laws must be paid for. Through the Atonement, Christ pays the penalty for sin by his personal suffering. He stands between the sinner and the demands of justice (Mosiah 15:9).

The atonement of Christ does something else relative to justice. It mitigates the demands of justice acting upon individuals, depending on their degree of accountability, which is based on their knowledge of red truths and the extent of their culpability. It pays for sins committed in ignorance (2 Nephi 9:25; Mosiah 3:11; Alma 42:21).

Alma summarized beautifully the intertwined principles of justice and mercy: "The plan of mercy could not be brought about except an atonement should be made; therefore God himself atoneth for the sins of the world, to bring about the plan of mercy, to appease the demands of justice, that God might be a perfect, just God, and a merciful God also. . . . But there is a law given, and a punishment affixed, and a repentance granted; which repentance mercy claimeth; otherwise, justice claimeth the creature. . . . For behold, justice exerciseth all his demands, and also mercy claimeth all which is her own; and thus, none but the truly penitent are saved" (Alma 42:15, 22, 24).

The Atonement not only appeases the demands of justice but also ensures that justice works on behalf of the righteous—that the injustices and unfairness that are sometimes a natural part of mortal life are overturned and made up to the faithful. The Savior taught this concept in the parable of the rich man and righteous Lazarus, in which the rich man looked up from his tormented situation in hell and asked for his circumstance to be changed—even a little bit. But father Abraham answered, "Son, remember that thou in thy lifetime receivedst thy good things, and likewise Lazarus evil [unjust] things: but now he is comforted, and thou art tormented" (Luke 16:25). Thus, justice is a friend to the righteous.

SOURCE
Lectures on Faith. Salt Lake City: Deseret Book, 1985.

ACS

JUSTIFICATION

To be justified is to be made clean, innocent, exonerated, or pardoned—to be forgiven of sins. It is to be brought into a right and proper relationship with God. After explaining to Adam that because of the Fall all men and women must be born of the Spirit, God said, "For by the water ye keep the commandment; by the Spirit ye are justified, and by the blood ye are sanctified" (Moses 6:60). At the time of the organization of the restored Church, the Prophet Joseph Smith wrote, "And we know that justification through the grace of our Lord and Savior Jesus Christ is just and true; and we know also, that sanctification through the grace of our Lord and Savior Jesus Christ is just and true, to all those who love and serve God with all their mights, minds, and strength" (D&C 20:30–31). That is to say, there is a true Christian doctrine of justification and sanctification, and both manifestations of the Atonement come to pass only through the mercy and grace of Christ the Redeemer.

"Just," or justified, men and women cannot be perfect of themselves but are "made perfect through Jesus the mediator of the new covenant, who wrought out this perfect atonement through the shedding of his own blood" (D&C 76:69). If men and women could keep the law of God perfectly—could do no wrong and commit no sin—they would be justified by works or by law. This may be hypothetically possible, but it is practically impossible. Those who commit sin turn to and lean on Jesus Christ (the One who did keep the law perfectly), and then seek forgiveness and exoneration through the power of his atoning blood may be justified by faith. Paul wrote that "all have sinned, and come short of the glory of God; therefore being justified only by his grace through the redemption that is in Christ Jesus; whom God hath set forth to be a propitiation [literally, a covering] through faith in his blood, to declare his righteousness for the remission of sins that are past, through the forbearance of God. . . . Therefore we conclude that a man is justified by faith alone without [apart from] the deeds of the law" (JST, Romans 3:23–25, 28). Truly, our only hope is to be justified by faith.

Joseph Smith taught, "Being born again, comes by the Spirit of God through ordinances" (3:392). In the same way, while being justified comes through the prerogative and power of the Lord, it is a gift that is received through covenant and ordinance. Baptism and confirmation of themselves do not justify or save us; Christ does. But these ordinances represent the outworking of the covenant, the extension of our faith, the demonstration of our reliance upon the Savior. Our covenant with Christ—our disclosure of our sinful plight, our recognition of the need for cleansing and renewal, our confession of Jesus Christ as Lord, and our surrender to him and his gospel plan—is personal and private, but the consummation of that covenant is the outward, public ordinances of water baptism and the laying on of hands for the gift of the Holy Ghost. From a Latter-day Saint perspective, to receive forgiveness of sin is to be restored to a justified state. To retain a remission of sins from day to day (Mosiah 4:11–12, 26) is to remain in a justified condition.

Moses 6:60 indicates that it is by the Spirit of God that we are justified and by the atoning blood of Christ that we are sanctified. Then what of the scriptural passages that suggest that we are sanctified by the Spirit (3 Nephi 27:20; D&C 84:33)? In point of fact, we are justified and sanctified by virtue of the atoning blood of our Lord, and this miraculous cleansing takes place through the medium of the Holy Ghost.

SOURCE

Smith, Joseph. *History of The Church of Jesus Christ of Latter-day Saints.* Edited by B. H. Roberts. 7 vols. 2d ed. rev. Salt Lake City: The Church of Jesus Christ of Latter-day Saints, 1932–51.

RLM

KEEPER OF THE GATE

Jesus Christ is the "keeper of the gate" who opens to the presence of God, and "he employeth no servant there" (2 Nephi 9:41). As the Gatekeeper, he ensures that "no man cometh unto the Father, but by me" (John 14:6; D&C 132:12), thereby honoring the Father's assignment that "all judgment" be committed "unto the Son" (John 5:22). Because the gate and the way to the gate are "narrow" (Matthew 7:14; Luke 13:24; 2 Nephi 9:41), only those whom he allows to enter will enter, and "he cannot be deceived" (2 Nephi 9:41).

The Prophet Joseph Smith saw in vision the "transcendent beauty of the gate through which the heirs of [the celestial] kingdom will enter." He reported that the gate "was like unto circling flames of fire," beyond which was the "blazing throne of God" (D&C 137:2–3). As Keeper of the Gate, Jesus is also the "door" to the sheepfold and the "good shepherd" who grants entrance to salvation with the Father (John 10:9, 11). Likening us to sheep, the Savior opens the sheepfold door only to those sheep who hear his voice and follow him. Those who try to enter into the sheepfold another way than by him—forgetting that there is only one narrow way to come into the presence of

God—will fail. Because he gave his life for his sheep and "did no sin," Jesus Christ—the Keeper of the Gate, the Door, the Judge—became our advocate with the Father and pleads, "Father, spare these my brethren that believe on my name, that they may come unto me and have everlasting life" (D&C 45:5).

CFO

KEYS

The word *keys* is used in at least two ways in scripture. First and in a broad sense, keys represent the authority to perform a particular assignment or oversee a specific work. Thus the Prophet Moroni holds the keys of the record of the stick of Joseph, the Book of Mormon (D&C 27:5); that is, he reveals it and provides direction for its care and use. Joseph Smith was given the keys of the gift of translation (D&C 6:28), the keys of the mysteries of the revelations that are sealed (D&C 28:7; 35:18), and the keys of the mysteries of the kingdom (D&C 64:5). Likewise, we are told that the Melchizedek Priesthood holds the keys of the mysteries of the knowledge of God (D&C 84:19; 128:14).

Second, the keys of the priesthood are the right of presidency, the directing power (D&C 107:8). Keys are held by the presidents of the deacons and teachers quorums, the bishop (the president of the priests quorum), the elders quorum president, the stake president, mission presidents, temple presidents, the president of the Quorum of the Twelve Apostles (D&C 112:16; 124:28), the members of the Quorum of the Twelve Apostles (D&C 112:30–32), the First Presidency of the Church (D&C 90:6), and the president of the Church. While such persons as the Sunday School president, the Relief Society president, the Primary president, the Young Women president, and the Young Men president all have the right to inspiration and divine guidance because of the responsibility they bear, they do not hold keys. Similarly, while a man may hold sufficient authority to confer the Melchizedek Priesthood upon a son or to baptize a daughter, such ordinances must be carried out under the direction of the stake president and the bishop, respectively.

RLM

KEYS OF THE KINGDOM

Matthew records that when Jesus called the Twelve Apostles, "he gave them power against unclean spirits, to cast them out, and to heal all manner of sickness and all manner of disease" (Matthew 10:1). Later, Jesus declared unto Peter, the senior apostle: "And I will give unto thee the keys of the kingdom of heaven: and whatsoever thou shalt bind on earth shall be bound in heaven: and whatsoever thou shalt loose on earth shall be loosed in heaven" (Matthew 16:19). These scriptures illustrate the difference between priesthood in general and priesthood keys in particular. Priesthood is God's power and the authority given to man to act in God's name. Priesthood keys, on the other hand, are the directing and governing power, the right of presidency (D&C 107:8) whereby that priesthood may be exercised. God's kingdom on earth is his church—The Church of Jesus Christ of Latter-day Saints. Hence, the "keys of the kingdom" are all the authority, rights, and powers at a given time to administer the Church and to unlock and open the doors (as the word *key* implies) of salvation for the children of God. President Joseph F. Smith clearly taught this principle when he declared: "The Priesthood in general is the authority given to man to act for God. Every man ordained to any degree of the Priesthood has this authority delegated to him. But it is necessary that every act performed under this authority shall be done at the proper time and place, in the proper way, and after the proper order. The power of directing these labors constitutes the keys of the Priesthood" (136).

Modern revelation teaches that "there is never but one on the earth at a time on whom this power and the keys of this priesthood are conferred" (D&C 132:7). The president of the Church holds and exercises all of the keys of the kingdom and has the right to govern and direct all of the Lord's affairs on earth. Counselors in the First Presidency and members of the Quorum of the Twelve Apostles also hold all the keys of the kingdom. For them, however, the keys are exercised only under the authorization and direction of the presiding high priest—the prophet, seer, and revelator (D&C 107:65–66, 91–92; 90:6; 107:24, 33).

The phrase "keys of the kingdom" generally refers to all of the governing and directing authorities and powers possessed by the president of the Church, the First Presidency, and the Twelve. Closely related is the phrase "keys of presidency." Under the direction of those who hold all the keys of the kingdom, a man called to a presiding office in the Church receives keys of presidency. This delegated authority allows him to direct and govern a particular part of the Lord's kingdom within certain parameters established by the president of the Church. Presidents of quorums and presiding officers of established Church units, such as temples, missions, stakes, wards, and branches have conferred upon them keys of presidency—authority to preside over and direct the affairs of a quorum or unit. "Thus, the president of a temple, the president of a stake, the bishop of a ward, the president of a mission, the president of a quorum each holds the keys of the labors performed in that particular body or locality," President Joseph F. Smith declared. "His Priesthood is not increased by this special appointment. . . . The president of an elders quorum, for example has no more Priesthood than any member of that quorum. But he holds the power of directing the official labors performed in that quorum, or in other words, the keys of that division of that work" (136).

SOURCE

Smith, Joseph F. *Gospel Doctrine.* Salt Lake City: Deseret Book, 1939.

BLT

KING FOLLETT SERMON

On 7 April 1844, less than three months before his martyrdom, Joseph Smith the Prophet delivered a funeral address for Brother King Follett, a Nauvoo resident and a member of the Church who had died in an accident while digging a well. The memorial service for Brother Follett was held in conjunction with the general conference of the Church, attended by thousands of Latter-day Saints. In the sermon the Prophet addressed the following doctrines:

1. God is an exalted man and once lived on an earth, just as we do now.

2. It is the responsibility and opportunity of every person to become, through the transforming powers of the Almighty extended to us, like our Heavenly Father.

3. To create is not to make out of nothing but rather to organize or form from existing materials.

4. In the premortal existence our Heavenly Father, the Head of the

gods, called a council of the gods to contemplate and prepare for the creation of the earth.

5. The mind of man is coeternal with God. God is a self-existent being and so is the eternal, uncreated part of man.

6. The greatest responsibility God has placed upon us is to seek after our dead.

7. The unpardonable sin is a grievous offense that will not be forgiven in this world or the next.

8. Little children who die before the age of accountability are saved in the highest heaven. Worthy parents who lose little children will have the privilege of raising these little ones to maturity.

Previous revelations had touched upon the doctrine of deification (item 2 above)—that mortals may, through the atonement of Jesus Christ, become as God is (D&C 76:58; 132:20; *Lectures,* 61)—a doctrine alluded to in the New Testament as well (Matthew 5:48; Romans 8:14–18; 2 Peter 1:4; 1 John 3:1–2). Previous revelations had also touched upon items 4 (Abraham 3:22–4:1), 5 (D&C 93:21–23, 29), 6 (D&C 128:15), 7 (D&C 76:31–37, 44–48; 132:27), and 8 (Mosiah 15:25; D&C 137:10) above. And while Latter-day Saints had been instructed that Adam was created in the image of God's body (Moses 6:9); that God is an exalted man, a Man of Holiness (Moses 6:57); and that our Father in Heaven has a body of flesh and bones as tangible as man's (D&C 130:22; *Words,* 60, 63–64), it seems that the specific information conveyed in item 1—that our Heavenly Father was once a mortal man who lived on an earth—had never been taught publicly prior to this sermon.

The King Follett sermon is, without doubt, the most memorable of all the addresses delivered by the Prophet Joseph Smith. For Latter-day Saints this sermon suggests a relationship with the being of Deity that expands our minds and broadens our perspectives on life here and hereafter. For those of other faiths, particularly traditional Christians, the discourse tends to elicit strong reactions: a theological antagonism, a cry of heresy. In this discourse, the Prophet Joseph dismissed as unsuitable and unacceptable the unknowable, unreachable, and unobtainable god of Plato. This sermon introduces us to a god who is God, who is, as the revelations affirm, "infinite and eternal, from everlasting to everlasting the same unchangeable God" who sits "enthroned, with glory, honor, power, majesty, might, dominion, truth, justice, judgment, mercy, and an infinity of fulness, from everlasting to everlasting" (D&C 20:17; 109:77). On the other hand, this glorious Being also delights to honor his children, is unselfish with his glory and power, and desires for the human family to become as he is.

Because the King Follett sermon is not a part of the canon of scripture and is not found within the standard works, it does not carry the same weight in determining and explaining doctrine as do the teachings in the Bible, the Book of Mormon, the Doctrine and Covenants, and the Pearl of Great Price. Also, because Joseph Smith died a short time after delivering this discourse, we do not have his singular, supplementary, prophetic insights into some of its more difficult doctrinal matters. For example, we have no problem as a people accepting the fact that God is an exalted man. But we do not know doctrinal details beyond what the Prophet taught. In addition, it remains for Joseph's apostolic and prophetic successors to set forth with greater clarity than we now possess how our Father in Heaven can be a man who became exalted (which we accept) *and* eternally God (which we also accept). In addition, we do not know specifically what it means to become as God, beyond gaining exaltation and eternal life, which entails receiving a fulness of the glory and power of the Father as well as enjoying the continuation of the family unit in eternity (D&C 132:19–20).

Because this sermon presents the Prophet Joseph Smith in a less formal mode, at times even playful while he seeks to expose the inconsistencies of false religion; because many of those who attended reported listening to a message that may have taken as long as two hours to give (we can read it in about thirty to forty-five minutes); and because there has been no official proclamation or declaration seeking to expand upon, clarify, or even refine the teachings of the sermon by those holding the keys of power, we read it as a significant historical address, one that in many ways illustrates the spiritual and intellectual heights to which the Saints in Nauvoo, the City of Joseph, aspired. We read it today as a people who are unafraid of engaging serious theological matters, at times being bold enough to think above and beyond where cautious, creedal Christians dare to go. And we read it as a body of believers who believe "all that God has revealed, all that He does now reveal, and we believe that He will yet reveal many great and important things pertaining to the Kingdom of God" (Articles of Faith 1:9).

SOURCES

Lectures on Faith. Salt Lake City: Deseret Book, 1985.

The Words of Joseph Smith. Compiled and edited by Andrew F. Ehat and Lyndon W. Cook. Provo, Utah: Brigham Young University Religious Studies Center, 1980.

RLM

KING JAMES VERSION OF THE BIBLE

The King James Version of the Bible was published in 1611 in England as a result of a convergence of events. The Puritans had crafted and delivered a petition to a newly acclaimed monarch, King James I (James VI of Scotland), when he ascended the English throne in 1603. They requested a new Bible and further reformation of the Church of England (Anglican). The king himself desired a new translation of the Bible, free of controversial annotations that divided the realm. Therefore, he approved its creation in 1604, and thus it also came to be known as the Authorized Version—though there is no official record of the king having formally approved the final product. The King James Version is the culmination of an interesting and inspiring history of English Bible translations.

The first complete Bible translated into English was produced by John Wycliffe (1328–84) and his associates sometime around 1382. It was translated solely from the Latin Vulgate (a fourth-century Latin version of the Bible), which was the work of Saint Jerome (347–420). Jerome undertook the translation of the Vulgate from Hebrew and Greek manuscripts—the original languages of the two testaments— because of errors in the existing Latin Bible of his day. In a letter to Pope Damasus in 383 seeking permission for the project, he outlined the problem with just the New Testament, let alone the Old Testament: "For if we are to pin our faith to the Latin texts, it is for our opponents to tell us which; for there are almost as many forms of texts as there are copies. If, on the other hand, we are to glean the truth from a comparison of many, why not go back to the original Greek and correct the mistakes introduced by inaccurate translators, and the blundering alterations of confident but ignorant critics, and further all that has been inserted or changed by copyists more asleep than awake?" (Stevenson, 183).

For almost a thousand years, the Vulgate was the *only* Bible available to most everyone in Christendom (with the exception of a few scholars who could read Hebrew or Greek manuscripts). But it was available only through the mediation of priests. That is, it was to be read and interpreted by Roman Catholic Church officials only. Wycliffe did more than just provide a new Bible in English. He also called attention to errant Church practices and doctrines. According to Wycliffe, scripture was to be the sole authority in Christian teaching. If an idea was not in the Bible, it should be rejected. The Church could not tolerate this kind of threat to its authority. Thus began an era of persecution and martyrdom. Anyone caught translating, possessing, or even reading the Bible in the vernacular, particularly English, was excommunicated or burned by decree of both church and state. Many gave the ultimate sacrifice to bring the word of God to the common people.

A little more than a century after Wycliffe died, William Tyndale (1492–1536) was born. He is recognized as the father of the English Bible. By the time he turned his considerable intellectual prowess to a new version of the Bible in English, Johann Gutenberg had invented printing with movable type and had produced his now-famous forty-two-line Vulgate Bible. In an April 1939 general conference address, Elder John A. Widtsoe stated that modern civilization really began with Gutenberg's invention of the movable-type printing press. In fact, "Latter-day Saints see even more in the coming of this great invention. To us it is part of the divine program to prepare the world for the restoration of the Gospel. . . . The new art of printing soon made the Bible available to all. . . . Had it not been for the invention of printing with its gift of more perfect knowledge of the holy scriptures . . . the coming of the Gospel might have long been delayed" (20).

Tyndale, an Oxford scholar, master of eight languages, and man of integrity, translated the New Testament from Greek and published it in Germany in 1526 because he was so actively persecuted by church and government leaders in England. It became an instant bestseller, with eighteen thousand copies sold in two years, even though they had to be smuggled into England. Tyndale then worked on the Old Testament, translating it from Hebrew. But before he could finish, he was arrested and imprisoned. After being condemned to die, he was tied to a stake, strangled to death, and then burned near Brussels. His contributions to subsequent English versions of the Bible were enormous, especially the future King James Version. About 84 percent of the King James New Testament is from Tyndale's earlier translation. About 76 percent of the Old Testament is Tyndale's language.

Tyndale's influence on the English language itself is hard to overstate. He coined or invented dozens of words and phrases to make his biblical translation more rich and understandable. These expressions include the following: Alpha and Omega; apple of his eye; beautiful; brother's keeper; busybody; cast the first stone; coat of many colors; eat, drink, and be merry; infidel; Jehovah; judge not; no man can serve two masters; Passover; stiff-necked; suffer fools gladly; two-edged sword; undergird; ungodly; and uproar. The very word *atonement* (at-one-ment) was created by Tyndale to signify the reconciliation that may occur between God and man through Christ's redemptive suffering. Those of us who share the English language speak much of what we speak because of William Tyndale. Many of these idioms are especially recognizable to Latter-day Saints because they are also found in Restoration scripture. We are the spiritual heirs of Tyndale. President Thomas S. Monson described Tyndale and other reforming pioneers as "honest men with yearning hearts, [who] at the peril of their very lives, attempted to establish points of reference, that they might find the true way. . . . The reformers were pioneers, blazing wilderness trails in a desperate search for those lost points of reference which, they felt, when found would lead mankind back to the truth Jesus taught. . . . Significant was the declaration of Tyndale to his critics: 'I will cause a boy that driveth the plough shall know more of the scripture than thou doest'" (51).

Tyndale left his unpublished Old Testament translation and notes to his friend John Rogers for safekeeping. Rogers finished the work and had the complete Bible published under the pseudonym of Thomas Matthew in 1537, just one year after Tyndale's death. At the insistence of English archbishop Thomas Cranmer, the "Matthews Bible" was officially recognized. But after Catholic Mary I, or "Bloody Mary" (reigned 1553–58), became queen, Rogers too was burned at the stake.

By the time King James succeeded Queen Elizabeth (1603), who had succeeded Queen Mary, several more versions of the Bible in English had appeared: the Coverdale Bible of 1535 (named after its editor), the Great Bible of 1539 (named for its size), the Geneva Bible of 1560 (named for its place of printing), the Bishop's Bible of 1568 (authorized by the clergy of the Church of England), and the Roman Catholic Douay-Rheims Bible of 1582 (named for its place of translation). But each of these Bibles favored a different viewpoint and was therefore not satisfactory to all.

The Geneva Bible was immensely popular; it seems to be the version Shakespeare used, and it was the version that came to America on the *Mayflower*. It was also the first version to use italics for words not found in the original manuscripts. But it was extremely perturbing to the clergy of the Church of England. It contained notes, annotations, and a kind of running commentary that was intensely antagonistic to the pope, Roman Catholic hierarchy, the Church of England, and the universities. Scholars called it "too protestant" even though the Puritans did want to "purify" the Church of England of all vestiges of Roman Catholicism (Miller, 178). The Anglican clergy answered the Geneva Bible by producing another Bible—the Bishops' Bible. But the latter was rejected by the Puritans, who said it was not accurate. When King James of Scotland went to London to become King of England as well, he was presented with the Millenary Petition (so called because it contained one thousand Puritan signatures).

In 1604 James agreed to hold a conference to review the state of the church in England and the Puritan requests. The king approved only one request—but it was monumental—a new Bible. That same year, the king announced that he had appointed a group of fifty-four scholars and churchmen, Anglicans and Puritans, to work on the new translation. They were divided into six companies and worked diligently on different biblical books for about three years to complete their initial drafts. The King James Version came off the press in London in 1611. The translators dedicated their work to the man who ordered the project, "the most high and mighty prince, James, by the grace of God, King of Great Britain, France, and Ireland, Defender of the Faith, etc" (preface, King James Bible).

The King James Version is an inspiring achievement. "Modern-day translators may rightly feel humble, knowing they can never produce a work that will so mold a language and shape an entire culture" (*Christian*, 44). Indeed, modern language and theology are filled with such immortal expressions as the following:

"The skin of my teeth" (Job 19:20)
"Woe is me" (Psalm 120:5)
"A drop of a bucket" (Isaiah 40:15)
"My brother's keeper" (Genesis 4:9)
"Holier than thou" (Isaiah 65:5)
"At their wits' end" (Psalm 107:27)
"The hair of my flesh stood up" (Job 4:15)
"Apple of the eye" (Psalm 17:8)
"Lily of the valleys" (Song of Solomon 2:1)
"Set thine house in order" (Isaiah 38:1)
"Can . . . the leopard [change] his spots?" (Jeremiah 13:23)
"Hollow of his hand" (Isaiah 40:12)

More than that, the restoration of the gospel is intimately tied to the King James Version. In a letter dated 22 May 1992 and addressed to all priesthood leaders in English-speaking units of the Church, the First Presidency—Ezra Taft Benson, Gordon B. Hinckley, and Thomas S. Monson—wrote the following:

"Many versions of the Bible are available today. Unfortunately, no original manuscripts of any portion of the Bible are available for comparison to determine the most accurate version. However, the Lord has revealed clearly the doctrines of the gospel in these latter-days. The most reliable way to measure the accuracy of any biblical passage is not by comparing texts, but by comparison with the Book of Mormon and modern-day revelations.

"While other Bible versions may be easier to read than the King James Version, in doctrinal matters latter-day revelation supports the King James Version in preference to other English translations. All of the Presidents of the Church, beginning with the Prophet Joseph Smith, have supported the King James Version by encouraging its continued use in the Church. In light of all the above, it is the English language Bible used by The Church of Jesus Christ of Latter-day Saints" (80).

SOURCES

Christian History: The 100 Most Important Events in Church History 28 (1 Oct. 1990): 43–44.

First Presidency. "First Presidency Statement on the King James Version of the Bible." *Ensign,* Aug. 1992, 80.

Miller, Stephen M., and Robert V. Huber. *The Bible: A History.* Intercourse, Pa.: Good Books, 2004.

Monson, Thomas S. "They Showed the Way." *Ensign,* May 1997, 50–52.

Stevenson, J., ed. *Creeds, Councils, and Controversies: Documents Illustrating the History of the Church* A.D. *337–461.* Nashville, Tenn.: Abingdon Press, 1990.

Widtsoe, John A. In Conference Report, Apr. 1939, 19–24.

ACS

KING OF THE JEWS

By virtue of his exalted station as the great Jehovah come to earth and his lineage as the son of Mary and stepson of Joseph, Jesus of Nazareth was the true and legitimate King of the Jews. Many Old Testament declarations testify that Jehovah was and is the great eternal King (Psalm 4:2; 10:16; 24:7–10; 44:4; 47:6–7; 89:18; Isaiah 6:5; 43:15; Jeremiah 46:18). Jesus Christ is Jehovah (3 Nephi 15:5). One of the early messianic prophecies declared that the scepter (symbol of kingship) would not depart from Judah, nor a lawgiver from among Judah's posterity "until Shiloh come" (Genesis 49:10). Shiloh is Christ (JST, Genesis 50:24). Furthermore, Jeremiah prophesied that "the days come, saith the Lord, that I will raise unto David a righteous Branch, and a King shall reign and prosper, and shall execute judgment and justice in the earth" (Jeremiah 23:5).

Jesus was born into that prophesied Davidic family through whom the line of Judah's legitimate kings was to come. Both Mary and Joseph were literal descendants of King David, through whose royal lineage kingship came (Talmage, 86, 89). "At the time of the Savior's birth, Israel was ruled by alien monarchs. The rights of the royal Davidic family were unrecognized; and the ruler of the Jews was an appointee of Rome. Had Judah been a free and independent nation, ruled by her rightful sovereign, Joseph the carpenter would have been the crowned king; and his lawful successor to the throne would have been Jesus of Nazareth, the King of the Jews" (Talmage, 87).

The gospel of Matthew affirms that Jesus was of the lineage of David (Matthew 1:1, 16–17). During Jesus' triumphal entry into

Jerusalem, the gathered multitude hailed him openly as the King of Israel (Matthew 21:1–11; Luke 19:29–38; John 12:12–16) in partial fulfillment of Jeremiah's prophecy (Jeremiah 23:5–6). When Jesus was arraigned before Pontius Pilate, the Roman governor asked him, "Art thou the King of the Jews?" Jesus responded affirmatively with the clarification, "To this end was I born" (John 18:33, 37). Finally, the placard on the cross placed above Jesus' head displayed the words "Jesus of Nazareth the King of the Jews." When requested by the chief priests to change the title to indicate that Jesus had *said* he was King of the Jews, Pilate responded, "What I have written I have written" (John 19:19, 22).

Modern revelation is clear that at the Second Coming, the Jews will look on the wounds in Jesus' hands and feet and ask about them. After he identifies himself, "then shall they lament because they persecuted their king" (D&C 45:51–53). Both prophecy and history declare Jesus of Nazareth to be the King of the Jews.

SOURCE

Talmage, James E. *Jesus the Christ.* Salt Lake City: Deseret Book, 1973.

ACS

KNOWLEDGE

God knows all things "and there is not anything save he knows it" (2 Nephi 9:20; see also D&C 38:2). Vital to our faith in God and his plan of salvation is that we know that he knows all things. "Without the knowledge of all things God would not be able to save any portion of his creatures; for it is by reason of the knowledge which he has of all things, from the beginning to the end, that enables him to give that understanding to his creatures by which they are made partakers of eternal life; and if it were not for the idea existing in the minds of men that God had all knowledge it would be impossible for them to exercise faith in him" (*Lectures,* 51–52).

Knowledge is a requirement for salvation: "It is impossible for a man to be saved in ignorance" (D&C 131:6). In his great Intercessory Prayer, the Savior revealed that to know God is to receive eternal life (John 17:3). In his commentary on the Savior's teachings, the apostle John explained that we can know God "if we keep his commandments" (1 John 2:3). Therefore, to love God, knowing that he first loved us, is at the foundation of knowledge (1 John 4; 1 Nephi 11:17). Additionally, coming "to the knowledge of the true Messiah, their Lord and their Redeemer" is the focus of the Book of Mormon definition of the gathering of Israel and a major purpose for God's work among his children (1 Nephi 10:14; 2 Nephi 6:11; Helaman 15:13).

At the beginning of man's sojourn on earth, God manifested the importance of gaining knowledge and teaching truths to the next generation. He also provided means by which we can receive this essential comprehension. First, he ensured that we were created with a basic understanding and capacity to learn: "I gave unto them their knowledge, in the day I created them" (Moses 7:32). Joseph Smith taught that the "relationship we have with God places us in a situation to advance in knowledge" (6:312). After Adam and Eve had left the Garden of Eden, God "saw that it was expedient that man should know concerning the things whereof he had appointed unto them." He therefore sent angels to teach Adam and Eve his plan of redemption and subsequently his commandments (Alma 12:28–32). Furthermore, God "has power to institute laws to instruct the weaker intelligences, that they may be exalted with himself" (Smith, 6:312). Without laws, there could be no punishment, no recognition of sin, and no realization of the need for a Redeemer (2 Nephi 2; Romans 3:20). God also gave his children the power of the Holy Ghost by which they "may know the truth of all things" (Moroni 10:5; D&C 35:19). The Spirit is the great teacher of both spiritual and temporal knowledge (Alma 18:35; D&C 107:71). In his mercy, God remembers those who do not receive an opportunity for learning in mortality. If a person does not gain knowledge of God in this life, that individual will have the opportunity to be taught in the spirit world (D&C 138:7, 32).

The Lord has directed us through the exercise of our agency and God-given abilities to add to this foundation of understanding throughout our mortal lives. Joseph Smith taught that "God has created man with a mind capable of instruction, and a faculty which may be enlarged in proportion to the heed and diligence given to the light communicated from heaven to the intellect; and that the nearer man approaches perfection, the clearer are his views, and the greater his enjoyments, till he has overcome the evils of his life and lost every desire for sin" (2:8). Jesus taught that by doing God's will—obeying his commandments—we can know the doctrine of Christ and that it comes from God (John 7:17). We are also promised that if we ask God in sincere prayer, he will grant us "knowledge upon knowledge," that we may know "the mysteries and peaceable things" (D&C 42:61). Gaining knowledge is a process; we learn line upon line, precept upon precept, not all at once (2 Nephi 28:30). Any knowledge and intelligence we gain in this life through our diligence and obedience to God will grant us greater advantage in the world to come (D&C 130:19).

As with any gift from God, warnings accompany the divine receipt of knowledge to remind us how we received our enlightened understanding. Vanity, failure to hearken to God's counsel, and foolishness result when we think we are wise because of our own accomplishments (2 Nephi 9:28–29). To continue to be taught God's wisdom and knowledge, we need to be humble and "consider [ourselves] fools before God." He will not open his treasures of knowledge to those "who are puffed up because of their learning, and their wisdom, and their riches" (2 Nephi 9:42).

SOURCES

Lectures on Faith. Salt Lake City: Deseret Book, 1985.

Smith, Joseph. *History of The Church of Jesus Christ of Latter-day Saints.* Edited by B. H. Roberts. 7 vols. 2d ed. rev. Salt Lake City: The Church of Jesus Christ of Latter-day Saints, 1932–51.

CFO

LAMB OF GOD

In the meridian dispensation of the gospel, John the Baptist was the first to refer to Jesus of Nazareth as "the Lamb of God, which taketh away the sin of the world" (John 1:29). Because John the Baptist trained and prepared several members of the original Quorum of the Twelve, including John the Beloved, who reported on the Baptist's work in his Gospel (John 1), it is not surprising that this same John the Beloved includes several references to Jesus' role as the Lamb in his other writings. John likens Jesus to "a Lamb as it had been slain" (Revelation 5:6)—an obvious reference to the central role that lambs played in Israel's sacrificial system, carried out first in the wilderness tabernacle and then in the Jerusalem temple to represent Christ's atonement for the sins of the covenant people. But the sacrificial system was only a type, shadow, and symbol of the actual atonement and redemption enacted through the great and last sacrifice of Jesus himself (Hebrews 9–10).

John the Revelator beheld in vision and heard the voices of one hundred million heavenly beings singing a new song, "saying with a loud voice, Worthy is the Lamb that was slain to receive power, and riches, and wisdom, and strength, and honour, and glory, and blessing. And every creature which is in heaven, and on the earth, and under the earth, and such as are in the sea, and all that are in them, heard I saying, Blessing, and honour, and glory, and power, be unto him that sitteth upon the throne, and unto the Lamb for ever and ever" (Revelation 5:11–13). Furthermore, John saw that those who are exalted "are they which came out of great tribulation, and have washed their robes, and made them white in the blood of the Lamb" (Revelation 7:14). Not coincidentally, the Savior himself said much the same thing to the Nephites in the New World after his resurrection. Only "those who have washed their garments in my blood," he said, can enter into God's rest, which rest is the fulness of his glory (3 Nephi 27:19; D&C 84:24).

John the Revelator also testified that the Saints overcome Satan by the power and blood of the Lamb (Revelation 12:11), which was already in operation in our premortal existence. In other words, the Atonement already operated in our behalf before Jesus physically enacted the Atonement in mortality. That is why John refers to Jesus Christ as "the Lamb slain from the foundation of the world" (Revelation 13:8), which is also the testimony of Enoch (Moses 7:47). If this were not so, Adam's transgression could not have already been forgiven him during the beginning phases of mortality. But it was (Moses 6:53–54)!

John saw numerous other scenes involving the Lamb of God: standing on Mount Zion, warring with the wicked and overcoming them, sharing his marriage supper with the righteous, and ultimately being enthroned as the Eternal King (Revelation 14:1; 17:14; 19:7, 9; 21:23; 22:3). There was no more important metaphor for John the Revelator than Christ as the Lamb of God.

Perhaps the greatest Old Testament prophecy of the Atonement invokes the imagery of a lamb being brought to the slaughter (Isaiah 53:7). Book of Mormon prophets also described the coming Messiah as "the Lamb of God" long before he came into mortality. Six hundred years before Christ, Nephi beheld in vision the blood of the Lamb of God purging sin and worldliness from the righteous, including the Twelve (1 Nephi 12:10–11). The imagery of the blood of the Lamb as the agent of cleansing was repeated by Alma and Ether (Alma 13:11; Ether 13:11).

An angel in the Doctrine and Covenants exults in the triumph of the Lamb of God over the demands of justice: "The Lamb of God hath overcome and trodden the wine-press alone, even the wine-press of the fierceness of the wrath of Almighty God" (D&C 88:106). Through the great power of the Lamb of God, "the graves of the saints shall be opened; and they shall come forth and stand on the right hand of the Lamb, when he shall stand upon Mount Zion, and upon the holy city, the New Jerusalem; and they shall sing the song of the Lamb, day and night forever and ever" (D&C 133:56). This is the sure destiny of all true followers of the Lamb of God.

ACS

LAW

All things are governed by law. The power of God—the Light of Christ—is the "law by which all things are governed" (D&C 88:13). "Unto every kingdom is given a law; and unto every law there are certain bounds also and conditions" (D&C 88:38). The Book of Mormon prophet Lehi likewise taught that without law there is no accountability or sin, no righteousness, no happiness, no misery. "And if these things are not there is no God," he declared. "And if there is no God we are not, neither the earth; for there could have been no creation of things, neither to act nor to be acted upon; wherefore, all things must have vanished away" (2 Nephi 2:13). Generally speaking, there are laws of God and laws of man. The laws of God are divine and eternal—fixed and unalterable. We usually think of the laws of God as being those commandments, ordinances, and principles that are given to guide and govern his children in their eternal progression. There are, however, other laws of God that likewise give order to and govern the universe. Those would include what we call laws of nature. Latter-day Saints believe that God created "worlds without number" (Moses 1:33) and governs them by eternal laws. He applies and organizes laws for the benefit of his children. The Prophet Joseph Smith taught that God "was the first Author of law, or the principle of it, to mankind" (2:13). The resurrected Christ referred to himself as "the law" (3 Nephi 15:9) and the "lawgiver" (Isaiah 33:22; D&C 38:22; see also 3 Nephi 15:5). God is the personification of divine law. There are consequences as eternal as law itself attached to obedience or disobedience of divine law (D&C 130:20–21; 132:5–12). People may choose to disregard God's laws, but they cannot choose or change the attendant consequences for such action or inaction. Laws and consequences, like agency and accountability, are inextricably linked. "I, the Lord, am bound when ye do what I say; but when ye do not what I say, ye have no promise" (D&C 82:10). That is God's divine law at work.

The laws of man are temporal and temporary—changing and adapted to the circumstances of our mortal existence. Latter-day Saints believe that "governments were instituted of God for the benefit of man; and that he holds men accountable for their acts in relation to them, both in making laws and administering them, for the good and safety of society" (D&C 134:1). Just as God will hold governments and leaders accountable for the laws they enact, he will hold us accountable for our actions in relationship to such laws—"obeying, honoring, and sustaining the law" (Articles of Faith 1:12). The Lord declared in this dispensation: "Let no man break the laws of the land, for he that keepeth the laws of God hath no need to break the laws of the land. Wherefore, be subject to the powers that be, until he reigns whose right it is to reign and subdues all enemies under his feet" (D&C 58:21–22).

SOURCE

Smith, Joseph. *History of The Church of Jesus Christ of Latter-day Saints*. Edited by B. H. Roberts. 7 vols. 2d ed. rev. Salt Lake City: The Church of Jesus Christ of Latter-day Saints, 1932–51.

BLT

LAW OF MOSES

The law of Moses was a comprehensive religious and legal system revealed to the prophet-lawgiver-deliverer Moses on Mount Sinai. It replaced, for a time, the higher law and fulness of the gospel that had operated from Adam to Moses and that the Lord had intended to reconfirm to Israel after their Egyptian sojourn had ended. But because Israel continued rebelling against sacred things, including the requirements of the higher law, the law of Moses, or lesser law, was "added because of transgression," as Paul taught (Galatians 3:19; see also JST, Exodus 34:1–2; JST, Deuteronomy 10:1–2).

Israel's rebellion and the origins of the law of Moses are well documented in modern revelation. In a powerful section of the Doctrine and Covenants on priesthood authority, the Lord emphasized Israel's tremendous loss:

"And this greater priesthood administereth the gospel and holdeth the key of the mysteries of the kingdom, even the key of the knowledge of God. Therefore, in the ordinances thereof, the power of godliness is manifest. And without the ordinances thereof, and the authority of the priesthood, the power of godliness is not manifest unto men in the flesh; for without this [the power of godliness] no man can see the face of God, even the Father, and live.

"Now this Moses plainly taught to the children of Israel in the wilderness, and sought diligently to sanctify his people that they might behold the face of God; but they hardened their hearts and could not endure his presence; therefore, the Lord in his wrath, for his anger was kindled against them, swore that they should not enter into his rest while in the wilderness, which rest is the fulness of his glory. Therefore, he took Moses out of their midst, and the Holy Priesthood also; and the lesser priesthood continued, which priesthood holdeth the key of the ministering of angels and the preparatory gospel; which gospel is the gospel of repentance and of baptism, and the remission of sins, and the law of carnal commandments, which the Lord in his wrath caused to continue with the house of Aaron among the children of Israel until John, whom God raised up, being filled with the Holy Ghost from his mother's womb" (D&C 84:19–27).

Thus, the law of Moses was administered by a lesser priesthood (the Aaronic order) and continued for several centuries until the first coming of Jesus Christ. It was not the fulness of the gospel but rather a preparatory gospel, a lesser law, a "schoolmaster" to point Israel to Christ (Galatians 3:24). It was a law of carnal commandments, suited to a spiritually immature people who required a step-by-step regimen. It consisted of "divers washings, and carnal ordinances, imposed on them until the time of reformation" (Hebrews 9:10). The time of reformation (Christ's advent) was also a time of restoration (JST, John 1:28), bringing back the fulness of the gospel, the Melchizedek Priesthood, and the higher law, which Jesus clearly contrasted with the lesser in his Sermon on the Mount (Matthew 5:21–48).

The Book of Mormon prophet Abinadi described the law of Moses and its intent as "a very strict law; for they [the children of Israel] were a stiffnecked people, quick to do iniquity, and slow to remember the Lord their God; therefore there was a law given them, yea, a law of performances and of ordinances, a law which they were to observe strictly from day to day, to keep them in remembrance of God and their duty towards him. But behold, I say unto you, that all these things were types of things to come. And now, did they understand the law? I say unto you, Nay, they did not all understand the law; and this because of the hardness of their hearts; for they understood not that there could not any man be saved except it were through the redemption of God" (Mosiah 13:29–32).

Abinadi taught that salvation is in Christ, not in the law of Moses: "And were it not for the atonement, which God himself shall make for the sins and iniquities of his people, . . . they must unavoidably perish, notwithstanding the law of Moses" (Mosiah 13:28). The Savior himself as well as his apostles, especially Paul, emphasized that humankind is justified, or put back into a right relationship with God, only through the atonement of Jesus Christ (John 5:39; Galatians 2:16; JST, Romans 3:24). The Savior's parables of the new patch on an old garment and new wine in old bottles teach that the gospel is not simply a bolstering of the law of Moses nor a refurbishing of Jewish tradition. Rather, the gospel of Jesus Christ is the foundation of salvation, and the law of Moses was fulfilled. King Benjamin boldly proclaimed that "the Lord God saw that his people were a stiffnecked people, and he appointed unto them a law, even the law of Moses. And many signs, and wonders, and types, and shadows showed he unto them, concerning his coming; and also holy prophets spake unto them concerning his coming; and yet they hardened their hearts, and understood not that the law of Moses availeth nothing except it were through the atonement of his blood" (Mosiah 3:14–15).

Besides prescribing moral, ethical, and physical behavior, the law of Moses contained an elaborate system of sacrifices that included animals, grains, and other commodities (Leviticus 1–7). These were to remind the Israelites of their duties to God and to point them to the great and last sacrifice of Jesus Christ, which ended sacrifice by the shedding of blood (Alma 34:13–14). Therefore, Abinadi prophesied that the time would come when it would "no more be expedient to keep the law of Moses" (Mosiah 13:27). When the resurrected Jesus appeared to the Nephites, he declared that the law of Moses was fulfilled:

"Behold, I say unto you that the law is fulfilled that was given unto Moses. Behold, I am he that gave the law, and I am he who covenanted with my people Israel; therefore, the law in me is fulfilled, for I have come to fulfil the law; therefore it hath an end. . . . For behold, the covenant which I have made with my people is not all fulfilled; but the law which was given unto Moses hath an end in me. Behold, I am the law, and the light. Look unto me, and endure to the end, and ye shall live; for unto him that endureth to the end will I give eternal life" (3 Nephi 15:4–5, 8–9).

Instead of animal sacrifice, from then on the Lord required the sacrifices of a broken heart and a contrite spirit. He declared: "I am the light and the life of the world. I am Alpha and Omega, the beginning and the end. And ye shall offer up unto me no more the shedding of blood; yea, your sacrifices and your burnt offerings shall be done away, for I will accept none of your sacrifices and your burnt offerings. And ye shall offer for a sacrifice unto me a broken heart and a contrite spirit. And whoso cometh unto me with a broken heart and a contrite spirit, him will I baptize with fire and with the Holy Ghost, even as the Lamanites, because of their faith in me at the time of their conversion, were baptized with fire and with the Holy Ghost, and they knew it not" (3 Nephi 9:18–20).

In truth, even before the Savior came and declared the law to be fulfilled, it had become dead to the Nephites because they had the gospel, operated under the Melchizedek (or higher) Priesthood, and looked to the Atonement as the means of their salvation. As they said: "For we labor diligently to write, to persuade our children, and also our brethren, to believe in Christ, and to be reconciled to God; for we know that it is by grace that we are saved, after all we can do. And, notwithstanding we believe in Christ, we keep the law of Moses, and look forward with steadfastness unto Christ, until the law shall be fulfilled. For, for this end was the law given; wherefore the law hath become dead unto us, and we are made alive in Christ because of our faith; yet we keep the law because of the commandment" (2 Nephi 25:23–25).

Perhaps this is why it appears to have been so much easier for the New World Israelites to shed the law of Moses once it was fulfilled than it was for those in the Old World. The single biggest controversy in the early apostolic Church centered on nominally Jewish Christians (Judaizers) who insisted that Gentile converts had to subscribe to certain provisions of the law of Moses before they could be considered full-fledged members of the Church of Jesus Christ. A general conference of the Church was held in Jerusalem, but the issue was not resolved for years (Acts 15; Galatians 2–3).

Faith, repentance, baptism by immersion, and remission of sins were part of the law of Moses. It is sometimes thought, erroneously, that the Ten Commandments are the basic equivalent of the law of Moses. The law of Moses emphasized the Ten Commandments (Exodus 20), but they are fundamental laws of the plan of salvation, are part of the gospel covenant revealed in the latter days, and have been repeated in various dispensations (JST, Exodus 34:1–2; Mosiah 12:32–37; 13:12–24; Matthew 19:17–19; D&C 42:18–28; 59:5–13).

Many Jewish authorities today maintain that alongside the written law of Moses, explicated in Exodus, Leviticus, Numbers, and Deuteronomy, an oral Torah, or oral law, was revealed to Moses on Mount Sinai. This oral law formed the "traditions of the elders" in Jesus' day (Matthew 15:2; Mark 7:3, 5). The oral tradition is believed to have been written down around A.D. 200 and is the law found in the Mishnah. The oral tradition has been viewed as constituting a kind of continuous revelatory element in Judaism, transforming the written Torah into a legal system "keeping pace with ages" (*Interpreter's*, 4:512).

SOURCE

The Interpreter's Dictionary of the Bible: An Illustrated Encyclopedia. Edited by George
   Arthur Buttrick. 5 vols. Nashville, Tenn.: Abingdon Press, 1962.

ACS

LECTURES ON FAITH

In the winter of 1834–35, the Prophet Joseph Smith and some of
his associates prepared and delivered a series of lectures to the men who
constituted the School of the Elders. These came to be known as the
Lectures on Faith. This collection is a systematic study of faith—what
it is, the objects on which it rests, and the fruits that flow from it.
These seven lectures contain some of the most profound and mind-
expanding teachings in our literature. They are worthy of serious and
sober reflection on the part of Latter-day Saints who desire to grow in
faith and come unto Christ. The Lectures on Faith were included in
the first edition (1835) of the Doctrine and Covenants. That edition
was made up of two parts. Part 1 was called "Doctrine" and consisted
of the Lectures on Faith; Part 2 was called "Covenants" and included
many of the revelations received to that point. The Lectures on Faith
remained in subsequent editions of the Doctrine and Covenants until
1921.

Lecture One is a discussion of the nature of faith. Faith is described as "the first principle in revealed religion, and the foundation
of all righteousness" (1). The lecture shows from scripture that faith is
not only the underlying principle behind all action but is also a "principle of power." As taught in Hebrews 11:3, "the principle of power
which existed in the bosom of God, by which the worlds were framed,
was faith; and . . . it is by reason of this principle of power existing in
the Deity, that all created things exist; so that all things in heaven,
on earth, or under the earth, exist by reason of faith as it existed in
Him. . . . It is the principle by which Jehovah works, and through
which he exercises power over all temporal as well as eternal things"
(3). This equation (faith as a principle of power) is an important one.
Faith thereby becomes more than an inert wish or even a strong long-
ing or yearning for some eventuality to occur. It helps us to understand
the Savior's statement: "If ye have faith, and doubt not, ye shall not
only do this which is done to the fig tree [cause it to wither], but also

if ye shall say unto this mountain, Be thou removed, and be thou cast into the sea; it shall be done. And all things, whatsoever ye shall ask in prayer, believing, ye shall receive" (Matthew 21:21–22).

Lecture Two is a statement of how faith comes—namely, by the power of human testimony. The lecture teaches that after Adam and Eve were cast from the Garden of Eden, they did not lose the knowledge they had gained in Eden. Although the knowledge of their premortal existence was veiled from their memory, Adam's "transgression did not deprive him of the previous knowledge with which he was endowed relative to the existence and glory of his Creator" (14). That is, Adam and Eve "retained a knowledge of [God's] existence, and that sufficiently to move them to call upon him" (15). Further, after their expulsion from Eden, God continued to reveal himself to our first parents. They in turn taught their children about the Almighty and the plan of salvation. "And the evidences which these men had of the existence of a God, was the testimony of their fathers in the first instance" (17). This knowledge was then transmitted from generation to generation "as a matter of tradition at least; for we cannot suppose that a knowledge of this important fact could have existed in the mind of any of the before-mentioned individuals, without their having made it known to their posterity" (23). And so "it was human testimony, and human testimony only, that excited this inquiry, in the first instance, in their minds. It was the credence they gave to the testimony of their fathers" that resulted "in the most glorious discoveries and eternal certainty" (24).

In Lecture Three, three prerequisites for the exercise of faith in God unto life and salvation are set forth:

1. The idea that God actually exists;

2. A correct idea of his character, attributes, and perfections;

3. An actual knowledge that the course in life one is pursuing is according to the will of God (38).

Lectures Three and Four deal with the character and attributes of God, establishing that God possesses all virtues, traits, and ennobling qualities in their perfection. That is what it means to be God. Thus, God is all-wise, all-caring, all-truthful, all-benevolent, all-patient, and forevermore consistent, constant, and dependable. Further, man must know that God embodies all of these attributes and qualities in order to exercise faith in him. How, for example, can one call upon the Almighty with confidence if there were any question about God's judgment, his sense of justice, or his approachability? How could one dare to call upon God for forgiveness if there were any doubt about God's willingness to forgive? "Such is the weakness of man, and such his frailties, that he is liable to sin continually, and if God were not long-suffering, and full of compassion, gracious and merciful, and of a forgiving disposition, man would be cut off from before him, in consequence of which he would be in continual doubt and could not exercise faith; for where doubt is, there faith has no power" (46).

In the same vein, consider the plight of man if he had any question as to God having all power or knowing all things. "Without the knowledge of all things God would not be able to save any portion of his creatures; for it is by reason of the knowledge which he has of all things, from the beginning to the end, that enables him to give that understanding to his creatures by which they are made partakers of eternal life; and if it were not for the idea existing in the minds of men that God had all knowledge it would be impossible for them to exercise faith in him" (51–52). Anyone, therefore, who doubts God's power, knowledge, or ability will never acquire the kind and quality of faith that leads unto life and salvation. Truly, "God is the only supreme governor and independent being in whom all fulness and perfection dwell; who is omnipotent, omnipresent and omniscient; without beginning of days or end of life; and . . . in him every good gift and every good principle dwell; and . . . he is the Father of lights" (10).

Lecture Five continues a discussion on the nature of God and focuses primarily on the perfections of Deity and the relationship of the Father and the Son. This lecture is particularly deep and penetrating and requires prayerful and serious reflection to grasp its message. Elder Bruce R. McConkie wrote of Lecture Five:

"Using the holy scriptures as the recorded source of the knowledge of God, knowing what the Lord has revealed to them of old in visions and by the power of the Spirit, and writing as guided by that same Spirit, Joseph Smith and the early brethren of this dispensation prepared a creedal statement on the Godhead. It is without question the most excellent summary of revealed and eternal truth relative to the Godhead that is now extant in mortal language. In it is set forth the mystery of Godliness; that is, it sets forth the personalities, missions, and ministries of those holy beings who comprise the supreme presidency of the universe. To spiritually illiterate persons, it may seem hard and confusing; to those whose souls are aflame with heavenly light, it is a nearly perfect summary of those things which must be believed to gain salvation" (*New*, 72). On an earlier occasion, Elder McConkie stated: "In my judgment, it is the most comprehensive, intelligent, inspired utterance that now exists . . . in one place defining, interpreting, expounding, announcing, and testifying what kind of being God is. It was written by the power of the Holy Ghost, by the spirit of inspiration. It is, in effect, eternal scripture; it is true" ("Lord").

As Latter-day Saints we go to great lengths to establish that the Father and the Son are separate and distinct personages, that they are not somehow intertwined or fused magically, that they are not merely two manifestations of the same person. And yet, our Heavenly Father and his Beloved Son are infinitely more unified than they are separate. They happen to be separate in person and being, but they are one in glory, one in purpose, one in focus and mission, and one in the sense that they both possess all of the attributes of godliness in perfection; they are one *in mind* and that oneness of mind is assured and maintained through the indwelling presence of the Holy Spirit. The Father and the Son possess "the same mind, the same wisdom, glory, power, and fulness—filling all in all; the Son being filled with the fullness of the mind, glory, and power; or, in other words, the spirit, glory, and power, of the Father." This lecture goes on to state how mortal man—frail and weak and in constant need of divine intervention—may grow and develop into a similar spiritual union with God. The Holy Spirit that conveys the mind of God "is shed forth upon all who believe on his name and keep his commandments; and all those who keep his commandments shall grow up from grace to grace, and become heirs of the heavenly kingdom, and joint heirs with Jesus Christ; possessing the same mind, being transformed into the same image or likeness, even the express image of him who fills all in all; being filled with the fullness of his glory, and become one in him, even as the Father, Son and Holy Spirit are one" (60).

Lecture Six discusses the third criterion for faith—a knowledge that the course in life we are pursuing is according to the divine will, which is the greatest challenge of all. The first two criteria require us to learn and understand something about *God.* The third requires that we know something about *ourselves.* That is to say, faith unto life and salvation depends upon *confidence*—a word the Prophet often used interchangeably with faith. We must have confidence that there is a God, confidence that he is who he says he is, and confidence that he has all power. And then we must have some degree of confidence in ourselves, a quiet assurance that the Lord is pleased with us. We who doubt our standing before God, who constantly question our own goodness and impugn our own righteousness, and who always feel inadequate and inferior cannot develop faith unto life and salvation. Though a certain measure of humility is typical of those who come unto Christ (2 Nephi 4:17–18; Ether 3:2), yet they must also have hope in Christ—the anticipation of divine acceptance because of him, assurance of eternal life through him, and expectation of glory with him—if they are to chart a course and follow it to salvation.

Lecture Six declares: "An actual knowledge to any person, that the course of life which he pursues is according to the will of God, is essentially necessary to enable him to have that confidence in God without which no person can obtain eternal life. It was this that enabled the ancient saints to endure all their afflictions and persecutions, and to take joyfully the spoiling of their goods, knowing (not believing merely) that they had a more enduring substance." Indeed, "such was, and always will be, the situation of the saints of God, that unless they have an actual knowledge that the course they are pursuing is according to the will of God they will grow weary in their minds and faint" (67–68). Stated another way, if the people of God are to have courage and the faith to overcome the world, they need to know that the Lord is pleased with them and that their acts and faith are acceptable to him. "For a man to lay down his all, his character and reputation, his honor, and applause, his good name among men, his houses, his lands, his brothers and sisters, his wife and children, and even his own life also—counting all things but filth and dross for the excellency of the knowledge of Jesus Christ—requires more than mere belief or supposition that he is doing the will of God; but actual knowledge, realizing that, when these sufferings are ended, he will enter into eternal rest, and be a partaker of the glory of God" (68).

And how do we gain such a knowledge? How do we come to know that we are on course, that our lives are in order and thus approved of the heavens? The members of the School of the Elders were taught—and this is one of the transcendent verities of the Restoration—that we must be willing to *sacrifice* all things for the gospel cause. If we would become inheritors of all that the Father has, we must be willing to give up all that we have. With us, it must be the kingdom of God or nothing. "Let us here observe," the Prophet declared, "that a religion that does not require the sacrifice of all things never has power sufficient to produce the faith necessary unto life and salvation" (69). Only a church that will ask everything of its members—everything!—is in a position to promise its members the riches of eternity. Total surrender is always prerequisite to total victory. Only those who reach the point in their spiritual development where they are at last able and willing to fully consecrate themselves to the Lord and his Church and kingdom, and to do so without hindrance, can gain that confidence before God of which the scriptures speak (D&C 121:45)—a confidence that results in the promise of eternal life.

Lecture Seven teaches of the fruits of faith; namely, spiritual gifts enjoyed by the faithful and ultimately complete salvation granted to the fully consecrated. Further, we learn that one of the benefits of true faith is that it develops in us a Christlike character, leading us onward toward the imitation of Christ our Master. Jesus is indeed the prototype of all saved beings. "Salvation consists in the glory, authority, majesty, power and dominion which Jehovah possesses and in nothing else; and no being can possess it but himself or one like him" (76). The plan of salvation is in fact "a system of faith—it begins with faith, and continues by faith; and every blessing which is obtained in relation to it is the effect of faith, whether it pertains to this life or that which is to come" (80).

Having established what faith is, what underlies that faith, and what is required of us in order to be counted among the favored of heaven, the lecture explains what it means to work by faith. "We understand that *when a man works by faith he works by mental exertion instead of physical force.* It is by words, instead of exerting his physical powers, with which every being works when he works by faith" (72; emphasis added). We are not to understand from this statement that working by faith is merely an intellectual exercise or that those with unusual mental capacities necessarily have more faith. Rather, the mental exertion seems to be the rigor and strenuous labor, the soul searching and personal denial associated with coming to know the mind and will of God and then acting upon it.

"There may be those," Elder McConkie observed, "whose mental powers and thought processes are greater than any of the saints, but only persons who are in tune with the Infinite can exercise the spiritual forces and powers that come from him. . . . He who is the Author of faith, he whose power faith is, he whose works are the embodiment of justice and judgment and wisdom and all good things, even he must approve the use of his power in the case at hand. Faith cannot be exercised contrary to the order of heaven or contrary to the will and purposes of him whose power it is. Men work by faith when they are in tune with the Spirit and when what they seek to do by mental exertion and by the spoken word is the mind and will of the Lord" (*New,* 192).

SOURCES

Lectures on Faith. Salt Lake City: Deseret Book, 1985.

McConkie, Bruce R. *The Lord God of Joseph Smith.* Brigham Young University Speeches of the Year. Provo, Utah, 4 Jan. 1972.

————. *A New Witness for the Articles of Faith.* Salt Lake City: Deseret Book, 1985.

RLM

LEVI/LEVITES

Levi was the third son of Jacob (Israel) and his first wife, Leah (Genesis 35:23), and one of the heads of the original twelve tribes of Israel. His Hebrew name means "joined" (Bible Dictionary, "Levi"), for as his mother said at his birth, "Now this time will my husband be *joined* unto me, because I have born him three sons: therefore was his name called Levi" (Genesis 29:34; emphasis added). Owing to his involvement in the slaughter of the Shechemites as revenge for Shechem's defilement of Dinah, his sister (Genesis 34), Levi was called an instrument of cruelty by his father, Jacob (Genesis 49:5). Levi and his brother, Simeon, were then cursed by Jacob for their anger and their "cruel" wrath. Foreshadowing future events, Jacob said, "I will divide them in Jacob, and scatter them in Israel" (Genesis 49:7).

Levi had three sons: Gershon, Kohath, and Merari (Genesis

46:11). They and their descendants constituted the Levites. They were generally righteous and sided with the Lord, as in the golden calf episode: "Then Moses stood in the gate of the camp, and said, Who is on the Lord's side? let him come unto me. And all the sons of Levi gathered themselves together unto him" (Exodus 32:26). On that occasion the Levites went throughout the camp of Israel, upon God's command, and slew about three thousand of the rebellious Israelites (Exodus 32:27–28).

To honor their righteousness, male members of the tribe of Levi were chosen to bear the lesser (Aaronic) priesthood, assigned to minister in the tabernacle and later the temple (Nehemiah 11:16), and to assist the priests—Aaron and his posterity (Numbers 3:5–10; 8:19; 18:1–7). They slaughtered the sacrifices and helped in other ways (2 Chronicles 29:34; 35:11; Ezra 6:20). The Levites were symbolically offered as a wave-offering, and were dedicated to the Lord and his service full-time in place of the firstborn males in Israel: "For they are wholly given unto me from among the children of Israel; instead of such as open every womb, even instead of the firstborn of all the children of Israel, have I taken them unto me. For all the firstborn of the children of Israel are mine, both man and beast: on the day that I smote every firstborn in the land of Egypt I sanctified them for myself. And I have taken the Levites for all the firstborn of the children of Israel" (Numbers 8: 16–18; see also Bible Dictionary, "Levites").

As holders of the Levitical Priesthood scattered throughout all the tribes of Israel, the Levites received no land inheritance in Canaan and were not counted as one of the twelve tribes in terms of allotment and assignments. Their lot was the priesthood and its duties. They were supported by the tithes of the people (Numbers 18:20–21, 23–24). Forty-eight cities belonged to them (Numbers 35:6), and they had claim on the alms given by Israelites during feasts (Deuteronomy 12:18–19; 14:27–29). The book of Leviticus was, in essence, the handbook of instructions for the holders of the lesser priesthood. Usually, the Levites are spoken of as separate from the priests (1 Kings 8:4; Ezra 2:70; John 1:19). They are mentioned three times in the New Testament (Luke 10:32; John 1:19; Acts 4:36).

In this last dispensation, it is expected that the sons of Levi will again perform their priesthood duties. When he restored the Aaronic

Priesthood, John the Baptist said of the lesser priesthood, "this shall never be taken again from the earth, until the sons of Levi do offer again an offering unto the Lord in righteousness" (D&C 13:1). Though this sounds as if the Levitical Priesthood will be removed at some point, it will not. Oliver Cowdery reported the words of John the Baptist slightly differently—changing the word "until" to "that": "Upon you my fellow-servants, in the name of Messiah, I confer this Priesthood and this authority, which shall remain upon earth, that the Sons of Levi may yet offer an offering unto the Lord in righteousness" (Joseph Smith–History 1:71, footnote). This is the sense in which Elder John A. Widtsoe understood the passage: "When, therefore, the sons of Levi accept Christ and His gospel, subject themselves to the ordinances of the Church, and become active in gospel requirements, they will offer the offering in righteousness of which has been spoken" (247). To bear the Levitical Priesthood anciently was a great honor, just as is the privilege of holding the Aaronic Priesthood in modern times.

SOURCE

Widtsoe, John A. *Evidences and Reconciliations.* Arranged by G. Homer Durham. Salt Lake City: Bookcraft, 1960.

ACS

LIAHONA

The Liahona was a tangible instrument that was prepared by the Lord to assist Lehi's family in their travels through the Arabian wilderness and across the seas to the promised land. By interpretation, the Liahona means "compass" (Alma 37:38). Upon arising one morning after his family's departure from Jerusalem, Lehi found a brass ball of "curious [skillful] workmanship" outside his tent (1 Nephi 16:10). Within the ball were two spindles that indicated the direction they should travel. Working according to the collective faith, heed, and diligence that Lehi's family gave to the Lord, the Liahona included various communications from God that appeared in clear, written form on the ball from time to time, granting them additional "understanding concerning the ways of the Lord" (1 Nephi 16:29).

Comparing Lehi's wilderness travels to the Israelites' sojourn with Moses, Nephi considered the Liahona their own "pillar of the cloud by day [and] . . . pillar of fire by night" to lead them to life-sustaining food, water, and protection from attack (Exodus 13:22). Just as the Israelites had but to look to the brazen serpent in order to live, the Lehites had but to give faith and diligence to the brass ball, which Nephi called a "small means" by which the Lord brought about "great things" (1 Nephi 16:29). Through the frequent, miraculous functioning of the Liahona, Lehi's family had daily opportunities to see the power of God in their lives (Alma 37:40). Because of their tendency toward slothfulness and forgetfulness, however, they suffered privations.

Although there is no evidence in the Book of Mormon that the Liahona operated as a miraculous compass for later generations, subsequent prophet-leaders preserved the curious ball and taught others of the lessons that could be gleaned from it. For example, Nephi took the compass with him when he separated from his brothers (2 Nephi 5:12), King Benjamin passed it on to his son Mosiah when he announced Mosiah as his successor (Mosiah 1:16), and in 1829 an angel showed Oliver Cowdery, David Whitmer, and Martin Harris the Liahona as well as the gold plates containing the Book of Mormon record (D&C 17:1). Additionally, more than five hundred years after Lehi left Jerusalem, Alma taught his son Helaman that the tangible Liahona was a shadow, type, or symbol, of spiritual guidance that was available to him if he would look (Alma 37:43–47). Alma likened the compass to the "word of Christ, which will point to you a straight course to eternal bliss" and taught that if we simply "look we may live forever." If we do not become slothful "because of the easiness of the way" in looking to Christ, God will "carry us beyond this vale of sorrow into a far better land of promise" (Alma 37:45).

Considering both the manner in which the Liahona functioned and Alma's teachings that the compass symbolized God's spiritual guidance, many important modern-day applications can be proposed. Each of these specific applications, however, must underscore that our faith in Christ and willing desires to heed his teachings are foundational to receiving the Lord's miraculous guidance. As the Liahona empowered Nephi to guide the ship safely to a land he had never known, so we are enabled by the grace of Christ to go wherever, do whatever, and say whatever he directs us. On the other hand, because Jesus Christ is the Bread of Life and the Living Water, failure to look to him because of our slothfulness or the easiness of the way will likewise produce hunger and thirst that no other source can satisfy. The same promise of spiritual direction is taught in Proverbs 3:5–6: "Trust in the Lord with all thine heart; and lean not unto thine own understanding. In all thy ways, acknowledge him, and he shall direct thy paths."

CFO

LIGHT OF CHRIST

We do not travel far in our study of the gospel before we read that Jesus Christ is "the true Light, which lighteth every man that cometh into the world" (John 1:9). Because Jehovah was the fore-ordained Redeemer and Savior of worlds (D&C 76:22–24; Moses 1:32–35) and the Lamb slain from the foundation of the world (Revelation 5:6; 13:8; Moses 7:47), the Father's plan became his by adoption; the gospel of God (Romans 1:1–3) thus became known as the gospel of Jesus Christ. Because Elohim has invested his Beloved Son with his own attributes and powers (Mosiah 15:3; D&C 93:17) and because the "Father of lights" (James 1:17) has ordained that Christ is to be the Light of lights and the Light of the world, those powers of life and light that we know as the power of God have come to be known as the Light of Christ or the Spirit of Jesus Christ.

Though there is but passing reference to the Light of Christ in the New Testament, the scriptures of the Restoration abound in detail, assisting us to understand how and in what manner the Light of Christ lights every man and woman born into mortality. We come to know first of all that that light is a manifestation of the glory of God, a divine influence that fills the immensity of space, and the means whereby God, a corporeal being who can be in only one place at one time, is omnipresent (D&C 88:12–13). Elder Charles W. Penrose declared that "this spirit which pervades all things, which is the light and life of all things, by which our heavenly Father operates, by which He is omnipotent, never had a beginning and never will have an end. It is the light of truth; it is the spirit of intelligence" (26:23).

The Light of Christ has both natural and redemptive functions. Elder Parley P. Pratt explained: "It is, in its less refined existence, the physical light that reflects from the sun, moon, and stars, and other substances, and, by reflection on the eye, makes visible the truths of the outward world. It is also in its higher degrees the intellectual light of our inward and spiritual organs, by which we reason, discern, judge, compare, comprehend, and remember the subjects within our reach. Its inspiration constitutes instinct in animal life, reason in man, and vision in the prophets, and is continually flowing from the Godhead throughout all his creations" (25). The Holy Ghost is a male personage of spirit and, like the Father, can be in only one place at a time. He draws upon the Light of Christ to communicate sacred truths and to dispense spiritual gifts to myriad beings separated in time and space (Moroni 10:17; Smith, 1:54; McConkie, 258–59).

The same power that makes it possible for us to see with our physical eyes also makes it possible for us to see with our spiritual eyes (D&C 88:6–13). Discernment, the innate ability to distinguish good from evil and the relevant from the irrelevant, also comes through this Spirit of Jesus Christ (Moroni 7:12–19). Further, those who are true to the Spirit within them—which includes their conscience and the canons of right and wrong and decency in society—will be led, either in this life or the next, to the higher light of the Holy Ghost that comes through the gospel covenant (D&C 84:44–53).

Elder Bruce R. McConkie wrote: "The light of Christ (also called the Spirit of Christ and the Spirit of the Lord) is a light, a power, and an influence that proceeds forth from the presence of God to fill the immensity of space. . . . It is the agency of God's power and the law by which all things are governed. It is also the agency used by the Holy Ghost to manifest truth and dispense spiritual gifts to many people at one and the same time. For instance, it is as though the Holy Ghost, who is a personage of spirit, was broadcasting all truth throughout the whole universe all the time, using the light of Christ as the agency by which the message is delivered. But only those who attune their souls to the Holy Spirit receive the available revelation. It is in this way that the person of the Holy Ghost makes his influence felt in the heart of every righteous person at one and the same time" (70).

SOURCES

McConkie, Bruce R. *A New Witness for the Articles of Faith.* Salt Lake City: Deseret Book, 1985.

Penrose, Charles W. In *Journal of Discourses.* 26 vols. London: Latter-day Saints' Book Depot, 1854–86.

Pratt, Parley P. *Key to the Science of Theology; A Voice of Warning.* Salt Lake City: Deseret Book, 1978.

Smith, Joseph Fielding. *Doctrines of Salvation.* Compiled by Bruce R. McConkie. 3 vols. Salt Lake City: Bookcraft, 1954–56.

RLM

LIGHT-MINDEDNESS/LOUD LAUGHTER

The Father's plan of salvation for his children is also known as the "great plan of happiness" (Alma 42:8). He wants his children to be happy and enjoy life. "Men are, that they might have joy," Father Lehi declared (2 Nephi 2:25). The Prophet Joseph Smith taught that "happiness is the object and design of our existence" (5:134). Humor and sociality are an important part of our existence. The Lord's command to avoid laughter and light-mindedness (D&C 88:121) does not mean that we are never to laugh aloud or find humor in ourselves or in the circumstances around us. Nor does it mean that we have to be somber and pensive all the time. In fact, many of the Lord's most spiritual and devoted servants enjoy a hearty laugh and are quick-witted, humorous, and fun. In the scriptures the term *light-mindedness* means making light of sacred things or failing to take seriously those eternally significant things that should be treated with reverence (D&C 84:54).

Likewise, the scriptures speak of laughter in a variety of contexts. From these passages we see that there are times and places that laughter is appropriate and expected, such as in social and entertainment settings. There are other times and places, however, when laughter is highly inappropriate and irreverent. Speaking of Sabbath day worship, the Lord urged the Saints to "do these things with thanksgiving, with cheerful hearts and countenances, *not with much laughter, for this is sin,* but with a glad heart and cheerful countenance" (D&C 59:15; emphasis added). Likewise, when worshipping and serving in the Lord's temples, we should "cease from [our] light speeches, *from all laughter,* from all [our] lustful desires, from all [our] pride and *light-mindedness,* and from all [our] wicked doings" (D&C 88:121; emphasis added). *Loud* laughter does not refer exclusively to volume, but also to content. It can be raucous, offensive, and dissonant. That which elicits loud laughter is always offensive to the Spirit of the Lord and antithetical to the attributes of godliness. In a similar way, the word *light* can mean empty, shallow, insignificant, and of little worth. Hence, light speeches and light-mindedness are at best empty in what they contribute to spirituality and righteousness, and at worst they are sin-inducing and spiritually destructive. In contrast, God invites us to "let the solemnities of eternity rest upon [our] minds" (D&C 43:34).

SOURCE

Smith, Joseph. *History of The Church of Jesus Christ of Latter-day Saints.* Edited by B. H. Roberts. 7 vols. 2d ed. rev. Salt Lake City: The Church of Jesus Christ of Latter-day Saints, 1932–51.

BLT

LORD

In the King James Version of the Bible, the word LORD, with the letters printed in small capitals, is generally used to denote the tetragrammaton (Greek, "four-letter word") when it appears in the Hebrew text. The tetragrammaton is the four-consonant name of God (ancient Hebrew was written without vowels) that non-Jews vocalize as Jehovah, though the original pronunciation has been lost. The convention of substituting LORD in its place follows the Jewish practice of refraining from pronouncing the name of God out of respect for its sanctity. When reading the Hebrew Bible, Jews most often substitute the term *Adonai*, which translates as "Lord," for the four-consonant name of Deity.

ACS

LORD OF SABAOTH

Sabaoth is a Hebrew word meaning "hosts" or "armies." It comes from a root word usually translated as "assembled for war" or "fought," though it is occasionally translated as "assembled for a service." The divine epithet "Lord of *Sabaoth*" or "Lord of Hosts" is the most common designation for God in the Old Testament, attested some 285 times (*New,* 3:687). Interestingly, the phrase is absent from Genesis through Joshua even though the Lord was well-known as "a man of war" (Exodus 15:3) after he explicitly and definitively defeated the Egyptian armies who came seeking Israel after the flight from Egypt (Exodus 14:27, 30). Most of the occurrences of the phrase "Lord of Hosts [Sabaoth]" are found in the prophetic books. Many passages directly connect "Lord of hosts" with Jehovah, noting that "the Lord of hosts is his name" (Isaiah 47:4; 48:2; 51:15; 54:5; Jeremiah 10:16; 31:35; Amos 5:27; and others).

Most often the phrase either implies or states Jehovah's role as commander of the armies of Israel (1 Samuel 17:45), but the phrase can also refer to his role as leader of unseen hosts. Indeed, much of the Old Testament demonstrates that Jehovah fights Israel's battles for them or that he delivers their enemies into their hands when they hearken to his voice (Judges 1:2, 4; 2:20–23). Joshua directly encountered Jehovah during the Israelite conquest, where he is called "captain of the host of the Lord" (Joshua 5:14). Just as the Lord promised he would fight Israel's battles in ancient times (2 Chronicles 20:17; 32:8), so too in the latter days the Lord has promised he will fight battles on behalf of his people if they are righteous (D&C 98:37–39). It has been prophesied that in the future the Lord will fight against and conquer those nations that rise up against the remnant of Israel or Judah in the last great battle known as Armageddon (Zechariah 14:3; Revelation 16:14; 20:8).

"Lord of hosts" is also a common epithet of God used in restoration scripture, with over fifty attestations in the Book of Mormon, and twelve in the Doctrine and Covenants. In four other instances in the Doctrine and Covenants, the actual transliterated Hebrew term, *Sabaoth,* is used: "Lord of Sabaoth." Two of these references occur in sections where war is the main focus (D&C 87:7; 98:2). The other two seem to use the term in its less-often attested meaning, which refers to an assemblage of heavenly beings, as in Doctrine and Covenants 88:2. In Doctrine and Covenants 95:7 ("Lord of Sabaoth, which is by interpretation, the creator of the first day, the beginning and the end"), the term *Sabaoth* may imply the "hosts" of elements that are being organized to form the universe and its myriad creations.

SOURCE

The New Interpreter's Dictionary of the Bible. 5 vols. Nashville, Tenn.: Abingdon, 2006–9.

ACS

LORD OF THE VINEYARD

Isaiah prophesied that the Lord of the vineyard would plant his "choicest vine" in the estate, but the vineyard would produce "wild grapes" (Isaiah 5:2). In this prophecy, the Lord of the vineyard is the Father, the vine is Christ, and the vineyard is Israel falling into apostasy because it cut itself off from the Vine (John 15:1–8). Centuries later Jesus related the parable of the wicked husbandmen, which echoes Isaiah's prophecy. The wicked husbandmen ignored the instructions from the Lord of the vineyard by beating the various servants the Lord had sent to gather the fruit and then killed the heir—the son of the Lord of the vineyard—and consequently the vineyard produced wild fruit (Matthew 21:33–46).

The Savior also related a parable in which the Lord God is the Lord of the vineyard. In the parable of the laborers in the vineyard, the Lord of the vineyard hires workers to labor in his vineyard throughout the day, giving them equal payment at the end of the day (Matthew 20:1–16). In Zenos's allegory of the olive tree, the Lord of the vineyard continues to send servants to prune and dig his vineyard in an effort to produce good fruit until his final visit, when he joins them in their work (Jacob 5:72). "And thus they labored, with all diligence, according to the commandments of the Lord of the vineyard, even until the bad had been cast away out of the vineyard, and the Lord had preserved unto himself that the trees had become again the natural fruit; and they became like unto one body; and the fruits were equal" (Jacob 5:74).

The Lord often warned Joseph Smith of the corrupted nature of his vineyard and the need to call eleventh-hour laborers to work together to see that the trees again produce good fruit (D&C 4; 33:2–7; 75:1–5). Because of priestcraft and slothful servants, the enemy had entered and overtaken the vineyard (D&C 101:44–62). In such dire circumstances, the Lord of the vineyard called the "residue" of his servants to go "straightway . . . and redeem my vineyard" because the vineyard is his, bought with the price of his blood (D&C 101:55–56). Today the Lord's servants are working to gather scattered Israel from the four corners of the earth, teaching them to come to the knowledge of their Redeemer and, in so doing, serving in the Lord's vineyard.

CFO

LOST SCRIPTURE

Internal evidence within the scriptures themselves indicates that some texts or documents, once well-known and considered authoritative, are missing from the current collections of books we call the Bible and the Book of Mormon. (The English word *bible* derives from the Greek *biblia,* meaning "books"; Bible Dictionary, "Bible"). Missing documents from the Old Testament include, at the very least, the following: the book of the Wars of the Lord (Numbers 21:14); the book of Jasher (Hebrew, "the upright"; Bible Dictionary, "Jasher"; Joshua 10:13; 2 Samuel 1:18); the book of the Acts of Solomon (1 Kings 11:41); the books of Samuel the Seer, Gad the Seer, and Nathan the Prophet (1 Chronicles 9:29; 29:29); the Visions of Iddo the Seer (2 Chronicles 9:29; 12:15; 13:22); the book of Shemaiah (2 Chronicles 12:15); the book of Jehu (2 Chronicles 20:34); and the Sayings of the Seers (2 Chronicles 33:19). In addition, a text called the "prophecy of Ahijah the Shilonite" is missing (2 Chronicles 9:29; see also Bible Dictionary, "Lost Books").

The New Testament makes reference to the following texts once extant but now apparently lost: an epistle written by Paul to the Corinthians, earlier than the present 1 Corinthians (1 Corinthians 5:9); an epistle to the Church at Laodicea (Colossians 4:16); and prophecies of Enoch known to Jude (Jude 1:14). In addition, there are probably other lost scriptural texts which are alluded to in our present biblical canon, including but not limited to "the rest of the acts of Uzziah" written by Isaiah (2 Chronicles 26:22; see also Bible Dictionary, "Lost Books").

Such data firmly support the fact that the Bible is not complete; it does not presently contain all that God ever revealed or all that prophets and apostles of different dispensations ever wrote. Such data flatly contradict the view that because the Bible is complete, perfect, and inerrant, there can be no additional scripture or that if any claim of canonicity or sacred authority is made for other texts, that claim must be false. The Prophet Joseph Smith declared that "[God] will yet reveal many great and important things pertaining to the Kingdom of God" (Articles of Faith 1:9).

Some scripture is lost due to wickedness. Missing scripture owing to deliberate sabotage was a great concern to Nephi in the Book of

Mormon because of the effect it would have on individuals. He saw in a vision that many plain and precious things, including covenants, had been removed from the Bible by wicked persons and organizations (1 Nephi 13:26–29, 32, 34). He further saw that as a result "an exceedingly great many do stumble, yea, insomuch that Satan hath great power over them" (1 Nephi 13:29).

The Book of Mormon, the "most correct of any book on earth" (Book of Mormon, Introduction), signals the existence of sacred authoritative texts that were either deliberately left out of the biblical canon or were lost due to carelessness. Some of these documents that were well-known and acknowledged in Old Testament times include the writings of Zenock, Zenos, and Neum (1 Nephi 19:10; Jacob 5; Alma 33:3–17; 3 Nephi 10:15–16). All three of those prophets testified of Christ and helped form the doctrinal foundation of Nephi's testimony. Zenock and Neum prophesied that Christ would yield himself to be crucified at the hands of wicked men, and Zenos prophesied of Christ's burial, the three days of darkness, and the destruction that ensued after Christ's death (1 Nephi 19:10). The Book of Mormon prophet Jacob also quoted Zenos's parable of the olive tree (Jacob 5).

Some scripture is lost from lack of care, as was the case with the book of Lehi. Included in the 116 manuscript pages translated by Joseph Smith, the book was lent to Martin Harris and lost thereafter. It can now be recovered in part only from quotations and synopses in the writings of Nephi and Jacob, Lehi's sons.

Additionally, our current Book of Mormon is an abridgment of many original records to which we do not presently have access. Some of these records are of monumental significance, including the plates of brass, which constituted the "standard works or the basic scriptures of the Nephites" (Millet, 643). They were like our Old Testament record but more extensive (1 Nephi 13:23). We know that Joseph Smith was not allowed to translate a part of the plates, now referred to as "the sealed portion." That part of the sacred record contains "a revelation from God, from the beginning of the world to the ending thereof" (2 Nephi 27:7). The Lord told Moroni that the sealed portion would be revealed when his people repented and exercised faith in him like that possessed by the brother of Jared (Ether 4:6–7). Thus, we see that some scripture is purposely withheld by the Lord because the people are not ready for it.

SOURCE

Millet, Robert L. "Plates of Brass." In Dennis L. Largey, ed., *Book of Mormon Reference Companion,* 643–44. Salt Lake City: Deseret Book, 2003.

ACS

LOST TRIBES OF ISRAEL

A major scattering of the tribes of Israel took place in 721 B.C. at the hands of the Assyrians, under Shalmaneser. As the people of the ten northern tribes of Israel were being deported, many of them escaped and spread themselves throughout the nations. Some remained in the land of Israel and intermarried with foreign peoples; these became known as the Samaritans. Others, such as Lehi's ancestors, settled in the land of Judah. The bulk of the people formerly of northern Israel were, however, scattered to the four winds. Six hundred years before the birth of Christ, Nephi explained that "the house of Israel, sooner or later, will be scattered upon all the face of the earth, and also among all nations. And behold, there are many who are already lost from the knowledge of those who are at Jerusalem. Yea, the more part of all the tribes have been led away; and they are scattered to and fro upon the isles of the sea; and whither they are none of us knoweth, save that we know that they have been led away" (1 Nephi 22:3–4).

These descendants of Abraham, Isaac, and Jacob are scattered and lost—lost to their covenant identity and to their spiritual birthright. They have been, are, and will be gathered as all others are gathered through the generations—as they hear the gospel of Jesus Christ preached, receive the message of salvation through baptism, associate with others of the covenant, and remain loyal through faithful discipleship. They are gathered first and foremost to a person, Jesus Christ—to his gospel, his doctrine, and his church and fold (1 Nephi 15:14; 2 Nephi 6:8–11; 10:5–8). Second, they are gathered to the lands of their inheritance, meaning to the congregations of the household of faith in our day.

In a sense we have been gathering the lost ten tribes since 1830. The tribe of Joseph is one of the ten northern tribes, and Joseph (Ephraim and Manasseh) was the principal tribe gathered during the twentieth century. Even today pockets of the tribe of Joseph are found throughout the world. "And then cometh the day when the arm of the Lord shall be revealed in power in convincing the nations, the heathen nations, *the house of Joseph*, of the gospel of their salvation. For it shall come to pass in that day, that every man shall hear the fulness of the gospel in his own tongue, and in his own language, through those who are ordained unto this power, by the administration of the Comforter, shed forth upon them for the revelation of Jesus Christ" (D&C 90:10–11; emphasis added).

But the great day of gathering for the ten tribes will be millennial. "And then shall the power of heaven come down among them," the risen Lord explained, "and I also will be in the midst. And then shall the work of the Father [the work of gathering Israel] commence at that day, even when this gospel shall be preached among the remnant of this people [the descendants of Lehi]. Verily I say unto you, at that day shall the work of the Father commence among all the dispersed of my people, yea, even the tribes which have been lost, which the Father hath led away out of Jerusalem" (3 Nephi 21:25–26; see also 2 Nephi 30:7–15).

It is interesting that the Savior chose the word *commence*, given that the work of gathering has been underway for a long time. The final great millennial gathering of Israel will commence in the sense that this marvelous missionary effort will be so vast, so expansive, so comprehensive in scope and effect as to cause all previous gatherings to fade into insignificance. Through Jeremiah comes the holy word regarding that glorious day when the King of kings reigns triumphant among his people: "Behold, the days come, saith the Lord, that I will make a new covenant with the house of Israel, and with the house of Judah: not according to the covenant that I made with their fathers . . . which my covenant they brake. . . . But this shall be the covenant that I will make with the house of Israel; . . . I will put my law in their inward parts, and write it in their hearts; and will be their God, and they shall be my people. And they shall teach no more every man his neighbor, and every man his brother, saying, Know the Lord: for they shall all know me, from the least of them unto the greatest of them, saith the Lord: for I will forgive their iniquity, and I will remember their sin no more" (Jeremiah 31:31–34).

RLM

MAN

In the scriptures the term *man* usually refers to all mankind—men *and* women. For example, the creation account of Genesis says, "So God created man in his own image, in the image of God created he him; male and female created he them" (Genesis 1:27). Likewise, the scriptures speak of the "fall of man"—meaning the mortal condition and spiritual estrangement that come upon all mankind—and the "salvation of man," meaning that Christ's atonement redeems all mankind from that fall and offers personal salvation to all, whether male or female (1 Nephi 10:6; 2 Nephi 9:5–24; Helaman 14:15–19).

In addition to this universal usage of the word *man,* the scriptures and teachings of the prophets and apostles show that man is unique among the creations of God—with a unique creation, a unique relationship to the Creator, and a unique stewardship over all other creations (Genesis 1:26–28; Moses 1:26–31; 6:8–10, 22). Man—all men and women—are thus unique in that they are offspring of God, the "Man of Holiness" (Moses 6:57). God "is an exalted man," the Prophet Joseph Smith declared. "If the veil were rent today, and the great God who holds this world in its orbit, and who upholds all worlds and all things by His power, was to make Himself visible,—I say, if you were to see Him today, you would see Him like a man in form—like yourselves in all the person, image, and very form as a man" (6:305). Within this context, we can see that man, as the Psalmist declared, is only "a little lower than the angels [in Hebrew the word is *Elohim,* the Gods], and [God] has crowned him with glory and honour" (Psalm 8:5). As the offspring of God, all men and women have the potential to become, through the principles and ordinances of the gospel of Jesus Christ and through his infinite mercy, exalted and like God—men and women of holiness in the most magnificent sense of the word.

Despite this lofty use of the term, *man* is also used in the scriptures to describe the fallen condition of the human family. Man, in this sense, is "an enemy to God" by reason of the spiritual estrangement resulting from Adam's fall and through each person's own sins (Mosiah 3:19). The term is sometimes used to illustrate the wide gap between God's perfection and the "carnal, sensual, and devilish" nature of men and the dependence of mortals upon Deity for sanctification and salvation (Romans 3:10, 23; 1 Corinthians 2:14; Mosiah 16:3–5; Alma 41:11; D&C 20:20). For this reason, the scriptures also speak of the necessity of becoming new men (and women) through Christ's atonement (Ephesians 2:15; 4:14; Colossians 3:10).

SOURCE

Smith, Joseph. *History of The Church of Jesus Christ of Latter-day Saints.* Edited by B. H. Roberts. 7 vols. 2d ed. rev. Salt Lake City: The Church of Jesus Christ of Latter-day Saints, 1932–51.

BLT

MANNA

Manna was the daily mainstay of the Israelites' diet during their forty-year sojourn in the wilderness (Exodus 16:35; Joshua 5:10–12). Several characteristics of this primary food source are given in the Bible. Manna was a fine, white, flaky substance that resembled coriander seed, was sticky and resinous in texture, and appeared on the ground like frost (Numbers 11:4–9; Exodus 16:1–36). It was sweet, tasting like wafers made with honey and oil. Each Israelite could gather an omer (two to four quarts) of manna early in the day, but any manna not gathered would disappear after the sun warmed the ground or would spoil if stored longer than a day. Manna could be boiled in pots or ground into meal and baked into cakes. The word *manna* is best translated as "What is it?" Even today we are not completely able to identify the substance.

Symbolically, however, manna typifies the living Bread of Life, or Jehovah. The Israelites' daily survival depended on the sustaining power of God. Like manna, Jesus Christ is the "true bread from heaven," given not to a few but to the world by God the Father. "For the bread of God is he which cometh down from heaven, and giveth life unto the world." For this reason, Jesus taught, "He that cometh to me shall never hunger; and he that believeth on me shall never thirst. . . . I am the living bread which came down from heaven: if any man eat of this bread, he shall live for ever: and the bread that I will give is my flesh, which I will give for the life of the world" (John 6:32–33, 35, 51).

CFO

MAN OF HOLINESS

Joseph Smith learned during his inspired translation of Genesis that one of the names of our Father in Heaven is Man of Holiness, and that God's Son is called the Son of Man of Holiness or, more succinctly, the Son of Man (Moses 6:57). This name-title obviously specifies two key realities about the Being who is the ultimate object of our worship: (1) He is a man, not merely a force, an influence, a law, a collection of laws, or a metaphorical master. He is a glorified, exalted man. (2) He is holy. Holiness is a grand, overarching category, one that comprehends or is closely associated with several divine characteristics. For example, Jacob, son of Lehi, declared, "And because of [Christ's] intercession for all, all men come unto God; wherefore, they stand in the presence of him, to be judged of him according to the truth and holiness which is in him" (2 Nephi 2:10). He added, "O how great the holiness of our God! For he knoweth all things, and there is not anything save he knows it" (2 Nephi 9:20). Clearly, Jacob intends in this latter passage to convey the priceless insight that a part of God's holiness is his omniscience. Likewise, virtue is properly linked with holiness (D&C 38:24; 46:33). The apostle Peter thus beckons to the Saints, "But as he which hath called you is holy, so be ye holy in all manner of conversation; because it is written, Be ye holy; for I am holy" (1 Peter 1:15–16; see also Leviticus 11:44).

RLM

MARRIAGE

The legal contract and covenant that binds a man and woman together as husband and wife is known as marriage. While customs and laws may vary around the world, every culture has some traditional rite or ceremony that is recognized as a legally and culturally binding union of a couple and the creation of a family unit. The institution of marriage has existed as long as man and woman have been upon the earth. In the Garden of Eden, God taught Adam and Eve that "it is not good that the man [or woman] should be alone" (Genesis 2:18). The Prophet Joseph Smith likewise taught that "marriage was . . . instituted in the garden of Eden" and that God commanded Adam and Eve to "multiply and replenish the earth" and pronounced blessings of "long life and prosperity" upon the heads of our first parents at that time (2:320). "Therefore shall a man leave his father and his mother," the Lord declared, "and shall cleave unto his wife: and they shall be one flesh" (Genesis 2:24; see also Moses 3:7, 18, 21–25). Thus, marriage between a man and a woman "is ordained of God unto man" (D&C 49:15) and is "essential to His eternal plan" (First Presidency, 102). It is, as President Boyd K. Packer has described, "the ideal pattern for human living" (15). So sacred is this institution that the Savior himself declared: "What therefore God hath joined together, let not man put asunder" (Matthew 19:6). In both the Old Testament and the New Testament, divine laws and commandments were given to protect the family and the institution of marriage. The apostle Paul wrote that "marriage is honourable" (Hebrews 13:4) and warned of those in the last days who would forbid marriage or seek to destroy marriage (1 Timothy 4:1–3).

Latter-day Saints believe strongly not only in the divine institution of marriage in general but also in the sacred responsibility that each husband and wife have to seek for marital happiness and fulfillment. Next to a personal relationship with God, we believe that the relationship between a husband and wife is our most significant and foundational relationship in life. While the Church recognizes that not all people will have the opportunity for a happy marriage in mortality, it should nonetheless be, as President Gordon B. Hinckley taught, "the hoped-for, the longed-for, the prayed-for desire—of men and women everywhere." God provided the institution of marriage "in His divine wisdom for the happiness and security of His children and the continuity of the race" (71).

In our day God has given direction through revelation and inspired counsel of latter-day prophets and apostles concerning how happiness in the marriage relationship—a happiness described by President Hinckley as "the sweetest feelings of life, the most generous and satisfying impulses of the human heart"—can be obtained and maintained. "Thou shalt love thy wife with all thy heart," the Lord declared to Joseph Smith in the revelation known as the Law of the Lord, "and shalt cleave unto her and none else" (D&C 42:22). Undoubtedly, this admonition applies equally to wives. President Spencer W. Kimball taught that the scriptural phrase "and none else" means "nothing else." He taught: "The words *none else* eliminate everyone and everything. The spouse then becomes preeminent in the life of the husband or wife, and neither social life nor occupational life nor political life nor any other interest nor person nor thing shall ever take precedence over the companion spouse" (143). Total fidelity—physical, emotional, and spiritual—is what the God-ordained, sacred institution of marriage deserves. Happiness in marriage also requires unselfishness and living the Golden Rule.

Prophets, apostles, and other Church leaders consistently teach that seeking to preserve happiness and harmony in marriage should be one of our most significant goals in life. As Latter-day Saints, we believe that endeavoring to have a happy marriage is not just a sociological benefit to our families and society but that it is also indeed a duty that affects our spiritual progression and our relationship with God in time and eternity.

SOURCES

First Presidency and Council of the Twelve Apostles. "The Family: A Proclamation to the World." *Ensign,* Nov. 1995, 102.

Hinckley, Gordon B. "What God Hath Joined Together." *Ensign,* May 1991, 71–74.

Kimball, Spencer W. *Faith Precedes the Miracle.* Salt Lake City: Deseret Book, 1972.

Packer, Boyd K. "Marriage." *Ensign,* May 1981, 13–15.

Smith, Joseph. *History of The Church of Jesus Christ of Latter-day Saints.* Edited by B. H. Roberts. 7 vols. 2d ed. rev. Salt Lake City: The Church of Jesus Christ of Latter-day Saints, 1932–51.

BLT

MARRIAGE, NEW AND EVERLASTING COVENANT OF

Latter-day Saints believe that marriage on earth not only is "ordained of God" (D&C 49:15) but also when contracted through the "new and everlasting covenant" (D&C 132:6) can be an enduring relationship throughout all eternity. Latter-day Saint marriages by those who have both civil authority and priesthood authority to "bind on earth" so that the marriages are also "bound in heaven" (Matthew 16:19) are performed in dedicated temples of God. This marriage ordinance is what President Howard W. Hunter called "the crowning gospel ordinance" (132) and is also known as sealing—sealing husband and wife together for time and all eternity. To Latter-day Saints, marriage in the new and everlasting covenant of the restored gospel—whether it is a temple marriage or a subsequent sealing after a civil marriage—is a requisite for exaltation in the highest glory or kingdom of God (D&C 131:1–4). In a revelation to the Prophet Joseph Smith, the Lord explained this ordinance and its implications in eternity:

"Therefore, if a man marry him a wife in the world, and he marry her not by me nor by my word, and he covenant with her so long as he is in the world and she with him, their covenant and marriage are not of force when they are dead, and when they are out of the world; therefore, they are not bound by any law when they are out of the world.

"Therefore, when they are out of the world they neither marry nor are given in marriage; but are appointed angels in heaven, which angels are ministering servants, to minister for those who are worthy of a far more, and an exceeding, and an eternal weight of glory. . . .

"And again, verily I say unto you, if a man marry a wife by my word, which is my law, and by the new and everlasting covenant, and it is sealed unto them by the Holy Spirit of promise, by him who is appointed, unto whom I have anointed this power and the keys of this priesthood; and it shall be said unto them—Ye shall come forth in the first resurrection; and if it be after the first resurrection, in the next resurrection; and shall inherit thrones, kingdoms, principalities, and powers, dominions, all heights and depths—then shall it be written in the Lamb's Book of Life, that he shall commit no murder whereby to shed innocent blood, and if ye abide in my covenant, and commit no murder whereby to shed innocent blood, it shall be done unto them in all things whatsoever my servant hath put upon them, in time, and through all eternity; and shall be of full force when they are out of the world; and they shall pass by the angels, and the gods, which are set there, to their exaltation and glory in all things, as hath been sealed upon their heads, which glory shall be a fulness and a continuation of the seeds forever and ever.

"Then shall they be gods, because they have no end; therefore shall they be from everlasting to everlasting, because they continue; then shall they be above all, because all things are subject unto them. Then shall they be gods, because they have all power, and the angels are subject unto them. Verily, verily, I say unto you, except ye abide my law ye cannot attain to this glory" (D&C 132:15–16, 19–21).

Abiding this new and everlasting covenant of marriage requires both receiving the priesthood ordinances and then faithfully keeping the associated temple covenants. Marrying or being sealed in the temple does not by itself guarantee the promised blessings of eternal families and celestial glory. "This gift, precious beyond all others," President Gordon B. Hinckley taught, "comes only with a price—with self-discipline, with virtue, with obedience to the commandments of God" (177–78). As with any ordinance of the gospel, realization of God's promises requires the keeping of covenants.

Temple marriage—the new and everlasting covenant of marriage—is required to enter the highest degree of celestial glory. God is mindful, however, that many in mortality—both in and out of the Church—will not have the privilege to receive this holy order of matrimony. Yet, the opportunity to do so will be made available at some future date for all who are faithful to the principles and ordinances of the gospel and who desire eternal marriage with all their hearts. "If you make yourselves worthy and ready to go to the house of the Lord and have faith in this sacred principle of celestial marriage for eternity, even though the privilege of marriage does not come to you now in mortality," President Harold B. Lee promised, "the Lord will reward you in due time and no blessing will be denied you. . . . The Lord knows the intent of your hearts, and in His own due time He will reward you with opportunities made possible through temple ordinances instituted in the Church for that purpose.

"Do all you can to comply with the laws of God pertaining to an exaltation in the kingdom of God. The Lord will judge you too by your works, as well as by the desires of your hearts, and your reward will be assured" (256).

SOURCES

Hinckley, Gordon B. *Teachings of Gordon B. Hinckley.* Salt Lake City: Deseret Book, 1997.

Hunter, Howard W. *The Teachings of Howard W. Hunter.* Edited by Clyde J. Williams. Salt Lake City: Bookcraft, 1997.

Lee, Harold B. *The Teachings of Harold B. Lee.* Edited by Clyde J. Williams. Salt Lake City: Bookcraft, 1996.

BLT

MARRIAGE SUPPER OF THE LAMB

The apostle John saw the marriage supper of the Lamb in vision, a symbolic view of the kingdom of heaven after the destruction of the wicked at the end of the world (Revelation 19:1–9). The Bridegroom at the wedding is the Lamb, or Jesus Christ (D&C 65:3; Luke 5:34–35); those "who are found faithful to the Lord" represent the bride and are therefore "found worthy to inherit a seat at the marriage supper" (Smith, 2:19).

The Savior related a parable about this marriage supper in which he was the king's son who was to be married (Matthew 22:1–14). Although all were summoned to the great celebration, many refused to come, even after receiving more than one invitation (Matthew 22:3–4). Some "made light" either of the invitation or of the feast itself, found other duties more important, or killed the messengers who relayed the invitation, and were therefore "not worthy" to come (Matthew 22:5–8).

To the Prophet Joseph Smith, the Lord specified that "all nations" would be invited, "first, the rich and the learned, the wise and the noble; and after that cometh the day of my power; then shall the poor, the lame, and the blind, and the deaf, come in unto the marriage of the Lamb, and partake of the supper of the Lord, prepared for the great day to come" (D&C 58:9–11).

In the parable, Jesus told of one man who was found among the wedding guests but was not covered with a "wedding garment." The king asked how he could have entered without this covering and, finding him thus unprepared, swiftly cast the speechless man into "outer darkness" (Matthew 22:11–13). John described the necessary covering for the bride, who "was granted" fine, clean, white linen, which represents the "righteousness of saints" (Revelation 19:8). In short, those who are covered by the atonement of Christ are made worthy to enter and feast with the Lamb.

SOURCE

Smith, Joseph. *History of The Church of Jesus Christ of Latter-day Saints.* Edited by

B. H. Roberts. 7 vols. 2d ed. rev. Salt Lake City: The Church of Jesus Christ of Latter-day Saints, 1932–51.

CFO

MARTYR/MARTYRDOM

The Greek word *martyr* means "witness." During the early Christian era, the term came to mean one who stood as a witness for his or her beliefs with such firmness as to be willing to forfeit life rather than renounce those beliefs. The church father Augustine of Hippo said, "It is not the pain but the purpose that makes a martyr" (*New*, 665). The greatest of all martyrs was Jesus Christ, whose perfect life and unjust death at the hands of wicked persons stands as an eternal witness of the truth of his gospel. He became a martyr so that all might live eternally (John 10:10; Romans 5:12–17). His martyrdom is also witness to his great love: "Greater love hath no man than this, that a man lay down his life for his friends" (John 15:13).

Jesus testified during his mortal life that martyrs for the truth would be greatly blessed and that standing firm for true principles was more valuable than life in this brief mortal sojourn. He said, "For whosoever will save his life shall lose it; but whosoever shall lose his life for my sake and the gospel's, the same shall save it. For what shall it profit a man, if he shall gain the whole world, and lose his own soul? Or what shall a man give in exchange for his soul? Whosoever therefore shall be ashamed of me and of my words in this adulterous and sinful generation; of him also shall the Son of man be ashamed, when he cometh in the glory of his Father with the holy angels" (Mark 8:35–38).

There have been many martyrs for the cause of truth since the days of Abel. Jesus spoke of "all the righteous blood shed upon the earth, from the blood of righteous Abel" that would testify against the wicked (Matthew 23:35–36; see also Luke 11:50). Jesus prophesied that many of his disciples would become martyrs (John 16:1–3). Stephen became the first Christian martyr after the death of the Savior (Acts 7:51–60). The apostle James, brother of John, was executed by King Herod Agrippa I (Acts 12:1–2). The chief apostle, Peter, and the apostle Paul were both executed in Rome (A.D. 67–68) during the Neronian persecution of Christianity—Peter being crucified upside down, according to tradition (Eusebius, 402–3).

As part of his great vision of earth's history, John the Revelator saw many martyrs when the fifth seal was opened (roughly the period from A.D. 1–999)—"them that were slain for the word of God, and for the testimony which they held" (Revelation 6:9). Churches were sometimes built over the graves or relics of martyrs in their honor. Such a church was called a *martyrium*. They are among the earliest churches in Christendom.

The age just prior to the Emperor Constantine (ca. A.D. 280–337) was "the classic period" of Christian martyrs (Cross, 1046). The certitude of martyrs gave great courage to, and strengthened the faith of, struggling Christians. A well-known adage attributed to Tertullian captures the outgrowth of such self-sacrifice: the blood of martyrs is the seed of faith. The lives of many martyrs in the Middle Ages and in the early modern era are documented by the great martyrologist of Oxford University, John Foxe, in his worthwhile volume *Foxe's Book of Martyrs.*

In the current dispensation, hundreds if not thousands have given their lives for the sake of the gospel of Jesus Christ. To all of those who give their all, even their very lives, the ancient promise of eternal life has been reiterated by Jesus Christ through the Prophet Joseph Smith. He said, "And whoso layeth down his life in my cause, for my name's sake, shall find it again, even life eternal" (D&C 98:13). The great martyrs of the dispensation of the fulness of times include Joseph and Hyrum Smith. Of them and their inclusion with other martyrs, President John Taylor wrote:

"Joseph Smith, the Prophet and Seer of the Lord, has done more, save Jesus only, for the salvation of men in this world, than any other man that ever lived in it. In the short space of twenty years, he has brought forth the Book of Mormon, which he translated by the gift and power of God, and has been the means of publishing it on two continents; has sent the fulness of the everlasting gospel, which it contained, to the four quarters of the earth; has brought forth the revelations and commandments which compose this book of Doctrine and Covenants, and many other wise documents and instructions for the benefit of the children of men; gathered many thousands of the Latter-day Saints, founded a great city, and left a fame and name that cannot be slain. He lived great, and he died great in the eyes of God and his people; and like most of the Lord's anointed in ancient times, has sealed his mission and his works with his own blood; and so has his brother Hyrum. In life they were not divided, and in death they were not separated!" (D&C 135:3).

Latter-day Saints owe a debt to the martyrs of our faith. What President Taylor said of Joseph and Hyrum Smith he also applied to honest and upright martyrs of every dispensation: "Their innocent blood, with the innocent blood of all the martyrs under the altar that John saw, will cry unto the Lord of Hosts till he avenges that blood on the earth" (D&C 135:7).

SOURCES

Cross, F. L., and E. A. Livingstone, ed. *The Oxford Dictionary of the Christian Church*. 3d ed. New York: Oxford University Press, 1997.

Eusebius. *The History of the Church*. Translated by G. A. Williamson. Rev. ed. London: Penguin Books, 1989.

The New Encyclopedia of Christian Quotations. Compiled by Mark Water. Grand Rapids, Mich.: Baker Books, 2000.

ACS

MARY

Mary's unique and vital mission as the mother of the Son of God was foretold centuries before she was born. Isaiah prophesied of her as the "virgin" who would bear a son called "Immanuel" (Isaiah 7:14). Young Nephi saw her in vision as a "virgin . . . exceedingly fair and white" who lived in Nazareth (1 Nephi 11:13). An angel explained to Nephi that "the virgin whom thou seest is the mother of the Son of God, after the manner of the flesh" (1 Nephi 11:18). Furthermore, Mary is one in a very short list of individuals whom prophets called by name before they were born (Mosiah 3:8). Clearly, this "precious and chosen vessel" was elected in premortality to give birth to and rear to adulthood the Only Begotten of the Father (Alma 7:10). No wonder she is called "blessed . . . among women" (Luke 1:28).

Mary's lineage is an important aspect of her mortal mission. As Elder James E. Talmage explained, "Since Jesus was to be born of Mary, yet was not begotten by Joseph, . . . the blood of David's posterity was given to the body of Jesus through Mary alone" (86). She descended from the tribe of Judah through the royal lineage of David, thereby reinforcing the literalness of the apostle Paul's testimony:

"Jesus Christ our Lord, which was made of the seed of David according to the flesh" (Romans 1:3).

The biblical account notes Mary's willingness to submit to the Father even though she was perplexed at Gabriel's announcement: "Fear not, Mary: for thou hast found favour with God. And, behold, thou shalt conceive in thy womb, and bring forth . . . the Son of the Highest" (Luke 1:30–32). With the only explanation being that "the Holy Ghost shall come upon thee, and the power of the Highest shall overshadow thee," Mary responded with straightforward and unwavering faith: "Behold the handmaid of the Lord; be it unto me according to thy word" (Luke 1:35, 38). In our desire to understand more about this sacred event, it is prudent to remember President Harold B. Lee's caution: "If teachers were wise in speaking of [the birth of the Savior] which the Lord has said but very little, they would rest their discussion on this subject with merely the words which are recorded on this subject in Luke 1:34–35. . . .

"Remember that the being who was brought about by [Mary's] conception was a divine personage. We need not question [God's] method to accomplish His purposes" (14).

If ever a mother could have extolled the virtues of her perfect child, it was Mary. But instead, she "kept all these things, and pondered them in her heart" (Luke 2:19). Hers was not the mission to announce to the world that the Savior was born. Her wisdom in knowing how to keep sacred that which is sacred allowed the Son of God to grow quietly to adulthood while the neighbors merely asked, "Is not this Joseph's son?" (Luke 4:22).

As a faithful observer of the law of Moses, Mary followed the customs of Jewish women in her day. At least forty-one days after giving birth to her first son, she went to the temple in Jerusalem, where she became ceremonially clean in the prescribed purification rite, including offering "a pair of turtledoves, or two young pigeons" (Luke 2:22–24). In the years following the birth of Jesus, Mary bore four more boys and an unidentified number of girls by her husband, Joseph (Matthew 13:55–56; Mark 6:3). One of these sons by Joseph, "James the Lord's brother," eventually became a Christian leader in Jerusalem (Galatians 1:19). We Latter-day Saints concur with the scripturally declared doctrine that as a virgin, Mary gave birth to the Messiah, but we reject the

Roman Catholic traditions of her perpetual virginity and of her own immaculate conception.

The New Testament provides glimpses of Mary when the young Jesus is teaching at the temple (Luke 2:41–51), at the wedding feast when Jesus turns water into wine (John 2:2–5), at the Savior's crucifixion (John 19:25–26), and among the faithful disciples after his ascension (Acts 1:14). Through these brief sightings of mother and Son together, we sense the Lord's great compassion for the woman who gave him mortal life but also the reminder that, like all of us mortals, she can return to the Father only through the atonement of her Son (Luke 8:19–21).

SOURCES

Lee, Harold B. *The Teachings of Harold B. Lee.* Edited by Clyde J. Williams. Salt Lake City: Bookcraft, 1996.

Talmage, James E. *Jesus the Christ.* Salt Lake City: Deseret Book, 1973.

CFO

MATTER

In God's vast kingdom there are, so far as has been revealed, two types of matter: the coarser, natural elements which constitute the physical world discernible by the five natural senses; and the "more fine or pure" matter which "can only be discerned by purer eyes" (D&C 131:7). The latter constitutes spirit substance, which we cannot presently see with the natural eye. But we are promised that "when our bodies are purified we shall see that it is all matter" (D&C 131:8), for "all spirit is matter" (D&C 131:7).

Revealed truth teaches that matter, or the elements, "are eternal" (D&C 93:33). This stands in stark contrast to the notion of creation *ex nihilo* ("out of nothing") that dominated men's thinking for centuries and was still widespread in the nineteenth century. Now, however, "modern scientific theories of matter . . . maintain the permanence of matter. . . . It is significant that the teachings of the restored gospel on the eternal nature of physical matter, along with a parallel in the spiritual realm, embody these conservation principles" (*Encyclopedia,* 2:868). It should be remembered that the revelations on the eternal nature of matter came *before* the scientific views of our modern world became well established.

The implications of the eternal existence of matter are truly significant, for they have a bearing on the nature of our existence as children of God. The Prophet Joseph Smith said, "The spirit of man is not a created being; it existed from eternity, and will exist to eternity. Anything created cannot be eternal; and earth, water, etc., had their existence in an elementary state, from eternity" (3:387). Furthermore, in one of his last sermons, the Prophet taught, "Now, the word create . . . does not mean to create out of nothing; it means to organize; the same as a man would organize materials and build a ship. Hence we infer that God had materials to organize the world out of chaos—chaotic matter, which is element. . . . Element had an existence from the time [God] had. The pure principles of element are principles which can never be destroyed; they may be organized and re-organized, but not destroyed. They had no beginning and can have no end" (6:308–9).

Creation is never a completely original act, but rather an organizing of preexisting realities. But even more important is the realization that inherent in the true doctrine of matter is the doctrine of becoming like God. "For man is spirit. The elements are eternal, and spirit and element, inseparably connected, receive a fulness of joy; and when separated, man cannot receive a fulness of joy. The elements are the tabernacle of God; yea, man is the tabernacle of God, even temples; and whatsoever temple is defiled, God shall destroy that temple" (D&C 93:33–35).

At the second coming of Jesus Christ, the physical matter of the earth will be changed. The elements will melt with fervent heat, and all things shall be made new (2 Peter 3:10–12; 3 Nephi 26:3; D&C 101:25). And when the earth receives its celestial glory another great change will affect the matter that constitutes this planet (D&C 77:1–2; 88:16–32; 130:9; Revelation 4:6).

SOURCES

Encyclopedia of Mormonism. Edited by Daniel H. Ludlow. 4 vols. New York: Macmillan, 1992.

Smith, Joseph. *History of The Church of Jesus Christ of Latter-day Saints.* Edited by B. H. Roberts. 7 vols. 2d ed. rev. Salt Lake City: The Church of Jesus Christ of Latter-day Saints, 1932–51.

ACS

MEDIATOR

A mediator is an intercessor, a conciliator, one who intercedes on behalf of another, who pleads for another, who reconciles persons or parties who are at odds with or estranged from each other, who intervenes to produce an agreement. In scripture, two principal mediators are mentioned who devoted their lives to reconciling the children of God with their God. The first, chronologically speaking, was a type and shadow of the second. The first interceded on behalf of the children of Israel. The second interceded on behalf of all humankind. The first was the mediator of a lesser law and covenant. The second was the Mediator of an eternal law and covenant. The first was mortal and temporary. The second was God, infinite and eternal. The first was Moses. The second was Jesus Christ.

Of these two mediators Paul wrote: "Wherefore then, the law was added because of transgressions, till the seed should come to whom the promise was made in the law given to Moses, who was ordained by the hand of angels to be a mediator of this first covenant (the law). Now this mediator was not a mediator of the new covenant; but there is one mediator of the new covenant, who is Christ, as it is written in the law concerning the promises made to Abraham and his seed. Now Christ is the mediator of life; for this is the promise which God made unto Abraham" (JST, Galatians 3:19–20).

The Old Testament contains illustrations of Moses interceding on behalf of the children of Israel. At the time of the golden calf episode, Moses told the people, "Ye have sinned a great sin: and now I will go up unto the Lord; peradventure I shall make an atonement for your sin" (Exodus 32:30). Indeed, Moses pled with God for forgiveness on behalf of the people, saying, "Yet now, if thou wilt forgive their sin—; and if not, blot me, I pray thee, out of thy book" (Exodus 32:32). Like the Mediator to come, Moses was willing to give his life for the people. In another instance, when Israel murmured against Moses, Aaron, and ultimately the Lord, the Lord tested Moses' integrity by indicating that he was ready to smite and disinherit Israel and "make of [Moses] a greater nation and mightier than they." The prophet again interceded on behalf of Israel and pled for the Lord to remember his own long-suffering, mercy, and forgiving nature. Israel was pardoned according to Moses's word and the Lord's mercy (Numbers 14:11–20).

These instances are powerful and real. But they pale in comparison to the mediation of Jesus Christ, the Holy Messiah, who came to earth to "make intercession for *all* the children of men" (2 Nephi 2:9; emphasis added), who was "the mediator of the new covenant, who wrought out this perfect atonement through the shedding of his own blood" (D&C 76:69). That is why the apostle Paul referred to Christ as the "one mediator between God and men" (1 Timothy 2:5). The old law and covenant administered under Moses "made nothing perfect, but was only the bringing in of a better hope" (JST, Hebrews 7:19). By the new covenant, or gospel of Jesus Christ, we are "made perfect" (D&C 76:69). Father Lehi observed that every individual is "free to choose liberty and eternal life, through the great Mediator of all men." He earnestly encouraged his sons to "look to the great Mediator, and hearken unto his great commandments; and be faithful unto his words, and choose eternal life" (2 Nephi 2:27–28).

It is only through the atonement of Jesus Christ that human beings can inherit eternal life. The Atonement is the very essence, the core, of Jesus' mediation and intercession, which he taught to the Prophet Joseph Smith: "Listen to him who is the advocate with the Father, who is pleading your cause before him—saying: Father, behold the sufferings and death of him who did no sin, in whom thou wast well pleased; behold the blood of thy Son which was shed, the blood of him whom thou gavest that thyself might be glorified; wherefore, Father, spare these my brethren that believe on my name, that they may come unto me and have everlasting life" (D&C 45:3–5).

Christ's mediation is also at the heart of the doctrine of justification. If left on their own, all people are lost. Only through the mediation of Jesus Christ can a person be brought back into a right relationship with God the Father. No one in mortality has any power to reconcile himself or herself to God the Father; such reconciliation comes only through the intercession of Jesus Christ. Paul was emphatic with the Galatian Saints when he said that one cannot be justified by the works of the law but only through Jesus Christ, who gave himself for each person (Galatians 2:16, 20). We are saved only by the grace, merits, and mercy of Christ—above and beyond all we can do (2 Nephi 25:23). As the Savior said, no one comes unto the Father except through him (John 14:6). Thus, the mediation of Christ is among the most important of subjects to be studied and appreciated by all who seek eternal life.

ACS

MELCHIZEDEK

The ancient patriarch Melchizedek was one of the greatest high priests who has ever lived. Alma testifies that of all of them, "none were greater" than Melchizedek (Alma 13:19). And "because Melchizedek was such a great high priest," the high priesthood to which he had been ordained—the "Holy Priesthood, after the Order of the Son of God"—was renamed in his honor in order to avoid the too frequent repetition of the name of Deity (D&C 107:2–4).

Melchizedek was a prototype, a type, a shadow of the Lord Jesus Christ to come. As Paul confirmed, "For that after the similitude of Melchisedec there ariseth another priest, who is made, not after the law of a carnal commandment, but after the power of an endless life" (Hebrews 7:15–16). Thus, Melchizedek possessed some of the very same name-titles Christ possessed, including "Prince of peace," "King of peace," and "king of heaven . . . or, in other words, the King of peace" (JST, Genesis 14:33, 36; Alma 13:18). Melchizedek's name (Hebrew, *malki-zedek*) means "king of righteousness," which likewise points to the Savior. Similarly, all those who are ordained to the high priesthood, like Melchizedek, are given the promise that they also can be "made like unto the Son of God, abiding a priest continually" (JST, Hebrews 7:3). Little wonder then that some errant ancient traditions confused Melchizedek with Jesus Christ, leaving people to believe them to be the same person (Robinson, 399–403).

Melchizedek served the people of his day as king over the land of Salem. But the people "had waxed strong in iniquity and abomination; yea, they had all gone astray" (Alma 13:17). Nevertheless, Melchizedek exercised mighty faith, preached repentance unto his people, and taught the ordinances that pointed to the Son of God (Alma 13:16–18). "And behold, they did repent; and Melchizedek did establish peace in the land in his days; therefore he was called the prince of peace, for he was the king of Salem; and he did reign under his father" (Alma 13:18). Joseph Smith's inspired translation of the Bible confirms that Melchizedek's people attained such a state of righteousness that they, like Enoch's Zion, "were translated and taken up into heaven. . . . And his people wrought righteousness, and obtained heaven, and sought for the city of Enoch which God had before taken" (JST, Genesis 14:32–34).

The Jewish historian Josephus wrote that Melchizedek was not only a powerful man among the people living in the land of Canaan but also "the Righteous King, for such he really was; on which account he was [there] the first priest of God, and first built a temple [there], and called the city Jerusalem, which was formerly called Salem" (6.10.1). In this regard, Elder Royden G. Derrick said, "We may assume that Melchizedek, as a holder of the Melchizedek Priesthood and builder of a temple, received his temple blessings—as one might also infer from reading Abraham 1:2–4" (26).

Obviously, Melchizedek was the Lord's presiding authority in the days of Abraham, for Abraham received the high priesthood from Melchizedek (D&C 84:14). Abraham himself tells us: "And, finding there was greater happiness and peace and rest for me, I sought for the blessings of the fathers, and the right whereunto I should be ordained to administer the same; having been myself a follower of righteousness, desiring also to be one who possessed great knowledge, and to be a greater follower of righteousness, and to possess a greater knowledge, and to be a father of many nations, a prince of peace, and desiring to receive instructions, and to keep the commandments of God, I became a rightful heir, a High Priest, holding the right belonging to the fathers. It was conferred upon me from the fathers" (Abraham 1:2–3). Certainly his quest for "righteousness," his desire to become "a prince of peace," led him to the one who was the "king of righteousness" and the "prince of peace" in his era.

It was Melchizedek to whom Abraham paid his tithes and offerings. "And Melchizedek king of Salem brought forth bread and wine: and he was the priest of the most high God. And he blessed him, and said, Blessed be Abram of the most high God, possessor of heaven and earth: and blessed be the most high God, which hath delivered thine enemies into thy hand. And he gave him tithes of all" (Genesis 14:18–20). Harking back to Josephus' comment, Sidney B. Sperry wrote of Abraham's tithes: "Such income would be used in part for erecting houses of worship and for building or maintaining a temple [of the

Lord] 'which my people are always commanded to build unto my holy name' [D&C 124:39]. . . . Abraham was acquainted with the sacred endowment and hence a temple or its equivalent in which they would be administered" (68).

Melchizedek is highly revered among the Jews. The rabbis taught that he acted as a great priest and handed down robes worn by Adam to Abram (Midrash). In two documents among the Dead Sea Scrolls, Melchizedek is presented as an angelic personage "who raises up God's holy ones for deeds of judgment" and "seems to officiate as the heavenly high priest, just as Jesus does in Hebrews" (VanderKam, 72–73).

Some authorities and writers believe that Melchizedek was the same person known as Shem, son of Noah (Genesis 5:29–32; 6:10; 7:13; 8:16; Moses 8:12; "Ancient Ruins," 746). Elder John A. Widtsoe believed this to be possible chronologically but questioned the notion because of the language of the Doctrine and Covenants: "Abraham received the priesthood from Melchizedek, who received it *through the lineage of his fathers, even till Noah*" (D&C 84:14; emphasis added). The first to articulate that Melchizedek was Shem may have been the great rabbinic commentator Rashi (d. 1105). Latter-day revelation refers to Shem as "the great high priest" (D&C 138:41), but no scriptural text explicitly connects Melchizedek and Shem. Be that as it may, several sources, historical and scriptural, ancient and modern, help Latter-day Saints to know more about the man Melchizedek, his greatness and honored status, than any other group of people today.

SOURCES

"Ancient Ruins." *Times and Seasons* 5, no. 23 (15 Dec. 1844): 744–48.

Derrick, Royden G. *Temples in the Last Days.* Salt Lake City: Bookcraft, 1988.

Josephus, Flavius. *The Wars of the Jews.* In *Josephus: Complete Works.* Translated by William Whiston. Grand Rapids, Mich.: Kregel Publications, 1960.

Midrash. Numbers Rabbah 4.8.

Robinson, James M., ed. *The Nag Hammadi Library in English.* San Francisco: Harper & Row, 1978.

Sperry, Sidney B. "Ancient Temples and Their Functions." *Ensign,* Jan. 1972, 67–72.

VanderKam, James. *The Dead Sea Scrolls.* Washington, D.C.: Biblical Archaeology Society, 2007.

ACS

MELCHIZEDEK PRIESTHOOD

As revealed to the Prophet Joseph Smith, the higher or Melchizedek Priesthood comprehends or encompasses the Aaronic or Levitical Priesthood (4:207) and "holds the right of presidency, and has power and authority over all the offices in the church in all ages of the world" (D&C 107:8). Thus, the Melchizedek Priesthood administers "the keys of all the spiritual blessings of the church" and "the mysteries of the kingdom of heaven" (D&C 107:18–19).

Like God himself, the Melchizedek Priesthood, which is his power, is eternal. The Prophet said, "The Priesthood is an everlasting principle, and existed with God from eternity, and will to eternity" (3:386). The Melchizedek Priesthood was instituted "prior to 'the foundation of this earth'" and "is the channel through which the Almighty commenced revealing His glory at the beginning of the creation of this earth, and through which He has continued to reveal Himself . . . and through which He will make known His purposes to the end of time" (Smith, *History,* 4:207). Hence, this priesthood was referred to in New Testament times as "without descent, having neither beginning of days, nor end of life" (JST, Hebrews 7:3). President Joseph Fielding Smith taught that Melchizedek Priesthood power and organization existed among our Heavenly Father's children before anyone came to this earth as mortal beings: "With regard to the holding of the priesthood in the preexistence, I will say that there was an organization there just as well as an organization here, and men there held authority. Men chosen to positions of trust in the spirit world held the priesthood" (84). In the Book of Mormon, Alma declared that all those ordained to the Melchizedek Priesthood in mortality were foreordained to hold that priesthood in their premortal existence (Alma 13:3–7).

The Melchizedek Priesthood and its highest ordinances were first revealed to Adam in the Garden of Eden ("A Facsimile from the Book of Abraham, No. 2," Explanation 3). Before the time of the patriarch Melchizedek, this higher priesthood was called "the Holy Priesthood, after the Order of the Son of God" (D&C 107:2). But out of respect or reverence for the name of Deity, its name was changed to the Melchizedek Priesthood on account of the greatness of the patriarch (D&C 107:4). When worthy men are ordained to this priesthood, they both emulate the Lord Jesus Christ and possess the power to come as he is: "And all those who are ordained unto this priesthood are made like unto the Son of God, abiding a priest continually" (JST, Hebrews 7:3). In fact, the Melchizedek Priesthood is the power by which men and women also may become like our Father in Heaven, heirs of his kingdom and joint-heirs with Jesus Christ, kings and priests, queens and priestesses, of the Most High God, possessing every blessing the Father and the Son possess (D&C 84:33–38; Romans 8:17; Revelation 1:5–6; Smith, *History,* 5:424, 554–55).

The Melchizedek Priesthood and its keys were held anciently by the chief apostles, Peter, James, and John (Smith, *History,* 3:387). After centuries of apostasy, these apostles restored to the Prophet Joseph Smith and Oliver Cowdery the Melchizedek Priesthood and the keys to direct its use. Though the exact date is unknown, this event probably occurred sometime shortly after the restoration of the Aaronic Priesthood on 15 May 1829 by John the Baptist, who said he acted under the direction of the chief apostles and that the restoration of the Melchizedek Priesthood was to follow "in due time" (Joseph Smith–History 1:72). That this promised restoration had taken place by August 1830 was made clear by the Lord himself when he spoke to the Prophet about "Peter, and James, and John, whom I have sent unto you, by whom I have ordained you and confirmed you to be apostles" (D&C 27:12). The best historical analysis indicates that "the restoration of the Melchizedek Priesthood and apostleship apparently occurred between 15 May 1829 and 1 June 1829, and certainly before the organization of the Church on 6 April 1830" (Porter, 6–7).

SOURCES

Porter, Larry C. "The Restoration of the Priesthood." *Religious Studies Center Newsletter* 9, no. 3 (May 1995), 1–12.

Smith, Joseph. *History of The Church of Jesus Christ of Latter-day Saints.* Edited by B. H. Roberts. 7 vols. 2d ed. rev. Salt Lake City: The Church of Jesus Christ of Latter-day Saints, 1932–51.

Smith, Joseph Fielding. In Conference Report, Oct. 1966, 83–84.

ACS

MERCY

Mercy is compassion, kindness, empathy, forgiveness. While grace might be described as blessings and favor from God that we do not necessarily deserve, mercy represents not receiving what we do deserve because of the patience and love of the Master. It is an attribute of Deity. Christ's mercy to man comes by reason of his infinite atoning sacrifice and perfect love. In the ancient tabernacle established by Moses, and subsequently in Solomon's temple, the ark of the covenant sat in the most sacred part of the sanctuary: the Holy of Holies. It represented the presence of God and was known as "the mercy seat" (Exodus 25:17–22).

Numerous scriptural passages speak of the mercy that the Father and the Son have for man. "The Lord thy God is a merciful God," declared Moses (Deuteronomy 4:31). Isaiah testified of the Messiah's "everlasting kindness," which manifests itself by his merciful Atonement (Isaiah 54:8). The apostle Paul testified that God is the "Father of mercies" (2 Corinthians 1:3) and that through Christ's redemptive love, both Jew and Gentile can "glorify God for his mercy" (Romans 15:9). God is, as Paul declared, "rich in mercy" (Ephesians 2:4), and it is by that divine mercy that Christ offers salvation to us (Titus 3:5). Likewise, the apostles James and Peter spoke of God as "full of mercy" (James 3:17; see also 5:11; 1 Peter 1:3). The Book of Mormon and modern revelation also testify of the Savior's "infinite mercy" (Mosiah 28:4; see also 2 Nephi 4:26; 9:53; Alma 9:26; 32:22; 42:15; D&C 84:102). God's kindness, compassion, and love are also characterized in the scriptural term "tender mercies," which, as Nephi taught in the Book of Mormon, "are over all" (1 Nephi 1:20). All humankind, universally and unconditionally, are beneficiaries of God's "tender mercies" in a general sense. The term *mercy*, however, is most often used in the scriptures to speak of the redemption and remission of sins that God extends to those "who [trust] in the Lord" (Psalm 32:10; Mosiah 29:20), are meek (D&C 97:2), fear God and obey him (Luke 1:50), exercise "faith unto repentance" (Alma 34:17), keep their covenants, and obey the commandments (D&C 54:6). The Prophet Joseph Smith taught: "Long-suffering, patience, and mercy have ever characterized the dealings of our heavenly Father towards the humble and penitent" (4:163). Thus, forgiveness of sins on earth and ultimate salvation in the next life come by reason of Christ's mercy but are accessed "on conditions of repentance" (Alma 42:13).

The Savior taught his disciples to be merciful—forgiving, kind, and compassionate—to others just as God is merciful toward us

(Matthew 5:7; 6:14–15; 18:21–35; Alma 41:14; D&C 64:7–10; 88:40). Receiving God's merciful pardon of our sins depends to a large degree on the mercy we extend to others and the extent to which our hearts and lives are like his. "Ever keep in exercise the principle of mercy," the Prophet Joseph Smith declared, "and be ready to forgive our brother on the first intimations of repentance, and asking forgiveness; and should we even forgive our brother, or even our enemy, before he repent or ask forgiveness, our heavenly Father would be equally as merciful unto us" (3:383).

SOURCE

Smith, Joseph. *History of The Church of Jesus Christ of Latter-day Saints.* Edited by B. H. Roberts. 7 vols. 2d ed. rev. Salt Lake City: The Church of Jesus Christ of Latter-day Saints, 1932–51.

BLT

MESSIAH

Messiah is the anglicized form of the Aramaic word *mashikha* or the Hebrew *mashiakh,* meaning "anointed one." The Greek equivalent is *christos* or Christ. Jesus of Nazareth is the Messiah—the Anointed One of God the Father, commissioned and empowered to bring about all the terms and conditions of the Father's plan (Acts 4:23–30). The apostle Peter testified that "God anointed Jesus of Nazareth" (Acts 10:38).

The word *mashiakh* occurs thirty-nine times in the Hebrew text of the Old Testament. It primarily designates the political king of Israel or Judah (*Interpreter's,* 3:360), though it is used once for a non-Israelite king, Cyrus of Persia, who restored the Jewish nation to its homeland and supported the rebuilding of the temple (Isaiah 45:1). Most of these occurrences point to an intimate connection between Jehovah and the king, as the following samples demonstrate: "the Lord's anointed" (used of Saul in 1 Samuel 24:6, 10; 26:9, 11, 16, 23; 2 Samuel 1:14, 16; used of David in 2 Samuel 19:21; and used of Zedekiah in Lamentations 4:20), "mine anointed" (used of David in 1 Samuel 2:35; Psalm 132:17), and "anointed of the God of Jacob" (used of David in 2 Samuel 23:1). Even the non-Israelite Cyrus is referred to as "his [the Lord's] anointed" (Isaiah 45:1).

These usages emphasize the intended symbolic nature of

anointing. They foreshadowed the coming of Jesus, *the* Anointed One, who is Lord, God, and King of the universe (Moses 7:53; McConkie, "Purifying," 11). Unfortunately, the important symbolic and typological aspect of anointing the kings of Israel and Judah seems to have been mostly lost or misunderstood by the time of the first century in Roman Judea.

In the general Jewish mind-set of Jesus' day, the Messiah was to be in the mold of King David. He was "a temporal deliverer who would throw off the yoke of Roman bondage and make Israel free again. They sought a ruler who would restore that glory and worldwide influence and prestige which was enjoyed when [David] sat on Israel's throne. The true concepts of deliverance from spiritual darkness, of being freed from the bondage of sin, of a kingdom which is not of this world—all made possible through an infinite and eternal atonement—all this was lost" among many Jews until Jesus taught powerfully of his messianic role (McConkie, *Promised,* 188).

In the New Testament, the Greek form of the Aramaic word for Messiah, *messias,* is used in John 1:41 and 4:25. Otherwise, the Greek *christos* is used. The Book of Mormon uses the word *Messiah* more than two dozen times, helping us to appreciate the rich and ancient meaning of the term and how Jesus of Nazareth is the fulfillment of messianic prophecies. Nephi prophesies the rejection of the Messiah by the Jews and testifies that there is only one Messiah (2 Nephi 25:18). Three revelations of the Doctrine and Covenants use *Messiah* (D&C 13:1; 19:27; 109:67).

SOURCES

McConkie, Bruce R. *The Promised Messiah: The First Coming of Christ.* Salt Lake City: Deseret Book, 1978.

———. "The Purifying Power of Gethsemane." *Ensign,* May 1985, 9–11.

The Interpreter's Dictionary of the Bible: An Illustrated Encyclopedia. Edited by George Arthur Buttrick. 5 vols. Nashville, Tenn.: Abingdon Press, 1962.

ACS

MILLENNIUM

The thousand-year Millennium begins when Jesus Christ, the King of kings and Lord of lords, returns to earth in power and glory. When the Lord of Hosts—literally, the Lord of armies—returns in glory, every corruptible thing will be destroyed (D&C 133:41, 49).

Those who are of a celestial or a terrestrial state will abide the day; all else will be cleansed from the surface of the earth. Those who lie and cheat and steal, those who revel in immorality and pervert the ways of righteousness, those who mock and point the finger of scorn at the Saints of the Most High will be burned at his coming, and their spirits will take up residence in the spirit world, there to await the last resurrection at the end of a thousand years. The Second Coming in glory is "the end of the world," meaning the end of the worldly, the destruction of the wicked (Joseph Smith–Matthew 1:4).

The Millennium does not begin when Christ comes to Adamondi-Ahman, when he appears at his temple in Independence, Missouri, or when he stands upon the Mount of Olives in the midst of Armageddon. The Millennium will not come because men and women on earth have become noble and good, because Christian charity has spread across the globe, or because goodwill has become the order of the day. The Millennium will not come because technological advancements and medical miracles have extended human life or because peace treaties among warring nations have soothed injured feelings and eased political tensions. The Millennium will be brought in by power, by the power of him who is Lord and Master and God. Satan will be bound by power, and the glory of the Millennium will be maintained by the righteousness of those who are permitted to live on earth (1 Nephi 22:15, 26).

At the beginning of the Millennium, the earth and all things upon it will be quickened, made alive, and transfigured—lifted spiritually to a higher plane for a season. The earth will be transformed from a telestial to a terrestrial glory, to that paradisiacal condition of which the scriptures and the prophets speak, that glorious condition that prevailed in Eden before the Fall (Articles of Faith 1:10). There will indeed be a new heaven and a new earth (Isaiah 65:17; Revelation 21:1).

When "the face of the Lord shall be unveiled," then in that day "the saints that are upon the earth, who are alive, shall be quickened and be caught up to meet him" (D&C 88:95–96). That quickening would seem to entail the accentuation of man's spiritual nature and the subduing of his fallen nature. Elder Orson Pratt explained that "all the inhabitants who are spared from this fire—those who are not proud, and who do not do wickedly, will be cleansed more fully and filled with the glory of God. A partial change will be wrought upon them"—a type of translation—"not a change to immortality, like that which all the Saints will undergo when they are changed in the twinkling of an eye, from mortality to immortality; but so great will be the change then wrought that the children who are born into the world will grow up without sin unto salvation [see D&C 45:48]. Why will this be so? Because *that fallen nature, introduced by the fall, and transferred from parents to children, from generation to generation, will be, in a measure, eradicated by this change*" (16:319; emphasis added).

The first resurrection began with the resurrection of Christ in the meridian of time. All of the prophets and those who gave heed to the words of the prophets, from the days of Adam to Christ—and, we would presume, all those who never had an opportunity to receive the gospel but would have received it had they been given the privilege (D&C 137:7–9)—came forth from the grave some time after the Savior rose to immortal glory (Mosiah 15:21–25; Alma 40:20). We have no indication that there has been a wholesale resurrection of Saints since the resurrection of the Savior.

"There are some who feel," President Ezra Taft Benson pointed out, "that the resurrection is going on continually and has been since that time. That is not scripturally true, but we do know that it is possible for our Father to call from the graves those whom He needs to perform special missions and special service. For example, we know of at least three [Peter, James, and Moroni] who have been called up since the resurrection of the Master and since that first mass resurrection when the graves were opened and many of the Saints arose" (18).

When the Master returns in glory to take charge of affairs on this earth, with him will come a host of the righteous dead. The First Resurrection will thereby resume. Those who died true to the faith, those who were valiant in the testimony of Jesus, and those who kept the celestial law will return to earth with resurrected, immortal bodies (D&C 88:97–98). Or according to the testimony of the apostle Paul, "they who are alive"—meaning, presumably, physically alive when the Lord comes—"shall be caught up together into the clouds with them who remain [the heavenly hosts], to meet the Lord in the air; and so shall we be ever with the Lord" (JST, 1 Thessalonians 4:17). That is the First Resurrection, or as we have come to call it, the morning of the First Resurrection, the resurrection of the celestial.

Although men and women who are alive at the time of Christ's second coming will be changed and quickened, they will yet continue to live as mortals. That is, for them death and immortality lie ahead. The mortal Saints will live to "the age of man" (D&C 63:50) during the Millennium, an age that Isaiah explained to be one hundred years (Isaiah 65:20). At that point they will pass from mortality through death into resurrected immortality instantly, "in the twinkling of an eye" (D&C 43:32; 63:51; 1 Corinthians 15:52; 3 Nephi 28:8). For these there will be no time for the body in the grave, no sojourn in the postmortal world of spirits, for they will be received into glory immediately after their death: "Wherefore, children shall grow up until they become old; old men shall die; but they shall not sleep in the dust, but they shall be changed in the twinkling of an eye" (D&C 63:51).

Not all who inhabit the earth during the beginning of the Millennium will be of one faith and one baptism. In that early hour of millennial splendor, not all will be converted to The Church of Jesus Christ of Latter-day Saints. President Brigham Young stated: "If the Latter-day Saints think, when the kingdom of God is established on the earth, that all the inhabitants of the earth will join the church called Latter-day Saints, they are egregiously mistaken. I presume there will be as many sects and parties then as now" (11:275.) On another occasion President Young said: "When Jesus comes to rule and reign King of Nations as he now does King of Saints, the veil of the covering will be taken from all nations, that *all flesh may see his glory together, but that will not make them all Saints.* Seeing the Lord does not make a man a Saint, seeing an Angel does not make a man a Saint by any means." President Young added that "kings and potentates of the nations will come up to Zion to inquire after the ways of the Lord, and to seek out the great knowledge, wisdom, and understanding manifested through the Saints of the Most High. They will inform the people of God that they belong to such and such a Church, and do not wish to change their religion" (2:316; emphasis added). In short, "in the millennium men will have the privilege of being Presbyterians, Methodists or Infidels, but they will not have the privilege of treating the name and character of Deity as they have done heretofore. No, but every knee shall bow and every tongue confess to the glory of God the Father that Jesus is the Christ" (12:274).

And yet the testimony of the scriptures and the prophets is consistent that as the power of God's Spirit continues to spread, eventually "the earth shall be full of the knowledge of the Lord, as the waters cover the sea" (Isaiah 11:9; see also Habakkuk 2:14). Truly "in that day when the Lord shall come, he shall reveal all things—things which have passed, and hidden things which no man knew, things of the earth, by which it was made, and the purpose and the end thereof—things most precious, things that are above, and things that are beneath, things that are in the earth, and upon the earth, and in heaven" (D&C 101:32–34). President Joseph Fielding Smith observed: "The gospel will be taught far more intensely and with greater power during the millennium, *until all the inhabitants of the earth shall embrace it. . . .* Through the revelations given to the prophets, we learn that during the reign of Jesus Christ for a thousand years *eventually all people will embrace the truth*" (3:64).

We can only imagine such an existence: a life without physical pain, premature death, an existence without the sorrow that accompanies sin and waywardness, without the disappointment associated with dishonesty and greed (Isaiah 11:6–9; 65:25). "In that day the enmity of man, and the enmity of beasts, yea, the enmity of all flesh"—the animosity, natural tension, and unrest that came as a result of the Fall—"shall cease from before my face" (D&C 101:26). And so it is that "violence shall no more be heard in thy land, wasting nor destruction within thy borders; but thou shalt call thy walls Salvation, and thy gates Praise" (Isaiah 60:18). It follows that because millions upon millions of souls will join themselves to the Saints in the Millennium, the work of temples will be among the most significant labors performed. President Wilford Woodruff taught that "this work of administering the ordinances of the house of God to the dead . . . will require the whole of the Millennium, with Jesus at the head of the resurrected dead to attend to it" (13:327).

The scriptures attest that the Lamb will make "unto our God kings and priests" from "every kindred, and tongue, and people, and nation" before the Lord Jesus comes in glory (Revelation 5:9–10). That implies that temples will dot the earth, that the fulness of priesthood blessings will be available to men and women everywhere, even before the ushering in of the Millennium. Such sacred labor will be intensified during the thousand-year era of peace and righteousness, for *"to accomplish this work there will have to be not only one temple but thousands of them,* and thousands and tens of thousands of men and women will go into those temples and officiate for people who have lived as far back as the Lord shall reveal" (Young, 3:372; emphasis added).

Our Lord and God will govern his people from two world capitals, "for out of Zion shall go forth the law, and the word of the Lord from Jerusalem" (Isaiah 2:3). "And he shall utter his voice out of Zion"—meaning, Independence, Missouri—"and he shall speak from Jerusalem, and his voice shall be heard among all people; and it shall be a voice as the voice of many waters, and as the voice of a great thunder, which shall break down the mountains, and the valleys shall not be found" (D&C 133:21–22). In that day the latter-day David, even Jesus Christ, the true son of David, will unite Ephraim and Judah and will preside over all Israel, from one end of the earth to the other. Thus will be fulfilled the divine decree: "Be subject to the powers that be, *until he reigns whose right it is to reign, and subdues all enemies under his feet"* (D&C 58:22; emphasis added). Christ and the resurrected Saints will dwell on earth—not permanently but periodically, "when they please, or when it is necessary to govern it" (Smith, *History,* 5:212).

At the end of the thousand years, we come to that time known as "the end of the earth" (D&C 88:101; Joseph Smith–Matthew 1:55), the final cleansing and celestialization of the planet. The earth will then be a fit abode for the true and faithful, "that bodies who are of the celestial kingdom may possess it forever and ever; for, for this intent was it made and created, and for this intent are they sanctified" (D&C 88:20). Unlike so many in the religious world, Latter-day Saints anticipate celestial life on a material world. Elder Orson Pratt eloquently and powerfully made this point:

"A Saint who is one in deed and in truth, does not look for an immaterial heaven, but he expects a heaven with lands, houses, cities, vegetation, rivers, and animals; with thrones, temples, palaces, kings, princes, priests, and angels; with food, raiment, musical instruments, etc., all of which are material. Indeed, *the Saints' heaven is a redeemed, glorified, celestial, material creation, inhabited by glorified material beings, male and female, organized into families,* embracing all the relationships of husbands and wives, parents and children, where sorrow, crying, pain, and death will be known no more. Or to speak still more definitely, *this earth, when glorified, is the Saints' eternal heaven. On it they expect to live, with body, parts, and holy passions; on it they expect to move and have their being;* to eat, drink, converse, worship, sing, play on musical instruments, engage in joyful, innocent, social amusements, visit neighboring towns and neighboring worlds; *indeed, matter and its qualities and properties are the only beings or things with which they expect to associate.* . . . Materiality is indelibly stamped upon the very heaven of heavens, upon all the eternal creations; it is the very essence of all existence" (in Lundwall, 62–63; emphasis added).

In the not-too-distant future, goodness and honesty and integrity will be the order of the day; morality and decency will characterize men and women across the globe. In that sense we look forward to the great millennial day. Though there are many tight places through which the Saints will be required to pass, though trials and difficulties will abound on every side, though disease and death and despair will be rampant prior to the Lord's coming in glory, yet we glory in the fact that one day the Lord of Hosts will wrest control of things, and this earth will be his.

SOURCES

Benson, Ezra Taft. *The Teachings of Ezra Taft Benson.* Salt Lake City: Bookcraft, 1988.
Lundwall, N. B. *Masterful Discourses of Orson Pratt.* Salt Lake City: Bookcraft, 1962.
Pratt, Orson. *In Journal of Discourses.* 26 vols. London: Latter-day Saints' Book Depot, 1854–86.
Smith, Joseph. *History of The Church of Jesus Christ of Latter-day Saints.* Edited by B. H. Roberts. 7 vols. 2d ed. rev. Salt Lake City: The Church of Jesus Christ of Latter-day Saints, 1932–51.
Smith, Joseph Fielding. *Doctrines of Salvation.* Compiled by Bruce R. McConkie. 3 vols. Salt Lake City: Bookcraft, 1954–56.
Woodruff, Wilford. In *Journal of Discourses.* 26 vols. London: Latter-day Saints' Book Depot, 1854–86.
Young, Brigham. In *Journal of Discourses.* 26 vols. London: Latter-day Saints' Book Depot, 1854–86.

RLM

MIRACLES

Elder Dallin H. Oaks defined a miracle as "a beneficial event brought about through divine power that mortals do not understand and of themselves cannot duplicate" (6). A miracle is a manifestation of the supremacy of God's law and will and is therefore impossible to explain on the basis of currently understood physical laws. The power to work miracles is a gift of the Spirit (D&C 46:21). Miracles are a part of the gospel of Jesus Christ, for unto as many as receive Jesus Christ is given "power to do many miracles" (D&C 45:8). The gospel of Jesus Christ, indeed Christianity itself, is founded on the greatest miracle of all—the bodily resurrection of Jesus Christ. True and lasting miracles are done in the name of Christ (Mark 16:17). Disciples of the Lord in this dispensation are not to be constantly desiring miracles. The Lord commanded, "Require not miracles, except I shall command you" (D&C 24:13).

Faith is the foundation of miracles. "For if there be no faith among the children of men God can do no miracle among them" (Ether 12:12). During his mortal ministry even the Son of God "could . . . do no mighty work" where faith was lacking (Mark 6:5–6). To the Nephites the resurrected Lord confirmed that to the Jews he "could not show unto them so great miracles, because of their unbelief" (3 Nephi 19:35). Modern revelation affirms that miracles and signs do not create faith. Rather, signs and miraculous events follow those who possess faith. "Yea, signs come by faith, unto mighty works, for without faith no man pleaseth God" (D&C 63:11). The working of miracles is also contingent upon an individual's spiritual purity. As Mormon noted of Nephi the son of Nephi, "For behold, it was a just man who did . . . many miracles in the name of Jesus; and there was not any man who could do a miracle in the name of Jesus save he were cleansed every whit from his iniquity" (3 Nephi 8:1).

The performance of miracles constituted a major part of Jesus' mortal ministry, and we learn much about miracles by reviewing the nature and circumstances of the miracles he performed. Jesus' miracles tell much about his divine character. His miracles were almost always beneficial and were always done to further God's plan and purposes. He never performed miracles for selfish reasons. On the one hand, he refused to turn stones to bread to gratify Satan (Matthew

4:3–4); on the other, he multiplied loaves and fishes to bless more than five thousand (John 6:5–14). On the one hand, he refused to save himself from death (Matthew 26:53–54) or come down from the cross (Mark 15:29–32); on the other, he raised at least three persons from the dead—a young woman (Mark 5:41–42), a young man (Luke 7:14–15), and Lazarus (John 11:43–44). Many of the miracles of Jesus do not seem to have been planned or premeditated, with notable exceptions, such as the raising of Lazarus (John 11:1–7, 21–26).

Jesus used a variety of methods in performing his miracles, especially miracles of healing. The Gospels record no instance of his using medicines or juices, but he did use clay made from spittle (Mark 7:33; 8:23; John 9:6). Jesus' use of oil is not mentioned, though his disciples' use of it is noted (Mark 6:13; James 5:14–15). Jesus sometimes touched those he healed (Matthew 8:1–4, 15; 9:29; 20:34; Mark 7:33; Luke 22:51). But sometimes he performed a miracle only by uttering "the word" (Matthew 8:8). On one occasion Jesus healed someone though he was far away and no physical contact was possible (Matthew 8:5–13).

Most of Jesus' miracles grew out of his compassion and love for humankind (Matthew 14:14–21; 15:29–38). But he also performed miracles to teach his disciples that he was the master of the elements (Mark 4:35–41). At least three times he performed miracles involving live fish (Matthew 17:24–27; Luke 5:1–11; John 21:1–14). He demonstrated that he had power over evil spirits (Mark 1:23–27; 9:17–27) and the ability to read men's innermost thoughts (Matthew 12:25; Luke 5:22; 6:8; 9:47; 11:17). On occasion he performed miracles to expose the narrow, self-righteous, self-centered views of Jewish leaders (Mark 3:1–6; Luke 13:10–17; 14:1–6). At least once Jesus used his power to destroy life—the fig tree—but again, it was done to teach profound lessons about faith, the condition of the Jewish nation, hypocrisy, and his absolute control over life and death (Matthew 21:18–22). Jesus' miracles demonstrate his ability and desire to heal the soul as well as the body (Mark 2:1–12). In all ways his miracles show disciples how to minister (Matthews, 2:11–12).

Miracles are one of the evidences of the Lord's Church, his work, and the identity of his true followers (Mark 16:14–20; Mormon 9:20–25). Miracles are very much a part of the Lord's kingdom in the latter days, showing that his power has not diminished in our time (D&C 35:8–9). "God has not ceased to be a God of miracles" (Mormon 9:15). Even the very creations that surround us are miracles (Mormon 9:17). If miracles have ceased or have ceased to be recognized, it is because faith has ceased and men and women have dwindled in unbelief and departed from the right way (Mormon 9:20). The rejection of miracles in the latter days was prophesied. The prophet Nephi foretold of those who would "put down the power and miracles of God" (2 Nephi 26:20). He prophesied that churches would be built up and teach that if someone should say, "There is a miracle wrought by the hand of the Lord, believe it not; for this day he is not a God of miracles" (2 Nephi 28:6).

As currently understood, miracles are wrought by two powers: the power of the priesthood through faith (James 5:14–15; D&C 42:43–48), and the power of faith without specifically calling upon the power of the priesthood. Elder Oaks noted that many of these kinds of miracles occur in the Church, "such as by the prayers of faithful women" (8). He also categorized miracles in a thoughtful way: macro-miracles (those that affect many people) and micro-miracles (those that affect few people). All miracles are subject to the Lord's will. "The priesthood of the Lord cannot be used to work a miracle contrary to the will of the Lord. We must also remember that even when a miracle is to occur, it will not occur on our desired schedule" (Oaks, 9). When the Lord directed his Saints that they should call for the elders of the Church to pray for and lay hands on the sick, he said, "And if they die they shall die unto me, and if they live they shall live unto me" (D&C 42:44).

In opposition to the truth, the devil possesses power to work miracles and attempts to deceive followers of the living God. The Lord warned that the adversary promotes false Christs and false prophets who are able to show great signs and wonders, just as their diabolical master is able to do, in order to lead away the elect (Matthew 7:15–23). Dramatic examples from scripture include Moses' encounter with Satan (Moses 1:12–22) and Joseph Smith's experience with the devil when he posed as an angel of light (D&C 128:20). But as both of these episodes demonstrate, the elect—those who hear the voice of the Lord "and harden not their hearts" (D&C 29:7)—have power over the adversary. In fact, Satan can have no power to deceive or tempt the Lord's people except as they allow him to (Smith, 4:358).

True miracles are those that have eternal significance. True miracles always point us to Christ, his Church, his apostles, and the ordinances of salvation performed by priesthood leaders (Mormon 9:18–26). This is a way the Lord's people can know if a miracle is from the divine source. All other miracles and miracle workers will fall by the wayside. Jesus said that in the end he will say to the deceivers and false miracle workers, "Depart from me, ye that work iniquity" (Matthew 7:23).

SOURCES

Matthews, Robert J. "The Miracles of Jesus." *Instructor,* May 1967, 211–13.
Oaks, Dallin H. "Miracles." *Ensign,* June 2001, 6–17.
Smith, Joseph. *History of The Church of Jesus Christ of Latter-day Saints.* Edited by B. H. Roberts. 7 vols. 2d ed. rev. Salt Lake City: The Church of Jesus Christ of Latter-day Saints, 1932–51.

ACS

MODESTY

From the beginning of man's creation, prophets have underscored the importance of dressing modestly to show respect and gratitude for our bodies, which God created, and to avoid feelings of superiority over others. Before Adam and Eve departed the Garden of Eden, the Lord clothed them in coats of skins, apparel that covered their nakedness and that is reminiscent of the Lamb of God, whose sacrifice would enable them to return to live with God (Moses 4:27; Genesis 3:21). The manner in which we choose to dress can likewise remind us of our need for the Savior's protection.

As much an attitude of humility as an outward show of decency, modesty is best described as "not [drawing] undue attention to yourself" (*True*, 106). For this reason we are often counseled in scripture to be "neat and comely" in our dress while avoiding visibly expensive or revealing apparel (Alma 1:27; 1 Timothy 2:9; D&C 42:40).

The principle of modesty is also reflected in respectful and uplifting language. Profaning the name of God, speaking with the intent to shock or offend, or indulging in irreverent expressions and behavior offend the Spirit and sow seeds of discord. Modesty is seeking after "anything virtuous, lovely, or of good report or praiseworthy" (Articles of Faith 1:13).

SOURCE

True to the Faith: A Gospel Reference. Salt Lake City: The Church of Jesus Christ of
Latter-day Saints, 2004.

CFO

MONOTHEISM

To be monotheistic is to hold to a belief in one God. From a Jewish perspective, that one God is Yahweh, or Jehovah. For Muslims it is Allah. For traditional, Trinitarian Christians, it is a God who is manifest in plurality and unity, a Trinity made up of three distinct persons in one being—Father, Son, and Holy Spirit of one essence or one substance.

Latter-day Saints are monotheistic. We are not deistic or polytheistic. Elder Bruce R. McConkie taught: "In the ultimate and final sense of the word, there is only one true and living God. He is the Father, the Almighty Elohim, the Supreme Being, the Creator and Ruler of the universe" (51). We believe in one God in that we believe in one Godhead, one divine presidency of the universe and in the supremacy of God the Father. The scriptures affirm that these three Gods, these three Beings, are one (2 Nephi 31:21; Alma 11:44; Mormon 7:7; D&C 20:28). How so? *Lectures on Faith* explains: "These three constitute the great, matchless, governing and supreme, power over all things; by whom all things were created and made that were created and made, and these three constitute the Godhead, and are one; the Father and the Son possessing the same mind, the same wisdom, glory, power, and fullness—filling all in all; the Son being filled with the fullness of the mind, glory, and power; . . . and all those who keep his commandments shall grow up from grace to grace, and become heirs of the heavenly kingdom, and joint heirs with Jesus Christ; possessing the same mind, being transformed into the same image or likeness" (60). The Father, Son, and Holy Ghost are infinitely more unified than they are separate.

SOURCES

Lectures on Faith. Salt Lake City: Deseret Book, 1985.

McConkie, Bruce R. *A New Witness for the Articles of Faith.* Salt Lake City: Deseret Book, 1985.

RLM

MORE SURE WORD OF PROPHECY

"The more sure word of prophecy means a man's knowing that he is sealed up unto eternal life, by revelation and the spirit of prophecy, through the power of the Holy Priesthood. It is impossible for a man to be saved in ignorance" (D&C 131:5–6). In other words, to receive the more sure word of prophecy is to receive the assurance that one's salvation is secure, that he or she will be exalted and will gain eternal life, that the tests of mortality have been successfully passed. One who receives this knowledge has made sure his calling and election to eternal life.

While wrestling with God for answers to vexing questions about how to deal with transgressors in the Church, Alma the Elder heard and recorded the following sweet assurance: "And blessed art thou because thou hast established a church among this people; and they shall be established, and they shall be my people. Yea, blessed is this people who are willing to bear my name; for in my name shall they be called; and they are mine. And because thou hast inquired of me concerning the transgressor, thou art blessed. Thou art my servant; and *I covenant with thee that thou shalt have eternal life*" (Mosiah 26:17–20; emphasis added). Similarly, the Lord spoke to Joseph Smith: "For I am the Lord thy God, and will be with thee even unto the end of the world, and through all eternity; for verily *I seal upon you your exaltation,* and prepare a throne for you in the kingdom of my Father, with Abraham your father. Behold, I have seen your sacrifices, and will forgive all your sins" (D&C 132:49–50; emphasis added).

The Prophet Joseph Smith declared, "I would exhort you to go on and continue to call upon God until you make your calling and election sure for yourselves, by obtaining this more sure word of prophecy, and wait patiently for the promise until you obtain it" (5:389). The more sure word of prophecy is therefore the highest form of revelation, the grandest manifestation of the Spirit unto men and women on earth (Romney, 43–45).

SOURCES

Romney, Marion G. "The Light of Christ." *Ensign,* May 1977, 43–45.

Smith, Joseph. *History of The Church of Jesus Christ of Latter-day Saints.* Edited by B. H. Roberts. 7 vols. 2d ed. rev. Salt Lake City: The Church of Jesus Christ of Latter-day Saints, 1932–51.

RLM

MORMON/MORMONISM

Like the word *Christian,* a name given to the followers of Jesus Christ by their enemies (Alma 46:13–14; 48:10; Acts 11:26), the word *Mormon* was used by critics of the early Latter-day Saints to identify the followers of Joseph Smith, who believed in and accepted the Book of Mormon as holy scripture. Since that time, however, the term has become a title, a badge of acknowledgment worn proudly by members of The Church of Jesus Christ of Latter-day Saints. Although members have been encouraged by their leaders to speak of the Church by its full title or as the Church of Jesus Christ and to refer to themselves as Latter-day Saints, we feel no shame or embarrassment in referring to the Mormon Tabernacle, the Mormon Tabernacle Choir, or the Mormon pioneers.

In that spirit, Mormonism is that system of revealed religion known also as the restored gospel, the fulness of the gospel, and the everlasting gospel. Mormonism refers to the doctrines, principles, precepts, beliefs, worship, covenants, ordinances, and way of life taught by the Savior and revealed and expanded upon by modern prophets and apostles. Mormonism is open to truth from every quarter. As the Prophet Joseph Smith explained: "In reality and essence we do not differ so far in our religious views [from other faith traditions], but that we could all drink into one principle of love. One of the grand fundamental principles of 'Mormonism' is to receive truth, let it come from whence it may" (5:499). Similarly, the Prophet declared, "Friendship is one of the grand fundamental principles of 'Mormonism'; [it is designed] to revolutionize and civilize the world, and cause wars and contentions to cease and men to become friends and brothers" (5:517).

Note the breadth of Brother Joseph's perspective: "Truth is 'Mormonism.' God is the author of it. He is our shield. It is by Him we received our birth. It was by His voice that we were called to a dispensation of His Gospel in the beginning of the fullness of times. It was by Him we received the Book of Mormon; and it is by Him that we remain unto this day; and by Him we shall remain, if it shall be for our glory; and in His Almighty name we are determined to endure tribulation as good soldiers unto the end" (3:297).

SOURCE

Smith, Joseph. *History of The Church of Jesus Christ of Latter-day Saints.* Edited by B. H. Roberts. 7 vols. 2d ed. rev. Salt Lake City: The Church of Jesus Christ of Latter-day Saints, 1932–51.

RLM

MORTALITY

The term *mortality* literally means "death." By reason of the fall of Adam, physical death was introduced into the world. But mortality, though it means death, is synonymous with life—life on earth with all of the conditions associated with it. The word, as used by Latter-day Saints, usually means the "second estate," or this probationary period of our eternal existence (2 Nephi 2:21). It is often used in connection with such other terms as *flesh* or *temporal,* which denote the fallen condition of humankind. Mortality will ultimately be swallowed up in immortality through the universal resurrection made possible through the atonement of Jesus Christ (1 Corinthians 15:53; 2 Corinthians 5:4; Alma 5:15; 12:12). The Book of Mormon prophet Mormon longingly looked forward to the resurrection when he declared, "And the day soon cometh that your mortal must put on immortality, and these bodies which are now moldering in corruption must soon become incorruptible bodies; and then ye must stand before the judgment-seat of Christ, to be judged according to your works; and if it so be that ye are righteous, then are ye blessed with your fathers who have gone before you" (Mormon 6:21).

BLT

MOSES, BOOK OF

In June 1830 Joseph Smith and Oliver Cowdery, working under the inspiration of God and as appointed by him, began an inspired translation of the King James Version of the Bible, known today as the Joseph Smith Translation. This work was a major prophetic undertaking and occupied the Prophet's mind and heart until he completed it in July 1833. The first material found on the handwritten manuscripts was a description of a vision given to Moses on an unnamed mountain sometime between his burning bush experience and his encounters with Pharaoh (Moses 1:17, 26). The vision has come to be known as Moses 1; it is the first chapter of Selections from the Book of Moses. Chapters 2–8 of the book of Moses are Joseph Smith's translation of the early chapters of Genesis—more precisely, Genesis 1:1–8:18 of the current edition of the Joseph Smith Translation, published by the Community of Christ (formerly the Reorganized Church of Jesus Christ of Latter Day Saints).

In the short chapters of the book of Moses are found some of the most profound and distinctive Latter-day Saint teachings anywhere: details on the Creation and the Fall (Moses 2–4), the premortal Council in Heaven (Moses 4:1–4), the rise of secret combinations and the establishment of the kingdom of Satan (Moses 5), the revelation of the gospel to Adam (Moses 6), the ministry of Enoch (Moses 6–7), and the life of Noah and his family before the Flood (Moses 8).

RLM

MOTHER IN HEAVEN

Little has been officially taught or revealed about our mother in heaven. Perhaps the earliest and best-known reference to her is in a poem by Eliza R. Snow. The exact date of the composition is unknown, although the date of first publication was 1845 in the *Times and Seasons* (1039). Identified today by its hymn title, "O My Father," the poem states:

> *In the heav'ns are parents single?*
> *No, the thought makes reason stare!*
> *Truth is reason; truth eternal*
> *Tells me I've a mother there.*
> *When I leave this frail existence,*
> *When I lay this mortal by,*
> *Father, Mother, may I meet you*
> *In your royal courts on high?*
> *Then, at length, when I've completed*
> *All you sent me forth to do,*

With your mutual approbation
Let me come and dwell with you.
(*Hymns,* no. 292)

In 1909 the First Presidency issued a statement entitled "The Origin of Man," which declared: "Man, as a spirit, was begotten and born of heavenly parents. . . . All men and women are in the similitude of the universal Father and Mother, and are literally the sons and daughters of Deity" (78, 80). More recently, the First Presidency and Council of the Twelve Apostles have affirmed that each human being "is a beloved spirit son or daughter of heavenly parents, and, as such, each has a divine nature and destiny" (102).

The existence of a female counterpart to our Father in Heaven is suggested in the scriptural narrative of the Creation: "And God said, Let us make man in our image, after our likeness. . . . So God created man in his own image, in the image of God created he him; male and female created he them. And God blessed them, and God said unto them, Be fruitful, and multiply, and replenish the earth" (Genesis 1:26–28).

SOURCES

First Presidency. "The Origin of Man." *Improvement Era,* Nov. 1909, 75–81; paragraphing altered; or *Ensign,* Feb. 2002, 26–30.

First Presidency and Council of the Twelve Apostles. "The Family: A Proclamation to the World." *Ensign,* Nov. 1995, 102.

"O My Father." *Hymns of The Church of Jesus Christ of Latter-day Saints,* no. 292. Salt Lake City: The Church of Jesus Christ of Latter-day Saints, 1985.

Snow, Eliza R. "My Father in Heaven." *Times and Seasons,* no. 17 (15 Nov. 1845): 1039.

CFO

MOUNTAIN OF THE LORD'S HOUSE

Isaiah prophesied that in the last days "the mountain of the Lord's house shall be established in the top of the mountains, and shall be exalted above the hills; and all nations shall flow unto it" (Isaiah 2:2). There is no question in the minds of Latter-day Saints that this prophecy was fulfilled through the building and dedication of the Salt Lake Temple and that the subsequent divine promises—that many people will go up "to the house of the God of Jacob" and there be taught his ways and learn thereby to "walk in his paths" (Isaiah 2:3)—are now happening and will yet see a future realization. In a revelation given to Joseph Smith and six elders of the Church, the word of the Lord came, "yea, the word of the Lord concerning his church, established in the last days for the restoration of his people, as he has spoken by the mouth of his prophets, and for the gathering of his saints to stand upon Mount Zion, which shall be the city of New Jerusalem" (D&C 84:1–2). And so Independence, Jackson County, Missouri, is named Mount Zion, where a temple is to be built in a future day (D&C 84:4–5). But is not Mount Zion the temple mount in Jerusalem (Isaiah 4:5; 8:18; 18:7; 27:13; Joel 2:32), a sacred location for Jews, Christians, and Muslims? Indeed it is.

"The mountain of the Lord's house" and "Mount Zion" are phrases that refer to high and holy places; points where we gain an elevated perspective; houses of worship where we enter into sacred, saving covenants and participate in redeeming and exalting ordinances; precious places where heaven intersects with earth and where the line separating time and eternity is often blurred and eventually dissolved. These phrases refer to the locations of holy temples, domiciles of holiness that, according to the prophetic promise, have begun to dot the earth.

RLM

MURDER

The sixth of the Ten Commandments given by Jehovah to Moses the lawgiver on Sinai was "Thou shalt not kill" (Exodus 20:13), meaning specifically "Thou shalt not *murder*." The command here is against what we in modern society would call premeditated murder. Consequently, the Almighty is particularly pained when the people of the covenant, those who have come out of the world into the gospel of Jesus Christ, sin against the light of conscience and inspiration and wantonly take another life. In such a situation, the perpetrator is guilty of what the scriptures call an *unforgivable* sin. Joseph Smith said, "A murderer, for instance, one that sheds innocent blood, cannot have forgiveness" (6:253).

In speaking to his son Corianton about the seriousness of sexual immorality, Alma declared: "Know ye not, my son, that these things are an abomination in the sight of the Lord; yea, most abominable above all sins save it be the shedding of innocent blood or denying the Holy Ghost? For behold, if ye deny the Holy Ghost when it once has had place in you, and ye know that ye deny it, behold this is a sin which is unpardonable; yea, and whosoever murdereth against the light and knowledge of God, it is not easy for him to obtain forgiveness; yea, I say unto you, my son, that it is not easy for him to obtain a forgiveness" (Alma 39:5–6). Again, speaking to those within the restored Church, the Lord affirms, "Thou shalt not kill; and he that kills shall not have forgiveness in this world, nor in the world to come" (D&C 42:18). "Murder is thus a sin unto death [see 1 John 5:16–17; D&C 64:7], at least concerning members of the Church, to whom this revelation, which is entitled 'the law of the Church,' was addressed. We do know that there are murders committed by Gentiles for which they at least can repent, be baptized, and receive a remission of their sins. (See 3 Nephi 30:1–2.)" (McConkie, 231).

SOURCES

McConkie, Bruce R. *A New Witness for the Articles of Faith.* Salt Lake City: Deseret Book, 1985.

Smith, Joseph. *History of The Church of Jesus Christ of Latter-day Saints.* Edited by B. H. Roberts. 7 vols. 2d ed. rev. Salt Lake City: The Church of Jesus Christ of Latter-day Saints, 1932–51.

RLM

MUSIC

"Music has boundless powers for moving families toward greater spirituality and devotion to the gospel" (First Presidency, in *Hymns,* x). Praises to God that are often inexpressible through words alone can be communicated through music. Likewise, "some of the greatest sermons are preached by the singing of hymns. Hymns move us to repentance and good works, build testimony and faith, comfort the weary, console the mourning, and inspire us to endure to the end" (First Presidency, in *Hymns,* ix).

Angelic choirs have announced singular events (Luke 2:17), communicated profound gratitude (Job 38:7), and borne witness of God through music (Revelation 14:2–3). Singing praises to God is often the natural reaction when we are delivered from a trial (D&C 101:18) and when we ultimately bow before the Lord at his second coming (D&C 133:32–33). Miriam and other Israelite women danced and sang before God in gratitude for their miraculous passage through the Red Sea (Exodus 15:20–21). Singing by the grateful Saints in celebration of the completion of the Kirtland Temple was accompanied by angels (Andrus, 32). Music can also be a powerful medium for strength in anticipation of challenges ahead. The Savior and his disciples sang a hymn before departing for Gethsemane (Matthew 26:30), Joseph Smith was fortified for his imminent martyrdom by John Taylor's singing in Carthage Jail, and the Saints found solace and hope through music in their challenging travels across the plains to their new home in the Rocky Mountains. Music can also be profoundly effective in missionary work—through the message that is conveyed but especially through the Spirit that is clearly manifested (D&C 66:11).

Because sacred music conveys such spiritual power, it is only reasonable that music can be created and used to offend the Spirit and cut us off from the influence of faith and goodness. We are therefore counseled to watch our thoughts, words, and deeds in choosing the music that will influence our lives.

For these and other reasons, the Lord invited Emma Hale Smith "to make a selection of sacred hymns, as it shall be given thee, which is pleasing unto me, to be had in my church." The Savior further explained, "For my soul delighteth in the song of the heart; yea, the song of the righteous is a prayer unto me, and it shall be answered with a blessing upon their heads" (D&C 25:11–12). Therefore, "inspirational music is an essential part of our church meetings. The hymns invite the Spirit of the Lord, create a feeling of reverence, unify us as members, and provide a way for us to offer praises to the Lord" (First Presidency, in *Hymns*, ix).

SOURCES

Andrus, Hyrum L., and Helen Mae Andrus. *They Knew the Prophet.* Salt Lake City: Deseret Book, 1999.

Hymns of The Church of Jesus Christ of Latter-day Saints. Salt Lake City: The Church of Jesus Christ of Latter-day Saints, 1985.

CFO

MYSTERIES

Something that is not understood by man when explained through natural means is usually referred to as a mystery. Some contend that mysteries, by their nature, can never be comprehended. In a gospel sense, however, the term *mysteries* refers to the things of God that can indeed be understood and experienced but only through revelation and the means God has appointed. "For my thoughts are not your thoughts, neither are your ways my ways," the Lord declared to Isaiah. "For as the heavens are higher than the earth, so are my ways higher than your ways, and my thoughts than your thoughts" (Isaiah 55:8–9). Because God's ways and thoughts are higher than man's, they can be obtained only by higher means, through God's way rather than man's way. The apostle Paul taught that God's mysteries are revealed "unto us by his Spirit; for the Spirit searcheth all things, yea, the deep things of God. For what man knoweth the things of man, save the spirit of man which is in him? Even so the things of God knoweth no man, but the Spirit of God" (1 Corinthians 2:10–11).

During his earthly ministry, the Savior taught his disciples that "it is given unto you to know the mysteries of the kingdom of heaven, but to them it is not given" (Matthew 13:11). Implicit in Jesus' statement is the notion that those who do not have faith and seek to know the things of God through natural eyes will not and cannot understand the "mysteries of the kingdom of heaven." Numerous other passages of scripture teach that understanding the things of God—"the mysteries of godliness" (1 Timothy 3:16; D&C 19:10)—is given to those who exercise faith in Christ and seek to live in accordance with the principles and ordinances of the everlasting gospel (Psalm 25:14; Romans 16:25; 1 Corinthians 2:14–16; 1 Nephi 10:19; Mosiah 2:9; Alma 12:9–11; D&C 42:65; 63:23). Through the ordinances of the holy priesthood, "which is after that holiest order of God" (D&C 84:18), men and women are given the "key of the mysteries of the kingdom, even the key of the knowledge of God. Therefore, in the ordinances thereof, the power of godliness is manifest" (D&C 84:19–20). Through faithful adherence to priesthood and temple covenants, for example, the Saints "have the privilege of receiving the mysteries of the kingdom of heaven, to have the heavens opened unto them" (D&C 107:19). Receiving mysteries is much more than just gaining deeper understanding of God's words and ways; it is also gaining greater *experience* with the miracle of spiritual transformation that the atonement of Jesus Christ affords. That is the great miracle of the gospel.

In addition to the promises of greater understanding of and experience with "the mysteries of godliness" in this life, the Lord has purposely withheld some things from our view. Many of these mysteries "which no man knew" will be revealed at his second coming and during his millennial reign (D&C 101:32–33). Ultimately, all faithful Saints will know all God's mysteries, for they will be like him. They will inherit all that he has, know all that he knows, and experience in their fulness the "riches of the glory of [God's] mystery" (Colossians 1:27).

BLT

————◈————

NATURAL MAN

Natural men and women are fallen beings who remain in that condition, living without God and godliness in the world. They are unredeemed creatures who live by their own light. On the one hand, natural men and women may be bent on lechery and lasciviousness; they may love Satan more than God and are therefore "carnal, sensual, and devilish" (Moses 5:13). After having preached to and pleaded with his son Corianton, teaching him that "wickedness never was happiness," Alma said, "And now, my son, all men that are in a state of nature, or I would say, in a carnal state, are in the gall of bitterness and in the bonds of iniquity." Now note how such persons are enemies to God: "They are without God in the world, and they have gone contrary to the nature of God; therefore, they are in a state contrary to the nature of happiness" (Alma 41:10–11).

On the other hand, natural men and women need not be what we would call degenerate. They may well be moral and upright men and women, bent on goodness and benevolence. Nevertheless, they operate in and are acclimated to the present fallen world. Such persons do not enjoy the enlivening powers of the Holy Ghost, have not received the revealed witness of the truth, and have not enjoyed the sanctifying powers of the blood of Christ. In 1867 President Brigham Young declared: "There is no doubt, if a person lives according to the revelations given to God's people, he may have the Spirit of the Lord to signify to him His will, and to guide and to direct him in the discharge of his duties, in his temporal as well as his spiritual exercises. I am satisfied, however, that in this respect, we live far beneath our privileges" (12:104).

Members of the Church who refuse to climb toward greater spiritual heights, who have no inclination to further anchor themselves in the truth, and who have become satisfied with their present spiritual state are natural men and women, persons generally of goodwill who do not understand that through their smugness and complacency they are aiding and abetting the cause of the enemy of all righteousness. "Fallen man," C. S. Lewis perceptively observed, "is not simply an imperfect creature who needs improvement: he is a rebel who must lay down his arms" (56).

What are some broad characteristics of natural men and women?

1. *They are unable or unwilling to perceive spiritual realities.* The apostle Paul explained that "the natural man receiveth not the things of the Spirit of God: for *they are foolishness unto him: neither can he know them,* because they are spiritually discerned" (1 Corinthians 2:14; emphasis added). In exulting over the Lord's infinite mercy—his willingness to snatch his children from evil and forgive their sins—Ammon said: "What natural man is there that knoweth these things? I say unto you, there is none that knoweth these things, save it be the penitent" (Alma 26:21). "No man has seen God at any time in the flesh, except quickened by the Spirit of God," a modern revelation teaches; "neither can any natural man abide the presence of God, neither after the carnal mind" (D&C 67:11–12; see also Moses 1:11).

2. *They are fiercely independent.* Joseph Smith taught that "all men are naturally disposed to walk in their own paths as they are pointed out by their own fingers and are not willing to consider and walk in the path which is pointed out by another, saying, This is the way, walk ye in it, although he should be an unerring director, and the Lord his God sent him" (1:408). Seeking to be independent, natural men and women ironically end up conforming to the trends of the day. Natural men and women, at least those who have "the carnal mind," are "not subject to the law of God" (Romans 8:7) but rather are subject to their

own whims, passions, and desires. Samuel the Lamanite expressed the tragic end of those whose natural view of reality causes them to spend their days struggling to climb the wrong spiritual ladder: "But behold, your days of probation are past; ye have procrastinated the day of your salvation until it is everlastingly too late, and your destruction is made sure; yea, for ye have sought all the days of your lives for that which ye could not obtain; and ye have sought for happiness in doing iniquity, which thing is contrary to the nature of that righteousness which is in our great and Eternal Head" (Helaman 13:38).

3. *They are proud, overly competitive, reactionary, and externally driven.* Natural men and women—be they the irreverent and ungodly or the well-meaning but spiritually unregenerate—are preoccupied with self and obsessed with personal aggrandizement. Their lives are keyed to the rewards of this ephemeral sphere; their values derive solely from pragmatism and utility. They take their cues from the world and the worldly. The central feature of pride, as President Ezra Taft Benson warned the Latter-day Saints, is enmity—enmity toward God and enmity toward man (4). The look of natural men and women is neither up (to God) nor over (to their fellow humans), except as the horizontal glance allows them to maintain a distance from others.

4. *They yield themselves to the harsh and the crude.* The Spirit of the Lord has a calming and quieting influence upon those who cultivate it and enjoy its fruits. As a sanctifier, the Holy Ghost "expands, and purifies all the natural passions and affections. . . . It inspires virtue, kindness, goodness, tenderness, gentleness, and charity" (Pratt, 61). On the other hand, as President Spencer W. Kimball declared, the natural man—the person who lives without this divine refinement—"is the 'earthly man' who has allowed rude animal passions to overshadow his spiritual inclinations" (112).

There is no escape for the natural man except into the arms of Jesus Christ. Only those who choose to be changed, who put off the natural man through putting on Christ and the Atonement, can ever hope to find comfort in the company of holy beings. Through the power of the blood of Christ, the natural man is transformed into the spiritual man and thereby becomes, over time and through the renovating powers of the Spirit, "submissive, meek, humble, patient," and "full of love" (Mosiah 3:19).

SOURCES

Benson, Ezra Taft. "Beware of Pride." *Ensign*, May 1989, 4–6.

Kimball, Spencer W. "Ocean Currents and Family Influences." *Ensign,* Nov. 1974, 110–13.

Lewis, C. S. *Mere Christianity.* New York: HarperCollins, 1980.

Pratt, Parley P. *Key to the Science of Theology; A Voice of Warning.* Salt Lake City: Deseret Book 1978.

Smith, Joseph. *History of The Church of Jesus Christ of Latter-day Saints.* Edited by B. H. Roberts. 7 vols. 2d ed. rev. Salt Lake City: The Church of Jesus Christ of Latter-day Saints, 1932–51.

Young, Brigham. In *Journal of Discourses.* 26 vols. London: Latter-day Saints' Book Depot, 1854–86.

RLM

NEW AND EVERLASTING COVENANT

Shortly after The Church of Jesus Christ of Latter-day Saints was organized, some new converts who had previously been baptized into other denominations wondered if it was necessary to be baptized again. The Prophet Joseph Smith inquired of the Lord and received the revelation recorded as section 22 of the Doctrine and Covenants. It is within that context that the phrase *"new and everlasting covenant"* was first used in this dispensation. Subsequent revelation further elaborated on the term. Eighteen months later at an important conference of Church leaders, the Lord stated that the new and everlasting covenant spoken of in the scriptures is "even the fulness of my gospel, sent forth unto the children of men, that they might have life and be made partakers of the glories which are to be revealed in the last days, as it was written by the prophets and apostles in days of old" (D&C 66:2).

Thus, the new and everlasting covenant is nothing more nor less than the gospel of Jesus Christ—all the laws, ordinances, principles, powers, and authority given from God to man for his salvation in the celestial kingdom. It is the plan by which all men and women may attain happiness in this life and eternal life in the world to come. The fulness of the gospel is both new and everlasting. It is everlasting, meaning that it is eternal, because it has no beginning and no end. It is the same gospel and plan of salvation that was received by Old Testament patriarchs and taught and testified of by prophets in all dispensations (Genesis 9:16; 17:7; Isaiah 55:3; Jeremiah 31:31; Ezekiel 37:26; Hebrews 8:13; 12:24; D&C 45:9; 101:39). Priesthood, like the gospel, is an everlasting covenant (Numbers 25:13). It is the means on earth by which the gospel plan is administered. And yet the gospel covenant is new, for it has been restored to the earth in this, the dispensation of the fulness of times.

There are some covenants and ordinances that are not eternal by nature but are practiced at a certain time and by specific people for distinctive purposes, such as circumcision (Genesis 17:9–14), as well as the carnal commandments and sacrifices included in the law of Moses (JST, Exodus 34:1–2; Galatians 3:19, 24; 2 Nephi 25:24–30; Mosiah 12:27–13:32; D&C 84:23–27).

The phrase *"new and everlasting covenant"* is most often used in connection with the ordinance of temple marriage (D&C 131:2; 132:6, 19). Temple marriage, however, is not the new and everlasting covenant. It is *one specific saving ordinance* within the overall plan of salvation—one component within the fulness of the gospel of Jesus Christ. Thus, in this way, every principle, ordinance, and covenant associated with the restored gospel could properly have the phrase *"new and everlasting covenant"* attached to it, such as "the new and everlasting covenant of baptism" or "the new and everlasting covenant of priesthood."

BLT

NEW JERUSALEM

One of the foundational doctrines of The Church of Jesus Christ of Latter-day Saints is that the latter-day city of Zion, also known in the scriptures as the New Jerusalem, "will be built upon the American continent; that Christ will reign personally upon the earth; and, that the earth will be renewed and receive its paradisiacal glory" (Articles of Faith 1:10). During the Millennium, there will be two world capitals of God's kingdom on earth—the city of Jerusalem on the eastern continent and the New Jerusalem on the American continent. Jerusalem will be a gathering place for the righteous descendants of Judah and other tribes of Israel, whereas the New Jerusalem will be primarily for the seed of Joseph. From both of these spiritual epicenters, as Isaiah prophesied, "shall go forth the law, and the word of the Lord" (Isaiah 2:3).

The scriptures, ancient and modern, speak of both of these cities as

Zion (1 Kings 8:1; Isaiah 60:14; Joel 2:32; D&C 45:66–67; 58:49–50). While numerous passages in the Old Testament speak of the latter-day Zion in dualistic ways, it is from modern revelation that the nature and location of the New Jerusalem is specifically identified. The Book of Mormon prophet Ether explicitly taught that the New Jerusalem "should be built up upon this land [the American continent], unto the remnant of the seed of Joseph" and that it will be as a "holy sanctuary"—a "holy city unto the Lord" where the inhabitants are sanctified "through the blood of the Lamb," never again to be scattered and confounded (Ether 13:6–10). The resurrected Christ taught the righteous Book of Mormon people that he would "establish in this land, unto the fulfilling of the covenant," a New Jerusalem, where "the powers of heaven shall be in the midst of this people; yea, even I will be in the midst of you" (3 Nephi 20:22). The righteous remnant of the seed of Joseph "and also as many of the house of Israel as shall come" will assist in the work of establishing this New Jerusalem, where "the power of heaven [shall] come down among them" (3 Nephi 21:23, 25).

One of the most important themes found in the revelations of the Doctrine and Covenants is that of establishing Zion, building the New Jerusalem, and having all things prepared to meet the Savior at his second coming to govern the earth during the Millennium (D&C 28:9; 42:9, 35–36; 84:2). The city of Zion—the New Jerusalem—was to be built as a "center place" (D&C 57:3) for the kingdom of God and for the gathering of the covenant people (D&C 42:36). The Lord revealed to the Prophet Joseph Smith that the location of this latter-day "City of Holiness" (Moses 7:19) is to be in Independence, Jackson County, Missouri (D&C 57:1–3; 84:3–4). Although the nineteenth-century Latter-day Saints who had longed for and worked diligently to establish this city were not able to build it because they "were hindered by their enemies" (D&C 124:51), we know that the New Jerusalem will yet be built in fulfillment of the ancient and modern declarations of the Lord. In the meantime, Saints are gathered to stakes throughout the world and seek to establish Zion through personal righteousness and devotion to the Lord. In that way all faithful Saints are assisting in the eventual establishment of the New Jerusalem, which will be a "land of peace, a city of refuge, a place of safety for the saints of the Most High God" (D&C 45:66). To the temple built in Jackson

County, the Savior will return to usher in his millennial reign and continue the gathering of his righteous seed, "and the glory of the Lord shall be there" (D&C 45:67).

In fulfillment of the words of prophets past, the millennial City of Holiness, the latter-day Zion, the New Jerusalem will greet the return of Enoch's City of Holiness. That remarkable community of Saints from a past dispensation will be, as the prophet Ether described, "the New Jerusalem, which should come down out of heaven" (Ether 13:3; see also Moses 7:60–64). From two millennial world capitals of God's earthly kingdom—the New Jerusalem in America and the rebuilt old city of Jerusalem, which will also be inhabited by righteous children of Father Abraham—"shall go forth the law, and the word of the Lord" (Isaiah 2:3). The Old and New Jerusalems will, at the end of the Millennium, give way for the City of Holiness, which will be the celestial city that will come as John the Revelator prophesied, "descending out of heaven from God: having the glory of God; and her light [will be] like unto a stone most precious. . . . And the city had no need of the sun, neither of the moon, to shine in it: for the glory of God did lighten it, and the Lamb is the light thereof. And the nations of them which are saved shall walk in the light of it" (Revelation 21:10–11, 23–24).

BLT

───●───

OATH

In the gospel sense, an oath is a solemn declaration or absolute promise. It calls on someone or something considered sacred by the oath-maker (often God) to witness the truth of the declaration or the binding nature of the promise being made. Throughout the ancient world, oaths carried an added measure of sanctity beyond a mere promise—even among nonbiblical peoples. In Roman culture, for example, oaths were sworn upon a special sacred stone established for that purpose in the temple of Jupiter, who was the head of the Roman pantheon. In ancient Israel oaths likewise were regarded as extraordinary promises, binding the oath maker's very soul: "If a man vow a vow unto the Lord, or swear an oath to bind his soul with a bond; he shall not break his word, he shall do according to all that proceedeth out of his mouth" (Numbers 30:2). We have reason to believe that even among dishonorable persons, oaths were regarded as inviolable. When the daughter of Herodias danced before Herod the tetrarch and his entourage, Herod "promised with an oath to give her whatsoever she would ask" (Matthew 14:7; see also Mark 6:25–29). She asked for the head of John the Baptist. "And the king was sorry: nevertheless for the oath's sake . . . he commanded it to be given her" (Matthew 14:9).

The first example recorded in the Bible of a righteous person to have taken an oath was Abraham's chief steward, Eliezer, when his master sent him to look for a wife for Isaac. "And Abraham said unto his eldest servant of his house, that ruled over all that he had, Put, I pray thee, thy hand under my thigh: and I will make thee swear by the Lord, the God of heaven, and the God of the earth, that thou shalt not take a wife unto my son of the daughters of the Canaanites, among whom I dwell: but thou shalt go unto my country, and to my kindred, and take a wife unto my son Isaac" (Genesis 24:2–4).

The patriarch Joseph made the Israelites swear an oath regarding the disposition of his remains after death, saying, "God will surely visit you, and ye shall carry up my bones from hence" (Genesis 50:25). The swearing of an oath was occasionally used to ensure loyalty and obedience to Israel's political leaders. King Solomon asked a certain Shimei why he had "not kept the oath of the Lord" to do what the king desired (1 Kings 2:43). Explicit acknowledgment of the penalty attached to breaking an oath was apparently part of the oath made by the righteous in Nehemiah's day. "And the rest of the people, the priests, the Levites, the porters, the singers, the Nethinims, and all they that had separated themselves from the people of the lands unto the law of God, their wives, their sons, and their daughters, every one having knowledge, and having understanding; they clave to their brethren, their nobles, and entered into a curse, and into an oath, to walk in God's law, which was given by Moses the servant of God, and to observe and do all the commandments of the Lord our Lord, and his judgments and his statutes" (Nehemiah 10:28–29).

With the coming of the gospel covenant in the meridian dispensation, Jesus Christ reoriented and redirected the actions of his disciples regarding the making of oaths. During the Sermon on the Mount, he said, "Again, ye have heard that it hath been said by them of old time, Thou shalt not forswear thyself, but shalt perform unto the Lord thine oaths: but I say unto you, Swear not at all; neither by heaven; for it is God's throne: nor by the earth; for it is his footstool: neither by Jerusalem; for it is the city of the great King. Neither shalt thou swear by thy head, because thou canst not make one hair white or black. But let your communication be, Yea, yea; Nay, nay: for whatsoever is more than these cometh of evil" (Matthew 5:33–37). James, half-brother of the Lord, repeated Jesus' command (James 5:12).

Though mortals were asked not to initiate oaths after the coming of the Messiah, God himself is not under the same restriction and has continued to make sacred oaths with his people. The first reason, perhaps, is that only he is fully righteous and fully capable of making and keeping oaths with exactness in this increasingly corrupt world. Second, all those who enter into the covenant of the higher law, which is the gospel, are in reality expected to live all aspects of their lives with the same level of sanctity inherent in oaths.

Among the most significant of all God's oaths is the one received by all who have the Melchizedek Priesthood conferred upon them. "And also all they who receive this priesthood receive me, saith the Lord; for he that receiveth my servants receiveth me; and he that receiveth me receiveth my Father; and he that receiveth my Father receiveth my Father's kingdom; therefore all that my Father hath shall be given unto him. And this is according to the oath and covenant which belongeth to the priesthood. Therefore, all those who receive the priesthood, receive this oath and covenant of my Father, which he cannot break, neither can it be moved" (D&C 84:35–40). For any oath to be valid, it must be ratified or "sealed by the Holy Spirit of promise" (D&C 132:7). Such validation comes only through righteous living.

In opposition to the Lord's oaths, and as a counterfeit to them, the adversary has manipulated many people and destroyed many lives through the imposition of his own system of oaths. These evil oaths were first administered by Satan to Cain, with their crowning purpose being to murder to get gain (Moses 5:29–31). From that time forward satanic oaths have been at the heart of establishing secret combinations, which in turn seek to overthrow agency, murder to get gain, establish awful wickedness, and destroy entire nations (Moses

5:49–51; Helaman 6:24–30). We are blessed to know that in the end, righteousness will prevail and Satan will fail—which he too knows (Revelation 12:10–12). Furthermore, Satan can have no power over us unless we allow him to (Smith, 214).

SOURCE

Joseph Smith [manual]. Teachings of Presidents of the Church series. Salt Lake City: The Church of Jesus Christ of Latter-day Saints, 2007.

ACS

OBEDIENCE

Obedience—willfully submitting to the commandments of God and seeking to conform one's life to his mind and will—is foundational and fundamental to one's Christian discipleship. Before the foundation of the world, the law of heaven decreed that "when we obtain any blessing from God, it is by obedience to that law upon which it is predicated" (D&C 130:20–21; see also *Words,* 232). One of the purposes of our earth life is to demonstrate our obedience to our Father in Heaven—"to see if [we] will do all things whatsoever the Lord [our] God shall command [us]" (Abraham 3:25; see also D&C 98:14). God does not expect obedience from his children as a cruel dictator would demand absolute submission, but rather he invites us to obey commands that are intended to protect, preserve, prosper, and guide us in our quest to become like him (Deuteronomy 6:24–25; D&C 25:15). As a result, he promises great blessings, both spiritual and temporal, to those who follow his loving counsel and seek to do his will (Leviticus 26:3–12; Deuteronomy 4:40; 1 Nephi 4:6–18; D&C 64:34; 93:1). "In obedience," the Prophet Joseph Smith taught, "there is joy and peace unspotted, unalloyed" (5:135). Those who choose disobedience, on the other hand, can expect consequences both in time and eternity (Leviticus 26:14–32; Jeremiah 11:3; Mosiah 2:32–33, 37; D&C 56:3; 58:32).

"If ye love me," Jesus taught his disciples, "keep my commandments" (John 14:15). Obedience to God is an expression of faith in and love for the Lord. There can be no obedience without freedom of choice; there are no blessings in compelled compliance. President Joseph F. Smith declared: "Obedience must be voluntary; it must not be forced, there must be no coercion. Men must not be constrained against their will to obey the will of God; they must obey it because they know it to be right, because they desire to do it, and because it is their pleasure to do it. God delights in the willing heart" (65). There are different levels of obedience, owing to individuals' varying levels of faith, commitment, knowledge, and motivation. Obeying out of tradition, external influences, temporal considerations, or other lesser motivations yields lesser blessings than obeying because of deep love for and faith in the Lord and a testimony of his work and commandments.

Obedience, President Boyd K. Packer has taught, not only yields great blessings but is also the key to freedom of the soul—perfect liberty that leads to eternal life. "Obedience—that which God will never take by force—He will accept when freely given. And He will then return to you freedom that you can hardly dream of—the freedom to feel and to know, the freedom to do, and the freedom to *be,* at least a thousand fold more than we offer Him" (256).

SOURCES

Packer, Boyd K. *That All May Be Edified.* Salt Lake City: Deseret Book, 1982.

Smith, Joseph. *History of The Church of Jesus Christ of Latter-day Saints.* Edited by B. H. Roberts. 7 vols. 2d ed. rev. Salt Lake City: The Church of Jesus Christ of Latter-day Saints, 1932–51.

Smith, Joseph F. *Gospel Doctrine.* Salt Lake City: Deseret Book, 1939.

The Words of Joseph Smith. Compiled and edited by Andrew F. Ehat and Lyndon W. Cook. Provo, Utah: Brigham Young University Religious Studies Center, 1980.

BLT

OMNIPOTENCE

God is omnipotent in the sense that he has all power, all might, and all dominion. There is no influence, no entity, no person, no organization, no empire, no location within our universe over which he does not exercise supreme authority. Holy scripture testifies:

- He is the Almighty God (Genesis 17:1; Revelation 1:8; Helaman 10:11).
- He has all power (Mosiah 4:9; Alma 26:35; Ether 3:4; D&C 61:1).
- He saves without restraint (1 Samuel 14:6).
- There is nothing too hard for him to do (Genesis 18:14; Jeremiah 32:17).

- There is nothing he takes "in his heart to do but what he will do it" (Abraham 3:17).
- With him all things are possible (Matthew 19:26; Mark 10:27; Luke 1:37; 18:27; 1 Nephi 7:12).
- He is mightier than all the earth (1 Nephi 4:1).
- He reigns (Revelation 19:6).

RLM

OMNIPRESENCE

God "has a body of flesh and bones as tangible as man's" (D&C 130:22). Consequently, he can be in only one place, one physical location, at a time. He is, however, omnipresent—everywhere present—by and through his Holy Spirit, meaning the Light of Christ or Spirit of Jesus Christ (D&C 84:45–46). Through that divine medium God can be in and through and round about all things in the same instant (D&C 88:6–13, 41). "The elements are the tabernacle of God," meaning the tabernacle of the Spirit of God, the Light of Christ; "yea, man is the tabernacle of God, even temples [see also 1 Corinthians 6:19]; and whatsoever temple is defiled, God shall destroy that temple" (D&C 93:35).

RLM

OMNISCIENCE

Omniscient (from Latin *omni,* "all," and *scientia,* "knowledge") means all-knowing. Jacob, son of Lehi, declared: "O how great the holiness of our God! For he knoweth all things, and there is not anything save he knows it" (2 Nephi 9:20; compare 2 Nephi 2:24; Mormon 8:17; Moroni 7:22; D&C 127:2). God searches all hearts and knows all (1 Chronicles 28:9; 2 Chronicles 6:30; Acts 1:24; 15:8; D&C 6:16); "his understanding is infinite" (Psalm 147:5); the Spirit knows all things (Alma 7:13; D&C 42:17); God comprehends all things (Alma 26:35); all things are present before his eyes (D&C 38:2; Smith, 4:597); all things are present with him, he knows them all (Moses 1:6), the end from the beginning (Abraham 2:8). "O the depth of the riches both of the wisdom and knowledge of God!

how unsearchable are his judgments, and his ways past finding out!" (Romans 11:33; compare D&C 76:2).

One of the great questions of the ages is how God can know all things and at the same time allow mortals to enjoy unfettered moral agency. Elder Neal A. Maxwell wrote that "for God to foresee is not to cause or even to desire a particular occurrence—but it is to take that occurrence into account beforehand, so that divine reckoning folds it into the unfolding purposes of God. . . . The actual determinations . . . are made by *us* mortals using *our* agency as to this or that course of action. For these determinations and decisions we are accountable. . . . Our agency is preserved . . . by the fact that as we approach a given moment we do not know what our response will be. Meanwhile, God has foreseen what we will do and has taken our decision into account (in composite with all others), so that His purposes are not frustrated. . . . In a very real sense, all we need to know is that God knows all!" (12–21).

SOURCE

Maxwell, Neal A. *All These Things Shall Give Thee Experience.* Salt Lake City: Deseret Book, 1979.

RLM

ONE HUNDRED FORTY-FOUR THOUSAND

The revelations declare, "Prepare ye the way of the Lord, and make his paths straight, for the hour of his coming is nigh—when the Lamb shall stand upon Mount Zion, and with him a hundred and forty-four thousand, having his Father's name written on their foreheads" (D&C 133:17–18; see also Revelation 7:4). This group of 144,000 are high priests after the holy order of God, men who have themselves received the promise of exaltation and whose mission it is to bring as many as will come into the Church of the Firstborn (D&C 77:11–12), into that inner circle of men and women who have passed the tests of mortality and have become the elect of God (Young, 14:242–43; Pratt, 16:325; 18:25). In the day of division, of unspeakable wickedness matched by consummate righteousness, temples will dot the earth and be accessible to the Lord's covenant people everywhere, and thus the fulness of temple blessings will be sealed upon millions upon millions of the faithful worldwide by those holding the keys of power.

SOURCE

Pratt, Orson. In *Journal of Discourses*. 26 vols. London: Latter-day Saints' Book Depot, 1854–86.

Young, Brigham. In *Journal of Discourses*. 26 vols. London: Latter-day Saints' Book Depot, 1854–86.

RLM

ONLY BEGOTTEN SON

Numerous scriptural passages found in all of the standard works refer to Jesus Christ as the "Only Begotten" (Moses 1:6, 33), "only begotten of the Father" (John 1:14; see also 2 Nephi 25:12; Moses 5:7–9) and "only begotten Son" of God (John 3:16; see also 1 John 4:9; Jacob 4:11; Alma 12:33; D&C 29:42; 76:13, 25, 57; 138:14). All of us are "literally the sons and daughters of Deity" who were "begotten and born of heavenly parents" (First Presidency, 78, 80). Yet Christ is the "Only Begotten" son of God *in the flesh*—meaning mortality, with Mary as his mother (D&C 93:11).

The phrase "Only Begotten Son" refers only to Jesus Christ (John 1:18; 3:16; Jacob 4:5, 11; Alma 12:33–34; D&C 20:21; 29:42; 49:5; 76:13, 25) and is both a description of his lineage as well as a name-title. All individuals who will ever live on this earth are spirit children of our Heavenly Father (Numbers 27:16; Hebrews 12:9), but Jesus is called the Only Begotten of the Father (Moses 5:9), meaning the Only Begotten in the flesh, because God is his physical father. Jesus' physical body was born into this fallen, mortal world the same way all other human beings come into this world. In making the announcement to Mary, the angel Gabriel said:

"And, behold, thou shalt conceive in thy womb, and bring forth a son, and shalt call his name JESUS. He shall be great, and shall be called the Son of the Highest: and the Lord God shall give unto him the throne of his father David: . . . And the angel answered and said unto her, The Holy Ghost shall come upon thee, and the power of the Highest shall overshadow thee: therefore also that holy thing which shall be born of thee shall be called the Son of God" (Luke 1:31–32, 35).

Elder James E. Talmage noted: "That Child to be born of Mary was begotten of Elohim, the Eternal Father, not in violation of natural law but in accordance with a higher manifestation thereof; and, the offspring from that association of supreme sanctity, celestial Sireship, and pure though mortal maternity, was of right to be called the 'Son of the Highest.' In His nature would be combined the powers of Godhood with the capacity and possibilities of mortality; and this through the ordinary operation of the fundamental law of heredity, declared of God, demonstrated by science, and admitted by philosophy, that living beings shall propagate—after their kind. The Child Jesus was to inherit the physical, mental, and spiritual traits, tendencies, and powers that characterized His parents—one immortal and glorified—God, the other human—woman" (81).

This is a fundamental doctrine of true Christianity. The Jews do not believe God (Elohim) would have a Son; the Muslims do not believe God (Allah) would have a Son in this world; and many Christians these days likewise deny the Savior's unique birth. Nevertheless, the doctrine of the divine Sonship of Christ is the foundation of our religion. With his unique parentage, Jesus had power over life and death. He said, "I lay down my life, that I might take it again. No man taketh it from me, but I lay it down of myself. I have power to lay it down, and I have power to take it again" (John 10:17–18). He could, and did, give his life and take it up again—providing the way for all of us to be resurrected.

President Ezra Taft Benson wrote: "A fundamental doctrine of true Christianity is the divine birth of the child Jesus. This doctrine is not generally comprehended by the world. The paternity of Jesus Christ is one of the 'mysteries of godliness' comprehended only by the spiritually minded. . . .

". . . The testimonies of appointed witnesses leave no question as to the paternity of Jesus Christ. God was the Father of Jesus' mortal tabernacle, and Mary, a mortal woman, was His mother. He is therefore the only person born who rightfully deserved the title 'the Only Begotten Son of God.' . . .

"The Church of Jesus Christ of Latter-day Saints proclaims that Jesus Christ is the Son of God in the most literal sense. The body in which He performed His mission in the flesh was sired by that same Holy Being we worship as God, our Eternal Father. Jesus was not the son of Joseph, nor was He begotten by the Holy Ghost. He is the Son of the Eternal Father. . . .

"He was the Only Begotten Son of our Heavenly Father in the flesh—the only child whose mortal body was begotten by our Heavenly Father. His mortal mother, Mary, was called a virgin, both before and after she gave birth" (6–7).

Symbolically, Paul refers to Abraham's son Isaac as Abraham's "only begotten son": "By faith Abraham, when he was tried, offered up Isaac: and he that had received the promises offered up his only begotten son" (Hebrews 11:17). This literary image was drawn as a likeness. The prophet Jacob in the Book of Mormon employed the same concept when he drew a comparison between God and Abraham, who offered up Isaac, "which is a similitude of God and his Only Begotten Son" (Jacob 4:5).

SOURCES

Benson, Ezra Taft. *The Teachings of Ezra Taft Benson.* Salt Lake City: Bookcraft, 1988.
First Presidency. "The Origin of Man." *Improvement Era,* Nov. 1909, 75–81; or *Ensign,* Feb. 2002, 26–30.
Talmage, James E. *Jesus the Christ.* Salt Lake City: Deseret Book, 1973.

ACS

ONLY TRUE CHURCH

In the first section of the Doctrine and Covenants, a revelation given to Joseph Smith in November 1831, The Church of Jesus Christ of Latter-day Saints is referred to as "the only true and living church upon the face of the whole earth" (D&C 1:30). Admittedly, this is strong language; it is hard doctrine, words that are offensive to persons of other faiths. It may be helpful to consider briefly what the phrase "the only true and living church" means and what it does *not* mean.

1. It does not mean that men and women of other Christian faiths are not sincere believers in truth and genuine followers of Christ.

2. It does not mean we believe that most of the doctrines in Catholic, Eastern Orthodox, or Protestant Christianity are false or that the leaders of the various branches of Christianity have improper motives. Joseph Smith stated: "The inquiry is frequently made of me, 'Wherein do you differ from others in your religious views?' In reality and essence we do not differ so far in our religious views, but that we could all drink into one principle of love. One of the grand fundamental principles of 'Mormonism' is to receive truth, let it come from

whence it may" (5:499). "Have the Presbyterians any truth?" he asked on another occasion. "Yes. Have the Baptists, Methodists, etc., any truth? Yes. . . . We should gather all the good and true principles in the world and treasure them up, or we shall not come out true 'Mormons'" (5:517; spelling standardized).

3. It does not mean that the Bible has been so corrupted that it cannot be relied upon to teach us sound doctrine and provide an example of how to live. While we do not subscribe to a doctrine of biblical inerrancy, we do believe that the hand of God has been over the preservation of the biblical materials such that what we have now is what the Almighty would have us possess. In the words of Elder Bruce R. McConkie, "we cannot avoid the conclusion that a divine providence is directing all things as they should be. This means that the Bible, as it now is, contains that portion of the Lord's word" that the present world is prepared to receive (280).

4. It does not mean that Latter-day Saints desire to face moral, social, and family challenges on their own. To be sure, we strive earnestly to work together with men and women of other faiths to stand up and speak out against the rising tide of immorality and ethical relativism that are spreading in our world. With most Christian groups, we are persuaded that the changes to be made in our society can come about only from the inside out—through the transforming power of Jesus Christ. Indeed, if we allow doctrinal differences, stereotyping, and demonizing of those who are different to prevent us from joining hands in halting the erosion of time-honored moral and family values, Lucifer will win a major victory.

What, then, does the revelation mean when it states that The Church of Jesus Christ of Latter-day Saints is "the only true and living church upon the face of the whole earth"?

"The word *only*," Elder Neal A. Maxwell wrote, "asserts a uniqueness and singularity" about the Church "as *the exclusive ecclesiastical, authority-bearing agent* for our Father in Heaven in this dispensation" (45; emphasis added).

Elder Maxwell pointed out: "When the Lord used the designation 'true,' he implied that the doctrines of the Church and its authority are not just partially true, but true as measured by divine standards. The Church is not, therefore, conceptually compromised by having been made up from doctrinal debris left over from another age, nor is it comprised of mere fragments of the true faith. It is based upon the *fullness* of the gospel of him whose *name* it bears, thus passing the two tests for proving his church that were given by Jesus during his visit to the Nephites (3 Nephi 27:8).

"When the word *living* is used," Elder Maxwell continued, "it carries a divinely deliberate connotation. The Church is neither dead nor dying, nor is it even wounded. The Church, like the living God who established it, is alive, aware, and functioning. It is not a museum that houses a fossilized faith; rather, it is a kinetic kingdom characterized by living faith in living disciples" (46).

It means that doctrinal finality rests with apostles and prophets, not theologians or scholars. There are simply too many ambiguous sections of scripture to let the Bible speak for itself. This was, in fact, young Joseph Smith's dilemma: "The teachers of religion of the different sects understood the same passages of scripture so differently as to destroy all confidence in settling [his religious questions] by an appeal to the Bible" (Joseph Smith–History 1:12). In many cases, neither linguistic training nor historical background will automatically produce the (divinely) intended meaning or clarification of challenging passages. What is the standard by which we judge and interpret? Who has the right to offer inspired commentary on words delivered by holy men of God who spoke or wrote anciently as they were moved upon by the Holy Spirit? (2 Peter 1:21). While each reader of holy writ should seek to be in tune with the Spirit enough to understand what the scripture intends, the final word on prophetic interpretation must rest with prophets.

SOURCES

Maxwell, Neal A. *Things as They Really Are.* Salt Lake City: Deseret Book, 1978.

McConkie, Bruce R. *Doctrines of the Restoration: Sermons and Writings of Bruce R. McConkie.* Edited by Mark L. McConkie. Salt Lake City: Bookcraft, 1989.

Smith, Joseph. *History of The Church of Jesus Christ of Latter-day Saints.* Edited by B. H. Roberts. 7 vols. 2d ed. rev. Salt Lake City: The Church of Jesus Christ of Latter-day Saints, 1932–51.

RLM

ORACLES

The word *oracle* literally means "to speak" and connotes the means whereby divine messages are conveyed to man. In the scriptures, the term is used in three different ways: (1) any sacred place where God speaks his will to his children, such as Mount Sinai, the Sacred Grove, temples, and other holy sites (D&C 124:39); (2) the inspired messages or revelations from God to man (Romans 3:2; D&C 124:126); and (3) the Lord's authorized servants who receive these revelations (2 Samuel 16:23; 1 Peter 4:11; D&C 90:4). "And all they who receive the oracles of God," the Lord has declared in this last dispensation, "let them beware how they hold them lest they are accounted as a light thing" (D&C 90:5). Clearly, God is reminding his people that his words and his servants who receive and teach his words are to be esteemed and heeded. To disregard or minimize the significance of the revelations and revelators is, as the Lord warned, accounting them as light things. Any man or woman who receives divine direction through the power of the Holy Ghost is an oracle in a general sense. The phrase "living oracles" is more specifically used in reference to modern-day prophets, seers, and revelators—those who hold all the keys of the kingdom and have the sacred right to declare the mind and will of God.

BLT

ORDINANCE

In a broad sense, a gospel ordinance is a law, statute, or commandment of God (D&C 52:15–16; 64:5). An act or ritual done with proper priesthood authority is known as an ordinance. All ordinances are instructive—designed to bring people closer to God and Christ and to bless them in some manner. "Therefore, in the ordinances [of the priesthood]," the Lord declared to the Prophet Joseph Smith, "the power of godliness is manifest. And without the ordinances thereof, and the authority of the priesthood, the power of godliness is not manifest unto men in the flesh" (D&C 84:20–21).

Some ordinances are essential for salvation in the celestial kingdom of God. In some religious traditions, the word *sacrament* is used synonymously with *ordinance.* Saving ordinances for Latter-day Saints include baptism for the remission of sins and the accompanying worthy partaking of the sacrament of the Lord's Supper, confirmation and receiving the gift of the Holy Ghost, ordination to the priesthood for all worthy males, and the temple ordinances of endowment and sealings. With each of these imperative ordinances, there are associated covenants by which the person receiving the ordinance promises to live his or her life. Accompanying these ordinances are also promises God makes to the faithful who live their lives in accordance with the covenants. For example, with the ordinance of baptism, persons covenant to repent of their sins, take upon themselves the name of Christ, and serve God by keeping his commandments and loving and serving their fellow men (2 Nephi 31:12–13; Mosiah 18:8–10; Moroni 6:2–3; D&C 20:37, 68–69). God in turn promises a remission of sins, the constant companionship of the Holy Ghost, and the power to obtain eternal life. All other saving ordinances are likewise linked to solemn covenants on the part of the person and divine promises from God. "Ordinances and covenants become our credentials for admission into His presence," President Boyd K. Packer has taught. "To worthily receive them is the quest of a lifetime; to keep them thereafter is the challenge of mortality" (24).

There are other priesthood ordinances performed within The Church of Jesus Christ of Latter-day Saints that are not essential for salvation but are for the benefit of the recipients. Such ordinances include naming and blessing newborn children, blessings of healing for the sick and afflicted, priesthood blessings of comfort and guidance, setting-apart blessings for officers and teachers of the Church, patriarchal blessings, and dedicating graves.

Not only do ordinances set things in order within the Church and kingdom of God but they also have real power in the lives of those who faithfully receive them. "Through the sacred ordinances of the gospel," Elder Dennis B. Neuenschwander taught, "we learn of His kingdom and learn of Him, we enter into holy and eternal covenants, and we receive an endowment of divine power in our lives. All of these things bring us to Christ that we may be perfected in Him" (26).

SOURCES

Neuenschwander, Dennis B. "Ordinances and Covenants." *Ensign*, Aug. 2001, 20–26.

Packer, Boyd K. "Covenants." *Ensign,* May 1987, 22–25.

BLT

ORIGINAL SIN

The concept of original sin holds that because of the disobedience of Adam and Eve in the Garden of Eden, because our first parents partook of the forbidden fruit, a taint of sin, the "curse of Adam"—what traditional Christendom has come to define as original sin—was transmitted by birth to all their posterity down to the end of time. Latter-day Saints reject the notion of original sin because (1) the idea did not originate with the prophets and is not set forth in scripture; rather, its roots may be traced largely to Saint Augustine (A.D. 354–430), the renowned doctor of the Christian church whose writings have affected Christian teachings for centuries. (2) Modern revelation attests that Adam and Eve were forgiven by God for their actions in Eden (Moroni 8:8; Moses 6:53–54) and that "men will be punished for their own sins, and not for Adam's transgression" (Articles of Faith 1:2).

To be sure, the effects of the Fall, including spiritual and temporal death, are significant and universal and can be overcome only through the gospel of Jesus Christ. The Fall and the Atonement were clearly foreseen and foreknown by God from eternity past; with the Creation, they are central to the Father's plan of salvation.

RLM

ORTHODOXY

The English terms *orthodox* and *orthodoxy* come from the combination of two Greek words, *orthos* ("right, straight, true") and *doxa* ("opinion," "thought," or "teaching"). Thus, the word *orthodox* means "right opinion" or "straight thinking." Something that is orthodox conforms to correct, established beliefs and doctrines as determined by Church leadership. Orthodoxy is the quality, practice, or position of being orthodox. Its opposite is *heterodoxy* (Greek, "other teaching"). Heterodox views lead to apostasy (from Greek, *apostasia,* "to stand apart from"), which is rebellion against the established beliefs, doctrines, principles, and practices of the Lord's Church.

Latter-day Saint orthodoxy is based on the pronouncements of living prophets and apostles, an expanded canon of written scripture called the standard works, heaven-sanctioned ordinances, and the teachings of those in authority when moved upon by the Holy Ghost (D&C 68:4). Latter-day Saint orthodoxy is true and living because it is found in The Church of Jesus Christ of Latter-day Saints, which is true and living (D&C 1:30). Orthodoxy is not static in the Lord's Church but is responsive to challenges presented by modernity. Latter-day Saint orthodox positions are ultimately determined by the prophet and senior apostle of the Church on earth, the only person who possesses and is authorized to exercise all priesthood keys (D&C 132:7). Teachers and leaders in the Church are to preach only that which is orthodox according to the Lord's standard (D&C 52:9). It seems self-evident that wise parents will do the same.

Any position, belief, or feeling that is not orthodox is out of harmony with the Lord's will. The twin pillars of Latter-day Saint orthodoxy have been succinctly summarized by President J. Reuben Clark Jr., a member of the First Presidency for twenty-eight years (1933–1961). In a landmark address titled "The Charted Course of the Church in Education," delivered 8 August 1938, President Clark stated:

"In all this there are for the Church, and for each and all of its members, two prime things which may not be overlooked, forgotten, shaded, or discarded:

"First—that Jesus is the Son of God, the Only Begotten of the Father in the flesh, the Creator of the world, the Lamb of God, the Sacrifice for the sins of the world, the Atoner for Adam's transgression; that He was crucified; that His spirit left His body; that He died; that He was laid away in the tomb; that on the third day His spirit was reunited with His body, which again became a living being; that He was raised from the tomb a resurrected being, a perfect Being, the First Fruits of the Resurrection; that He later ascended to the Father; and that because of His death and by and through His resurrection every man born into the world since the beginning will be likewise literally resurrected. . . .

"The second of the two things to which we must all give full faith is that the Father and the Son actually and in truth and very deed appeared to the Prophet Joseph in a vision in the woods; that other heavenly visions followed to Joseph and to others; that the gospel and the Holy Priesthood, after the Order of the Son of God were in truth and fact restored to the earth from which they were lost by the apostasy of the primitive Church; that the Lord again set up His Church, through the agency of Joseph Smith; that the Book of Mormon is just what it professes to be; that to the Prophet came numerous revelations for the guidance, upbuilding, organization, and encouragement of the Church and its members; that the Prophet's successors, likewise called of God, have received revelations as the needs of the Church have required, and that they will continue to receive revelations as the Church and its members, living the truth they already have, shall stand in need of more; that this is in truth The Church of Jesus Christ of Latter-day Saints; and that its foundation beliefs are the laws and principles laid down in the Articles of Faith. These facts also, and each of them, together with all things necessarily implied therein or flowing therefrom, must stand, unchanged, unmodified, without dilution, excuse, apology, or avoidance; they may not be explained away or submerged. Without these two great beliefs the Church would cease to be the Church.

"Any individual who does not accept the fulness of these doctrines as to Jesus of Nazareth or as to the restoration of the gospel and holy priesthood is not a Latter-day Saint" (56).

Orthodoxy is much like the path that the Lord declared to be strait and narrow; it is constricted (3 Nephi 14:13–14; Matthew 7:13–14). It makes no difference whether someone goes off the path to the left or to the right, being either too liberal or too conservative. It is still off the path. The Lord has commanded all to enter in at the strait gate (3 Nephi 14:13; Matthew 7:13). The prophet Nephi knew the challenges of orthodoxy in his day and ours, and so he prayed: "May the gates of hell be shut continually before me, because that my heart is broken and my spirit is contrite! O Lord, wilt thou not shut the gates of thy righteousness before me, that I may walk in the path of the low valley, *that I may be strict in the plain road*" (2 Nephi 4:32; emphasis added).

Father Lehi saw in vision the strait and narrow path; he saw many that were lost because they strayed from that safe path of orthodoxy and wandered in strange roads (1 Nephi 8:20, 32). Both Lehi and Nephi saw the mists of darkness—the devil's temptations that lead individuals away from the strait and narrow path into broad roads, which may be termed heterodoxy (1 Nephi 12:17). Pride often leads individuals into the realm of heterodoxy. Teachers constantly face the temptation of priestcraft, which is "that men [and women] preach and set themselves up for a light unto the world, that they may get gain and praise of the world; but they seek not the welfare of Zion" (2 Nephi 26:29). Only by praying and striving to eliminate pride from our lives, to follow the strait and narrow path, to remain orthodox in all we think and do, can our faith and our beliefs "divide asunder all the cunning and the snares and the wiles of the devil, and lead the man [or woman] of Christ in a strait and narrow course across that everlasting gulf of misery which is prepared to engulf the wicked—and land their souls . . . at the right hand of God in the kingdom of heaven" (Helaman 3:29–30).

It must be remembered that there are some matters and issues for which there is no orthodox position in the Lord's Church. We have the Lord's promise, however, that there is "a time to come in the which nothing shall be withheld" (D&C 121:28). Until that time comes, the Lord's people must be wise regarding what they say and do with respect to matters that fall outside of orthodoxy. As a wise man said, "In the mouth of the foolish is a rod of pride: but the lips of the wise shall preserve them" (Proverbs 14:3; see also v. 16).

SOURCE

Clark, J. Reuben, Jr. "Excerpts from the Charted Course of the Church in Education." *Ensign,* Sept. 2002, 54–61.

ACS

OUTER DARKNESS

Alma referred to that portion of the postmortal spirit world that is often known as hell or spirit prison as "outer darkness," a place where there will be among "the spirits of the wicked . . . weeping, and wailing, and gnashing of teeth, and this because of their own iniquity, being led captive by the will of the devil. Now this is the state of the souls of the wicked, yea, in darkness" (Alma 40:13–14). From this condition individuals will be released after they have paid the penalty for their sins and met the requisite demands of justice, all before coming forth in the last resurrection at the end of the Millennium.

Outer darkness is also used to describe the final state of the sons of perdition, the only ones who will be subject to the second death, meaning the second spiritual death, and who will suffer over their denial, defiance, and defection for eternity (D&C 76:31–32).

RLM

PARABLE/PARABLES

A parable is a succinct story that describes one thing in the guise of another, attempting to convey a deeper understanding of a concept, principle, or moral lesson. The word derives from the Greek *parabolē*, meaning "to set side by side." Thus, a parable is essentially a comparison or analogy, sometimes described as an extended metaphor. Unlike a simile, a parable's parallel meaning is unspoken and implicit. However, parables may have layers of meaning. They depict images common to members of a particular society. Thus, parables are usually specific to the culture in which they are presented. They are based on the fundamental values and norms of that society. Each parable is drawn from life, a short story that encompasses a spiritual message. Parables are a well-known teaching method. They are found in many cultures of the world, and most great teachers, especially in the ancient Near East, have used them.

The parables of Jesus use the same method of teaching that was familiar to ancient Israel from the time of the judges onward and that was constantly used by rabbis of late antiquity. The written Jewish collections known as the Talmud and Midrash, though appearing long after the Savior's ascension, contain many parables and narratives derived from an earlier period involving sowing and harvesting, farming and building, stewards, landlords, tenants, and peasants. There are rabbinic stories of hidden treasure, a Pharisee and a publican, a prodigal son, a feast given to the poor but meant for others, and so on. In short, many of the stories told by Jesus were familiar to the great Jewish teachers of that period, but their uniqueness came in the way Jesus used them: the messages, the lessons, and the doctrines he illustrated and emphasized centered on him and his gospel.

Parables constitute a significant portion of Jesus' teaching ministry, making up about one-third of his recorded teachings. The parables of Jesus are recorded in the synoptic Gospels. Many scholars agree that parables, as such, are noticeably absent from John's Gospel. The Gospel of Luke contains both the greatest total number of parables as well as the greatest number of unique parables—those not found in the other Gospels. At a certain point in his Galilean ministry, Jesus did not teach without using parables. But then when he was alone with the Twelve, he "expounded all things" to them (Mark 4:34).

The Prophet Joseph Smith presented a key interpretive principle by which to understand the meaning of the scriptures in general and parables in particular. "I enquire, what was the question which drew out the answer, or caused Jesus to utter the parable?" (5:261).

Jesus taught with parables for several reasons.

1. *Parables were part of the world in which he grew up and lived as an adult.* The greatest teachers and rabbis of Jesus' era used parables, even some of the very same elements found in the parables presented by the Savior. Perhaps Jesus used both the general outline as well as specific elements of parables taught by others precisely because they were so well known and his listeners already knew, or at least knew about, the stock-in-trade stories he presented. With Jesus' parables, however, there was not only something new, a singular application, but as with all his teachings, "he taught them as one having authority, and not as the scribes" (Matthew 7:29). Perhaps people "were astonished at his doctrine" (Matthew 7:28) because his parables were unique, even though they sometimes may have contained the same elements, subjects, and objects as the stories of other great teachers.

2. *Parables teach by analogies that are not easily forgotten.* Because parables compare or set principles of the gospel side by side with ordinary objects, common events, or familiar circumstances of life, they could be readily identified and understood. Each parable was drawn from life, a short story that encompassed a spiritual message. By placing real-life stories familiar to all people side by side with gospel principles, the Savior could stimulate his hearers' thinking and give ordinary, easily visualized reminders of the eternal principles he taught.

3. *Parables have a double use in communicating messages*—they can simultaneously veil or unveil concepts, reveal or conceal meaning, according to an individual's spiritual capacity and ability to receive. Thus, the Savior could simultaneously teach truths to those ready to receive them and withhold truths from those unprepared to receive

them. As the Savior explained to his disciples, "Therefore speak I to them in parables: because they seeing see not; and hearing they hear not, neither do they understand" (Matthew 13:13). Every person could be taught a different but true lesson, depending on each one's understanding of the objects used in the parable. A parable conveys truth to the listener in direct proportion to his or her faith and intelligence.

The prophet Alma taught: "It is given unto many to know the mysteries of God; nevertheless they are laid under a strict command that they shall not impart only according to the portion of his word which he doth grant unto the children of men, according to the heed and diligence which they give unto him. And therefore, he that will harden his heart, the same receiveth the lesser portion of the word; and he that will not harden his heart, to him is given the greater portion of the word, until it is given unto him to know the mysteries of God until he know them in full" (Alma 12:9–10).

4. *By teaching in parables, the Lord protected unprepared individuals from more truth than they could live—a merciful way to teach.* In premortality "we were duly informed that in this mortal life we would have to walk by faith. Previously we had walked by sight, but now was to come a period of trial to see if by faith we would be true to every covenant and commandment our Father required at our hands" (Smith, *Doctrines,* 1:57–58).

The parables can be understood on different levels. A veiled view of them would render only the lesser portion of what was meant. If individuals with veiled minds had been listening to the Savior teach, they would have heard a few simple stories about common, familiar things. But those same individuals, listening by the Spirit, would have understood that each story was given to teach an eternal principle or truth. And if they were sensitive to the Spirit's promptings, they would have readily perceived that parables have multiple levels of meaning and may simultaneously teach more than one principle. Certainly, parables reach people on more than one level and even reach people living in different periods of time.

5. *On occasion the Savior taught in parables so that his listeners could not possibly misunderstand his intention.* At one point he said, "I speak in parables; that your unrighteousness may be rewarded unto you" (JST, Matthew 21:34). This is specifically true of the Jewish leaders

of Jesus' day, some of whom were responsible for his death. They were condemned because they understood but refused to act accordingly. "Woe unto you, scribes and Pharisees, hypocrites! for ye are like unto whited sepulchres, which indeed appear beautiful outward, but are within full of dead men's bones, and of all uncleanness. Even so ye also outwardly appear righteous unto men, but within ye are full of hypocrisy and iniquity" (Matthew 23:27–28).

Of particular interest to Latter-day Saints are the parables of Matthew 13. The Prophet Joseph Smith believed that Jesus uttered these parables to teach the singular message of the gathering of Israel in the latter days and that these parables afford us "as clear an understanding upon the important subject of the gathering, as anything recorded in the Bible" (2:264). Following are the eight parables of Matthew 13 along with a synopsis of their meaning in relation to the doctrine of the gathering as described by Joseph Smith (2:264–72).

The sower and the soils. Jesus and the apostles sowing the seeds of the gospel in the meridian of time.

The wheat and the tares. The Great Apostasy.

The mustard seed. Restoration—the kingdom rolls forth to fill the earth (Daniel 2).

The three measures of leaven. Witnesses of the Book of Mormon, testimony by revelation, and ordinances that raise sinners to become Saints.

The treasure hidden in a field. Missionary work in the latter days (D&C 123:7–8, 12–14); people gathering to the kingdom.

The pearl of great price. Saints sacrificing to establish Zion in all places.

The net. Gathering to the gospel net; separating good from bad at the Second Coming.

The householder. The millennial day.

As Joseph Smith concluded his instruction to the Saints about these parables, he affirmed the importance they have to us today: "'Jesus saith unto them, Have you understood all these things? They say unto Him, Yea, Lord.' And we say, yea Lord; and well might they say, yea, Lord; for these things are so plain and so glorious that every Saint in the last days must respond with a hearty Amen to them" (2:272).

SOURCES

Smith, Joseph. *History of The Church of Jesus Christ of Latter-day Saints.* Edited by B. H. Roberts. 7 vols. 2d ed. rev. Salt Lake City: The Church of Jesus Christ of Latter-day Saints, 1932–51.

Smith, Joseph Fielding. *Doctrines of Salvation.* Compiled by Bruce R. McConkie. 3 vols. Salt Lake City: Bookcraft, 1954–56.

ACS

PARADISE

At death, we pass instantaneously into the postmortal spirit world. There we undergo a kind of partial judgment, after which our spirit goes either to spirit prison or to paradise. Spirit prison, or hell, is a temporary abode of disembodied spirits at various levels of preparation, knowledge, and goodness who are given an opportunity to acknowledge their wrongdoing on earth, repent of sin, learn the principles of the gospel of Jesus Christ, choose whether they will receive that gospel, and prepare for resurrection. Paradise is a temporary sphere of existence into which the faithful and obedient are received at the time of death, a world in which their spirits continue to grow, expand in understanding, become more refined, and prepare for the resurrection of the just. In short, paradise is "a state of happiness, . . . a state of rest, a state of peace, where they shall rest from all their troubles and from all care, and sorrow" (Alma 40:12).

We learn from President Joseph F. Smith's vision of the redemption of the dead (D&C 138) that after His death on the cross, our Lord and Savior entered paradise and was there greeted by "an innumerable company of the spirits of the just, who had been faithful in the testimony of Jesus while they lived in mortality. . . . All these had departed the mortal life, firm in the hope of a glorious resurrection, through the grace of God the Father and his Only Begotten Son, Jesus Christ" (vv. 12, 14). Jesus "preached to them the everlasting gospel, the doctrine of the resurrection and the redemption of mankind from the fall, and from individual sins on conditions of repentance" (v. 19). Further, the Lord organized the faithful in paradise and empowered them to bridge the gulf that had separated the righteous from the wicked in the spirit world (Luke 16:26; 1 Nephi 15:28–30; Alma 26:20). In other words, the inhabitants of paradise were commissioned to enter the other realm of the spirit world to minister where the Savior "could not go personally, because of their rebellion and transgression, that they through the ministration of his servants might also hear his words" (D&C 138:37).

One frequently misunderstood New Testament passage is the account of the Savior's exchange with the thief on the cross during the final moments of our Lord's mortal existence: "And one of the malefactors which were hanged railed on [Jesus], saying, If thou be Christ, save thyself and us. But the other answering rebuked him, saying, Dost not thou fear God, seeing thou art in the same condemnation? And we indeed justly; for we receive the due reward of our deeds: but this man hath done nothing amiss. And he said unto Jesus, Lord, remember me when thou comest into thy kingdom. And Jesus said unto him, Verily I say unto thee, *To day shalt thou be with me in paradise*" (Luke 23:39–43; emphasis added).

A prevalent misperception of this dialogue hinges on the word *paradise*, and that is the idea of deathbed repentance, the notion that a person can postpone until just before death a confession of the Lord Jesus Christ, the acknowledgment of his divine sonship, and the outward fruits of conversion. Though we must never discount the value of sincere repentance, no matter how late it occurs in a person's earthly life (Matthew 20:1–16), yet the word of the Lord is clear that "he that repents and *does the commandments of the Lord* shall be forgiven" (D&C 1:32; emphasis added). "Not every one that saith unto me, Lord, Lord, shall enter into the kingdom of heaven," the Master taught, "but he that doeth the will of my Father which is in heaven" (Matthew 7:21). Confession and repentance prompted by the imminence of death hardly prepare an individual's soul for a place with the sanctified.

In discoursing upon our Lord's words on the cross, the Prophet Joseph Smith observed: "I will say something about the spirits in prison. There has been much said by modern divines about the words of Jesus (when on the cross) to the thief, saying, 'This day shalt thou be with me in paradise.' King James' translators make it [presumably the Greek word *Hades*] out to say paradise. But what is paradise? It is a modern word: it does not answer at all to the original word that Jesus made use of. Find the original of the word paradise. You may as easily find a needle in a haymow. . . . There is nothing in the original word in Greek from which this was taken that signifies paradise; but it was—*This day thou shalt be with me in the world of spirits*" (5:424–25; emphasis added). Joseph Smith also taught: "Hades, the Greek, or Shaole, the Hebrew: these two significations mean a world of spirits. *Hades, Shaole, paradise, spirits in prison, are all one: it is a world of spirits*" (5:425; emphasis added).

Not discounting in any way, therefore, the feelings of contrition that may have existed in the heart of the thief on the cross, Elder Parley P. Pratt explained that this man went into the world of spirits "in a state of ignorance, and sin, being uncultivated, unimproved, and unprepared for salvation. He went there to be taught, and to complete that repentance, which in a dying moment he commenced on the earth" (1:9). As the Prophet said, our Savior "knows the situation of both the living and the dead, and has made ample provision for their redemption, according to their several circumstances, and the laws of the kingdom of God, whether in this world, or in the world to come" (4:597).

SOURCES

Pratt, Parley P. In *Journal of Discourses*. 26 vols. London: Latter-day Saints' Book Depot, 1854–86.

Smith, Joseph. *History of The Church of Jesus Christ of Latter-day Saints*. Edited by B. H. Roberts. 7 vols. 2d ed. rev. Salt Lake City: The Church of Jesus Christ of Latter-day Saints, 1932–51.

RLM

PASSOVER

Passover was both a feast and an ordinance (Exodus 12:14) instituted by Jehovah among the Israelites to commemorate their deliverance from Egyptian bondage as well as the deliverance of their first born from physical death (Exodus 12:27; 13:15). It derives its name (Hebrew, *pesach*) from God's act of passing over those houses marked with blood from the Passover or paschal lambs that Israelite households were commanded to slay and eat (Exodus 12:6–7, 13). Passover became one of three pilgrimage or sanctuary festivals that Israel was commanded to observe (Exodus 23:14–17; Deuteronomy 16:16). Thus, three times a year all males of the covenant were required to appear before the Lord at the place he chose—first the tabernacle and later the Jerusalem temple.

The deeper symbolic intent of Passover was to point to the ministry and sacrifice of the Lamb of God, who is Jesus Christ. Most elements of the Passover do just that in one way or another. In fact, ancient and modern prophetic references to Jesus Christ as the Lamb of God hark back to the Passover. But there is more:

- Passover marked a new beginning (Exodus 12:2), just as Jesus Christ brought a new beginning (2 Corinthians 5:17; Romans 6:3–4).

- The lamb chosen to be killed was to be a male without blemish (Exodus 12:3, 5), just as Jesus was the Lamb without blemish, chosen in premortality to be humankind's Redeemer (1 Peter 1:18–20).

- The firstborn in Egypt perished because of the sins and obstinacy of others (Exodus 11:5; 12:12), just as the Firstborn of God perished because of the sins of others (Colossians 1:12–15; 2 Corinthians 5:21).

- The blood of the Passover lamb caused death to pass by (Exodus 12:13; Leviticus 17:11), just as the blood of Christ causes physical and spiritual death to pass by and brings eternal salvation (Hebrews 9:12–15).

- No bone of the paschal lamb was to be broken (Exodus 12:46), just as no bone of Christ was broken (John 19:36).

- The Israelites ate the flesh of the paschal lamb to fulfill the commandment (Exodus 12:8), just as disciples of Jesus Christ must symbolically "eat" his flesh through the ordinance of the sacrament to fulfill the commandment (John 6:51–58).

- No stranger was to partake of the paschal lamb (Exodus 12:43), just as no unworthy person is to partake of the sacrament (3 Nephi 18:28–30).

- Hyssop was used in performance of the Passover ritual (Exodus 12:22), just as hyssop was used during Christ's crucifixion (John 19:29).

- Leaven was purged from the houses of the Israelites (Exodus 12:15), just as the "old leaven" is to be purged from the lives of the disciples who are under the new covenant (1 Corinthians 5:6–8).

- The Israelites who were poor became rich, and the Egyptians who were rich became poor as a result of Passover (Exodus 12:35–36), just as disciples who are "poor in spirit" (Matthew 5:3) become rich as a result of the Atonement (Luke 16:25; D&C 38:39). There will be a great reversal of fortunes through Jesus Christ.

Though some elements of Passover in Jesus' day appear to have been added, changed, or emphasized, they still pointed to the Savior. For example, the four cups of wine consumed during different stages of the Passover feast in New Testament times represented the spilled blood of Christ, especially the third cup, "the cup after supper" (Luke 22:20), which was mixed with water and pointed to the event recorded in John 19:34: "But one of the soldiers with a spear pierced his side, and forthwith came there out blood and water." It seems to have been at this juncture—the cup after supper during the last Passover Jesus celebrated with his disciples in the upper room—that the Passover feast was fully transformed into the sacrament of the Lord's Supper.

Luke records that after Jesus had broken bread and given it to the disciples, he purposely changed the intent for which they had met: "This is my body which is given for you: this do in remembrance of me" (Luke 22:19). No longer were the disciples to remember the blood of paschal lambs, the Exodus, and corporate deliverance from physical and spiritual bondage. Now they must remember in a personal way Jesus Christ, the One who instituted Passover, the One who delivers from physical and spiritual death, the One who would work out the infinite and eternal Atonement through the shedding of his blood. "Likewise also the cup after supper, saying, This cup is the new testament in my blood, which is shed for you" (Luke 22:20). At that moment, and forever after, Jesus became "our passover . . . sacrificed for us" (1 Corinthians 5:7). In other words, Passover as such ended for the disciples of Jesus Christ, and a new aspect of the permanent ordinance (Exodus 12:17, 24) began to be observed.

Jews today still celebrate Passover, though it has changed for them as well. Since the destruction of the temple in A.D. 70, a paschal lamb is no longer sacrificed, nor is one eaten at celebrations of the feast. Recounting the Exodus story is a major element of the modern Passover. The Passover feast is also referred to as the Seder (Hebrew, "order, arrangement") meal. As in ancient times, Passover in the land of Israel is a seven-day observance called the Feast of Unleavened Bread (Luke 22:7). Outside of Israel an extra day was added, a second "first day" of observance, because communications officially announcing the start of Passover could be delayed.

For centuries many Jews have waited for the appearance of Elijah during their yearly Passover celebration. A place setting is even reserved for him. From a sample Jewish Passover narrative we read: "For our legends tell us that Elijah enters every house where a Seder is taking place. Why Elijah? Of all our Biblical Prophets, it is Elijah who became the kindly mediator between Heaven and Earth. The Bible stories tell us of a fiery chariot sent to carry him up to Heaven. And from Heaven, he was to return to help prepare mankind for the dreamed-of time of the coming of the Messiah, the time of judgment and redemption. The Prophet Malachi foretold this about Elijah, when he said,

> Behold, I will send you Elijah the Prophet
> Before the coming of the great and terrible day of the Lord,
> And he shall turn the hearts of the fathers to the children,
> And the hearts of the children to their fathers. (Levin, 93–94)

Significantly, Elijah did return at Passover time (along with Jehovah, Moses, and Elias) to the Kirtland Temple to restore priesthood keys to fulfill Malachi's prophecy (D&C 110). That day, 3 April 1836, was the second "first day" of Passover for Jews living outside the land of Israel. Elder Joseph Fielding Smith, in his April 1936 general conference address, stated: "It was, I am informed, on the third day of April, 1836, that the Jews, in their homes at the Paschal feast, opened their doors for Elijah to enter. On that very day Elijah did enter—not in the home of the Jews to partake of the Passover with them, but he appeared in the House of the Lord" (75).

In modern revelation the Lord graphically linked the Word of Wisdom to the first Passover observed anciently: "And all saints who remember to keep and do these sayings, walking in obedience to the commandments, shall receive health in their navel and marrow to their bones; and shall find wisdom and great treasures of knowledge, even hidden treasures; and shall run and not be weary, and shall walk and not faint. And I, the Lord, give unto them a promise, that the destroying angel shall pass by them, as the children of Israel, and not slay them. Amen" (D&C 89:18–21).

SOURCES

Levin, Meyer. *An Israel Haggadah for Passover.* New York: Harry N. Abrams, 1970.
Smith, Joseph Fielding. In Conference Report, Apr. 1936, 72–76.

ACS

PATRIARCH

There are two main uses of the term *patriarch* within the teachings of The Church of Jesus Christ of Latter-day Saints. First, in a broad sense, a patriarch is a father—the presiding officer over a family unit. In the family setting, a father has the right and responsibility to provide for, protect, teach, and spiritually guide his family. This role could properly be called a "natural patriarch"—a role that comes with the covenant of marriage and fathering children. It becomes even more spiritually significant when coupled with the ordinances of the temple. Elder Bruce R. McConkie taught, "Every holder of the higher priesthood who has entered into the patriarchal order of celestial marriage—thereby receiving for himself the blessings of the patriarchs Abraham, Isaac, and Jacob—is a natural patriarch to his posterity" (560). We refer to great prophets and spiritual leaders that preceded Moses, such as Abraham, Isaac, and Jacob, as "the patriarchs." Their age is referred to as the patriarchal period because they not only presided as natural patriarchs over their families but they also held the keys of the priesthood and administered the principles and ordinances of the gospel for their respective generations (D&C 107:40–53).

A second and more restricted usage of the term *patriarch* is an ordained office of the Melchizedek Priesthood. Doctrine and Covenants 107 refers to the office of patriarch as "evangelist" (v. 39). The Prophet Joseph Smith explained that "an evangelist is a Patriarch" and that "wherever the Church of Christ is established in the earth, there should be a Patriarch for the benefit of the posterity of Saints, as it was with Jacob in giving his patriarchal blessing unto his sons" (140). "The calling of a patriarch is the calling of revelation," President Boyd K. Packer explained. "The patriarch in a sense is a prophet to give blessings which really in effect are a prophecy for each individual" (142).

In the early days of the Church, a patriarch for the entire Church was called to have the responsibility to give patriarchal blessings to the members. As the Church expanded and stakes were organized, patriarchs were called and ordained under the direction of the Quorum of the Twelve and set apart to give blessings to members within a geographical stake of Zion (D&C 107:39). With virtually every member of the Church having access to an ordained stake patriarch for blessings, the office of patriarch to the Church was eliminated in 1979. As with other offices in the priesthood, once a man is ordained to an office he retains that office (except in the case of excommunication). Thus, a man who is released from his specific service as a stake patriarch is not released from the priesthood office of patriarch. An ordained patriarch is also a high priest and is a member of a stake or district high priests quorum. As such, except as he pronounces patriarchal blessings, he serves in the office of high priest in the Melchizedek Priesthood.

SOURCES

Joseph Smith [manual]. Teachings of Presidents of the Church series. Salt Lake City: The Church of Jesus Christ of Latter-day Saints, 2007.

McConkie, Bruce R. *Mormon Doctrine.* 2d ed. Salt Lake City: Bookcraft, 1966.

Packer, Boyd K. *Mine Errand from the Lord: Selections from the Sermons and Writings of Boyd K. Packer.* Salt Lake City: Deseret Book, 2008.

BLT

PATRIARCHAL BLESSING

"Wherever the Church of Christ is established in the earth," Joseph Smith declared, "there should be a Patriarch for the benefit of the posterity of the Saints, as it was with Jacob in giving his patriarchal blessings unto his sons" (3:381). Every worthy member of the Church has the right and is encouraged to receive a blessing under the hands of an ordained patriarch. From the beginning of time, this Melchizedek Priesthood office has played a unique role in the kingdom of God (Genesis 49:11–28; Ephesians 4:11; 2 Nephi 4:3–11; D&C 107:39, 42–56; 124:91–92). "The office of patriarchy is one of the great separate priesthood offices of the Melchizedek Priesthood," Elder James E. Faust explained. "The patriarchal office is one of blessing, not of administration, nor of counseling" (53–54). There are two main purposes for patriarchal blessings: (1) the declaration of lineage and (2) the pronouncement of specific blessings and inspired, personal direction for the individual receiving the blessing.

Declaration of lineage. Abraham was promised of God that his descendants would "bear this ministry and Priesthood unto all nations" by bringing to "all the families of the earth" the gospel of Jesus Christ and the "blessings of salvation, even of life eternal" (Abraham 2:9, 11). Descendants of Abraham, through the lineage of Israel, have been promised not only the blessings of the patriarchs but also a birthright responsibility. A declaration of lineage in a patriarchal blessing speaks of this sacred responsibility and provides a glimpse of what the descendants were like before they were born into mortality. Moses taught that the house of Israel was established even before the foundation of the earth (Deuteronomy 32:7–9). As a result, patriarchal blessings may help individuals know that they were tested, tried, and proven before they were born into mortality.

Elder Melvin J. Ballard explained: "Through this lineage were to come the true and tried souls that had demonstrated their righteousness in the spirit world before they came here. . . . Our particular branch is the house of Joseph through his son Ephraim. That is the group whence shall come the majority of the candidates for celestial glory" (218–19). Every member of the Church, whether descended from the bloodline of Israel or adopted into the lineage through baptism and conversion, takes upon himself or herself the birthright covenants. The declaration of lineage reminds us of who we were before we came to earth, what our spiritual responsibilities are while we are here, and what rewards await those who are true to the covenants of Abraham, Isaac, and Jacob.

Pronouncement of blessings and direction. To assist his children in fulfilling their missions in mortality and to realize their eternal potential, God gives his faithful children the opportunity to receive personal guidance in the form of patriarchal blessings. The revelation received therein is, President Thomas S. Monson taught, "a white line down the middle of the road, to protect, inspire, and motivate activity and righteousness. A patriarchal blessing literally contains chapters from your book of eternal possibilities" (66). Patriarchal blessings are recorded and carefully transcribed, with copies sent to the recipient and to LDS

Church archives. A patriarchal blessing is a sacred, personal revelation and should be viewed reverently and not spoken of widely or lightly. Because of the individualized nature of such blessings, many of the promises and counsel will not be applicable to others or generalizable to the Church as official doctrine. As President Monson taught, this official, written blessing serves as "a personal Liahona" that "will see you through the darkest night," "guide you through life's dangers," and "chart your course and guide your way" (66). Because of the individual nature of these blessings, recipients are counseled to read and review them prayerfully and frequently, pondering on the meaning of the counsel and promises. Many of the promises may not be fully understood until after they are fulfilled during the course of one's life; some promises may not even be realized in mortality but will be fulfilled beyond the veil of death. As with all promised blessings, their realization is conditioned upon personal worthiness and obedience to the principles and ordinances of the gospel. "I, the Lord, am bound when ye do what I say; but when ye do not what I say, ye have no promise" (D&C 82:10; see also D&C 58:31–32; 130:20–21).

SOURCES

Ballard, Melvin J. "The Three Degrees of Glory." In *Crusader for Righteousness*. Salt Lake City: Bookcraft, 1966.

Faust, James E. "Patriarchal Blessings." In *1980 BYU Devotional and Fireside Addresses*. Provo, Utah: Brigham Young University Press, 1981, 53–57.

Monson, Thomas S. "Your Patriarchal Blessing: A Liahona of Light." *Ensign*, Nov. 1986, 65–67.

Smith, Joseph. *History of The Church of Jesus Christ of Latter-day Saints*. Edited by B. H. Roberts. 7 vols. 2d ed. rev. Salt Lake City: The Church of Jesus Christ of Latter-day Saints, 1932–51.

BLT

PATRIARCHAL ORDER

Joseph Smith taught, "All Priesthood is Melchizedek; but there are different portions or degrees of it" (109). One of the degrees or orders of the Melchizedek Priesthood is the patriarchal order, a family-centered system of government that operated from the days of Adam until the time of Moses. In our day we enter into the patriarchal order through the new and everlasting covenant of marriage in the temple. In speaking of the blessings of holding the priesthood, Elder Bruce R.

McConkie stated, "We can enter into the patriarchal order, the order of eternal marriage, the order which enables the family unit to continue everlastingly in celestial glory" (34).

President Howard W. Hunter warned husbands and fathers: "A man who holds the priesthood accepts his wife as a partner in the leadership of the home and family with full knowledge of and full participation in all decisions relating thereto. Of necessity there must be in the Church and in the home a presiding officer (see D&C 107:21). By divine appointment, the responsibility to preside in the home rests upon the priesthood holder (see Moses 4:22). The Lord intended that the wife be a helpmeet for man (*meet* means equal)—that is, a companion equal and necessary in full partnership. Presiding in righteousness necessitates a shared responsibility between husband and wife; together you act with knowledge and participation in all family matters. For a man to operate independently of or without regard to the feelings and counsel of his wife in governing the family is to exercise unrighteous dominion" (49–51). Indeed, the husband or father is counseled to lead his family as Christ leads the Church (Ephesians 5:21–33; Colossians 3:18–22).

SOURCES

Hunter, Howard W. "Being a Righteous Husband and Father." *Ensign,* Nov. 1994, 49–51.

Joseph Smith [manual]. Teachings of Presidents of the Church series. Salt Lake City: The Church of Jesus Christ of Latter-day Saints, 2007.

McConkie, Bruce R. "The Ten Blessings of the Priesthood." *Ensign,* Nov. 1977, 33–35.

RLM

PEACE

In one sense, peace is the absence of war, conflict, or contention. Such conditions have rarely been experienced for any length of time on the earth (4 Nephi 1:1–17; Moses 7:13–16). True peace, however, is not the mere absence of war or even a condition of our fallen world but depends on our accepting and following Christ, the Prince of Peace. Isaiah observed that there is no peace for the wicked (Isaiah 48:22; 1 Nephi 20:22). This is because God is the author of peace (1 Corinthians 14:33), and peace is a gift of God made available only through the atonement of Christ and the companionship of the Spirit (John 14:27; 16:33).

Being "spiritually minded" is the key to living in peace (Romans 8:6). When we are at peace with God, we can be at peace even when the world is in turmoil around us. We will not be unduly concerned about the cares of the world because "the peace of God, which passeth all understanding, shall keep [our] hearts and minds through Christ Jesus" (Philippians 4:7).

Following Christ encourages a proactive approach to peace; we are often reminded to promote peaceful relationships with others, including those who believe differently than we do (Mark 9:50; Romans 12:18–21). King Benjamin taught his people not to "have a mind to injure one another, but to live peaceably, and to render to every man according to that which is his due" (Mosiah 4:13). The Savior admonished us to be "peacemakers" (Matthew 5:9; 3 Nephi 12:9). One way we can make peace is by "publishing peace," as Isaiah counseled (Isaiah 52:7). In a stirring testimony to those who held him captive, Abinadi explained Isaiah's writings to mean that all those who preach Christ's words, who carry the gospel of the "founder of peace" to the world are those who publish peace or are peacemakers (Mosiah 15:11–18). Through our actions as much as through our words, we can influence others to invite the Prince of Peace and his gospel into their lives (D&C 6:33–37).

CFO

PEARL OF GREAT PRICE

The Pearl of Great Price is one of the books within the Latter-day Saint canon of scripture known as the standard works. When Elder Franklin D. Richards of the Quorum of the Twelve Apostles was called to preside over the European Mission (headquartered in England), he discovered that the Saints in England had little Church literature in their possession. He decided to produce a mission pamphlet that contained many of his favorite resources of the Restoration, including selections from the Joseph Smith Translation of the Bible (what we know today as the book of Moses and Joseph Smith–Matthew), revelations that had been given through the Prophet (D&C 20, 77, 107, and 87 [the first time this 1832 prophecy on war had been published]), the translation of the Egyptian papyri that had come into the possession of the Saints in July 1835 and was published in the *Times and Seasons* in 1842 (the book of Abraham and the facsimiles), a portion of Joseph Smith's history of the Church (Joseph Smith–History), thirteen statements of LDS belief (Articles of Faith), and a poem written by British convert John Jaques titled "Truth" (what we would later sing as the hymn "Oh Say, What Is Truth?"). This mission pamphlet was published in Liverpool in 1851 and carried the name *Pearl of Great Price.*

As the British Saints emigrated to Utah, many of them carried with them their copies of the *Pearl of Great Price.* In 1878 Elder Orson Pratt, who had been assigned to prepare a new edition of the Book of Mormon and the Doctrine and Covenants, was similarly charged to prepare the first American edition of the Pearl of Great Price. Elder Pratt organized the materials from the Prophet's translation of the Bible (Moses), deleted from the pamphlet the sections of the Doctrine and Covenants and the poem by John Jaques, and prepared the text to be more reader friendly. All three books that now constitute the triple combination—the Book of Mormon, the Doctrine and Covenants, and the Pearl of Great Price—were presented to the Church in the general conference assembled in October 1880 and accepted as holy scripture. In subsequent years, questions arose concerning the scriptural status of the Articles of Faith. In October 1890 Elder Richards, by then a senior member of the Twelve, presented the Articles of Faith to the Saints, who sustained by vote the decision to consider them as scripture and part of the standard works. In 1921 Elder James E. Talmage prepared an edition of the Pearl of Great Price, which served the Church well for sixty years. In the 1970s teams of Church officers and employees worked tirelessly to prepare an LDS edition of the King James Bible (published in 1977). A new edition of the triple combination, including the Pearl of Great Price, followed in 1981.

In this short sixty-one-page collection, we learn about seven major dispensations—those of Adam, Enoch, Noah, Abraham, Moses, Jesus Christ, and Joseph Smith. We read in this sacred volume of the premortal Council in Heaven, the nature of God, the reality of Satan, the Creation and the Fall, the rise of the kingdom of Satan, the revelation of the gospel to Adam, the ministry and translation of Enoch and his city, the early life of the family of Noah, Abraham and the covenant

Jehovah made with him, the early ministry of Joseph Smith, and the choice selection of doctrinal statements we treasure as the Articles of Faith. The Pearl of Great Price is indeed everything its name implies. What began as one mission president's genuine effort to meet a pressing need in 1850–51 has become a godsend—scriptural manna from heaven that now blesses millions of people worldwide.

RLM

PECULIAR PEOPLE

The apostle Peter taught that through the atonement of Jesus Christ and by obedience to the principles and ordinances of the gospel, faithful disciples become "a chosen generation, a royal priesthood, an holy nation, a *peculiar people;* that ye should shew forth the praises of him who hath called you out of darkness into his marvellous light" (1 Peter 2:9; emphasis added). Peter's words reflect those of the Lord uttered to Moses and the children of Israel in commanding them to prepare themselves to come into the presence of God. "Now therefore, if ye will obey my voice indeed, and keep my covenant, then ye shall be a *peculiar treasure* unto me above all people: for all the earth is mine: and ye shall be unto me a kingdom of priests, and an holy nation" (Exodus 19:5–6; emphasis added).

The Hebrew word for "peculiar" is *segullah,* which signifies a property or a treasure that is exceedingly precious, diligently cared for, and painstakingly preserved. In our modern vernacular, *peculiar* has come to mean "strange," "weird," or "odd" and almost always connotes something negative—a characteristic that is feared, scorned, or avoided. In the scriptural context, however, *peculiar* is a highly valued trait—a positive attribute that bespeaks one's love of God that is noticeably different in righteous ways from the worldly. Being a *peculiar people*—a royal priesthood, a holy nation—requires one to maintain high standards of worthiness in order to fulfill sacred responsibilities and covenantal obligations of the Abrahamic covenant to bless the nations of the earth (Abraham 2:9, 11). For this reason, the Lord often reminded ancient Israel that they could not remain *segullah* and be like everyone else, adopting the wicked and worldly practices of their pagan neighbors.

One of the interesting connotations of the Hebrew word *segullah* is that of a special possession or treasure that has been *purchased.* This idea is even more evident in the Greek word *peripoiesis,* from which the word *peculiar* is translated in the New Testament. Becoming a peculiar people, or a precious treasure, comes through the everlasting covenant and the atonement of Jesus Christ. "For ye are bought with a price," the apostle Paul declared (1 Corinthians 6:20).

For covenant Israel today, it is the same. Through faith in the saving power of Christ and by obedience to the principles and ordinances of his gospel, we become and remain a *peculiar people.* In order for the Church, individually and institutionally, to fulfill its obligation to be the "salt of the earth" (Matthew 5:13)—the preservative or saving agent—it cannot be polluted, diluted, or tainted by impure, foreign elements or by anything that would cause one to be unworthy and abandon the protective covenants of the Lord. Elder Neal A. Maxwell said that peculiar people are "different [from the world] in order to make a difference in the world" (13). As the standards of the world continue to decline, faithful disciples of the Savior who strive to embody in word and deed the teachings of the gospel will increasingly be seen as unique, peculiar, or different. Remaining *segullah*—a unique, untainted spiritual treasure—enables covenant people to bless and sanctify the world. To the Prophet Joseph Smith the Lord declared:

"When men are called unto mine everlasting gospel, and covenant with an everlasting covenant, they are accounted as the salt of the earth and the savor of men; they are called to be the savor of men; therefore, if that salt of the earth lose its savor, behold it is thenceforth good for nothing only to be cast out and trodden under the feet of men" (D&C 101:39–40).

SOURCE

Maxwell, Neal A. "Why Not Now?" *Ensign,* Nov. 1974, 12–13.

BLT

PERDITION, SONS OF

Lucifer, the father of all lies (John 8:44; Moses 4:4), is Perdition, meaning ruin or destruction. It is his work, his whole purpose, to oppose, undermine, and defy the work and glory of God (Moses 1:39) and to proselyte as many to that nefarious effort as possible. Cain became the father of Satan's lies, the devil's earthly counterpart, or

Perdition (Moses 5:24). Those who have accepted the gospel of Jesus Christ through baptism, have received the gift of the Holy Ghost, have had the heavens opened, have come to know God, and who then spurn that supernal knowledge and witness and become an enemy to the cause of righteousness are they whom the scriptures designate as sons of perdition (Smith, 6:314). These are they about whom Jesus spoke when he taught of sin that was unpardonable, of sin or blasphemy against the Holy Ghost, of those who would not be forgiven in this world or the next (Matthew 12:31; Alma 39:6). These were "once enlightened, and have tasted of the heavenly gift, and were made partakers of the Holy Ghost." They have "tasted the good word of God, and the powers of the world to come." They shed the only truly innocent blood; they essentially "crucify to themselves the Son of God afresh, and put him to an open shame" (Hebrews 6:4–6; see also D&C 132:27).

The ultimate fate of the sons of perdition has not been revealed, nor will it be save to those who so qualify; we know only that the sons of perdition who have mortal bodies will be resurrected to a kingdom of no glory (Alma 11:41; D&C 88:32). They "go away into everlasting punishment, which is endless punishment, which is eternal punishment" (D&C 76:44), from which there is no return (Smith, 1:366). They are the only ones who suffer the second death, meaning the second spiritual death (D&C 76:37).

SOURCE

Smith, Joseph. *History of The Church of Jesus Christ of Latter-day Saints.* Edited by B. H. Roberts. 7 vols. 2d ed. rev. Salt Lake City: The Church of Jesus Christ of Latter-day Saints, 1932–51.

RLM

PERFECTION

Because "there is none that doeth good, no, not one" and because "all have sinned and come short of the glory of God" (Romans 3:12, 23), we conclude that no man or woman, save Jesus only (2 Corinthians 5:21; Hebrews 4:15; 1 Peter 2:22), has lived on earth without committing sin. No person has kept the law of God perfectly. In his Sermon on the Mount, Jesus challenged each of us: "Be ye therefore perfect, even as your Father which is in heaven is perfect"

(Matthew 5:48). How do we reconcile the daunting task before us with the fact that no person except the sinless Son of Man has ascended to that height?

For one thing, the Lord does expect us to do our best in life, strive to keep the commandments, and follow God's counsel to the best of our ability. Though we will inevitably fall (D&C 117:13), we keep trying. We draw upon every ounce of strength and willpower we possess to do what's right. On the one hand, we become aware that all things must be done in wisdom and in order, "for it is not requisite that a man should run faster than he has strength." On the other hand, as King Benjamin explained, "it is expedient that [we] should be diligent, that thereby [we] might win the prize" (Mosiah 4:27). While it may be hypothetically possible for a mortal to keep the law of God perfectly (*Lectures,* 59–60), it is practically impossible.

In both the Old Testament (written in Hebrew) and the New Testament (written in Greek), the charge for us to be perfect is in reality a charge for us to become whole, complete, finished, mature, fully formed, and full of integrity. To be perfect is to be focused on one grand end. To be perfect is to be wholly committed to an enterprise. In a gospel sense, then, to be perfect is to be riveted to righteousness, to have cast our lot with the Lord Jesus Christ, to have enlisted wholeheartedly in his army, to have charted a course leading to eternal life, to have made a significant decision to keep our covenants and endure faithfully until death.

We become perfect *in Christ,* in covenant with him, in conjunction with him, and in cooperation with him through the means and by the power of his mighty arm. The invitation of the Savior's Church is always and forevermore for men and women to "come unto Christ, and be perfected in him" (Moroni 10:32). We as finite mortals are empty while he is full. Together we are full. We are incomplete while he is complete. Together we are complete. We are partial while he is whole. Together we are whole. And we are imperfect while he is marvelously perfect. *Together we are perfect.* This background will assist us to understand the language of the vision of the glories regarding those who inherit the celestial kingdom: "These are they who are just men [and women] *made perfect through Jesus the mediator of the new covenant,* who wrought out this perfect atonement through the shedding of his own blood" (D&C 76:69; emphasis added).

Moses wrote that "Noah was a just man, and perfect in his generations, and Noah walked with God" (Genesis 6:9). The scriptures also tell us that "there was a man in the land of Uz, whose name was Job; and that man was perfect and upright, and one that feared God, and eschewed evil" (Job 1:1). In the scriptural sense, therefore, people may be perfect and yet not flawless; their eye may be single to the glory of God (D&C 88:67), and yet they are not without shortcomings or sins. Neither Noah nor Job was without sin, but they loved the Lord with all their heart and made a decision, a life's decision, to follow him and be loyal to the gospel cause all the days of their lives.

SOURCE

Lectures on Faith. Salt Lake City: Deseret Book, 1985.

RLM

PHYSICAL BODY

The scriptures clearly teach that we cannot lay hold upon exaltation and a fulness of joy without coming to earth and receiving mortal physical bodies (D&C 45:17; 93:33–34; 138:15–17). The Prophet Joseph Smith taught that "no person can have this salvation except through a tabernacle" (*History*, 5:388). Having a physical body, the Prophet taught, is a key element in the plan of happiness.

"We came to this earth that we might have a body and present it pure before God in the celestial kingdom. The great principle of happiness consists in having a body. The devil has no body, and herein is his punishment. He is pleased when he can obtain the tabernacle of man, and when cast out by the Savior he asked to go into the herd of swine, showing that he would prefer a swine's body to having none" (*Joseph Smith*, 211).

The apostle Paul taught that the body is a "temple of God" (1 Corinthians 3:16; see also 6:19). It is the earthly tabernacle of the immortal, divine spirit of human beings. These two—the body and the spirit—combined "are the soul of man" (D&C 88:15). It is the spirit that gives life to the body. "Take the spirit from the body," President Brigham Young taught, "and the body is lifeless" (9:287). Although the physical body is dependent upon the spirit for life, the body, nonetheless, can affect spiritual sensitivities. Addictions and sinful behaviors can dull one's ability to feel and respond to the promptings of the Spirit of God. For this reason, the Lord has commanded us to care for and treasure our body as a "tabernacle of God" (D&C 93:35). The Latter-day Saint health code known as the Word of Wisdom is an example of how caring for the physical body brings not only good health and temporal blessings—"health in [the] navel and marrow to [the] bones"—but also spiritual blessings such as "wisdom and great treasures of knowledge, even hidden treasures" (D&C 89:18–19).

The physical body also plays an important role in the testing and experiential purposes of mortality. Because of the fall of Adam, all mankind is subject to pains, sicknesses, temptations, and the natural appetites of the physical body. All of these are necessary to our earthly probation and provide us with opportunities to learn and grow in ways we could not in our first estate. They are also essential as a part of the testing during our earthly probation. The great challenge of mortality is, as the Prophet declared, "to present [our body] pure before God in the celestial kingdom" (*Joseph Smith,* 211). Learning to control our body—subjugating the physical to the spiritual—is the great test of life. President Young taught:

"When you are tempted, buffeted, and step out of the way inadvertently; when you are overtaken in a fault, or commit an overt act unthinkingly; when you are full of evil passion, and wish to yield to it, then stop and let the spirit, which God has put into your tabernacles, take the lead. If you do that, I will promise that you will overcome all evil, and obtain eternal lives. But many, very many, let the spirit yield to the body, and are overcome and destroyed. . . .

"But let the body rise up with its passions, with the fallen nature pertaining to it, and let the spirit yield to it, your destruction is sure. On the other hand, let the spirit take the lead, and bring the body and its passions into subjection, and you are safe" (2:256).

At death the earthly physical body returns to the dust of the earth (Genesis 3:19) as the spirit lives on in the spirit world. Separated from their physical bodies, spirits cannot experience a fulness of joy or achieve the measure of their creation. This can be accomplished only through the reunion of body and spirit known as resurrection. The physical body that is raised from the dead at resurrection is complete, whole, and perfected (Alma 11:43; 40:23). Through the holy resurrection, a vital aspect of the atonement of Jesus Christ, the "corruptible" nature of the mortal physical body will be replaced with "incorruption" (1 Corinthians 15:53–54). At that point our resurrected physical bodies will, as Paul taught, "bear the image of the heavenly" (1 Corinthians 15:49); that is, our glorified bodies will be adapted and capacitated to dwell in a kingdom suited to their nature and according to the law by which we governed our lives (D&C 88:28–31).

SOURCES

Joseph Smith [manual]. Teachings of Presidents of the Church series. Salt Lake City: The Church of Jesus Christ of Latter-day Saints, 2007.

Smith, Joseph. *History of The Church of Jesus Christ of Latter-day Saints.* Edited by B. H. Roberts. 7 vols. 2d ed. rev. Salt Lake City: The Church of Jesus Christ of Latter-day Saints, 1932–51.

Young, Brigham. In *Journal of Discourses.* 26 vols. London: Latter-day Saints' Book Depot, 1854–86.

BLT

PLURAL MARRIAGE

The Church of Jesus Christ of Latter-day Saints teaches that marriage is more than a civil ordinance. It is first and foremost an institution ordained of God (D&C 49:15). Marriage between a man and a woman is sacred. Further, Latter-day Saints believe that marriage and the family were intended to last forever, to survive death. We teach, therefore, that marriages performed in temples by the proper authority do not end with the death of the marriage partners but rather can endure for time and all eternity.

During the ministry of Joseph Smith and continuing for more than fifty years, Latter-day Saints practiced plural marriage because God commanded them to do so. Plural marriage was a religious principle, and this is the only valid explanation as to why the practice was maintained despite decades of opposition and persecution. Introduced by Joseph Smith on a selective basis during his administration as president of the Church (1830–44), the practice of plural marriage was first announced publicly in a general conference of the Church in April 1852 during the administration of President Brigham Young. In 1890, during the administration of President Wilford Woodruff, the practice was officially discontinued. Present-day Church leaders teach that monogamy is the rule. Unauthorized practice of the principle of plural marriage is condemned in the Book of Mormon (Jacob 2:23–30, 34; 3:5), the Doctrine and Covenants (D&C 132:38–39), the sermons of Joseph Smith himself (6:46), and the teachings of current Church leaders.

Most of those who became Latter-day Saints during the nineteenth century had been associated with other religious societies before their conversion and had been reared in traditional, monogamous homes. The idea of having more than one wife came into sharp contrast with all they had been brought up to believe. Therefore plural marriage was at first extremely difficult for many of the Saints to accept, including Church presidents Joseph Smith, Brigham Young, and John Taylor. President Taylor said, "It was the one of the greatest crosses that ever was taken up by any set of men since the world stood" (11:221). President Brigham Young declared: "It was the first time in my life that I had desired the grave, and I could hardly get over it for a long time. And when I saw a funeral I felt to envy the corpse its situation, and to regret that I was not in the coffin" (3:266). Nevertheless, these and other early Latter-day Saints believed that whatever God commanded was right and that plural marriage, when properly performed by authorized persons, was both legal and acceptable to God. Men and women within a plural marriage family were expected to demonstrate loyalty and devotion to spouse and to observe the highest standards of fidelity and morality.

There is scriptural precedent for plural marriage in the lives of noble and faithful men and women in the Old Testament. For example, Abraham, Jacob, and Moses took additional wives (Genesis 16:1–11; 29:28; 30:4, 9, 26; Exodus 2:21; Numbers 12:1), and there is no indication that God disapproved of their actions in any way. In fact, Jesus declared, "I say unto you, That many shall come from the east and west, and shall sit down with Abraham, and Isaac, and Jacob, in the kingdom of heaven" (Matthew 8:11). Nonetheless, God did condemn King David's unauthorized relationship with Bathsheba (2 Samuel 11–12) and King Solomon's marriages to foreign women who turned his heart away from the worship of Jehovah (1 Kings 11).

Members of the Church in this dispensation who entered into this order of matrimony did so under the direction of the presiding authorities of the Church. Elder Orson Pratt, one of the early Latter-day Saint apostles who at first opposed the principle, stated later: "How are these things to be conducted? Are they to be left at random? Is every servant of God at liberty to run here and there, seeking out the daughters of men as wives unto themselves without any restrictions, law, or condition? No. We find these things were restricted in ancient times. Do you not recollect the circumstances of the Prophet Nathan's coming to David? He came to reprove him for certain disobedience. . . . Nathan the Prophet, in relation to David, was the man that held the keys concerning this matter in ancient days; and it was governed by the strictest laws.

"So in these days . . . there is but one man in all the world, at the same time, who can hold the keys of this matter, but one man has power to turn the key to inquire of the Lord, and to say whether I, or these my brethren, or any of the rest of this congregation, or the Saints upon the face of the whole earth, may have this blessing of Abraham conferred upon them; he holds the keys of these matters now, the same as Nathan, in his day" (1:63–64).

Faced with a national antipolygamy campaign, many Latter-day Saint women startled their Eastern sisters (who had equated plural marriage with the oppression of women) by publicly demonstrating in favor of their right to live plural marriage as a religious principle. In January 1870 thousands of women met in the Salt Lake Tabernacle in what they called the Great Indignation Meeting to protest against antipolygamy laws. Nevertheless, public opposition in the United States to the practice of plural marriage grew during the last quarter of the nineteenth century. A number of Church officials were incarcerated, and the government threatened to confiscate Church property, including the temples. In the wake of oppressive laws that had been enacted, President Wilford Woodruff sought the will of the Lord on the matter, and it was revealed to him that plural marriage should be discontinued. President Woodruff issued what has come to be known as the Manifesto, which announced the discontinuation of the practice and which was accepted during general conference in October 1890.

Regarding those who practice polygamy today, President Gordon B. Hinckley said: "I wish to state categorically that this Church has nothing whatever to do with those practicing polygamy.

They are not members of this Church. Most of them have never been members. . . . If any of our members are found to be practicing plural marriage, they are excommunicated, the most serious penalty the Church can impose. . . . More than a century ago God clearly revealed . . . that the practice of plural marriage should be discontinued, which means that it is now against the law of God" (71).

Latter-day Saints believe in "obeying, honoring, and sustaining the law" (Articles of Faith 1:12). While the Church stands firmly against the practice of plural marriage today, Latter-day Saints leave to local magistrates the enforcement of civil law. In speaking of those who continue the practice, President Hinckley added: "They are in violation of the civil law. They know they are in violation of the law. They are subject to its penalties. The Church, of course, has no jurisdiction whatever in this matter" (71).

SOURCES

Hinckley, Gordon B. "What Are People Asking about Us?" *Ensign,* Nov. 1998, 70–72.

Pratt, Orson. In *Journal of Discourses.* 26 vols. London: Latter-day Saints' Book Depot, 1854–86.

Smith, Joseph. *History of The Church of Jesus Christ of Latter-day Saints.* Edited by B. H. Roberts. 7 vols. 2d ed. rev. Salt Lake City: The Church of Jesus Christ of Latter-day Saints, 1932–51.

Taylor, John. In *Journal of Discourses.* 26 vols. London: Latter-day Saints' Book Depot, 1854–86.

Young, Brigham. In *Journal of Discourses.* 26 vols. London: Latter-day Saints' Book Depot, 1854–86.

RLM

PREDESTINATION

At the time of the Protestant Reformation in the sixteenth century, Martin Luther rebelled against what he perceived to be theological and ecclesiastical abuses of the Roman Catholic Church. Luther focused a great deal in his ministry and teachings upon such tenets as *sola scriptura* (scripture alone) and *sola gratia* (salvation by grace alone) and emphasized strongly that men and women are justified or made right with God *sola fides* (through faith alone). John Calvin, though largely in doctrinal agreement with Luther, tended to emphasize much more strongly the divine sovereignty of God—of God being totally and completely in control of all things. This latter teaching led Calvin and his followers to adopt the doctrine of the unconditional election, or predestination, of men and women to either salvation or damnation, heaven or hell—a teaching he revived and resuscitated from the writings of Saint Augustine more than a millennium earlier.

The reasoning behind the teaching is that because of humankind's depravity, no one deserves to be saved. But the Almighty is ever loving and generous, and so, before the foundations of the world, God predetermined that a certain portion of his children would be saved (the elect) and a large portion would be damned (the reprobate). The saved would be born, come to faith at the appropriate time, and manifest their election through righteous living. The damned would wander in the morass of uncertainty and spiritual darkness, never receive Jesus Christ as Lord and Savior, and receive hereafter the just consequences of their waywardness.

In one sentence the Prophet of the Restoration denounced such teachings: "We believe that through the Atonement of Christ, *all mankind may be saved,* by obedience to the laws and ordinances of the Gospel" (Articles of Faith 1:3; emphasis added). In the Book of Mormon, Lehi explained to his son Jacob that because of the Atonement, men and women "are redeemed from the fall" and have "become free forever, knowing good from evil; to act for themselves and not to be acted upon" (2 Nephi 2:26). Similarly, Samuel the Lamanite taught a wicked generation that "whosoever perisheth, perisheth unto himself; and whosoever doeth iniquity, doeth it unto himself; for behold, ye are free; ye are permitted to act for yourselves; for behold, God hath given unto you a knowledge and he hath made you free" (Helaman 14:30). Likewise in our day the Lord has decreed that "men should be anxiously engaged in a good cause, and do many things of their own free will, and bring to pass much righteousness; for the power is in them, wherein they are agents unto themselves" (D&C 58:27–28).

Joseph Smith observed that "unconditional election of individuals to eternal life was not taught by the Apostles. God did elect or predestinate, that all those who would be saved, should be saved in Christ Jesus, and through obedience to the Gospel" (4:360). In other words, it is decreed throughout time and eternity, predestined if you will, that the only way salvation can and will come to individuals and whole nations is through the name and holy work of Jesus the Christ (Acts 4:12; Mosiah 3:17); there is no other way (JST, Romans 8:29–30). But Christ and the gospel of Jesus Christ must be chosen by each individual.

SOURCE

Smith, Joseph. *History of The Church of Jesus Christ of Latter-day Saints.* Edited by B. H. Roberts. 7 vols. 2d ed. rev. Salt Lake City: The Church of Jesus Christ of Latter-day Saints, 1932–51.

RLM

PREMORTAL EXISTENCE

Prior to their birth into mortality, all people were begotten spirit children of God and lived with him. This condition is commonly referred to as the premortal existence. The First Presidency and Council of the Twelve Apostles declared that "in the premortal realm, spirit sons and daughters knew and worshipped God as their Eternal Father and accepted His plan by which His children could obtain a physical body and gain earthly experience to progress toward perfection and ultimately realize [their] divine destiny as [heirs] of eternal life" (102). The scriptures and teachings of latter-day prophets and apostles give us a glimpse into what principles governed and what conditions prevailed in our premortal home. To the Prophet Joseph Smith the Lord declared that "that which is temporal [is] in the likeness of that which is spiritual" (D&C 77:2). Generally, the earthly kingdom of God, or the Church, is patterned after the premortal kingdom. The Lord has yet to lift the veil of forgetfulness concerning the exact conditions there, but he has revealed that order, agency, and the principles of the gospel prevailed in that realm.

A house of order. Wherever the kingdom of God exists—in premortality, in mortality, and in postmortality—order, organization, priesthood keys, offices, assignments, and instruction are in place. This order and organization is eternally intertwined with priesthood. "The Priesthood is an everlasting principle, and existed with God from eternity," Joseph Smith taught. "Its institution was prior to 'the foundation of this earth'" (3:386; 4:207). Alma taught that priesthood leaders on earth were "called and prepared from the foundation of the world" (Alma 13:3). The eternal priesthood is the channel by which come the knowledge and instruction necessary to prepare the spirit children of God for eventual exaltation. This pattern applies to premortal lives as well as to this life and the postmortal world of spirits. Through the power of the priesthood and by the administration of some form of Church organization, premortal spirits "received their first lessons in the world of spirits and were prepared to come forth in the due time of the Lord" (D&C 138:56). President Joseph Fielding Smith taught:

"There must be leaders, presiding officers, and those who are worthy and able to take command. During the ages in which we dwelt in the pre-mortal state we not only developed our various characteristics and showed our worthiness and ability, or the lack of it, but we were also where such progress could be observed. It is reasonable to believe that there was a Church organization there. The heavenly beings were living in a perfectly arranged society. Every person knew his place. Priesthood, without any question, had been conferred and the leaders were chosen to officiate. Ordinances pertaining to that pre-existence were required and the love of God prevailed" (*Way*, 50–51).

A house of agency. Agency was one of the fundamental conditions in the premortal existence for all of the Father's spirit children. Agency is an eternal principle and is essential to the entire plan of salvation. The spirit children of God exercised agency as they chose either to follow the plan of salvation outlined by the Father with Christ as the Savior or to reject that plan and follow Lucifer in premortal rebellion (D&C 29:36–37; Moses 4:3). Undoubtedly, spirits used their agency and made many other choices that affected not only their premortal condition but also their future mortal existence. Knowing that men and women exercised agency in the premortal world can give insight into what other conditions prevailed there. The Book of Mormon prophet Lehi teaches that four fundamental principles must always exist for agency to operate: (1) laws (2 Nephi 2:13), (2) opposition (2 Nephi 2:11), (3) knowledge of good and evil (2 Nephi 2:5), and (4) the power or freedom to choose (2 Nephi 2:16, 27).

The Prophet Joseph Smith clearly taught that the laws, principles, and ordinances of the gospel were ordained, established, and taught before the earth came into existence (5:308; 6:50–51). Premortal councils ensured that all were sufficiently instructed in the laws of God in order to choose wisely. In order for agency to operate in the premortal world, there had to be opposition or enticements—good and evil, virtue and vice, righteousness and wickedness. Likewise, it is necessary to know the difference between the alternatives. In the premortal spirit world, this knowledge came in two ways: instruction and experience. Complete understanding of good and evil could not be obtained by instruction alone; we needed to make choices and experience the consequences of those choices. Premortal experience of good and evil was, however, limited. Spirits could not experience all aspects of righteousness and wickedness—some things could be learned only with physical bodies in a temporal world. Nevertheless, the premortal world did provide sufficient opportunities through effective instruction and by important, albeit limited, experience for the children of God to learn and progress.

Because of individual agency and accountability among the children of God in the premortal spirit world, there were, as there are on earth, varying levels of obedience, faithfulness, service, and devotion, as well as differing degrees of understanding of gospel principles and adherence to them. Abraham saw in vision that premortal spirits were not equally intelligent or "noble and great" (Abraham 3:22–24). These differences resulted from the eternal principle of agency, as taught by President Joseph Fielding Smith:

"God gave his children their free agency even in the spirit world, by which the individual spirits had the privilege, just as men have here, of choosing the good and rejecting the evil or partaking of the evil to suffer the consequences of their sins. Because of this, some even there were more faithful than others in keeping the commandments of the Lord. Some were of greater intelligence than others, as we find it here, and were honored accordingly. . . .

"*The spirits of men were not equal. They may have had an equal start,* and we know they were all innocent in the beginning; but the right of free agency which was given to them enabled some to outstrip others, and thus, through the eons of immortal existence, to become more intelligent, more faithful, for they were free to act for themselves, to think for themselves, to receive the truth or rebel against it" (*Doctrines,* 1:58–59).

Because there must be opposition in order for agency to operate fully and because there was premortal goodness, there was also premortal wickedness. If there was premortal diligence and faithfulness, there must have been premortal slothfulness and disobedience. Undoubtedly, then, sin was possible—ranging from seemingly small sins of omission to blatant, unforgivable rebellion, as in the case of Lucifer and his followers. Gospel principles such as faith in the Lord Jesus Christ and repentance were not only taught but also practiced in the premortal world (Alma 13:3). This would indicate that the Atonement of Jesus Christ was in full effect there (D&C 93:38).

We do not know every detail, but we can in general see that God's kingdom on earth—with its attendant priesthood, Church organization, plan of salvation, and application of gospel principles here and now—is after the pattern of our spirit existence then and there.

SOURCES

First Presidency and Council of the Twelve Apostles. "The Family: A Proclamation to the World." *Ensign,* Nov. 1995, 102.

Smith, Joseph. *History of The Church of Jesus Christ of Latter-day Saints.* Edited by B. H. Roberts. 7 vols. 2d ed. rev. Salt Lake City: The Church of Jesus Christ of Latter-day Saints, 1932–51.

Smith, Joseph Fielding. *Doctrines of Salvation.* Compiled by Bruce R. McConkie. 3 vols. Salt Lake City: Bookcraft, 1954–56.

———. *The Way to Perfection.* Salt Lake City: Deseret Book, 1975.

BLT

PRIESTHOOD

Priesthood is the power of God manifest on earth and in the heavens. "The Priesthood is an everlasting principle," the Prophet Joseph Smith taught, "and existed with God from eternity, and will to eternity, without beginning of days or end of years" (104). It is the power by which worlds, the sun, moon, and stars were created. It is the power that gives life and light to all things. It is the power by which all things are governed. Priesthood is, as President Brigham Young taught, "the means [God] employs to save and exalt his obedient children to the possession with him of the same glory and power to be crowned with crowns of glory, immortality and eternal lives" (5). President John Taylor stated that priesthood "is the government of God, whether on the earth or in the heavens, for it is by that power . . . that all things are upheld and sustained. It governs all things—it directs all things—it sustains all things—and has to do with all things that God and truth are associated with" (321).

Priesthood is the power and authority God gives to others to assist in his work and glory "to bring to pass the immortality and eternal life of man" (Moses 1:39). "Wherever the ordinances of the Gospel are administered," the Prophet Joseph Smith taught, "there is the Priesthood" (105). Adam was the first man on earth to receive this authority from God. Others were likewise authorized with priesthood power to administer the kingdom of God on earth in every dispensation (D&C 84:6–18; 86:8). The Hebrew concept of priesthood, as evidenced in the Old Testament, placed the authorized priesthood leader as a mediator between God and man (Bible Dictionary, 753). Priesthood gives power and authority to God's servants to teach the gospel, to prepare men for salvation, to perform ordinances of salvation, to administer the Church (the earthly kingdom of God), to heal the sick, to cast out devils, and to say what God wants said and do what God wants done (Matthew 10:1–2; 3 Nephi 12:1–2; Mosiah 18:17–20; Moroni 2:1–3; D&C 1:17–30; 84:18–21; 107:18–21). Priesthood is, as President Joseph F. Smith taught, "nothing more nor less than the power of God delegated to man by which man can act in the earth for the salvation of the human family, in the name of the Father and the Son and the Holy Ghost, and act legitimately; not assuming that authority, nor borrowing it from generations that are dead and gone" (5).

God's house—his kingdom in heaven and his Church on earth—is a house of order. As such, the priesthood, as the governing power of that house, is conferred and controlled in an orderly and systematic way. Speaking to his authorized apostles, Jesus said, "Ye have not chosen me, but I have chosen you, and ordained you" (John 15:16). Likewise, the apostle Paul clearly understood and taught that one does not assume priesthood authority on his own but rather receives it from God, in his ordained way and time: "No man taketh this honour unto himself, but he that is called of God, as was Aaron" (Hebrews 5:4; see also Exodus 28:1). Thus, "we believe that a man must be called of God, by prophecy, and by the laying on of hands by those who are in authority, to preach the Gospel and administer in the ordinances thereof" (Articles of Faith 1:5).

God's power is priesthood. The specific vehicle by which that power is manifest on earth is "the Holy Priesthood, after the Order of the Son of God," or what came to be called the Melchizedek Priesthood (D&C 107:3). "All priesthood is Melchizedek," the Prophet Joseph Smith taught, "but there are different portions or degrees of it" (109). The different "portions or degrees" of priesthood are enumerated in modern revelation: "There are, in the church, two priesthoods, namely the Melchizedek and Aaronic, including the Levitical Priesthood" (D&C 107:1). Each of these has unique roles, responsibilities, and powers—all working together to bring the power of God into the lives of his children and by that power to lead them back to his presence.

There is a difference between priesthood power and priesthood office. Ideally, one who has been called and ordained to a priesthood office would also possess God's power. Although one may hold authority, office, and rights of the priesthood, the "powers of heaven" can be "controlled [or] handled only upon the principles of righteousness" (D&C 121:36). Thus, to fully exercise the priesthood of God, one must not only possess the right to use the priesthood, obtained through proper ordination, but also be faithful to the oath and covenant of the priesthood and be worthy to "bear the vessels of the Lord" (D&C 38:42).

SOURCES

Joseph Smith [manual]. Teachings of Presidents of the Church series. Salt Lake City: The Church of Jesus Christ of Latter-day Saints, 2007.

Smith, Joseph F. In Conference Report, Oct. 1904, 1–6.

Taylor, John. "On Priesthood." *Millennial Star* 9, no. 21 (1 Nov. 1847): 321–26.

Young, Brigham. *Discourses of Brigham Young.* Selected and arranged by John A. Widtsoe. Salt Lake City: Deseret Book, 1954.

BLT

PRIESTHOOD, FULNESS OF

In explaining to the early Saints why they were to begin the construction of the Nauvoo Temple, the Lord declared that "there is not a place found on earth that he may come to and restore again that which was lost unto you, or which he hath taken away, even the fulness of the priesthood" (D&C 124:28). President Gordon B. Hinckley reminded us that "the blessings of the temple represent that fulness of the priesthood of which the Lord spoke when He revealed His will unto the Prophet Joseph Smith. With the location of temples much nearer to the homes of our people, there is made more available to them all of the ordinances to be had in the Lord's house for both the living and the dead" (5).

The Prophet Joseph Smith pointed out: "If a man gets a fullness of the priesthood of God, he has to get it in the same way that Jesus Christ obtained it, and that was by keeping all the commandments and obeying all the ordinances of the house of the Lord" (5:424). President Joseph Fielding Smith likewise explained, "I do not care what office you hold in the Church—you may be an apostle, you may be a patriarch, a high priest, or anything else—but you cannot receive the fullness of the priesthood and the fullness of eternal reward unless you receive the ordinances of the house of the Lord" (58). Men and women "who become heirs of God and joint heirs with Jesus Christ," Brother Joseph said, "will have to receive the fulness of the ordinances of [God's] kingdom" (5:424) Those who hold the fulness of the Melchizedek Priesthood "are kings and priests of the Most High God, holding the keys of power and blessings" (5:555).

SOURCES

Hinckley, Gordon B. "The Work Goes On." *Ensign,* May 2001, 4–6.
Smith, Joseph. *History of The Church of Jesus Christ of Latter-day Saints.* Edited by B. H. Roberts. 7 vols. 2d ed. rev. Salt Lake City: The Church of Jesus Christ of Latter-day Saints, 1932–51.
Smith, Joseph Fielding. In Conference Report, Apr. 1970, 58–60.

RLM

PRIESTHOOD, OATH AND COVENANT OF

The priesthood is the power of God, delegated to man on earth, to act in all things for the salvation of humankind. "The Priesthood is an everlasting principle, and existed with God from eternity, and will to eternity, without beginning of days or end of years" (Smith, 3:386). Every man who has the Melchizedek Priesthood conferred upon him enters into a covenant with God. President Boyd K. Packer has explained:

"The covenant rests with man; the *oath* with God. The Melchizedek Priesthood is received by covenant. A man's covenant with God is: to be faithful and magnify his callings in the priesthood; to give heed to the words of eternal life; and to live by every word that proceedeth forth from the mouth of God. (See D&C 84:33, 43, 44.)

"God, for his part, declares with an everlasting oath that all who receive the priesthood and obey the covenants that pertain to that priesthood shall receive 'all that [the] Father hath. . . . And this is according to the oath and covenant which belongeth to the priesthood'" (153; emphasis added).

In other words, when we are faithful to our priesthood covenant, "the Lord—to show the binding nature of his promise—swears with an oath that the promised reward shall be obtained. This oath, as it pertained to the Son of God himself, is spoken of in these words: 'The Lord hath sworn, and will not repent, Thou art a priest for ever after the order of Melchizedek.' (Ps. 110:4.) And with reference to all others who also receive the Melchizedek Priesthood, the scripture saith: 'And all those who are ordained unto this priesthood are made like unto the Son of God, abiding a priest continually.' (JST, Heb. 7:3.) That is to say, they will be kings and priests forever; their priesthood will continue to all eternity; they will have eternal life" (McConkie, 33–35).

SOURCES

McConkie, Bruce R. "The Ten Blessings of the Priesthood." *Ensign,* Nov. 1977, 33–35.

Packer, Boyd K. *The Things of the Soul.* Salt Lake City: Bookcraft, 1996.

Smith, Joseph. *History of The Church of Jesus Christ of Latter-day Saints.* Edited by B. H. Roberts. 7 vols. 2d ed. rev. Salt Lake City: The Church of Jesus Christ of Latter-day Saints, 1932–51.

RLM

PRIESTHOOD, REVELATION ON

There have been times throughout the history of the world that God's holy priesthood has been both granted to or restricted from certain groups of people. Prior to the time of Moses, priesthood was conferred upon men in a patriarchal manner from righteous father to righteous son (D&C 84:6–16; 107:40–53). When the disobedient Israelites of Moses' day hardened their hearts against God and his laws, the higher priesthood was taken out of their midst generally, and a lesser priesthood was administered by the descendants of Aaron through the tribe of Levi (D&C 84:24). When the higher priesthood was conferred on anyone, it came by special dispensation, requiring revelation from God through his prophets. Centuries later, the apostle Peter received a revelation that directed that the blessings of the gospel, and undoubtedly priesthood authority, be made available to Jew and Gentile, based on personal worthiness and faithfulness alone. Restrictions on priesthood and the lifting of these restrictions throughout the centuries occurred by revelation from God to his anointed servants, the ones who held and exercised all the keys of the priesthood. As in ancient days, modern revelations control the dispensing and administration of the authority to act in God's name on earth.

On 9 June 1978, the First Presidency announced a change in a long-standing Church practice. "Aware of the promises made by the prophets and presidents of the Church who have preceded us that at some time in God's eternal plan, all of our brethren who are worthy may receive the priesthood," Presidents Spencer W. Kimball, N. Eldon Tanner, and Marion G. Romney wrote, "and witnessing the faithfulness of those from whom the priesthood has been withheld, we have pleaded long and earnestly in behalf of these, our faithful brethren, spending many hours in the Upper Room of the Temple supplicating the Lord for divine guidance." The official declaration goes on to declare: "He has heard our prayers, and by revelation has confirmed that the long-promised day has come when every faithful, worthy man in the Church may receive the holy priesthood, with power to exercise its divine authority, and enjoy with his loved ones every blessing that flows therefrom, including the blessings of the temple. Accordingly, all worthy male members of the Church may be ordained to the priesthood without regard for race or color" (Official Declaration 2).

This revelation on priesthood is one of the most significant revelations of the Restoration. It is a latter-day revelation akin in its significance to Peter's revelation from God that extended the blessings of the gospel to all worthy males in the meridian of time (Acts 10). Why those of African descent were denied the blessings of the priesthood and the temple for nearly a century and a half has not been revealed. Just as the scriptures are virtually silent concerning why men from only a certain lineage in ancient times held the priesthood, there is precious little detail as to the practice of restricting the priesthood in the modern Church. Numerous members of the Church have suggested possible explanations, but their views do not constitute the doctrine of the Church.

"There are statements in our literature by the early brethren which we have interpreted to mean that [those of African descent] would not receive the priesthood in mortality," Elder Bruce R. McConkie explained after the revelation and subsequent change in policy were announced. "I have said the same things. . . . Forget everything that I have said, or what President Brigham Young or President George Q. Cannon or whomsoever has said in days past that is contrary to the present revelation. We spoke with limited understanding and without the light and knowledge that now has come into the world. We get our truth and our light line upon line and precept upon precept. We have now added a new flood of intelligence and light on this particular subject, and it erases all the darkness and all the views and all the thoughts of the past. They don't matter anymore" ("Alike," 3–4).

Years before the revelation, leaders of the Church had extensively studied and fervently prayed about the matter of who should and should not hold the priesthood. "There [were] members of the Church who had brought to President David O. McKay their reasons why it should be changed," President Kimball explained. "Others had gone to Joseph Fielding Smith and Harold B. Lee and to all the former presidents and it had not been accepted because the time had not come for it" (15). The "long-promised day" came on 1 June 1978 in a meeting of the First Presidency and Quorum of the Twelve Apostles in the Salt Lake Temple. Several of the Brethren who were eyewitnesses to this event recorded their feelings concerning the experience.

Elder David B. Haight described the process: "Humbly . . . the prophet asked each of us to express his feelings regarding the matter, and we did so. As each responded we witnessed an outpouring of the Spirit which bonded our souls in perfect unity—a glorious experience. . . .

"President Kimball then suggested that we have our prayer at the altar. . . .

". . . The prophet of God pour[ed] out his heart, pleading eloquently for the Lord to make his mind and will known to his servant, Spencer W. Kimball. The prophet pleaded that he would be given necessary direction which could expand the Church throughout the world by the offering the fullness of the everlasting gospel to all men, based solely upon their personal worthiness without reference to race or color" (in Tate, 279–80).

Elder McConkie testified: "The Lord could have sent messengers from the other side to deliver [the revelation], but he did not. He gave the revelation by the power of the Holy Ghost.

"The Spirit of the Lord rested mightily upon us all; we felt something akin to what happened on the day of Pentecost and at the dedication of the Kirtland Temple. From the midst of eternity, the voice of God, conveyed by the power of the Spirit, spoke to his prophet. . . . And we all heard the same voice, received the same message, and became personal witnesses that the word received was the mind and will and voice of the Lord. . . .

"On this occasion, because of the importuning and the faith, because the hour and the time had arrived, the Lord in his providences poured out the Holy Ghost upon the First Presidency and the Twelve in a miraculous and marvelous manner, beyond anything that any then present had ever experienced" ("New," 128, 133–35).

President Gordon B. Hinckley likewise testified: "There was a hallowed and sanctified atmosphere in the room. For me, it felt as if a conduit opened between the heavenly throne and the kneeling, pleading prophet of God who was joined by his Brethren. . . . Not one of us who was present on that occasion was ever quite the same after that. Nor has the Church been quite the same" (70).

Within hours after the official announcement, worthy men of African descent received the priesthood of God. Within days and weeks black members of the Church received their temple ordinances, and families were sealed for time and all eternity. Within months scores of congregations of the Church were established on the African continent with black priesthood leadership. The impact of this revelation can hardly be comprehended. Tens of thousands of members of the Church from African descent have received the blessings of priesthood and temple ordinances, and millions on the other side of the veil have likewise had the doors of salvation opened to them through family history and temple work made possible by the revelation on priesthood. This was a revelation, Elder McConkie observed, "that would reverse the whole direction of the Church, procedurally and administratively; one that would affect the living and the dead; one that would affect the total relationship that we have with the world" ("New," 134).

SOURCES

Hinckley, Gordon B. "Priesthood Restoration." *Ensign,* Oct. 1988, 69–72.

Kimball, Spencer W. In Gerry Avant, "Pres. Kimball Says Revelation Was Clear." *Church News,* 6 Jan. 1979, 15.

McConkie, Bruce R. "All Are Alike unto God." *Second Annual Church Educational System Religious Educators' Symposium,* 18 Aug. 1978. Salt Lake City: The Church of Jesus Christ of Latter-day Saints, 1979, 3–5.

———. "The New Revelation on Priesthood." In *Priesthood.* Salt Lake City: Deseret Book, 1981.

Tate, Lucille C. *David B. Haight: The Life Story of a Disciple.* Salt Lake City: Bookcraft, 1987.

BLT

PRINCE OF PEACE

A choir of angels announced to shepherds watching over their sheep that the possibility of consummate peace and goodwill had come to the earth with the birth of the Savior (Luke 2:13–14). This nativity was prophesied more than seven hundred years before when Isaiah wrote, "For unto us a child is born, unto us a son is given . . . and his name shall be called . . . The Prince of Peace" (Isaiah 9:6). As the Prince of Peace, Jesus Christ offers those who believe on him a comfort and serenity that the wicked cannot know (Isaiah 48:22; 1 Nephi 20:22). Furthermore, there is no end to his peace (Isaiah 9:7).

CFO

PRINCE OF THE WORLD

Jesus often referred to Satan as the "prince of this world" (John 12:31; 14:30; 16:11). The world in which God allows Satan influence and power is the carnal and corruptible world, the world that rejects and spurns the Savior and his disciples (John 7:7; 17:14–16). Satan is the prince of the figurative Babylon that stones the prophets and convolutes the doctrine of Christ. As prince of the world, Satan shares nothing with Jesus Christ (John 14:30) and is therefore cast out from God's presence and is not "lifted up" with Christ (John 12:32). As Christ is the "chief cornerstone" of the only sure foundation, the prince of the world is the "prince of the power of the air," or the edifice that has no foundation whatsoever (Ephesians 2:2, 20; 1 Nephi 8:26). We "cannot fall" when we are built on the Rock that is "broad as eternity," but we will undeniably fall if we worship at the feet of him who

509

claims ownership of the world (Helaman 5:12; Moses 7:53; Matthew 4:8–10).

CFO

PROCREATION

"The family is central to the Creator's plan for the eternal destiny of His children," the First Presidency and Council of the Twelve Apostles declared in "The Family: A Proclamation to the World." The proclamation adds: "The first commandment that God gave to Adam and Eve pertained to their potential for parenthood as husband and wife. We declare that God's commandment for His children to multiply and replenish the earth remains in force. We further declare that God has commanded that the sacred powers of procreation are to be employed only between man and woman, lawfully wedded as husband and wife" (102).

An earlier First Presidency likewise affirmed the sacred nature of the commandment to procreate within the divine institution of marriage. "The Lord has told us that it is the duty of every husband and wife to obey the command given to Adam to multiply and replenish the earth, so that the legions of choice spirits waiting for their tabernacles of flesh may come here and move forward under God's great design to become perfect souls, for without these fleshly tabernacles they cannot progress to their God-planned destiny. Thus, every husband and wife should become a father and mother in Israel to children born under the holy, eternal covenant" (in Conference Report, 11–12).

While leaders of the Church have unequivocally and consistently taught the principle that procreation is a solemn parental responsibility, they also acknowledge and are deeply sensitive to the fact that there are many couples who desire with all their hearts to have children but are unable to do so for a variety of reasons. Likewise, there are many couples who, although physically able to conceive, may not be able to have as many children as they would desire. In each of these cases, the Lord will judge according to the desires of the heart, not according to the number of children. The doctrine of procreation teaches us that, as the Old Testament psalmist declared, "children are an heritage of the Lord," and "happy is the man [and woman] that hath his [and her] quiver full of them" (Psalm 127:3, 5). Because personal circumstances and factors related to procreation are unique and varied, individual couples must seek the inspiration of the Lord as to how to apply to their own situations the divine commandment to "be fruitful and multiply" (Abraham 4:22, 28; see also Genesis 1:22; Moses 2:22).

"Much has been said . . . about birth control," President Gordon B. Hinckley taught. "I like to think of the positive side of the equation, of the meaning and sanctity of life, of the purpose of this estate in our eternal journey, of the need for the experiences of mortal life under the great plan of God our Father, of the joy that is to be found only where there are children in the home, of the blessings that come of good posterity. When I think of these values and see them taught and observed, then I am willing to leave the question of numbers to the man and the woman and the Lord" (35).

Principles, like those mentioned by President Hinckley, do not change over time, but policies and practices may be altered as cultural conditions and technologies change. As a result, official policies of the Church or specific counsel given by its leaders at one particular time in the past may not have the same application to the present. Therefore, Latter-day Saints are taught that when it comes to issues of family planning—family size, spacing of children, forms of contraception or conception, or adoption—couples should carefully consider both the spiritual dimensions of the commandment along with other related issues, including the physical and emotional well-being of parents, family circumstances, medical conditions, potential side effects of contraception or fertility treatments, and other factors. Additionally, inspired counsel and direction from Church leaders can help in the decision-making process. Ultimately, however, each couple must prayerfully make the decision for themselves. Because such decisions affect not only our lives here on earth but also our families in eternity, God has promised his Holy Spirit to help us make wise choices if we faithfully seek his will. The guiding principle in all this is that our greatest desires should be for the things of God, keeping his commandments and seeking those things that have eternal significance, not that which is fleeting and will not, in the eternal scheme of things, satisfy our souls.

SOURCES

First Presidency. In Conference Report, Oct. 1942, 7–17.

First Presidency and Council of the Twelve Apostles. "The Family: A Proclamation to the World." *Ensign,* Nov. 1995, 102.

Hinckley, Gordon B. *Teachings of Gordon B. Hinckley.* Salt Lake City: Deseret Book, 1997.

BLT

PROFANITY

The opposite of revering sacred things, profanity is disrespect or contempt for the name and things of God. Something that is profane is unholy, impure, and ungodly. The term *profanity* usually refers to speech that is crude, coarse, or improperly and irreverently uses the names of Deity. The scriptures, both ancient and modern, warn against profanity. From Mount Sinai, God declared, "Thou shalt not take the name of the Lord thy God in vain" (Exodus 20:7; see also Mosiah 13:15; D&C 136:21). In the New Testament, James spoke of the hypocrisy of one who speaks blessings and then with the same mouth utters curses (James 3:10). Profanity is the antithesis of the "tongue of angels" and is repulsive to the Spirit of God (2 Nephi 31:13). "Do angels take the Lord's name in vain?" asked President George Q. Cannon. "The idea is so ridiculous that we scarcely like to ask the question. . . . How dare we do that which angels dare not do? Is it possible for us to argue that that which is forbidden in heaven is praiseworthy on earth?" Profanity is "unnecessary and consequently foolish; it lessens our respect for holy things and leads us into the society of the wicked; it brings upon us the disrespect of the good who avoid us; it leads us to other sins, for he who is willing to abuse his Creator is not ashamed to defraud his fellow creature; and also by so doing we directly and knowingly break one of the most direct of God's commandments" (156).

Profanity is much more than merely profaning God's name. It is swearing. It is using coarse and crude language, whether in anger or jest. It is the attempt of a feeble mind to express itself. Such language reflects the "corrupt communication" (Ephesians 4:29) of the natural man rather than the communication of one whose thoughts and words are garnished with virtue unceasingly (D&C 121:45). Profanity is also filthy and foul talk manifest in dirty jokes, slang, euphemisms, "bathroom talk," and sexual innuendoes. These forms of corrupt communication are as grievous to the Spirit of the Lord as swearing is. Both

512

indicate what is in the mind *and* the heart. Profane, filthy, and foul talk, if not checked by repentance, will lead to profane behaviors. As a man thinks—and speaks—so is he (Proverbs 23:7). President Gordon B. Hinckley testified: "I know that the Lord is pleased when we use clean and virtuous language, for He has set an example for us. His revelations are couched in words that are affirmative, that are up-lifting, that encourage us to do what is right and to go forward in truth and goodness. Don't swear. Don't profane. Stay away from conversa-tion that is sprinkled with foul and filthy words. You will be happier if you do so, and your example will give strength to others" (48).

SOURCES

Cannon, George Q. "Editorial Thoughts." *Juvenile Instructor* 8, no. 20 (27 Sept. 1873): 156.

Hinckley, Gordon B. "Take Not the Name of God in Vain." *Ensign,* Nov. 1987, 44–48.

BLT

PROPHECY

Prophecy is one of the gifts of the Spirit (1 Corinthians 12:10; Moroni 10:13; D&C 46:22). It is the power to profess or bear wit-ness of Jesus Christ, as directed by the Holy Ghost (Revelation 19:10). This spirit of prophecy is available to men and women, children and adults in assisting the Lord in spreading his gospel to all peoples of the earth. The prophet Joel declared the Lord's promise: "I will pour out my spirit upon all flesh; and your sons and your daughters shall prophesy, your old men shall dream dreams, your young men shall see visions: and also upon the servants and upon the handmaids in those days will I pour out my spirit" (Joel 2:28–29; see also Numbers 11:29). Those with the gift of prophecy bring forth their witness of Jesus Christ, born of the Spirit. In scripture, they are at times called prophets and prophetesses.

The apostle Paul deemed the gift of prophecy to be among the greatest gifts of God because "he that prophesieth speaketh unto men to edification, and exhortation, and comfort. . . . If all prophesy, and there come in one that believeth not, or one unlearned, he is convinced of all, he is judged of all. . . . For ye may all prophesy one by one, that all may learn, and all may be comforted" (1 Corinthians 14:3, 24, 31).

Men called by the Lord to be prophets, seers, and revelators have additional gifts of prophecy, including the authorization to speak for God (Exodus 4:16), foretell future events (Isaiah 9:6), and receive revelation for new or forgotten truths. As Amos said, "Surely the Lord God will do nothing, but he revealeth his secret unto his servants the prophets" (Amos 3:7). The inspired writings and teachings of prophets constitute prophecy.

CFO

PROPHET

"Would God that all the Lord's people were prophets," Moses declared, "and that the Lord would put his spirit upon them!" (Numbers 11:29). From this and other scriptural passages, it is clear that the term *prophet* has both general and specific applications. All of God's children may be prophets in a broad way, whereas in a precise way— that of being president of the Church—"there is never but one on the earth at a time" (D&C 132:7) who is the Lord's anointed prophet (D&C 21:4–7; 28:2–7; 43:1–6). The word *prophet* (Hebrew, *nabi*; Greek, *prophetes*) means "one who speaks on behalf of God" to "announce" or "proclaim" the mind and will of God. While many think of a prophet in terms of someone receiving revelations that predict or foretell future events, the ancient usage of the term did not always or even generally connote prediction. Prophecy is more about proclaiming than predicting, more about teaching and testifying than foretelling. A prophet speaks forthrightly and is a "preacher of righteousness" (Bible Dictionary, 754). "A prophet is a teacher," Elder John A. Widtsoe said. "That is the essential meaning of the word. He teaches the body of truth, the gospel, revealed by the Lord to man; and under inspiration explains it to the understanding of the people. He is an expounder of truth" (257). In this manner, all who teach and testify of truth are prophets.

In addition to the prophetic roles of preacher of righteousness, one who tells forth rather than foreteller, and expounder of truth, a prophet is one who has the testimony of Jesus, which is, as John the Revelator declared, "the spirit of prophecy" (Revelation 19:10). Having that testimony, according to the Prophet Joseph Smith, "constitutes a prophet" (5:215). Hence, all who possess a testimony of the divinity of the Lord

Jesus Christ, as revealed to them by the power of the Holy Ghost, are prophets. Faithful members of the Church can be prophets, not only as they teach truth and possess a testimony of Jesus but also as they receive spiritual guidance within their own stewardships. President Harold B. Lee testified, "Anyone who enjoys the gift by which he may have God revealed has the spirit of prophecy, the power of revelation, and, in a sense, is a prophet within the sphere of responsibility and authority given to him" (155).

There is a more specific aspect of the word *prophet* that must also be understood and put in its proper context. It stems from the ancient Hebrew root of the word that means "the called one" or "one who is anointed." This implies a more restricted usage of the term *prophet,* referring to those who have been given a particular calling or office with specialized responsibilities above and beyond the general prophetic roles of teaching and testifying. "A true prophet is one who holds the holy priesthood," Elder Bruce R. McConkie wrote, "*who is a legal administrator;* who has power and authority from God to represent him on earth" (*Mortal,* 2:169; emphasis added). This definition of a prophet as a "legal administrator" differentiates between those faithful men and women who love and proclaim the truth, have testimonies of the Savior, and receive spiritual guidance in their lives and those who are called, sustained, ordained, and set apart as prophets to the people. Even though Moses prayed that all the Lord's people could be prophets, there was still a fundamental difference between what they could be as prophets in a general sense and what he could do as *the* prophet.

The Church as the kingdom of God on earth is governed at various levels under the direction of priesthood authority by men and women who are guided by inspiration and the spirit of prophecy in their respective service in the Church. While this means that there may be many prophets within the Church, at a given time there are only fifteen men whom the Lord has designated as prophets, seers, and revelators. These ordained prophets have been given what President J. Reuben Clark Jr. characterized as "a special spiritual endowment" different from all others. "They are sustained as prophets, seers, and revelators, which gives them a special spiritual endowment in connection with their teaching of the people," he explained. "They have the right, the power, and authority to declare the mind and will of God to his people, subject to the over-all power and authority of the President of the Church. Others of the General Authorities are not given this special spiritual endowment . . . , and the resulting limitation upon their power and authority in teaching applies to every other officer and member of the Church, for none of them is spiritually endowed as a prophet, seer, and revelator" (9–10).

Although all members of the First Presidency and Quorum of the Twelve Apostles are prophets, seers, and revelators, the president of the Church, as God's senior apostle, is exclusively designated as *the prophet*. Modern revelation explains that he is the "Presiding High Priest" (D&C 107:56–66) and the "President of the office of the High Priesthood" who "preside[s] over the whole church" and has "all the gifts of God which he bestows upon the head of the Church" (D&C 107:91–92). As such, he holds all the keys of the kingdom, and by that authority all things necessary for the salvation of men are made available. "He alone can give direction to all others," taught Elder McConkie, "direction from which none is exempt" ("Keys," 23).

SOURCES

Clark, J. Reuben, Jr. "When Are Church Leaders' Words Entitled to Claim of Scripture?" *Church News,* 31 July 1954, 9–11.

Lee, Harold B. *Stand Ye in Holy Places.* Salt Lake City: Deseret Book, 1974.

McConkie, Bruce R. "The Keys of the Kingdom." *Ensign,* May 1983, 21–23.

———. *The Mortal Messiah: From Bethlehem to Calvary.* 4 vols. Salt Lake City: Deseret Book, 1979–81.

Smith, Joseph. *History of The Church of Jesus Christ of Latter-day Saints.* Edited by B. H. Roberts. 7 vols. 2d ed. rev. Salt Lake City: The Church of Jesus Christ of Latter-day Saints, 1932–51.

Widtsoe, John A. *Evidences and Reconciliations.* Arranged by G. Homer Durham. Salt Lake City: Bookcraft, 1987.

BLT

PROPITIATION

To propitiate is to appease, to conciliate, to win the goodwill of a party, or to cause someone to become favorably inclined toward someone else. In the gospel sense, a *propitiation* is an appeasement or a satisfying of the demands of divine justice; it is a reversal of the righteous wrath of God resulting from broken laws and commandments that he instituted. To appease the demands of divine justice, a full payment is required. This payment has been provided by Christ for all mortals who will repent (D&C 19:16–19). "Jesus Christ the righteous . . . is the propitiation for our sins: and not for ours only, but also for the sins of the whole world" (1 John 2:1–2). Thus the concept of propitiation is closely related to the doctrine of substitution as taught by Paul. "For [God] hath made [Jesus] to be sin for us, who knew no sin; that we might be made the righteousness of God in him" (2 Corinthians 5:21).

The concept of propitiation is also intimately tied to the doctrines of justification and reconciliation. Christ's conciliatory act puts each individual who so desires back in a right relationship with God—which is the meaning of justification. By accepting Jesus' ultimate act of propitiation, each person may stand justified before God and continue on the path of sanctification—the actual transformation of a person's nature and character. As Paul taught, "All have sinned, and come short of the glory of God." But each may be justified by the grace of Jesus Christ, "whom God hath set forth to be a propitiation through faith in his blood" (Romans 3:23–25). We are justified, or reconciled to God, *only* through the act of propitiation carried out by Jesus (Galatians 2:16).

Paul taught that each individual must be "reconciled to God" (2 Corinthians 5:20). Nephi explained that his people expended great effort "to persuade our children, and also our brethren, to believe in Christ, and to be reconciled to God" (2 Nephi 25:23). Jacob implored, "Wherefore, beloved brethren, be reconciled unto him through the atonement of Christ" (Jacob 4:11).

The concept of propitiation is at the core of God's great plan of happiness. To the Nephites, the resurrected Lord declared that "no unclean thing can enter into [his Father's] kingdom; therefore nothing entereth into his rest save it be those who have washed their garments in my blood" (3 Nephi 27:19). Entrance into the Father's kingdom is made possible by the propitiation of Jesus Christ. Propitiation, reconciliation, and mediation are all related and are part of the grand doctrine of the Atonement.

ACS

PUNISHMENT

One of the fundamental laws of physics states, "For every action, there is an equal or opposite reaction." Spiritually, the law is much the same. For every action—every choice, every desire, every deed, every use of the eternal law of agency—there is a reaction or consequence. Righteousness yields rewards and blessings. Sin and disobedience yield punishment. In the eternal scheme of things, no righteous deed goes unrewarded and no wickedness goes unpunished (2 Nephi 9:25; Alma 42:1, 16). The principle of punishment—the penalty imposed for wrongdoing—is both earthly and eternal. From the beginning of time there have been laws, both spiritual and temporal, which if violated bring punishment. For example, one who murdered anciently was usually punished by the forfeiture of his life (Genesis 9:6; Exodus 21:12). The Book of Mormon peoples were likewise governed by a system of laws and punishments whereby a man was "punished according to the crime which he has committed, according to the law which has been given to us by our fathers" (Mosiah 29:15; see also Words of Mormon 1:15–16). Even today, all civil laws have attendant punishments prescribed for the violation of the law—punishment commensurate with the crime.

Violation of spiritual laws brings spiritual punishments that may be much different than criminal punishments. For example, a person who has immoral and lustful thoughts may not be prosecuted by civil law, but he invariably will be punished with the loss of the Spirit and the loss of blessings and opportunities that he could have enjoyed had he been obedient. Not all spiritual punishments are observable. Yet there is always some earthly punishment for sin. "The punishment may, for the most part, consist of the torment we inflict upon ourselves," observed President Boyd K. Packer. "It may be the loss of privilege or progress. We are punished *by* our sins, if not *for* them" (19; see also Mormon 4:5).

For some, however, justice may not fully come in this life, but it will come eventually. Throughout the history of the world, God has warned through his prophets of the eternal punishments that surely will come upon the wicked. "I will punish the world for their evil," the Lord declared through the prophet Isaiah, "and the wicked for their iniquity" (Isaiah 13:11). The apostle Peter said, "The Lord knoweth how to deliver the godly out of temptations, and to reserve the unjust unto the day of judgment to be punished" (2 Peter 2:9). King Benjamin in the Book of Mormon taught that he "who listeth to obey [the evil] spirit" and then "dieth in his sins, the same drinketh damnation to his own soul; for he receiveth for his wages an everlasting punishment, having transgressed the law of God contrary to his own knowledge" (Mosiah 2:33). In modern revelation the Lord has reiterated that eternal punishment—which is God's punishment—awaits those who will not turn to the Holy One and repent of their sins. This divine punishment, the Lord declared, is sure and sore—"how sore you know not, how exquisite you know not, yea, how hard to bear you know not" (D&C 19:15).

The Lord has provided a way whereby we can escape the full punishment required by eternal law for every sin and evil deed. Deliverance is through repentance. Christ has satisfied the law of justice through his infinite suffering. He took the punishment upon himself so that he can extend mercy and forgiveness to those who have faith in him, repent of their sins, and submit to the principles and ordinances of his gospel. Of this he declared in our day:

"For behold, I, God, have suffered these things for all, that they might not suffer if they would repent; but if they would not repent they must suffer even as I; which suffering caused myself, even God, the greatest of all, to tremble because of pain, and to bleed at every pore, and to suffer both body and spirit—and would that I might not drink the bitter cup, and shrink—

"Nevertheless, glory be to the Father, and I partook and finished my preparations unto the children of men. Wherefore, I command you again to repent, lest I humble you with my almighty power; and that you confess your sins, lest you suffer these punishments of which I have spoken, of which in the smallest, yea, even in the least degree you have tasted at the time I withdrew my Spirit" (D&C 19:16–20).

SOURCE

Packer, Boyd K. "The Brilliant Morning of Forgiveness." *Ensign,* Nov. 1995, 18–21.

BLT

PURITY

God desires that we have a pure mind and a pure heart. We cannot purify ourselves, but we are made pure through faith in Jesus Christ and "in obeying the truth through the Spirit" (1 Peter 1:21–22; Acts 15:9). We are made "pure and spotless before God" when our "garments [are] washed white through the blood of the Lamb . . . after being sanctified by the Holy Ghost" (Alma 13:11–12). Through the atoning blood of Christ we are "clothed with purity, . . . even with the robe of righteousness" (2 Nephi 9:14).

Purity connotes submission to the Lord in all he requires: A person "putteth off the natural man and becometh a saint through the atonement of Christ the Lord" (Mosiah 3:19). Purity is seen and felt in those who have "spiritually been born of God," who have God's image in their countenances, and who are stripped of pride and envy (Alma 5:14, 28–29). We become a Zion community when we are "pure in heart," a state of being that occurs when we yield our hearts unto God (D&C 97:21; Helaman 3:35).

One of the blessings that accompanies the pure in heart is that they will "see God," not only in the eternities but also in mortality (Matthew 5:8; D&C 97:16). God's gift of purity enables us to see him in those around us and in all of his creations. Furthermore, we are made free from guilt and eventually have "no more disposition to do evil, but to do good continually" (Mosiah 4:2–3; 5:2). Having pure desires, we seek after those things that are just, lovely, and pure, which in turn strengthen our faith and devotion to the Giver of all that is pure and beautiful (Philippians 4:8). Finally, being cleansed from all stain enables us to be examples of purity to unbelievers, thereby attracting them to the love and goodness of Christ (1 Timothy 4:12).

CFO

———◦◦◦———

RACE

Latter-day Saints believe that all mankind, regardless of race, culture, and ethnicity, are brothers and sisters in the human family, "the offspring of God" (Acts 17:27–29; see also Romans 8:16). Prior to being born on earth into specific families, races, and nations, every one of us lived with God as his begotten spirit daughter or son and was "reared to maturity in the eternal mansions of the Father" (First Presidency, 80). Because of this sacred familial relationship with the universal Father and with every other person on earth, there is no place for racism, prejudice, or discrimination in the restored gospel of Jesus

Christ. "We are all children of God," President Howard W. Hunter taught. "In the eyes of the Church and in the followers of Christ there are no differences. . . . Nationality makes no difference. We are all children of God, and we are brothers and sisters" (97).

The Book of Mormon teaches that Christ invites "all to come unto him and partake of his goodness; and he denieth none that come unto him, black and white, bond and free, male and female . . . all are alike unto God" (2 Nephi 26:33). The First Presidency of The Church of Jesus Christ of Latter-day Saints—sustained as prophets, seers, and revelators—has admonished us to follow the Savior's example in showing "special love and concern for the eternal welfare of all men and women regardless of religious belief, race, or nationality" (in Morrison, 16). Likewise, President Spencer W. Kimball taught that "racial prejudice is of the devil. Racial prejudice is of ignorance. There is no place for it in the gospel of Jesus Christ" (237).

SOURCES

First Presidency. "The Origin of Man." *Improvement Era,* Nov. 1909, 75–81; or *Ensign,* Feb. 2002, 26–30.

Hunter, Howard W. *The Teachings of Howard W. Hunter.* Edited by Clyde J. Williams. Salt Lake City: Bookcraft, 1997.

Kimball, Spencer W. *The Teachings of Spencer W. Kimball.* Edited by Edward L. Kimball. Salt Lake City: Deseret Book, 1982.

Morrison, Alexander B. "No More Strangers." *Ensign,* Sept. 2000, 16–20.

BLT

RECONCILE

To reconcile is to reunite formerly estranged parties. Because of the Fall and our sins, we become distanced from Deity and from things of righteousness. The atonement of Jesus Christ has been provided as a consummate gift so that through faith and repentance, our sins may be forgiven. Further, the immortality of the soul and the hope for life after death is ensured through Christ's rise from the tomb. Finally, the Atonement makes it possible for fallen men and women to be redeemed, to be brought back into the divine presence, to enjoy sweet fellowship with God and Christ once again. From the Latin, *reconcile* means "to sit again with." Jacob counseled, "Wherefore, beloved brethren, be reconciled unto [God] through the atonement of Christ, his Only Begotten Son" (Jacob 4:11).

There is another related sense in which *reconcile* is used in scripture. While the process of reconciliation with God is accomplished through our incorporation of the Atonement and the first principles and ordinances of the gospel, we become reconciled to God and to the will of God when we determine that we will follow the Lord and do things his way. This seems to be the meaning of Jacob's words in 2 Nephi 10:24: "Wherefore, my beloved brethren, reconcile yourselves to the will of God, and not to the will of the devil and the flesh; and remember, after ye are reconciled unto God, that it is only in and through the grace of God that ye are saved."

RLM

REDEEM

Isaiah warned ancient Israel that because of their iniquities, they had "sold themselves" (Isaiah 50:1) and thereby forfeited the blessings of the covenant that might have been theirs. Often those who are of infinite worth to God (D&C 18:10) auction themselves off to the cheapest bidder through foolish transgression. The promise of forgiveness and of spiritual restoration and royal reinstatement is a promise of redemption. *Redeem* means to purchase, to buy back, to restore one's status. The worth of souls is indeed great. That is why "the Lord your Redeemer suffered death in the flesh; wherefore he suffered the pain of all men, that all men might repent and come unto him" (D&C 18:11). We have been bought with a price—the infinite price of the precious blood of Jesus Christ (1 Peter 1:18–20)—and we are not our own (1 Corinthians 6:19–20; 7:23).

Redeem is used several ways in scripture: redemption associated with moral agency (2 Nephi 2:26); forgiveness of sin and spiritual rebirth (Mosiah 27:24–26; Alma 11:40; Helaman 5:10); release from the curse of the law, the curse of disobedience (Galatians 3:13); release from spiritual death (Mosiah 27:29; Helaman 14:16; Mormon 9:13); cleansing from sin through being washed in the blood of the Lamb (Revelation 5:9; Alma 5:21); the blessings of the resurrection (Mosiah 15:22–26; Alma 11:41; 12:25; Helaman 14:17; Mormon 9:13); the adoption of sonship and daughterhood (Galatians 4:5); and becoming a pure and peculiar people (1 Peter 2:9).

RLM

RELIGION

Generally, the word *religion* refers to any set of beliefs concerning the nature of Deity, the purpose of life, moral imperatives, and the nature and destiny of the soul. In more specific usage, *religion* also refers to the rituals and practices that are accepted by a group, such as the "Buddhist religion" or the "Christian religion." Those who adhere to doctrines and practices of a specific religion would be referred to as members or adherents of that religion. Sometimes the word *religion* is used in reference to worship, whether it be public or private. Likewise, the word *religion* usually connotes a system of beliefs and practices that yields a better life here and salvation hereafter.

The root word from which the word *religion* comes is *ligare,* which means to "tie," "fasten," or "bind." The word *ligament,* which means to "hold together," comes from the same word. Thus, in the truest sense of the word, religion is more than mere affiliation with a church or organization. It is more than professed beliefs, accepted doctrines, or ritual. It is a divine process of being tied to God and held together in the faith. It is a deep conviction of the validity of those things as manifest in one's life and in one's relationships with others. Thus, religion, if it is to have real power in one's life, must permeate all aspects of one's existence. In the New Testament, James defined "pure religion" thus: "to visit the fatherless and widows in their affliction, and to keep himself unspotted from the world" (James 1:27).

BLT

REPENTANCE

In the scriptures the word *repentance* is translated from the Hebrew word *shuv* (Old Testament) and the Greek word *metanoia* (New Testament) and generally means "to turn" or to "turn around" by turning *from* sin and turning *to* God. Repentance is a comprehensive turning or changing of one's heart (desires), mind (attitudes), and behavior (deeds). "Repent, and turn yourselves from all your transgressions," the prophet Ezekiel declared. "Cast away from you all your transgressions, whereby ye have transgressed; and make you a new heart and a new spirit" (Ezekiel 18:30–31; see also Isaiah 55:7; Jeremiah 35:15).

Repentance is one of the fundamental principles of the gospel of

Jesus Christ, and therefore all accountable persons must repent of their sins and be cleansed through the atonement of Jesus Christ in order to enter into God's celestial glory (Luke 13:3; Acts 2:38; 2 Nephi 31:10–20; Mosiah 3:12; Alma 9:12; Helaman 12:23; D&C 133:62). It is only by faith in the Lord Jesus Christ that enduring, profound repentance is made possible (Alma 34:14–17). "True repentance is based on and flows from faith in the Lord Jesus Christ," President Ezra Taft Benson taught. "There is no other way" (71). It was faith in Christ that brought Enos a remission of sins (Enos 1:3–8). Likewise, it was Alma's fervent faith in the saving power of Christ that liberated him, through repentance, from the "gall of bitterness" and the "everlasting chains of death" and replaced them with "marvelous light" and "joy as exceeding as was [his] pain" (Alma 36:18, 20).

"Faith is the starting point—the foundation and cause of our repentance," Elder Orson Pratt wrote ("Faith," 76–77). Actions or efforts to repent that are not firmly founded in faith in Christ will not produce a true repentance that results in a remission of sins. Without fully comprehending that repentance must be a fruit of faith, we may go through a series of steps of repentance or actions that may result in a change of behavior, only to sadly discover that the spiritual gift of peace of conscience that accompanies the remission of sins has eluded us. Willpower can change behavior, but only the atonement of Jesus Christ changes the entire being. An overemphasis, however well intended, on an enumerated list of steps or *actions* that one must complete in order to repent may actually unwittingly deemphasize "faith unto repentance" or *attitudes* of true repentance. Turning from evil and turning to God requires *both* actions *and* attitudes, faith *and* works, behavior *and* one's whole being. The Lord has not in scripture given us a simplistic checklist, but he has revealed the simple but profound way whereby a person may manifest repentance of his sins: "Behold, he will confess them and forsake them" (D&C 58:43). This definition—confession and forsaking—encompasses all other essential attitudes and actions of repentance.

Confession. The scriptures, both ancient and modern, teach that confession of sins is an integral part of true repentance (Leviticus 5:1, 5–6; 26:40–42; Psalm 32:5; James 5:16; 1 John 1:9; Mosiah 26:29, 32–36; Moroni 6:7; D&C 42:88–89; 59:12). Speaking of acceptance of Christ as the Savior of the world, the apostle Paul said, "For with the heart man believeth unto righteousness; and with the mouth confession is made unto salvation" (Romans 10:10). In a similar manner, confession unto salvation through sincere repentance requires an *attitude* of confession in the heart as well as an *action* of confession from the mouth. This important principle is reflected in the dogma of virtually all Christian denominations, although there is great diversity in the specific applications and rituals of confession. Whether it be a private, personal confession of sins, confession to clergy, or a more public confession to a congregation, the ritual or act of confession serves as a mirror whereby sinners can examine themselves spiritually and recognize their dependence upon the cleansing power of Christ. The scriptures speak of the attitude of confession as "godly sorrow" that "worketh repentance to salvation" (2 Corinthians 7:10)—a "broken heart and a contrite spirit" (2 Nephi 2:7; 3 Nephi 9:20; Moroni 6:2). This deep, inner yearning to be clean leads one to recognize his inability to overcome sinfulness on his own and his total need to rely "wholly upon the merits of him who is mighty to save" (2 Nephi 31:19; see also Mosiah 4:5). Godly sorrow is "an awful view" of one's "own guilt and abominations" (Mosiah 3:25) that strips away rationalization and self-justification (Alma 42:29–30). It is a willingness to "submit to all things which the Lord seeth fit to inflict upon him" (Mosiah 3:19). A "broken heart and a contrite spirit" will lead to the necessary action of confession.

The scriptures speak of two major acts of confession. Alma taught that sins were to be confessed both to the Lord and to his anointed representative (Mosiah 26:29). Elder Bruce R. McConkie wrote: "There are thus two confessions and two sources of forgiveness. A sinner must always confess all sins, great and small, to the Lord; in addition, any sins involving moral turpitude and any serious sins for which a person might be disfellowshipped or excommunicated must also be confessed to the Lord's agent, who in most instances is the bishop. The bishop is empowered to forgive sins as far as the church is concerned, meaning that he can choose to retain the repentant person in full fellowship and not impose [disciplinary council] penalties upon him. Ultimate forgiveness in all instances and for all sins comes from the Lord and from the Lord only" (236).

Confession to the Lord and in some cases to the appropriate priesthood leader is not merely for cathartic release. Rather, confession of sins has a two-fold purpose. First, confession is a covenant. It is an opportunity to vow to make necessary adjustments in our lives. Disclosure without a sincere commitment to change does not produce enduring effects. "To confess our sins before God, would be of no particular benefit, unless we were determined to forsake them," wrote Elder Orson Pratt. "Without a covenant or promise before God, that we will forsake sin with an unshaken determination, that we will henceforth yield to no evil, our confession and repentance will be vain. . . . Confession of sins, unaccompanied with the resolution to forsake, is a solemn mockery before Him. . . . Such a confession must be accompanied with a solemn covenant or promise to sin no more; and the heart should be fixed and immovable in this covenant" ("Repentance," 31–32). In addition to making a covenant through confession of sins, we open the door to be taught and to receive inspired counsel, correction, comfort, and direction that are only available from the Lord and his authorized servants. When we cast our burdens upon the Lord through complete confession and commitment to forsake sin, we are in a position to be taught from on high. This divine guidance far surpasses any well-meant advice from mortals. Confession as a personal covenant and means to receive direction gives the transgressor strength to do the next and most important aspect of true repentance—forsake sin.

Forsaking sin. The scriptures teach that forsaking requires the abandonment of sinfulness, not just a particular sin. One cannot in the spirit of true repentance merely forsake one specific sin and yet cling tenaciously to other sins. Forsaking sin cannot be fragmented or selective. It requires a total surrender—a comprehensive change in one's disposition and desire for sin. "True repentance is not only sorrow for sins, and humble penitence, and contrition before God," President Joseph F. Smith taught, "but it involves the necessity of turning away from them, a discontinuance of all evil practices and deeds, a thorough reformation of life, a vital change from evil to good, from vice to virtue, from darkness to light" (100). Such forsaking involves a "mighty change in [our] hearts" (Alma 5:14)—our desires and deeds—and a mighty change of direction and devotion.

The apostle Paul taught King Agrippa that repentance means to "turn to God, and do works meet for repentance" (Acts 26:20). Works "meet for repentance" are naturally (1) greater love for God and commitment to his kingdom and (2) greater devotion and service to fellow men. President Spencer W. Kimball declared, "Though one may have abandoned a particular sin and even confessed it to his bishop, yet he is not repentant if he has not developed a life of action and service and righteousness" (7). Alma the Younger and the sons of Mosiah are great examples of that principle (Alma 36:24). True repentance requires restitution—not just a literal repayment or restoration of that which was lost through sin (Exodus 22:1–6; Leviticus 6:2–5) but also a lifelong devotion to the Lord.

While it is true that we can in no way of ourselves repay the Savior, we can show our appreciation for his atoning sacrifice, which makes a remission of sins possible, by making a symbolic restitution through lifelong commitment to serve God and our fellowmen. Thus, making restitution requires more than paying money and doing transitory deeds. There is no shortcut to repentance. It requires our very lives—our changed *being* as well as our changed *behavior*. When we view repentance this way, we see that each of us should be living in a perpetual state of repentance (2 Nephi 31:13). That is the message of the gospel—the invitation of the Savior. To choose Christ is to choose change. "Behold, he sendeth an invitation unto all men, for the arms of mercy are extended towards them, and he saith: Repent, and I will receive you. Yea, he saith: Come unto me and ye shall partake of the fruit of the tree of life; yea, ye shall eat and drink of the bread and waters of life freely; yea, come unto me and bring forth works of righteousness" (Alma 5:33–35).

SOURCES

Benson, Ezra Taft. *The Teachings of Ezra Taft Benson.* Salt Lake City: Bookcraft, 1988.

Kimball, Spencer W. "What Is True Repentance?" *New Era,* May 1974, 4–7.

McConkie, Bruce R. *A New Witness for the Articles of Faith.* Salt Lake City: Deseret Book, 1985.

Pratt, Orson. "The True Faith." In *A Series of Pamphlets by Orson Pratt.* 1852.

———. "True Repentance." In *A Series of Pamphlets by Orson Pratt.* 1852.

Smith, Joseph F. *Gospel Doctrine.* Salt Lake City: Deseret Book, 1939.

BLT

REST OF THE LORD

In one sense a person enters the rest of God in the present, in the here and now, when he or she gains a testimony of the gospel and is brought out of worldly confusion into the peace and security that come only from God. Truly, the rest of God is "the spiritual rest and peace which are born from a settled conviction of the truth in the minds of [individuals]." To enter into God's rest here and now is to enter into "the knowledge and love of God, having faith in his purpose and in his plan, to such an extent that we know we are right, and that we are not hunting for something else, we are not disturbed by every wind of doctrine, or by the cunning and craftiness of men who lie in wait to deceive." The rest of the Lord that we gain in this life is thus "rest from doubt, from fear, from apprehension of danger, rest from the religious turmoil of the world" (Smith, 126, 58). It is to know the peace of the Spirit, to enjoy the blessing of the Comforter. It is what Jesus promised to his disciples when he said: "Come unto me, all ye that labour and are heavy laden, and I will give you rest" (Matthew 11:28).

A second way spirits enter the rest of God is when they enter paradise, the abode of the righteous in the postmortal spirit world, at death. Alma explained to Corianton, "Then shall it come to pass, that the spirits of those who are righteous are received into a state of . . . paradise, *a state of rest,* a state of peace, where they shall rest from all their troubles and from all care, and sorrow" (Alma 40:12; emphasis added). Indeed, it is a place and a condition wherein men and women "expand in wisdom, where they have respite from all their troubles, and where care and sorrow do not annoy" (Smith 448). "The Lord suffereth the righteous to be slain," Captain Moroni wrote to Pahoran, "that his justice and judgment may come upon the wicked; therefore ye need not suppose that the righteous are lost because they are slain; but behold, they do enter into the rest of the Lord their God" (Alma 60:13).

A third dimension of the rest of the Lord follows the resurrection and judgment, when we enter the celestial kingdom and receive exaltation. It is interesting that Mormon, speaking to the members of the Church in his day, uses *rest* in at least two ways. "Wherefore," he said, "I would speak unto you that are of the church, that are the peaceable followers of Christ, and that have obtained a sufficient hope by which ye can enter into the rest of the Lord"—meaning here in mortality—"from this time henceforth until ye shall rest with him in heaven" (Moroni 7:3). Abiding in the rest of the Lord in this life comes in anticipation of the ultimate rest and peace to be had in eternal glory. There is yet another sense in which the word *rest* is used in scripture: the fulness of God's glory (D&C 84:24).

Alma's invitation to the people of Ammonihah to enter into the rest of the Lord is built upon the notion that ancient Israel provoked God and proved themselves unworthy of this blessing (Alma 12:36–37). Moses desired to make available the highest privilege of the priesthood to Israel—the privilege of seeing the face of God, of coming directly into the divine presence. Of the Israelites, Jehovah said, "I have sworn in my wrath, that they shall not enter into my presence, *into my rest,* in the days of their pilgrimage" (JST, Exodus 34:2; emphasis added). Here the rest of the Lord is equated with being received into the presence of the Lord while the recipients are still mortal.

So many scriptural terms that describe life hereafter also describe a dimension of that life here. We need not wait until the resurrection to enjoy redemption in Christ; we may be redeemed here and now, in the present, through repentance, forgiveness, rebirth, and divine submission. We long for that glorious day when we will be received into the highest heaven, but we rejoice in the truth that the sacred and settling peace we know as the rest of the Lord may be experienced during our days of probation. Amulek meant what he said when he taught that "this life is the time for men to prepare to meet God" (Alma 34:32). Redemption here prepares us for redemption hereafter. Rest and peace here are harbingers of the glory that is to be.

SOURCE
Smith, Joseph F. *Gospel Doctrine.* Salt Lake City: Deseret Book, 1939.

RLM

RESTORATION

To restore means to return to a former condition or to bring back. The term *restoration* and its synonym *restitution* have multiple meanings in the scriptures and in Latter-day Saint teachings. The most common use of the term refers to the series of events and divine revelations whereby the fulness of gospel principles, ordinances, priesthood authority, and the true Church of Jesus Christ were restored to the earth.

These events, beginning with Joseph Smith's First Vision in 1820, the translation and publication of the Book of Mormon, and the organization of the Church in 1830, are all part of what Latter-day Saints refer to as the Restoration—the fulfillment of Peter's prophecy of "the times of restitution" that will precede the second coming of Christ (Acts 3:21; see also Matthew 17:11; Ephesians 1:10; Revelation 14:6–7; 1 Nephi 13:20–34; 2 Nephi 9:2; D&C 1; 110; 112:30; Joseph Smith–History 1).

Numerous scriptural passages also use the term *restoration* in the context of restoring the tribes of Israel to their former knowledge of God and his gospel and their covenants with him. This restoration of the house of Israel is a fundamental part of the Restoration and the latter-day work of The Church of Jesus Christ of Latter-day Saints (1 Nephi 10:14; 15:12–18; 2 Nephi 25:17–18; 29:1–2; 30:7; 3 Nephi 20–21; D&C 29:7; 110:11).

The Book of Mormon prophet Alma uses the term *restoration* to refer to the literal resurrection of the body. Speaking of the resurrection, Alma states: "Yea, this bringeth about the restoration of those things of which has been spoken by the mouths of the prophets. The soul shall be restored to the body, and the body to the soul; yea, and every limb and joint shall be restored to its body; yea, even a hair of the head shall not be lost; but all things shall be restored to their proper and perfect frame" (Alma 40:22–23).

In addition to teaching of the physical resurrection as a restoration, Alma taught that in the Final Judgment there is a spiritual restoration of deeds and desires "requisite with the justice of God" (Alma 41:3). "For that which ye do send out," he taught concerning this restoration, "shall return unto you again, and be restored; therefore, the word restoration more fully condemneth the sinner, and justifieth him not at all" (Alma 41:15).

"And now behold, is the meaning of the word restoration to take a thing of a natural state and place it in an unnatural state, or to place it in a state opposite to its nature? O, my son, this is not the case; but the meaning of the word restoration is to bring back again evil for evil, or carnal for carnal, or devilish for devilish—good for that which is good; righteous for that which is righteous; just for that which is just; merciful for that which is merciful.

"Therefore, my son, see that you are merciful unto your brethren; deal justly, judge righteously, and do good continually; and if ye do all these things then shall ye receive your reward; yea, ye shall have mercy restored unto you again; ye shall have justice restored unto you again; ye shall have a righteous judgment restored unto you again and ye shall have good rewarded unto you again" (Alma 41:12–14).

The scriptures also use the terms *restoration* and *restitution* as an essential part of the repentance process. A thorough transformation of one's life through faith unto repentance requires a restoration—a repayment or reparation, as far as is possible, for the damages incurred by transgression. The prophet Ezekiel said: "If the wicked *restore the pledge,* give again that he had robbed, walk in the statutes of life, without committing iniquity; he shall surely live, he shall not die. None of his sins that he hath committed shall be mentioned unto him: he hath done that which is lawful and right; he shall surely live" (Ezekiel 33:15–16; emphasis added). Restitution—restoring that which has been lost—has always been part of repentance. The literal nature of this restoration is delineated in the Old Testament. The law required a repayment or restoration of that which was stolen or lost through someone else's sin. Often this payment meant paying back more than was originally lost (Exodus 22:1–6; Leviticus 6:2–5).

In the Church today we are still required to pay back that which was lost as a result of transgression. Sometimes restitution is easy to make, as when paying for something that was stolen or simply returning it. Such restitution, however, is possible only in a few instances. Much more common are deeply damaging consequences for which restitution is not so simple or clear-cut. It is true that we can in no way of ourselves repair all the damage done through sin or repay the Savior for his atonement in our behalf. Therefore, sometimes all we can do to make proper restoration is to devote our lives to a lifetime of restitution through righteousness, relying upon the grace of Christ to rectify that which we could never correct ourselves. In that sense, Jesus fixes the otherwise unfixable, repairs the otherwise irreparable (Packer, 18–21). Because we all have an eternal indebtedness to the Lord for his mercy, forgiveness, and goodness, we need continual restitution—daily living in repentance and faithfulness, seeking always to "restore the pledge" and "zealously striving to repair all the injuries" (Ezekiel 33:15; Mosiah

27:35) caused by our sins. Thus, the restoration or restitution required by the Lord demands our very lives—our changed being as well as our changed behavior.

SOURCE

Packer, Boyd K. "The Brilliant Morning of Forgiveness." *Ensign,* Nov. 1995, 18–21.

BLT

RESURRECTION

"For as in Adam all die," the apostle Paul declared, "even so in Christ shall all be made alive" (1 Corinthians 15:22). Because Jesus Christ, the Only Begotten Son of God, forever broke the bands of death and as the risen Lord became "the firstfuits of them that slept" (1 Corinthians 15:20), all mankind will be literally resurrected from death to immortality, from corruptibility to incorruptibility (1 Corinthians 15:54). The Prophet Joseph Smith taught that the resurrection of the dead is so foundational to our beliefs that it should be taught "among the first principles of the Gospel of Jesus Christ" (3:379). While some in the Christian world question the reality of a universal resurrection and others question whether such a resurrection is truly physical or merely spiritual, Latter-day Saints believe and declare that just as Jesus was resurrected to a tangible, glorified body of flesh and bones (Luke 24; 3 Nephi 11:1–15), so too will all men. The Book of Mormon prophet Alma taught, "The soul [spirit] shall be restored to the body, and the body to the soul; yea, and every limb and joint shall be restored to its body; yea, even a hair of the head shall not be lost; but all things shall be restored to their proper and perfect frame" (Alma 40:23). Likewise, the prophet Amulek testified:

"Now, there is a death which is called a temporal death; and the death of Christ shall loose the bands of this temporal death, that all shall be raised from this temporal death. The spirit and the body shall be reunited again in its perfect form; to its proper frame, even as we now are at this time. . . .

"Now, this restoration shall come to all, both old and young, both bond and free, both male and female, both the wicked and the righteous; and even there shall not so much as a hair of their heads be lost; but every thing shall be restored to its perfect frame, as it is now, or in the body, and shall be brought and be arraigned before the bar of

Christ the Son, and God the Father, and the Holy Spirit, which is one Eternal God, to be judged according to their works, whether they be good or whether they be evil.

"Now, behold, I have spoken unto you concerning the death of the mortal body, and also concerning the resurrection of the mortal body. I say unto you that this mortal body is raised to an immortal body, that is from death, even from the first death unto life, that they can die no more; their spirits reuniting with their bodies, never to be divided, thus the whole becoming spiritual and immortal, that they can no more see corruption" (Alma 11:42–45).

The Old Testament also testifies of a literal resurrection. Job declared, "And though after my skin worms destroy this body, yet in my flesh shall I see God" (Job 19:26). The prophet Ezekiel saw the resurrection in vision and heard the word of the Lord declare:

"I will cause breath to enter into you, and ye shall live: and I will lay sinews upon you, and will bring up flesh upon you, and cover you with skin, and put breath in you, and ye shall live; and ye shall know that I am the Lord. . . . I will open up your graves, and cause you to come up out of your graves, and bring you into the land of Israel" (Ezekiel 37:5–6, 12).

Exactly how the corruptible, mortal body is resurrected to an incorruptible, immortal body has not been made known. Nor could the mortal mind comprehend how it is done. We do, however, know that just as Jesus changed the composition of the elements of water to become wine, so the Almighty has power to cause an elemental recomposition of our bodies. "The particles of this earth that now compose this body will be re-arranged," President Brigham Young taught, "and the spirit will be clothed with an immortal tabernacle" (8:43). He also taught: "In the resurrection everything that is necessary will be brought from the elements to clothe and to beautify the resurrected Saints, who will receive their reward" (9:192).

The "proper and perfect frame" spoken of by Alma and Amulek is more glorious than anything mortal. It is a new creation of a perfect body that has, as President Spencer W. Kimball explained, "every organ perfect, every limb intact, with every injury or deformity restored and put right; with the infirmities of mortality replaced with strength and vigor and power and beauty of virile maturity" (45).

Latter-day prophets have also taught that resurrection is effected by the power of the priesthood. "Some person holding the keys of the resurrection, having previously passed through that ordeal," explained President Young, "will be delegated to resurrect our bodies[,] and our spirits will be there and prepared to enter into their bodies" (9:139).

All who have ever lived in mortality will be resurrected with immortal bodies of flesh and bones because of the mercy and grace of the Savior, but not all will receive the same glory in the resurrection. Jesus spoke of two resurrections—a "resurrection of life" for the righteous and a "resurrection of damnation" for those "that have done evil" (John 5:29). The apostle Paul, in a similar vein, taught that resurrected bodies would differ in glory as much as do the sun, moon, and stars. "There are also celestial bodies, and bodies terrestrial. . . . There is one glory of the sun, and another glory of the moon, and another glory of the stars: for one star differeth from another star in glory. So also is the resurrection of the dead" (1 Corinthians 15:40–42). From additional revelations on the resurrection given by God in this dispensation, Latter-day Saints believe that the different resurrections spoken of by Christ and Paul are both qualitative and chronological. First, "the resurrection of the just" (JST, John 5:29) with the righteous and the celestial receiving more glory, and last, "the resurrection of damnation" (John 5:29) for those who receive less glory and for the sons of perdition, who receive no glory.

The first resurrection began when the risen Lord came forth from the tomb. The literal nature of his resurrection was witnessed by his disciples, hundreds in the Old World, and thousands in the New World (Matthew 28; Mark 16; Luke 24; John 20–21; 3 Nephi 11). With the bands of death broken through Christ's Atonement, "many bodies of the saints which slept arose, and came out of the graves after his resurrection, and went into the holy city, and appeared unto many" (Matthew 27:52–53; see also Mosiah 15:20–24; Alma 40:16–21; Helaman 14:25; 3 Nephi 23:8–13). Among those who rose from the dead were Moses, Elijah, Elias, John the Baptist, and the righteous Saints of Enoch's city of Zion (D&C 133:54–55). Later, Peter, James, the Book of Mormon prophet Moroni, and perhaps others were also resurrected.

From the Doctrine and Covenants we learn that at Christ's second coming, the first resurrection will resume (D&C 29:11–13; 45:44–46; 88:95–98; 133:56). Latter-day Saints refer to this as the "morning of the first resurrection." Although the term is not scriptural, it is used to denote the glorious resurrection of the righteous—those who have been sanctified through the law of Christ, the law of the celestial kingdom (D&C 88:20–26). These are they who are resurrected and "caught up to meet [the Savior] in the midst of the pillar of heaven" (D&C 88:97) and "shall come forth and stand on the right hand of the Lamb, when he shall stand upon Mount Zion" (D&C 133:56). The resurrection will continue throughout the Millennium as those who are mortal at Christ's coming and those who are born during the thousand years of peace and righteousness will live to "the age of a tree" and then die and be resurrected in the "twinkling of an eye" (D&C 101:30–31; see also Isaiah 65:17–20).

Latter-day Saints do not use the term "afternoon of the first resurrection," but it would aptly apply to the resurrection of those who have lived a lesser, terrestrial law but who also have part in the first resurrection, or the "resurrection of the just" (D&C 76:17, 50, 65). President Joseph Fielding Smith explained:

"Following [the Second Coming], and after the Lord and the righteous who are caught up to meet him have descended upon the earth, there will come to pass another resurrection. This may be considered as a part of the first, although it comes later. In this resurrection will come forth those of the terrestrial order, who were not worthy to be caught up to meet him, but who are worthy to come forth to enjoy the millennial reign" (2:296).

Those who would not abide by the celestial law of Christ or a terrestrial law—those who are "liars, and sorcerers, and adulterers, and whoremongers, and whosoever loves and makes a lie" (D&C 76:103)—remain in the spirit world until the end of the Millennium, "when Christ shall have subdued all enemies under his feet and shall have perfected his work" (D&C 76:106; see also 1 Corinthians 15:24–26). Those who "have willfully rebelled against God, that have known the commandments of God, and would not keep them; these are they that have no part in the first resurrection" (Mosiah 15:26). This is the last resurrection, or the "resurrection of damnation" of which Jesus spoke.

With the resurrection complete, the effects of the fall of Adam are swallowed up in Christ. All are brought back into the presence of God to be judged. The Book of Mormon prophet Samuel taught that Christ died "to bring to pass the resurrection of the dead, that thereby men may be brought into the presence of the Lord" and that he "redeemeth all mankind from the first death—that spiritual death" (Helaman 14:15–16). By the power of God and by virtue of Christ's infinite atonement, all mankind—righteous and wicked—will be resurrected to immortality. Death will be forever destroyed (2 Nephi 9:10–12). "O death, where is thy sting? O grave, where is thy victory?" the apostle Paul asked. "But thanks be to God which giveth us the victory through our Lord Jesus Christ" (1 Corinthians 15:55, 57; see also Mosiah 16:7–8).

Like Ezekiel of old, the Prophet Joseph Smith saw the resurrection in vision and testified of the greatness of that coming day: "Would you think it strange if I relate what I have seen in vision in relation to this interesting theme [of resurrection]? Those who have died in Jesus Christ may expect to enter into all that fruition of joy when they come forth, which they possessed or anticipated here.

"So plain was the vision, that I actually saw men, before they had ascended from the tomb, as though they were getting up slowly. They took each other by the hand and said to each other, 'My father, my son, my mother, my daughter, my brother, my sister.' And when the voice calls for the dead to arise, suppose I am laid by the side of my father, what would be the first joy of my heart? To meet my father, my mother, my brother, my sister; and when they are by my side, I embrace them and they me. . . .

". . . All your losses will be made up to you in the resurrection, provided you continue faithful. By the vision of the Almighty I have seen it" (5:361–62).

SOURCES

Kimball, Spencer W. *The Teachings of Spencer W. Kimball*. Edited by Edward L. Kimball. Salt Lake City: Deseret Book, 1982.

Smith, Joseph. *History of The Church of Jesus Christ of Latter-day Saints*. Edited by B. H. Roberts. 7 vols. 2d ed. rev. Salt Lake City: The Church of Jesus Christ of Latter-day Saints, 1932–51.

Smith, Joseph Fielding. *Doctrines of Salvation*. Compiled by Bruce R. McConkie. 3 vols. Salt Lake City: Bookcraft, 1954–56.

Young, Brigham. In *Journal of Discourses.* 26 vols. London: Latter-day Saints' Book Depot, 1854–86.

BLT

REVELATION

Any divine communication from God to man is called revelation. Revelation comes in many different forms. Scriptures record the messages of God delivered through holy prophets. The Light of Christ, "given to every man, that he may know good from evil" (Moroni 7:16), is a universal revelation. All true revelation comes by the power of the Spirit of God. By this power, the Almighty speaks to our minds and hearts (D&C 8:2). The Prophet Joseph Smith taught that the principle of revelation can be observed in one's life "when you feel pure intelligence flowing into you" as "sudden strokes of ideas" (3:381). Revelation comes not only as thoughts but also as feelings. To Oliver Cowdery the Lord said: "I will cause that your bosom shall burn within you; therefore, you shall feel that it is right" (D&C 9:8). Divine messages from God can also come in the form of visions, visitations, inspired dreams, and other direct and miraculous means. Revelation in its many forms comes to us from God for the purpose of instruction, exhortation, comfort, direction, warning—all designed to help us now in our various responsibilities and challenges on earth and to prepare us for ultimate exaltation in the presence of God. By revelation, we can "know the truth of all things" (Moroni 10:5) "which are expedient unto the children of men" (D&C 18:18).

To Latter-day Saints, revelation from God comes through two different but related lines of communication. These are what Elder Dallin H. Oaks called "the personal line and the priesthood line." Each is essential in coming to know the mind and will of God. Personal revelation is, as Elder Oaks taught, "an essential feature of [God's] marvelous gospel plan which allows each one of His children to receive a personal witness of its truth. . . . The personal line is of paramount importance in personal decisions and in the governance of the family" (83). Personal revelation can guide us in our unique circumstances and responsibilities. The gift of revelation, President Joseph F. Smith taught, "belongs to every individual member of the Church; and it is the right and privilege of every man, every woman, and every child who has reached the years of accountability, to enjoy the spirit of revelation, and to be possessed of the spirit of inspiration in the discharge of their duties as members of the Church. It is the privilege of every individual member of the Church to have revelation for his own guidance, for the direction of his life and conduct" (34).

President Boyd K. Packer has taught: "All inspiration does not come from God. The evil one has the power to tap into those channels of revelation and send conflicting signals which can mislead and confuse us" (144). There are eternal principles that govern true revelation and serve as a protection against false revelation. Because the Spirit is the power by which all revelation comes, one must be worthy to receive such revelation, for "the Spirit of the Lord doth not dwell in unholy temples" (Helaman 4:24). Faithful obedience to the principles and covenants of the gospel opens the door to personal revelation, while unworthiness and disobedience slams it shut. Another important principle to remember is that revelation always stays within certain, divinely mandated parameters—stewardship, established doctrine, and channels of authority. "If we are worthy, we are entitled to receive revelations for ourselves, parents for their children, and members of the Church in their callings," President James E. Faust explained. "But the right of revelation for others does not extend beyond our own stewardship" (4). Likewise, only the president of the Church, as God's sole mouthpiece and revelator on earth, has the right and authority to receive revelation and declare God's mind and will for the entire Church, even the whole world. This is what Elder Oaks referred to as the "priesthood line." Additionally, no true revelation for others or for ourselves under our stewardship will be contrary to the teachings of scripture, established doctrines of the Church, or counsel and teachings of living prophets. President Spencer W. Kimball taught:

"The one who receives revelation for any part of the Church, if his revelations are from God, will always be in the same direction as the general program the Lord has revealed to his prophets. . . .

". . . If one does receive revelations, which one may expect if he is worthy, they will always be in total alignment with the program of the Church; they will never be counter. And they will always be within his own jurisdiction and never beyond" (453, 458).

Latter-day Saints believe in revelation—through both personal lines and priesthood lines, both individually and institutionally. "We believe all that God has revealed, all that He does now reveal, and we believe that He will yet reveal many great and important things pertaining to the Kingdom of God" (Articles of Faith 1:9). Without revelation we cannot know the Father and his Only Begotten Son and lay claim to eternal life (John 17:3). "[W]e never can comprehend the things of God and of heaven, but by revelation," the Prophet Joseph Smith declared (5:344). "Salvation cannot come without revelation; it is in vain for anyone to minister without it" (3:389). To each of us, if we are worthy and faithful, God promises, "If thou shalt ask, thou shalt receive revelation upon revelation, knowledge upon knowledge, that thou mayest know the mysteries and peaceable things—that which bringeth joy, that which bringeth life eternal" (D&C 42:61).

SOURCES

Faust, James E. "Communion with the Holy Spirit." *Ensign,* Mar. 2002, 2–7.

Kimball, Spencer W. *The Teachings of Spencer W. Kimball.* Edited by Edward L. Kimball. Salt Lake City: Deseret Book, 1982.

Oaks, Dallin H. "Two Lines of Communication." *Ensign,* Nov. 2010, 83–86.

Packer, Boyd K. *Mine Errand from the Lord: Selections from the Sermons and Writings of Boyd K. Packer.* Salt Lake City: Deseret Book, 2008.

Smith, Joseph. *History of The Church of Jesus Christ of Latter-day Saints.* Edited by B. H. Roberts. 7 vols. 2d ed. rev. Salt Lake City: The Church of Jesus Christ of Latter-day Saints, 1932–51.

Smith, Joseph F. *Gospel Doctrine.* Salt Lake City: Deseret Book, 1939.

BLT

REVELATOR

The term *revelator* has multiple meanings in the scriptures. The ultimate revelator is God himself, who reveals his word and will to man through the power of his Holy Spirit. The Prophet Joseph Smith declared, "The Holy Ghost is a revelator" (6:58; see also 2 Nephi 33:1; Moroni 10:5). Both Deity and mortal men can be revelators, though each in a different way. God is the giver of revelation, and man is the receiver and expounder. In a general sense, any person who receives revelation from God, applies those truths, and conveys them to another could be characterized as a revelator. All can receive revelation for themselves and for others within the bounds of their stewardship. The more common and precise use of the term *revelator* in the Church today, however, refers to those sustained as prophets, seers, and revelators—the First Presidency and Quorum of the Twelve Apostles. More specifically, *the* revelator is the president of the Church. He alone has the right and keys to be, as Elder John A. Widtsoe said, "a bearer of new truth." A revelator "makes known, with the Lord's help, something before unknown. It may be new or forgotten truth, or a new or forgotten application of known truth to man's need. Always, the revelator deals with truth, certain truth (D&C 100:11) and always it comes with the divine stamp of approval" (258).

With this definition as the foundation, it is clear that only the president of the Church can receive and declare as revelation truths and doctrines that have never previously been revealed. The Lord's law of revelation declares that "there is none other [besides the president of the Church] appointed unto you to receive commandments and revelations" for the entire Church and the world (D&C 43:3; see also D&C 28:1–7). As the revelator on earth, the prophet-president of the Church is "like unto Moses" (D&C 107:91) in that he "alone has the right to receive revelations for the Church, either new or amendatory, or to give authoritative interpretations of scriptures that shall be binding on the Church, or change in any way the existing doctrines of the Church. He is God's sole mouthpiece on earth for The Church of Jesus Christ of Latter-day Saints, the only true Church. He alone may declare the mind and will of God to his people. No [other officer] has this high right and lofty prerogative" (Clark, 10).

SOURCES

Clark, J. Reuben, Jr. "When Are Church Leaders' Words Entitled to Claim of Scripture?" *Church News,* 31 July 1954, 9–11.

Smith, Joseph. *History of The Church of Jesus Christ of Latter-day Saints.* Edited by B. H. Roberts. 7 vols. 2d ed. rev. Salt Lake City: The Church of Jesus Christ of Latter-day Saints, 1932–51.

Widtsoe, John A. *Evidences and Reconciliations.* Arranged by G. Homer Durham. Salt Lake City: Bookcraft, 1960.

BLT

REVERENCE

Recognition of, deference toward, and awe for the grandeur, greatness, and majesty of the Lord constitute reverence. We experience reverence through feelings of profound respect for all members of the Godhead, as well as all they create, consecrate, or set apart as holy. To fear God, as is often encouraged in scripture, is to know true reverence for Deity.

Loss of reverence for the sacred is evident when we treat lightly or casually the things of God. It occurs when we know God but neither glorify him nor show gratitude to him because of our pride and vain imaginations (Romans 1:21). We destroy the power of reverence within us when we change "the glory of the uncorruptible God into an image made like to corruptible man" or bring Almighty God down to our carnal level and speak of him as common (Romans 1:23). President J. Reuben Clark Jr. warned of losing reverence for the Savior by merely focusing on his role as a great teacher, saying, "It is all right to speak of the Savior and the beauty of his doctrines, and the beauty of the truth. But . . . this is the thing I wish you to . . . always carry with you, the Savior is to be looked at as the Messiah, the Redeemer of the world. His teachings were ancillary and auxiliary to that great fact" (187). Likewise, we cannot feel reverence for God if we defame any edifice that has been erected to honor or worship Deity, whether by marring the building in any way or speaking ill of another while within its walls. Sincere reverence extends to showing similar respect for religious edifices of those not of our faith. President Marion G. Romney observed: "Reverence is the soul of true religion. Its seedbed is sincerity. Its quality is determined by the esteem in which one holds the object of his reverence as evidenced by his behavior toward that object. When that object is *God,* the genuinely reverent person has a worshipful adoration coupled with a respectful behavior toward him and all that pertains to him" (2).

The Book of Mormon prophet Enos exemplified reverence when he desired forgiveness of his sins and went into the forest, reflecting on his father's words concerning "eternal life and the joy of the saints" (Enos 1:3). Enos reported, "And my soul hungered; and I kneeled down before my Maker, and I cried unto him in mighty prayer, and supplication for mine own soul" (Enos 1:4). When the resurrected Christ appeared to the Nephites, the multitude cried out: "Hosanna! Blessed be the name of the Most High God! And they did fall down at the feet of Jesus, and did worship him" (3 Nephi 11:17). Eventually, "every knee shall bow, and every tongue confess" that Jesus is the Christ, thereby extending to him the reverence that is rightfully his (Mosiah 27:31).

SOURCES

Clark, J. Reuben, Jr. *Selected Papers of J. Reuben Clark.* Edited by David H. Yarn Jr. Provo, Utah: Brigham Young University Press, 1984.

Romney, Marion G. "Reverence." *Ensign,* Oct. 1976, 2–3.

CFO

RIGHTEOUS

One is righteous when he or she is spiritually sound, on course, pointed to, and moving toward the grand goal of eternal life. Although a perfect person (such as Jesus) is certainly righteous, a righteous person is not necessarily free of sin or flaws. Hugh Nibley, one of the greatest defenders of the faith in the twentieth century, wrote: "Who is righteous? Anyone who is repenting. No matter how bad he has been, if he is repenting, he is a righteous man. There is hope for him. And no matter how good he has been all his life, if he is not repenting he is a wicked man. The difference is which way you are facing. The man on the top of the stairs facing down is much worse off than the man on the bottom step who is facing up. The direction we are facing, that is repentance; and that is what determines whether we are good or bad" (301–2).

One definition of sin is "missing the mark," meaning, missing the target or bull's-eye. One Christian writer has explained: "One of the Hebrew words for a righteous person suggests 'one whose aim is true.' Set beside the word that defines sin as 'missing a mark,' this gives me an image of righteousness as 'target practice.' Whether my arrow finds its mark or falls a hundred feet away, the daily practice of right relationship is how I improve my aim. I will continue to sin, no doubt about it, but that is not my aim. My true aim is to live as God wants me to live" (Taylor, 71–72). A righteous person is a just person, one who is in a proper relationship with God. This status, this spiritual condition does not come by hard work, grit, and willpower alone, although true discipleship always entails a measure of discipline. The apostle Paul explained that "a man is justified [made right with God] by faith alone, without the deeds of the law" (JST, Romans 3:28).Thus, persons who qualify for a celestial resurrection are "just [meaning justified] men made perfect through Jesus the mediator of the new covenant, who wrought out this perfect atonement through the shedding of his own blood" (D&C 76:69). Just men and women are righteous men and women.

SOURCES

Nibley, Hugh. *Approaching Zion.* Edited by Don E. Norton. Salt Lake City: Deseret Book, 1989.

Taylor, Barbara Brown. *Speaking of Sin: The Lost Language of Salvation.* Lanham, Md.: Cowley Publications, 2001.

RLM

ROCK

In scripture the prophets often use the word *rock* to refer to that which is solid, enduring, immovable, steady, and sure. When the apostle Peter bore his powerful testimony of the Savior at Caesarea Philippi—declaring, "Thou art the Christ, the Son of the living God"—the Master responded: "Blessed art thou, Simon Bar-jona: for flesh and blood hath not revealed it unto thee, but my Father which is in heaven. And I say also unto thee, That thou art Peter, and upon this rock I will build my church" (Matthew 16:16–18). The Prophet Joseph Smith taught, "Jesus in His teachings says, 'Upon this rock I will build my Church, and the gates of hell shall not prevail against it.' What rock? Revelation" (5:258).

Elder Bruce R. McConkie explained: "And how could it be otherwise? There is no other foundation upon which the Lord could build his Church and kingdom. The things of God are known only by the power of his Spirit. God stands revealed or he remains forever unknown. No man can know that Jesus is the Lord but by the Holy Ghost.

"*Revelation*: Pure, perfect, personal revelation—this is the rock! Revelation that Jesus is the Christ: the plain, wondrous word that comes from God in heaven to man on earth, the word that affirms the divine Sonship of our Lord—this is the rock! . . .

"All this is the rock, and yet there is more. Christ is the Rock: the Rock of Ages, the Stone of Israel, the Sure Foundation—the Lord is our Rock!" (77).

In a broader sense, the doctrine of Christ (3 Nephi 11:39–40), the gospel of Jesus Christ itself (1 Nephi 13:36; D&C 11:24; 18:4–5, 17), is the rock upon which discerning people build their houses of faith. Christ is the Rock of our righteousness, the Rock of our salvation (1 Nephi 15:15; 2 Nephi 4:30, 35; 9:45), the Rock of Heaven (Moses 7:53).

SOURCES

McConkie, Bruce R. "Upon This Rock." *Ensign,* May 1981, 75–77.
Smith, Joseph. *History of The Church of Jesus Christ of Latter-day Saints.* Edited by B. H. Roberts. 7 vols. 2d ed. rev. Salt Lake City: The Church of Jesus Christ of Latter-day Saints, 1932–51.

RLM

SABBATH

The English word *Sabbath* comes from the Hebrew word *Shabbat,* which means "to rest" or "cease" (from work). In the Creation accounts found in scripture, we learn that God "rested" on the seventh "day," when "the heavens and the earth were finished, and all the host of them" (Genesis 2:1–2; see also Moses 3:1–3). From the dawn of creation, a Sabbath was set aside as a blessed and sanctified day for men to worship God, praise his goodness, and, by taking "rest" from their temporal labors, to keep themselves attuned to eternal purposes and priorities (Genesis 2:3). From Mount Sinai, Moses delivered to the children of Israel the tablets containing the Ten Commandments, which had been etched in stone by the finger of the Lord God Jehovah (Exodus 20). Those commandments were a profound expression of God's tender mercies and loving-kindness. The remaining nine commandments are directly related to the first—to have no other gods before ("in place of") our Heavenly Father. That is for our benefit, not merely to satisfy God's vanity; nor is it an autocratic demand for exclusive devotion.

There is no one and nothing else that can preserve and protect like our Father—the Almighty God of Abraham, Isaac, and Jacob. Hence, every other commandment ties us back to him—to his watchful care and infinite love. The fourth commandment declares, "Remember the sabbath day, to keep it holy" (Exodus 20:8). We are commanded to keep the Sabbath holy in order to remember God and our relationship with him. To keep our heartstrings firmly fastened to God, he gave the Sabbath as a regular reminder of the need for exclusive devotion in order to be protected, preserved, and prospered. Sabbath observance is a sign between covenant Israel and the Lord and a continual reminder that "rest"—real, lasting rest, both here and hereafter—is not found in the world or worldly ways but only through a deep and abiding relationship with the Almighty. So important was this eternal principle that specific laws and expectations served to remind the ancients of the sanctity of the day. Work both by master and servant was to cease (Exodus 23:12), and even seemingly small tasks requiring little or no effort were forbidden (Numbers 15:32–35). The penalty for violation of this sacred commandment was death (Exodus 31:14), the same punishment as for idolatry, because failing to honor the Sabbath was a form of infidelity toward God and a form of false worship. The death penalty served as a symbolic reminder that failure to remember God in all aspects of life constitutes a kind of death—a spiritual death in which one is cut off from the life-giving powers of God. In contrast, obedience and devotion to God, as symbolized by Sabbath observance, means life, the abundant life. The prophet Isaiah declared:

"If thou turn away thy foot from the sabbath, from doing thy pleasure on my holy day; and call the sabbath a delight, the holy of the Lord, honourable; and shalt honour him, not doing thine own ways, nor finding thine own pleasure, nor speaking thine own words: then shalt thou delight thyself in the Lord; and I will cause thee to ride upon the high places of the earth, and feed thee with the heritage of Jacob thy father: for the mouth of the Lord hath spoken it" (Isaiah 58:13–14).

Old Testament prophets rebuked the ancient Israelites at times for their failure to properly keep and remember the Sabbath day as the Lord had commanded. They reminded Israel that Sabbath observance was a sign of the covenant God had made with them—one of the main ways by which the Lord's chosen people would be known (Isaiah 56:2; Jeremiah 17:21–27; Ezekiel 46; Nehemiah 13:15–22). Sabbath observance was viewed as a visible, outward way of dividing the righteous from the wicked.

By the time of Jesus, "fences around the law" (Ludlow, 26) had been established by the doctors of the law to prevent people from ever coming close to breaking the Sabbath. These regulations focused on behavior more than devotion. The Sabbath had become burdensome rather than a day of delight, of which Isaiah spoke. It became more about *what* one does on the Sabbath than *why* one should remember to keep the day sacred. It was more about acceptable or unacceptable activities than about true worship. Condemning this perversion of the true purpose of the Sabbath, Jesus taught, "Wherefore the Sabbath was given unto man for a day of rest; and also that man should glorify God, and not that man should not eat; for the Son of Man made the Sabbath day, therefore the Son of Man is Lord also of the Sabbath" (JST, Mark 2:26–27).

Sabbath observance is not merely a matter of doing or not doing certain things. It involves our attitudes and innermost desires and feelings—our love, devotion, and appreciation for the Lord and his infinite sacrifice. It reminds us that there is no rest, no peace, and no salvation in the world or in following after its many false gods. The Sabbath is a constant reminder of our unique relationship to God.

To early Christians the Sabbath commemorated not only the creation of the earth and the fact that God rested from his labors but also the resurrection and atonement of Jesus Christ, whereby mankind and all the earth would be able to fill the measure of their creation (Acts 20:7; 1 Corinthians 16:2; Revelation 1:10). The "Lord's day" (D&C 59:12), or Sabbath, was celebrated on the first day of the week in remembrance of the resurrection of Christ. Thus, honoring the Sabbath day is an expression of one's worship, love, and gratitude for the Lord Jesus Christ. Elder Mark E. Petersen taught:

"Our observance or nonobservance of the Sabbath is an unerring measure of our attitude toward the Lord personally and toward his suffering in Gethsemane, his death on the cross, and his resurrection from the dead. It is a sign of whether we are Christians in very deed, or whether our conversation is so shallow that commemoration of his atoning sacrifice means little or nothing to us" (49).

In this dispensation the Lord has reminded us of two divine purposes of the Sabbath:

"And that thou mayest more fully keep thyself unspotted from the world, thou shalt go to the house of prayer and offer up thy sacraments upon my holy day; for verily this is a day appointed unto you to rest from your labors, and to pay thy devotions unto the Most High" (D&C 59:9–10).

We remain "unspotted from the world" not just by our reverential reflection on the Savior's atonement and our resting from temporal labors on the Sabbath day but also by worthily partaking of the sacrament of the Lord's Supper. The Sabbath as a holy day is inextricably linked to the sacrament. A remission of our sins and the companionship of the Holy Ghost are part of the "rest" promised by the Lord. Thus, the sacrament should be the very essence of our Sabbath worship. When honoring the Sabbath as a day of delight rather than viewing it merely as a day of don'ts, as did the Pharisees of old, we receive spiritual strength, "rest," and temporal blessings (Leviticus 26:2–13). The Sabbath is an oasis in the spiritual deserts of life.

SOURCES

Ludlow, Victor L. "Major Jewish Groups in the New Testament." *Ensign,* Jan. 1975, 26–29.

Petersen, Mark E. "The Sabbath Day." *Ensign,* May 1975, 47–49.

BLT

SACRAMENT

A sacrament is "a very special kind of symbol. . . . A sacrament could be any one of a number of gestures or acts or ordinances that unite us with God and his limitless powers. We are imperfect and mortal; he is perfect and immortal. But from time to time—indeed, as often as is possible and appropriate—we find ways and go to places and create circumstances where we can unite symbolically with him and, in so doing, gain access to his power. Those special moments of union with God are sacramental moments, such as kneeling at a marriage altar, or blessing a newborn baby, or partaking of the emblems of the Lord's Supper. This latter ordinance is the one we in the Church have come to associate most traditionally with the word *sacrament,* though it is technically only one of many such moments when we formally take the hand of God and feel his divine power" (Holland, 193–94).

SOURCE

Holland, Jeffrey R., and Patricia T. Holland. *On Earth As It Is in Heaven.* Salt Lake City: Deseret Book, 1989.

RLM

SACRAMENT OF THE LORD'S SUPPER

On the eve of his passion, or great suffering, Jesus of Nazareth instituted the sacrament of the Lord's Supper in an upper room in the city of Jerusalem during Passover. Often called simply the sacrament by Latter-day Saints, the term refers to the partaking of bread and water (originally wine) in remembrance of Christ's atoning sacrifice. The apostle Paul explained the symbolic significance of the sacrament to the Corinthian Saints:

"For I have received of the Lord that which also I delivered unto you, That the Lord Jesus the same night in which he was betrayed took bread: And when he had given thanks, he brake it, and said, Take, eat: this is my body, which is broken for you: this do in remembrance of me. After the same manner also he took the cup, when he had supped, saying, This cup is the new testament in my blood: this do ye, as oft as ye drink it, in remembrance of me. For as often as ye eat this bread, and drink this cup, ye do shew the Lord's death till he come. Wherefore whosoever shall eat this bread, and drink this cup of the Lord, unworthily, shall be guilty of the body and blood of the Lord. But let a man examine himself, and so let him eat of that bread, and drink of that cup. For he that eateth and drinketh unworthily, eateth and drinketh damnation to himself, not discerning the Lord's body" (1 Corinthians 11:23–29).

So fundamental is the sacrament to the Lord's postresurrection Church that he personally instituted this ordinance among the Nephites on the first day of his three-day visit to them. After they had partaken of the bread, Jesus stated in language similar to Paul's: "And this shall ye always observe to do, even as I have done, even as I have broken bread and blessed it and given it unto you. And this shall ye do in remembrance of my body, which I have shown unto you. And it shall be a testimony unto the Father that ye do always remember me. And if ye do always remember me ye shall have my Spirit to be with you" (3 Nephi 18:6–7). This experience would have been graphic and memorable to the people because they had just felt the wounds of his suffering (3 Nephi 11:14–15).

Likewise, after consuming wine, Jesus reminded the people of the symbolism involved: "And when the disciples had done this, Jesus said unto them: Blessed are ye for this thing which ye have done, for this is fulfilling my commandments, and this doth witness unto the Father that ye are willing to do that which I have commanded you. And this shall ye always do to those who repent and are baptized in my name; and ye shall do it in remembrance of my blood, which I have shed for you, that ye may witness unto the Father that ye do always remember me. And if ye do always remember me ye shall have my Spirit to be with you" (3 Nephi 18:10–11).

Jesus also commanded the Nephites to partake of the sacrament worthily. "And now behold, this is the commandment which I give unto you, that ye shall not suffer any one knowingly to partake of my flesh and blood unworthily, when ye shall minister it; for whoso eateth and drinketh my flesh and blood unworthily eateth and drinketh damnation to his soul; therefore if ye know that a man is unworthy to eat and drink of my flesh and blood ye shall forbid him" (3 Nephi 18:28–29). Then, as now, those who partake of the sacrament in worthiness enter into a covenant with God the Father. According to the prayers offered by priesthood holders when blessing the sacrament, followers promise to always remember the broken body and spilled blood of God's Only Begotten Son, to take upon themselves the name of God's Son, and to keep his commandments. God, in turn, promises that worthy disciples of his Son will always have his Spirit to be with them (D&C 20:75–79; Moroni 4–5). During his mortal ministry Jesus said that those who consumed the emblems of his body and blood worthily would be given eternal life and their bodies would be raised up (John 6:54; compare 3 Nephi 27:14–15).

To the Nephites the resurrected Lord also taught that his bodily sacrifice fulfilled the need for blood sacrifices involving animals. Instead of looking forward to his death through sacrificial offerings, his disciples were now to look back, to remember his suffering through new symbols, including the sacrament, during which worshippers "offer for a sacrifice unto [him] a broken heart and a contrite spirit" (3 Nephi 9:19–20).

In this dispensation we have been reminded that the bread and water are "the emblems of the flesh and blood of Christ" (D&C 20:40). The emblems are symbolic and do not physically change into the actual body and blood of Christ, as is believed to be the case with the concept of transubstantiation. Though wine was originally used for the sacrament in the early days of the Restoration, the Lord revealed to the Prophet Joseph Smith that it does not matter what is used for the sacrament as long as the ordinance is done with an eye single to God's glory and in remembrance of the Savior's body and blood sacrificed for our sins. The Lord then commanded his leaders not to purchase wine or strong drink from their enemies (D&C 27:2–3).

The sacrament of the Lord's Supper was instituted when Jesus transformed the nature of the Passover feast he had been celebrating with his disciples in the upper room. The Passover feast in Jesus' day required that certain food and drink—unleavened bread, four cups of wine, and other items—be consumed according to an arranged order during the evening. Luke records that after Jesus had broken bread and given it to the disciples, he changed the intent of the evening's celebration. Said he, "This is my body, which is given for you: this do in remembrance of me" (Luke 22:19). Thus, by this command, his disciples were no longer to focus on the blood of the paschal lambs, the Exodus from Egypt, and the corporate deliverance from physical and spiritual bondage. Now they must remember in a personal way Jesus Christ, the One who instituted Passover, the One who delivers from physical and spiritual death, the One who would work out the infinite and eternal Atonement through the shedding of his own blood. Then Jesus took the third cup of wine, the cup after supper, and said, "This cup is the new testament in my blood, which is shed for you" (Luke 22:20). The transformation was complete. At that moment and forever after, Jesus became "our passover . . . sacrificed for us" (1 Corinthians 5:7). In other words, a new, permanent ordinance began to be observed.

At the beginning of the evening, when Jesus reclined with his disciples in the upper room, he made reference to the future. "And he said unto them, With desire I have desired to eat this passover with you before I suffer: For I say unto you, I will not any more eat thereof, until it be fulfilled in the kingdom of God" (Luke 22:15–16). Through modern revelation (D&C 27:5–14), we understand that at some point there will be a great gathering of the Saints from all ages at Adam-ondi-Ahman. The Lord himself will be there. Adam, the Ancient of Days, will give an accounting of his stewardship. Others in attendance will include Moroni, Elias, John the Baptist, Elijah, Abraham, Isaac, Jacob, Joseph, Peter, James, and John. At that time, a grand sacrament service will be convened, and all will partake of the sacrament with the Lord. Moreover, every faithful person in the history of the world who has lived to inherit eternal life will be present for the fulfillment of the Savior's promise, made two thousand years ago, that he will partake of the sacrament again when "it be fulfilled in the kingdom of God" (Luke 22:16). All of this awaits the faithful.

Sacrament meetings in the Lord's Church today are holy gatherings. Worthiness is requisite for full participation. As was said of animal sacrifices in ancient times, so too it must be said of the sacrament of the Lord's Supper: "This thing is a similitude of the sacrifice of the Only Begotten of the Father" (Moses 5:7).

ACS

SAINT

The scriptures use the word *Saint* to refer to those who have come out of the darkness of the world into the "marvellous light" of Christ (1 Peter 2:9), have accepted Jesus Christ as their Lord and Savior, and have come into his Church. Saints are striving to put off the natural man and put on Christ (Mosiah 3:19). Saints are members of the Church of Jesus Christ and will ultimately "inherit the kingdom of God" (2 Nephi 9:18; see also Acts 9:13, 32, 41; Romans 1:7; 1 Corinthians 1:2; Philippians 1:1; 1 Peter 1:14–15; 1 Nephi 14:12; Moroni 8:26). They are "the sanctified ones" who are being cleansed and purified from sin and its effects by the blood of the Redeemer. They are the separated ones who have chosen to distance themselves from evil and deny themselves of ungodliness. They are those with whom the devil makes war (D&C 76:29) and whom the mother of abominations persecutes (D&C 88:94). True Saints will be delivered "from that awful monster the devil, and death, and hell, and that lake of fire and brimstone, which is endless torment" (2 Nephi 9:19) and will dwell with God forever on the celestialized earth (Moroni 8:26; D&C 103:7).

RLM

SALEM

The first mention of Salem in the scriptures occurs in Genesis 14:18 as the place where Melchizedek ruled as king. *Salem* derives from the Hebrew root meaning "peace" and has been identified as Jerusalem. Thus, "Melchisedec, king of Salem, [was] priest of the most high God, . . . first being by interpretation King of righteousness [the literal meaning of the name Melchizedek], and after that also King of Salem, which is, King of peace" (Hebrews 7:1–2). The Prophet Joseph Smith said, "Salem is designed for a Hebrew term. It should be Shiloam [Shalom], which signifies righteousness and peace" (5:554).

The earliest undisputed mention of Jerusalem in nonbiblical records comes from Egypt shortly after 2000 B.C., wherein it is called *Rushalimum* or *Urusalimum.* Half a millennium later, *circa* 1400 B.C., in diplomatic correspondence (Tell el-Amarna letters) between the ruling power, Egypt, and local city-states to the northeast, the land of Jerusalem is mentioned as a non-Israelite entity called *Urusalim.* In the days of the Assyrian king Sennacherib (705–681 B.C.), it was called *Ursalimmu* or *Uruslimmu.* Subsequent Nabataean, Syriac, and Arabic texts refer to it as *Ursalem, Urishlem,* and *Ursalimu,* respectively. "For two thousand years, then, the texts, whether in Egyptian, Akkadian, or West Semitic languages, consistently present Jerusalem under the name meaning 'City of Shalem,' or 'City of Peace or Perfection,'" (Galbraith, 26).

Although Jerusalem has known much unrest, it is justly called the city of peace and perfection on account of who sojourned there as well as what will happen there. Salem's former inhabitants and visitors included prophets (beginning with Melchizedek), apostles, and Jesus Christ himself, the Prince of Peace, who will return to the city at the Second Coming (Zechariah 14:4; Isaiah 2:3). As a result of the return of the Prince of Peace, millennial Jerusalem will truly become a city of peace and perfection—a condition it has seldom enjoyed throughout its long history. On this point, the word of the Lord is sure: "And men shall dwell in it, and there shall be no more utter destruction; but Jerusalem shall be safely inhabited" (Zechariah 14:11).

Another name for Salem anciently was Jebus (Judges 19:10). It is possible that it was also known as Jebus-salem, and under the influence of its name elsewhere (*Urusalimum, Ursalem,* and so forth) became contracted to Jerusalem. King David conquered the city of Jebus, from a Canaanite tribe called the Jebusites, and made it the capital of the united monarchy by moving there from Hebron. It came to be known as the City of David as well as Jerusalem from that time on (1 Chronicles 11:1–5).

Early on, Salem was the host city for the house of the Lord. It is likely that the first temple at Salem existed during the time of Melchizedek and Abraham. The Jewish historian Josephus wrote that "he who first built it [meaning Jerusalem] was a potent man among the Canaanites, and is in our tongue called [Melchisedek] the Righteous King, for such he really was; on which account he was [there] the first priest of God, and first built a temple [there], and called the city Jerusalem, which was formerly called Salem" (6.10.1). From the time of King Solomon onward, Salem became the site of three more temples of the Lord—Solomon's, Zerubbabel's, and Herod's. Currently, the presumed site of those temples, or close to it, is occupied by the Muslim holy shrine known as the Dome of the Rock. It is from there that Muslims believe the prophet Muhammad made his journey through the seven heavens (Galbraith, 61, 275).

Even more important than Salem's past glory and sanctity will be her role in the Millennium. Salem will be the site of yet another temple of the Lord and will become one of two world capitals of peace and safety, "for out of Zion shall go forth the law, and the word of the Lord from Jerusalem" (Isaiah 2:3). At the Second Coming, Jerusalem will reclaim her intended environment of peace as comprehended in the city's original name: Salem.

SOURCES

Galbraith, David B., D. Kelly Ogden, Andrew C. Skinner. *Jerusalem, the Eternal City.* Salt Lake City: Deseret Book, 1996.

Josephus, Flavius. *The Jewish Wars.* Translated by H. St. J. Thackeray. Cambridge, Mass.: Harvard University Press, 1928.

Smith, Joseph. *History of The Church of Jesus Christ of Latter-day Saints.* Edited by B. H. Roberts. 7 vols. 2d ed. rev. Salt Lake City: The Church of Jesus Christ of Latter-day Saints, 1932–51.

ACS

SALT OF THE EARTH

Jesus Christ used this phrase on two continents to remind his disciples of their covenantal connections to him and their covenantal obligations to the rest of the earth (Matthew 5:13; Luke 14:34–35; 3 Nephi 12:13). Salt was a symbol of God's permanent covenant with Israel, "a covenant of salt" (Numbers 18:19). If members of the covenant community have lost their "savor," if they have abandoned to any degree their commitment to the covenant, if they have deviated from or become lax toward covenantal promises, if they have lost their ability to influence those around them because of wickedness or sloth, they are "good for nothing, but [are] to be cast out" (3 Nephi 12:13; Matthew 5:13). "Salt will not lose its savor with age. Savor is lost through mixture and contamination" (Asay, 42). The Lord's metaphor is a warning to avoid contamination by the world, to remain pure and undefiled, to be in the world but not of the world.

According to the terms of the Abrahamic covenant, "all the families of the earth" are to be blessed through members of the covenant (Abraham 2:11). If covenant participants have lost their savor, they cannot fulfill the aims of the covenant. It is against this backdrop that the Lord in this dispensation continued the salt analogy: "When men are called unto mine everlasting gospel, and covenant with an everlasting covenant, they are accounted as the salt of the earth and the savor of men; they are called to be the savor [influence or Lord's agents] of men; therefore, if that salt of the earth lose its savor, behold, it is thenceforth good for nothing only to be cast out and trodden under the feet of men" (D&C 101:39–40).

Salt is such a significant element and symbol that it is mentioned in the Old and New Testaments, the Book of Mormon, and the Doctrine and Covenants. Anciently salt was a vital part of everyday life as well as religious practice. It was a condiment or seasoning agent, a preservative, a purgative, a medicine, and a crucial element in the sacrificial system of Mosaic law. Job asked, "Can that which is unsavoury [tasteless] be eaten without salt?" (Job 6:6). It was the custom to rub newborn babies with salt for medicinal as well as religious reasons (Ezekiel 16:4). The reputation of the life-giving and curative powers of salt prompted Elisha to use it to purify the spring at Jericho. "And he went forth unto the spring of the waters, and cast the salt in there, and said, Thus saith the Lord, I have healed these waters; there shall not be from thence any more death or barren land" (2 Kings 2:21). Scholars have argued that the declared cure of barrenness applied not to the land but rather to miscarriage, that is, "neither death nor miscarriage shall come from it [the waters]" (*Interpreter's*, 4:167). The fact that the word *land* in 2 Kings 2:21 is in italics in the King James Version and thus not in the original Hebrew text makes this reading plausible.

Perhaps most significant was the role salt played in the tabernacle and temple sacrifices. Salt was used with every grain offering (Leviticus 2:13), and Ezekiel saw in his vision of the temple that salt was to be scattered on all burnt offerings (Ezekiel 43:24). The Hebrew text of Exodus 30:35 states that the incense of the sanctuary was to be mixed with salt. (The King James Version reads "tempered together pure and holy.") Salt also appears in the list of temple supplies (Ezra 6:9). The sacrificial system was a type, shadow, and symbol of the great atoning sacrifice made by our Savior (Hebrews 9–10). Thus, salt not only is a token of the covenant that the Lord made with his followers but also points to the Savior.

Little wonder that Jesus referred to salt as the great symbol of membership in the covenant community. As salt would season the temple sacrifices, so disciples of the Lord who are promulgators of the covenant would season the world and preserve it by spreading the truths of his covenant. And just as salt was a powerful curative and healing agent, so too it pointed to the greatest healing agent in the world—the atonement of Jesus Christ, the very being who used the metaphor of salt in the meridian dispensation and in ours. In addition to describing disciples as the savor and salt of the earth in Doctrine and Covenants 101:39–40, the Lord uses a play on words in another modern revelation to refer to true disciples as the *savor* and *saviors* of others in the world. "For they were set to be a light unto the world, and to be the saviors of men; and inasmuch as they are not the saviors of men, they are as salt that has lost its savor, and is thenceforth good for nothing but to be cast out and trodden under foot of men" (D&C 103:9–10).

Our Savior will never lose his savor. True disciples must not lose theirs.

SOURCES

Asay, Carlos E. "Salt of the Earth: Savor of Men and Saviors of Men." *Ensign,* May 1980, 42–44.

The Interpreter's Dictionary of the Bible: An Illustrated Encyclopedia. Edited by George Arthur Buttrick. 5 vols. Nashville, Tenn.: Abingdon Press, 1962.

ACS

SALVATION

To be saved is to be delivered. It is to be healed, to be made well. "Salvation is nothing more nor less," Joseph Smith declared, "than to triumph over all our enemies and put them under our feet"(5:387). He also said, "Salvation means a man's being placed beyond the power of all his enemies" (5:392). The apostle Paul wrote that Christ must reign until he has "put all enemies under his feet. The last enemy that shall be destroyed is death" (1 Corinthians 15:25–26; see also Hebrews 2:8). The Prophet Joseph added that "until a man can triumph over death, he is not saved. A knowledge of the priesthood alone will do this" (5:403). Further, "salvation consists in the glory, authority, majesty, power and dominion which Jehovah possesses and in nothing else; and no being can possess it but himself or one like him" (*Lectures,* 76).

Salvation is "the greatest of all the gifts of God" (D&C 6:13). Elder Bruce R. McConkie wrote: "Salvation is free. (2 Nephi 2:4.) Justification is free [JST, Romans 3:28]. Neither of them can be purchased; neither can be earned; neither comes by the Law of Moses, or by good works, or by any power or ability that man has. . . . Salvation is free, freely available, freely to be found. It comes because of [Christ's] goodness and grace, because of his love, mercy, and condescension toward the children of men. . . . The questions then are: What salvation is free? What salvation comes by the grace of God? With all the emphasis of the rolling thunders of Sinai, we answer: All salvation is free; all comes by the merits and mercy and grace of the Holy Messiah; there is no salvation of any kind, nature, or degree that is not bound to Christ and his atonement" (346–47).

Given all that we have and enjoy, all that the Lord Jesus Christ has done to redeem our souls, we ask with Paul, "How shall we escape, if we neglect so great salvation . . . ?" (Hebrews 2:3).

SOURCES

Lectures on Faith. Salt Lake City: Deseret Book, 1985.

McConkie, Bruce R. *The Promised Messiah: The First Coming of Christ.* Salt Lake City: Deseret Book, 1978.

Smith, Joseph. *History of The Church of Jesus Christ of Latter-day Saints.* Edited by B. H. Roberts. 7 vols. 2d ed. rev. Salt Lake City: The Church of Jesus Christ of Latter-day Saints, 1932–51.

RLM

SALVATION FOR THE DEAD

Joseph Smith taught that some time during or just following the mortal ministry of Jesus, the doctrine of salvation for the dead was revealed to the Saints of the first century. In testifying of the resurrection of the Lord, the apostle Paul presents the glad tidings that Christ suffered for our sins, died, rose again the third day, and ascended into heaven (1 Corinthians 15:1–4). If Christ had not risen from the dead, Paul asserted, the preaching of the apostles and the faith of the Saints would be in vain. "If in this life only we have hope in Christ," he said, "we are of all men most miserable" (1 Corinthians 15:19). After establishing that the Lord had conquered all enemies, including death, Paul added: "And when all things shall be subdued unto him, then shall the Son also himself be subject unto him [the Father] that put all things under him, that God may be all in all. *Else what shall they do which are baptized for the dead, if the dead rise not at all? why are they then baptized for the dead?*" (1 Corinthians 15:28–29; emphasis added). This passage has given rise to a host of interpretations by biblical scholars of various faiths.

On 21 January 1836 Joseph Smith and many of the leaders of the Church were gathered together in the upper story of the Kirtland Temple. The heavens were opened, light and knowledge filled the Prophet's mind, and he beheld what we know now as the Vision of the Celestial Kingdom (D&C 137). In this vision Joseph was given a glimpse of the highest heaven, where he saw such ancient prophets as Adam and Abraham. In addition, he saw his mother, Lucy Mack Smith, and his father, Joseph Smith Sr. Clearly this was a vision of a future celestial world, for Father Smith would live another four years and Mother Smith would live another twenty years.

Joseph then saw someone whose presence in the celestial kingdom surprised him—his elder brother Alvin, who had died in 1823 (Joseph Smith–History 1:56). Alvin had passed away six years before the priesthood was restored and seven years before the Church was organized. The Smith family had grieved his passing, and that grief was only intensified by a strong suggestion on the part of the minister preaching his funeral sermon that Alvin had gone to hell because he had not been baptized (Peterson, 11). Joseph wondered how Alvin was able to inherit the celestial kingdom. The divine voice declared: "All who have died without a knowledge of this gospel, who would have received it if they had been permitted to tarry, shall be heirs of the celestial kingdom of God; also all that shall die henceforth without a knowledge of it, who would have received it with all their hearts, shall be heirs of that kingdom; for I, the Lord, will judge all men according to their works, according to the desire of their hearts" (D&C 137:7–9). This vision opened the door to an understanding of the doctrine of salvation for the dead.

More than two years later, on Tuesday, 8 May 1838, the Prophet Joseph answered a series of questions about the faith and practices of the Latter-day Saints. One of the questions was "If the Mormon doctrine is true, what has become of all those who died since the days of the Apostles?" His response: "All those who have not had an opportunity of hearing the Gospel, and being administered unto by an inspired man in the flesh, must have it hereafter, before they can be finally judged" (*History,* 3:29). Joseph Smith delivered his first public sermon on baptism for the dead on 15 August 1840 at the funeral of Seymour Brunson. Simon Baker described the occasion: "He read the greater part of the 15th chapter of Corinthians and remarked that the Gospel of Jesus Christ brought glad tidings of great joy, and then remarked that he saw a widow in that congregation that had a son who died without being baptized, and this widow in reading the sayings of Jesus 'except a man be born of water and of the spirit he cannot enter the kingdom of heaven,' and that not one jot nor tittle of the Savior's words should pass away, but all should be fulfilled. He then said that this widow should have glad tidings in that thing. He also said the apostle [Paul] was talking to a people who understood baptism for the dead, for it was practiced among them. He went on to say that people could now act for their friends who had departed this life, and that the plan of salvation was calculated to save all who were willing to obey the requirements of the law of God. He went on and made a very beautiful discourse" (*Words,* 49).

Two months later Joseph stated: "I presume the doctrine of 'baptism for the dead' has ere this reached your ears, and may have raised some inquiries in your minds respecting the same. . . . I would say that it was certainly practiced by the ancient churches." He then quoted from 1 Corinthians 15:29 and continued, "The Saints have the privilege of being baptized for those of their relatives who are dead, whom they believe would have embraced the Gospel, if they had been privileged with hearing it, and who have received the Gospel in the spirit, through the instrumentality of those who have been commissioned to preach to them while in prison" (*History,* 4:231). Additional details on how vicarious baptisms were to be carried out and witnessed as well as how this supernal doctrine provides a missing puzzle piece in the Father's great plan of happiness came through letters from Joseph Smith to the Saints in Nauvoo in 1842 (D&C 127–128).

What then of those who never have the opportunity in this life to know of Christ and his gospel or who never have the opportunity to be baptized for a remission of sins and for entrance into the kingdom? Latter-day Saints teach of an omnipotent God who truly loves all his children and will reach even beyond the grave to make the fulness of his blessings available to them. As the Prophet said, "It is no more incredible that God should *save* the dead, than that he should *raise* the dead" (*Joseph Smith,* 471).

SOURCES

Joseph Smith [manual]. Teachings of Presidents of the Church series. Salt Lake City: The Church of Jesus Christ of Latter-day Saints, 2007.

Peterson, J. W. "Statement of William Smith, Concerning Joseph, the Prophet." *Deseret Evening News,* 20 Jan. 1894, 11.

Smith, Joseph. *History of The Church of Jesus Christ of Latter-day Saints.* Edited by B. H. Roberts. 7 vols. 2d ed. rev. Salt Lake City: The Church of Jesus Christ of Latter-day Saints, 1932–51.

The Words of Joseph Smith. Compiled and edited by Andrew F. Ehat and Lyndon W. Cook. Provo, Utah: Brigham Young University Religious Studies Center, 1980.

RLM

SANCTIFICATION

To be sanctified is to be cleansed, purified, made holy. The Lord affirmed in modern revelation that both justification and sanctification are true and real and that they are significant features of the gospel of Jesus Christ (D&C 20:30–33). When a person is forgiven of sin, pardoned of misdeeds, pronounced innocent, and decreed righteous, that person has been justified; justification represents a change in the person's standing before God. The process by which the children of God are purified and made free from the effects of sin, by which their *state* is changed, is sanctification. Elder D. Todd Christofferson explained that "to be sanctified through the blood of Christ is to become clean, pure, and holy. If justification removes the punishment for past sin, then sanctification removes the stain or effects of sin. . . . This marvelous pardon that relieves us of the punishment that justice would otherwise exact for disobedience and the purifying sanctification that follows are best described as gifts. . . . Given the magnitude of the gift of grace, we would never suppose, even with all the good we could possibly do in this life, that we had earned it. It is just too great" (22). It is a lifetime process, one in which we gradually notice changes in our nature and disposition: we come to love the things we before hated (we begin to warm to and be attracted by goodness) and hate the things we before loved (we begin to find distasteful and to abhor such things as sin, uncleanness in its many forms, and the harsh, the crude, and the violent).

As the Saints of the Most High strive to cultivate the gift of the Holy Ghost, they feel the need and the desire to yield their hearts unto God and thereby be sanctified (Helaman 3:35). Such Saints are touched by innocence, delighted by simple truths, made meek in the midst of provocation or hardship, and moved to the very core by beauty and drawn regularly to righteousness. Over time such persons have "no more disposition to do evil but to do good continually" (Mosiah 5:2) and no longer see the commandments of God as burdensome or oppressive (1 John 5:3). Rather, they look upon the commandments and divinely given instructions as a vital means of being sanctified (D&C 43:8–9). Similarly, those who magnify their callings are "sanctified by the Spirit unto the renewing of their bodies" (D&C 84:33). The sanctified are those who surrender their will to the Almighty and submit to his chastening and correcting hand (D&C 101:5). It is the sanctified who will stand before God's throne and worship him forever (D&C 76:21); these are they who will not see death any more (D&C 88:116). Truly, "unto him that repenteth and sanctifieth himself before the Lord shall be given eternal life" (D&C 133:62).

Elder B. H. Roberts taught that the forgiven soul may still continue to "feel the force of sinful habits bearing heavily upon him. He who has been guilty of habitual untruthfulness, will at times find himself inclined, perhaps, to yield to that habit. He who has stolen may be sorely tempted, when opportunity arises, to steal again. While he who has indulged in licentious practices may again find himself disposed to give way to the seductive influence of the siren. So with drunkenness, malice, envy, covetousness, hatred, anger, and in short all the evil dispositions that flesh is heir to.

"There is an absolute necessity for some additional sanctifying grace that will strengthen poor human nature, not only to enable it to resist temptation, but also to root out from the heart concupiscence—the blind tendency or inclination to evil. The heart must be purified, every passion, every propensity made submissive to the will, and the will of man brought into subjection to the will of God.

"Man's natural powers are unequal to this task; so, I believe, all will testify who have made the experiment. Mankind stand in some need of a strength superior to any they possess of themselves, to accomplish this work of rendering pure our fallen nature. Such strength, such power, such a sanctifying grace is conferred on man in being born of the Spirit—in receiving the Holy Ghost. Such, in the main, is its office, its work" (170).

SOURCES

Christofferson, D. Todd. "Justification and Sanctification." *Ensign,* June 2001, 18–25.

Roberts, B. H. *The Gospel and Man's Relationship to Deity.* Salt Lake City: Deseret Book, 1965.

RLM

SATAN

Satan is the adversary of God and of all righteousness (1 Peter 5:8). He is the "father of all lies" (2 Nephi 2:18; see also John 8:44), and he "seeketh that all men might be miserable like unto himself" (2 Nephi 2:27). Just as the Father is the author of the plan of salvation, Satan is the "author of all sin," whose "works of darkness" lead to "an entire destruction, and to an everlasting hell" (Helaman 6:28, 30). He is also known in the scriptures as Perdition (D&C 76:26), Beelzebub (Matthew 12:24), the destroyer (D&C 61:19), the wicked one (Matthew 13:19, 38; 1 John 3:12), and the tempter (Matthew 4:3). He is portrayed as a devouring dragon, a dangerous and deceptive serpent, and a frightening beast with horns that consumes and kills—all symbolic of his diabolical intent to thwart the work of God and destroy the souls of men. Peter described Satan "as a roaring lion, [who] walketh about, seeking whom he may devour" (1 Peter 5:8). Likewise, Old Testament prophets often used the most ruthless, wicked, and destructive kingdoms of their day, such as Assyria, Egypt, and Babylon, as types for the devil and his nefarious ways (Isaiah 13; 14:4–16; 31:1–4; Jeremiah 50; 51:6–8; Ezekiel 17; 29–32).

Additional insight into the nature and designs of Satan is found in modern revelation. Latter-day Saints believe that in the premortal existence Lucifer was a spirit son of God who angrily rebelled against the Father and the plan of salvation and as a result was thrust down from heaven along with those rebellious spirits that followed him, becoming "the devil and his angels" (D&C 29:37; see also Moses 7:26; Abraham 3:23–28; D&C 76:25–29). "An angel of God who was in authority in the presence of God" (D&C 76:25), Lucifer, whose name means "the Shining One" and "Lightbringer" (Bible Dictionary, 726), was overcome by jealousy, covetousness, and contempt for the Father and the chosen Son of God and became "the accuser of our brethren," (Revelation 12:10), making open war against the plan of salvation with "eyes open to the truth of it" (Smith, *History,* 6:314). The Prophet Joseph Smith taught further: "The contention in heaven was—Jesus said there would be certain souls that would not be saved; and the devil said he would save them all, and laid his plans before the grand council, who gave their vote in favor of Jesus Christ. So the devil rose up in rebellion against God, and was cast down, with all who put up their heads for him" (*History,* 6:314).

Lucifer—"that old serpent, even the devil, who rebelled against God . . . and his Christ"—continues his rebellion against righteousness on earth. He seeks to destroy the kingdom of God and all who would be drawn unto it. "Wherefore, he maketh war with the saints of God, and encompasseth them round about" (D&C 76:29). President Wilford Woodruff testified of Satan's efforts in the continuing conflict between good and evil:

"[Satan] has great influence over the children of men; he labors continually to destroy the worlds of God in heaven, and he had to be cast out. He is here, mighty among the children of men. There is a vast number of fallen spirits, cast out with him, here on the earth. They do not die and disappear; they have not bodies only as they enter the tabernacles of men. They have not organized bodies, and are not to be seen with the sight of the eye. But there are many evil spirits amongst us, and they labor to overthrow the church and kingdom of God. . . .

"Do you suppose these devils are around us without trying to do something? . . . I say . . . we have got a mighty warfare to wage with these spirits. We cannot escape it. What will they do to you? They will try to make us do anything and everything that is not right" (238, 240).

Although Satan possesses great knowledge and power, as evidenced by his seeking to imitate and counterfeit God's miraculous powers (Exodus 7:9–22; 2 Corinthians 11:13–15; 2 Nephi 9:9), his powers are limited. "All beings who have bodies have power over those who have not," the Prophet Joseph Smith taught. "The devil has no power over us only as we permit him; the moment we revolt at anything which comes from God, the devil takes power" (*Joseph Smith*, 211, 214). With this assurance, we recognize that although Satan has power to tempt and deceive, he cannot compel us do anything against our will. Protection from Satan's powers is found in faith in God, obedience to his commandments, and yielding to the Holy Spirit. "Submit yourselves therefore to God," the apostle James declared. "Resist the devil, and he will flee from you" (James 4:7).

Just as Lucifer and his hosts were defeated in the war in heaven, they will yet be defeated on earth and ultimately banished to "everlasting punishment . . . where their worm dieth not, and the fire is not quenched" (D&C 76:44; see also Revelation 20:10). God will reign victorious over Satan and his minions. The victory must, however, be won personally on the same conditions as it was in heaven—"by the blood of the Lamb, and by the word of their testimony" (Revelation 12:11). By putting on the armor of God, we are able to "quench all the fiery darts of the wicked" (D&C 27:17). Ultimately, Satan is defeated both in the world and in our own individual hearts and souls through the atonement of Jesus Christ.

SOURCES

Joseph Smith [manual]. Teachings of Presidents of the Church series. Salt Lake City: The Church of Jesus Christ of Latter-day Saints, 2007.

Smith, Joseph. *History of The Church of Jesus Christ of Latter-day Saints.* Edited by

B. H. Roberts. 7 vols. 2d ed. rev. Salt Lake City: The Church of Jesus Christ of Latter-day Saints, 1932–51.

Woodruff, Wilford. *Discourses of Wilford Woodruff.* Compiled by G. Homer Durham. Salt Lake City: Bookcraft, 1946.

BLT

SAVIORS ON MOUNT ZION

We become saviors on Mount Zion when we contribute to the salvation of those who have passed away without a knowledge of the gospel or without having received the ordinances of salvation. "[W]e are commanded to be baptized for our dead," Joseph Smith said, "thus fulfilling the words of Obadiah, when speaking of the glory of the latter-day: 'And saviors shall come upon Mount Zion to judge the remnant of Esau, and the kingdom shall be the Lord's.' [See Obadiah 1:21.] A view of these things reconciles the Scriptures of truth, justifies the ways of God to man, places the human family upon an equal footing, and harmonizes with every principle of righteousness, justice and truth" (4:599). On another occasion Brother Joseph declared: "The keys are to be delivered, . . . the Saints of God gathered, Zion built up, and the Saints to come up as saviors on Mount Zion.

"But how are they to become saviors on Mount Zion? By building their temples, erecting their baptismal fonts, and going forth and receiving all the ordinances, baptisms, confirmations, washings, anointings, ordinations and sealing powers upon their heads, in behalf of all their progenitors who are dead, and redeem them that they may come forth in the first resurrection and be exalted to thrones of glory with them; and herein is the chain that binds the hearts of the fathers to the children, and the children to the fathers, which fulfills the mission of Elijah" (6:184).

SOURCE

Smith, Joseph. *History of The Church of Jesus Christ of Latter-day Saints.* Edited by B. H. Roberts. 7 vols. 2d ed. rev. Salt Lake City: The Church of Jesus Christ of Latter-day Saints, 1932–51.

RLM

SCATTERING OF ISRAEL

The scriptures, especially the Old Testament and the Book of Mormon, affirm that individuals and whole nations are scattered whenever they reject the true Messiah, refuse to accept his gospel and its doctrines and Church, and do not align themselves with the people of the covenant, the household of faith (1 Nephi 15:13–16; 2 Nephi 6:8–11; 10:5–7). They are then scattered, as much to their covenant identity as to their location. Scattering also occurs whenever the Lord sees fit to lead away certain branches of his chosen people to various parts of the earth to accomplish his larger purpose—to spread the blood and influence of Abraham's descendants throughout the globe. This was exactly the case with the Lehites, a branch of Joseph that was led away from their homeland to another hemisphere because of wickedness in the land of Israel (1 Nephi 17:36–38; 2 Nephi 10:20–22; see also Jeremiah 23:1–4).

RLM

SCRIPTURE

As set forth in latter-day revelation, "whatsoever [the leaders of the Church] shall speak when moved upon by the Holy Ghost shall be scripture, shall be the will of the Lord, shall be the mind of the Lord, shall be the word of the Lord, shall be the voice of the Lord, and the power of God unto salvation" (D&C 68:4). Peter taught that "no prophecy of the scripture is of any private interpretation. For the prophecy came not in old time by the will of man: but holy men of God spake as they were moved by the Holy Ghost" (2 Peter 1:20–21). In a more limited and restrictive sense, we might speak also of *canonized scripture,* that which was spoken and recorded by the power of the Spirit and is included within the canon, meaning the standard works, by a vote of the Church. For example, Joseph Smith's Vision of the Celestial Kingdom and Joseph F. Smith's Vision of the Redemption of the Dead were both true, doctrinally sound, and scriptural from the time they were received by the first (1836) and sixth (1918) presidents of the Church, respectively. At the April 1976 conference of the Church, however, these two revelations were presented to the Saints and received by vote to be a part of the standard works, where they now reside as sections 137 and 138 of the Doctrine and Covenants. As such, they are now binding upon all members of The Church of Jesus Christ of Latter-day Saints.

RLM

SEALING POWER

At Caesarea Philippi, the Savior promised Peter "the keys of the kingdom of heaven." With this apostolic authority and priesthood power, the senior apostle was told that "whatsoever thou shalt bind on earth shall be bound in heaven: and whatsoever thou shalt loose on earth shall be loosed in heaven" (Matthew 16:19). To Latter-day Saints, the power of which Jesus spoke is known as the sealing power. To seal an ordinance is to make it valid and binding, both on earth and in heaven, both in mortal and postmortal life. In this dispensation the prophet Elijah restored the sealing keys to Joseph Smith (D&C 2:1–3; 110:13–16). "There is never but one on the earth at a time on whom this power and the keys of this priesthood are conferred," the Lord declared (D&C 132:7). Without authorization by the Lord's anointed through the keys of sealing, "all covenants, contracts, bonds, obligations, oaths, vows, performances, connections, associations, or expectations" are "of no efficacy, virtue, or force in and after the resurrection from the dead; for all contracts that are not made unto this end have an end when men are dead" (D&C 132:7).

"The keys of the sealing power are synonymous with the keys of the everlasting priesthood," President Boyd K. Packer taught. "Those keys belong to the President of the Church—to the prophet, seer, and revelator. That sacred sealing power is with the Church now. Nothing is regarded with more sacred contemplation by those who know the significance of this authority. Nothing is more closely held" (148–49). The president of the Church administers the sealing power on earth. He may delegate to others the power to perform in temples the sacred sealing ordinances of husbands to wives and children to parents. However, those who are given the sealing power do not necessarily hold the keys to that power and may not give to others the power to perform sealings unless specifically authorized to do so by the president of the Church.

Although the sealing power is essential for all ordinances to endure in eternity, it is most commonly seen as the authority to perform the aforementioned sealing ordinances in holy temples. There is, however, another dimension of the sealing power that resides with the First Presidency and Quorum of the Twelve Apostles, who hold all of the keys of the kingdom. Ordinances of salvation performed by the power of the priesthood may be *loosed* as well as *bound* on earth and in heaven. For example, a person who is excommunicated from the Church is, under the direction of the First Presidency, loosed from all previously performed ordinances and covenants. After a period of repentance and demonstrated faithfulness and upon the authorization of the First Presidency, those previous blessings may be restored or *sealed* anew. Likewise, a sealing of a husband to a wife may be canceled or loosed for exceptional reasons such as transgression and divorce. Only the First Presidency has the right and authority to cancel sealing ordinances and authorize the couple to be sealed to another. In these examples, we see how the sealing power, residing in the president of the Church, can both bind and loose on earth and in heaven.

The sealing power gives life and meaning to all priesthood ordinances and gospel covenants. Without it, as both Moroni and Malachi declared, "the whole earth would be utterly wasted at [the Savior's second] coming" (D&C 2:3; see also Malachi 4:5–6). It is only through the grace of God and the sealing power that family relationships may continue beyond the grave and exaltation in the celestial kingdom be made possible.

SOURCE

Packer, Boyd K. *The Shield of Faith*. Salt Lake City: Bookcraft, 1998.

BLT

SECOND ADAM

The expression "second Adam" refers to Jesus Christ. The apostle Paul used it to illustrate the inseparable link between Adam's fall and Christ's atonement in our Heavenly Father's eternal plan for all of his children on this earth. Adam's fall, ironically, is a type and shadow of Jesus Christ in that through the Fall, all humankind, the earth, and all life thereon became mortal. Adam's fall provided the way for all of our Heavenly Father's children who kept their first estate to receive a physical body (Abraham 3:26, 28). The atonement of Jesus Christ gives life yet again (after physical death) and provides a resurrected physical body for every soul initially given life through Adam (1 Corinthians 15:22). Thus, the actions of both Adam and Jesus Christ gave life to the entire human family, each in his proper order, and each inextricably linked to the other. The apostle Paul discussed this similitude in two of his most significant theological discourses—his letters to the Corinthians and the Romans:

"And so it is written, The first man Adam was made a living soul; the last Adam [Christ] was made a quickening spirit. . . . And as we have borne the image of the earthy [man], we shall also bear the image of the heavenly [being]" (1 Corinthians 15:45, 49).

"Death reigned from Adam to Moses, even over them that had not sinned after the similitude of Adam's transgression, who is the figure of him that was to come" (Romans 5:14).

The Hebrew word *'adam* means, literally, "man" or "human." Paul, a scholar of the Hebrew scriptures, or Old Testament, created a play on words to teach his readers the doctrine of our first father's similitude and typifying of Jesus Christ. Just as Christ is the "second" or "last" Adam (or man), so the reverse is also true: Adam, the first man, is the prefiguring of the second Adam, Jesus Christ. And just as every human is in the image of the first Adam, "the earthy," through birth, so every human will also bear the image of Jesus, "the heavenly," through the rebirth of resurrection.

ACS

SECOND COMFORTER

Once a person has made his or her calling and election sure—has passed the tests of mortality and received the assurance of eternal life hereafter—that person may yet receive additional blessings. The Prophet Joseph Smith taught:

"After a person has faith in Christ, repents of his sins and is baptized for the remission of his sins and receives the Holy Ghost, (by the laying on of hands), which is the first Comforter, then let him continue to humble himself before God, hungering and thirsting after righteousness, and living by every word of God, and the Lord will soon say unto him, Son, thou shalt be exalted. When the Lord has thoroughly proved him, and finds that the man is determined to serve Him at all hazards, then the man will find his calling and his election made sure, then it will be his privilege to receive the other Comforter, which the Lord hath promised the Saints, as is recorded in the testimony of Saint John, in the 14th chapter [John 14:18, 21, 23]. . . .

"Now what is this other Comforter? It is no more nor less than the Lord Jesus Christ Himself; and this is the sum and substance of the whole matter; that when any man obtains this last Comforter, he will have the personage of Jesus Christ to attend him, or appear unto him from time to time, and even He will manifest the Father unto him, and they will take up their abode with him, and the visions of the heavens will be opened unto him, and the Lord will teach him face to face, and he may have a perfect knowledge of the mysteries of the Kingdom of God; and this is the state and place the ancient Saints arrived at when they had such glorious visions—Isaiah, Ezekiel, John upon the Isle of Patmos, Saint Paul in the three heavens, and all the Saints who held communion with the general assembly and Church of the Firstborn" (3:380–81).

The members of the School of the Elders were given a similar ideal after which to seek: "Let us here observe, that after any portion of the human family are made acquainted with the important fact that there is a God, who has created and does uphold all things, the extent of their knowledge respecting his character and glory will depend upon their diligence and faithfulness in seeking after him, until, like Enoch, the brother of Jared, and Moses, they shall obtain faith in God, and power with him to behold him face to face" (*Lectures,* 24).

And yet this higher blessing will come to us not according to when we think we are prepared to receive it but rather when God, who knows best our bearing capacity, chooses. "Therefore, sanctify yourselves that your minds become single to God, and the days will come that you shall see him; for he will unveil his face unto you, and it shall be in his own time, and in his own way, and according to his own will" (D&C 88:68).

In speaking of the need for further striving, a modern apostle has written: "There are, of course, those whose callings and election have been made sure who have never exercised the faith nor exhibited the righteousness which would enable them to commune with the Lord on the promised basis. There are even those who neither believe nor know that it is possible to see the Lord in this day, and they therefore are without the personal incentive that would urge them onward in the pursuit of this consummation so devoutly desired by those with spiritual insight" (McConkie, 586).

SOURCES

Lectures on Faith. Salt Lake City: Deseret Book, 1985.

McConkie, Bruce R. *The Promised Messiah: The First Coming of Christ*. Salt Lake City: Deseret Book, 1978.

Smith, Joseph. *History of The Church of Jesus Christ of Latter-day Saints*. Edited by B. H. Roberts. 7 vols. 2d ed. rev. Salt Lake City: The Church of Jesus Christ of Latter-day Saints, 1932–51.

RLM

SECOND COMING OF CHRIST, SIGNS OF

Shortly before his crucifixion and resurrection, the disciples asked Jesus, "What shall be the sign of thy coming, and of the end of the world?" (Matthew 24:3). These questions have been asked in virtually every dispensation. In response, the Lord has spoken of the signs that would precede the glorious Second Coming and the Savior's millennial reign. These signs, declared by prophets, apostles, and the Lord himself, are given to warn the inhabitants of the earth, call the wicked to repentance, comfort the righteous, and prepare believers for the apocalyptic events of the last days. Numerous signs, types, and shadows of the Second Coming are found in the scriptures, both ancient and modern. Some are plain and straightforward, while others are cryptic. "Ye shall hear of wars and rumours of wars," the Savior declared. "For nation shall rise against nation, and kingdom against kingdom: and there shall be famines, and pestilences, and earthquakes, in divers places" (Matthew 24:6–7). The scriptures speak of other signs:

- "The sun shall be darkened, and the moon shall be turned into blood, and the stars shall fall from heaven, and there shall be greater signs in heaven above and in the earth beneath" (D&C 29:14).
- "A great hailstorm sent forth to destroy the crops of the earth" (D&C 29:16).
- "An overflowing scourge" and "desolating sickness" that will cover the earth (D&C 45:31).
- "False Christs, and false prophets shall show great signs and wonders, insomuch, that, if possible, they shall deceive the very elect, who are the elect according to the covenant" (Joseph Smith–Matthew 1:22).

- "All things shall be in commotion; and surely, men's hearts shall fail them; for fear shall come upon all people" (D&C 88:91).
- Flies and maggots will eat the flesh of people, and "their flesh shall fall from off their bones, and their eyes from their sockets" (D&C 29:18–19).
- "And the land of Jerusalem and the land of Zion shall be turned back into their own place, and the earth shall be like as it was in the days before it was divided" (D&C 133:24).

In addition to these signs that could be viewed as negative or fearful, numerous others testify of hopeful and positive events that will likewise precede our Lord's glorious return. The First Vision, the coming forth of the Book of Mormon, the establishment of the Church, and the restoration of all priesthood keys are also important signs of the last days (2 Nephi 27–30). "And again, this Gospel of the Kingdom shall be preached in all the world, for a witness unto all nations, and then shall the end come" (Joseph Smith–Matthew 1:31). Temples will dot the earth, and the kingdom will "roll forth until it has filled the whole earth" (D&C 65:2; see also Isaiah 2:2–3; Daniel 2:34–45). The Lord's elect and the remnant of the house of Israel will be gathered to the stakes of Zion (D&C 109:57–67; see also D&C 133:7–11; Jeremiah 16:15–21; Ezekiel 36). The discovery of America and the establishment of a free nation governed by an inspired constitution are also signs of the last days—transformational events that are forerunners to the great spiritual events that will precede the Second Coming. Advancements in technology and knowledge that further the work of the Lord—such as the remarkable developments in family history, temple work, and translation and distribution of scriptures and Church materials—are less commonly viewed as signs of the Second Coming but are no less significant.

The primary purpose of the signs and prophecies concerning the last days—inspired writings in the scriptures and teachings uttered by prophets and apostles—is more about preparation than identification, more about conversion than chronology. The Savior gave specific signs to his disciples in response to their inquiry, but he reminded them to "watch therefore: for ye know not what hour your Lord doth come" (Matthew 24:42). This admonition is repeated many times, not only in the New Testament account but also in modern revelation. It is clear that we are to look to the signs and prophecies not in an effort to identify with precision when the Second Coming will occur but to be spiritually and temporally vigilant—ever prepared and worthy. In fact, Jesus made it abundantly clear that "of that day and hour knoweth no man, no, not the angels of heaven, but my Father only" (Matthew 24:36). Despite this, many of the disciples seemed to assume that the Second Coming would occur in their lifetime because they saw signs all around them.

In this dispensation, the Saints likewise have assumed that the establishment of the New Jerusalem, the Second Coming, and the Millennium were imminent. There is a tendency to view prophecies and signs within our own limited context of time as opposed to the Lord's eternal timetable. Elder Joseph Young explained that many of the Saints of the nineteenth century misconstrued or miscalculated the prophecies on a number of matters, including the building of the city of Zion and the Second Coming. "The Holy Spirit brought many things close to their minds," Elder Young declared. "They appeared right by and hence many were deceived. . . . I knew that faith and the Holy Ghost brought the designs of Providence close by, and by that means we were enabled to scan them, . . . but we had not knowledge enough to . . . fully comprehend those things" (9:230). This is evidenced in the Doctrine and Covenants. The Lord declared that his coming "is near, even at the doors" (D&C 110:16). Thirteen times in the Doctrine and Covenants the Savior states, "I come quickly," meaning suddenly. He describes the Second Coming as "nigh at hand" another twelve times and as "soon" six more times. It is easy to understand why the early Saints felt that the Second Coming would occur shortly. Despite these declarations and the accompanying signs and prophecies, the Lord clearly taught that no one knows exactly when that great event will occur (D&C 39:21; 49:7; 51:20; 61:38; 124:10; 133:11).

Because of the differences between man's perspective and God's omniscience, it is virtually impossible for one to put the signs that will precede the Second Coming in a specific chronological sequence or to identify an exact timeline. Besides, that is not the Lord's purpose. Signs are to help us prepare, not to identify exact dates. "Can we use

. . . scientific data to extrapolate that the Second Coming is likely to occur during the next few years, or the next decade, or the next century?" Elder M. Russell Ballard asked. "Not really. I am called as one of the apostles to be a special witness of Christ in these exciting, trying times, and I do not know when He is going to come again. As far as I know, none of my brethren in the Council of the Twelve or even in the First Presidency know. And I would humbly suggest to you . . . that if we do not know, then nobody knows, no matter how compelling their arguments or how reasonable their calculations. The Savior said that 'of that day and hour knoweth no man, no, not the angels of heaven, but my Father only' (Matthew 24:36).

"I believe that when the Lord says 'no man' knows, it really means that no man knows. You should be extremely wary of anyone who claims to be an exception to divine decree" (186).

In the Savior's Olivet discourse (Matthew 24), he not only spoke of the signs of the last days but even more important, he also taught the disciples about the need for constant readiness. They asked, "When shall these things be?" (Matthew 24:3). Jesus' response answered the unasked question: "What must we do to be prepared for the Second Coming?" By using parables, the Master taught the disciples that though they will "know neither the day nor the hour" of the Second Coming, they must be ever vigilant, worthy, and spiritually prepared. That is what he meant when he said, "Watch therefore" (Matthew 25:13). The parable of the ten virgins (Matthew 25:1–13) teaches that spiritual preparation cannot be done hastily or at the last minute. It requires consistent, continual, conscientious effort. The oil in the parable represents a state of worthiness that cannot be purchased or borrowed, the readiness that the Holy Spirit supplies (D&C 45:57) that must be acquired individually through worthy living and faithful service. President Spencer W. Kimball taught:

"The foolish asked the others to share their oil, but spiritual preparedness cannot be shared in an instant. The wise had to go, else the bridegroom would have gone unwelcomed. They needed all their oil for themselves; they could not save the foolish. The responsibility was each for himself. This was not selfishness or unkindness. The kind of oil that is needed to illuminate the way and light up the darkness is not shareable. . . . Each must obtain that kind of oil for himself. . . .

"In the parable, oil can be purchased at the market. In our lives the oil of preparedness is accumulated drop by drop in righteous living. Attendance at sacrament meetings adds oil to our lamps, drop by drop over the years. Fasting, family prayer, home teaching, control of bodily appetites, preaching the gospel, studying the scriptures—each act of dedication and obedience is a drop added to our store. Deeds of kindness, payment of offerings and tithes, chaste thoughts and actions, marriage in the covenant for eternity—these, too, contribute importantly to the oil with which we can at midnight refuel our exhausted lamps" (255–56).

From modern revelation we learn what the oil represents and how the wise virgins were able to be prepared. "For they that are wise and have received the truth, and *have taken the Holy Spirit for their guide,* and have not been deceived—verily I say unto you, they shall not be hewn down and cast into the fire, but shall abide the day" (D&C 45:57; emphasis added). Living our lives in such a way as to be worthy of the companionship of the Holy Ghost is the best way to be prepared for the Second Coming. Living worthy of and hearkening to the Spirit keeps our lamps continually full of the oil of spiritual preparation.

In the parable of the talents (Matthew 25:14–30) and the parable of the sheep and goats (Matthew 25:31–46), Jesus teaches us that another way in which we can watch and be ready is through being anxiously engaged in service to God and our fellow men. We may have differing gifts, and the sizes of our tasks may vary, but the Lord expects us not to bury our talents—either by idling away our talents in "all is well in Zion" complacency (2 Nephi 28:21) or by failing to be faithful because of hand-wringing anxiety about the future. In the parable of the talents, the servant who was condemned did nothing because he was consumed by worldly fear. Those who were rewarded were found faithfully doing what they could—whether much or little—to further the kingdom. Whether we are apostles or nursery workers, we prepare for the Second Coming by doing our respective duties, serving the Lord the best we can, blessing our families, and serving our neighbors.

From the parable of the sheep and the goats, we are taught that those who inherit the great reward at the Master's return are those who fed him when he was hungry, clothed him when he was naked, strengthened him when he was sick, and befriended him when he was lonely. How did they do that? "Inasmuch as ye have done it unto c of the least of these my brethren," the Savior declared, "ye have done unto me" (Matthew 25:40). We prepare joyfully to meet Christ upon his glorious return with every act of service, compassion, kindness, and mercy. The degree to which we love and serve our fellow men is the degree to which we are prepared for the Second Coming.

In Joseph Smith's translation of Matthew 24, the Savior warned of false Christs and false prophets who could potentially deceive and destroy, and he taught of the means whereby the elect could be protected and preserved: "And whoso treasureth up my word, shall not be deceived" (Joseph Smith–Matthew 1:37). Treasuring up the words of the Lord means much more than simply reading the scriptures. It means embracing them—studying and pondering their words and living by their precepts. It means making the words of the Lord our words, the words we live by, the compass that guides our steps in life. Treasuring up the words of the Lord requires us to internalize the doctrines of Christ. They become living, vibrant parts of us that can protect us from danger and guide us with light in an ever-darkening world.

The world will be in commotion prior to the Second Coming, but faithful believers can stand firm and steadfast. Christ declared that even when we see the fulfillment of the prophesied signs around us—a desolating scourge, earthquakes and famines, blood, smoke, failing hearts, and love that waxes cold—"my disciples shall stand in holy places, and shall not be moved" (D&C 45:32). Standing in holy places is not so much about geography as it is about personal righteousness. Being a holy edifice—pure in heart, spiritually prepared—will enable faithful disciples to stand when others fall and are consumed by the "glory of his presence" (D&C 133:49).

The Lord's teachings about the signs that will precede his coming and the reasons for those signs are distilled in the following verses, found in modern revelation:

"Behold, now *it is called today until the coming of the Son of Man.* . . . For after today cometh the burning—this is speaking after the manner of the Lord—for verily I say, *tomorrow all the proud and they that do wickedly shall be as stubble;* and I will burn them up, for I am the Lord of Hosts; and I will not spare any that remain in Babylon.

Wherefore, if ye believe me, *ye will labor while it is called today"* (D&C 64:23–25; emphasis added).

If we live each day as if it were the day the Savior will come, we will be ready for *tomorrow,* when he does come—whenever that tomorrow will be. President Gordon B. Hinckley gave this wise counsel concerning recognizing the signs of the times and preparing for the Savior's glorious return:

"Certainly there is no point in speculating concerning the day and the hour. Let us rather live each day so that if the Lord does come while we yet are upon the earth we shall be worthy of that change which will occur as in the twinkling of an eye and under which we shall be changed from mortal to immortal beings. And if we should die before he comes, then—if our lives have conformed to his teachings—we shall arise in that resurrection morning and be partakers of the marvelous experiences designed for those who shall live and work with the Savior in that promised Millennium. We need not fear the day of his coming; the very purpose of the Church is to provide the incentive and the opportunity for us to conduct our lives in such a way that those who are members of the kingdom of God will become members of the kingdom of heaven when he establishes that kingdom on the earth" (576).

SOURCES

Ballard, M. Russell. "When Shall These Things Be?" In *Brigham Young University 1995–96 Speeches,* 185–93. Provo, Utah: Brigham Young University, 1996.

Hinckley, Gordon B. *Teachings of Gordon B. Hinckley.* Salt Lake City: Deseret Book, 1997.

Kimball, Spencer W. *Faith Precedes the Miracle.* Salt Lake City: Deseret Book, 1972.

Young, Joseph. In *Journal of Discourses.* 26 vols. London: Latter-day Saints' Book Depot, 1854–86.

BLT

SECOND COMING(S) OF CHRIST

The phrase "second coming of Christ" usually refers to the Savior's return to earth in glory, a day when the wicked are destroyed, the righteous are caught up to meet him, the general resurrection of the just commences, and the paradisiacal Millennium begins. It is referred to as "the great and dreadful day of the Lord" (Malachi 4:5; D&C 2)—a great day of joy and spiritual rewards for the righteous who have faithfully "waited upon the Lord" (JST, Matthew 3:24; see also Isaiah 25:7–9; D&C 133:45–56) and a dreadful day of guilt, fear, and "vengeance on them that know not God, and that obey not the gospel of our Lord Jesus Christ" (2 Thessalonians 1:7–8; see also Isaiah 30:27–33; D&C 1:9; 29:17; 133:64). There are, however, other meanings of the phrase "second coming" used in the scriptures. Many scriptural passages refer to various events in the last days that, when viewed together, describe the second coming of Christ. Elder Bruce R. McConkie wrote: "The second coming of the Son of Man consists not of one but of many appearances. Our blessed Lord will come—attended by all the hosts of heaven, and in all the glory of his Father's kingdom—not to one but to many places. He will stand on one continent after another . . . and work his will among succeeding groups of mortals. Allusions to and some explanations concerning these various appearances are found in the ancient word. These, however, might well go unnoticed or remain without proper interpretation if it were not for the clarifying views found in latter-day revelation" (575).

Numerous Old Testament prophets spoke of a glorious event that would precede the end of times, when the Lord "shall appear in his glory" (Psalm 102:16) and usher in a millennial period of peace and righteousness on earth (Isaiah 40:3–5; 63:1–4; Ezekiel 21:27; 38–39; Daniel 7; Joel 3; Micah 4; Haggai 1:6–9; Zechariah 12–14; Malachi 3–4). Most devout Jews in Jesus' day expected the Messiah to appear in glory and power and thus could not accept Jesus of Nazareth as the promised Messiah. They did not understand that the Old Testament prophecies referred to Christ's second coming at the end of days, not his earthly ministry in the meridian of time.

Jesus taught his disciples of the Second Coming (Matthew 16:27), which prompted their questions concerning the signs that would precede that event (Matthew 24). Upon the Savior's ascension into heaven after his resurrection, angels declared to the disciples that "this same Jesus, which is taken up from you into heaven, shall so come in like manner as ye have seen him go into heaven" (Acts 1:11). Preparing for the Second Coming, therefore, became a major theme in the teachings of the New Testament apostles (1 Thessalonians 4:16; 2 Thessalonians 1:7; 2:8; 2 Peter 3:10; Jude 1:14; Revelation 1:7; 3:11; 14; 20–22). The Book of Mormon also testifies of the events of the last days that will prepare the earth for the Second Coming and the Millennium. The resurrected Christ reviewed with the Nephites the prophecies of Malachi concerning the "great and dreadful day of the Lord," when "all that do wickedly, shall be as stubble; and the day that cometh shall burn them up" (3 Nephi 25:1, 5). The appearance of the risen Lord in the New World, with its attendant signs and events, serves as a type and shadow of the Savior's second coming.

Numerous passages in the Doctrine and Covenants also testify of the glorious return of Jesus Christ, the destruction of the wicked, and the commencement of the millennial reign of the Lord (D&C 5:19; 29:8–11; 34:6–9; 43:29; 45:39–46; 63:34; 88:87–97; 101:23–33). Clearly, the scriptures point to Christ's appearance to the world, when "all flesh shall see [him] together" (D&C 101:23), as the Second Coming. As a result, it is common to think of the Second Coming as one glorious event. Other latter-day revelations, however, help us to understand that there are several appearances of the Savior to various groups and at various times that precede the culminating appearance to the world and the destruction of the wicked. Prior to that event, Christ appears to at least two groups of people at different times—the Saints and the Jews. Together, these appearances in the dispensation of the fulness of times—to the Saints, the Jews, and the entire world—constitute the Second Coming.

The Lord's appearances to the Saints. It could be said that the Second Coming began with the appearance of the Father and the Son to Joseph Smith in the spring of 1820. Subsequent visitations and visions were preparatory for the work of the last days and the Millennium. The scriptures speak of a future appearance of the Savior at the council that will convene at Adam-ondi-Ahman, where all previous dispensation heads will "render up their stewardships to the first Patriarch of the race, who holds the keys of salvation" and when "Christ will take over the reins of government, officially on this earth" (Smith, *Way,* 289–90; see also D&C 116). This event of the Second Coming will not be known to the world, but faithful and spiritually sensitive Latter-day Saints will come to know of this sacred council and understand the transfer of power that is taking place.

A second promised coming of the Lord will occur when he comes "suddenly . . . to [his] temple" (D&C 36:8) in the city of Zion, the

New Jerusalem. Elder Charles W. Penrose taught: "He will come to the temple prepared for him, and his faithful people will behold his face, hear his voice, and gaze upon his glory. From his own lips they will receive further instructions for the development and beautifying of Zion and for the extension and sure stability of his kingdom" (582–83). The scriptures are silent concerning the time that separates the Savior's appearance at Adam-ondi-Ahman from his appearance to the Saints in the temple at the New Jerusalem.

The Lord's appearance to the Jews. The Old Testament prophet Zechariah foresaw a day when "all nations" are gathered "against Jerusalem to battle." The city will be taken, "and the houses rifled, and women ravished." At the moment of impending and utter destruction of Jerusalem, Zechariah prophesied, "then shall the Lord go forth, and fight against those nations" (Zechariah 14:3). The Mount of Olives will split in two, the Jews will escape their enemies, "and the Lord shall be king over all the earth" (Zechariah 14:9). The Lord revealed clarification of these passages to the Prophet Joseph Smith. In the Doctrine and Covenants, we learn that the resurrected Christ will appear on the Mount of Olives after it cleaves in two. The Jews will escape their enemies and will then ask their Liberator, "What are these wounds in thine hands and in thy feet?" Jesus will teach them that he is the Messiah, the Son of God, the Redeemer of the world. "And then shall they weep because of their iniquities; then shall they lament because they persecuted their king" (D&C 45:51, 53). Christ's appearance to them will begin the millennial work of restoring Judah to the covenant and the knowledge of their Redeemer, including their acceptance of the principles and ordinances of the gospel and their ultimate gathering to their homeland. This appearance of the Savior on the Mount of Olives in Jerusalem will precede the glorious Second Coming, when the Savior "shall be red in his apparel, and his garments like him that treadeth in the wine-vat. And so great shall be the glory of his presence that the sun shall hide his face in shame, and the moon shall withhold its light, and the stars shall be hurled from their places. . . . And the graves of the saints shall be opened; and they shall come forth and stand on the right hand of the Lamb, when he shall stand upon Mount Zion, and upon the holy city, the New Jerusalem; and they shall sing the song of the Lamb, day and night forever" (D&C 133:48–49, 56).

The scriptures teach and testify of the reality of the different appearances of the Lord as part of the second coming of Christ, but there is no precise scriptural sequence or timetable. The Master gave general signs that would precede his coming, but he clearly taught that "of that day and hour knoweth no man, no, not the angels of heaven, but my Father only" (Matthew 24:36). The apostle Paul compared the Second Coming to a woman giving birth. When she feels signs within her body, she knows that the time of delivery is near, though she may not know when the exact moment will be (1 Thessalonians 4:15–16; 5:1–9). Likewise, in modern revelation the Lord states that his coming is "near, even at the doors," "nigh at hand," and that he is coming "quickly" or "soon" (D&C 110:16; 43:17; 29:9; 51:20; 61:38; 124:10; 133:11). He repeatedly declares, as he did anciently, that "the day or the hour no man knoweth; but it surely shall come" (D&C 39:21; see also D&C 49:6–7). The Prophet Joseph Smith taught: "Jesus Christ never did reveal to any man the precise time that He would come. Go and read the Scriptures, and you cannot find anything that specifies the exact hour He would come; and all that say so are false teachers" (6:254).

The Lord's message is clear—knowing when the Savior will come is not as important as being spiritually prepared for it.

SOURCES

McConkie, Bruce R. *The Millennial Messiah: The Second Coming of the Son of Man.* Salt Lake City: Deseret Book, 1982.

Penrose, Charles W. "The Second Advent." *Millennial Star* 21, no. 37 (10 Sept. 1859): 581–84.

Smith, Joseph. *History of The Church of Jesus Christ of Latter-day Saints.* Edited by B. H. Roberts. 7 vols. 2d ed. rev. Salt Lake City: The Church of Jesus Christ of Latter-day Saints, 1932–51.

Smith, Joseph Fielding. *The Way to Perfection.* Salt Lake City: Deseret Book, 1949.

BLT

SEED OF CHRIST

The word *seed* is used in the scriptures both literally and symbolically. In the literal sense, descendants of earthly parents are known as their seed. In the symbolic spiritual sense, people who accept covenants, such as the Abrahamic covenant, are received into the covenantal family and are thus viewed as the *seed,* or rightful heirs. The oath and covenant of the priesthood speaks of the faithful as "sons of Moses and of Aaron and the *seed of Abraham*" (D&C 84:34; emphasis added; see also D&C 103:17). In the Book of Mormon, Abinadi refers to those who have hearkened unto the words of the "holy prophets who have prophesied concerning the coming of the Lord" and "have looked forward to that day for a remission of their sins" as Christ's "seed, or they are the heirs of the kingdom of God" (Mosiah 15:11). Thus, the *seed of Christ* are those who have embraced Christ's gospel, taken his name upon themselves, partaken of the covenants and ordinances, and lived their lives so as to be born again—spiritually begotten sons and daughters unto Christ, joint-heirs with him of the Father's glory (Mosiah 5:7; 27:25; D&C 76:24; Romans 8:17). "We are adopted into a state of sonship by the Father. Christ is his natural heir [seed], and as adopted sons [and daughters], we become joint-heirs, receiving, inheriting, and possessing as does the Natural Heir" (McConkie, 287).

SOURCE

McConkie, Bruce R. *A New Witness for the Articles of Faith.* Salt Lake City: Deseret Book, 1985.

BLT

SEER

The Old Testament Hebrew word for *seer* is *ro'eh,* which means "one who sees" or "one who looks." The ancient usage of the term designated seers as a distinct class of prophets. From that usage of the word, we see that while there is a close relationship in function, seers were in some special way different from prophets as proclaimers or teachers of truth. As evidenced in the scriptures, two unique gifts belong to seers: (1) to use the Urim and Thummim, if necessary, to translate records or receive revelation; and (2) to prophesy of or foretell future events. The Book of Mormon clearly teaches these distinctions. When King Limhi asked Ammon whether he could translate the twenty-four gold plates that contained the Jaredite records, Ammon said no but that Mosiah, the prophet, seer, and king could.

"Now Ammon said unto him: I can assuredly tell thee, O king, of a man that can translate the records; for he has wherewith that he can look, and translate records that are of ancient date; and it is a gift from God. And the things are called interpreters, and no man can look in them except he be commanded, lest he should look for that he ought not and he should perish. And whosoever is commanded to look in them, the same is called seer. . . . And the king said that a seer is greater than a prophet. And Ammon said that a seer is a revelator and a prophet also; and a gift which is greater can no man have, except he should possess the power of God, which no man can; yet a man may have great power given him from God" (Mosiah 8:13, 15–16).

In Old Testament times the high priest in the Levitical Priesthood carried the Urim and Thummim in a pocket in the breastplate of his garment, known as an ephod. The Old Testament does not explain this instrument in great detail, but we see examples of its function in the Book of Mormon (Mosiah 28:13–16) and in the ministry of Joseph Smith, who was not only a prophet and seer but also a translator (D&C 21:1). Using the Urim and Thummim to translate records is one of the roles of a seer—a role that has been relatively rare and limited throughout history.

"A seer is one who sees with spiritual eyes," Elder John A. Widtsoe wrote. "He perceives the meaning of that which seems obscure to others; therefore he is an interpreter and clarifier of eternal truth. . . . In short, he is one who sees, who walks in the Lord's light with open eyes" (258). As one who "walks in the Lord's light," a seer not only tells forth God's truths but is also a foreteller. Ammon taught, "But a seer can know of things which are past, also of things which are to come" (Mosiah 8:17). This gift of prophecy is a characteristic of prophets who are also seers (1 Samuel 9:9; 2 Samuel 24:11). The seeric responsibility and gift to see with "spiritual eyes" (Moses 1:11) things that are not "visible to the natural eye" (Moses 6:36) is no ordinary gift or ecclesiastical duty within the Church. Rather, it is what Elder Orson F. Whitney called a "supernatural endowment" belonging to those who have been sustained as prophets, seers, and revelators and who hold seeric keys (39–40).

SOURCES

Whitney, Orson F. *Saturday Night Thoughts: A Series of Dissertations on Spiritual, Historical and Philosophic Themes.* Salt Lake City: The Deseret News, 1921.

Widtsoe, John A. *Evidences and Reconciliations.* Arranged by G. Homer Durham. Salt Lake City: Bookcraft, 1960.

BLT

SERVICE

Service to God and our neighbor is the natural expression of our love for the Lord, evidence that we are sincere disciples of Christ, and a nonverbal witness to the truthfulness of the gospel of Jesus Christ (D&C 42:29; John 14:15; Matthew 22:37–40). When we are baptized, we enter into a covenant to serve God for the rest of our lives (Mosiah 18:13). The desire to serve God with all our heart, might, mind, and strength opens to us limitless opportunities to serve in meaningful ways (D&C 4:2–3). Ammon, one of King Mosiah's missionary sons, exemplified the power of teaching the gospel through service when he encountered his first Lamanite community (Alma 17). Selfless service typifies Christ, our great Exemplar in this and all virtues (Luke 22:27; Matthew 20:26–28).

The Savior taught that "no man can serve two masters" (Matthew 6:24). We have our agency to choose whom we will serve—God or the world (Joshua 24:15). Claiming we can devote our lives to both of these through our service and love is duplicitous and makes hypocrites of us. That is why the Lord asks us to "serve him with a perfect heart" and in all humility (1 Chronicles 28:9; Isaiah 38:1–5; Acts 20:9). The apostle Paul counseled that sincere service occurs when we "present [our] bodies a living sacrifice, holy, acceptable unto God" (Romans 12:1). The apostle James taught that a testimony of Jesus Christ without willing obedience or service to God is merely an expression of belief comparable to that held by "devils" (James 2:19).

Our motives for service may vary widely from personal reward to selfless concern for others. Elder Dallin H. Oaks taught that the highest motive for service is inspired by the pure love of Christ (15). For this reason, serving others out of genuine love for them is also a form of worshipping the Lord (Mosiah 2:16–17; Matthew 25:40). Charitable service, or service motivated by the pure love of Christ, also reflects that we are empowered to serve selflessly because of the atonement of Christ; through his grace, we are enabled to "serve God acceptably" (Hebrews 12:28). King Benjamin recognized this necessary dynamic when he taught that even if we served God continually (which none of us do), we would still be "unprofitable servants" (Mosiah 2:21). But we "can do all things through Christ which strengtheneth" us (Philippians 4:13).

SOURCE
Oaks, Dallin H. "Why Do We Serve?" *Ensign,* Nov. 1984, 12–15.

CFO

SEVENTY

Seventy is an office in the Melchizedek Priesthood. Its historical and scriptural roots can be found in both the Old and New Testaments. Moses took "seventy of the elders of Israel" (Exodus 24:1) up into the mount with him, where "they saw the God of Israel" (Exodus 24:9–10). These seventy witnesses of God were thus given responsibility to assist Moses in bearing witness of God and his teachings and in leading and directing the children of Israel. In New Testament times Jesus "appointed other seventy also, and sent them two and two before his face into every city and place, whither he himself would come" (Luke 10:1). These authorized disciples not only taught the gospel to the people but also performed miracles in the name of the Lord (Luke 10:17).

In this dispensation, the Lord has revealed additional knowledge concerning the role and responsibilities of the Seventy. In 1835 the Lord revealed that, as with the Twelve Apostles, "the Seventy are also called to preach the gospel, and to be especial witnesses unto the Gentiles and in all the world—thus differing from other officers in the church in the duties of their calling" (D&C 107:25). At the organization meeting of the First Quorum of the Seventy in Kirtland, Ohio, on 28 February 1835, the Prophet Joseph Smith taught: "The Seventies are to constitute traveling quorums, to go into all the earth, whithersoever the Twelve Apostles shall call them" (2:202). The primary responsibility of the seventies in the early days of the Church was to preach the gospel as missionaries. They were presided over by seven presidents (D&C 107:93–94). The revelation further stipulated that others may be called "if the labor in the vineyard of necessity requires it" (D&C 107:96). In fact, the Prophet Joseph Smith stated that if necessary, many additional seventies could be called, even "seven times seventy, and even until there are one hundred and forty-four thousand thus set apart for the ministry" (2:221).

As Church membership grew and with the gathering of the Saints to Nauvoo, there were ten or more quorums of the seventy, all presided over by the seven presidents. When the Saints moved west and settled the Great Basin area, it became virtually impossible to maintain the quorums as they had been organized in Nauvoo. Therefore, quorums of seventies were organized in the stakes, and subsequently seventies served primarily as stake missionaries. General Authorities acted as the seven presidents of the seventy and directed the missionary labors of the stake seventies. In 1986 stake quorums of seventies were dissolved, leaving only General Authority Seventies to act in this capacity "in the name of the Lord, under the direction of the Twelve" (D&C 107:34). Today there are two kinds of seventies—those who are General Authority Seventies and those who are Area Seventies. General Authorities, as the name implies, have general authority to serve anywhere in the Church under the direction of the First Presidency and the Twelve. Area Seventies are authorized to serve within specific geographical areas and are organized into quorums based on geography. Each Seventy has all the necessary authority for the "building up the church and regulating the affairs of the same in all nations, first unto the Gentiles and then to the Jews" (D&C 107:34).

Whereas the first seventies of this dispensation were primarily missionaries, the Seventies of today administer all the affairs of the kingdom as called upon by the Quorum of the Twelve (D&C 107:38). The Prophet Joseph Smith taught that "the Seventies are not called to serve tables, or preside over churches to settle difficulties, but are to preach the Gospel and build them up, and set others, who do not belong to these quorums, to preside over them, who are High Priests" (2:431–32). Explaining how this is done today in the Church, Elder Earl C. Tingey, who served as the senior president of the quorums of the Seventy, stated:

"The Seventy do not receive additional priesthood keys, but with each assignment they receive from the First Presidency or the Quorum of the Twelve Apostles, they are delegated authority to accomplish the assignment given.

"The General Authority Seventies meet in regular quorum meetings. Those assigned at Church headquarters meet weekly. These quorum meetings may consist of doctrinal and Church history instruction and training and, from time to time, counsel from the Twelve Apostles and the Presidency of the Seventy. . . .

"Area Seventies live at home and serve on a Church-service basis, much like a bishop or a stake president, for a designated number of years. They receive assignments similar to those received by General Authority Seventies, with the exception that they serve in their local areas rather than worldwide. . . .

"Members of these . . . quorums meet in quorum meetings annually in Salt Lake City during April general conference and also annually somewhere in the designated geographical part of the Church where they live" (48–49).

SOURCES

Smith, Joseph. *History of The Church of Jesus Christ of Latter-day Saints.* Edited by B. H. Roberts. 7 vols. 2d ed. rev. Salt Lake City: The Church of Jesus Christ of Latter-day Saints, 1932–51.

Tingey, Earl C. "The Quorums of the Seventy." *Ensign,* Aug. 2005, 48–50.

BLT

SHEOL

The Hebrew term *she'ol* is the equivalent of the Greek *hades* and in a general sense refers to the place of departed spirits. The Prophet Joseph Smith taught: "Hades, the Greek, or Shaole, the Hebrew . . . mean a world of spirits. Hades, Shaole, paradise, spirits in prison are all one: it is a world of spirits. The righteous and the wicked all go to the same world of spirits until the resurrection" (5:425). Of course, the Prophet was here using the broad definition of Sheol, for there certainly exist different places within the world of spirits. The righteous "are received into a state of happiness, which is called paradise, a state of rest, a state of peace, where they shall rest from all their troubles and from all care, and sorrow" (Alma 40:12). On the other hand, the spirits of the wicked are "in darkness, and a state of awful, fearful looking for the fiery indignation of the wrath of God . . . [a] state of misery" (Alma 40:14–15). This latter description of the place where the spirits of the wicked go after death is the specific meaning of the term *Sheol,* the place of hell, and the sense in which it is used elsewhere in scripture, as when modern revelation speaks of "the dark and benighted dominion of Sheol" (D&C 121:4). In a few instances the King James translators rendered *she'ol* as "grave" (Genesis 44:29, 31; Job 7:9; Psalm 30:3) or "pit" (Numbers 16:30, 33; Job 17:16).

Most of the terms used for the world of departed spirits have a broad, general meaning attached to them as well as a specific meaning. The Savior used the broad, general meaning of the term *paradise* when he spoke to the criminal hanging next to him on a cross: "To day shalt thou be with me in paradise" (Luke 23:43). Jesus was not promising the thief an abode with the righteous but only that the man would soon join Jesus in a place where departed spirits go after death and that it would be a better place than this world. The Prophet Joseph Smith taught that Jesus was simply saying, "This day thou shalt be with me in the world of spirits" (5:424–25). Alma, however, uses the specific meaning of *paradise* in his prophetic discourse: the place in the spirit world where the righteous are separated from the wicked, the place of peace, rest, and cessation of cares and sorrows (Alma 40:11–12).

SOURCE

Smith, Joseph. *History of The Church of Jesus Christ of Latter-day Saints.* Edited by B. H. Roberts. 7 vols. 2d ed. rev. Salt Lake City: The Church of Jesus Christ of Latter-day Saints, 1932–51.

ACS

SHILOH

According to the Joseph Smith Translation, Shiloh is Christ (JST, Genesis 50:24). The term *Shiloh* constitutes one of the earliest messianic prophecies in the Old Testament and is found in the patriarchal blessing that Jacob bestowed upon his son Judah. He said, "The sceptre shall not depart from Judah, nor a lawgiver from between his feet, until Shiloh come; and unto him shall the gathering of the people be" (Genesis 49:10). That is, leadership of the family of Israel, symbolized by the scepter, would reside in the tribe of Judah and descend through his posterity (those "from between his feet") until the arrival of one named Shiloh, Jesus Christ, "whose right it is to reign" (D&C 58:22).

The word *Shiloh* is a Hebrew contraction and is literally translated as "which is to him," thus conveying the sense of a person to whom rightfully belongs power and authority. "This authority was to be that of kingly rule or exercise of authority in making and enforcing the law. . . . And Judah had the scepter in Israel or Judah, until the days of Christ" (Smith, 3:21, 20; paragraphing altered).

SOURCE

Smith, Joseph Fielding. *Doctrines of Salvation.* Compiled by Bruce R. McConkie.
3 vols. Salt Lake City: Bookcraft, 1954–56.

ACS

SIGN OF THE DOVE

"And Jesus, when he was baptized, went up straightway [immediately] out of the water: and, lo, the heavens were opened unto him, and he saw the Spirit of God descending like a dove, and lighting upon him: and lo a voice from heaven, saying, This is my beloved Son, in whom I am well pleased" (Matthew 3:16–17). The baptism of Jesus at the hands of John the Baptist is one of the many scriptural evidences for three separate personages within the Godhead: God the Son being baptized, the presence of God the Holy Spirit being manifested by the token or sign of the dove, and the voice of God the Father being heard on this sacred occasion. John and Jesus did in fact see a dove, but the dove was not the Holy Ghost but rather a sign of the Holy Ghost. "The sign of the dove was instituted before the creation of the world, a witness for the Holy Ghost, and the devil cannot come in the sign of the dove. The Holy Ghost is a personage, and is in the form of a personage. It does not confine itself to the *form* of the dove, but in *sign* of the dove. The Holy Ghost cannot be transformed into a dove; but the sign of a dove was given to John to signify the truth of the deed, as the dove is an emblem or token of truth and innocence" (Smith, 5:261).

SOURCE

Smith, Joseph. *History of The Church of Jesus Christ of Latter-day Saints.* Edited by
B. H. Roberts. 7 vols. 2d ed. rev. Salt Lake City: The Church of Jesus Christ of
Latter-day Saints, 1932–51.

RLM

SIGNS

Any evidence—event, experience, or teaching—that validates or proves something to be true is a sign. Signs are both predictive and instructive. In the scriptures God often gives signs through miraculous manifestations. At other times, however, signs are subtle and symbolic. In his efforts to liberate the captive Israelites, Moses gave dramatic signs to Pharaoh to demonstrate God's almighty power (Exodus 7–11).

Joshua brought down the walls of Jericho as a divine sign to both the children of Israel and their enemies (Joshua 6). Elijah sealed the heavens (1 Kings 17) and called down fire from heaven (1 Kings 18) as a testimony against those who had forsaken Jehovah and worshipped idols. The scriptures are filled with such miraculous events, which are signs of God's power and the truthfulness of his prophets' words. In fact, every prophecy uttered by holy prophets is a sign from God. Isaiah gave a simple, dualistic prophecy, of a virgin giving birth to a child, that predicted not only the future virgin birth of the Messiah but also the impending destruction of the ancient kingdom of Israel (Isaiah 7:14–16). Malachi prophesied of the latter-day coming of the prophet Elijah "before the coming of the great and dreadful day of the Lord: and he shall turn the heart of the fathers to the children, and the heart of the children to their fathers" (Malachi 4:5–6). Jesus admonished his disciples to look for the signs that would precede the destruction of Jerusalem and his second coming (Matthew 24; Joseph Smith–Matthew).

Signs—both in the prophetic word and by wonders in heaven and on earth (Daniel 6:27)—announced the birth of the Savior (Matthew 2; Helaman 14; 3 Nephi 1) and the Crucifixion and Resurrection (3 Nephi 8). Numerous events in the scriptures are direct signs of the fulfillment of prophecy and attest to God's power and the truthfulness of his gospel. In fact, as Alma declared in response to Korihor's demand for a convincing sign of the existence of God, "all things denote there is a God; yea, even the earth, and all things that are upon the face of it, yea, and its motion, yea, and also all the planets which move in their regular form do witness that there is a Supreme Creator" (Alma 30:44). Similarly, Luke spoke of "many infallible proofs" as signs of the divinity of Jesus Christ and the reality of his resurrection (Acts 1:3). To those who truly believe, signs—wonders, miracles, prophecies, types and shadows—are "infallible proofs," but to those who refuse to see the hand of God, no sign has convincing and converting power. For this reason, the Lord has declared that "an evil and adulterous generation seeketh after a sign" (Matthew 12:39). In contrast to the way of the world that demands proof before belief—"show unto us a sign . . . ; then we shall believe" (Alma 32:17)—the Lord has promised that signs and "infallible proofs" come after one first believes.

"Signs follow them that believe" (Mark 16:17; see also Mormon 9:24; Ether 4:18; D&C 84:65).

Those who seek for faith unto salvation will inevitably see signs and wonders all about them—answers to prayers, miracles, witnesses of the Spirit, spiritual experiences, gospel knowledge, and personal testimony. But seeking to test God by demanding signs or proofs before we believe and submit our will to God's is the antithesis of faith that saves. Those who do so may indeed see signs "but not unto salvation"—for signs guarantee neither faith nor salvation (D&C 63:7).

"Faith cometh not by signs," the Lord declared in our dispensation, "but signs follow those that believe. Yea, signs come by faith, not by the will of men, nor as they please, but by the will of God. Yea, signs come by faith, unto mighty works, for without faith no man pleaseth God; and with whom God is angry he is not well pleased; wherefore, unto such he showeth no signs, *only in wrath unto their condemnation.* Wherefore, I, the Lord, am not pleased with those among you who have sought after signs and wonders for faith, and not for the good of men unto my glory" (D&C 63:9–12; emphasis added).

Seeking for Christ by faithfully following him, we will indeed see signs but not because we need them for our faith. We will come to intimately know the Master. On the other hand, those who demand signs before they will follow Christ will neither find him nor know him. Faith is never found in signs but can be rewarded and strengthened thereby.

BLT

SIN

There are two different contexts in which the word *sin* is used in the scriptures: (1) an action (defiance of God's commandments) and (2) a state of being (sinfulness, or living in a fallen, sinful condition).

Action. "Therefore to him that knoweth to do good, and doeth it not," the apostle James wrote, "to him it is sin" (James 4:17). Likewise, Lehi taught that having knowledge of God's laws is requisite for sin to exist (2 Nephi 2:13). Mormon taught that little children need no baptism for the remission of sins because they lack necessary knowledge and accountability and are "whole, for they are not capable of committing sin" (Moroni 8:8; see also D&C 29:47). Thus, to sin is to willfully, knowingly, and with accountability disobey the commandments of God.

State of being. "And the whole world lieth in sin," the Lord has declared in this dispensation, "and groaneth under darkness and under the bondage of sin" (D&C 84:49). The fall of Adam introduced sin to the world. In addition to experiencing physical death, all mankind experiences spiritual death—an estrangement from God by reason of the Fall. It is of this spiritual condition that the apostle Paul spoke when he taught that "there is none righteous, no, not one. . . . For all have sinned, and come short of the glory of God" (Romans 3:10, 23; see also Galatians 3:22). Only the Perfect One, even Jesus Christ, lived without sin and spiritual death. Only he, through his atoning sacrifice, can save mankind from sin—both the fallen, sinful world and our own sinfulness, which we bring about ourselves through our actions (2 Corinthians 5:21; 1 Peter 2:22–24; 2 Nephi 2:5–10; Alma 34:8–15).

BLT

SIN AGAINST THE HOLY GHOST

"The sin against the Holy Ghost" is the unpardonable sin, the offense that "cannot be forgiven in this world or in the world to come" (Smith, 6:314, 317; see also Matthew 12:31; Hebrews 6:4–6; 10:26–28; D&C 132:27). Only a person who has received the gift of the Holy Ghost can commit such a crime. Only a person who has sought for and obtained a divine witness of the truth, has had the heavens opened and enjoyed the sweet fruits of the faith, and has for one reason or another taken offense and become embittered toward the Lord and his Church and kingdom and fought against them—only this kind of person can commit the sin against the Holy Ghost. The Prophet Joseph Smith declared:

"Strange as it may appear at first thought, yet it is no less strange than true, that notwithstanding all the professed determination to live godly, apostates after turning from the faith of Christ, unless they have speedily repented, have sooner or later fallen into the snares of the wicked one, and have been left destitute of the Spirit of God, to manifest their wickedness in the eyes of multitudes. From apostates the faithful have received the severest persecutions. Judas was rebuked and

591

immediately betrayed his Lord into the hands of His enemies, because Satan entered into him.

"There is a superior intelligence bestowed upon such as obey the Gospel with full purpose of heart, which, if sinned against, the apostate is left naked and destitute of the Spirit of God, and he is, in truth, nigh unto cursing, and his end is to be burned. When once that light which was in them is taken from them they become as much darkened as they were previously enlightened, and then, no marvel, if all their power should be enlisted against the truth, and they, Judas-like, seek the destruction of those who were their greatest benefactors.

"What nearer friend on earth, or in heaven, had Judas than the Savior? And his first object was to destroy Him" (2:23).

SOURCE

Smith, Joseph. *History of The Church of Jesus Christ of Latter-day Saints.* Edited by B. H. Roberts. 7 vols. 2d ed. rev. Salt Lake City: The Church of Jesus Christ of Latter-day Saints, 1932–51.

RLM

SON OF DAVID

That Jesus Christ is "the son of David" is well documented in scripture. Matthew begins his testimony by recounting the family history of Jesus of Nazareth and immediately confirms that Jesus is "the son of David" (Matthew 1:1). The angel Gabriel declared to Mary that she would conceive, bear a son, call his name Jesus, and that God would give unto him the throne of "*his father David:* And he shall reign over the house of Jacob for ever; and of his kingdom there shall be no end" (Luke 1:32–33; emphasis added). Both Joseph and Mary were literal descendants of King David (Talmage, 86, 89). In fact, the angel of the Lord addressed Joseph as "thou son of David" (Matthew 1:20). So there is no question that Jesus was legally and lineally the son of David.

As Gabriel's announcement implies, the name-title "son of David" means not only that Jesus was a literal descendant of the great monarch but also that he was *the* son of David, the Messiah, the Son of God. The highest legal authority in Judaism, the high priest, acknowledged the exact equivalence of these terms, though not their fulfillment in the person of Jesus (Matthew 26:63). Jesus was recognized as the son of David, the Messiah, and the Son of God by all who possessed spiritually discerning eyes, whether Jew or Gentile, whether sighted or sightless. For example, as Jesus passed by two blind men, they cried out, "Have mercy on us, O Lord, thou Son of David" (Matthew 20:30). The non-Israelite or Gentile "woman of Canaan" came to Jesus seeking a special blessing and addressed him, "O Lord, thou Son of David" (Matthew 15:22). At his triumphal entry into Jerusalem on the last Sunday of his mortal life, Jesus was greeted with acclamations of his messiahship: "Hosanna to the Son of David" (Matthew 21:9).

It was well known by the Jewish leaders in Jesus' day that the promised Messiah would be a literal descendant of King David. When Jesus asked the Pharisees about the Messiah, "Whose son is he?" they answered, "The Son of David" (Matthew 22:42). But when he quoted Psalm 110:1 and tried to get them to acknowledge that the son of David was also the Lord Jehovah and that he was that very Being, they would say no more (Matthew 22:43).

Thus, the phrase "son of David" was filled with meaning in ancient times. It was a designation for the Messiah, but it also implied the right to rule as king of the Jews, which office Jesus also rightfully possessed. To him should have devolved all honor, power, dominion, and authority. Had the Lord's own people, the Jews, set aside their prideful and prejudicial ways and accepted the Savior, their blessings could have been innumerable.

SOURCE

Talmage, James E. *Jesus the Christ.* Salt Lake City: Deseret Book, 1973.

ACS

SON OF MAN

The phrase "son of man" has differing meanings. First, it can refer to a mortal human being (Numbers 23:19; Job 25:6; Psalm 8:4; 80:17). In the book of Ezekiel alone, Jehovah refers to his children on earth as "son of man" ninety times. Second, and more specifically, because God the Father was known by Adam as the Man of Holiness, Jesus Christ came to be known as the Son of the Man of Holiness or, succinctly, as the Son of Man (Moses 6:57). Jesus refers to himself almost a hundred times in the New Testament Gospels as the Son of

Man, although there is no record of anyone else referring to him by that title during his mortal ministry.

RLM

SON OF THE MORNING

The archenemy of God and all that is good is Lucifer ("torch bearer"), also known as Satan ("slanderer" [Bible Dictionary, "Satan"] or "accuser of our brethren" [Revelation 12:10]), the father of all lies (John 8:44; Moses 4:4), "the author of all sin" (Helaman 6:30). Satan is also known in scripture, ancient and modern, as a son of the morning (Isaiah 14:12; 2 Nephi 24:12; D&C 76:26). "This name-title of Satan indicates he was one of the early born spirit children of the Father" (McConkie, 744).

SOURCE

McConkie, Bruce R. *Mormon Doctrine*. 2d ed. Salt Lake City: Bookcraft, 1966.

RLM

SOUL

The narrowest scriptural use of *soul* is spirit, meaning the human spirit (Alma 36:15; 40:15, 19–21, 23; D&C 101:37). Additionally, in scores of scriptural passages *soul* refers to the whole person and, more directly, to the spirit and the body united (2 Nephi 9:13; D&C 88:15). We may enjoy a measure of peace and happiness and contentment in this life, but only in the resurrection, when "spirit and element [are] inseparably connected"—constituting our complete soul—can we "receive a fulness of joy" (D&C 93:33).

RLM

SPIRIT BODY

From modern revelation we learn that all things, man included, were created spiritually before they were created temporally (D&C 29:31–32; Moses 3:5–7). Every man and woman is created in the image and likeness of God (Genesis 1:26–27; Moses 2:26–27; 6:8–9; Abraham 4:26–27; Mosiah 7:27; Ether 3:15). These references to mankind's creation in the image of God's body apply just as much to the spirit bodies of mankind as to their physical bodies. The 1909 First

Presidency statement titled "The Origin of Man" states: "'God created man in His own image.' This is just as true of the spirit as it is of the body, which is only the clothing of the spirit, its complement; the two together constituting the soul. The spirit of man is in the form of man, and the spirits of all creatures are in the likeness of their bodies" (78).

Examples in the scriptures illustrate that spirits, both premortal and postmortal, have form and likeness similar to physical bodies. When the premortal Christ appeared to the brother of Jared, he learned that the Savior's earthly body would be in the likeness of his spirit body.

"And the veil was taken from off the eyes of the brother of Jared, and he saw the finger of the Lord; and it was as the finger of a man, like unto flesh and blood. . . . Seest thou that ye are created after mine own image? . . . Behold, this body, which ye now behold is the body of my spirit; and even as I appear unto thee to be in the spirit will I appear unto my people in the flesh" (Ether 3:6, 15–16).

The Prophet Joseph Smith likewise learned through revelation from God that "that which is spiritual [is] in the likeness of that which is temporal; and that which is temporal in the likeness of that which is spiritual; the spirit of man in the likeness of his person" (D&C 77:2). Speaking of the nature of the spirit body, the Prophet declared that "spirit is a substance; that it is material, but that it is more pure, elastic and refined matter than the body; that it existed before the body, can exist in the body; and will exist separate from the body, when the body will be mouldering in the dust; and will in the resurrection, be again united with it" (4:575).

Elder Orson Pratt elaborated: "We, as Latter-day Saints, believe that the spirits that occupy these tabernacles have form and likeness *similar* to the human tabernacle. Of course there may be deformities existing in connection with the outward tabernacle which do not exist in connection with the spirit that inhabits it. These tabernacles become deformed by accident in various ways, sometimes at birth, but this may not altogether or in any degree deform the spirits that dwell within them, therefore we believe that the spirits which occupy the bodies of the human family are *more or less in the resemblance of the tabernacles*" (15:242–43; emphasis added).

All spirit children of our Heavenly Parents were reared to maturity in the premortal world of spirits prior to coming to earth and obtaining physical bodies (First Presidency, 80). Thus, a mature spirit enters mortality by occupying an earthly tabernacle as a baby. The physical body grows to maturity, but the spirit has already attained that state. Therefore, when a child dies, the physical body that is small and not yet fully grown is laid in the grave, but the spirit that enters the postmortal spirit world is a mature, adult spirit. This doctrine was taught by President Joseph F. Smith: "The spirits of our children are immortal before they come to us, and their spirits, after bodily death, are like they were before they came. They are as they would have appeared if they had lived in the flesh, to grow to maturity, or to develop their physical bodies to the full stature of their spirits" (455).

SOURCES

First Presidency. "The Origin of Man." *Improvement Era,* Nov. 1909, 75–81; or *Ensign,* Feb. 2002, 26–30.

Pratt, Orson. In *Journal of Discourses.* 26 vols. London: Latter-day Saints' Book Depot, 1854–86.

Smith, Joseph. *History of The Church of Jesus Christ of Latter-day Saints.* Edited by B. H. Roberts. 7 vols. 2d ed. rev. Salt Lake City: The Church of Jesus Christ of Latter-day Saints, 1932–51.

Smith, Joseph F. *Gospel Doctrine.* Salt Lake City: Deseret Book, 1939.

BLT

SPIRIT PRISON

The term *spirit prison* is used by Latter-day Saints to refer to that portion of the postmortal spirit realm where men and women are taught the gospel of Jesus Christ. This use of the expression probably derives from the words of Peter regarding our Lord's ministry to the spirit world following his death (1 Peter 3:18–19).

In a broader sense, the entire postmortal spirit world is a spirit prison. We are told in modern revelation that all spirits, not just the wicked, look upon the long absence of their bodies from their spirits as a bondage; they are as captives, and they yearn for deliverance and liberty from the chains of death (D&C 45:17; 138:15–18). "Hades, the Greek, or Shaole, the Hebrew: these two significations mean a world of spirits," taught the Prophet Joseph Smith. "Hades, Shaole, paradise, spirits in prison, are all one: it is a world of spirits.

"The righteous and the wicked all go to the same world of spirits until the resurrection" (5:425).

"When our spirits leave these bodies, will they be happy?" Orson Pratt asked. "Not perfectly so. Why? Because the spirit is absent from the body; it cannot be perfectly happy while a part of the man is lying in the earth. . . . You will be happy, you will be at ease in paradise; but still you will be looking for a house where your spirit can enter and act as you did in former times" (1:289). President Brigham Young was most emphatic on this matter: "I know it is a startling idea to say that the Prophet [Joseph Smith] and the persecutor of the Prophet, all go to prison together. . . . But *they have not got their bodies yet, consequently they are in prison*" (3:95; emphasis added).

SOURCES

Pratt, Orson. In *Journal of Discourses.* 26 vols. London: Latter-day Saints' Book Depot, 1854–86.

Smith, Joseph. *History of The Church of Jesus Christ of Latter-day Saints.* Edited by B. H. Roberts. 7 vols. 2d ed. rev. Salt Lake City: The Church of Jesus Christ of Latter-day Saints, 1932–51.

Young, Brigham. In *Journal of Discourses.* 26 vols. London: Latter-day Saints' Book Depot, 1854–86.

RLM

SPIRITUALITY

In direct contrast to the carnality, sensuality, and devilishness that characterize the "natural man," who "is an enemy to God" (Mosiah 3:19) with a disposition to do evil (Ether 3:2), spirituality is holiness, love for the things of God, and sensitivity to the promptings of the Holy Spirit. Natural men love wickedness and worldliness. Spiritual men "hunger and thirst after righteousness" (Matthew 5:6) and have "an eye single to the glory of God" (D&C 4:5; 82:19). Spirituality is having "a broken heart and a contrite spirit" (2 Nephi 2:7) as opposed to hard-heartedness, pride, and disobedience. Spirituality is much more than what one *feels*; it is what one *is* to the very core. Spirituality is that which motivates one to follow the Master. One does not automatically have true spirituality. It must be cultivated and developed by loving and living the principles of the gospel. Spirituality is increased each time a person recognizes and responds to instruction received by the power and gift of the Holy Ghost.

Some feel that they lack spirituality because they do not see angels, speak in tongues, or live in a state of continual spiritual experiences. This is false. "I have learned that strong, impressive spiritual experiences do not come to us very frequently," President Boyd K. Packer taught. "And when they do, they are generally for our own edification, instruction, or correction" (53). A person may actually witness spiritual experiences without necessarily being a spiritual person. While some do indeed experience profoundly spiritual events or feelings, true spirituality is not determined by such experiences. Spiritual experiences may bring a temporary feeling, but spirituality yields a lasting transformation of life. The reverence with which one speaks of such experiences is also a manifestation of spiritual maturity and true spirituality. Sometimes people confuse sentimentality with spirituality. Emotion evoked by sensational stories may bring a tear to the eye and a lump to the throat, but it may not necessarily be true spirituality, which brings a deep, quiet inner peace and a personal devotion. Spirituality is not always manifest by speaking in hushed tones or using pious phrases. Long-faced solemnity and an overserious manner are not required to make us truly spiritual individuals, either. Satan sometimes seeks to counterfeit spirituality by contrived emotions and actions. President George A. Smith warned, "When a man professes a great deal of sanctity—a great deal of holiness and piety—when he can scarcely speak without a pious groan, he is to be suspected; for such hypocrisy is in itself the most cursed corruption that can exist" (7:116).

President David O. McKay explained, "Spirituality is the consciousness of victory over self and of communion with the Infinite" (390). Strict observance of the commandments alone does not necessarily mean spirituality, as demonstrated in the lives of the scribes and Pharisees of Jesus' day. Spirituality is an inward devotion to God that is manifest in one's outward behavior and being—how one lives the gospel and loves God and his children. Spirituality is doing the right things for the right reasons. The following statement by Frederic W. Farrar, author of the classic work *The Life of Christ,* describes spirituality as a defining characteristic of true disciples.

"It is easy to be a slave to the letter, and difficult to enter into the spirit; easy to obey a number of outward rules, difficult to enter intelligently and self-sacrificingly into the will of God; easy to entangle the soul in a network of petty observances, difficult to yield the obedience of an enlightened heart; easy to be haughtily exclusive, difficult to be humbly spiritual; easy to be an ascetic or a formalist, difficult to be pure, and loving, and wise, and free; easy to be a Pharisee, difficult to be a disciple; very easy to embrace a self-satisfying and sanctimonious system of rabbinical observances, very difficult to love God with all the heart, and all the might, and all the soul, and all the strength" (289).

The apostle Paul taught that charity—the pure love of Christ—is the ultimate manifestation of true spirituality. "Though I speak with the tongues of men and of angels, and have not charity, I am become as sounding brass, or a tinkling symbol. And though I have the gift of prophecy, and understand all mysteries, and all knowledge; and though I have all faith, so that I could remove mountains, and have not charity, I am nothing" (1 Corinthians 13:1–2). Thus, the pure love of Christ—loving Christ with a perfect love, loving others as Christ would love them, and embracing Christ's atoning love for us—is the very essence of the gospel and the very essence of true spirituality.

SOURCES

Farrar, Frederic W. *The Life of Christ*. New York: E. P. Dutton & Company, 1883.
McKay, David O. *Gospel Ideals: Selections from the Discourses of David O. McKay*. Salt Lake City: Improvement Era, 1953.
Packer, Boyd K. "The Candle of the Lord." *Ensign,* Jan. 1983, 51–56.
Smith, George A. In *Journal of Discourses*. 26 vols. London: Latter-day Saints' Book Depot, 1854–86.

BLT

SPIRIT WORLD, POSTMORTAL

"All men know that they must die," Joseph Smith explained to the Latter-day Saints in Nauvoo. "And it is important that we should understand the reasons and causes of our exposure to the vicissitudes of life and of death, and the designs and purposes of God in our coming into the world, our sufferings here, and our departure hence. . . . It is but reasonable to suppose that God would reveal something in reference to the matter, and it is a subject we ought to study more than any other. We ought to study it day and night, for the world is ignorant in reference to their true condition and relation [to God]. If we have any claim on our Heavenly Father for anything, it is for knowledge on this important subject" (6:50). As a part of the Restoration, the God of heaven chose to make known, line upon line, precept upon precept, the soul-warming verities associated with the third phase of our eternal journey we know as the postmortal existence.

Death passes upon all men and women to fulfill "the merciful plan of the great Creator" (2 Nephi 9:6). It is merciful in the sense that it delivers us from the toils and agonies of this life. "When men are prepared," the Prophet observed, "they are better off to go hence" (6:52). In speaking of little children who depart this life before they arrive at the age of accountability, he said: "The Lord takes many away, even in infancy, that they may escape the envy of man, and the sorrows and evils of this present world; they were too pure, too lovely, to live on the earth; therefore, if rightly considered, instead of mourning we have reason to rejoice as they are delivered from evil, and we shall soon have them again" (4:553).

Death is merciful too because it opens to us a new phase of life, a time wherein the restrictions of this mortal coil are gone. President Brigham Young, in speaking of the glory of what lies ahead, remarked: "I can say with regard to parting with our friends, and going ourselves, that I have been near enough to understand eternity so that I have had to exercise a great deal more faith to desire to live than I ever exercised in my whole life to live. The brightness and glory of the next apartment is inexpressible. It is not encumbered . . . so that when we advance in years we have to be stubbing along and to be careful lest we fall down. We see our youth, even, frequently stubbing their toes and falling down. But yonder, how different! They move with ease and like lightning" (14:231; see also Pratt, 2:243–46).

Modern revelation attests that the transition from time into eternity is immediate. As we breathe our last breath, our spirit leaves our body and takes up its abode in the world of spirits. Joseph Smith taught, "The righteous and the wicked all go to the same world of spirits until the resurrection" (5:425). He added: "The spirits of the just are exalted to a greater and more glorious work; hence they are blessed in their departure to the world of spirits. Enveloped in flaming fire, they are not far from us, and know and understand our thoughts, feelings, and motions, and are often pained therewith" (6:52). President Young asked: "Is the spirit world here? It is not beyond the sun, but is on this earth that was organized for the people that have lived and that do and will live upon it" (3:372).

At the time of one's entrance into the spirit world, the individual experiences what President Joseph F. Smith called a "partial judgment" (449). Paradise is the abode of the faithful, a state of happiness, "a state of rest, a state of peace, where they shall rest from all their troubles and from all care, and sorrow" (Alma 40:12). Paradise is a place where spirits "expand in wisdom, where they have respite from all their troubles, and where care and sorrow do not annoy" (Smith, *Gospel*, 448). On the other hand, the spirits of the wicked, as Alma observed, "shall be cast out into outer darkness; there shall be weeping, and wailing, and gnashing of teeth, and this because of their own iniquity, being led captive by the will of the devil" (Alma 40:13).

Surely in the postmortal spirit world, men and women will have the burdens of abuse, neglect, false teachings, and improper traditions—all of which can deter one from embracing the truth—torn away as a film. Then perhaps they will in that sphere, free from Lucifer's taunts, see as they are seen and know as they are known. President Wilford Woodruff stated: "I tell you when the prophets and apostles go to preach to those who are shut up in prison, . . . thousands of them will there embrace the Gospel. They know more in that world than they do here" (341). President Lorenzo Snow, presumably speaking of the honest-hearted individual who enters the spirit world, also pointed out: "I believe, strongly too, that when the Gospel is preached to the spirits in prison, the success attending that preaching will be far greater than that attending the preaching of our Elders in this life. I believe there will be very few indeed of those spirits who will not gladly receive the Gospel when it is carried to them. The circumstances there will be a thousand times more favorable. . . . I believe there will be very few who will not receive the truth. They will hear the voice of the Son of God; they will hear the voice of the Priesthood of the Son of God, and they will receive the truth and live" (50).

The postmortal spirit world is an intermediate stop for all men and women. It is a place of waiting, of remorse and repentance, of peace and rest, and of instruction and preparation. Mortality is behind. Resurrected immortality lies ahead. The restored gospel sounds a trump of triumph—life and love and learning are forever.

SOURCES

Pratt, Orson. In *Journal of Discourses.* 26 vols. London: Latter-day Saints' Book Depot, 1854–86.

Smith, Joseph. *History of The Church of Jesus Christ of Latter-day Saints.* Edited by B. H. Roberts. 7 vols. 2d ed. rev. Salt Lake City: The Church of Jesus Christ of Latter-day Saints, 1932–51.

Smith, Joseph F. *Gospel Doctrine.* Salt Lake City: Deseret Book, 1939.

Snow, Lorenzo. "Discourse by President Lorenzo Snow." *Millennial Star* 56, no. 4 (22 Jan. 1894): 49–53.

Woodruff, Wilford. "Discourse by President Wilford Woodruff." *Millennial Star* 56, no. 22 (28 May 1894): 337–41.

Young, Brigham. In *Journal of Discourses.* 26 vols. London: Latter-day Saints' Book Depot, 1854–86.

RLM

STANDARD WORKS

The volumes of scripture accepted as the official canon of The Church of Jesus Christ of Latter-day Saints are collectively known as the standard works. Included are the Holy Bible (the King James Version of the Old and New Testaments), the Book of Mormon, the Doctrine and Covenants, and the Pearl of Great Price. These canonized writings are the standard by which all other teachings in the Church are measured. The written word of God as found in the four standard works "fixes permanently the general truths which God has revealed," wrote Elder B. H. Roberts. "It preserves, for all time and for all generations of men, the great frame-work of the plan of salvation—the Gospel. There are certain truths that are not affected by ever-changing circumstances; truths which are always the same, no matter how often they may be revealed; truths which are elementary, permanent, fixed; from which there must not be, and cannot be, any departure without condemnation. The written word of God preserves the people of God from vain and foolish traditions, which, as they float down the stream of time, are subject to changes by distortion, by addition or subtraction, or by the fitful play of fancy in fantastic and unreliable minds. It forms a standard by which even the living oracles of God may instruct themselves, measure themselves, and correct themselves. It places within the reach of the people, the power to confirm the oral words, and the ministry of the living oracles, and thus to add faith to faith, and knowledge to knowledge" (576–77).

The standard works—those fundamental revelations, doctrines, principles—are universally applicable and binding upon the entire Church. In a revelation "embracing the law of the Church," given to the Prophet Joseph Smith in 1831, the Lord declared: "Thou shalt take the things which thou hast received, which have been given unto thee in my scriptures for a law, to be my law to govern my church" (D&C 42:59). President Joseph Fielding Smith elaborated upon the role of canonized scripture as this governing law, or standard: "It makes no difference what is written or what *anyone* has said, if what has been said is in *conflict* with what the Lord has revealed, we can set it aside. *My words, and the teachings of any other member of the Church, high or low, if they do not square with the revelations, we need not accept them.* Let us have this matter clear. We have accepted the four *standard works* as the measuring yardsticks, or balances, by which we *measure every man's doctrine*" (3:203).

Resting upon each individual is the personal responsibility to search the scriptures and obtain an in-depth, sound understanding of the doctrines of the gospel as found in the standard works. Only when we have devoted ourselves to serious, extensive, and continual study of the scriptures can they serve as measuring rods in helping others and ourselves discern truth and dispel error. Thus, the responsibility to know, teach, and judge truth by the standard works is an individual as well as an institutional obligation and blessing.

SOURCES

Roberts, B. H. "A Nephite's Commandments to His Three Sons." *Improvement Era,* June 1900, 570–78.

Smith, Joseph Fielding. *Doctrines of Salvation.* Compiled by Bruce R. McConkie. 3 vols. Salt Lake City: Bookcraft, 1954–56.

BLT

STEWARDSHIP

As the Creator and Savior of the world, Jehovah aptly proclaims, "The world is mine, and the fulness thereof" (Psalm 50:12). In his role as Supreme Being over the earth, Jehovah made his sons and daughters stewards over his creations. He blessed his male and female children and declared, "Have dominion over the fish of the sea, and over the fowl of the air, and over every creeping thing that creepeth upon the earth" (Genesis 1:26; D&C 104:13–17). Additionally, the Lord made his disciples stewards over his Church and its covenants and ordinances "to prepare my people for the time when I shall dwell with them" (D&C 104:59). "In time and in eternity," we will be required to give "an account" of our stewardship to the Lord, including how we imparted his "abundance" (D&C 104:18) "to the poor and the needy" (D&C 72:12).

As faithful, just, and wise stewards of God's abundance, we subsequently remember that all that we possess and enjoy comes from our Creator and Redeemer. Elder Neal A. Maxwell explained: "The submission of one's will is really the only uniquely personal thing we have to place on God's altar. The many other things we 'give' . . . are actually the things He has already given or loaned to us" (24). To all those who are true to their assigned stewardship, Jesus Christ has promised eternal life and "the joy of his Lord" (D&C 51:19; 72:3–4).

SOURCE

Maxwell, Neal A. "'Swallowed Up in the Will of the Father.'" *Ensign,* Nov. 1995, 22–24.

CFO

SUCCESSION, APOSTOLIC

With the death of the Prophet Joseph Smith on 27 June 1844, the pattern for succession to the office of president of The Church of Jesus Christ of Latter-day Saints was established. Prior to his death, the Prophet taught important principles relating to this process. Because Brigham Young became the rightful successor to Joseph Smith, the pattern has followed fundamental principles, and it proceeds "in an orderly systemized way" (McConkie, 25).

1. *Keys of the kingdom are conferred upon the Quorum of the Twelve.* In the months preceding his death, Joseph Smith taught the Twelve concerning their roles in carrying forth the kingdom of God (the Church) after his death and gave them the necessary authority to do so. The Prophet conferred upon the apostles every key, power, and principle that had been conferred upon him. With all of the keys conferred upon the Twelve, Joseph declared, "Now if they kill me you have got all the keys, and all the ordinances and you can confer them upon others, and the hosts of Satan will not be able to tear down the

kingdom, as fast as you will be able to build it up; and . . . on your shoulders will the responsibility of leading this people rest" ("Trial," 5:651). Today, each key of priesthood authority is given when a man is called, ordained, and set apart as a member of the Quorum of the Twelve Apostles. Hence, the first principle in succession is the conferral of all the keys. It is, as President Harold B. Lee taught, "the beginning of the call of one to be President of the Church" (123).

2. *The order of apostolic seniority determines presiding authority.* When a man is ordained an apostle and becomes a member of the Twelve, he receives not only the keys of the kingdom but also his place of seniority. The seniority in the first Quorum of the Twelve established in 1835 was arranged by age. Since then seniority has been determined by dates of ordination, the apostle who has served the longest being the senior. Seniority determines who presides over the Quorum of the Twelve. Although each apostle is "equal in authority" (D&C 107:24), the senior apostle presides and actively exercises the keys. The matter of seniority is, as Elder John A. Widtsoe wrote, "a wise procedure. It places as the head of the Church the apostle who has been the longest in service." This principle "eliminates the shadow of politics from the operations of the Council" (264).

3. *At the president's death, there is no First Presidency.* In 1836, Joseph Smith taught the Twelve that "where I am not, there is no First Presidency over the Twelve" (2:374). At the death of the president of the Church, the quorum of the First Presidency is automatically dissolved, and the counselors return to their respective places of seniority in the Twelve. The Quorum of the Twelve becomes, as it were, the presidency of the Church. At this moment the Twelve truly become "equal in authority . . . to the three presidents" (D&C 107:24).

4. *The senior apostle presides over the Quorum and the Church.* With the First Presidency dissolved, the Quorum of the Twelve become the presidency of the Church, and the senior apostle, by virtue of that seniority, becomes the presiding high priest (D&C 107:65–66). As the president of the presiding quorum, he "automatically becomes the presiding officer of the Church" and actively holds and exercises all the keys of the kingdom (Smith, *Doctrines,* 3:156). He is not only the acting president but in very deed, by virtue of those keys, the prophet and president of the Church.

5. *The First Presidency is reorganized, and its members are set apart.* As the presiding officer, the senior apostle has the prerogative, in consultation with the Quorum of the Twelve, as to when to reorganize the First Presidency and to call counselors in that newly reorganized quorum. When it is determined that the time for reorganization has arrived, the senior apostle is ordained and set apart as the president of the Church by the members of the Quorum of the Twelve, who hold the keys and authority to fulfill this important function. Upon that setting apart, the First Presidency, as the presiding quorum, is reorganized and the counselors are then set apart under the direction of the president of the Church, with the Quorum of the Twelve assisting. With the senior apostle ordained as the new president of the Church, the next apostle in seniority is then set apart as the president of the Quorum of the Twelve Apostles. If he is called as a counselor in the First Presidency, as has occurred several times, the next senior member of the Twelve is set apart as the acting president of the Twelve. With the reorganization of the First Presidency, it again assumes its revealed role as "the highest council of the church" (D&C 107:80), with the Quorum of the Twelve Apostles again serving under the direction of the First Presidency.

With these actions completed, the pattern and precedent followed, the leading quorums are again fully organized and operative. Members of the Church are given the opportunity at the next general conference of the Church, in solemn assembly, to formally sustain the action and commit themselves to follow the newly ordained prophet-president of the Church, the newly reorganized First Presidency, and the Quorum of the Twelve as prophets, seers, and revelators. Any vacancy in the Quorum of the Twelve is filled by revelation to and under the direction of the president of the Church.

SOURCES

Lee, Harold B. In Conference Report, Apr. 1970, 122–26.

McConkie, Bruce R. "Succession in the Presidency." In *Speeches of the Year, 1974,* 17–27. Provo, Utah: Brigham Young University Press, 1975.

Smith, Joseph. *History of The Church of Jesus Christ of Latter-day Saints.* Edited by B. H. Roberts. 7 vols. 2d ed. rev. Salt Lake City: The Church of Jesus Christ of Latter-day Saints, 1932–51.

Smith, Joseph Fielding. *Doctrines of Salvation.* Compiled by Bruce R. McConkie. 3 vols. Salt Lake City: Bookcraft, 1954–56.

Top, Brent L., and Lawrence R. Flake. "'The Kingdom of God Will Roll On': Succession in the Presidency." *Ensign*, Aug. 1996, 22–35.

"Trial of Elder Rigdon." *Times and Seasons* 5, no. 17 (15 Sept. 1844): 647–55; (1 Oct. 1844): 660–67.

Widtsoe, John A. *Evidences and Reconciliations.* Arranged by G. Homer Durham. Salt Lake City: Bookcraft, 1960.

BLT

SUICIDE

Suicide is the deliberate taking of one's own life. In some languages the meaning of the word for *suicide* is "self-murder." The sanctity of life—one's own and the lives of others, born and unborn—is clearly taught and carefully guarded by the commandments of God. "Thou shalt not kill," God declared on Mount Sinai (Exodus 20:13). In modern times the Lord has reiterated this prohibition against the taking of life. "And now . . . I speak unto the church. Thou shalt not kill; and he that kills shall not have forgiveness in this world, nor in the world to come" (D&C 42:18; see also D&C 59:6; Smith, 6:253–54). Modern prophets and apostles have likewise spoken clearly about the seriousness of murder, including self-murder and the severity of consequences associated therewith. "It is a terrible criminal act for a person to go out and shorten his life by suicide," President Spencer W. Kimball said (187). President George Q. Cannon, counselor in the First Presidency, said in 1886: "Man did not create himself. He did not furnish his spirit with a human dwelling place. It is God who created man, both body and spirit. Man has no right, therefore, to destroy that which he had no agency in creating. They who do so are guilty of murder, self-murder it is true; but they are no more justified in killing themselves than they are in killing others" (25).

It is abundantly clear that suicide is indeed an abhorrent thing—a grievous sin. What is not so clear is if the eternal penalty for suicide is the same as for murder. Does the scriptural injunction "he that kills shall not have forgiveness in this world, nor in the world to come" apply equally to all killing? The answer appears to be no. Just as there are differing levels of accountability for killing another person, such as accidents, self-defense, war, and so forth, so is there with regard to suicide. Elder M. Russell Ballard has taught:

"I feel that judgment for sin is not always as cut and dried as some of us seem to think. I feel that the Lord also recognizes differences in intent and circumstances: Was the person who took his life mentally ill? Was he or she so deeply depressed as to be unbalanced or otherwise emotionally disturbed? Was the suicide a tragic, pitiful call for help that went unheeded too long or progressed faster than the victim intended? Did he or she somehow not understand the seriousness of the act? Was he or she suffering from a chemical imbalance that led to despair and a loss of self-control?

"Obviously, we do not know the full circumstances surrounding every suicide. Only the Lord knows all the details, and he it is who will judge our actions here on earth. When he does judge us, I feel he will take all things into consideration: our genetic and chemical makeup, our mental state, our intellectual capacity, the teachings we have received, the traditions of our fathers, our health, and so forth" (7–8).

Because we do not understand all the circumstances surrounding someone's suicide, the level of the person's accountability, and the penalty that the Lord, in his infinite love and wisdom, may see fit to inflict upon the person, we must avoid judgment. Regardless of those circumstances and the Lord's divinely imposed punishment, followers of Christ are to be loving and compassionate to those who are hurt by a loved one's act of suicide. They are real victims themselves. Therefore, nothing in our comments or actions should inflict additional pain or add to the heavy emotional burdens they already bear. Let the Lord be the judge, but let us as disciples of Christ "bear one another's burdens, that they may be light" and be "willing to mourn with those that mourn; yea, and comfort those that stand in need of comfort" (Mosiah 18:8–9).

SOURCES

Ballard, M. Russell. "Suicide: Some Things We Know, and Some We Do Not." *Ensign*, Oct. 1987, 6–9.

Cannon, George Q. *Gospel Truth: Discourses and Writings of George Q. Cannon.* Edited by Jerreld L. Newquist. 2 vols. in 1. Classics in Mormon Literature series. Salt Lake City: Deseret Book, 1987.

Kimball, Spencer W. *The Teachings of Spencer W. Kimball.* Edited by Edward L. Kimball. Salt Lake City: Deseret Book, 1982.

Smith, Joseph. *History of The Church of Jesus Christ of Latter-day Saints.* Edited by

B. H. Roberts. 7 vols. 2d ed. rev. Salt Lake City: The Church of Jesus Christ of Latter-day Saints, 1932–51.

BLT

TELESTIAL KINGDOM

Celestial persons receive the testimony of Jesus and also the gospel covenant. Terrestrial persons receive the testimony of Jesus but not the gospel covenant. We learn concerning the inhabitants of the telestial world: "These are they who received not the gospel of Christ, neither the testimony of Jesus" (D&C 76:82; see also D&C 76:101). They "deny not the Holy Spirit" (D&C 76:83). That is, their wickedness is not such as to lead to complete perdition; they do not qualify to become sons of perdition, but they are "thrust down to hell" (D&C 76:84). At the time of their mortal death, they enter into that realm of the postmortal sphere we know as hell and are confronted with their sinfulness. These do not come forth from the grave until the "last resurrection," until the end of the Millennium, "until the Lord, even Christ the Lamb, shall have finished his work" (D&C 76:85).

As is the case with the other kingdoms of glory, there are broad classifications of telestial people. "These are they who are of Paul, and of Apollos, and of Cephas. These are they who say they are some of one and some of another—some of Christ and some of John, and some of Moses, and some of Elias, and some of Esaias, and some of Isaiah, and some of Enoch; but received not the gospel, neither the testimony of Jesus, neither the prophets, neither the everlasting covenant" (D&C 76:99–101). They are divided and also divisive in their loyalties.

Further, the telestial kingdom is the final abode of "liars, and sorcerers, and adulterers, and whoremongers" (D&C 76:103), and, as John the Revelator learned, murderers (Revelation 21:8; 22:15).

Finally, the vision of the glories adds the sobering detail that the inhabitants of the telestial world, "as innumerable as the stars in the firmament of heaven, or as the sand upon the seashore," will be "servants of the Most High; but where God and Christ dwell they cannot come, worlds without end" (D&C 76:109, 112). In short, the celestial body is qualitatively different from the terrestrial body or the telestial body.

Elder Melvin J. Ballard pointed out that "one who gains possession of the lowest degree of the telestial glory may ultimately rise to the highest degree of that glory, but no provision has been made for the promotion from one glory to another. . . .

". . . Those who come forth in the celestial glory with celestial bodies have a body that is more refined. It is different. The very fibre and texture of the celestial body is more pure and holy than a telestial or terrestrial body, and a celestial body alone can endure celestial glory. . . . When we have a celestial body it will be suited to the celestial conditions and telestial bodies could not endure celestial glory. It would be torment and affliction to them. I have not read in the scripture where there will be another resurrection where we can obtain a celestial body for a terrestrial body. What we receive in the resurrection will be ours forever and forever" (224–25; see also Smith, 2:31–34). President Spencer W. Kimball wrote: "After a person has been assigned to his place in the kingdom, either in the telestial, the terrestrial or the celestial, or to his exaltation, he will never advance from his assigned glory to another glory. That is eternal! That is why we must make our decisions early in life and why it is imperative that such decisions be right" (243–44).

The telestial kingdom is the lowest of the kingdoms of glory, but the inhabitants of that glory will be "heirs of salvation" in a world that "surpasses all understanding" (D&C 76:88–89). Generally speaking, the word *salvation* means in scripture exactly the same thing as exaltation or eternal life (D&C 6:13; 14:7; Alma 11:40). A few times in scripture, however, salvation refers to something less than exaltation (D&C 132:17), and this is one of those times. Our Lord seeks to save all his children with an everlasting salvation (D&C 43:25). And he does so, in that all but the sons of perdition eventually inherit a kingdom of glory (D&C 76:43). In fact, Elder Charles W. Penrose observed about the telestial kingdom:

"While there is one soul of this race, willing and able to accept and obey the laws of redemption, no matter where or in what condition it may be found, Christ's work will be incomplete until that being is brought up from death and hell, and placed in a position of progress, upward and onward, in such glory as is possible for its enjoyment and the service of the great God.

"The punishment inflicted will be adequate to the wrongs performed. In one sense the sinner will always suffer its effects. When the debt is paid and justice satisfied; when obedience is learned through the lessons of sad experience; when the grateful and subdued soul comes forth from the everlasting punishment, thoroughly willing to comply with the laws once rejected; there will be an abiding sense of loss. The fulness of celestial glory in the presence and society of God and the Lamb are beyond the reach of that saved but not perfected soul, forever. The power of increase, wherein are dominion and exaltation and crowns of immeasurable glory, is not for the class of beings who have been thrust down to hell and endured the wrath of God for the period allotted by eternal judgment. . . .

"Those who were cast down to the depths of their sins, who rejected the gospel of Jesus, who persecuted the saints, who reveled in iniquity, who committed all manner of transgressions except the unpardonable crime, will also come forth in the Lord's time, through the blood of the Lamb and the ministry of His disciples and their own repentance and willing acceptance of divine law, and enter into the various degrees of glory and power and progress and light, according to their different capacities and adaptabilities. They cannot go up into the society of the Father nor receive of the presence of the Son, but will have ministrations of messengers from the terrestrial world, and have joy beyond all expectations and the conception of uninspired mortal minds. They will all bow the knee to Christ and serve God the Father, and have an eternity of usefulness and happiness in harmony with the higher powers. They receive the telestial glory" (72, 74–75).

SOURCES

Ballard, Melvin J. "The Three Degrees of Glory." In *Crusader for Righteousness.* Salt Lake City: Bookcraft, 1966.

Kimball, Spencer W. *The Miracle of Forgiveness.* Salt Lake City: Bookcraft, 1969.

Penrose, Charles W. *"Mormon" Doctrine, Plain and Simple; or, Leaves from the Tree of Life.* Salt Lake City: Geo. Q. Cannon & Sons, 1897.

Smith, Joseph Fielding. *Doctrines of Salvation.* Compiled by Bruce R. McConkie. 3 vols. Salt Lake City: Bookcraft, 1954–56.

RLM

TEMPLE

Latter-day Saint temples are literally houses of the Lord (D&C 97:10–16), just as ancient temples were (1 Kings 8:11; Isaiah 2:2–3). Therein sacred ordinances are administered that enable worshippers to receive eternal life and exaltation and reside in the presence of the Father and the Son. President Gordon B. Hinckley explained that "the ordinances administered [in the temple] represent the ultimate in our worship. These ordinances become the most profound expressions of our theology" (*Teachings,* 638). The temple is central to all that is done in the Lord's true Church. The Prophet Joseph said, "We need the temple more than anything else" (6:230).

The English word *temple* derives from the Latin *templum,* which anciently meant "sacred space," a place marked out for the observation of the heavens, where signs and portents originated and from where gods answered humans. A temple was a place where sacred matters occurred involving gods and mortals. So too in true temples of God in the latter days, sacred matters take place involving God and his children. A word related to temple is *template.* Both come from the same Latin root. A template is a pattern, which is a helpful way to think about the temple. The temple is a pattern for our journey back to God's presence.

The Lord has declared in modern revelation that his people are "always commanded" to build temples to his holy name "for the glory, honor, and endowment" of all the Saints through special doctrines and ordinances revealed there (D&C 124:39–40). In addition, Joseph Smith taught that the purpose in gathering God's people in *every* dispensation has always been for the building of temples in which to administer the ordinances of salvation. He said: "What was the object of gathering the . . . people of God in any age of the world? . . . The main object was to build unto the Lord a house whereby He could reveal unto His people the ordinances of His house and the glories of His kingdom, and teach the people the way of salvation" (5:423).

The sacred ordinances of the temple were first revealed to Adam and Eve and then to succeeding patriarchs. President Ezra Taft Benson taught: "When our Heavenly Father placed Adam and Eve on this earth, He did so with the purpose in mind of teaching them how to regain His presence. Our Father promised a Savior to redeem them from their fallen condition. He gave to them the plan of salvation and told them to teach their children faith in Jesus Christ and repentance. Further, Adam and his posterity were commanded by God to be baptized, to receive the Holy Ghost, and to enter into the order of the Son of God. To enter into the order of the Son of God is the equivalent today of entering into the fullness of the Melchizedek Priesthood, which is received only in the house of the Lord. Because Adam and Eve had complied with these requirements, God said to them, 'Thou art after the order of him who was without beginning of days or end of years, from all eternity to all eternity' (Moses 6:67)" (8).

In addition, the explanations of figures 3, 7, and 8 of Facsimile 2 of the book of Abraham testify of the longevity of temple ordinances on the earth. The explanation for figure 3, for example, states: "Is made to represent God, sitting upon his throne, clothed with power and authority; with a crown of eternal light upon his head; representing also the grand Key-words of the Holy Priesthood, as revealed to Adam in the Garden of Eden, as also to Seth, Noah, Melchizedek, Abraham, and all to whom the Priesthood was revealed." The Jewish historian Josephus stated that the patriarch Melchizedek actually built a temple: "[Melchizedek], the Righteous King, for such he really was; on which account he was [there] the first priest of God, and first built a temple, [there], and called the city Jerusalem, which was formerly called Salem" (6.10.1). President Marion G. Romney corroborated the fact that later patriarchs possessed temple ordinances. He said, "Pondering upon the subject of temples and the means therein provided to enable us to ascend into heaven brings to mind the lesson of Jacob's dream. . . . Temples are to us all what Bethel was to Jacob" (16).

The concept of temples, even those not authorized by the Lord, was at the core of almost all ancient Near Eastern civilizations. Examples abound in the ancient world of endowment-like ceremonies being practiced, including special washings, anointings, and the clothing of participants in ritual garments. Perhaps the most impressive exhibit is in Egypt, the huge temple precinct along the Nile River at Karnak, which clearly portrays initiation ceremonies, with the above-mentioned elements inscribed on walls in plain view.

After Moses led the children of Israel out of Egyptian bondage, he received detailed instructions on the construction of a portable temple, the tabernacle, for the performance of special sacred ordinances (Exodus 25–31; 35–40). King David was not permitted to build a permanent temple, but his son Solomon was—from materials David had collected (1 Kings 5:13–18; 1 Chronicles 22:5–19; 2 Chronicles 3–7). Following Judah's return from the Babylonian exile (538 B.C.), King Cyrus of Persia sponsored the construction of a new sanctuary to replace Solomon's temple, which had been destroyed. Called the temple of Zerubbabel, this new temple was dedicated in 516 B.C. (Ezra 1–6). King Herod rebuilt and expanded this temple on the same site, a temple with which Jesus and his disciples were familiar (John 2:20). After the destruction of Herod's temple by the Romans in A.D. 70, no more temples were built in the Old World.

Thirty years after their arrival in the New World, the Nephites built a temple in the land of Nephi (2 Nephi 5:16; Jacob 1:17; 2:2, 11). King Benjamin gathered his people at the temple in Zarahemla to instruct them, with "every man having his tent with the door thereof towards the temple" (Mosiah 2:6). That temples existed there for many hundreds of years is evident from the fact that the resurrected Savior ministered to the people assembled at the temple in the land Bountiful (3 Nephi 11:1).

The first temple to be built by commandment in the current dispensation was at Kirtland, Ohio (D&C 88:119). Dedicatory services began on 27 March 1836. Keys of both knowledge and authority were restored by heavenly messengers, including Jesus Christ, Moses, Elias, and Elijah (D&C 110). A partial endowment (consisting of washings, anointing, sealing of anointing, and the washing of feet) was administered therein, and miraculous, even Pentecostal outpourings, occurred. Other temples followed. The dedication of the Salt Lake Temple fulfilled in part Isaiah's prophecy that "it shall come to pass in the last days, that the mountain of the Lord's house shall be established in the top of the mountains, and shall be exalted above the hills; and all nations shall flow unto it" (Isaiah 2:2). The prophet Ezekiel saw in vision that a future glorious temple would be rebuilt in Jerusalem as part of the Lord's return (Ezekiel 37:21–28; D&C 133:13). The Prophet Joseph Smith also testified of this event (5:336–37). John the Revelator saw in vision that the time would come when the earth would be celestialized, including the eternal city of Jerusalem, but that a temple would no longer be needed there, "for the Lord God Almighty and the Lamb are the temple of it" (Revelation 21:22).

Today, as in ancient times, the Lord has commanded that temples be kept pure and undefiled. Only worthy members of the covenant community are allowed entrance. The prophet Ezekiel recorded, "Thus saith the Lord God; No stranger, uncircumcised in heart, nor uncircumcised in flesh, shall enter into my sanctuary, of any stranger that is among the children of Israel" (Ezekiel 44:9). The great blessings deriving from keeping each temple pure were outlined to the Prophet Joseph Smith. The Lord said, "And inasmuch as my people build a house unto me in the name of the Lord, and do not suffer any unclean thing to come into it, that it be not defiled, my glory shall rest upon it; yea, and my presence shall be there, for I will come into it, and all the pure in heart that shall come into it shall see God" (D&C 97:15–16). Because of the Lord's presence in temples, they are places of accelerated learning and superior means of instruction. Elder John A. Widtsoe taught:

"The wonderful pedagogy of the temple service, especially appealing to me as a professional teacher, carries with it evidence of the truth of temple work. We go to the temple to be informed and directed, to be built up and to be blessed. How is all this accomplished? First by the spoken word, through lectures and conversations, just as we do in the class room, except with more elaborate care, then by the appeal to the eye by representations by living, moving beings; and by pictorial representations in the wonderfully decorated rooms. . . . Meanwhile the recipients themselves, the candidates for blessings, engage actively in the temple service. . . . Altogether our temple worship follows a most excellent pedagogical system. I wish instruction were given so well in every school room throughout the land, for we would then teach with more effect than we now do.

"For these reasons, among many others, I have always felt that temple work is a direct evidence of the truth of the word re-established by the Prophet Joseph Smith. It may be that the temple endowment and the other temple ordinances form the strongest available evidence of the divine inspiration of the Prophet Joseph Smith" (59).

Temples are places of missionary labor for those who have passed on. President Spencer W. Kimball said: "The more clearly we see eternity, the more obvious it becomes that the Lord's work . . . is one vast and grand work with striking similarities on each side of the veil. . . .

". . . I hope to see us dissolve the artificial boundary line we so often place between missionary work and temple and genealogical work, because it is the same great redemptive work!" (3).

Temples are places of personal reflection and revelation. President Hinckley stated: "The temple is also a place of personal inspiration and revelation. Legion are those who in times of stress, when difficult decisions must be made and perplexing problems must be handled, have come to the temple in a spirit of fasting and prayer to seek divine direction. Many have testified that while voices of revelation were not heard, impressions concerning a course to follow were experienced at that time or later which became answers to their prayers" ("Temple," 6).

Temples are places of security and protection in mortality. At the dedication of the cornerstone of the Logan Utah Temple, President George Q. Cannon stated, "Every foundation stone that is laid for a Temple, and every Temple completed according to the order the Lord has revealed for his holy Priesthood, lessens the power of Satan on the earth, and increases the power of God and Godliness, moves the heavens in mighty power in our behalf, invokes and calls down upon us the blessings of the Eternal Gods, and those who reside in their presence" (743).

Temples are places of eternal linking: families are linked together forever; the living are linked to their kindred dead; heaven and earth are linked as one; worshippers are linked to the Savior. "Each new Temple forms an additional bond between the heavens and the earth, marking a new epoch in the mighty work of vicarious redemption by the living for the dead—enabling the Saints to be indeed saviors upon Mount Zion" (Clark, 5:256).

President Hinckley urged Latter-day Saints everywhere, "with all of the persuasiveness of which [he was] capable, to live worthy to hold a temple recommend, to secure one and regard it as a precious asset, and to make a greater effort to go to the house of the Lord and partake of the spirit and the blessings to be had therein" (*Teachings*, 638).

SOURCES

Benson, Ezra Taft. "What I Hope You Will Teach Your Children about the Temple." *Ensign,* Aug. 1985, 6–10.

Cannon, George Q. "The Logan Temple." *Millennial Star* 39, no. 46 (12 Nov. 1877): 693–95, 708–11, 726–27, 742–43, 747–49.

Clark, James R., comp. *Messages of the First Presidency of The Church of Jesus Christ of Latter-day Saints.* 6 vols. Salt Lake City: Bookcraft, 1965–75.

Hinckley, Gordon B. "The Salt Lake Temple." *Ensign,* Mar. 1993, 2–6.

———. *Teachings of Gordon B. Hinckley.* Salt Lake City: Deseret Book, 1997.

Josephus, Flavius. *The Wars of the Jews.* In *Josephus: Complete Works.* Translated by William Whiston. Grand Rapids, Mich.: Kregel Publications, 1960.

Kimball, Spencer W. "The Things of Eternity—Stand We in Jeopardy?" *Ensign,* Jan. 1977, 3–7.

Romney, Marion G. "Temples—The Gates to Heaven." *Ensign,* Mar. 1971, 12–16.

Smith, Joseph. *History of The Church of Jesus Christ of Latter-day Saints.* Edited by B. H. Roberts. 7 vols. 2d ed. rev. Salt Lake City: The Church of Jesus Christ of Latter-day Saints, 1932–51.

Widtsoe, John A. "Temple Worship." *The Utah Genealogical and Historical Magazine* 12 (1921), 49–64.

ACS

TEN COMMANDMENTS

God provided foundational, governing principles to his children from the beginning. This divine guidance includes the Ten Commandments, which were given twice to Moses, first as part of the higher law (Exodus 20:3–17), and then in the law of Moses after the first tables of stone containing the higher law were broken (JST, Exodus 34:1–2; Deuteronomy 5:7–21). Abinadi recited the Ten Commandments to King Noah and his wicked priests to remind them of their complete disregard for the law (Mosiah 13:12–24). He taught that "if ye keep the commandments of God ye shall be saved," but "salvation doth not come by the law alone; and were it not for the atonement, which God himself shall make for the sins and iniquities of his people, that they must unavoidably perish, notwithstanding the law of Moses" (Mosiah 12:33; 13:28).

President Spencer W. Kimball illustrated ways that we more deeply internalize the Ten Commandments when we desire to live them according to a higher-law perspective. For example, for the sixth commandment, "Thou shalt not kill," President Kimball explained, "It is not enough to refrain from killing. We are rather under solemn obligation to respect life and to foster it. Far from taking a life, we must be generous in helping others to enjoy the necessities of life. And when this has been accomplished, we seek to improve the mind and the spirit.

"We refrain from taking harmful substances into our body. Through wisdom and moderation in all things, we seek good health and a sense of physical well-being" (6).

The Ten Commandments are as relevant to our day as they were in the day they were given. They are a deeply significant part of the fulness of the gospel (D&C 42:18–24). Obedience to these commandments is an indication that we are becoming more like the Savior. The Lord's desire for his children is that rather than always being taken by the hand to be shown how to obey commandments, they on their own "put my law in their inward parts, and write it in their hearts; and will be their God, and they shall be my people" (Jeremiah 31:33). With such mature faith, we will learn that God gives us commandments to inspire us (D&C 20:7). "For this is the love of God, that we keep his commandments: and his commandments are not grievous [burdensome or oppressive]" (1 John 5:3).

SOURCE

Kimball, Spencer W. "Hold Fast to the Iron Rod." *Ensign,* Nov. 1978, 4–6.

CFO

TERRESTRIAL KINGDOM

The vision of the glories gives a broad description of terrestrial beings: "Behold, these are they who died without law" (D&C 76:72). We know from Joseph Smith's vision of the celestial kingdom that those who did not have the opportunity to receive the fulness of the gospel but who would have accepted it had the opportunity been extended to them are heirs of the celestial kingdom (D&C 137:7–10). Those who "knew no law" who are assigned to the terrestrial glory are those of the heathen nations (D&C 45:54) who choose not to accept the gospel, as explained in the poetic version of the vision the Prophet prepared in 1843:

> Behold, these are they that have died without law;
> The heathen of ages that never had hope.
> ("Vision," 84.)

The Prophet Joseph and his scribe Sidney Rigdon witnessed the final state of those who choose to abide by goodness and equity and decency in their second estate but choose not to receive and incorporate the fulness of the light and power that derive from receiving the everlasting gospel. The terrestrial glory is made up of those who in this life did not receive the testimony of Jesus—the testimony that he is the Savior and Redeemer of mankind—but afterward received it; that is, they received the witness in the postmortal spirit world (D&C 76:73–74). The terrestrial world is also inhabited by those who knew in this life that Jesus was the Christ but who were not valiant enough in that witness to receive the fulness of the gospel when it was presented to them. Or, as the Prophet rendered it poetically:

> Not valiant for truth, they obtain'd not the crown,
> But are of that glory that's typ'd by the moon:
> They are they, that come into the presence of Christ,
> But not to the fulness of God, on his throne.
> ("Vision," 84.)

For that matter, those who receive the fulness of the gospel of Jesus Christ—in our day, those who have joined The Church of Jesus Christ of Latter-day Saints—and then do not prove valiant in their testimony are candidates for the terrestrial degree of glory hereafter. "Not to be valiant in one's testimony," President Ezra Taft Benson stated, "is a tragedy of eternal consequence. These are members who know that this latter-day work is true but who fail to endure to the end. Some may even hold temple recommends, but they do not magnify their callings in the Church. Without valor, they do not take an affirmative stand for the kingdom of God. Some seek the praise, adulation, and honors of men; others attempt to conceal their sins; and a few criticize those who preside over them" (13–14).

SOURCES

Benson, Ezra Taft. *Come unto Christ.* Salt Lake City: Deseret Book, 1983.
"A Vision." *Times and Seasons* 4, no. 6 (1 Feb. 1843): 81–85.

RLM

TESTAMENT

The English term *testament* in the scriptural sense is derived from the Latin Vulgate word *testamentum,* which in turn is a translation of the Greek word *diatheke.* The latter has a number of meanings, but especially "covenant," "last will," or "testament." Thus, *diatheke* was used to translate the Old Testament Hebrew term *berith,* which means "covenant" or, by extension, any two-way promise, even "treaty." So when Latin translators of the Bible replaced *diatheke* with *testamentum,* they were technically correct in that both words can mean "testament," but they misunderstood the primary intended meaning behind *diatheke,* which is "covenant." Therefore, "it would be far better . . . to speak of the Hebrew scriptures as the Old Covenant than as the Old Testament. It should be remembered that the idea of a covenant between God and a chosen group of people is one of the outstanding characteristics of the Hebrew scriptures" (Sperry, 2).

The New Testament also ought to be regarded as the New Covenant, for it derives its name and significance in relation to the Old. The Old Testament prophet Jeremiah spoke of a new covenant that would someday replace the old.

"Behold, the days come, saith the Lord, that I will make a new covenant with the house of Israel, and with the house of Judah: not according to the covenant that I made with their fathers in the day that I took them by the hand to bring them out of the land of Egypt; which my covenant they brake, although I was an husband unto them, saith the Lord: but this shall be the covenant that I will make with the house of Israel; after those days, saith the Lord, I will put my law in their inward parts, and write it in their hearts; and will be their God, and they shall be my people. And they shall teach no more every man his neighbour, and every man his brother, saying, Know the Lord: for they shall all know me, from the least of them unto the greatest of them, saith the Lord: for I will forgive their iniquity, and I will remember their sin no more" (Jeremiah 31:31–34).

This new covenant is the gospel covenant, centered explicitly in Jesus Christ. The scriptures speak of "Jesus the mediator of the new covenant" (Hebrews 12:24). The "new covenant," rooted in the atonement of Jesus Christ is *the* message, the essence, of the New Testament. The fulness of the new covenant includes many "covenants, contracts, bonds, obligations, oaths, vows, performances, connections, associations, [and] expectations" and is called in modern revelation the "new and everlasting covenant" (D&C 132:4, 7).

Modern disciples of the Lord regularly remember "the new and everlasting covenant," with all of its associated promises and principles, by partaking of the sacrament of the Lord's Supper. When Jesus instituted the sacrament during the last night of his mortal life, he spoke of his "blood of the new *testament*" (Greek, *diatheke*), which should be translated as "new *covenant*" (Matthew 26:28; Mark 14:24; emphasis added; see also Luke 22:20; 1 Corinthians 11:25). This new covenant of his blood replaced the old covenant, which was administered and remembered through the ordinances of animal sacrifice.

SOURCE

Sperry, Sidney B. *The Spirit of the Old Testament.* 2d ed. Salt Lake City: Deseret Book, 1980.

ACS

TESTIMONY

A testimony is an inner witness, a conviction, an affirmation—borne of the Spirit of God—of the truthfulness of the gospel or of any matter associated with that gospel. Acquiring a testimony of the gospel of Jesus Christ is a remarkable thing. It is a miracle—an instance in which the Infinite impacts the finite, the heavens touch the earth, the Spirit speaks to our spirit, and God manifests truth to mortals. To gain a testimony is to be reborn as to what we know and feel and value. One who has received such a manifestation is a new creature in Christ. President Marion G. Romney explained, "To know God our Eternal Father and Jesus Christ, whom he sent, one must, as did the Apostles of old, learn of them through the process of divine revelation. One must be born again. . . . Church members have, of course, been through the process. They have been baptized and confirmed members of the Church and have had hands laid upon their heads for the gift of the Holy Ghost. Through these ordinances the door is unlocked. Submission to this is absolutely essential to rebirth" (14–15). Testimonies are fortified as we immerse ourselves in holy scripture and in the words of living apostles and prophets, as we pray to our Father in Heaven to bless us with that certainty that defies all doubt, and as we declare with conviction that which has come to us by the power of God's Holy Spirit.

SOURCES

Lee, Harold B. *Stand Ye in Holy Places.* Salt Lake City: Deseret Book, 1974.
Romney, Marion G. "Except a Man Be Born Again." *Ensign,* Nov. 1981, 14–15.

RLM

THEOCRACY

A theocracy is a government by God. While individuals within the community of faith are free to express their own views and make their own choices as a part of their moral agency, in a theocratic system God speaks through his chosen servants, who declare the mind and will of God. The people then elect either to obey or disobey, to follow counsel or reject it. Joseph Smith taught:

"When Egypt was under the superintendence of Joseph it prospered, because he was taught of God; when they oppressed the Israelites, destruction came upon them. When the children of Israel were chosen with Moses at their head, they were to be a peculiar people, among whom God should place His name; their motto was: 'The Lord is our lawgiver; the Lord is our Judge; the Lord is our King; and He shall reign over us.' While in this state they might truly say, 'Happy is that people, whose God is the Lord.' Their government was a theocracy; they had God to make their laws, and men chosen by Him to administer them; He was their God, and they were His people. Moses received the word of the Lord from God Himself; he was the mouth of God to Aaron, and Aaron taught the people, in both civil and ecclesiastical affairs; they were both one, there was no distinction; so will it be when the purposes of God shall be accomplished: when 'the Lord shall be King over the whole earth' and 'Jerusalem His throne.' 'The law shall go forth from Zion, and the word of the Lord from Jerusalem'" (5:64).

In the restored Church today, portions of the government of God remain intact as the prophets, seers, and revelators dispense truth and provide divine counsel regularly and consistently, and the people are left to choose as they will. The law of common consent, as set forth in latter-day revelation (D&C 20:65; 26:2; 28:13) and in which Church members are called by inspiration and members of the congregation are invited to sustain them, is another illustration of a theocratic practice.

SOURCE

Smith, Joseph. *History of The Church of Jesus Christ of Latter-day Saints.* Edited by B. H. Roberts. 7 vols. 2d ed. rev. Salt Lake City: The Church of Jesus Christ of Latter-day Saints, 1932–51.

RLM

THEODICY

Theodicy, which means "God's justice," is the attempt to philosophically and theologically reconcile the existence of evil and suffering in the world with the existence of an all-loving and all-powerful God. Why do bad things happen to good people? Why would a merciful and compassionate Heavenly Father allow his children to suffer all manner of trials, tragedies, and tribulations? Why would he create a world designed for the happiness of man to be enveloped in crime, corruption, pain, and poverty? Such questions are not new. Great philosophers and theologians throughout the world's history have wrestled with these paradoxes and ironies. Even prophets of God have struggled to receive answers.

"Wherefore doth the way of the wicked prosper?" Jeremiah queried. "Wherefore are all they happy that deal very treacherously?" (Jeremiah 12:1). Amidst his own unspeakable suffering, Job wondered aloud why righteous people—those who love and seek to serve the Lord—must often suffer so much affliction in life (Job 10:1–3). Similarly, Alma cried out at Ammonihah, "How long shall we suffer these great afflictions, O Lord?" (Alma 14:26). The Prophet Joseph Smith—who had communed with the Eternal Father and His Only Begotten Son and had received countless revelations—in the agony of his own suffering at Liberty Jail cried out: "O God, where art thou? And where is the pavilion that covereth thy hiding place? How long shall thy hand be stayed . . . ?" (D&C 121:1–2). Even within the context of the restored gospel, there are often more questions than answers, because as the Lord explained to the prophet Isaiah: "For my thoughts are not your thoughts, neither are your ways my ways. . . . For as the heavens are higher than the earth, so are my ways higher than your ways, and my thoughts than your thoughts" (Isaiah 55:8–9).

In response to such questions as "If there is a loving God in heaven, why would he allow such terrible things to happen on earth?" President Spencer W. Kimball taught: "I wish I could answer these questions with authority, but I cannot. I am sure that sometime we'll understand and be reconciled. But for the present we must seek understanding as best we can in the gospel principles. . . .

"Did the Lord cause the man to suffer a heart attack? Was the death of the missionary untimely? Answer if you can. I cannot, for though I know God has a major role in our lives, I do not know how much he causes to happen and how much he merely permits. Whatever the answer to this question, there is another I feel sure about.

"Could the Lord have prevented these tragedies? The answer is Yes. The Lord is omnipotent, with all power to control our lives, save us pain, . . . protect us, save us from labor, effort, sickness, even from death, if he will. But he will not" (96).

A Latter-day Saint explanation recognizes that not all things have yet been revealed. Yet the restored gospel of Jesus Christ does provide many answers and an eternal perspective. From the standard works and teachings of modern prophets and apostles, three general causes or explanations for what some have called the problem of pain emerge— laws of nature, agency, and the works of God.

Laws of nature. The Savior taught in the Sermon on the Mount about the impartiality of the laws of nature (Matthew 5:45). The fallen world in which we live is governed by laws such as weather, gravity, sickness, death, cause and effect, and so forth. These laws are essential to the plan of salvation and ensure that there is an opposition in all things. The conditions of mortality provide all of Heavenly Father's children with opportunities to learn, progress, and be tested. As a result, many of the pains and problems we encounter in life are part of the natural order of things, merely part of living in an imperfect and fallen world. The Prophet Joseph Smith taught that suffering and afflictions are an inherent part of life. Speaking of the trials and tribulations associated with the last days and the second coming of the Savior, he said:

"It is a false idea that the Saints will escape all the judgments, whilst the wicked suffer; *for all flesh is subject to suffer,* and 'the righteous shall hardly escape;' still many of the Saints will escape, for the just shall live by faith; yet many of the righteous shall fall a prey to disease, to pestilence, etc., *by reason of the weakness of the flesh,* and yet be saved in the Kingdom of God. So that it is an unhallowed principle to say that such and such have transgressed because they have been preyed upon by disease or death, *for all flesh is subject to death"* (4:11; emphasis added).

Agency. Just as the laws of nature are fundamental to our mortal probation, so is the law of agency. "Without this divine power to choose," President David O. McKay taught, "humanity cannot progress" (1073). Because of its supreme significance, agency is a protected principle. God does not infringe upon the free exercise of agency to safeguard the purposes of mortality and the principle of accountability. While this promotes accountability and progression, it also carries with it side effects that may bring suffering and sorrow in life. Sometimes suffering and adversity come as a direct consequence of someone else's use or misuse of agency. While God allows his children to choose for themselves, he does not shield all others from the results of those choices. For example, Alma, Amulek, and the righteous Saints of Ammonihah suffered unspeakable afflictions because of the agency of the wicked inhabitants of the city. Alma explained that the Lord "doth suffer that they may do this thing, or that the people may do this thing unto them, according to the hardness of their hearts, that the judgments which he shall exercise upon them in his wrath may be just" (Alma 14:11). The afflictions the early Saints in Missouri suffered at the hands of their persecutors are another example of how God allowed the misuse of agency of others to bring pain upon the innocent in order to hold the wicked accountable (D&C 103:1–3).

Some suffering and sorrow in life is self-inflicted. Just as others can bring pain into our lives through their bad choices, so too can we. Agency is thus a two-edged sword. The scriptures are filled with examples of people who experienced all kinds of heartache and hardships on account of their own foolishness, disobedience, and wickedness. President Joseph Fielding Smith taught that many of the problems men experience in life come "because man himself . . . will not walk in righteousness," and so "the Lord permits all of these evils to come upon him" (3:28).

Acts of God. Whether the pains and problems of life come to us by reason of agency—our own as well as that of others—or the natural laws and conditions of mortality, our Father in Heaven often permits suffering to bring about his own purposes in our lives. We came to earth to obtain a physical body, to have our faith and devotion tested, to develop eternal relationships, and to gain necessary experience and education to prepare us for eternity. Thus, suffering and sorrows, trials and tribulations are part of the probationary and refining processes of life. Many scriptural passages witness of the merciful designs of God in allowing and causing adversity and afflictions in people's lives so as to turn them to him in greater faith and humility (1 Kings 8:35–36; Hosea 5:15; Isaiah 30:20; 48:10; Hebrews 12:5–8; Mosiah 1:17). Mormon taught "that except the Lord doth chasten his people with many afflictions, yea, except he doth visit them with death and with terror, and with famine and with all manner of pestilence, they will not remember him" (Helaman 12:3; see also Psalm 78:17–18, 28–35). In this manner, suffering can be redemptive in nature—leading us back to God, the ultimate source of strength, peace, comfort, and prosperity. President Joseph F. Smith taught that adversities and afflictions have the potential to be "for the good of [God's] children, to quicken their devotion to others, and to bring out their better natures. . . . They are the heralds and tokens of his final judgment, and the schoolmasters to teach the people to prepare themselves by righteous living for the coming of the Savior" (55).

Latter-day Saints recognize that much of the pain and suffering we experience in life serves to chasten and purify us. Life's tests and ordeals involve a stripping away of undesirable traits and false allegiances. The scriptures speak of this process as the "refiner's fire" (Malachi 3:2; D&C 105:6). Refining implies a melting away or an elimination of the dross, of things undesirable or unnecessary. After the refining there must also be a reshaping. Adversity and affliction can become important tools whereby this spiritual remodeling can be accomplished. When approached with courage, patience, faith in the Lord, and determination to endure valiantly, adversity—though not sought for—brings blessings both now and eternally.

"For verily I say unto you, blessed is he that keepeth my commandments, whether in life or in death; and he that is faithful in tribulation, the reward of the same is greater in the kingdom of heaven. Ye cannot behold with your natural eyes, for the present time, the design of your God concerning those things which shall come hereafter, and the glory which shall follow after much tribulation. For after much tribulation come the blessings" (D&C 58:2–4).

SOURCES

Kimball, Spencer W. *Faith Precedes the Miracle*. Salt Lake City: Deseret Book, 1972.

McKay, David O. "Man's Free Agency—An Eternal Principle of Progress." *Improvement Era,* Dec. 1965, 1072–73, 1096–98.

Smith, Joseph. *History of The Church of Jesus Christ of Latter-day Saints*. Edited by B. H. Roberts. 7 vols. 2d ed. rev. Salt Lake City: The Church of Jesus Christ of Latter-day Saints, 1932–51.

Smith, Joseph F. *Gospel Doctrine*. Salt Lake City: Deseret Book, 1939.

Smith, Joseph Fielding. *Doctrines of Salvation*. Compiled by Bruce R. McConkie. 3 vols. Salt Lake City: Bookcraft, 1954–56.

BLT

THEOLOGY

The word *theology* means "God talk," "sayings about God," or "the study of God." Theology is the serious intellectual investigation into such matters as who and what God is, why he is, how he may be approached, and the manner in which he and his ways may be, at least in a measure, comprehended. Sometimes we use the words *theology* and *doctrine* interchangeably in casual exchanges, but theology is actually the means, whereas doctrine is the end; theology is the endeavor, whereas doctrine is the result; theology is the exercise, whereas doctrine is the product; theology is the search, whereas doctrine is the find. Theological methods and undertakings are often extremely useful, but strictly speaking, members of The Church of Jesus Christ of Latter-day Saints have been instructed to "teach one another the *doctrine* of the kingdom" (D&C 88:77; emphasis added). Theology may be fascinating and certainly worth engaging, but doctrine is foundational and fundamental to the faith. True doctrine, when understood, changes attitudes and behavior (Packer, 16–18).

SOURCE

Packer, Boyd K. "Little Children." *Ensign,* Nov. 1986, 16–18.

RLM

TITHING

Tithing is God's law and system for the financing of his earthly kingdom. From the earliest days of recorded history, God's people have been commanded to give a tithe of their annual increase, whether it be in livestock or fruits of the field or cash income. Tithing was an essential element of the Lord's law of sacrifice. Abraham paid tithes to Melchizedek, the king of Salem (Genesis 14:18–20). The law of Moses specified that a tithe consists of a tenth of one's increase—"whether of the seed of the land, or of the fruit of the tree" (Leviticus 27:30). The tithing donation was to be the best of one's flocks or fruits of the field, for "it is holy unto the Lord" (Leviticus 27:30; Deuteronomy 14:22–29). These sacred tithing offerings were designated for the caring of the poor and needy (Deuteronomy 15:7–15), supporting the Levites who labored in the temple (Numbers 18:21–32), and building and maintaining the temple (1 Kings 12:25–33).

Part of the reforms instituted by Ezra and Nehemiah upon the return from the Babylonian captivity was a return to strict observance of the law of tithing (Nehemiah 10:37–38). In giving offerings of tithing, the worshipper was to make the sacrifice with a willing and joyful heart. Obedience to the law was to be both internal—the spirit of worship and sacrifice—and external—the actual donation of an honest tithe. Old Testament prophets rebuked the people when either the heart or the donation was not right. Amos was critical of those who paid tithes yet failed to live just and righteous lives (Amos 4:4–5). Malachi condemned those who would "rob God" by refusing to give unto the Lord the sacred tenth (Malachi 3:8). As with each of God's commandments, blessings are pronounced for obedience to this law. "Bring ye all the tithes into the storehouse," the Lord declared through Malachi, "that there may be meat in mine house, and prove me now herewith, saith the Lord of hosts, if I will not open you the windows of heaven, and pour you out a blessing, that there shall not be room enough to receive it" (Malachi 3:10).

In this last dispensation, the Lord has reminded the Saints that "it is a day of sacrifice, and a day for the tithing of my people; for he that is tithed shall not be burned at his coming" (D&C 64:23). While the biblical concept of tithing was generally understood, the early Saints viewed tithing not so much as an exact tenth of their increase but rather as any freewill offering given unto the Lord. In an effort to address the significant temporal needs of the Saints, the law of consecration and stewardship was given to the Church by revelation in 1831 (D&C 42:30–36). Many members of the Church, however, did not respond well to the call for total consecration. As a result, the difficult financial situation of the Church and individual members did not improve significantly. Amidst these challenges and the revealed mandate to build a temple and a city at Far West, Missouri, the Prophet Joseph prayed to know how to raise the necessary revenues to do the work of the Lord. "O! Lord, show unto thy servants how much thou requirest of the properties of thy people for a Tithing" (2:257). The answer came by revelation and is found in Doctrine and Covenants 119:4: "Those who have thus been tithed shall pay one-tenth of all their interest annually and this shall be a standing law unto them forever," the Lord declared. The term *interest* as used in the revelation has been authoritatively interpreted by the First Presidency to mean "income" (Letter).

Like Malachi in ancient times, modern-day prophets and apostles have repeatedly promised blessings for obedience to the law of tithing. The windows of heaven will indeed be opened and temporal and spiritual blessings poured out upon the heads of the faithful and obedient. "Pay your tithes that you may be worthy of the Lord's blessings," President Gordon B. Hinckley stated. "I will not promise that you will become wealthy. But I bear testimony that the Lord does reward generously in one way or another, those who keep His commandments." He further declared: "I do not say that if you pay an honest tithing you will realize your dream of a fine house, a Rolls Royce, and a condominium in Hawaii. *The Lord will open the windows of heaven according to our need, and not according to our greed.* If we are paying tithing to get rich, we are doing it for the wrong reason. The basic purpose for tithing is to provide the Church with the means needed to carry on the Lord's work. The blessing to the giver is an ancillary return, and that blessing may not be always in the form of financial or material benefit" (657–58).

Although the Lord has promised temporal blessings as we obey this law, the spiritual blessings that come from faithful payment of tithes and offerings are more significant and usually what we need most in our lives. "Then shall thy light break forth as the morning,"

Isaiah promised, "and thy righteousness shall go before thee; the glory of the Lord shall be thy rereward. Then shalt thou call, and the Lord shall answer; thou shalt cry, and he shall say, Here I am. . . . And the Lord shall guide thee continually, and satisfy thy soul in drought, and make fat thy bones; and thou shalt be like a watered garden, and like a spring of water whose waters fail not" (Isaiah 58:8-9, 11).

SOURCES

First Presidency Letter. The Church of Jesus Christ of Latter-day Saints. 19 Mar. 1970.

Hinckley, Gordon B. *Teachings of Gordon B. Hinckley*. Salt Lake City: Deseret Book, 1997.

Smith, Joseph. *The Papers of Joseph Smith*. Edited by Dean C. Jessee. 2 vols. Salt Lake City: Deseret Book, 1989–92.

BLT

TONGUES, GIFT OF

There are differing manifestations of the gift of tongues.

1. There have been occasions in the Church in this dispensation when persons have been moved upon by the Spirit to speak the language of God, the Adamic language described in modern revelation as "pure and undefiled" (Moses 6:6). In September 1832, when Brigham Young first met the Prophet Joseph Smith, Brother Young was called upon by the Prophet to pray in an evening meeting. "In my prayer," he said, "I spoke in tongues. As soon as we arose from our knees the brethren flocked around [Joseph], and asked his opinion concerning the gift of tongues that was upon me. He told them it was the pure Adamic language. Some said to him they expected he would condemn the gift brother Brigham had, but he said, 'No, it is of God, and the time will come when brother Brigham Young will preside over this Church'" (439). On numerous occasions thereafter, especially during the Pentecostal season surrounding the dedication of the Kirtland Temple, people spoke in tongues and interpreted them (Smith, 2:428).

2. On the day of Pentecost in the meridian of time, when the Holy Ghost was poured out in an unusually powerful manner, men and women were empowered by the Spirit to speak and understand a foreign but known language (Acts 2:1–6). In that same spirit, the servants of the Lord throughout the world are granted special privileges on a regular basis in learning languages, speaking them fluently, and

communicating the message of salvation to those of every nation, kindred, tongue, and people.

3. People speak in tongues when they speak by the power of the Holy Ghost, when they speak with "the tongue of angels," or, in other words, the "words of Christ" (2 Nephi 31:13; 32:2–3).

Joseph Smith offered words of caution regarding the gift of tongues: "As to the gift of tongues, all we can say is, that in this place, we have received it as the ancients did: we wish you, however, to be careful lest in this you be deceived. . . . Satan will no doubt trouble you about the gift of tongues, unless you are careful; you cannot watch him too closely, nor pray too much" (1:369).

"Tongues were given for the purpose of preaching among those whose language is not understood; as on the day of Pentecost, etc., and it is not necessary for tongues to be taught to the Church particularly, for any man that has the Holy Ghost, can speak of the things of God in his own tongue as well as to speak in another; for faith comes not by signs, but by hearing the word of God" (3:379).

"If you have a matter to reveal, let it be in your own tongue; do not indulge too much in the exercise of the gift of tongues, or the devil will take advantage of the innocent and unwary. You may speak in tongues for your own comfort, but I lay this down for a rule, that if anything is taught by the gift of tongues, it is not to be received for doctrine" (4:607).

"Be not so curious about tongues, do not speak in tongues except there be an interpreter present; the ultimate design of tongues is to speak to foreigners, and if persons are very anxious to display their intelligence, let them speak to such in their own tongues. The gifts of God are all useful in their place, but when they are applied to that which God does not intend, they prove an injury, a snare and a curse instead of a blessing" (5:31–32).

SOURCES

"History of Brigham Young." *Millennial Star* 25, no. 28 (11 July 1863): 295–96, 310–11, 326–28, 360–61, 374–76, 390–92, 406–8, 423–24, 438–40.

Smith, Joseph. *History of The Church of Jesus Christ of Latter-day Saints.* Edited by B. H. Roberts. 7 vols. 2d ed. rev. Salt Lake City: The Church of Jesus Christ of Latter-day Saints, 1932–51.

RLM

TRANSFIGURATION

Transfiguration is the process by which a person is raised temporarily to a higher spiritual plane in order to be able to abide an intense spiritual presence or environment. Moses was transfigured as he stood in the presence of God (Moses 1:11–14), as were Peter, James, and John on the holy mount (Matthew 17:1–8; Mark 9:2–8; Luke 9:28–36; D&C 63:20–21). The Three Nephites, as they were caught up to heaven (3 Nephi 28:15), as well as Joseph Smith in his First Vision (Joseph Smith–History 1:15–17), were transfigured. To be transfigured in this sense is to be infused with an added measure of divine strength and power. The process is described in modern revelation:

"And again, verily I say unto you that it is your privilege, and a promise I give unto you that have been ordained unto this ministry, that inasmuch as you strip yourselves from jealousies and fears, and humble yourselves before me, for ye are not sufficiently humble, the veil shall be rent and you shall see me and know that I am—not with the carnal neither natural mind, but with the spiritual. For no man has seen God at any time in the flesh, except quickened by the Spirit of God. Neither can any natural man abide the presence of God, neither after the carnal mind. Ye are not able to abide the presence of God now, neither the ministering of angels; wherefore, continue in patience until ye are perfected" (D&C 67:10–13).

RLM

TRANSFIGURATION, MOUNT OF

Approximately one week after Peter's great confession to the Lord that "thou art the Christ, the Son of the living God" and of Jesus' promise that the keys of the kingdom would be given (Matthew 16:16), the Master took Peter, James, and John to a high mountain to pray (Luke 9:28). It was the fall of the year, a time when the Feast of Tabernacles was celebrated among the Jews. It was half a year before Passover, six months before the Redeemer would be crucified and resurrected. It was a time of sober reflection for the Lord and of inquiry for the apostles. Mark writes that Jesus took "Peter, and James, and John, who asked him many questions concerning his sayings" (JST, Mark 9:2).

The Spirit of God was poured out abundantly on this occasion. Christ and his meridian First Presidency were transfigured—lifted spiritually to a higher plane in preparation for what they were about to see and receive (Smith, *History,* 3:387). According to the synoptic Gospels, Moses and Elias (Elijah) appeared. Luke points out that they "appeared in glory, and spake of [Jesus'] death, and also his resurrection, which he should accomplish at Jerusalem" (JST, Luke 9:31). Elder James E. Talmage observed: "In faithfully treading the path of His life's work, He had reached the verge of the valley of the shadow of death; and the human part of His nature called for refreshing. As angels had been sent to minister unto Him after the trying scenes of the forty days' fast and the direct temptation of Satan, and as, in the agonizing hour of His bloody sweat, He was to be sustained anew by angelic ministry, so at this critical and crucial period, the beginning of the end, visitants from the unseen world came to comfort and support Him" (373).

These ancient prophets appeared not only to comfort and prepare our Lord for what lay ahead but also to join with him in conferring priesthood keys or directing powers; these keys would enable the Twelve to lead the Church of Jesus Christ after the Savior's mortal ministry was completed. Both Moses and Elijah had been translated in their own day, taken from the earth without tasting death. They came to the holy mount with physical bodies in order to confer sacred authority. Moses the lawgiver, the one who had gathered and led ancient Israel for forty years, appeared. Drawing upon modern revelation as a commentary on ancient scripture, we would conclude that Moses conferred upon Peter, James, and John the keys of the gathering of Israel. This is precisely what Moses did during the Pentecostal season in Kirtland, Ohio, at the time of the dedication of the temple (D&C 110:11).

Elias appeared. As we know, the name *Elias* in the New Testament generally refers to the Old Testament prophet Elijah. Again, extrapolating from modern revelation, we understand that Elijah assisted the Savior in conferring upon Peter, James, and John the sealing powers, the right of presidency associated with binding and sealing on earth and in heaven, the very power Jesus had promised earlier and that he would soon deliver to all the Twelve (Matthew 16:19; 18:18).

The Prophet Joseph Smith explained, "The spirit, power, and calling of Elijah is, that ye have power to hold the key of the revelation, ordinances, oracles, powers and endowments of the fullness of the Melchisedeck Priesthood and of the kingdom of God on the earth; and to receive, obtain, and perform all the ordinances belonging to the kingdom of God." He taught further, "Then what you seal on earth, by the keys of Elijah, is sealed in heaven; and this is the power of Elijah, and this is the difference between the spirit and power of Elias and Elijah; for while the spirit of Elias is a forerunner, the power of Elijah is sufficient to make our calling and election sure" (6:251, 252).

The messenger Elias who appeared in 1836, whose specific identity is not mentioned in the record of the vision, "committed the dispensation of the gospel of Abraham, saying that in us and our seed all generations after us should be blessed" (D&C 110:12). That is, in modern times Elias restored the Abrahamic covenant, the patriarchal order, the keys associated with that order of the Melchizedek Priesthood we know as the new and everlasting covenant of marriage (D&C 131:1–4). Elias conferred the power whereby men and women who have been gathered out of the world may, through temples, be organized into eternal family units.

Mark adds the fascinating detail that John the Baptist was also present on the Mount of Transfiguration (JST, Mark 9:4). Whereas Moses and Elijah, both of whom had been translated and taken to heaven without tasting death, would have come with physical bodies to confer priesthood authority, the Baptist was still a spirit. He, like myriad others, would wait but six months more before his "sleeping dust was to be restored unto its perfect frame" (D&C 138:17). Peter, James, and John were apostles. They held the Melchizedek Priesthood. There would therefore be no need for John to confer any authority upon those who led the Twelve. "Perhaps he was there, as the last legal administrator under the Old Covenant, to symbolize that the law was fulfilled and all old things were done away, thus contrasting his position with that of Peter, James, and John who were then becoming the 'first' legal administrators of the New Kingdom" (McConkie, 1:404).

Modern prophets have suggested that Peter, James, and John may have received the temple endowment on the mount. President Joseph Fielding Smith taught that "when there is no house of the Lord and the work is urgent, the Lord makes it possible that . . . the ordinances that pertain to the house of the Lord may be performed in the wilderness, on a mountain top, or in a lake or a stream of water. I am convinced in my own mind that when the Savior took the three disciples up on the mount, . . . he there gave unto them the ordinances that pertain to the house of the Lord and that they were *endowed*. That was the only place they could go. That place became holy and sacred for the rites of salvation which were performed on that occasion" (2:170).

In speaking of this supernal experience many years later, the apostle Peter stated: "We have not followed cunningly devised fables, when we made known unto you the power and coming of our Lord Jesus Christ, but were eyewitnesses of his majesty. For he received from God the Father honour and glory, when there came such a voice to him from the excellent glory, This is my beloved Son, in whom I am well pleased. And this voice which came from heaven we heard, when we were with him in the holy mount. We have also a more sure word of prophecy; whereunto ye do well that ye take heed, as unto a light that shineth in a dark place, until the day dawn, and the day star arise in your hearts" (2 Peter 1:16–19). Joseph Smith, in offering prophetic commentary on this passage, said:

"And though they had heard an audible voice from heaven bearing testimony that Jesus was the Son of God, yet [Peter] says we have a more sure word of prophecy. . . . Now, wherein could they have a more sure word of prophecy than to hear the voice of God saying, This is my beloved Son. . . .

"Now for the secret and grand key. Though they might hear the voice of God and know that Jesus was the Son of God, this would be no evidence that their election and calling was made sure, that they had part with Christ, and were joint heirs with Him. They then would want that more sure word of prophecy, that they were sealed in the heavens and had the promise of eternal life in the kingdom of God. Then, having this promise sealed unto them, it was an anchor to the soul, sure and steadfast. Though the thunders might roll and lightnings flash, and earthquakes bellow, and war gather thick around, yet this hope and knowledge would support the soul in every hour of trial, trouble, and tribulation" (5:388–89).

A bright cloud overshadowed the three chief apostles, followed by a voice: "This is my beloved Son, in whom I am well pleased; hear ye him. And when the disciples heard it, they fell on their face, and were sore afraid. And Jesus came and touched them, and said, Arise, and be not afraid. And when they had lifted up their eyes, they saw no man, save Jesus only" (Matthew 17:5–8). It was the voice of the Eternal Father bearing record of the Word of his power. The *Shekinah,* or dwelling cloud, manifested the glory and presence of God, even as it had in ancient Israel (Exodus 33:9–11; Numbers 9:15–22; 11:25).

Finally, a modern revelation speaks of a vision that came to Peter, James, and John on the mount. "He that endureth in faith and doeth my will," the holy word attests, "the same shall overcome, and shall receive an inheritance upon the earth when the day of transfiguration shall come"—that day we know as the Millennium, initiated by the second coming of the Son of Man in glory. "When the earth shall be transfigured, even according to the pattern which was shown unto mine apostles upon the mount; of which account the fulness ye have not yet received" (D&C 63:20–21).

And so the three chief apostles descended the holy mount different from when they had ascended it. They were lifted spiritually, empowered, endowed, sealed, and prepared. Theirs was a perspective of what was, a view of what was to be, and a confidence in the God of heaven that would enable them to lead the Church of Jesus Christ into a difficult and uncertain future.

SOURCES

McConkie, Bruce R. *Doctrinal New Testament Commentary.* 3 vols. Salt Lake City: Deseret Book, 1966–73.

Smith, Joseph. *History of The Church of Jesus Christ of Latter-day Saints.* Edited by B. H. Roberts. 7 vols. 2d ed. rev. Salt Lake City: The Church of Jesus Christ of Latter-day Saints, 1932–51.

Smith, Joseph Fielding. *Doctrines of Salvation.* Compiled by Bruce R. McConkie. 3 vols. Salt Lake City: Bookcraft, 1954–56.

Talmage, James E. *Jesus the Christ.* Salt Lake City: Deseret Book, 1973.

RLM

TRANSGRESSION

In the scriptures the term *transgression* is generally used synonymously with *sin*—a willful violation of God's laws and commandments (Exodus 23:21; Isaiah 43:25; Ezekiel 18:30; Hebrews 9:15;

Mosiah 15:9; Alma 34:8; D&C 104:52). The word, however, can also mean to violate or go against a law, custom, rule, or socially accepted practice. This kind of violation, although a transgression, would not necessarily be the same as sin. For example, an ill-mannered person who may chew with his mouth open transgresses laws of etiquette, but this annoying and even offensive behavior would not be a sin. In a theological sense, some violations of God's laws, when done without malice, knowledge, or accountability, would likewise be classified as transgressions rather than sins. For example, little children or others who are not "capable of repentance" (D&C 20:71) may do something that is forbidden in God's or even man's laws, such as lying, stealing, or being unkind and hurtful. Yet committed without accountability, the act that would under other circumstances be sinful, would not be in this circumstance. Thus, all sins are transgressions, but not all transgressions are sins. Perhaps this is what the Prophet Joseph Smith meant when he said, "What many people call sin is not sin" (4:445). This distinction likewise applies to Adam and Eve partaking of the forbidden fruit while in the Garden of Eden. Certainly they transgressed a law and became mortal, but that action was not the same as a willful sin (2 Nephi 2:22–25; Moses 5:10–12).

SOURCE

Smith, Joseph. *History of The Church of Jesus Christ of Latter-day Saints*. Edited by
B. H. Roberts. 7 vols. 2d ed. rev. Salt Lake City: The Church of Jesus Christ of
Latter-day Saints, 1932–51.

BLT

TRANSLATED BEINGS

In the overall scheme of things, and under the divine superintendence of our God, who knows perfectly well when and under what circumstances to send his servants to earth, the Lord occasionally has chosen to translate his servants. That is, he has caused a change to come upon their bodies such that they are "sanctified in the flesh," no longer subject to sin, pain, bodily decay, and death, but are not resurrected (3 Nephi 28:7–9, 39). "Wherefore, I will that all men shall repent, for all are under sin, except those which I have reserved unto myself, holy men that ye know not of" (D&C 49:8).

Translated beings are still mortal, but their bodies have been transformed from a telestial to a terrestrial order (Smith, 4:210). They are given great power and are able to appear and disappear as they choose (3 Nephi 28:27–30). The nature of their activities is determined and governed by the Lord, and only he knows their whereabouts. The Three Nephites "did go forth upon the face of the land, and did minister unto all the people, uniting as many to the church as would believe in their preaching; baptizing them, and as many as were baptized did receive the Holy Ghost" (3 Nephi 28:18). They remain in this condition until the second coming of Christ in glory, at which time they will undergo a change equivalent to death, being changed from mortality to resurrected and glorified immortality (3 Nephi 28:7–8, 39–40). Indeed, as the Prophet Joseph Smith explained: "Translated bodies cannot enter into rest until they have undergone a change equivalent to death" (4:425).

Persons in scripture who have been translated include Enoch and his city (Genesis 5:21–24; D&C 107:48–49; Moses 7:68–69), Melchizedek and the city of Salem (Alma 13:14–19; JST, Genesis 14:25–40), Moses (Alma 45:19), Elijah (2 Kings 2; D&C 110:13), Alma the Younger (Alma 45:18–19), Nephi the son of Helaman (3 Nephi 1:2–3; 2:9), John the Beloved (John 21:20–23; D&C 7), and the Three Nephite apostles (3 Nephi 28).

SOURCE

Smith, Joseph. *History of The Church of Jesus Christ of Latter-day Saints.* Edited by B. H. Roberts. 7 vols. 2d ed. rev. Salt Lake City: The Church of Jesus Christ of Latter-day Saints, 1932–51.

RLM

TREE OF LIFE

God "made . . . to grow the tree of life also in the midst of the garden" of Eden (Genesis 2:9). After Adam and Eve partook of the fruit of the tree of knowledge, God placed "cherubims, and a flaming sword which turned every way, to keep the way of the tree of life . . . lest [man] put forth his hand, and take also of the tree of life, and eat, and live for ever" (Genesis 3:24, 22). Adam fell by partaking of the forbidden fruit and, consequently, "all mankind became a lost and fallen people" (Alma 12:22). If it had been possible for Adam to partake of the fruit of the tree of life at that time, there would have been no death and no "space" of time to repent and "prepare to meet God." Adam and Eve "would have been forever miserable, having no preparatory state; and thus the plan of redemption would have been frustrated, and the word of God would have been void, taking none effect" (Alma 12:24, 26; see also 42:2–6).

Through the mercy and grace of the Lord, the way is opened during this preparatory state whereby we may access the tree of life. The Lord invites: "Come unto me and ye shall partake of the fruit of the tree of life. . . . Come and be baptized unto repentance, that ye also may be partakers of the fruit of the tree of life" (Alma 5:34, 62). But "if [we] will not nourish the word, looking forward with an eye of faith to the fruit thereof, [we] can never pluck of the fruit of the tree of life" (Alma 32:40). The apostle John taught that the "gates into the city" of God are opened to those who are given the "right to the tree of life" because they keep the commandments of God (Revelation 22:14). These are they who overcome the pull of the fallen world through the atonement of Christ and are thereby permitted to "eat of the tree of life" (Revelation 2:7), which means everlasting life.

A representation of the tree of life as a tree and "the love of God" was reported in Lehi's dream and Nephi's vision of the dream (1 Nephi 11:22). Although the tree was the focal point of the dream, Lehi did not see it until he acknowledged his lost and fallen state and prayed to God for mercy (1 Nephi 8:7–10). He described the representative fruit as "desirable to make one happy"—the most sweet and white to exceed all other whiteness. Furthermore, tasting it filled him with a tremendous desire to share it with others (1 Nephi 8:10). The multitudes that arrived at the tree and remained there in the dream did so by "continually holding fast to the rod of iron," and then they "fell down" at the tree to partake (1 Nephi 8:30).

In response to Nephi's request to understand the interpretation of the tree of life as "the love of God" (1 Nephi 11:25), the Spirit showed Nephi the mortal life and ministry of Jesus Christ, including times when people fell "down at his feet and worship[ped] him," as was symbolized at the tree of life (1 Nephi 11:24). "For God so loved the world, that he gave his only begotten Son" (John 3:16). As the apostle John likened the Savior to the "word of God," so Alma likened the "word of God" (Alma 32:1, 16) to a seed that becomes the tree of everlasting life, whose fruit is likewise "sweet above all that is sweet, and which is white above all that is white, yea, and pure above all that is pure; and ye shall feast upon this fruit even until ye are filled, that ye hunger not, neither shall ye thirst" (Alma 32:42).

The tree of life, further, is a representation of Jesus Christ, our Redeemer and Savior. Alma implored: "Cast about your eyes and begin to believe in the Son of God, that he will come to redeem his people, and that he shall suffer and die to atone for their sins; and that he shall rise again from the dead, which shall bring to pass the resurrection, that all men shall stand before him, to be judged at the last and judgment day, according to their works. . . . I desire that ye shall plant this word in your hearts, and as it beginneth to swell even so nourish it by your faith. And behold, it will become a tree, springing up in you unto everlasting life" (Alma 33:22–23). Only by coming in faith to the tree, which is Christ, do we in this life taste the sweetness of which Alma spoke and enjoy exaltation in the life to come.

CFO

TRIBES OF ISRAEL

The patriarch Jacob, grandson of Abraham, was also called Israel, a new name he received from a divine messenger after seeing God face to face (Genesis 32:28–30; 35:10). Jacob had twelve sons with his four wives: Reuben, Simeon, Levi, Judah, Issachar, and Zebulun (by Leah), Dan and Naphtali (by Bilhah), Gad and Asher (by Zilpah), and Joseph and Benjamin (by Rachel; Genesis 29:32–30:24; 35:16–18). As patriarch of the family, Jacob passed his new name on to his descendants. His sons and their posterity constitute the twelve tribes of Israel.

Jacob gave patriarchal blessings to his sons, prophesying their destinies and their families' destinies (Genesis 49; Deuteronomy 33). The two richest blessings were given to Judah and Joseph, leaders of the family (Richards, 9–10). Judah was blessed with political leadership of Israel until the advent of the Messiah (Genesis 49:10). Joseph's posterity would prevail to the "utmost bound of the everlasting hills" (Genesis 49:26)—the Americas. Jacob also gave blessings to the two sons of Joseph—Ephraim and Manasseh—and adopted them as his own sons: "And now, of thy two sons, Ephraim and Manasseh, which were born unto thee in the land of Egypt, before I came unto thee into Egypt; behold, they are mine, and the God of my fathers shall bless them; even as Reuben and Simeon they shall be blessed, for they are mine; wherefore they shall be called after my name. (Therefore they were called Israel.) And thy issue which thou begettest after them, shall be thine, and shall be called after the name of their brethren in their inheritance, in the tribes; therefore they were called the tribes of Manasseh and of Ephraim" (JST, Genesis 48:5–6).

Thus, the tribe of Joseph received a double portion of the inheritance of Israel. Joseph's inheritance was divided between his two sons. Ephraim and Manasseh came to be reckoned as two of the twelve tribes of Israel in terms of inheritance. Levites received no land inheritance because they were set apart for priesthood service throughout the other tribes (Genesis 49:7; Numbers 3:1–4, 49). Furthermore, as the chronicler notes, Reuben lost the birthright, or leadership of the family, through wickedness, and Ephraim became the leader of the tribes of Israel: "Now the sons of Reuben the firstborn of Israel, (for he was the firstborn; but, forasmuch as he defiled his father's bed, his birthright was given unto the sons of Joseph the son of Israel: and the genealogy is not to be reckoned after the birthright. For Judah prevailed above his brethren, and of him came the chief ruler; but the birthright was Joseph's:)" (1 Chronicles 5:1–2; see also Jeremiah 31:9).

After the death of King Solomon, the once-united kingdom of the twelve tribes split into two factions, the kingdom of Judah in the south (922–586 B.C.) and the kingdom of Israel in the north, also called Ephraim (922–721 B.C.). Because of continual wickedness the ten tribes in the north (with their capital at Samaria) were conquered by the Assyrians and deported from their lands. They became known as the lost ten tribes of Israel. But as he promised, the Lord will begin to gather scattered Israel and bring them back to their ancestral home in the last days in preparation for the millennial reign of Christ (Articles of Faith 1:10; Isaiah 5:26; 54:7; 1 Nephi 15:12–17; 2 Nephi 10:8).

In the last days the tribe of Ephraim will be gathered first to the gospel covenant and then will bear the message of the restored gospel to the world. Ephraim will preside over the gathering of Israel and administer the ordinances of salvation. The Lord revealed to the Prophet Joseph Smith that "they [the scattered tribes of Israel] shall bring forth their rich treasures unto the children of Ephraim, my servants. . . . And there shall they fall down and be crowned with glory, even in Zion, by the hands of the servants of the Lord, even the children of Ephraim. And they shall be filled with songs of everlasting joy. Behold, this is the blessing of the everlasting God upon the tribes of Israel, and the richer blessing upon the head of Ephraim and his fellows" (D&C 133:30, 32–34).

John the Revelator also saw that in the preparation for Christ's millennial reign 144,000 high priests would perform a special mission on the earth. Twelve thousand will be called out of each of the tribes of Israel. They "are ordained out of every nation, kindred, tongue, and people, by the angels to whom is given power over the nations of the earth, to bring as many as will come to the church of the Firstborn" (D&C 77:11).

SOURCE

Richards, LeGrand. *Israel! Do You Know?* Salt Lake City: Deseret Book: 1954.

ACS

TRINITY

Latter-day Saints believe in the Trinity in the sense that we believe in the Father, the Son, and the Holy Ghost, the three members of the Godhead. We do not, however, subscribe to all the teachings of the post-New Testament church councils and creeds that set forth what some have called the ontological oneness of the Father, the Son, and the Holy Spirit—that these three, while three in person, are yet one in being. Eleven days before his death Joseph Smith testified, "I have always declared God to be a distinct personage, Jesus Christ a separate and distinct personage from God the Father, and . . . the Holy Ghost a distinct personage and a Spirit: and these three constitute three distinct personages and three Gods" (4:474). These three glorious persons are one in every way we might conceive (mind, might, power, majesty, glory, purpose, and attributes), but Latter-day Saint scripture and prophetic teaching counsel us against shrouding the Godhead in mystery and creating a theological and spiritual chasm between God and man that will never be spanned, a divide that is both doctrinally unnecessary and practically unfruitful.

SOURCE

Smith, Joseph. *History of The Church of Jesus Christ of Latter-day Saints.* Edited by
B. H. Roberts. 7 vols. 2d ed. rev. Salt Lake City: The Church of Jesus Christ of
Latter-day Saints, 1932–51.

RLM

TRUE VINE

In an allegory related during the Last Supper, Jesus portrayed his
Father as the Husbandman of the vineyard; himself as the True Vine,
or main trunk of the vineyard; and his apostles as the branches, or the
dependent vines that grow from the True Vine (John 15:1–8). The
True Vine depends on the Husbandman, and the branches depend on
the True Vine. If the branches "abide" in the True Vine, they will produce "much fruit." If a branch is separated from the True Vine, it "cannot bear fruit of itself" (John 15:4), any more than any of the apostles
can bring about righteousness except they abide in Christ. Taking a
broader view, none of us can hope for eternal life unless we are connected or grafted into the True Vine, "for without [Jesus Christ] ye can
do nothing" (John 15:5; see also 1 Nephi 15:15).

CFO

TRUTH

The Lord has defined *truth* as "knowledge of things as they are,
and as they were, and as they are to come" (D&C 93:24; see also
Jacob 4:13). President Brigham Young declared:

"God has revealed all the truth that is now in the possession of the
world, whether it be scientific or religious. The whole world is under
obligation to him for what they know and enjoy; they are indebted to
him for it all. . . .

"I want to say to my friends that we believe in all good. If you can
find a truth in heaven, earth, or hell, it belongs to our doctrine. We believe it; it is ours; we claim it. . . . Our religion is simply the truth. It is
all said in this one expression—it embraces all truth, wherever found,
in all the works of God and man that are visible or invisible to mortal
eye. . . . 'Mormonism' embraces all truth that is revealed and that is
unrevealed, whether religious, political, scientific, or philosophical. . . .

"It comprehends all true science known by man, angels, and the gods. There is one true system and science of life; all else tends to death. That system emanates from the Fountain of life" (2).

Truth—that which really is, was, and will be—is absolute, fixed, unchanging, and eternal (Psalm 117:2; D&C 1:39; 88:66). In contrast, theories, opinions, perspectives, and applications of truth may be relative and changing. The Lord has said, "All things unto me are spiritual" (D&C 29:34); however, that we "may naturally understand" (D&C 29:33), he sometimes refers to some truths that are temporal and some truths that are spiritual by nature. President J. Reuben Clark Jr. stated:

"In a way and speaking generally, temporal truths relate to the materials, forces, compositions that are universe-wide, and to matters that generally are covered as matters of science, economics, sociology, politics, and like matters—I am not listing, I am only indicating—they are essentially non-scriptural, except where the Lord has declared the truth.

"Spiritual truths include all matters relating to the principles and doctrines of religion, as generally termed, and all matters of scriptures dealing therewith, and all matters affecting the progress, development, and destiny of the soul of man. Again I am not listing, but indicating.

"The first matters, temporal truths, are not normally controlled by the revelations of the Lord concerning them and are, so to say, in the public domain. They may be discussed, investigated, experimented upon, theorized about, and handled in any way we wish, with the exception noted.

"Spiritual truths, on the other hand, are to be found in and are governed and controlled by the revelations of our Heavenly Father as contained in the scriptures and in inspired utterances of his prophets" (145).

As Latter-day Saints, we are commanded to seek after and learn as much truth as we can in both temporal and spiritual fields (D&C 88:78–84). Yet we understand that not all truth is of equal value, either on earth or in eternity. Elder Neal A. Maxwell insightfully observed: "As, more and more, we brush against truth, we sense that it has a hierarchy of importance. Some truths are salvationally significant and others are not" (69). Therefore, the Lord has commanded us to seek truth both "by study and also by faith" (D&C 88:118). Some truths can be obtained merely by the intellect, but saving truths—the truths of the gospel—cannot be obtained without faith, obedience, and "bending of the whole soul through worthy living to become attuned to the Holy Spirit of the Lord, the calling up from the depths of one's own mental searching, and the linking of our own efforts to receive the true witness of the Spirit" (Lee, 92–93).

Knowing the truth about some things may make our lives better on earth and are important. But in the ultimate sense, knowledge of one dimension of truth is imperative. Jesus referred to himself as "the truth" (John 14:6) and said, "The truth shall make you free" (John 8:32). Jesus makes us free (D&C 98:8). He is the source of salvation—the embodiment of God's glory, even light and truth (D&C 93:36, 37, 39, 40, 42). He is the means whereby we can become free from death and hell. Knowing "the truth" through obedience to his laws and ordinances and by studying his gospel makes it possible ultimately to acquire all truth and know all things (D&C 88:66–67; 93:28; Alma 12:9–11).

SOURCES

Clark, J. Reuben, Jr. *Selected Papers on Religion, Education, and Youth.* Edited by David H. Yarn Jr. Provo, Utah: Brigham Young University Press, 1984.

Lee, Harold B. *The Teachings of Harold B. Lee.* Edited by Clyde J. Williams. Salt Lake City: Bookcraft, 1996.

Maxwell, Neal A. "The Inexhaustible Gospel." *Ensign,* Apr. 1993, 68–73.

Young, Brigham. *Discourses of Brigham Young.* Selected and arranged by John A. Widtsoe. Salt Lake City: Deseret Book, 1954.

BLT

TYPE

A type is something that represents or exemplifies something else. Types are symbols and usually involve something physical to represent something spiritual. They may be in the form of an object, such as the blemish-free male lamb slain on the altar of the temple that symbolically points to the infinite atoning sacrifice of the Lamb of God. Similarly, the brazen serpent that Moses raised for the Israelites to gaze upon and be healed from fiery serpent bites was a prophetic type of the Savior being lifted up upon the cross to spiritually heal all mankind (Numbers 21:6–9; John 3:14; Alma 37:44–47; Helaman 8:13–15; 3 Nephi 15:9). Alma taught that the Liahona was a type for the "word of Christ" (Alma 37:44). A person may be a type. For example, we see Christ's redemptive role in the lives and ministries of prophets such as

Joseph, son of Jacob, who redeemed his own family while in Egypt, and Moses, who gave the law to the children of Israel, delivered them from bondage, and acted as a mediator between the people and God. In a manner, all prophets are types of the Savior. Likewise, historical events can symbolize and foreshadow other, even more spiritually significant occurrences.

For example, Abraham's willingness to sacrifice his son Isaac on Mount Moriah pointed to the ultimate sacrifice that would occur on that same mountain in the meridian of time with the crucifixion of the Son of God (Jacob 4:5). The Book of Mormon prophet Abinadi taught that his death as a martyr at the hands of wicked men would be "a type and a shadow of things which are to come" (Mosiah 13:10; see also Alma 25:10). Likewise, the destruction on the American continent after the death of Christ in the Old World and the subsequent appearance of the resurrected Savior to the "more righteous part" of the people (3 Nephi 10:12) at the temple in Bountiful are types of the events that will precede the second coming of Jesus Christ.

Types that represent future events are called shadows because they foreshadow or symbolically prophesy of the future. Innumerable types and shadows are found in the scriptures. "All things have their likeness, and all things are created and made to bear record of me," the Savior declared to Father Adam, "both things which are temporal, and things which are spiritual; things which are in the heavens above, and things which are on the earth, and things which are in the earth, and things which are under the earth, both above and beneath: all things bear record of me" (Moses 6:63; see also 2 Nephi 11:4; Mosiah 3:15). Elder Bruce R. McConkie taught: "To crystallize in our minds the eternal verities which we must accept and believe to be saved, to dramatize their true meaning and import with an impact never to be forgotten, to center our attention on these saving truths again and again and again, the Lord uses similitudes. Abstract principles may easily be forgotten or their deep meaning overlooked, but visual performances and actual experiences are registered on the mind in such a way as never to be lost" (377).

Symbols help us to comprehend and appreciate deep, spiritual concepts. "Spiritual truths are sometimes very difficult to teach," President Boyd K. Packer has explained. "The reason the teaching of the gospel ofttimes is so difficult is that ideals in the gospel are such intangible things as faith, repentance, love, humility, reverence, obedience, modesty, and so forth. The dimensions of size and shape and color and texture just do not serve us there. In teaching the gospel we do not re-create the material world around us; we deal with the intangible world within us" (40; paragraphing altered). As in ancient times, symbolic types and shadows can be found today in the ordinances of the gospel and in Church teachings and practices. Baptism by immersion is a shadow of the death, burial, and resurrection of Christ. It is a type of a newness of life that comes to one who embraces the gospel and partakes of the Savior's redemptive atonement. The emblems of the sacrament are types of the broken body and spilt blood of the Redeemer and symbolic reminders of our own covenants. Perhaps nowhere is the use of symbolism—of types and shadows—more profound than in the ordinances of the temple. Types are all around us—symbols that remind us of God and beckon us to him, teach us of his gospel, and testify of spiritual realities. "All things which have been given of God from the beginning of the world, unto man," the Book of Mormon prophet Jacob testified, "are the typifying of him" (2 Nephi 11:4).

SOURCES

McConkie, Bruce R. *The Promised Messiah: The First Coming of Christ.* Salt Lake City: Deseret Book, 1978.

Packer, Boyd K. *The Holy Temple.* Salt Lake City: Bookcraft, 1980.

BLT

URIM AND THUMMIM

The Hebrew plural nouns *urim* and *thummim* mean "lights" and "perfections." However, the two words together denote a physical object, described by Joseph Smith as "two stones in silver bows . . . fastened to a breastplate" (Joseph Smith–History 1:35). The Urim and Thummim is an instrument used to receive revelation. It was deposited with the gold plates given to Joseph Smith, "and the possession and use of these stones were what constituted 'seers' in ancient or former times; . . . God had prepared them for the purpose of translating the book [of Mormon]" (Joseph Smith–History 1:35). The Lord testified that the

Prophet Joseph Smith was given power to translate the ancient records by means of the Urim and Thummim (D&C 10:1), and he received several revelations through this instrument (D&C 3, 6, 11, 14).

The history of the Urim and Thummim indicates that there was likely more than one. Chronologically, the first scriptural reference to the Urim and Thummim, though not explicitly named, appears to be in connection with the visions and revelations given to the brother of Jared. At that time, "two stones" were mentioned that he was to seal up along with the revelations he had written down. The Lord then indicated how the stones would be used: "For behold, the language which ye shall write I have confounded; wherefore I will cause in my own due time that these stones shall magnify to the eyes of men these things which ye shall write" (Ether 3:24). Later, "the people of Limhi brought to Mosiah a record, 'engraven on plates of ore,' [Mosiah 21:27] which record Mosiah translated, by the aid of 'two stones which were fastened into the two rims of bow,' and which gave an account of the Jaredites [Mosiah 28:11–19]" (Smith, 3:224). This was the Urim and Thummim hidden by Moroni and received by Joseph Smith—the same Urim and Thummim possessed by the brother of Jared (D&C 17:1).

The patriarch Abraham also possessed a Urim and Thummim and learned about the nature of the physical universe by using it. "And I, Abraham, had the Urim and Thummim, which the Lord my God had given unto me, in Ur of the Chaldees. . . . And the Lord said unto me, by the Urim and Thummim, that Kolob was after the manner of the Lord, according to its times and seasons in the revolutions thereof; that one revolution was a day unto the Lord, after his manner of reckoning, it being one thousand years according to the time appointed unto that whereon thou standest. This is the reckoning of the Lord's time, according to the reckoning of Kolob" (Abraham 3:1, 4).

Biblical references to the Urim and Thummim show it to be the means by which the Aaronic high priest inquired of the Lord. Aaron and the priests in Israel possessed it from generation to generation (Exodus 28:30; Leviticus 8:8; Numbers 27:21; Deuteronomy 33:8; 1 Samuel 28:6). Apparently, the breastplate containing the Urim and Thummim was worn over the chest, specifically the heart. Some scholars take Ezra 2:63 and Nehemiah 7:65 to mean that the Urim and Thummim was not found in ancient Israel after the Babylonian exile.

Though Lehi and Nephi do not speak of the Urim and Thummim, they are referred to from the days of Mosiah as "interpreters," requiring divine authorization to use them and being passed down from prophet to prophet (Mosiah 8:13, 19; 28:20; Alma 37:21; Ether 4:5). A comment from the Ammon who led an expedition to the land of Nephi helps us understand the connection between the Urim and Thummim and those authorized to use it: "And the things are called interpreters, and no man can look in them except he be commanded, lest he should look for that he ought not and he should perish. And whosoever is commanded to look in them, the same is called seer" (Mosiah 8:13).

The Prophet Joseph Smith received the same Urim and Thummim "given to the brother of Jared upon the mount, when he talked with the Lord face to face" and that the Three Witnesses were promised a glimpse of if they trusted the Lord (D&C 17:1). President Joseph Fielding Smith stated that this Urim and Thummim was "separate and distinct" from the one possessed by the patriarch Abraham and the Aaronic Priesthood leaders in ancient Israel (3:222).

When Joseph received the Book of Mormon plates and the Urim and Thummim, he said he was commanded to show them "only to those to whom I should be commanded to show them" (Joseph Smith–History 1:42). As late as 1842 several sources indicate that he once again had access to the Urim and Thummim and that several individuals saw it. In his journal dated 19 February 1842, Wilford Woodruff wrote, "The Lord is blessing Joseph with power to reveal the mysteries of the kingdom of God; to translate through the Urim and Thummim ancient records and hieroglyphics as old as Abraham or Adam which causes our hearts to burn within us while we behold their glorious truths opened unto us" (2:155).

From the life of Wilford Woodruff, we read that in December 1841, on the 26th and 27th the Twelve visited the home of the Prophet. On one of these days Elder Woodruff says in his journal that the Prophet showed him and others for the first time the Urim and Thummim (Cowley, 157).

In July 1842 the editors of the *Millennial Star* wrote, "The record (Book of Abraham) is now in course of translation by the means of the Urim and Thummim, and proves to be a record written partly by the father of the faithful, Abraham, and finished by Joseph when in

Egypt" (47). The revelatory function of a Urim and Thummim, its use as an instrument of personal revelation in a day yet future, has been described in latter-day scripture: "The angels do not reside on a planet like this earth; but they reside in the presence of God, on a globe like a sea of glass and fire, where all things for their glory are manifest, past, present, and future, and are continually before the Lord. The place where God resides is a great Urim and Thummim. This earth, in its sanctified and immortal state, will be made like unto crystal and will be a Urim and Thummim to the inhabitants who dwell thereon, whereby all things pertaining to an inferior kingdom, or all kingdoms of a lower order, will be manifest to those who dwell on it; and this earth will be Christ's. Then the white stone mentioned in Revelation 2:17, will become a Urim and Thummim to each individual who receives one, whereby things pertaining to a higher order of kingdoms will be made known; and a white stone is given to each of those who come into the celestial kingdom, whereon is a new name written, which no man knoweth save he that receiveth it. The new name is the key word" (D&C 130:6–11).

SOURCES

Cowley, Matthias F. *Wilford Woodruff: History of His Life and Labors as Recorded in His Daily Journals.* Salt Lake City: Bookcraft, 1964.

"Editorial Remarks." *Millennial Star* 3, no. 3 (1 July 1842): 44–47.

Smith, Joseph Fielding. *Doctrines of Salvation.* Compiled by Bruce R. McConkie. 3 vols. Salt Lake City: Bookcraft, 1954–56.

Woodruff, Wilford. *Wilford Woodruff's Journal.* Edited by Scott G. Kenney and Susan Staker. 9 vols. Midvale, Utah: Signature Books, 1984–91.

ACS

USURY

The term *usury* comes from the Latin *usura,* meaning "interest" charged on loans. The Mosaic law forbade charging interest to fellow Israelites or to sojourners, a term that might be better translated as "resident aliens"—those non-Israelites living in the land (Exodus 22:25; Leviticus 25:35–37; Deuteronomy 15:7–11). The prohibition extended to money, food, or anything else that might earn interest. The law did permit, however, the charging of interest to a complete stranger or foreigner (Deuteronomy 23:20).

The law regarding usury assisted the worthy poor who embraced

Jehovah's true religion and parallels the welfare program of the Lord's Church in modern times. The Jewish historian Josephus stated: "Let no one lend to any one of the Hebrews upon usury, neither usury of what is eaten or what is drunken; for it is not just to make [take] advantage of the misfortunes of one of thy own countrymen; but when thou hast been assistant to his necessities, think it thy gain, if thou obtainest their gratitude to thee; and withal that reward which will come to thee from God, for thy humanity towards him" (4.8.25).

Nehemiah condemned the practice of nobles in his day who, ironically, exacted usury from their own countrymen after they bought or redeemed them from the Gentiles to whom they had been sold. This human chattel was being sold again, as it were, to their fellow Israelites through exorbitant interest rates they could not pay (Nehemiah 5:7–8). Job described the poverty that caused the orphan and infant of the poor to be seized for payment of debt (Job 24:3–10). Not surprisingly, Ezekiel condemns usury, saying the righteous man does not lend to charge interest (Ezekiel 18:8). He also puts usury in the same category with extortion and accepting bribes to shed blood (Ezekiel 22:12).

During his mortal ministry, Jesus Christ recognized the practice of usury and crafted parables that portrayed the concept (Matthew 25:14–30; Luke 19:12–27). There is no indication that he explicitly condemned it; however, he certainly preached an expansive kind of generosity, urging his followers to "lend, hoping for nothing again" (Luke 6:35). Interestingly, the Koran states in fairly strong terms that God condemns usury and blesses generous charitable giving (Sura Al-Baqara 2:275–76). In modern times Latter-day Saint Church leaders have not condemned the business practice of charging reasonable and fair interest. But what the scriptures describe as exorbitant interest to get "unjust gain" may be a different matter (Proverbs 28:8).

SOURCE

Josephus, Flavius. *The Antiquities of the Jews*. In *Josephus: Complete Works*. Translated by William Whiston. Grand Rapids, Mich.: Kregel Publications, 1960.

ACS

VANITY

Vain means "empty," "futile," or "worthless." We commonly think of vanity as "conceit," "self-absorption," and "pride." All of these meanings are used in the scriptures. The Lord condemned "vain repetitions" in prayer—superfluous phrases uttered more to impress others than to worship God, and empty words unaccompanied by devotion and obedience (Matthew 6:7). Likewise the Master condemned those who "in vain . . . do worship me" because they draw "nigh unto me with their mouth, and honoureth me with their lips; but their heart is far from me" (Matthew 15:8). Taking the name of God in vain would include more than profaning the name of God. In this way, the covenant becomes vain—empty and without effect.

Vanity is an attribute of the "natural man," and truly all fallen men and women are vain—in all meanings of the word—until they overcome the "natural man" through the atonement of Jesus Christ (Mosiah 3:19). "All are subjected to vanity," the Prophet Joseph Smith declared, "while they travel through the crooked paths and difficulties which surround them. Where is the man that is free from vanity? None ever were perfect but Jesus" (4:358). In Lehi's vision, the great and spacious building represented the "vain imaginations . . . of men" (1 Nephi 12:18). The vanities of the world can be anything or anyone that becomes more important than God and his ways. "Ye cannot serve God and mammon," Jesus warned (Matthew 6:24). Satan promotes vanity among men by "puffing them up with pride, tempting them to seek for power, and authority, and riches, and the vain things of the world" (3 Nephi 6:15). Wealth, worldliness, ambition, and the honors of men will not bring immortality and eternal life. Thus, they are vain—empty, shallow, futile, and worthless—in the eternal scheme of things (Alma 39:14). For this reason the Book of Mormon prophet Jacob, paraphrasing the words of Isaiah, declared, "Do not spend money for that which is of no worth, nor your labor for that which cannot satisfy," but instead "come unto the Holy One of Israel, and feast upon that which perisheth not, neither can be corrupted" (2 Nephi 9:51; see also vv. 30–39).

Vanity is trusting "in the arm of flesh" (2 Nephi 4:34)—whether it be the philosophies and learning of men or our own desires, including an inordinate desire to be accepted by others—instead of trusting in the Lord and "relying wholly upon the merits of him who is mighty to save" (2 Nephi 4:34; 31:19). God's ways are always higher and better than man's ways (Isaiah 55:9). Vanity—pride, conceit, and self-deception—can cause us to think otherwise (2 Nephi 9:28–29). In the end, however, our vanity will always be vain—frail, futile, fruitless.

SOURCE

Smith, Joseph. *History of The Church of Jesus Christ of Latter-day Saints.* Edited by B. H. Roberts. 7 vols. 2d ed. rev. Salt Lake City: The Church of Jesus Christ of Latter-day Saints, 1932–51.

BLT

VIRGIN BIRTH

Eighty-three years before the Savior's birth, Alma declared, "And behold, [Jesus] shall be born of Mary, at Jerusalem which is the land of our forefathers, she being a virgin, a precious and chosen vessel, who shall be overshadowed and conceive by the power of the Holy Ghost, and bring forth a son, yea, even the Son of God" (Alma 7:10). Gabriel announced to Mary, "The Holy Ghost shall come upon thee, and the power of the Highest shall overshadow thee: therefore also that holy thing which shall be born of thee shall be called the Son of God" (Luke 1:35). Jesus Christ is the Son of God—the firstborn spirit Son of God the Father and the Only Begotten of the Father in the flesh. This expression, declaration, and doctrine of the divine Sonship of Christ is neither mythical nor metaphorical. From Mary, a mortal woman who had never had sexual relations with any man (Luke 1:34), Jesus inherited mortality, including the capacity to die; from God, the immortal Man of Holiness, Jesus inherited immortality, the capacity to live forever. He is the Son of God, and he is God the Son.

RLM

VISIONS

One of the means by which God speaks to man and reveals things of eternal import is through visions. By the power of the Holy Ghost, a person may have his "spiritual eyes" opened and see things not discernible by the natural man. These may include seeing past or future events, symbolic images and representations, heavenly beings and kingdoms. The scriptures are replete with examples of each. Enoch and Abraham saw the premortal spirit world (Moses 6:36; Abraham 3:22–25). Moses beheld the grandeur of all of God's creations (Moses 1:8, 27–28). Daniel saw four beasts, representing the kingdoms of the world, that would be destroyed by the kingdom of God (Daniel 7). Peter received a symbolic view of unclean beasts, whereby he learned that the gospel was to go to the Gentiles (Acts 10:9–18). John's apocalyptic visions are recorded in the book of Revelation. In the Book of Mormon we read of Nephi's vision of the future ministry of Jesus Christ and his crucifixion and resurrection, the coming forth of the Bible and the Book of Mormon, the discovery and founding of America, and the latter-day Restoration (1 Nephi 11–14). We also read of the vision by the brother of Jared of "all the inhabitants of the earth which had been, and also all that would be" (Ether 3:25). In this dispensation important visions have likewise been received and recorded in holy writ, commencing with Joseph Smith's First Vision (Joseph Smith–History 1:14–20). In the Doctrine and Covenants we read of Joseph's visions of heavenly messengers (D&C 2, 110), the kingdoms of glory (D&C 76, 137), Lucifer's premortal rebellion and the war in heaven (D&C 76:25–39), and "the glory of the Son, on the right hand of the Father" (D&C 76:20). President Joseph F. Smith's vision of the Savior's postmortal ministry to the spirit world and the great redemptive work for the dead is found in Doctrine and Covenants 138.

While visitations are often considered visions, the distinction could be made that visions are seen in the mind and understood by the power of the Spirit, while visitations occur when heavenly ministrants appear in person to a mortal. Such was the case with the visitation of the Father and the Son to Joseph Smith in the First Vision; the visitation of Moroni and the delivery of the gold plates to the Prophet; the restoration of the priesthood by John the Baptist and Peter, James, and John; and the restoration of priesthood keys in the Kirtland Temple by Moses, Elias, and Elijah (D&C 110). In each of these "visions," heavenly beings visited the earth in person and delivered their messages to mortals. An interesting account from Church history illustrates the difference between visions and visitations. While in the Kirtland Temple, the Prophet Joseph Smith saw in vision the transcendent beauty and glory of the celestial kingdom. Upon the "blazing throne of God" were seated the Father and the Son. In addition, the Prophet said he saw "Father Adam and Abraham; and my father and my mother; my brother Alvin, that has long since slept" (D&C 137:3, 5). What is unique is that Joseph's father and mother were still alive. In fact, Joseph Smith Sr. attended the meeting where his son had this vision.

In a similar manner, inspired dreams can also be visions. They come when we are sleeping, but we still *see* and understand important spiritual messages by this means of communication. Whenever God by the power of the Holy Ghost conveys a spiritual message through visual means—whether we are awake or asleep or even unconscious—it is a vision and a revelation from God. Joseph in Egypt had inspired dreams. So did the Babylonian king Nebuchadnezzar. Lehi had an inspired dream of the tree of life. Nephi saw and understood the same images by way of a vision. Latter-day Saints believe that in fulfillment of Joel's prophecy of the last days, "old men shall dream dreams" and "young men shall see visions" (Joel 2:28). We believe that God continues to convey inspired messages of hope, love, instruction, and correction to his prophets and apostles and to all his faithful children by the power of the Holy Ghost through dreams, visions, visitations, and impressions to the soul.

BLT

WAR

War originated in our premortal existence when Lucifer sought to overthrow God and destroy the moral agency that God had given to man (Revelation 12:7–9; D&C 29:36; Moses 4:3). War in this world is a continuation of the war in heaven and usually involves agency or freedom. The Prophet Joseph Smith and Sidney Rigdon beheld in vision that "Satan, that old serpent, even the devil, who rebelled against God . . . maketh war with the saints of God, and encompasseth them round about. And we saw a vision of the sufferings of those with whom he made war and overcame" (D&C 76:28–30). James, the brother of the Lord, taught that fighting is pervasive among men because of their "lusts that war in [their] members." He continued, "Ye lust, and have not: ye kill, and desire to have, and cannot obtain: ye fight and war, yet ye have not" (James 4:1–2).

War is fundamentally incompatible with the Prince of Peace, his gospel, and associated sacred things. Anciently the Lord prohibited King David from building a temple at Jerusalem because he "made great wars" and "shed much blood upon the earth" (1 Chronicles 22:8). In a revelation given through Joseph Smith on 6 August 1833, the Lord declared that the Saints were to "renounce war and proclaim peace, and seek diligently to turn the hearts of the children to their fathers, and the hearts of the fathers to the children" (D&C 98:16). He also articulated principles of what might be called a policy of "just war" or "defensive war." He exhorted his covenant people to bear patiently the attacks inflicted upon them by their enemies and "not go out unto battle against any nation, kindred, tongue, or people" unless the Lord commanded it (D&C 98:33). He also recapitulated the law of warfare that he gave to his "ancients" and reminded the Latter-day Saints that he justified the ancients in going out to battle only after a standard of peace had been offered three times to their enemies (D&C 98:32–36).

In all of this the Lord declared that such principles are "an ensample unto all people" and that he "would fight their battles, and their children's battles," unto the fourth generation if they would do as he taught (D&C 98:38, 37). The Lord also promised great rewards to those who follow his counsel and instructions regarding warfare, where readiness to forgive far outweighs readiness to go to war (D&C 98:24–26, 39–43).

Other scriptures teach that the Lord has used war for his purposes, including the protection of liberty and agency. When Captain Moroni inspired and rallied the Nephites to battle for the cause of freedom and family, he did so with the Lord's approval (Alma 43:47). He rent his coat and lifted a banner of liberty and righteous action: "In memory of our God, our religion, and freedom, and our peace, our wives, and our children" (Alma 46:12). Certainly the Lord supported the American Revolutionary War. The power of God was with the colonists, while "the wrath of God was upon all those that were gathered together against them to battle" (1 Nephi 13:18).

In this final dispensation it is understood that wars and rumors of wars are part of the signs of the times, incident to the end of the world and the second coming of Christ (Joseph Smith–Matthew 1:23–31).

The Prophet Joseph Smith's Civil War prophecy, uttered in 1832, foretold increasing conflict and destruction from that time forward, until the Lord made "a full end of all nations" (D&C 87:6).

During the twentieth century, Church leaders spoke about the tragedy of war and condemned its use to further state policies at the expense of moral agency. At the outbreak of World War I, President Joseph F. Smith exhorted Church members serving in the armed forces to keep cruelty, hate, and murder out of their hearts, even during battle. Less than a week after the attack on Pearl Harbor during World War II, the First Presidency's Christmas message echoed similar sentiments, insisting that only adherence to the gospel of Jesus Christ could bring peace to the world. President J. Reuben Clark Jr. of the First Presidency declared that "nothing is more unrighteous, more unholy, more ungodly than man-declared mass slaughter of his fellow man for an unrighteous cause" (in Cowan, 188). President Spencer W. Kimball was particularly emphatic in his denunciation of warlike tendencies among even the Lord's covenant people:

"We are a warlike people, easily distracted from our assignment of preparing for the coming of the Lord. When enemies rise up, we commit vast resources to the fabrication of gods of stone and steel—ships, planes, missiles, fortifications—and depend on them for protection and deliverance. When threatened, we become anti-enemy instead of pro-kingdom of God; we train a man in the art of war and call him a patriot, thus, in the manner of Satan's counterfeit of true patriotism, perverting the Savior's teaching:

"'Love your enemies, bless them that curse you, do good to them that hate you, and pray for them which despitefully use you, and persecute you;

"'That ye may be the children of your Father which is in heaven' (Matthew 5:44–45).

"We forget that if we are righteous the Lord will either not suffer our enemies to come upon us . . . or he will fight our battles for us (Exod. 14:14; D&C 98:37, to name only two references of many)" (6).

At the same time, Church leaders have also mentioned the need for citizens to support the country to which they owe their allegiance, adding that leaders of warring nations are responsible and not individual citizens or soldiers. The First Presidency has promoted peace and relief of suffering from war in tangible ways. In 1915, for example, the First Presidency encouraged Church members to contribute to the Zion's Emergency Fund to aid needy Church members in Europe. In the wake of World War II, the Church shipped food, clothing, and other supplies to war-torn countries outside the United States. War has deeply affected the Church around the world, including the curtailing or halting of construction projects, activities, and missionary work in some countries. War has taken many lives and caused much misery. It will continue on the earth until Satan is vanquished. The battle of Armageddon will usher in the Second Coming and the millennial reign of Christ.

SOURCES

Cowan, Richard O. *The Church in the Twentieth Century.* Salt Lake City: Bookcraft, 1985.

Kimball, Spencer W. "The False Gods We Worship." *Ensign,* June 1976, 3–6.

ACS

WAR IN HEAVEN

Before the foundation of the world, while all the children of God were yet in their premortal home, a conflict occurred that has become known as the war in heaven. Lucifer, "an angel of God who was in authority in the presence of God" (D&C 76:25), sought to save the children of God in a way that was contrary to eternal law and the will of the Father. He wanted to be the Savior instead of Jehovah, who was the "Lamb slain from the foundation of the world" (Revelation 13:8; see also 1 Peter 1:19–20). Rejected in his attempts, Lucifer angrily sought to overthrow the plan of the Father. His proposal, or amendatory offer, had it been accepted, would have destroyed mankind's agency (Moses 4:3). Although Lucifer made a false offer of salvation without individual responsibility, he gained many followers, and the war in heaven ensued. Michael the archangel (later named Adam) led the forces of Jehovah in a battle for the loyalties of the Father's children (Revelation 12:7). The exact nature of this war is not detailed in the scriptures, but we know it involved the principles of the gospel of Jesus Christ and how humankind was to be saved. The Prophet Joseph Smith explained:

"The contention in heaven was—Jesus said there would be certain souls that would not be saved; and the devil said he would save them

658

all, and laid his plans before the grand council, who gave their vote in favor of Jesus Christ. So the devil rose up in rebellion against God" (6:314). The result was that Lucifer and "a third part of the hosts of heaven" (D&C 29:36) who followed and supported him in the rebellion were cast out of heaven (Isaiah 14:12–15; Jude 1:6; Revelation 12:4–9; Moses 4:1–4; Abraham 3:27–28; D&C 76:25–29), eternally deprived of being born into mortality with physical bodies, never to have salvation (Smith, 5:388). Because they "rebelled against God, and sought to take away the kingdom of our God and his Christ" and make "war with the saints of God," they became sons of perdition—"vessels of wrath doomed to suffer the wrath of God . . . in eternity" (D&C 76: 28–29, 33). So great was the fall of Lucifer that "the heavens wept over him" (D&C 76:26). So great is the punishment of those who follow him that the Lord said of those who become sons of perdition in this life that it would have "been better for them never to have been born" (D&C 76:32).

Known on earth as Satan or the devil, Lucifer and his "angels" still continue to war against the work and people of God. Thus, the war in heaven continues on earth as Satan still seeks to destroy the agency of man and desires "that all men might be miserable like unto himself" (2 Nephi 2:27). Just as Lucifer was defeated in the premortal war in heaven, he will be defeated again. Victory over Satan, now and eternally, is won on the same conditions as it was in heaven—"by the blood of the Lamb, and by the word of [our] testimony" (Revelation 12:11).

SOURCE

Smith, Joseph. *History of The Church of Jesus Christ of Latter-day Saints.* Edited by B. H. Roberts. 7 vols. 2d ed. rev. Salt Lake City: The Church of Jesus Christ of Latter-day Saints, 1932–51.

BLT

WEAKNESS

In speaking through the prophet Moroni, Jesus Christ declared: "And if men come unto me I will show unto them their weakness. I give unto men weakness that they may be humble; and my grace is sufficient for all men that humble themselves before me; for if they humble themselves before me, and have faith in me, then will I make weak things become strong unto them" (Ether 12:27; see also 2 Corinthians 12:9–10). God allows us to wrestle with weakness and toil with troubles, all as a part of the learning and growth experience of this second estate. In many cases we give ourselves weaknesses through yielding to sin and thus weakening our resolve and our resistance to evil.

Obviously the Lord can and will reveal unto us, if we seek in diligent prayer, our individual weaknesses and specific sins that deserve our attention and merit our repentance. The above passage, however, instructs us that the Lord will, if we are teachable, show us our weakness—our mortality, our fallenness, our utter inability to achieve peace and happiness on our own, our need for divine strength. Our weakness is our plight, a divine dilemma that points us always and forever to the Savior.

RLM

WICKED/WICKEDNESS

Those who are characterized in the scriptures as wicked are those who defies God's will and disobeys his commandments. The term *wicked* is often used interchangeably with *sinful, iniquitous, proud, rebellious.* The Prophet Joseph Smith defined wickedness as "pride, high-mindedness, and unbelief" and living in such a way as to warrant the withdrawal of the Holy Spirit (1:314). While there are certainly varying levels of wickedness, just as there are myriad sins, all wickedness is enmity against God and his laws—whether big sins or small ones, for God "cannot look upon sin with the least degree of allowance" (D&C 1:31). It is the state of those who have not repented of their sins and put off the "natural man" through the atonement of Jesus Christ (Mosiah 3:19). Interestingly, the Lord characterizes Martin Harris as a "wicked man" because he did not keep his covenant to protect the 116 pages of the Book of Mormon manuscript (D&C 10:1). Violating promises and sacred covenants, whether maliciously or carelessly, is wickedness.

Wickedness is the opposite of holiness, which is the very nature of God. Wickedness is the nature of Satan, who rebelled against God. Wickedness is worldliness—that which is unholy, unclean, carnal, sensual, and devilish. Righteousness is holiness—that which is "honest, true, chaste, benevolent, virtuous" (Articles of Faith 1:13)—that which is of God and like God. For this reason, the Lord, both in ancient and modern times, commands his disciples to "come ye out from the wicked, and be ye separate, and touch not their unclean things" (Alma 5:57; see also D&C 38:42). Wickedness can never be happiness, as Alma declared, because it is "contrary to the nature of God" (Alma 41:11).

At the end of the world, those who are destroyed when the Son of God comes will be the wicked—those who refuse to repent of their sins, "for they love darkness rather than light, and their deeds are evil" (D&C 29:45; see also D&C 63:34–37, 54). The wicked are they who "received not the gospel, neither the testimony of Jesus, neither the prophets, neither the everlasting covenant. . . . These are they who are liars, and sorcerers, and adulterers, and whoremongers, and whosoever loves and makes a lie. These are they who suffer the wrath of God on earth. These are they who suffer the vengeance of eternal fire" (D&C 76:101, 103–5).

SOURCE

Smith, Joseph. *History of The Church of Jesus Christ of Latter-day Saints.* Edited by B. H. Roberts. 7 vols. 2d ed. rev. Salt Lake City: The Church of Jesus Christ of Latter-day Saints, 1932–51.

BLT

WOMAN

In the divine plan of salvation, women and men are equally yoked, making it difficult to speak of the contributions of one without reference to the other. As the apostle Paul taught, "Neither is the man without the woman, neither the woman without the man, in the Lord" (1 Corinthians 11:11). We therefore find that women have an essential, leading role in creation, in the patriarchal order as equal partners with their husband, as prophetesses, as types of Christ, and as mothers.

Man and woman were God's final creations, made after his own image (Genesis 1:26-27; Moses 2:26-27). At the time of creation, God gave "them" (man and woman) dominion over all living things (Genesis 1:26, 28; Moses 2:26, 27; D&C 20:18). Given the responsibility to be stewards over God's other creations, all men and women are to use and care for his creations, remembering that all creation

ultimately belongs to God. Nowhere in scripture is man given dominion over woman; nor is woman given dominion over man. Figuratively
speaking, woman was created from the rib of man so that together
they could be one flesh. The imagery of the rib, or side, further symbolizes that man and woman are made of the same substance and are
to exist together, side by side, not beneath or above one another (Moses
3:21-25).

Woman is an equal partner with her husband in the Melchizedek
Priesthood. This ideal form of governing is patterned after God's
government, which he, as the Father, operates through families here
on earth. As "The Family: A Proclamation to the World" declares,
"Fathers and mothers are obligated to help one another as equal partners" (First Presidency, 102). In this patriarchal order, home is the
center of the community, and religion is woven into the family's
daily life. Children are viewed as a divine gift, and parents are stewards for God in rearing their children to love and serve him. Family,
rather than man or woman, is the foundation of the patriarchal order. The priesthood therefore blesses families in important ways. Elder
Dallin H. Oaks has explained: "A most important difference in the
functioning of priesthood authority in the family and in the Church
results from the fact that the government of the family is patriarchal,
whereas the government of the Church is hierarchical. The concept of
partnership functions differently in the family than in the Church"
(26). Likewise, President Boyd K. Packer has taught: "In the Church
there is a distinct line of authority. We serve where called by those who
preside over us. In the home it is a partnership with husband and wife
equally yoked together, sharing in decisions, always working together"
(73).

In recent decades feminist movements have pushed to establish
and defend equal political, economic, and social rights for women.
Feminism argues for laws and cultural mores that permit equal opportunities for women in place of legislation that consigns women to a
subservient or silent role. Many devoted, believing, and participating
members of The Church of Jesus Christ of Latter-day Saints have embraced and promoted these fundamental causes of feminism. Likewise,
many converted, dedicated, and faithful members of the Church have
rejected the radical feminist political agenda, which often skews the

meaning of feminism in order to promote rejection and censure of men.

The restored gospel teaches that God does not favor men over women. This foundational truth invites our acceptance of policies that provide equal opportunities and remuneration for a job regardless of gender and other rights that have not always existed in society for women. A person's standing in the Church is not judged by that person's feminist philosophy but rather by devotion to the restored gospel of Jesus Christ. The doctrines of the Church encourage the essential inclusion and participation of women in its highest ordinances, teachings, and blessings of salvation. Despite these teachings, there are still those in the Church who inappropriately or ignorantly allow their limited perspective to diminish or exclude the contribution of women in the Church and community. Such attitudes and conduct contradict sincere Christian discipleship.

Some women in the Bible are called prophetesses, meaning they were endowed with the spiritual knowledge that Jesus is the Christ and bore that witness by the same spirit (Revelation 19:10; Smith, 3:28, 390; 5:215–16). Elder James E. Talmage observed: "No special ordination in the Priesthood is essential to man's receiving the gift of prophecy. . . . The ministrations of Miriam and Deborah show that this gift may be possessed by women also" (228–29). Latter-day Saints, therefore, are not confused by the apostle Paul's writings to the Corinthian Saints: "Let your women keep silence in the churches: for it is not permitted unto them to rule" (JST, 1 Corinthians 14:34). Latter-day Saint women are not ordained to "rule," or administer ordinances and preside as priesthood leaders in the Church, but they have the God-given privilege to teach the doctrines of the gospel to the Church, preside as leaders of Church auxiliaries, pray and preach in all general meetings of the Church, and officiate in temple ordinances. Set apart by the power of priesthood, women are called by God "to expound scriptures, and to exhort the church, according as it shall be given [them] by my Spirit" (D&C 25:7). By virtue of being daughters of God and through the atonement of Christ, women have divine rights to pray directly to the Father and receive answers, which he communicates specifically to them (Genesis 25:22-23; 1 Samuel 2:1; Alma 32:23). No priesthood ordination is required for communion with the Father, application of the Atonement, receipt of the companionship of the Holy Ghost, and the enjoyment of spiritual gifts.

Various images symbolize and typify Jesus Christ in scripture, including those that portray female imagery. Our Savior is the pained woman in childbirth, crying in anguish as she brings forth life (Isaiah 42:14), the mother who caresses and comforts her troubled child (Isaiah 66:13), and the mother hen who gathers her chicks under her wings (Luke 13:34; 3 Nephi 10:4-6; D&C 10:65). The Redeemer's merciful mission of salvation is further linked to the pains and unselfishness of motherhood by the same Hebrew root (*rhm*) that produces both the word for Christ's compassion and the word for a woman's womb.

Motherhood is a gift of God to all women but does not depend on a woman's giving birth. Mother Eve was called "the mother of all living" before she ever bore a child (Genesis 3:20), and the Israelite judge Deborah called herself "a mother in Israel" after she had helped deliver the Israelites from oppression (Judges 5:7). As a mother figure for her people, Deborah manifested characteristics that are equally valued in parenting. She loved the people she served just as a mother loves her biological children. She nurtured, protected, taught, and inspired the people to trust in God and act in faith to restore freedom, peace, and opportunity in the land. Duties of mothers in this context are not focused on cleaning and cooking but on leading charges to the Source of salvation. Mothers recognize that they cannot save their children—but God can and will.

A mother's love can therefore expand beyond her immediate family to eventually unite cities and nations. Such mothers see family in community, where all are welcomed and offered nourishment and compassion. Certainly, Christ's perfect love has that boundless capacity to encircle all those who come to him. Responding to their God-given assignment of being mothers, women emulate and typify the selfless love that the Savior demonstrates to each of us.

SOURCES

First Presidency and Council of the Twelve Apostles. "The Family: A Proclamation to the World." *Ensign,* Nov. 1995, 102.

Oaks, Dallin H. "Priesthood Authority in the Family and the Church." *Ensign,* Nov. 2005, 24–27.

Packer, Boyd K. "The Relief Society." *Ensign,* May 1998, 72–74.

Smith, Joseph. *History of The Church of Jesus Christ of Latter-day Saints.* Edited by B. H. Roberts. 7 vols. 2d ed. rev. Salt Lake City: The Church of Jesus Christ of Latter-day Saints, 1932–51.

Talmage, James E. *The Articles of Faith.* Classics in Mormon Literature series. Salt Lake City: Deseret Book, 1981.

CFO

WORD OF GOD

The scriptures use the phrase "word of God" in two different ways: (1) the message of salvation that God delivers to humankind through scriptures, revelations to prophets and apostles, and the power of the Holy Ghost; (2) a title for Jesus Christ that signifies that the words of salvation are found in him. He is the means whereby God's word and will is manifest to the world. Christ, as the "word of [God's] power" (Moses 1:33; 2:5, 16; 3:7; D&C 29:30), is the means by which worlds are created, maintained, and redeemed. Thus, John the Beloved begins his Gospel by saying: "In the beginning was the Word, and the Word was with God, and the Word was God. . . . All things were made by him; and without him was not any thing made that was made" (John 1:1, 3). Later in the same chapter, John identifies the Word of God as Christ, the One who "was made flesh and dwelt among us, (and we beheld his glory, the glory as of the only begotten of the Father,) full of grace and truth" (John 1:14). The Joseph Smith Translation more directly identifies the Word as Jesus Christ, the Son of God (JST, John 1:16). In the book of Revelation, John records a symbolic vision of Christ's ultimate triumph over evil with this interesting description: "And he was clothed with a vesture dipped in blood: and his name is called *The Word of God. . . .* And out of his mouth proceedeth the word of God, and with it he will smite the nations; and he will rule them with the word of his mouth; and he treadeth the winepress in the fierceness and wrath of Almighty God. And he hath on his vesture, and on his thigh a name written, KING OF KINGS, AND LORD OF LORDS" (JST, Revelation 19:13, 15–16; emphasis added).

Both scriptural uses of the phrase "word of God" are represented by the rod of iron in Lehi's and Nephi's visions of the tree of life (1 Nephi 8, 11). The rod provides safe passage for those who press forward in faith and remain near the tree of life, which represents God's love and eternal life. The words of God, the scriptures, the prophets, the Spirit, the fulness of the gospel all bring us to Christ. He is the Word of God. He is the means and end of our salvation. He is the embodiment of God's word and will.

BLT

WORD OF WISDOM

In the 1830s there was widespread abuse of alcohol in the United States, and tobacco use in its many forms was prevalent. Owing to this social problem, many societies and organizations actively advocated temperance—either the moderate use of or total abstinence from alcohol and tobacco. As the temperance movement gained greater popularity in American society, questions arose among Latter-day Saints concerning the appropriateness of tobacco and alcohol usage by Church members. Considering the widely differing views even among the Prophet Joseph Smith's peers in the leadership of the Church, the Prophet took his questions and concerns to the Lord and on 27 February 1833 received a revelation known as the Word of Wisdom (D&C 89). More than just a health code for Latter-day Saints, the Word of Wisdom (and the prophetic commentary that has come in the decades since the revelation was received) teaches foundational principles upon which its health proscriptions are based, and it promises both temporal and spiritual blessings to all who follow its precepts. The stated objective of this revelation is "the temporal salvation of all saints in the last days" and to protect against the "evils and designs which do and will exist in the hearts of conspiring men in the last days" (D&C 89:2, 4).

Latter-day Saints believe that the physical body is, as the apostle Paul taught, a temple of God wherein the Spirit of God dwells (1 Corinthians 6:15). The physical body, as a temple of God and the fleshly tabernacle of a divine spirit (D&C 88:15), is to be kept pure and free from physical and spiritual defilement. That is a governing, overarching principle in the Word of Wisdom. As a result, the revealed code of health not only prohibits certain substances, such as alcohol, tobacco, "hot drinks" (which have been authoritatively interpreted to mean tea and coffee), but it also encourages the partaking of healthy foods that will strengthen the body and preserve good health, such as "wholesome herbs," fruits, vegetables, and grains. Likewise, the Lord declared that meat should "be used sparingly" (D&C 89:10, 12).

The Word of Wisdom was given as a revelation to the Prophet Joseph Smith in 1833, but not until many decades later was full observance of the Word of Wisdom—meaning total abstinence from alcohol, tobacco, tea, and coffee—a requirement for men to be called to responsible positions of priesthood leadership and women and men to be considered worthy to participate in temple ordinances. Although Joseph Smith expected the Saints to live the Word of Wisdom in his day, it was difficult for many to rid themselves of bad habits, and the leaders of the Church continued to urge the Saints toward total abstinence rather than mere moderation. President Joseph F. Smith explained: "The reason undoubtedly why the Word of Wisdom was given—as not 'by commandment or restraint' was that at that time, at least, if it had been given as a commandment it would have brought every man addicted to the use of these noxious things, under condemnation; so the Lord was merciful and gave them a chance to overcome, before He brought them under the law" (14).

Just as in the early days of the Church, today some members seek to interpret the Word of Wisdom to justify their questionable behavior or to condemn the practices of others who may not conform to their view. Some seek to establish the Word of Wisdom as a legal code—a law of Moses list of exactly what foods, drinks, or substances should or should not be consumed. Questions, interpretations, judgments, and criticisms abound, but that was never the intent of the Lord's Word of Wisdom. President Boyd K. Packer has taught:

"The Word of Wisdom was 'given for a principle with promise' (D&C 89:3). That word *principle* in the revelation is a very important one. A principle is an enduring truth, a rule you can adopt to guide you in making decisions. Generally principles are not spelled out in detail. That leaves you free to find your way with an enduring truth, a principle as your anchor.

"Members write in [to Church headquarters] asking if this thing or another is against the Word of Wisdom. It's well known that tea, coffee, liquor, and tobacco are against it. It has not been spelled out in more detail. Rather, we teach the principle together with the promised blessings. There are many habit-forming, addictive things that one can drink or chew or inhale or inject which injure both body and spirit which are not mentioned in the revelation. Everything harmful is not specifically listed; arsenic, for instance—certainly bad, but not habit-forming! He who must be commanded in all things, the Lord said, 'is a slothful and not a wise servant' (D&C 58:26)" (17).

As important as it is as a health code that promotes physical well-being, the Word of Wisdom is even more important as a spiritual law. To Latter-day Saints, the spirit and the body constitute the soul (D&C 88:15). Living the Word of Wisdom not only helps the body but also yields spiritual blessings—those who observe it "find wisdom and great treasures of knowledge, even hidden treasures" (D&C 89:19). The wisdom and hidden treasures promised come to a person through personal revelation—the guiding and protecting power of the Holy Ghost. Worthily adhering to the Word of Wisdom opens the door to enjoying the companionship of the Holy Ghost.

SOURCES

Packer, Boyd. K. "The Word of Wisdom: The Principle and the Promises." *Ensign,* May 1996, 17–19.

Smith, Joseph F. In Conference Report, Oct. 1913, 14.

BLT

WORK

Physical labor is a blessing that God instituted in his plan from the beginning for all of his children. He greatly multiplied Eve's sorrow (or gave her repeated challenges) throughout mortality (Genesis 3:16) and cursed the ground for Adam's sake so that he would eat "in the sweat of [his] face" (Genesis 3:19). Therefore Adam and Eve labored together "by the sweat" of their brows for the well-being of their family (Moses 5:1).

Scriptures repeatedly show that spiritual and temporal prosperity accompany sustained, honest work (Mosiah 5:10). The Book of Mormon prophet Nephi "caused his people to be industrious" (2 Nephi 5:17). The apostle Paul, who saw the temptations that arise from idleness, reminded his new converts that if they did not work, they should not expect to eat. Furthermore, they were instructed to find joy and fulfillment in work and "be not weary in well doing" (2 Thessalonians 3:13). In his years of effort to bring souls unto Christ, Alma the

Younger found that "the Lord doth give me exceedingly great joy in the fruit of my labors" (Alma 36:25). Honest work is a reward in itself.

Jesus was often criticized by some of the Jewish leaders for his work ethic. He went about doing good on the Sabbath and was rebuked. The Savior responded, "My Father worketh hitherto, and I work" (John 5:17). He never forgot that he was on his Father's errand: "I must work the works of him that sent me" (John 9:4). In his Intercessory Prayer, the Savior reported to the Father, "I have finished the work which thou gavest me" (John 17:4). In summary, his work is to "bring to pass the immortality and eternal life of man" (Moses 1:39).

The Lord invites each of us to participate in his great work. "Say nothing but repentance unto this generation. Keep my commandments, and assist to bring forth my work, according to my commandments, and you shall be blessed" (D&C 11:9). The commandment to "work out our own salvation with fear and trembling" (Philippians 2:12; see also Alma 34:37) is a reminder of our dependence on the Savior's mercy, grace, and merits for salvation rather than an inference that we earn exaltation through our labors, "for it is God which worketh in you both to will and to do of his good pleasure" (Philippians 2:13). The Savior's gift of salvation is personal and intimate—between him and each one of us. His sacrifice for us enables and fortifies our ability to work and succeed.

CFO

WORSHIP

From the beginning God gave Adam and Eve commandment to worship him and instructions on how to do so (Moses 5:5–9). In our day "we know that all men must repent and believe on the name of Jesus Christ, and worship the Father in his name, and endure in faith on his name to the end, or they cannot be saved in the kingdom of God" (D&C 20:29). Specifically, we worship the "infinite and eternal, from everlasting to everlasting . . . unchangeable God," who framed heaven and earth and created men and women in his own image (D&C 20:17). Furthermore, when we honor or worship the Son of God, we worship the Father (John 5:23), and we worship the Father in the name of his Only Begotten Son (Jacob 4:5).

True worship of God evokes loving service to him with all of our heart, mind, and strength (Deuteronomy 10:12–13; Matthew 4:10; 2 Nephi 25:29). If we worship him with all our heart and mind, then he is the only Being we will worship; we will have no other gods before him (Exodus 34:14). We need no specific place or circumstance in which to worship God, for we are free to worship him "in whatsoever place [we] may be in" (Alma 34:38). We can worship God through offering sincere prayer, singing songs of praise and gratitude, teaching his gospel, bearing testimony of him, making and keeping sacred covenants, participating in holy ordinances, visiting "the fatherless and widows in their affliction," and keeping ourselves "unspotted from the world" (James 1:27). We worship when we "live in thanksgiving daily" (Alma 34:38) and give the Lord the glory because of his name (Psalm 29:2).

The Lord warned that worship becomes vain or fruitless when a people honor "me with their lips, but their heart is far from me," or when they teach commandments of men as though these false ideas were doctrines from God (Mark 7:6). Worship becomes a mockery of God when we convolute the sacred ordinances or knowingly offer them to those who are unworthy or who deny Christ (4 Nephi 1:27).

In addition to being given commandments for direction in our worship, we, as disciples of Christ, are instructed as were the Nephites "that there should not any man, belonging to the church, arise and persecute those that did not belong to the church" (Alma 1:21). When our first love is for the Lord, we allow people of other faiths to worship how they choose. As is clearly stated in the Articles of Faith, "We claim the privilege of worshiping Almighty God according to the dictates of our own conscience, and allow all men the same privilege, let them worship how, where, or what they may" (1:11).

CFO

WORTHY

In one sense, to be worthy is to be deserving. A student receives the highest score on an exam, and she is said to be deserving or worthy of the highest grade. A person conducts himself with dignity and poise in the midst of very trying circumstances, and he is said to be worthy of praise. In the gospel sense, however, none of us deserves the highest heaven hereafter as a result of our own works, and none of us is worthy of the celestial kingdom because we have worked ourselves into glory. As Aaron, son of King Mosiah taught, "Since man had fallen he could not merit anything of himself; but the sufferings and death of Christ atone for their sins, through faith and repentance" (Alma 22:14). The restored gospel declares that "the worth of souls is great in the sight of God" (D&C 18:10). Why? Because men and women have earned such worth? Because people by nature deserve the highest rewards? No. "Remember the worth of souls is great in the sight of God; for, behold, the Lord your Redeemer suffered death in the flesh; wherefore he suffered the pain of all men, that all men might repent and come unto him" (D&C 18:10–11). As the apostles Paul and Peter explained, we are not our own; we have been "bought with a price," even the "precious blood" of the sinless Son of Man (1 Corinthians 6:19–20; 7:23; 1 Peter 1:18–19).

To be worthy is to be appropriate, suitable, to possess worth, and to have qualities suited to a given requirement, standard, or level of attainment. To be worthy to attend the holy temple does not mean we are morally perfect, that we are without flaw, or that we walk each day without sin. It means that we are *striving* to keep the commandments of God, striving to be true to our covenants, striving to cultivate the sweet influence of the Spirit. To be worthy of the celestial kingdom hereafter requires that we strive in this life to be "quickened by a portion of the celestial glory" so that in the resurrection we "shall then receive of the same, even a fulness" (D&C 88:29). Moroni exhorted us: "See that ye do all things in worthiness, and do it in the name of Jesus Christ, the Son of the living God; and if ye do this, and endure to the end, ye will in no wise be cast out" (Mormon 9:29).

RLM

WRATH

From a mortal perspective, wrath is intense, vengeful anger or an action carried out in great anger. It is probably not possible for us to fully comprehend wrath from a divine perspective. Nevertheless, the scriptures speak of two kinds of wrath: that possessed by humans and that possessed by God. Wrath in humans is almost never a good thing. "For the wrath of man worketh not the righteousness of God" (James 1:20). Therefore, counsels James, "let every man be swift to hear, slow to speak, slow to wrath" (James 1:19). Paul describes wrath as one of the "works of the flesh" or as one of the characteristics of fallen, unregenerate man (Galatians 5:19). Wrath does not allow the Spirit of the Lord to flourish. Wrath breeds strife (Proverbs 15:18). Therefore, Paul encouraged fathers not to provoke their children to wrath (Ephesians 6:4). Wise parents and leaders know that "a soft answer turneth away wrath" (Proverbs 15:1).

The book of Proverbs, especially, contains much good counsel for followers of God regarding wrath. "Wrath is cruel, and anger is outrageous" (Proverbs 27:4). "Wise men turn away wrath" (Proverbs 29:8). "He that is slow to wrath is of great understanding" (Proverbs 14:29). "A man of great wrath shall suffer punishment" (Proverbs 19:19). Ultimately, says Job, "wrath killeth the foolish man" (Job 5:2).

Quite different from the wrath of mortals is the wrath of God. Indeed, wrath is one of his divine attributes. Because he is perfectly righteous, God kindles his wrath against willful disobedience and wickedness. By commanding us to be holy like himself (Leviticus 11:44; 19:2; 20:26), he expects that we will kindle our own wrath against wickedness. Alma taught that iniquity provokes God to send down his wrath (Alma 12:36). And Paul reminded the Colossian Saints that "the wrath of God cometh on the children of disobedience" (Colossians 3:6). Ancient Israel so provoked the Lord that "in his wrath, for his anger was kindled against them, [he] swore that they should not enter into his rest while in the wilderness, which rest is the fulness of his glory" (D&C 84:24). So too in the latter days the Lord has decreed that his wrath should be "poured out upon the wicked without measure" (D&C 1:9). The wicked are defined as "the unbelieving and rebellious" (D&C 1:8). But they are not the only ones who experience God's wrath: "In nothing doth man offend God, or against none is his wrath kindled, save those who confess not his hand in all things, and obey not his commandments" (D&C 59:21).

Thus, God's wrath is an extension of his divine justice. Ironically, his wrath affected the mortal Jesus more than anyone else. Through the Atonement, Jesus delivered his followers "from the wrath to come" (1 Thessalonians 1:10). That is, through his infinite sacrifice humankind was released from the grasp of justice. But the demands of justice and the punishments affixed for broken laws still had to be met, and they were met and satisfied by Jesus Christ (Alma 42:14–15). He was, therefore, forced to face "the fierceness of the wrath of Almighty God" all alone (D&C 76:107; 88:106). Jesus took upon himself the full force of justice, the full force of the punishment deserved by each individual who has lived or ever will live. As Elder Neal A. Maxwell explained: "Jesus always deserved and always had the Father's full approval. But when He took our sins upon Him, of divine necessity required by justice He experienced instead 'the fierceness of the wrath of Almighty God' [Isaiah 53:10]" (13).

Because Jesus faced the wrath of Almighty God, mortals may repent of the sinful wrath they may sometimes possess in their moments of weakness. And because Jesus absorbed the wrath of Almighty God, deserved by each of us, God will remember only mercy toward us in the coming "day of wrath," provided we repent (D&C 101:9).

SOURCE

Maxwell, Neal A. *Lord, Increase Our Faith.* Salt Lake City: Bookcraft, 1994.

ACS

YOKE OF CHRIST

During his mortal ministry, Jesus taught: "Come unto me, all ye that labour and are heavy laden, and I will give you rest. Take my yoke upon you, and learn of me; for I am meek and lowly in heart: and ye shall find rest unto your souls. For my yoke is easy, and my burden is light" (Matthew 11:28–30). The most commonly recognized yoke is a wooden beam and collar that are placed on the shoulders of oxen or other draft animals. Working together as a team, two oxen can pull extremely heavy loads with their massive, broad shoulders. With a yoke and a partner, they can pull far more than one of them could pull alone. In a similar way, when we partner with the Savior, wearing his yoke, we can do what we never could accomplish if left to our own strength and resources.

A similar yoke is worn by humans rather than work animals. This kind of yoke is a crossbar fitted to a person's shoulders with ropes or cables hanging from the ends to which buckets or baskets are attached for carrying loads. A yoke allows a person to carry heavy burdens for a longer period of time. In reality, every one of us wears a figurative yoke as we attempt to carry the responsibilities and burdens of life. That load is nearly always oppressive. The Savior therefore invited us to take his yoke upon us, learn of him, and follow him. Only then will our burdens become light, and we will find rest. With the yoke of Christ, "his commandments are not grievous" (1 John 5:3) but rather inspire those who honor them (D&C 20:7).

Since the days of antiquity, yokes have at times symbolized bondage because they have also been used to oppress and enslave others. Moses warned of consequences that would follow the Israelites if they forgot their God: "Therefore shalt thou serve thine enemies which the Lord shall send against thee, in hunger, and in thirst, and in nakedness, and in want of all things: and he shall put a yoke of iron upon thy neck, until he have destroyed thee" (Deuteronomy 28:48). Only through the power of the Atonement are we freed from the yoke of bondage to again follow the Lord in faith (Isaiah 14:25). "Thus saith the Lord. . . . Though I have afflicted thee, I will afflict thee no more. For now will I break his yoke from off thee, and will burst thy bonds in sunder" (Nahum 1:12–13).

CFO

———◦◉◦———

ZION

Joseph Smith seems to have first encountered the concept of Zion (in a sense other than the holy mount or holy city in Jerusalem) in his translation of the Book of Mormon. The Book of Mormon prophets spoke of Zion as a holy commonwealth, a *society* of the Saints, *a way of life* that was to be established or brought forth under God's direction; those who fought against it would incur God's displeasure, and the laborers in Zion who labored for money rather than for Zion would perish (2 Nephi 26:31). In addition, in the words of the resurrected Savior, Zion was identified as a specific *place* in the land of America, a land of promise and inheritance for the descendants of Joseph of old (1 Nephi 13:37; 2 Nephi 10:11–13; 26:29–31; 28:20–24; 3 Nephi 16:16–18).

By December 1830, as the Prophet undertook his inspired translation of the Bible, he learned particulars concerning the patriarch Enoch and his ancient city of Zion. A King James text of three verses on Enoch and his people was expanded to more than one hundred verses, uncovering knowledge of such things as the manner in which an entire society of antediluvians was spiritually awakened and motivated to transcendent righteousness; the means by which this ancient people, formerly bent on selfishness and pride, had their souls changed, saw to the needs of the poor, and became "of one heart and one mind"; and how, through the application of such a divine philosophy, they were translated, taken from the earth into the bosom of God (Moses 7:18). Enoch's Zion became the pattern, the scriptural prototype for Latter-day Saints. In the months that followed Joseph's inspired translation, several revelations now in the Doctrine and Covenants spoke of the ancient Zion of Enoch and provided guidelines whereby the Latter-day Saints, through the principles of consecration and stewardship of properties, could lay the foundation for a modern society of Zion (D&C 38; 42).

In some of the earliest revelations recorded was the repeated command: "Now, as you have asked, behold, I say unto you, keep my commandments, and seek to bring forth and establish the cause of Zion" (D&C 6:6; see also 11:6; 12:6; 14:6). Zion thus came to be associated with the restored Church and the grand work of the Restoration; the faithful could take heart in the midst of their troubles, for Zion was the city of God (D&C 97:19). Indeed, in speaking of the sacred spot where the people of God congregated, the Lord said: "Behold, the land of Zion—I, the Lord, hold it in mine own hands" (D&C 63:25). Surely the King of Zion (Moses 7:53) would deal mercifully with his subjects.

The idea that there was a specific location for the city of Zion within North and South America was made known to Joseph Smith early in his ministry. In 1830 some of the Saints were called to preach among "the Lamanites," or native Americans. At that point in time, "it is not revealed, and no man knoweth where the city Zion shall be built, but it shall be given hereafter"; the Saints were told, however, that the location "shall be on the borders by the Lamanites" (D&C 28:9). Then on 20 July 1831, just as the leaders of the Church had begun to arrive in Missouri, word came concerning the specific location of Zion. The Saints were told that "the land of Missouri" was "the land which I [God] have appointed and consecrated for the gathering of the saints. Wherefore, this is the land of promise, and the place for the city of Zion. . . . The place which is now called Independence [Missouri] is the center place" (D&C 57:1–3).

Zion is spoken of in scripture as a banner or *ensign* around which a weary people may rally. It is also a *standard* against which the substance and quality of all things are to be evaluated. The Saints were expected to judge all things by guidelines obtained from a source beyond that of unenlightened man. Note the language of one of the revelations: "Behold, I, the Lord, have made my church in these last days like unto a judge sitting on a hill, or in a high place, to judge the nations. For it shall come to pass that the inhabitants of Zion shall judge all things pertaining to Zion" (D&C 64:37–38). As an illustration of this principle, Elder Joseph Young, brother of President Brigham Young, explained that Joseph Smith "recommended the Saints to cultivate as high a state of perfection in their musical harmonies as the standard of the faith which he had brought was superior to sectarian religion. To obtain this, he gave them to understand that the refinement of singing would depend upon the attainment of the Holy Spirit. . . .

". . . 'When these graces and refinements and all the kindred attractions are obtained that characterized the ancient Zion of Enoch, then the Zion of the last days will become beautiful, she will be hailed by the Saints from the four winds, who "will gather to Zion with songs of everlasting joy"'" (14–15).

In addition, Zion was to be the focus, the convergence, and the concentration of all that is good, all that is ennobling, all that is instructive and inspirational. In Zion all things are to be gathered together in one in Christ (Ephesians 1:10). In short, according to President Brigham Young, "every accomplishment, every polished grace, every useful attainment in mathematics, music, in all science and art belong to the Saints" (10:224). The Saints "rapidly collect the intelligence that is bestowed upon the nations," he said on another occasion, "for all this intelligence belongs to Zion" (8:279).

Zion is people, the people of God, the people who have come out of the world into the marvelous light of Christ. The early Saints were encouraged: "Verily, thus saith the Lord, let Zion rejoice, for this is

Zion—THE PURE IN HEART; therefore, let Zion rejoice, while all the wicked shall mourn" (D&C 97:21). Thus, Zion is *a state of being,* a state of purity of heart that entitles us to be known as members of the household of faith. President Young therefore spoke of the Saints having Zion in their hearts: "Unless the people live before the Lord in the obedience of His commandments, they cannot have Zion within them." He added, "As to the spirit of Zion, it is in the hearts of the Saints, of those who love and serve the Lord with all their might, mind, and strength" (2:253). On another occasion he affirmed: "Zion will be redeemed and built up, and the Saints will rejoice. This is the land of Zion; and who are Zion? The pure in heart are Zion; they have Zion within them. Purify yourselves, sanctify the Lord God in your hearts, and have the Zion of God within you" (8:198). Finally, he asked: "Where is Zion? Where the organization of the Church of God is. And may it dwell spiritually in every heart; and may we so live as to always enjoy the Spirit of Zion" (8:205).

Seven hundred years before Christ, Isaiah spoke of the "mountain of the Lord's house" being "established in the top of the mountains" (Isaiah 2:2). In July 1840 Joseph Smith declared that "the land of Zion . . . consists of all North and South America, but that any place where the Saints gather is Zion" (*Words,* 415). The latter part of this statement—that Zion represented any locus of gathering—is significant. It broadens the notion of Zion to include areas around the world where people of the covenant congregate. A larger vision of Zion was manifest in some of Joseph's earliest revelations, especially in one recorded during a particularly difficult time of persecution in Missouri:

"Zion shall not be moved out of her place, notwithstanding her children are scattered. They that remain, and are pure in heart, shall return, and come to their inheritances, they and their children, with songs of everlasting joy, to build up the waste places of Zion—and all these things that the prophets might be fulfilled. And, behold, there is none other place appointed than that which I have appointed; neither shall there be any other place appointed than that which I have appointed, for the work of the gathering of my saints—until the day cometh when there is found no more room for them; and then I have *other places which I will appoint unto them, and they shall be called stakes,* for the curtains or the strength of Zion" (D&C 101:17–21; emphasis added).

In the dedicatory prayer of the Kirtland Temple, the Prophet pleaded in behalf of the Saints "that they may come forth to Zion, or to her stakes, the places of thine appointment, with songs of everlasting joy" (D&C 109:39). The Saints came to understand that safety and refuge are to be found in the stakes of Zion. "Arise and shine forth, that thy light may be a standard for the nations; and that the gathering together upon the land of Zion, and upon her stakes, may be for a defense, and a refuge from the storm, and from wrath when it shall be poured out without mixture upon the whole earth" (D&C 115:5–6).

Like the Church itself, the concept of Zion has grown and expanded. In 1884 Elder Erastus Snow pointed out that when the early Saints "first heard the fullness of the Gospel preached by the first Elders, and read the revelations given through the Prophet Joseph Smith, our ideas of Zion were very limited. But as our minds began to grow and expand, why we began to look upon Zion as a great people, and the Stakes of Zion as numerous. . . . We ceased to set bounds to Zion and her Stakes" (25:30–31).

Zion is a place. Zion is a people. Zion is a holy state of being. In the words of President Spencer W. Kimball, Zion is the "highest order of priesthood society" (78). It is the heritage of the Saints. Joseph Smith taught:

"The building up of Zion is a cause that has interested the people of God in every age; it is a theme upon which prophets, priests and kings have dwelt with peculiar delight; they have looked forward with joyful anticipation to the day in which we live; and fired with heavenly and joyful anticipations they have sung and written and prophesied of this our day; but they died without the sight; we are the favored people that God has made choice of to bring about the Latter-day glory." In that sense, as the Prophet stated, "We ought to have the building up of Zion as our greatest object" (4:609–10; 3:390).

SOURCES

Kimball, Spencer W. "Welfare Services: The Gospel in Action." *Ensign,* Nov. 1977, 76–79.

Smith, Joseph. *History of The Church of Jesus Christ of Latter-day Saints.* Edited by B. H. Roberts. 7 vols. 2d ed. rev. Salt Lake City: The Church of Jesus Christ of Latter-day Saints, 1932–51.

Snow, Erastus. In *Journal of Discourses*. 26 vols. London: Latter-day Saints' Book Depot, 1854–86.

The Words of Joseph Smith. Compiled and edited by Andrew F. Ehat and Lyndon W. Cook. Provo, Utah: Brigham Young University Religious Studies Center, 1980. Spelling and punctuation standardized.

Young, Brigham. In *Journal of Discourses*. 26 vols. London: Latter-day Saints' Book Depot, 1854–86.

Young, Joseph. *History of the Organization of the Seventies*. Salt Lake City: Deseret Steam Printing Establishment, 1878.

RLM

INDEX OF TOPICS